Time Out

Venice

timeout.com/venice

Published by Time Out Guides Ltd, a wholly owned subsidiary of Time Out Group Ltd.
Time Out and the Time Out logo are trademarks of Time Out Group Ltd.

© Time Out Group Ltd 2007
Previous editions 1999, 2001, 2003, 2005.

10 9 8 7 6 5 4 3 2 1

This edition first published in Great Britain in 2007 by Ebury Publishing
A Random House Group company
20 Vauxhall Bridge Road, London SW1V 2SA

Random House Australia Pty Limited 20 Alfred Street, Milsons Point, Sydney, New South Wales 2061, Australia
Random House New Zealand Limited 18 Poland Road, Glenfield, Auckland 10, New Zealand
Random House South Africa (Pty) Limited Isle of Houghton, Corner Boundary
Road & Carse O'Gowrie, Houghton 2198, South Africa

Random House UK Limited Reg. No. 954009

For details of distribution in the Americas, see www.timeout.com

ISBN 10: 1-84670007-8
ISBN 13: 978-1-84670007-1

A CIP catalogue record for this book is available from the British Library

Colour reprographics by Wyndeham Icon, 3 & 4 Maverton Road, London E3 2JE

Printed and bound in Germany by Appl

Papers used by Ebury Publishing are natural, recyclable products made from wood grown in sustainable forests

Piazza San Marco: the drawing room of Europe. *See p77.*

Time Out Guides Limited
Universal House
251 Tottenham Court Road
London W1T 7AB
Tel + 44 (0)20 7813 3000
Fax + 44 (0)20 7813 6001
Email guides@timeout.com
www.timeout.com

Editorial

Editor Anne Hanley
Deputy Editor Daniel Smith
Listings Editor Patrizia Lerco
Proofreader Patrick Mulkern
Indexer Lesley McCave

Managing Director Peter Fiennes
Financial Director Gareth Garner
Editorial Director Ruth Jarvis
Deputy Series Editor Lesley McCave
Assistant Series Editor Holly Pick
Accountant Kemi Olufuwa

Design

Art Director Scott Moore
Art Editor Pinelope Kourmouzoglou
Senior Designer Josephine Spencer
Graphic Designer Henry Elphick
Digital Imaging Simon Foster
Ad Make-up Jenni Prichard

Picture Desk

Picture Editor Jael Marschner
Deputy Picture Editor Tracey Kerrigan
Picture Researcher Helen McFarland

Advertising

Sales Director Mark Phillips
International Sales Manager Fred Durman
International Sales Executive Simon Davies
Advertising Sales (Venice) Fabio Giannini
International Sales Consultant Ross Canadé
Advertising Assistant Kate Staddon

Marketing

Group Marketing Director John Luck
Marketing Manager Yvonne Poon
Marketing & Publicity Manager, US Rosella Albanese

Production

Group Production Director Mark Lamond
Production Manager Brendan McKeown
Production Coordinator Caroline Bradford

Time Out Group

Chairman Tony Elliott
Financial Director Richard Waterlow
Time Out Magazine Ltd MD David Pepper
Group General Manager/Director Nichola Coulthard
Time Out Communications Ltd MD David Pepper
Time Out International MD Cathy Runciman
Group Art Director John Oakey
Group IT Director Simon Chappell

Contributors

Introduction Anne Hanley. **History** Anne Hanley. **Today** Anne Hanley. **Venetian Painting** Frederick Ilchman. **Architecture** Anne Hanley. **Music in Venice** Nicky Swallow. **Where to Stay** Nicky Swallow. **Sightseeing** Gregory Dowling (*Hampered in the Ghetto*; *Pinault at the Punta?* Anne Hanley; *Murano glass* Nicolò Scibilia). **Eating Out** Lee Marshall; Michela Scibilia. **Cafés, Bars & *Gelaterie*** Jill Weinreich. **Shops & Services** JoAnn Titmarsh. **Festivals & Events** Anne Hanley; Daniel Smith. **Children** Patrizia Lerco. **Film** JoAnn Titmarsh. **Galleries** Chiara Barbieri. **Gay & Lesbian** Salvatore Mele. **Music & Nightlife** Kate Davies. **Performing Arts** Kate Davies. **Sport & Fitness** JoAnn Titmarsh. **The Veneto: Getting Started** Anne Hanley (*Not Venice but trying*, *Chioggia* Gregory Dowling). **Padua** Charlotte Thomas. **Verona** Kate Davies. **Vicenza** Charlotte Thomas. **Treviso & The Northern Veneto** JoAnn Titmarsh. **Directory** Charlotte Thomas (*Glossary, Vocabulary, Further Reference* Anne Hanley).

Maps LS International Cartography, via Decemviri 8, 20138 Milan, Italy. www.geomaker.com

Photography by Olivia Rutherford except: page 12 akg-images/Nimatallah; pages 14, 22, 32 akg-images/Cameraphoto; pages 19, 20 The Art Archive/Museo Correr Venice/Dagli Orti; pages 27, 28 Cameraphoto Arte Venezia/The Bridgeman Art Library; page 40 Alinari/The Bridgeman Art Library; page 203 Vito Arcomano/Fototeca ENIT; page 278 Tri-Star/The Kobal Collection.

The Editor would like to thank Patrizia Lerco, Michela Scibilia, Fulvio Marsigliani, Lee and Clara Marshall, and all contributors to previous editions of *Time Out Venice*, whose work forms the basis for parts of this book.

Contents

Introduction

How do you introduce Venice without lapsing into cliché? We've seen the documentaries. We've gasped at reproductions of the art works. We've heard – perhaps too often – the *Four Seasons*. The odd thing is, that when you get there, it really is like that. The streets *are* full of water. The colours are rich and ineffably Titianesque. And even if they don't bring vicious red dwarves to mind, the narrow, tortuous alleyways do have a strong, quiver-inducing magic all of their own. It's instantly recognisable, and utterly unique.

The city can also, of course, seem to be a cliché in itself, especially if you stick to the well-trodden routes and the well-known experiences. However romantic that gondola ride may be, it's never going to avoid being kitsch. And great as Vivaldi's masterpiece is, should a mediocre rendition by hack musicians in crumpled sateen be the definitive, Venetian way of appreciating it?

In this fifth edition of *Time Out Venice* we have looked in particular into music-making in Venice, on both the composing and performing sides. This is where the Gabrielis invented a whole new 'surround sound' way of raising church rafters by placing choirs at strategic points around St Mark's basilica; and this is, arguably, where the opera form was born (for more information, *see pp40-2* **Music in Venice**). Vivaldi, you will find, is the tip of a musical iceberg; and concealed in Venice today are excellent musicians (none clad in sad wigs) whose repertoire goes well beyond this over-exploited crowd pleaser. (For where to find them, *see p224-30* **Performing Arts**.)

But that's Venice all over. On the surface, *La Serenissma* – the Most Serene Republic of Venice – comes on like a historical theme park, frayed slightly at the edges by the onslaught of tourist hordes, and offering little in the way of that heart-warming 'authenticity' which is considered so essential an element of any other Italian destination.

But real, workaday Venice is there, beneath the surface, and it's well worth seeking out. You'll need to muster all your map-reading skills, and be prepared to get very, very lost. But as a reward, you'll find that Venice is a lived-in, working city punctuated by glorious churches, gleaming art works and locals who make the alleyways ring not with the inappropriate Neapolitan favourites crooned by gondoliers but with outbursts of genuine Venetian exuberance.

ABOUT TIME OUT CITY GUIDES

This is the fifth edition of *Time Out Venice*, one of an expanding series of Time Out guides produced by the people behind the successful listings magazines in London and New York. Our guides are all written by resident experts who have striven to provide you with all the most up-to-date information you'll need to explore the city or read up on its background, whether you're a local or a first-time visitor.

THE LIE OF THE LAND

Many visitors never make it further than St Mark's and the Rialto, but there is a rich world of cultural treasures to discover in the streets beyond. Finding your way around this maze-like city is never easy. We have divided this book according to the *sestieri*, Venice's historic neighbourhoods. House numbers don't begin and end in each street: they start at an arbitrary point in each *sestiere* and continue, apparently at random, to the last house in that district. Addresses, therefore, are almost useless for locating your goal. To make navigation easier,

our listings include the official address (ie *sestiere* plus number), followed by the name of the street that the sight or venue is located in. The nearest vaporetto (water ferry) stop is also given, and each listing has a map reference to help you locate your target on the maps that begin on p316. Each establishment listed in our **Where to Stay** (❶), **Eating Out** (❶), and **Cafés, Bars & Gelaterie** (❶) chapters is marked on our maps with colour-coded dots.

ESSENTIAL INFORMATION

For all the practical information you might need for visiting the area – including visa and customs information, details of local transport, a listing of emergency numbers, information on local weather and a selection of useful websites – turn to the Directory at the back of this guide. It begins on page 284.

THE LOWDOWN ON THE LISTINGS

We have tried to make this book as easy to use as possible. Addresses, phone numbers, public transport information, opening times

and admission prices are all included in the listings. However, businesses can change their arrangements at any time. Before you go out of your way, we'd strongly advise you to phone ahead to check opening times and other particulars. While every effort and care has been made to ensure the accuracy of the information contained in this guide, the publishers cannot accept responsibility for any errors it may contain.

PRICES AND PAYMENT

We have noted where venues such as shops, hotels, restaurants and theatres accept the following credit cards: American Express (AmEx), Diners Club (DC), MasterCard (MC) and Visa (V). Some will also accept travellers' cheques, and/or other cards.

The prices we've listed in this guide should be treated as guidelines, not gospel. If prices vary wildly from those we've quoted, ask whether there's a good reason. If not, go elsewhere. Then

please let us know. We aim to give the best and most up-to-date advice, so we want to know if you've been badly treated or overcharged.

TELEPHONE NUMBERS

The area code for Venice is 041. All landline numbers listed in this guide take this code unless stated. This code must be dialled, *with* the initial zero, whether you are calling from inside or outside Venice. The country code for Italy is 39. For more on telephones and codes, *see p301*.

MAPS

The map section at the back of this book (*see p316*) includes street maps of central Venice and the larger outlying islands, and a map showing vaporetto (water ferry) routes around the city. They now pinpoint specific locations of hotels (❶), restaurants (❶) and cafés and bars (❶). Maps for destinations in our **Veneto** section (*see p327-81*) are in the chapters themselves.

LET US KNOW WHAT YOU THINK

We hope you enjoy *Time Out Venice*, and we'd like to know what you think of it. We welcome tips for places that you consider we should include in future editions and we take note of your criticism of our choices. You can email us at guides@timeout.com.

There is an online version of this book, along with guides to over 100 international cities, at **www.timeout.com**.

In Context

Features

Teatro La Fenice. *See p91*.

Justinian I: bought Venetian loyalty.
See p13.

History

How Venice went to the doges.

The origins of *La Serenissima*, as Venice would come to be known, were far from serene: rampaging Visigoths, Huns, Ostrogoths and Lombards drove thousands of terrified inhabitants of mainland towns out on to the muddy, flood-prone islets and sand banks of the lagoon in the fifth century AD. But this ignominious start was easily forgotten, as the hamlets on the mudflats grew into a maritime republic that would have total control over the shipping routes of the eastern Mediterranean for almost six centuries.

Enormous public works were necessary almost from the beginning to shore up and consolidate the islands of the lagoon (*see p39* **How to build a house on mud**). Huge amounts of timber had to be cut down and transported here from coastal forests. The trunks were sunk deep into the mud as foundations for the buildings – mainly wooden – of the villages scattered on islands. But above all, the rivers – including the fast-flowing Brenta and Piave, which drain the eastern Dolomites and which threatened to silt up the lagoon – had to be tamed and diverted.

And yet this battle against nature helped to unite the early lagoon dwellers into a close-knit community and eventually into a republic that was to become one of the strongest and most stable states in European history. The fight against the sea never ended, however. Even in the 18th century, when the French army was advancing on the lagoon and the Venetian Republic was near the end of its own decline and fall, the government invested its last resources in the construction of the *murazzi*, the massive sea walls that run between the Lido, Pellestrina and Chioggia.

THE MAROONED LAGOON

Until the collapse of the Roman Empire, the islands of the lagoon hosted only transient fishing hamlets. But the cities around – Padua, Verona, Aquileia and Altino – were among the most prosperous in Roman Italy; many smaller towns – among them Vicenza, Concordia and Belluno – were of almost equal importance. With the final disintegration of any semblance of public order and security in the late sixth century, their inhabitants finally fled for their lives. Aquileians and Concordians gravitated towards the islands of the Grado lagoon, between Venice and Trieste. Inhabitants of Altino and Treviso made for the islands of Murano, Burano, Mazzorbo and Torcello in the northern section of the lagoon. Paduans pitched up on the central island of Rivo Alto ('high banks'), later abbreviated to Rialto, the first nucleus of historical Venice. Chioggia drew fugitives from Este and Monselice.

These influxes were meant to be temporary, but as economic life on the mainland collapsed, the lagoon islands came to be thought of as permanent homes. They offered enormous potential in the form of fish and salt – basic necessities. Once settled in the lagoon, the fugitives could also enjoy the relative peace and tranquillity that would be denied to the peoples of mainland Europe for centuries to come.

BETWEEN A GOTH AND A HARD PLACE

In 552 Justinian I, the emperor of Byzantium, was determined to reconquer Italy from the barbarians. His first object was the city of Ravenna. But his troops were confronted with an almost insuperable problem: they had made their way overland, via the Dalmatian coast on the eastern side of the Adriatic, but were blocked by the barbarian Goths who controlled the mainland to the north of Venice. The only way they could attack and take Ravenna was to bypass the Goths, crossing the lagoon from the town of Grado. Justinian's commander Narsete requested help to transport his men.

Already by this time, the lagoon communities had adopted a practice that was to denote Venetian diplomacy for 1,250-years: staying as far as possible from and, where possible, profiting by, other people's quarrels. Justinian's request presented a dilemma: helping him would be seen as a declaration of war against the Ostrogoths in Ravenna, with whom the lagoon communities had reached a comfortable *modus vivendi* assuring safety on the mainland for their traders. Yet the Eastern emperor was offering vast monetary and political rewards for transporting his troops.

The communities eventually threw in their lot with Byzantium. Justinian conquered Ravenna and marched on to Rome. From this time on the communities of the lagoon became vassals of the Eastern Empire; Venice would remain technically subject to the Byzantine emperors until considerably later than the Sack of Constantinople – an attack led by Venetians – during the Fourth Crusade in 1204.

THE DUCHY AND THE DOGE

It was not until AD 697, under the growing threat of the barbarian Lombards who then controlled the mainland, that the communities scattered around the lagoon – now officially recognised by Byzantium as a duchy – decided to convert their fragile confederation into a stronger, more centralised state. In this year (or maybe not: some historians have dismissed the story as a Venetian myth) they elected one Paoluccio Anafesto to be their first doge, as the

Attila the Hun's stone throne in Torcello.

dukes of Venice became known. Yet right from the beginning *il doge* was very different from the other feudal strongmen of Europe.

In the first application of a system that would be honed into shape over the centuries (*see p15* **Machinery of state**), the doge was elected for life by a council chosen by an assembly that represented all the social groups and trades of the island communities. Technically, therefore, the leadership was elected democratically, although the strongest groups soon formed themselves into a dominant oligarchy. Yet democracy of a kind survived in the system of checks and balances employed to ensure that no single section of the ruling elite got its hands on absolute power. Venetians, fearing the creation of an immovable hereditary monarchy, hedged the office of doge with all kinds of limitations.

The first ducal power struggle took place in 729. The doge in question, Ipato Orso, achieved the duchy's first outstanding military victory when he dislodged Lombard forces from Ravenna. Success, though, went to Orso's head, and he attempted to transform the doge's office into a hereditary monarchy. Civil war racked the lagoon for two years, ending only when a furious mob forced its way into Orso's house and cut his throat. Troubles continued with the two succeeding doges: both were accused of tyranny, and were not only deposed and exiled but also ceremonially blinded.

Despite moments of near-anarchy, the lagoon dwellers were already becoming a commercial power to be seriously reckoned with in the upper Adriatic, the eastern Mediterranean, the Black Sea and North Africa. Craftsmen were sent abroad to Dalmatia and Istria to study the art of shipbuilding; they learnt so swiftly that by the seventh century the construction and fitting out of seagoing vessels had become a thriving industry. Mercantile expansion and technical advances went hand in hand, as tradesmen brought back materials and techniques from afar – especially the Middle and Far East, where technical and scientific culture was far in advance of the West.

'Two succeeding doges accused of tyranny were not only deposed and exiled but also ceremonially blinded.'

In 781 Pepin, son of the Frankish king Charlemagne, invaded Italy and attacked the Lombards. Wariness of mainland struggles still dominated the duchy's policy and it played for time, unsure whether to sacrifice the alliance with Byzantium to this new and powerful player on the European scene. In the end, however, Pepin's designs on Istria and Dalmatia – part of the Venetian sphere of influence – caused relations to turn frosty. Exasperated by the duchy's fence-sitting, Pepin attacked its ally Grado on the mainland, executing its cardinal by hurling him from the town's highest tower. He then proceeded to take all the mainland positions around Venice, and besieged the lagoon communities from the sea.

Enrico Dandolo: old, blind, and supremely cunning. *See p17.*

Machinery of state

The longevity of the Venetian republic was due to a large extent to a finely honed system of checks and balances that kept the powerful merchant aristocracy closely involved in the machinery of state without allowing any one person or dynasty to lord it over the others. Rules, numbers and duties changed. At the end of the 13th century, what had started out as something close to a democracy became an oligarchy, with only members of the 200-odd powerful clans included in the *Libro d'oro* (Golden Book) eligible for office. Later, anyone with the necessary funds could buy into the machinery of state.

The main ruling bodies were:
Collegio dei savi (College of Wise Men) – a group of experts, elected by the *senato*, who staffed special committees to oversee all aspects of internal, marine and war policy.
Consiglio dei dieci (Council of Ten) – appointed by the *senato*, the council's extensive network of spies brought any would-be subversives to a closed-door trial in which defence lawyers were forbidden. In time, the increasingly powerful *Consiglio dei dieci* would have the Inquisition to assist it in its task.
Il doge (the Duke) – elected for life in a complicated, cheat-proof system of multiple ballots, the sumptuously robed Duke of Venice was glorious to behold. He could not, however, indulge in business of his own, receive foreign ambassadors alone, leave Venice without permission, or accept personal gifts. If his city state tired of him,

he could be deposed. With his extended family banned from high office for the term of his reign, many doges hailed from less politically adept Venetian clans. Most, moreover, were very old by the time they donned the *biretta*, the distinctive horned hat – the average age of doges between 1400 and 1570 was 72. However, the doge was the only official privy to all state secrets and eligible to attend all meetings of state organs; he could, if he played his cards right, have a determining effect on Venetian policy.
Maggior consiglio (Great Council) – the Republic's parliament – made up of all voting-age males from the clans included in the *Libro d'oro* – which elected (and provided the candidates for) most other state offices, including that of doge.
Minor consiglio (Lesser Council) – elected by and from the *maggior consiglio*, this six-man team advised – or kept tabs on – the doge.
Pien collegio (Full College) – made up of the *minor consiglio* and the *collegio dei savi*, this became Venice's real government, eventually supplanting the senato.
Quarantie – the three supreme courts; the l40 members were chosen by the *senato*.
Senato (Senate) – known until the late 14th century as the *pregadi*, the *senato* was the upper house of the Venetian parliament; by the 16th century it had some 300 members.
Serenissima signoria (Most Serene Lordships) – the *minor consiglio*, the heads of the three *quarantie* courts and the doge; this body was vested with ultimate executive power.

In the mid eighth century the confederation had moved its capital from Heraclea in the northern lagoon to Malamocco on the Adriatic coast, where it was at the mercy of Frankish naval forces. At this crucial juncture, in 810, a strong leader emerged in the form of an admiral, Angelo Partecipazio. He abandoned the besieged capital of Malamocco; almost overnight the capital was moved to the island archipelago of Rialto in the centre of the lagoon.

Partecipazio's next move was a stroke of military genius. He ordered his fleet to head out of the lagoon through the strait of Malamocco to attack Pepin's ships, then to feign terror and retreat. In hot pursuit, the deep-keeled Frankish ships ran aground on the sandbanks of the lagoon; the locals, with their knowledge of deep-water channels, picked off the crews with ease: thousands were massacred.

THE THEFT OF ST MARK

After his great victory against the Franks, Partecipazio was elected doge. During his reign, work began on a ducal palace on the site of the current one, and the confederation of islands that made up the lagoon duchy was given the name 'Venetia'. Around the same time the flourishing city of Torcello began to decline, as the surrounding lagoon waters silted up and malarial mosquitoes took over.

It was also around this time that Venice set about embroidering a mythology worthy of its ambitions. After Venetian merchants stole the body of St Mark from Alexandria and brought it back with them to their city – traditionally in the year 829 – the city's previous patron, the Byzantine St Theodore, was unceremoniously deposed and the Evangelist – symbolised by a winged lion

Daniele Manin led a final, ill-fated revolt against the Austrians. *See p23.*

History

– set up in his place. A shrine to the saint was erected in the place where St Mark's basilica (*see p78*) would later rise.

Angelo Partecipazio's overwhelming success in both military and civic government led to another tussle for power. Before he died in 827, he made certain that his son Giustiniano would succeed him. When Giustiniano died two years later, his younger brother Giovanni was elected doge, despite dissent and jealousy from rival families. It was a measure of Partecipazio's importance that his surname was to feature repeatedly in the ducal roll of honour over the next century; the family was never allowed to achieve the hegemony that the Medici dynasty enjoyed in Renaissance Florence, though. In Venice, any sign of dynastic ambition was greeted either with banishment or worse; one doge with aspirations beyond the role assigned to him, Pietro Candiano, was thrown to the dogs at the end of the tenth century.

BLIND CUNNING

The development of the vast Venetian empire grew out of the mercantile pragmatism that dominated Venetian political thinking. They embarked upon territorial expansion for two main reasons: to secure safe shipping routes and to create permanent trading bases. Harassed by Slav pirates in the upper Adriatic, the Venetians established bases around the area from which to attack the pirate ships: gradually they took over the ports of Grado and Trieste, then expanded along the coastlines of Istria and Dalmatia. In some cases, Venetian protection against pirates was requested; in others, 'help' arrived unbidden – though it was often less than helpful.

With the coast well defended, the Venetians rarely bothered to expand their territories into the hinterland. There was, for many centuries, a certain mistrust of *terra firma*; Venetian citizens were not even allowed to own land outside the lagoon until 1345.

The crusades presented Venice with its greatest opportunity yet for expanding trade routes while reaping a profit. Transporting crusaders to the Holy Land became big business for the city. More importantly, the naïve crusaders were easy prey for the professional generals – the *condottieri* – who commanded Venice's army of highly trained mercenaries: the eager defenders of the faith were, as often as not, used to extend and consolidate the Venetian empire. Never was this more true than in the case of the Fourth Crusade, which set off proudly from Venice in 1202 to reconquer Jerusalem. The Venetian war fleet was under the command of Doge Enrico Dandolo who, though 80 and completely blind,

was a supremely cunning leader, outstanding tactician and accomplished diplomat. Other European crusader leaders were persuaded to take time out to conquer the strategic Adriatic port of Zara, thus assuring Venice's control of much of the Dalmatian coastline. Even more surprisingly, they allowed themselves to be talked into attacking Constantinople.

Venice's special relationship with the Eastern Empire had always had its ups and downs. In 1081 and 1082 Venice had done the Byzantine emperor a favour when it trounced menacing Normans in the southern Adriatic; they were granted duty-free trading rights throughout the Empire in return. But in 1149 those trading privileges were withdrawn in disgust at Venetian arrogance during a siege of Corfu.

As the Fourth Crusade set out, Dandolo saw that this was an ideal opportunity to remove the Byzantine challenge to Venetian trade hegemony once and for all. He pulled the wool over his fellow crusaders' eyes, with the apparently noble argument that the Eastern emperor must be ousted and replaced by someone willing to reunite the eastern Orthodox and western Roman churches.

They acquiesced, but there was nothing noble about the brutal, bloody, Venetian-led sacking of the city on 13 April 1204, nor about the horrendous pillaging that ensued. Far outstripping their colleagues in greed and callousness, the Venetians looted the city's greatest treasures, including the celebrated quartet of antique Greek horses that was transported back to Venice and placed above the entrance of St Mark's basilica. Innumerable other artefacts – jewellery, enamels, golden chalices, statuary, columns, precious marbles and much more – were plundered: they are now an inseparable part of the fabric of the *palazzi* and churches of Venice.

But the booty was only a minor consideration for the Venetians and their pragmatic doge: the real prize was the one handed out when the routed Byzantine empire was carved up. The Venetians were not interested in grabbing huge swathes of territory that they knew they couldn't hold. This was left to the French and German knights, who, indeed, lost it within a few decades. Putting their intimate knowledge of eastern trade routes to excellent use, the Venetians hand-picked those islands and ports that could guarantee their merchant ships a safe passage from Venice to the Black Sea and back. These included almost all the main ports on the Dalmatian coast, certain strategic Greek islands, the Sea of Marmara and a number of strategic Black Sea ports.

For many years after the conquest of Constantinople, Venetian ships could sail from

La virtuosissima cantatrice

Barbara Strozzi was born in Venice in 1619, the illegitimate offspring of Giulio Strozzi who named her as his adoptive heir in his will. Giulio – himself the illegitimate son of one of Florence's powerful Strozzi clan – was a member of a leading intellectual circle, the *Accademia degli incogniti*, and a champion of education for women; he arranged for his musically gifted daughter to study under Francesco Cavalli, a *maestro di cappella* at St Mark's and a leading composer of the popular new genre – opera.

Barbara played the *viola da gamba* – a forerunner of the 'cello – but it was for her extraordinary soprano voice that she was best known. Indeed, her father formed a new club for music-lovers – called the *Accademia degli unisoni* – at which Barbara was the main attraction.

Which of her attractions were the biggest draw remains a moot point: a portrait of her by Genoese painter Bernardo Strozzi (no relation) shows a dishevelled Barbara with a precipitous *decolleté* which has led some historians to presume that she was a courtesan much along the lines of Veronica Franco (*see p21* **La più onorata cortigiana**). But Barbara lived at home with her parents until their deaths, and had four children by the same father – whom, admittedly, she never married – Giovanni Paolo Vidman.

More importantly, she dedicated what free time she had to churning out an impressive body of music: recitatives, arias, ariettas, madrigals and cantatas, mostly for soprano voices. Though 125 pieces still remain, many more are known to have been lost. Dedications of her works to the Austrian Emperor Ferdinand II, to the Duke of Mantua and to the Grand Duchess of Tuscany bear witness to her fame in her day.

Popular composer Nicolò Fontei, on the other hand, dedicated his first collection of *Bizzarrie poetiche* to Barbara in 1635, describing her as *la virtuossimima cantatrice* (the most virtuosic – and virtuous – singer).

Venice to Byzantium without ever leaving waters controlled by the city. The Serene Republic, *La Serenissima*, had finally become a major imperial power. The city marked the turn of events by conferring a new title upon its doge: *Quartae Partis et Dimidiae Totius Imperii Romaniae Dominator* – Lord of a Quarter and Half a Quarter of the Roman Empire.

AGE OF UPRISINGS

In 1297, in what came to be known as the *Serrata del Maggior Consiglio*, the leaders of the Venetian merchant aristocracy decided to limit entry to the Grand Council to those families already in the club. Membership of the *maggior consiglio* was restricted to those who had held a seat there in the previous four years, or to descendants of those who had belonged at any point since 1172. Under these rules, only around 150 extended families were eligible for a place, but the number of council members leapt to some 1,200.

Up-and-coming clans were understandably indignant at the thought of being forever excluded from power and from a coveted place in the *Libro d'oro* – the Golden Book – of the Venetian aristocracy. In 1310 a prosperous merchant, Baiamonte Tiepolo, harnessed the growing discontent in a rebellion against the aristocratic oligarchy. Had Tiepolo's standard-bearer not been felled by a loose brick knocked carelessly out of its place by an old lady watching the shenanigans from her window in the Merceria, the uprising may have succeeded. However, as it was, his troops fled in panic, and the uprising was savagely crushed, and the much-feared Council of Ten was granted draconian police and judicial powers. An extensive network of spies and informers was set up to suppress any future plots.

In 1354 Doge Marino Faliero made a bid to undermine the powers of the Venetian oligarchy while increasing and consolidating his own powers as a permanent hereditary leader. This plot too was mercilessly suppressed and Faliero was beheaded.

LAVISH LOVE AND LUXURY

The Council of Ten – along with the Venetian Inquisition that was also established after the Tiepolo plot of 1310 – wielded its special powers most effectively after the Faliero incident, ensuring that this was the last serious attempt to attack the principle of rule by elite. It was at this time that lion's-head postboxes first appeared at strategic points around the city: Venetians were encouraged to drop written reports of any questionable activity that they noticed through their marble mouths.

While Venice's mercantile power was at its zenith from the 13th to the 15th centuries, vast fortunes were built up and lavished on building, furnishing and decorating great *palazzi* and churches. It was at this time that the city took on the architectural form still visible today. For sheer luxury, Venice's lifestyle was unequalled anywhere else in Europe.

In the 14th and 15th centuries Venice was one of the largest cities in Europe, with an estimated population of between 150,000 and 200,000, many connected with the city's booming mercantile activities. International visitors were generally astounded by *La Serenissima*'s legendary opulence and phenomenal economic dynamism.

'Venetians were dedicated to love and earthly pleasures; nuns were banned from going out at night in ordinary clothes.'

The salt which had been the mainstay of Venice's economy in the early days had long ceased to be Venice's main trading commodity. When ships set sail from Venice for the Middle East, their holds were crammed with Istrian pine wood, iron ore, cereals, wool and salted and preserved meats. These were traded for finely woven textiles, exotic carpets, perfumes, gold and silverware, spices, precious stones of all kinds, ivory, wax and slaves: with a virtual monopoly on all these much sought after commodities, Venice was able to act as broker and sell them on to the rest of Europe's moneyed-classes at enormous profit.

The Venetian aristocracy certainly liked to live in comfort. 'The luxury of any ordinary Venetian house,' wrote one traveller in 1492, 'is so extraordinary that in any other city or country it would be sufficient to decorate a royal palace.' Domestic luxury was not confined to the city. The Venetians were also investing huge amounts of money in their summer villas on the mainland, which often surpassed their city establishments in magnificence, designed and decorated as they were by the leading Veneto architects and painters.

Venetians lavished the same kind of attention on their appearance. Fortunes were spent on the richest and most gorgeous textiles and jewellery. Venetian women were famous for the unbridled luxury of their clothing, of their furs and of their fabrics woven with gold and silver thread. Their perfumes and cosmetics were the envy of all Europe, as were the beauty and fascination of the courtesans (*see p21* **La Più onorata cortigiana**) who dominated much of the social and cultural life of the city.

So dedicated were Venetians to the cult of love and earthly pleasures, that the Patriarch, Venice's cardinal, was compelled to issue orders forbidding the city's nuns from going out on the town at night in ordinary clothes.

Sumptuous festivals of music, theatre and dance were almost daily occurrences during these wild times. The visit of a foreign ruler, a wedding or funeral of a member of the aristocracy, a religious festival, a naval or military victory, or delivery from an epidemic – all these were excuses for public celebrations involving days of festivities and huge sums of money. The city's foreign communities – Jews, Armenians, Turks, Germans, French and Mongols, many of them permanent residents in this truly cosmopolitan city – would also celebrate their national or religious feast days with enormous pomp.

Despite the wealth of the city and the full employment created by its many trades and industries (at full stretch, the shipyard was capable of launching one fully equipped ship every day), life was not easy for the city's poorest residents, who often lived in damp, filthy conditions. Epidemics of disease were also frequent: indeed, more than half the city's population is estimated to have died in the Black Death of 1348-9. Partly as a result, social tension and discontent were rife.

Francesco Morosini: a brilliant strategist. *See p23.*

GENOESE JEALOUSY

Meanwhile the enormous wealth of the Venetian Republic and its rapidly expanding empire inevitably provoked jealousy among the other trading nations of the Mediterranean – above all with the powerful city state of Genoa, Venice's main rival to trade with the East.

In 1261 the Genoese had clashed with the Venetians when the former obliged the Byzantine emperor by helping to evict Venice's high-handed merchants from Constantinople. Skirmishes between the two Italian powers continued throughout most of the 14th century, regularly flaring up into major battles or periods of open warfare, and often resulting in disastrous defeats for Venice.

By 1379 the situation had become desperate for *La Serenissima*. The Genoese fleet and army had moved into the Gulf of Venice in the upper Adriatic and, after a long siege, had taken Chioggia, at the southern end of the lagoon. From here the Genoese attacked and occupied much of the lagoon, including Malamocco and the passage to the open sea. Venice was under siege and began to starve.

Then, in 1380, the city worked another of its miracles of level-headed cunning. Almost the whole of the Genoese fleet was anchored inside the fortified harbour of Chioggia. Vittor Pisani, the admiral of the Venetian fleet, ordered hundreds of small boats to be filled with rocks. Panicked by a surprise Venetian attack on the mouth of the port, the Genoese failed to notice that the small boats were being sunk in the shallow port entrance, preventing any escape. The tables had been well and truly turned, and Venice besieged the trapped Genoese fleet until it was forced to surrender unconditionally. Genoa's days as a great naval power were over, and Venice exulted.

Ironically, however, this victory was to spell the beginning of the end for *La Serenissima*. For though the Republic had reached the climax of its prosperity and had re-acquired its supremacy in the East, concentrating its energies on fighting Genoa was to prove a bad foreign policy mistake. Venice's leaders badly underestimated the threat posed by the emergence of the Turks as a military power in Asia Minor and the Black Sea area. Convinced – wrongly and ultimately fatally – that diplomacy was the way to deal with the threat from the East, Venice turned its attention to conquering other powers on the Italian mainland.

VENETIAN EXPANSION

For centuries Venice had followed a conscious policy of steady neutrality towards the various powers that had carved up the Italian mainland. The European political upheavals from the end of the 12th century to the end of the 14th century put paid to that neutrality. The bitter rivalry between Venice and the other Italian maritime states, especially Pisa and Genoa, inevitably brought it into conflict with their powerful mainland allies: the Pope, the Scaligera dukes of Verona and a succession of Holy Roman emperors.

The defeat of the vast Scaligera empire (which included much of the Venetian hinterland) by Count Gian Galeazzo Visconti of Milan in 1387 brought the Milanese much too close to the lagoon for comfort. It was not only Venetian security which was under threat, but also access to all-important trade routes through north-eastern Italy and across the Alps into northern Europe beyond. Venice began a series of wars that led to the conquest of Verona and its enormous territories in 1405, and also of Padua, Vicenza and a number of other significant towns.

By 1420 Venice had annexed Friuli and Udine; by 1441 *La Serenissima* controlled Brescia, Bergamo, Cremona and Ravenna. The land campaign continued until 1454, when Venice signed a peace treaty with Milanese ruler Francesco Sforza. Though Ravenna soon slipped from Venice's grasp, the rest of the Republic's immense mainland territories were to remain more or less intact for almost 300 years.

Lodovico Manin: threw in his hat.
See p23.

La più onorata cortigiana

It's estimated that at one point in the 16th century, 12,000 of Venice's 100,000 residents were prostitutes. Perhaps it was to be expected, then, than such a significant social grouping should break down into sub-classes. At the very top of the pyramid – living lives which differed from those of other wealthy women only in the small matter of virtue – were *le più honorate cortigiane*: 'most honoured courtesans'.

In a world where wives were part and parcel of mercantile dealings, bringing dowries and/or prestige, and haggled over in the matrimonial market place, it was to the honoured courtesans that rich Venetian men turned for cultured company and entertainment, as well as sex.

Veronica Franco made her appearance in the *Catalogo di tutte le principale et più honorate cortigiane di Venezia* in 1565, when she was 20. Her fees, the catalogue stated, were to be paid to her mother. By that time, she had married, had a child and left her husband, demanding her dowry back so that she could set up her own household.

A well-read polyglot and skilled player of the spinnet and lute, Veronica published poetry and other writings that rubbished the concept of ideal love for an ideal woman – so popular since Petrarch – in favour of a more down-to-earth assessment of the lot of women, and in particular those women who earn their own way with their wits.

So highly esteemed was this meretrix that France's King Henri III sought her company when he visited Venice in 1573. But her most assiduous patron was Domenico Venier, a nobleman whose literary salon was the city's most renowned and illustrious. Venier stood by her when she was driven from Venice during a bout of plague in 1577, when superstitious locals alleged the disease was punishment for the city's vices. (Her absence gave those same locals a chance to ransack her richly-appointed home.) And he spoke in her defence in 1580 when the Inquisition charged her with, and acquitted her of, witchcraft .

It's not clear what happened to Veronica between Venier's death in 1582 and her own in 1610. Deprived of her wealth and of her patron, she no doubt discovered the other feature that set the courtesan apart from the 'honest' married woman: security.

PORTUGUESE SPICE THINGS UP

Even as Venice expanded its operations on the mainland, events were conspiring to bring *La Serenissima*'s reign as a political power and trading giant to a close. In 1453 the Ottoman Turks swept into Constantinople, and Venice's crucial trading privileges in the former Byzantine Empire were almost totally lost. In 1487 Vasco da Gama rounded the Cape of Good Hope; in 1489 he became the first European to reach Calcutta by sea, shattering Venice's monopoly on the riches of the East. The arrival of Portuguese ships laden with spices and textiles in Portuguese ports caused a sensation in Europe and despair in Venice. The Venetians hastily drew up plans to open a canal at Suez to beat the Portuguese at their own game, but the project came to nothing.

Instead, cushioned by the spoils and profits of centuries and exhausted by 100 years of almost constant military campaigning, the city sank slowly over the next two centuries into dissipation and decline.

But, as was only to be expected from a city as lavish as Venice, the decline was glorious. For most of the 16th century few Venetians behaved as if the writing were on the wall. Such was the enormous wealth of the city that the economic fall-out from the Turks' inexorable progress through the Middle East went almost unnoticed at first. Profits were not as massive as before, but the rich remained very rich and the setbacks in the East were partly counterbalanced by exploitation of the newly acquired *terra firma* territories.

As revenue gradually declined through the 16th century, spending on life's little pleasures increased, producing an explosion of art, architecture and music. Titian, Tintoretto, Veronese and Giorgione were hard at work in the city (*see chapter* **Venetian Painting**). Meanwhile, Palladio (*see p266* **Andrea Palladio**), Sanmicheli and Scamozzi were changing the face of architecture (*see chapter* **Architecture**) and *litterati* dazzled with their wit and learning in elite clubs such as the Accademia degli Incogniti. The city rang with music, by composers raging from the Gabrielis (*see p41*) whose fame was Europe-wide, to Venetian prodigies such as Barbara Strozzi (*see p18* **La virtuosissima cantatrice**).

On the mainland, however, Venice's arrogant annexation of territory had not been forgotten by the powers that had suffered at her hands.

When Venice took advantage of the French invasion of Italy in the final years of the 15th century to extend its territories still further, the Habsburgs, France, Spain and the papacy were so incensed that they clubbed together to form the League of Cambrai, with the sole aim of annihilating Venice.

They came very close to doing so. One Venetian military rout followed another, a number of Venetian-controlled cities defected to the enemy, and others that did not were laid waste by the hostile forces. Only squabbling within the League of Cambrai stopped Venice itself from being besieged. By 1516 the alliance had fallen to pieces and Venice had regained almost all its territories.

TURKISH DELIGHT

Its coffers almost empty, its mainland dominions in tatters, Venice was now forced to take stock of the damage that was being done by the Turks. A short-sighted policy of trying to keep the Ottoman Empire at bay by diplomacy had already had devastating effects on Venice's once-supreme position in the eastern Mediterranean.

In 1497, as the Ottomans stormed through the Balkans, coming almost within sight of the bell towers of Venice, *La Serenissima* had been obliged to give up several Aegean islands and the port of Negroponte; two years later it lost its forts in the Peloponnese, giving the Turks virtually total control of the southern end of the

Adriatic. And if Venice felt jubilant about securing Cyprus in 1489 – won by pressuring the king's Venetian widow Caterina Cornaro into bequeathing control of the island – the legacy was marred by the side-effect fact that it involved the Republic in almost constant warfare to keep the Turks away from this strategically vital strip of land.

In 1517 Syria and Egypt fell to the Turks; Rhodes followed in 1522; and by 1529 the Ottoman Empire had spread across the southern Mediterranean as far as Morocco. The frightened European powers turned to Venice to help repulse the common foe. But mistrust of the lagoon republic by its new allies was deep and, in their determination to keep Venice from deriving too much financial profit from the war against the Turks, the campaign itself was botched.

In 1538 a Christian fleet was trounced at Preveza in western Greece; in 1571 Venice led a huge European fleet to victory against hundreds of Turkish warships in the Battle of Lepanto, in what is now the Gulf of Corinth. But despite the massive propaganda campaign of self-congratulation and self-glorification that followed, it became apparent that the victory was hollow and that the Turks were as strong as ever. In a treaty signed after the battle in 1573, Venice was forced ignominiously to hand over Cyprus, its second-last major possession in the eastern Mediterranean. (Crete, the final one, held out until 1669.)

Venetians rise up against the Austrians. *See p23.*

TRADE DEFICIT

By the 17th century Venice was no longer under any illusion about the gravity of its crisis. The *Savi alla Mercanzia* (state trading commission) noted on 5 July 1610 that 'Our commerce and shipping in the West are completely destroyed. In the East only a few businesses are still functioning and they are riddled with debt, without ships and getting weaker by the day. Moreover, and this must be emphasised, only a small quantity of goods is arriving in our city, and it is becoming increasingly difficult to find buyers for them. The nations which used to buy from us now have established their businesses elsewhere. We are facing the almost total annihilation of our commerce.'

> **'These moments of glory, celebrated with colossal pomp and ceremony in Venice itself, were invariably short-lived.'**

Venice was down but not quite out. In 1617 a successful campaign was fought against the Uskoks – pirates financed by the Austrian Habsburg rulers in Istria and the Dalmatian coast; in the process, some resounding blows were struck against the Turks of the region too. Between 1681 and 1687 Francesco Morosini, the brilliant strategist then in command of the Venetian fleet, reconquered much of the territory taken by the Turks in the preceding century, including Crete and the Peloponnese. But these moments of glory, celebrated with colossal pomp and ceremony in Venice itself, were invariably short-lived.

Exhausted by debts and the sheer effort of its naval campaigns, the Venetian Republic lacked the resources needed to consolidate its victories. In 1699 the Treaty of Carlowitz had rewarded Francesco Morosini's naval and military victories, restoring much of Venice's possessions in the East and many of its trading privileges. But by 1718 the Republic was struggling to keep its head above water as the Austrians and Turks forced it to cede most of its gains in the humiliating Treaty of Passarowitz.

By the time the Venezia Trionfante café (now Caffè Florian, *see p171*) opened for business in piazza San Marco in 1720, the Republic was virtually bankrupt; its governing nobility had grown decadent and politically inert. But decadence was good for the city's growing status as the party capital of Europe.

Aristocratic women of all ages and marital states were accompanied in their gadding by handsome young *cisibei* (male escorts), whose professions of chastity fooled nobody. Masked nuns were a common sight at the city's gambling houses and theatres; party-pooping church officials who tried to confine nuns to barracks at the convent by the church of San Zaccaria would be met with a barrage of bricks.

Priests too were not slow to join in the fun: composer-prelate Antonio Vivaldi's supposed affairs with members of his famous female choir were well publicised (*see p99* **Vivaldi walk**). Father Lorenzo Da Ponte (*see p229* **Mozart's libertine librettist**), Mozart's great Venetian librettist, was better known for his amorous conquests than for his sanctity. And though Giacomo Casanova, the embodiment of sexual excess, never actually donned a cassock, he had been a promising student of theology before he realised where his true vocation lay.

THROWING IN THE CAP

Bankrupt, politically and ideologically stagnant and no longer a threat to its former enemies, Venice directed its final heroic effort to survive not against those erstwhile foes but against the forces of nature. Even as Napoleon prepared to invade Venice in 1797, the city was spending the meagre funds left in its coffers on building the vast *murazzi*, the long stone and marble dyke designed to protect the city from the worst ravages of unpredictable Adriatic tides.

On 12 May 1797 the last doge, Lodovico Manin, was deposed by the French who, even before the Republic bowed to the inevitable and voted itself out of existence, had handed control of the lagoon city over to Austria. Manin gave his doge's cap to the victors, saying, 'Take this, I don't think I'll be needing it any more.'

In 1805 Napoleon absorbed Venice back into his Kingdom of Italy. Until 1815, when the French emperor's star waned and Venice once again found itself back under Austrian control, Napoleon's Venetian plenipotentiaries were given free rein to dismantle churches, dissolve monasteries and redesign bits of the city, including the wide thoroughfare now known as via Garibaldi and its adjoining public gardens.

The last spark of Venice's ancient independent spirit flared up in 1848, when lawyer Daniele Manin (no relation of the last doge) led a popular revolt against the Austrians. An independent republican government was set up, holding out valiantly against siege for five heroic months. It was doomed to failure from the outset, however, and the Austrians were soon firmly back in the saddle, keeping their grip on this insignificant backwater until 1866, when a weakened Austria, badly beaten on other fronts by the Prussians, handed the city over to the newly united kingdom of Italy.

Venice's visitors follow predictable routes.

Venice Today

A city keeping its head above the water.

In a June 2006 article in the *Financial Times*, respected UK economist John Kay argued that Venice could only be saved by Disney – or some corporation with a solid grasp of organising tourist masses. Irate Venetians threw their hands up in horror, Venice habitués moaned in despair. But here and there there were self-satisfied smirks. For beneath the headline-grabbing rhetoric, Kay had put his finger in a long-festering wound: how can a city which relies almost totally on tourism for its livelihood be quite so bad at handling tourists?

'Venice is already a theme park,' Kay argued. 'As a centre of business, politics and culture, it died centuries ago and only the flow of visitors brought it back to life. Today, most people in the city are tourists and most people who work there have come for the day to service the needs of tourists... The economics of the city are the economics of Yosemite and Disneyland, not the economics of Bologna or Los Angeles.'

This is, in part, a gross over-simplification. Most people in Venice at any given moment are Venetian residents. A new generation of young professionals finds this unique city very congenial for their IT- or design-oriented purposes. And people *do* (occasionally) come to Venice for reasons other than tourism.

But lose yourself in the St Mark's square maelstrom, and you'd never know it. Or wander across the Rialto bridge and along the road at its north-western foot and you may find yourself asking what *are* these mounds of the tackiest possible souvenirs doing in one of the world's most perfectly preserved artistic and architectural treasure troves?

Is it inertia, or are the City Fathers actively encouraging the kind of hit-and-run tourism in which droves of package-tour day-trippers are herded into the most heavily touristed spots in the *centro storico*, never ploughing any more back into the local economy than the price of a musical plastic gondola? Even those visitors who choose to bed down in *La Serenissima* stay for an average 2.5 days, against a considerably healthier average in Rome of 3.5 days.

Cynics might say that this state of affairs suits Venetians, for whom St Mark's square is another country, and who know alternative routes into the glorious fruit, vegetable and fish market that lurks just behind the Rialto. Having utterly predictable madding crowds in easily avoidable areas means they can get on with life.

Mask maker Sergio Boldrin has a shop by the Rialto but returns home to a very different world: 'The tourists are only on a few *calli*, the main arteries. Where I live, over in Santa Marta, many people never see a tourist except when they ride the vaporetto. There are people in my neighbourhood who get to piazza San Marco once a year.'

One exasperated hotelier describes arriving over an hour late for an appointment because bewildered tourists hampered her progress on the raised walkways put up during *acqua alta*. There's no point arguing that in Rome or Naples, traffic snarl-ups, protest marches and transport strikes make getting to appointments on time well-nigh impossible several times a week. 'That's different,' she snaps, hissing with rage. 'This is Venice!'

And indeed it is. It's a city that raises problems that few are willing to address; a city that lives on tourism but considers its visitors annoying obstacles; of unimaginable beauty with no quality control; a Byzantine-Gothic-Renaissance city which would like to present a contemporary front but which backs down at the last moment (*see p36* **Where are they now?**); and that, despite these drawbacks, continues to be the most captivating, most breath-takingly beautiful on the globe.

ACROSS THE WATER

Beyond island Venice is another world again, that of the Veneto. While *La Serenissima* continues to hold the world in her thrall, the *terra firma* side of the lagoon has come quietly but steadily into its own. And besides being one of Italy's biggest economic success stories, it now has a burgeoning tourist industry as well. Visitors spent more than 50 million nights in the hotels and alternative accommodation of the Veneto region in 2003; this figure is expected to rise over the next few years, to make the Veneto Italy's most visited region – with Venice itself drawing only a fraction of the total.

The success story of Venice and the Veneto is a very recent one. Venice had slipped far into decline before the city capitulated to Napoleon's troops in 1797, putting an end to the longest-running independent republic in history – more than 1,000 years. Under Austrian rule (1815-66), it was relegated to the status of a picturesque, inconsequential backwater. But if the city suffered, the fate of its former mainland territories was even worse: with no industry to speak of, and agriculturally behind the times, the Veneto ran the semi-feudal south a close race for the title of Italy's own Third World. Between 1876 and 1901, almost 35 per cent of the 5.2 million desperate Italians who sought a better life abroad were fleeing from the crushing poverty of the Veneto and the neighbouring Friuli region.

Massive industrialisation in Venice's mainland Porto Marghera area after World War I and – more extensively – World War II shifted the more impoverished sectors of the population from agricultural to urban areas. But the poverty remained. As recently as 1961, 48 per cent of homes in the north-east had no running water, 72 per cent had no bathroom and 86 per cent had no heating.

What the people of the Veneto did have, however, was a deep-rooted attachment to their traditional crafts, and a cussedness of character unmatched anywhere else in Italy. In the past both proved detrimental: when captains of heavy industry sought meek vassals to man the furnaces, many of the natives of the Veneto who protested were forcibly deported to populate Fascist new towns in the malarial swamps south of Rome.

RIDING OUT THE BAD TIMES

It was not, in fact, until the 1970s that north-eastern determination came into its own. With a growing trend towards industrial downscaling, those family-run workshops that had ridden out the bad times gradually became viable business concerns. Giuliana Benetton's humble knitting machine gave birth to a global clothing empire centred in Treviso; the metalworking lessons that Leonardo del Vecchio learned in an orphanage spawned Luxottica, the world's biggest producer of spectacle frames, based in Belluno; and Ivano Beggio progressed from tinkering with bikes in his father's cycle shop in Noale to running Aprilia, one of Europe's largest manufacturers of motorcycles and scooters. Through the mid to late 1990s a third of the country's huge balance of trade surplus was generated in the north-east and the region now boasts some of Italy's lowest unemployment rates – under five per cent.

The 21st century has seen a slight tarnishing of the Veneto's Midas touch. The competitive edge for exports created by a weak lira was lost with the introduction of the single European currency. Crippling labour costs have forced many businesses to relocate to eastern Europe and a manpower shortfall has been bridged by hiring immigrant workers (in 2005, 11 per cent of the Veneto's workforce was non-Italian), resulting in an unprecedented ethnic pot pourri: learning to live with social and cultural differences is one of the biggest challenges the famously insular Veneto must face today.

The post-war parabola described by island Venice, which for centuries was one of the richest commercial centres in the world, was, if anything, bleaker. As the *terra firma* became industrialised, blue-collar workers looked across the water for employment. Realising housing on the mainland was cheaper, drier and easier to park in front of, they moved out in an exodus that brought the resident population of island Venice plunging from around 170,000 in 1946 to less than 62,000 today.

For an area about the size of New York's Central Park, however, that's still a respectable figure. Few such small cities, moreover, can lay claim to a population comprising gondoliers, mask makers, glass-blowers, fishermen, monks, nuns, musicians, artists, writers, architects, historians, academics, restoration experts and many of Italy's rich and famous. Add to that a sizeable student population, a dedicated group of expats and part-time residents and the result is a solid base of 'locals' that gives Venice its distinct flavour.

Because there *is* a 'real' city where Venice-worshipping residents are prepared to persevere – despite exorbitant prices, grocers turning into mask shops and the chance that *acqua alta* may cause irreparable damage to their carpets.

And there *are* initiatives under way to keep Venice above water – both literally and figuratively – in the 21st century. For every headline-grabbing problem project – Santiago Calatrava's fourth bridge over the Grand Canal (constantly postponed), David Chipperfield's San Michele cemetery island refurbishment/extension (years behind schedule), the Miralles-Tagliabue makeover of the old port area (postponed indefinitely?), the underground train line from the airport to the Fondamenta Nuove (shelved?), the MoSE moveable flood barriers at the mouths of the lagoon (one of Italy longest-running stop-go farces) – others carry on with no fanfare and much success. Take Insula (www.insula.it) for example: a consortium that has doggedly worked its way around Venice since 1997, dredging clogged canals, removing hundreds of thousands of cubic metres of mud, and rebuilding footpaths in a quiet but positive maintenance programme on this 'sinking' city.

(VERY) SMALL BLESSINGS

On the mainland too things are on the move. In Mestre, the piazza and *campanile* have been restored. Among the high-tech businesses attracted to the rapidly developing Venice Gateway for Science and Technology park (VEGA) at the northern end of Porto Marghera, is a nanotechnologies laboratory, placing Venice in the running for title of world leader in the technology that manipulates matter on a scale below 100 nanometres. Equally impressive, San Giuliano (*see p329* **Not Venice but trying**) has been converted from a dumping ground for industrial and urban waste into the largest city park in Europe.

Dazzled, disorientated and besieged by pigeons, the average visitor to *La Serenissima* may not even realise that a traipse from St Mark's to the Rialto tells them as much about the city as a guided tour of the Tower of London or a lift to the top of the Empire State Building tell about those other great metropoli. Much of Venetian life takes place behind closed doors, concealed from the casual observer.

Venetians have always maintained their unique code of conduct and ethics, their particular sense of time and place. An isolated culture, hedged about by water, one that remained an independent republic for over a millennium, one that once lorded it over the entire Mediterranean, cannot be easily penetrated by an outsider, although everyone and anyone is welcome to try. Otherwise, feel free to sit back and enjoy the show.

Venice by numbers

	1990	2000	2002	2005
Population – *centro storico*	78,165	66,386		61,820
Population – all Venice	317,837	275,368		268,980
Population – Veneto region (01)			4,527,694	
Hotels – *centro storico*		205	209	226
Hotel beds – *centro storico*		11,997	12,118	13,512
Foreign tourists in hotels – *centro storico* (average stay)		1,197,643 (2.31 days)	1,121,632 (2.35)	1,336,356 (2.51 days)
Total tourists in hotels – *centro storico* (average stay)				1,521,062 (2.5 days)
Tourists in hotels etc – *centro storico*	1,250,840			1,902,470
Tourists in hotels etc – all Venice	2,550,004			3,237,620
Total tourists – Veneto region		11,504,835		12,468,600
Tides above 80cm		81	108	61
Tides above 100cm		19	19	2

Sebastiano del Piombo's
San Giovanni Cristostomo. See p31.

Venetian Painting

Artists so great they name cocktails after them.

Venetian pride takes many forms. Locals know their dialect to be the wittiest in Italy, and are confident in the superiority of their cuisine and stand-up rowing. Without self-consciousness, Venetians still speak in the first-person plural about defeating the Turks at Lepanto (1571; *see p22*) or building the church of the Salute in gratitude for the end of the plague (1630).

But their pride in their painters goes even deeper. Venetian gastronomic specialities – from the Bellini to *carpaccio* – are named after local artists. Parishioners shed tears of joy when an altarpiece like Giovanni Bellini's in San Zaccaria (*see p96*) returns home after a lengthy period *in restauro*. And a rich literature of art writing, stretching from Ludovico Dolce in 1557 to the learned professors at the Università di Ca' Foscari publishing today, assuredly asserts the supremacy of Venetian *colorito* (colouring) over Florentine *disegno*.

But appreciation for this rich tradition needn't be restricted to Venetian citizens. Thanks to significantly longer opening hours in churches and museums, determined travellers can today understand with relative ease the reasons for such bursting pride.

One element in the effectiveness of Venetian painting is that many great pictures remain in the buildings for which they were painted. The attentive art pilgrim can maximise enjoyment by observing carefully a painting's technique and its setting, since the two are intertwined more in Venice than almost anywhere else on the globe. Leave the madding crowd at San Marco behind, and you'll soon come across superb pictures in obscure churches: glowing altarpieces and pulsating canvas *laterali*

► For artistic terms, *see p304* **Glossary**.

In Context

(paintings for side walls of chapels). Seeing these pictures in their original sites reveals how aware painters were of the relation of their works to the surrounding architecture, light and existing artwork. Yet, exceptionally, the paintings also relate to the physical context of Venice itself. What makes Venetian painting distinctive – the decorated surfaces, asymmetry, shimmering light effects and, above all, warm tonalities – can also be found in the lagoon environment. Renaissance Venice's visual culture encompassed the richness of Islamic art and Byzantine mosaics, the haphazard arrangement of streets and canals with their strong shadows, and light experienced through haze or reflected off moving water.

THE END OF ANONYMITY

Venetian church interiors were once covered with frescoes; the damp climate means that very few of these earliest works survive today. The official history of Venetian painting begins in the 1320s with the first painter to emerge from medieval anonymity, **Paolo Veneziano** (c1290-1362), who worked in egg tempera and gold leaf on wood panel. He championed the composite altarpiece, which would become one of the key formats of Venetian painting. His polyptychs, such as the newly cleaned *The Coronation of the Virgin* in the Accademia gallery (*see p132*), were ornately framed, compartmentalised works featuring sumptuous fabrics, a preference for surface decoration and pattern over depth, and a seriousness – or stiffness – derived from Byzantine icons. A love of drapery and textile patterns proved to be a Venetian constant, still visible in Veronese's paintings in the 16th century and even beyond that in Tiepolo's 18th century works.

Although many painters worked in Venice in the century after Paolo, the next major legacy was that of a team, **Giovanni d'Alemagna** (John of Germany) and his brother-in-law **Antonio Vivarini**, active in the mid 15th century. Their three altarpieces in San Zaccaria (*see p96*) dated 1443, one in San Pantalon (*see p124*) and an imposing canvas triptych in the Accademia demonstrate the transition from Gothic to Renaissance. All have benefited from recent restorations that recapture the original courtly elegance and three-dimensional details in *pastiglia* (raised ornament).

Although Italian art historians give precedence to Antonio, the sudden decline in the quality of his works after Giovanni's death in 1450 suggests his partner was the brains behind the operation. Antonio's younger brother **Bartolomeo Vivarini**, who ran the family workshop from the 1470s until about 1491, learned Renaissance style from both

Tiepolo was the greatest painter of the Venetian rococo. *See p33.*

painting and sculpture, as seen in the lapidary figures in the altarpiece (1474) in the Cappella Corner of the Frari (*see p123*).

By the next generation, the main players had become more clearly defined. From around 1480 **Giovanni Bellini** directed the dominant workshop in Venice. Most of Bellini's sizeable output, stretching from the late 1450s until his death in 1516, was painted on wood panel rather than the newer canvas. He cornered the market in small, devotional panels commissioned by cultivated private clients.

The important group of early Bellini pictures in the Museo Correr (*see p83*) and the many variations on the Madonna and Child theme in the Accademia show how varied and moving these subjects could be.

Equally impressive is Bellini's stunning series of altarpieces. In these he perfected the subject of the *Sacra conversazione* (Sacred Conversation), where standing saints flank a seated figure, usually the Virgin Mary, within a setting that evokes the gold mosaics and costly marbles of the Basilica di San Marco (*see p78*). The inner glow afforded by the new medium of oil paint allowed Bellini to model his figures with an astonishing delicacy of light and shadow. One can follow his progress through a series of altarpieces that remain *in situ*: in Santi Giovanni e Paolo (*see p95*), the Frari, San Zaccaria and San Giovanni Crisostomo (*see p104*). A letter home by German painter Albrecht Dürer in 1506 shows that Bellini's fame was great in his own lifetime: 'Giovanni Bellini is very old but he is still the best painter of all.'

Giovanni's elder brother, **Gentile Bellini**, enjoyed even greater official success: from 1474 until his death in 1507 he directed the decoration of the Palazzo Ducale (*see p84*), replacing crumbling frescoes with huge canvases. He also performed a diplomatic role for the Venetian government, travelling to Constantinople in 1479 to paint for the Ottoman sultan. Although his Palazzo Ducale canvases were destroyed by fire in 1577, his *Procession in Piazza San Marco* (1496), now in the Accademia, shows his ability to depict sumptuous public spectacle with choreographed verve.

Three painters born in the second half of the 15th century and who were active in the 16th were worth seeking out. **Cima da Conegliano** (c1459-1517) offers a stiffer style than Bellini, depicting figures standing in dignified repose against crisp landscapes. Cima's best altarpieces, in the Accademia, and at San Giovanni in Bragora (*see p101*), the Madonna dell'Orto (recently restored, *see p109*) and the Carmini (*see p130*), all demonstrate a mastery of light.

Vittore Carpaccio (c1465-1525) specialised in narrative works for the *scuole* (*see p67*). These canvases tell a story from left to right, and offer enough miscellaneous detail to immerse the viewer in the daily life of Renaissance Venice. Two intact cycles from around 1500 are among the treasures of Venetian painting: the grand St Ursula cycle in the Accademia and that of St George and St Jerome in the intimate Scuola di San Giorgio degli Schiavoni (*see p101*).

Lorenzo Lotto (c1480-1556), active throughout the first half of the 16th century, spent much of his career outside Venice: he was an entrepreneur who knew how to create markets in provincial centres. His best altarpieces in Venice, in the Carmini and Santi Giovanni e Paolo, combine an uncanny accuracy – in rendering landscape or cloth, for example – with a deeply felt spirituality. His impressive portraits, such as the *Portrait of a Youth*, displayed in the Accademia, employ an unusual horizontal format and convey a seemingly modern melancholy.

SECULAR SUBJECTS

At the beginning of the 16th century Venetian painting took a dramatic turn. Three of Bellini's pupils – Giorgione, Sebastiano del Piombo and Titian – experimented with new secular subject matter and new ways of handling paint. **Giorgione** (c1477-1510) remains one of the great enigmas of art. No other reputation rests on so few surviving pictures. The hard contours and emphasis on surface pattern seen in earlier Venetian painting have softened in his work, and for the first time the atmosphere becomes palpable, like damp lagoon air. Two haunting pictures in the Accademia, *La Tempesta* and *La Vecchia*, may be deliberately enigmatic, more concerned with mood than story. It can be argued that the modern concept of the painting was born in Venice around 1500. For the first time three conditions that we now take for granted were met: these works were all oil on canvas, painted at the artist's initiative, and not intended for a specific location.

Sebastiano del Piombo (c1485-1547) left his mark with a similar emphasis on softened contour and tangible atmosphere. His major altarpiece, which was painted around 1507 and can still be seen in San Giovanni Crisostomo, shows a *Sacra conversazione* in which some of the figures are seen in profile, rather than head on, and hidden in shadow. Even more exciting is a set of standing saints painted as organ shutters, now in the Accademia, which show an unprecedented application of thick paint (*impasto*).

TITIAN AND TINTORETTO

Events conspired to boost the early career of **Titian** (Tiziano Vecellio, c1488-1576) when, in the space of only six years (1510-16), Giorgione fell victim to the plague, Sebastiano del Piombo moved to Rome and Giovanni Bellini died. Titian soon staked his claim with a dynamic *Assumption of the Virgin* (1518) for the high altar of the Frari. There he dominated the enormous space by creating the largest panel painting in the world. Although Titian gained fame throughout Europe for his portraits and mythological paintings, no examples of these survive in Venice.

The lagoon city is, however, the place to appreciate *in situ* the nearly 70-year span of the master's religious work. These include a second, glorious altarpiece in the Frari (the *Madonna di Ca' Pesaro*, which is essentially a *Sacra conversazione* rotated on its axis), the virile St Christopher fresco in the Palazzo Ducale and the ceiling paintings in the sacristy of the Salute (*see p134*).

For a decade (c1527-39) Titian had a true rival in **Pordenone** (c1483-1539), a painter of muscular figures engaged in violent action. Now, for the first time in decades, Pordenone's work can be appreciated in Venice. The recently restored *Saints Christopher and Martin* in the church of San Rocco (*see p125*) shows an urgent style that had great appeal. Even more interesting is the confrontation in the reopened church of San Giovanni Elemosinario (*see p115*), where Pordenone's bulging figures on the right altar square off against the soft contours of Titian's high altar. Yet once again Titian found his road cleared of obstacles when his adversary suddenly died.

By the 1560s, in works such as the extraordinary *Annunciation* in San Salvador (*see p87*), Titian's handling of paint had become so loose that his forms were not so much defined by contours as caressed into being. Line was replaced by quivering patches of warm colouring. Canvas, which had originally been seen as a cheap and durable substitute for fresco or wood, was now a textured surface to exploit.

Contemporaries swore that the old artist painted as often with his fingers as with the brush. Nowhere is this tactile quality more apparent than in Titian's final painting, a *Pietà* originally intended for his tomb, and now in the Accademia. Left unfinished at his death during the plague of 1576, this picture summarises the Venetian artistic tradition, with its glittering mosaic dome and forms so dissolved as to challenge the very conventions of painting.

Instead of mourning Titian's death, Jacopo Robusti (c1518-94) – better known as **Tintoretto** – probably breathed a sigh of relief. Though he rose to fame in the late 1540s, he had to wait until he was 58 years old before he could claim the title of Venice's greatest living painter. Yet Tintoretto was canny enough to learn from his rival. He supposedly inscribed the motto 'The drawing of Michelangelo and the colouring of Titian' on the wall of his studio.

Tintoretto's breakthrough work, *The Miracle of the Slave* (1548), now in the Accademia, offered a brash attempt at this synthesis, combining Michelangelo's confident muscular anatomies with Titian's glistening paint surface. Borrowing the figure types and violent compositions of Pordenone, Tintoretto's aggressive and tumultuous canvases marked the end of the decorative narrative painting tradition perfected by Carpaccio.

As Ruskin noted in *The Stones of Venice*, Tintoretto, unlike Titian, is an artist who can only be appreciated in Venice. Among the dozens of works in his home town, the soaring choir paintings in the Madonna dell'Orto (c1560) or the many canvases at the Scuola Grande di San Rocco (*see p125*), executed 1564-87, amaze in their scale and complexity. Tintoretto offered his clients free pictures or discounts, revealing a knack for marketing.

His many workshop assistants, including two sons and a daughter, allowed him to increase production to unprecedented quantities. Like his contemporaries Bassano and Veronese, Tintoretto went even further than Titian in the liberation of the brush stroke. Rough brushwork and *impasto* served as a sort of signature for these artists. The tradition of bravura handling that goes from Rubens to Delacroix to De Kooning begins with the action painters of 16th-century Venice.

Paolo Veronese (1528-88) made his impact in Venice with a love of rich fabrics and elegant poses that contrasts with Tintoretto's agitated figures. Veronese's savoir faire is best seen in the overpopulated feasts he painted for monastery refectories. The example now in the Accademia got its painter in hot water. When confronted by the Inquisition in 1573 over a *Last Supper* in which figures of 'buffoons, drunkards, Germans, dwarves' apparently insulted church decorum, Veronese cleverly got around the Inquisition's command to alter the picture by changing the title to *Feast in the House of Levi*. Veronese's wit can also be seen in one of the few great 16th-century mythological paintings remaining in Venice: *The Rape of Europa* in the Palazzo Ducale, with its leering, slightly comical bull. His supreme ensemble piece is in San Sebastiano (*see p127*), a church that features altars, ceilings, frescoes and organ shutters all painted by Veronese, as well as the artist's tomb.

Venetian painting was also practised outside Venice: **Jacopo Bassano** (c1510-92) was an artist based in a provincial centre who kept pace with the latest innovations. Although his work is best seen in his home town of Bassano del Grappa (*see p276*), a number of canvases in the Accademia and an altarpiece in San Giorgio Maggiore (*see p140*) display characteristic Venetian flickering brush work and dramatic chiaroscuro.

With the following generation, the golden age of Venetian painting drew to a close. The super-prolific **Palma il Giovane** (c1548-1628), who completed Titian's *Pietà*, now in the Accademia,

Deadly rivals

The artistic climate in Renaissance Venice was anything but *serenissimo*. Although the city prospered throughout the 15th and 16th centuries (minus the hiccup of near-invasion in 1509) – meaning a growing market for paintings – the competition between artists only grew fiercer. Searching for prestigious commissions not available in the provinces, painters both confident and desperate flocked to Venice, bringing the names of their hometowns with them (Veronese, Bassano, Pordenone) and crowding the local artists.

Others came from farther afield and sparked jealousy among Venetians. In 1506 **Albrecht Dürer**, fresh from Nuremberg, complained about rough treatment to a German buddy back home: 'I have many good friends among the Italians who warn me not to eat and drink with their painters. Many of them are my enemies, and they copy my work in the churches and wherever they find it, and then sneer at it…'

Sometimes the enmity became physical. **Niccolò Pizzolo**, who collaborated (and quarrelled) with Mantegna in the church of the Eremitani in Padua, was reputed to have preferred weapons to painting, and was murdered on the way home from work in 1453. A 17th-century biographer tells the story of how **Tintoretto** sought revenge when slandered by the writer Pietro Aretino, a staunch supporter of Titian.

Aretino had asked Tintoretto to paint his portrait, but at the sitting, Tintoretto suddenly pulled out a huge knife. Aretino thought the worst. But Tintoretto told him to calm down: he was only 'measuring' him. Tintoretto held the blade alongside Aretino's head and then moved toward the feet, concluding: 'you are two and half daggers tall.' Aretino never disparaged Tintoretto again.

Even when Venetian painters didn't draw their swords, they faced off in their art. Contemporary sources say that **Pordenone** always tried, out of rivalry, for commissions

in places where **Titian** had already worked. Titian probably accepted a minor altarpiece commission in San Sebastiano in order to insert himself into a church that **Veronese** was busy transforming, through his canvases and frescoes, into a personal monument. Tintoretto outfoxed his rivals and won the competition for a ceiling painting in the Scuola di San Rocco by installing a finished canvas instead of submitting the requested preparatory sketch. Veronese triumphed in turn when he was awarded the commission for the gargantuan painting *Paradise* for the Great Council Hall of the Doge's Palace (*see p84*). But Veronese's early death meant that this prestigious commission fell to his arch-rival Tintoretto, who completed the massive task only with help from his son.

A fascinating showdown can be seen in San Giovanni Crisostomo, where the elderly **Giovanni Bellini** outshone his former pupil **Sebastiano del Piombo**, some 50 years his junior. Sebastiano struck first, around 1507, with the high altarpiece (**photo p27**), boldly setting the central figure of St John Chrysostom in profile and immersed in shadow. The painter contrasted the aged saint with a particularly lyrical John the Baptist (note how the scroll winding around his staff mimics the turning of the saint's body and the drapery swirls). Not to be outdone, Bellini's 1513 altarpiece (**photo p32**) in the right chapel includes similar chessboard paving and a twisting St Christopher, clearly critiquing Sebastiano's Baptist. Moreover, St Alvise at the right displays the dreamy, fairytale mood of Giorgione's style. Above all, the central figure is presented as a seated and bearded geriatric saint holding a tome, literally facing off against Sebastiano's prototype. Bellini made sure viewers knew that this was not the work of a young trendy: he signed and dated the painting prominently near Christopher's knee. Although Bellini was pushing 80, he proved an old dog could still learn new tricks.

created works loosely in the style of Tintoretto. His finest pictures, such as the *Crucifixion* in the Madonna dell'Orto or those in San Giacomo dell'Orio (*see p119*) or the Oratorio dei Crociferi (*see p110*), all date from the 1580s.

After the deaths of Veronese and Tintoretto it seems that the pressure was gone and the quality of Palma's work took a nosedive. The decline of Venetian painting at the end of the

Renaissance can be seen at San Giovanni Elemosinario, now finally open again after decades *in restauro*. Although outsized canvases by painters active at the end of the 16th century crowd the church's walls, the aforementioned small altarpieces by Titian and Pordenone executed more than half a century earlier outshine their progeny and dominate the space.

Giovanni Bellini: facing off across
San Giovanni Crisostomo. *See p31.*

BAROQUE AND ROCOCO

In the following years, baroque in Venice was represented largely by out-of-towners (**Luca Giordano**, whose restored altarpieces adorn the Salute) or by bizarre posturing (**Gian Antonio Fumiani**'s stupefying canvas ceiling in San Pantalon). Exaggerated light effects ruled the day. It was only at the beginning of the 18th century that Venetian painting experienced a resurgence. **Giambattista Piazzetta** (1683-1754) produced a ceiling painting in Santi Giovanni e Paolo and a sequence of altarpieces (particularly those in Santa Maria della Fava, *see p88*, the Gesuati, *see p136*, and San Salvador), all demonstrating restrained elegance and a muted palette of gold, black and brown. He enlivened his by placing the figures in a zigzag arrangement.

Giambattista Tiepolo (1696-1770), the greatest painter of the Venetian rococo, adapted Piazzetta's zigzag scheme for use with warm pastel colours. In his monumental ceilings in the Gesuati, the Pietà (*see p101*) and Ca' Rezzonico (*see p129*), Tiepolo reintroduced frescoes on a large scale after more than two centuries of canvas ceilings. Perhaps the most satisfying place to view his work is the upper room of the Scuola Grande dei Carmini (*see p130*), where the disproportionately low ceiling provides a close-up view of his technique. The depth of Venetian talent in the 18th century is demonstrated by the painters of impressive facility overshadowed by the dazzling Tiepolo, starting with his own son, **Giandomenico Tiepolo** (1727-1804).

Though frequently his father's top assistant, Giandomenico can be seen at his independent best in an eerie cycle of 14 *Stations of the Cross* in San Polo (*see p115*), which he executed as a 20-year-old. **Gaspare Diziani** (1689-1767) deserves credit for three gorgeous ceiling canvases on the life of St Helen, recently cleaned, in the former meeting room of the Scuola del Vin (wine merchants' confraternity), entered through the church of San Silvestro (*see p116*). Above all, the essence of the Venetian rococo is to be found in the sites where architecture, sculpture and painting were employed to form a unified whole: the Gesuati, Santa Maria della Fava, San Stae (*see p120*) and the furnished rooms of Ca' Rezzonico.

In the 18th century collectors provided a constant demand for portraits and city views. A woman artist, **Rosalba Carriera** (1675-1757), developed a refined portrait style using pastels. **Canaletto** (1697-1768) and **Guardi** (1712-93) offered views of Venice, respectively in sharp focus and softly blurred. The popularity of these landscape paintings as Grand Tour souvenirs means that although examples exist in the Accademia and Ca' Rezzonico, both artists are seen at their best in Britain. A different aspect of 18th-century painting, and perhaps Guardi's masterpiece, can be seen in the astonishingly delicate *Stories of Tobias* (1750-3) decorating the organ loft in the church of Angelo Raffaele (*see p126*). **Pietro Longhi** (1702-85) created amusing genre scenes which gently satirised the social life of his day.

By the time of Napoleon's conquest in 1797, Venetian painting, like Venetian military power, was a spent force. The capital of the art world in the 19th century was Paris. Over the following 200 years, however, Venice's unique setting and lavish collections have remained a magnet for foreign visitors, including artists.

Venice now exhibits painters, rather than producing them. The city's contemporary art scene is increasingly vibrant, with a handful of smaller players and three major institutions: the somewhat rudderless but still prestigious Biennale (*see p215* **La Biennale**), the Peggy Guggenheim Collection (*see p133*), which has expanded and is flourishing, and the newly refurbished Palazzo Grassi (*see p90*).

This last venue, after two decades of lavish historical exhibitions, reopened in 2006 with a selection of works from the private post-war collection of its new owner, French magnate François Pinault in a sober, even severe interior designed by Tadao Ando. Surveys dedicated to *Europe 1967* and *Arte povera* will undoubtedly be beautifully presented, but it remains unclear how the public will take to the new Palazzo Grassi. Pinault may be granted yet more space to indulge his exhibiting whims when the future of the Punta della Dogana warehouses is decided (*see p131* **Pinault at the Punta?**).

The biggest transformation, however, will arrive in a few years with the opening of the Grandi Gallerie dell'Accademia. The ground floor of the present Accademia building – used by the art school from 1807 to 2003 – is currently being converted into additional galleries so that nearly 650 works (instead of the present 400) can be displayed, many of them specially restored for the opening. Projected amenities include a café, a better bookshop and a less congested entrance. The final result should be worthy of the tremendous collections.

Given that the Italian government funded this makeover, we might conclude that the high local opinion of Venetian painting has spread throughout the peninsula. When the foundation stone was laid in February 2005, then-culture minister Giuliano Urbani emphasised how the Grandi Gallerie dell'Accademia will 'contribute in a decisive manner to elevate the prestige of our nation in the world'. With 'told-you-so' smiles on their faces, the Venetians concurred.

Time Out
Travel Guides

Italy

Time Out
Florence
& the best of Tuscany

Time Out
Milan

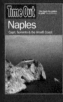
Time Out
Naples
Capri, Sorrento & the Amalfi Coast

Time Out
Rome

Time Out
Turin

Time Out
Venice
Verona, Treviso & the Veneto

The slaughterhouse-turned-economics faculty. *See p39*.

Architecture

A feast of buildings... but not much that's new.

Venice's history is written in masonry, from its unlikely beginnings on foundations placed upon wooden piles driven into inhospitable marshes, via its heyday when commerce and conquest furnished the city's lush ornamentation, to its decline and fall when former glories flaked, chipped, peeled and began subsiding into the muddy lagoon.

As befits a thriving commercial *entrepôt*, Venice produced few architectural geniuses of its own, preferring to import talent from elsewhere to design its cityscape. Of the four architects who altered the fabric of the city, three are out-of-towners: Tuscan-born Jacopo Sansovino; Vicenza-based Andrea Palladio; and early Renaissance master Mauro Codussi from Bergamo. The only native talent is baroque wonderboy Baldassare Longhena.

MEDIEVAL AND BYZANTINE

It all started in Torcello, where the cathedral of Santa Maria Assunta (*see p148*), founded in 639, is the oldest surviving building on the lagoon. It has been remodelled since then – notably in the ninth and 11th centuries – but still retains the simple form of an early Christian basilica. Next door, the 11th-century church of Santa Fosca (*see p148*) has a Greek cross plan – also found in San Giacomo al Rialto (*see p114*), traditionally considered the earliest church in Venice. The portico of Santa Fosca exhibits a feature that recurs in the first-floor windows of 12th-century townhouses on the Grand Canal: stilted arches, with horseshoe-shaped arches supported on slender columns.

The history of Venetian architecture can be charted by following the development of the arch, the most typically Venetian of all structural devices. This is understandable in a city built on mud, where load-bearing capabilities were a prime consideration. In the latter part of the 13th century the pure, curved Byzantine arch began to sport a point at the top, under the influence of Islamic models – an early example of this can be seen in the heavily restored Albergo del Selvadego in calle dell'Ascensione (San Marco). Soon this point developed into a fully fledged ogee arch – a northern Gothic trait.

Meanwhile, St Mark's basilica (*see p78*) was into its sixth century of growth. Founded in 829-32, the original church was modelled on the

Where are they now?

On paper, Venice has developed a passion for the most contemporary of architecture. On the ground, however, you'll have to look hard to find it. When 16th-century city fathers finally selected a plan for the Rialto bridge, it took just three years to erect the massive thing. By the 20th century, however, such decisive action was as hazy a memory as the Serene Republic herself.

In 1963, **Le Corbusier** was handed the job of planning a new city hospital in Cannaregio; not until 1978 – after the architect's death – was the plan shelved in favour of a structure on the Lido.

More recently, acclaimed Catalan architect **Enric Miralles** (www.mirallestagliabue.com) also died before learning the fate of his project for the redevelopment of the port area in Dorsoduro, to create new spaces for the architecture university IUAV. He and his partner, **Benedetta Tagliabue**, presented a winning blueprint in a competition in 2002 – stuck firmly on the drawing board ever since.

The Venetian saga of fellow Catalan **Santiago Calatrava** has lasted even longer. His plan for a fourth bridge over the Grand Canal got the go-ahead in 1997; the glass structure was, he said, to be a 'shining path of light'. Obscured by a series of problems – such as the architect's oversight in not making it wheelchair-accessible and, reportedly, the particularly unstable nature of the canal banks at the designated point – the bridge had still not been erected as this guide went to press, and locals scoff each time a new unveiling date is announced.

British architect **David Chipperfield**'s (www.davidchipperfield.co.uk) plan for refurbishment and extension of the San Michele cemetery island (*see p143*) was approved in 1998, with an ETA for the finished product of 2013. Finally, the refurbishment is going ahead. But quizzed recently on the chances of completing the work in the allotted timescale Chipperfield sighed and said, 'this is Italy'.

Optimists in high places predicted that **Frank O Gehry**'s curvy design – given the thumbs up in 1999 – for the new Gateway hotel, conference centre and boat dock across on the mainland by Venice's airport might be ready in 2007-8. Pessimists on the lagoon scoff and make their own predictions: it won't.

Church of the Apostles in Constantinople. This first building burnt down, to be replaced with the one we see today. The main body of the church – with its Greek cross plan surmounted by five domes – dates from the 11th century; but it was embellished extensively over the next four centuries, sometimes with curious results (note the curved Byzantine arches on the façade surmounted by hopeful Gothic ogees). Two humbler 12th-century churches, San Giacomo dell'Orio (*see p119*) and San Nicolò dei Mendicoli (*see p126*), both feature squat bell towers detached from the church – a key feature of the Veneto-Byzantine style.

GOTHIC AND LATE GOTHIC
In the 14th and 15th centuries Venetian architecture developed an individual character unmatched before or since. It was at this time – when Venice had beaten Genoa for control of eastern Mediterranean sea routes, and when the Republic was engaged in large-scale *terra firma* expansion – that the city's own Arab-tinged version of Gothic came into its own.

By the mid 14th century the ogee arch (two concave-convex curves meeting at the top) had sprouted a point on the inside of its concave edge – producing the cusped arch, which distributes the forces pressing down on it so efficiently that the Victorian critic art John Ruskin decreed that 'all are imperfect except these'.

By the beginning of the 15th century this basic shape had been hedged around with elaborate tracery and trefoils (clover-shaped openings) and topped with Moorish-looking pinnacles in a peculiarly Venetian take on the flamboyant Gothic style, which reached its apotheosis in the façades of the Palazzo Ducale (*see p84*) and the Ca' d'Oro (*see p103*) – both completed by 1440. The Palazzo Ducale was a prime example of the Venetian faith in tradition: a design first initiated in the 1340s was adhered to faithfully over the following century; the florid Porta della Carta (1438) marks this passage of time most dramatically.

CHURCHES AND SCUOLE
Outside of St Mark's, church architecture mainly reflected the traditional building styles of the large religious orders which commissioned the work: the cavernous brick monuments of Santi Giovanni e Paolo (1430; *see p95*) and the Frari (1433; *see p123*) are classic examples of, respectively, the Dominican and

Franciscan approaches. Both have a Latin cross plan, a façade pierced by a large rose window and a generous sprinkling of pinnacles.

More individual are churches such as Santo Stefano (*see p90*), with its wooden ship's-keel roof, and the first *scuole* (*see p67*), such as the Scuola Vecchia della Misericordia (*see p107*), with its ogee windows and Flemish-style roof gable. Both involved the collaboration of **Giovanni** and **Bartolomeo Bon**, who also worked on the Ca' d'Oro. These 15th-century sculptors and masons are among the first named 'architects'.

THE VENETIAN PALAZZO
Majestic Grand Canal palaces such as Ca' Foscari (begun in 1452 and Palazzo Pisani Moretta continued to indulge the yen for elaborate tracery windows, but behind the façade the structure went back centuries. The Venetian palazzo was not only a place of residence; it was also the family business headquarters, and the internal division of space reflects this, with loading and storage space below a magnificent first floor *piano nobile*.

On the roof, between those funnel-shaped chimneys, there was often a raised wooden balcony or *altana*, where clothes were dried and Titianesque beauties bleached their hair in the sun. In a city where space was at a premium, courtyards were almost unheard of.

EARLY RENAISSANCE
Venetians were so fond of their own gracefully oriental version of Gothic that they held on to it long after the new classicist orthodoxy had taken over central Italy. For the second half of the 15th century emergent Renaissance forms existed alongside the Gothic swansong. Sometimes they merged or clashed in the same building, as in the church of San Zaccaria (*see p96*), which was begun by **Antonio Gambello** in 1458 in the purest of northern Gothic styles but completed by **Mauro Codussi** in the local Renaissance idiom he was then elaborating.

Next to nothing is known about Codussi's background, save that he may have trained under Giovanni Bon. In 1469 he was appointed *protomagister* (works manager) for the church of San Michele (*see p143*). Within ten years he had completed the first truly Renaissance building in the city. The austere Istrian marble façade with its classical elements has something Palladian about it, though the curves of the pediment and buttresses are pure Codussi, adapted from a late Gothic model.

LOMBARDESQUE STYLE
Codussi took over a number of projects begun by **Pietro Lombardo**, who represents the other strand of early Renaissance architecture in northern Italy. This was based on the extensive

use of inlaid polychrome marble, Corinthian columns and decorated friezes. Lombardo's masterpiece is Santa Maria dei Miracoli (*see p111*), but he also designed – with his sons Tullio and Antonio – the lower part of the façade of the Scuola Grande di San Marco (*see p97*), with its *trompe l'oeil* relief. The Lombardesque style, as it was known, was all the rage for a while, producing such charmers as tiny, lopsided Ca' Dario (1487-92) on the Grand Canal.

HIGH RENAISSANCE
Codussi's influence lingered well into the 16th century in the work of architects such as **Guglielmo dei Grigi** and **Scarpagnino**, both of whom have been credited with the design of the Palazzo dei Camerlenghi (1525-8) next to the Rialto bridge. It was around this time that piazza San Marco took on the shape we see today, with the construction of the Procuratie Vecchie (*see p77*) and the Torre dell'Orologio (*see p87*), both to designs by Codussi and both demonstrating that in the centre of civic power, loyalty to the myth of Venice tended to override architectural fashions and impose a faintly antiquarian style harking back to the city's Veneto-Byzantine origins. It was not until the late 1520s that something really new turned up, in the form of **Jacopo Sansovino**, a Tuscan sculptor.

'Loyalty to the myth of Venice tended to override architectural fashions.'

Perhaps it was the influence of his new-found friends Titian and the poet Pietro Aretino that secured him the prestigious position of *protomagister* of St Mark's only two years after his arrival, despite his lack of experience; certainly the gamble paid off, as Sansovino went on to create a series of buildings that changed the face of the city. He began to refine his rational, harmonious Renaissance style in designs for the church of San Francesco della Vigna (begun in 1532; *see p94*) and Palazzo Corner della Ca' Grande on the Grand Canal, Venice's first Roman-style palazzo.

But it was in piazza San Marco that Sansovino surpassed himself. La Zecca (*see p87*) – the state mint – with its heavy rustication and four-square solidity, is a perfect financial fortress. The Biblioteca Marciana (*see p83*; completed in 1554, also known as the Libreria Sansoviniana) is his masterpiece, disguising its classical regularity beneath a typically Venetian wealth of surface detail. Finally, the little Loggetta at the base of the Campanile (*see p82*) showed that Sansovino was also capable of a lightness of touch that derived from his sculptural training.

PALLADIAN PRE-EMINENCE

Michele Sanmicheli, primarily a military architect, built the imposing sea defences on the island of Le Vignole, and two hefty Venetian *palazzi*, the Palazzo Corner Mocenigo (1559-64) in campo San Polo and the Palazzo Grimani (1556-75) on the Grand Canal. But it was another out-of-towner, **Andrea Palladio**, who would set the agenda for what was left of the 16th century (*see p266* **Palladio**).

The man who invented the post-Renaissance found it difficult to get a foothold in a city that valued flexibility above critical rigour. But he did design two influential churches: San Giorgio Maggiore (begun in 1562; *see p140*) and the Redentore (1577-92; *see p138*). The church of Le Zitelle (*see p138*), also on the Giudecca, was built to Palladio plans after the architect's death.

Palladio's disciple **Vincenzo Scamozzi** designed the Procuratie Nuove (*see p77*) in piazza San Marco. At the same time, **Antonio Da Ponte** was commissioned to design a stone bridge at the Rialto in 1588 after designs by Michelangelo and Palladio had been rejected.

BAROQUE

The examples of Sansovino and Palladio continued to be felt well into the 17th century, though buildings such as Palazzo Balbi (1582-90) on the Grand Canal, by **Alessandro Vittoria**, showed the first signs of a transition to baroque opulence. But it wasn't until the arrival on the scene of **Baldassare Longhena** in the 1620s that Venice got twirly bits in any abundance. Longhena was a local boy who first made his mark with the Duomo in Chioggia. But it was with the church of Santa Maria della Salute (*see p134*) that he pulled out all the stops, creating perhaps the greatest baroque edifice outside of Rome. Commissioned in 1632, and 50 years in the making, this highly theatrical church dominates the southern reaches of the Grand Canal.

Longhena was also busy designing a series of impressive *palazzi*, including the huge Grand Canal hulk of Ca' Pesaro (1652; *see p118*). He also designed the façade of the Ospedaletto (1667-74; *see p85*), with its grotesque telamons.

This was a taste of things to come: the overwrought façade developed in the 1670s through the exuberance of the Scalzi (*see p106*) and Santa Maria Del Giglio (*see p91*) – both the work of Longhena's follower **Giuseppe Scalzi** – to the bombast of San Moisè (*see p90*), a kitsch collaboration between **Alessandro Tremignon** and sculptor **Heinrich Meyring**.

NEO-CLASSICISM

During the 18th-century decline, limp variations on Palladio and Longhena dominated the scene. **Domenico Rossi** adorned Palladian orders with swags and statuary in the façades he designed for the churches of San Stae (1709-10; *see p120*) and the Gesuiti (1715-28; *see p110*). Sumptuous palaces continued to go up along the Grand Canal; one of the last was the solid Palazzo Grassi (*see p90*), built between 1748 and 1772. It was designed by **Giorgio Massari**, the most successful of the city's 18th-century architects. Massari also designed the church of La Pietà (*see p100*) – the Vivaldi church – the oval floorplan of which strikes a rare note of originality (though it may have been copied from a church by Sansovino that was swept away by Napoleon). The Palazzo Venier dei Leoni – now home to the Peggy Guggenheim Collection (*see p133*) – also dates from the mid 18th century. If it had ever been finished, this huge palazzo would have been as boring as Palazzo Grassi, but funds ran out after the first storey, giving Venice one of its most bizarrely endearing landmarks.

'The city became an architectural sacred cow.'

Giannantonio Selva's La Fenice opera house (1790-2; *see p90*) was one of the Serene Republic's last building projects. Napoleon's arrival in 1797 marked the destruction of many churches and convents, but also began a series of clearances that allowed for the creation of the city's first public gardens, the *Giardini pubblici* (*see p98*), and the nearby thoroughfare now known as via Garibaldi. Piazza San Marco took on its present-day appearance at this time too, when the Procuratie Vecchie and Nuove were united by the neoclassical Ala Napoleonica.

Though one project – the railway bridge linking Venice to Mestre (1841-2) – put an end to the city's history of isolation, restoration rather than building dominated the Austrian occupation of Venice (1815-66). This trend was reinforced by Victorian art critic John Ruskin in his influential book the *Stones of Venice* (1853). Ruskin set out to discredit 'the pestilent art of the Renaissance' in favour of 'healthy and beautiful' Gothic. Such was the clout of Ruskin and his stiff-collared Victorian cronies that the city became an architectural sacred cow, untouchable by the unclean hand of innovation.

SINCE THE RISORGIMENTO

Little wonder then, that the years when Venice became a part of modern Italy were also the years when it began to recreate its Gothic and Byzantine past. An example is the Palazzo Franchetti next to the Ponte dell'Accademia, a 15th-century edifice redesigned in neo-medieval style (1878-82). One of the city's most elegant neo-Gothic constructions is the cemetery of San Michele (1872-81), the pinnacle-and-arch brick facing of which dominates the northern lagoon. Another landmark from the period is the Molino Stucky (1897-1920; *see p140*), a mill at the western end of the Giudecca designed in Hanseatic Gothic style by **Ernest Wullekopf**. The turn of the 20th-century was also a boom time for hotels, with the Excelsior on the Lido (1898-1908) setting the eclectic, Moorish-Byzantine agenda.

MODERNITY CATCHES UP

Venice's modern architecture is limited, though things are looking up. To date, only locally born modernist **Carlo Scarpa** (1906-78) – a master of multi-faceted interiors – has had a chance to build up a body of work, with the entrance and garden patio of the Biennale gardens (1952; *see p98*), the Olivetti showroom (1957-8) in piazza San Marco, the entrance lobby of the IUAV architecture faculty near piazzale Roma and the ground-floor reorganisation of the Museo Querini Stampalia (1961-3; *see p93*). Scarpa's student **Mario Botta** has recently overhauled the top-floor exhibition rooms of this last establishment.

The 1970s and '80s brought one or two adventurous public housing projects around outlying areas of the city or lagoon, such as **Giancarlo De Carlo**'s low-income housing on the island of Mazzorbo (1979-86). A new high-tech airport terminal by local architect **Giampaolo Mar** was inaugurated in summer 2002 and the 70Ha Parco di San Giuliano, designed by Boston-based urban planner

Antonio Di Mambro, opened on the mainland by Mestre in 2004. Vittorio Gregotti and others worked on the revamp of industrial areas in north-western Cannaregio, including a former slaughterhouse which now houses the university's economics faculty. Japanese superstar Tadao Ando refurbished Palazzo Grassi (*see p90*) in record time for its reopening in spring 2006, and is said to have designs ready for the new contemporary art gallery planned for the Punta della Dogana (*see also p131* **Pinault at the Punta?**).

Projects currently in the pipeline include an extension of the cemetery at San Michele by London-based architect David Chipperfield; the Venice Gateway hotel and convention complex by Frank Gehry; and a revamp Enric Miralles and Benedetta Tagliabue of the old port authority area near Santa Marta for the IUAV (*see p36* **Where are they now?**).

Despite all this, an air of foot-dragging and lack of commitment hangs over this new-look Venice. The usual excuse given for architectural stasis – shortage of space – no longer convinces. And the 'Ruskin effect' is wearing off fast. But the port authority area remains eerily inactive, a negligible amount has been achieved across on the cemetery island since Copperfield won his competition in 1998. And – the longest-running farce in Venice – as this guide went to press the long-awaited fourth bridge over the Grand Canal – to a design by Santiago Calatrava – had still not been erected despite an original ETA of 2004.

How to build a house on mud

If you absolutely must build a city on a squishy base of 100-odd marshy islets in an inhospitable lagoon, it's clear you're going to have to think about foundations. Especially if, in time, you want this city to grow into more than a collection of wooden huts on stilts, to become a flourishing trade empire, acquiring some stunning marble-clad churches and *palazzi* en route.

Beneath the Venetian lagoon is a layer of compacted clay called *caranto*, the remains of the ancient Venetian plain which subsided aeons ago. On top of this firm base are silt deposits which vary in depth – from very shallow by the mainland to many metres deep out by the Adriatic.

As the builders of this unlikely city soon realised, nothing of any size would stay up unless it was standing on the *caranto*. So great trunks of larch and oak – taken first

from forests on the Italian mainland and later from lands on the far side of the Adriatic conquered by Venice – were driven down through the mud, to bear the weight of what would then be built above. Lack of oxygen in the clay saved the wood from decomposition, turning the stakes as hard as rock. As you walk through Venice's *calli*, you are, in effect, striding over a petrified forest.

The solution is good, but not perfect. As the sea level rises and the *caranto* level subsides – at an estimated one millimetre per year – there's no way that the trunks can be stretched to keep the floor above water. And occasionally the wood rots, especially if the piles are shaken – with the risk of oxygen sneaking in – by passing motorized water traffic. At which point, those wooden piles will need to be replaced – and it's no fun having a forest dragged through your living room floor.

Antonio Vivaldi, Venice's most famous virtuoso. *See p42.*

Music in Venice

From madrigals to arias, Venice led the way.

Compared with other northern Italian cities, Venice was a late developer in terms of its musical life. No formal musical establishment existed in the basilica of San Marco, it would seem, until around 1312, when an organ was installed and an organist appointed. Nearly 100 years were to pass before a singing school was founded. But by the end of the 15th century, signs of a modest musical culture were emerging in *La Serenissima* when San Marco's musical activities expanded and the religious confraternities of the *scuole grandi* (*see p67*) began employing singers and instrumentalists.

The first significant step in Venice's rise as a great musical centre was the appointment of the Flemish composer **Adrian Willaert** to the job of *maestro di cappella* at San Marco in 1527. This was the most prestigious musical job in town – indeed, in all Italy. Willaert was an excellent teacher and, along with his followers, he ensured that Venice became a centre for composition and performance that set the stage for the outstanding musicians of the future.

San Marco was the heart and soul of musical life in the city at this time and it had a large 'music department'; the *maestro di cappella* employed two organists plus a number of singers and instrumentalists. The post of organist was a highly prestigious one; each had charge of a separate instrument, as San Marco had two choir lofts facing each other, a feature that was to play an important part in the development of Venetian compositional style. The basilica and the vast square that it stood on were the scene of lavish ceremonies honouring both Church and State. It was part of the maestro's duties to produce suitable music for such occasions.

The city's rise to musical prominence was complemented by the emergence of numerous publishing houses, many of which specialised in the printing of music. By the mid-16th century, Venetian music publishers were the most important in Italy, and one of the greatest in the world, and attracted composers from far and wide who came to oversee the printing of their works, providing a richly cosmopolitan element to musical life in the city.

Six years after Willaert's death in 1562, the musical directorship of San Marco passed to **Andrea Gabrieli** (born c1515). A permanent instrumental ensemble was appointed for the first time to complement the choir. This small nucleus of paid-up musicians was added to as and when required; a particularly lavish piece to celebrate an important festival might require around 20 instrumentalists and 30 singers – pretty impressive numbers for those days. Such forces allowed the use of *cori spezzati* (divided choirs), a device whereby groups of instruments and voices were placed in different galleries and choir lofts. Composers exploited San Marco's peculiar acoustical properties to create dramatic dynamic contrast (by placing larger groups to one side and smaller groups to the other) and impressive spatial effects, devices that were an integral feature of Venetian church music at the time.

SURROUND SOUND

After his death in 1586, Andrea Gabrieli's baton passed to his nephew and star pupil **Giovanni Gabrieli** (1557-1612) who was to outshine his uncle by far in terms of his compositional ability. He frequently wrote for double choirs of voices and instruments, or three, four or even five groups of musicians placed in the galleries around the church. In these works of richness and grandeur, the *cori*

spezzati technique is perfected; the resulting 'surround sound' effect produced in the great basilica must have been stunning.

By now, the Venetian school of composition was admired as the most progressive in Italy, and was influential throughout Europe into the late 16th and early 17th centuries. Full, rich harmonies along with varied and colourful sonorities were the hallmarks of its musical style, while Venetian composers were particularly celebrated for their madrigal writing and organ music.

> ## 'The librettist's aim was to introduce as many elements of disguise, murder, madness and suicide as possible.'

A year after Giovanni Gabrieli's death, Cremona-born **Claudio Monteverdi** was invited to take up the post of *maestro di cappella* at San Marco. However, the basilica was beginning to lose its dominance over musical life in Venice. Music was now everywhere: in the streets and on the canals, in private palaces and in brothels. With the opening of the San Cassiano theatre in 1637 – a milestone in musical history – the focus of musical life continued its shift away from San Marco and into the opera houses.

Reviving Vivaldi

The award-winning, globetrotting **Venice Baroque Orchestra** (www.venicebaroque orchestra.net) is so busy touring nowadays it no longer plays regularly in the ensemble's native city, except during the Venice Music Festival (*see p230*). The orchestra, once resident at the Scuola di San Rocco (*see p125*), was formed in 1997 by its conductor, harpsichordist, organist and baroque scholar, Andrea Marcon. It is dedicated to the recovery of neglected works of the Venetian baroque, which its outstanding players perform on period instruments.

As a true baroque orchestra, its size and composition varies from a small chamber ensemble to a classic orchestra, as the repertoire requires. It has won widespread acclaim for its performances of previously unpublished works by Claudio Monteverdi, Benedetto and Francesco Marcello and Antonio Vivaldi and for its modern-day

premieres of fully staged operas, including *L'Orione* by Francesco Cavalli (1998), Handel's *Siroe* (2000), *L'Olimpiade* (2006) by Baldassare Galuppi and the Venetian serenata, *Andromeda liberata* (2004), which was partly or fully composed by Vivaldi; academics are divided on this.

The orchestra's revolutionary playing technique does away with the mechanical and tinkly, so-called 'sewing machine' style usually used for baroque music, and aims to recapture the spirit of the period and revitalise its music with the energy, emotion and extravagance so evident in its art and architecture. Listening to their interpretation of well-known works by Vivaldi, with the brilliant violinist Giuliano Carmignola, is like hearing them for the first time – even *The Four Seasons*. In 2002 they were snapped up by Deutsche Grammophon, so you can experience baroque Venice on your iPod.

A NEW ART FORM IS BORN

Venice was the birthplace of opera as public entertainment. It soon became the opera capital of Italy – a distinction it was to retain until well into the 18th century. Numerous opera houses opened whose fame spread far and wide and there was an ample choice of new productions on offer for opera-goers at any given time.

Celebrated madrigalist Claudio Monteverdi was the principal opera composer of his day, producing his last operas for Venice, *Il ritorno di Ulisse in patria* (1641) and *L'incoronazione di Poppea* (1642). Arguably his greatest achievement, *L'incoronazione* is remarkable for its musical characterisation and has been called the first 'human' opera. When he died in 1643, Monteverdi was given a grand funeral and buried in the Frari church (*see p123*).

> ## 'Sickly young Vivaldi became a virtuosic violinist, a fine teacher – and a skilful seducer of young girls.'

Opera was by now the craze of the day and composers churned out new works to satisfy the public's thirst; **Francesco Cavalli** (1602-76) wrote 42, for example. Opera houses were not only music venues, but also social hubs for all walks of life, from the aristocracy and foreign dignitaries to the *barcaiuoli* (gondoliers) who got in for free. Tickets were available either by way of subscription for boxes, or by single-ticket admission to the stalls and pit. It was usual for the leading families to rent or even buy boxes at opera houses, thus becoming part-owners of the theatres themselves.

LIBRETTISTS TAKE TO THE STAGE

Operas' *libretti* were specially printed for each production and read by the audience by little wax candles. Productions were visually and musically splendid – the more special effects the better, and audiences loved to see floating clouds, gods, angels and spirits, moving ships, live animals, vehicles and trap doors. One of the librettist's main aims was to introduce as many elements of intrigue, mistaken identity, disguise, murder, madness and suicide as possible within a standard (and very unlikely) plot featuring several pairs of lovers involved in alternating serious and comic storylines. Musically, solo singing was of the utmost importance; there was virtually no chorus and the orchestra had a purely accompanying role. What the audience wanted above all was to hear beautifully sung arias.

Meanwhile, a further challenge to San Marco's hold on musical life in Venice emerged in the form of the *ospedali* (charitable institutions founded to care for orphans and illegitimate children) where music was an important part of the school curriculum. The Ospedale della Pietà (*see p100*) was particularly well known for its concerts, which drew large audiences not only because of its high musical standards but also because the orchestra and choir was made up mainly of teenage girls.

Teaching posts at the *ospedali* attracted a series of distinguished musicians, the most famous of whom was, of course, **Antonio Vivaldi** (1678-1741) who was employed at the Pietà between 1704 and 1740. Known as *il prete rosso* (the red priest) thanks to his colourful head of hair, the sickly young Antonio had been ordained, but practised music from an early age, becoming a virtuosic violinist and a fine teacher (and, by all accounts, a skilful seducer of young girls). Under his guidance, the Pietà gained a reputation as the best music school in northern Italy.

It was here that Vivaldi composed much of the vast output of instrumental music that is so well known today, including the *Quattro stagioni* (the now ubiquitous *Four Seasons*). The often fiendishly difficult solo parts were played either by himself or by his star pupils. A virtuosic technique was a prerequisite for a soloist and gave rise to a true Venetian style of solo concerto of which Vivaldi and **Tomaso Albinoni** were outstanding exponents.

THE OUTSIDERS MOVE IN

Although best known for his instrumental music, Vivaldi also wrote some 46 operas, but with his death Venice lost the last of her great composers; with little local talent left, outsiders took the stage. Still a richly cosmopolitan cultural centre, Venice attracted composers from all over to have their works produced.

A new style of opera imported from Naples – the intermezzo (a comic interlude) – soon became enormously popular, eventually giving way to *opera buffa* (comic opera) at which Venetian composers excelled, notably **Baldassare Galuppi**. His collaboration with **Carlo Goldoni** (*see p123*) was perceived as a huge success.

With the decline of the Venetian Republic in the late 18th century came the fall in fortunes of the city's musical institutions. A chink of light amid the cultural gloom was the inauguration in 1792 of the new Teatro La Fenice (*see p91*) which soon became the most important theatre in town, hosting premieres of works by internationally acclaimed composers such as **Cimarosa**, **Bellini** and **Donizetti**. Rossini wrote several of his most successful operas for Venice (including *Tancredi* and *L'italiana in*

Algeri, both 1813) and first performances of Verdi's *Rigoletto* and *La Traviata* were given at La Fenice in 1851 and 1853 (*see p226* **Viva Verdi!**). After the Unification of Italy in 1866, however, the focus shifted to Rome and Milan. *La Serenissima* would never again attain the staggering heights of the glorious age when she was the most celebrated musical centre in Europe, but she has continued to inspire composers such as Richard Wagner, Igor Stravinsky, Pyotr Ilyich Tchaikovsky and Benjamin Britten over the years.

Few tourists today see the great basilica of San Marco in a musical context, but try going in there armed with an iPod loaded with Giovanni Gabrieli's *Sonata pian' e forte*; look up at the now-empty choir galleries and the vacant organ lofts. Turn up the volume and imagine…

In Context

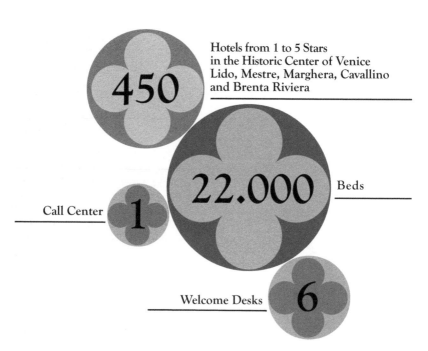

Where to Stay

Al Ponte Mocenigo. *See p59.*

Where to Stay

Visitors keep arriving, and so do new hotels.

Judging by the number of new hotels that have opened in Venice since the last edition of this guide, the post-9/11, post-recession slump in visitor numbers would appear to be over. Venetian hoteliers have reported a bumper season for 2006 and indeed, the *calli* and *campi* around the city's most popular sights are once again heaving with humanity.

You wouldn't think that Venice could take more new hotels, but with some three million people per year staying here, there are plenty of high profile openings in the pipeline. The most eagerly awaited is probably the vast **Molino Stucky** flour mill (*see p140* **Stucky on you**), which is finally due to open sometime late 2006/early 2007 as a 380-room hotel with conference centre and luxury apartments under the management of Hilton International.

The past few years have witnessed a significant increase in the number of small hotels, guest houses and Bed & Breakfasts; punters these days seem more interested in an intimate, homely atmosphere and personalised service than long lists of hotel facilities. B&Bs now number more than 200 in Venice, ranging from simple, clean rooms in modern apartments to glorious antique-filled *palazzi*; prices reflect position and facilities. Some rooms can be quite spartan, so check when booking whether, for example, your room has a bathroom. We have listed a few B&Bs here; the APT tourist office (*see p302*) has a complete list, or look at the excellent www.bed-and-breakfast.it website.

Aside from the establishments included in our main listings below, two other places caught our eye. **Ca' Miani** (San Marco 2865, calle del Frutarol, 041 241 1868), was one of Venice's very first B&Bs and surely the only such place where you can get an in-house hair-do (Pascal, the French owner, is a hairdresser), while the prize for the most unusual B&B experience in town goes to **Boat & Breakfast**, a lovely 1930s yawl with three cabins moored on the southern side of the Giudecca (Giudecca 212A, 335 666 6241/www.realvenice.it/shaula).

LOCATION

Choosing your location carefully will enhance your enjoyment of the city. Plush hotels and tourist action centre around St Mark's square and the riva degli Schiavoni. But despite the luxury indoors, remember that the crowds thronging outside the door can seriously tarnish

that pampered feel – particularly on the riva. On the other side of the Grand Canal, in the *sestieri* of Dorsoduro, Santa Croce and San Polo, chic little hideaways are springing up for those who seek style without the glam trappings of grandes dames such as the **Gritti** (*see p49*) and the **Danieli** (*see p51*).

See our Sightseeing section for more detail about the city's *sestieri*.

WHAT TO EXPECT

Price category and star rating reflect an establishment's facilities rather than character, so it can be difficult to judge a place on paper. The modern annexe or extreme refurbishment will provide more mod cons than the old palazzo but may be short on Venetian magic.

For a city with no cars, Venice is surprisingly noisy; water traffic carries a high decibel level and echoes bouncing off the walls of narrow *calli* can be very loud if the alley is an important thoroughfare. Rooms overlooking a garden or courtyard are the best bet for light sleepers.

Any kind of watery vista will push up the price of your room, but in some cases, your 'canal view' involves craning to catch a glimpse of water at the end of a calle. Or your dreams of romantic evening light playing on a gently-flowing rio may dissolve in a slick of murky water with an oppressive brick wall on the other side. Check this ahead.

By and large, most hotels will exchange currency (although the rate will not be favourable) and, for an extra charge, organise babysitting, laundry and dry-cleaning. Baby cots or supplementary beds can often be squeezed into bedrooms for a supplement.

Not all rooms in the lower price category hotels have their own bathroom. We have stated when this is the case, but check when booking that you have been given what you want – those without will obviously be cheaper.

Facilities for the disabled are shamefully lacking in Venetian hotels, partly due to the nature of the buildings. A number of smaller establishments do not even have lifts; always check first. Where we have stated that disabled

---

❶ Blue numbers given in this chapter correspond to the location of each hotel as marked on the street maps. *See pp317-328.*

rooms are available, this means that the room (and bathroom) is fully wheelchair accessible.

Italy's anti-smoking legislation means that you can only smoke in officially designated bedrooms. The majority of hotels have simply banned smoking altogether.

Breakfast is usually included in the price of the room; if it's not, opt out of what will almost certainly be a disappointment and head to the local bar or *pasticceria*.

LAST-MINUTE OPTIONS

Don't ever risk turning up in Venice with no hotel room booked, even in what elsewhere would count as the low season. If you have nowhere to lay your head, make for an AVA (Venetian Hoteliers Association) bureau at the Santa Lucia railway station, piazzale Roma or the airport; staff will help you track down a room, charging a small commission that you can claim back on the price of your first night.

If you're not fussy about the state of your room, try the cheaper hotels in the area around the station (which is cleaner and safer than its equivalent in most cities). If you're really desperate, there's always Mestre on the mainland – by no means a bad bet if you're travelling by car; hotels are usually cheaper and it's only a ten-minute hop across to Venice by train or bus. But don't let anyone try to convince you that it's the same as staying in Venice: it very definitely isn't.

For last-minute bookings from home, AVA has a detailed online information and booking service online too: www.veniceinfo.it. On the www.venicehotel.com site is a directory of hotels, B&Bs and campsites that can be booked online.

CUTTING COSTS

One thing has not changed in *La Serenissima*: a bargain is a relative concept. Prices remain as high as – often higher than – anywhere in Italy.

The best way to cut costs in Venice is to visit out of season – August, and from November to the pre-Lenten Carnevale, excluding Christmas and the New Year – when some great bargains are to be had, especially at the larger hotels. Throughout the year, midweek stays can sometimes mean that even the swankiest five-star hotels approach affordability for many. Check hotel websites for special offers.

Some hotels such as **La Calcina** (*see p63*) or **Messner** (*see p63*) have apartments for longer stays, as do some of the B&Bs; these are true money-saving options, especially for groups or families. Cleaning and breakfast are not always included in the price. Also, www.viewsonvenice.com and www.veniceapartment.com are good resources if you fancy a residential approach to the city. *See also p291*.

LOCATING YOUR HOTEL

Even old Venice hands get lost in the city. Make sure you obtain detailed directions before you arrive: check for a map on the website or call to ask your hotel for the nearest vaporetto stop, easily identifiable campo (square) and/or landmark (such as a church). Alternatively, you'll need an excellent map and a fiendishly good sense of direction.

The best Hotels

For breakfast in the garden
Accademia. See p60.
Ca' Nigra Lagoon Resort. See p58.
Flora. See p50.
Metropole. See p51.
Oltre il Giardino. See p60.

For breakfast with a bird's-eye view
Ai Due Fanali. See p59.
Danieli. See p51.
Locanda Vivaldi. See p53.

For a really good breakfast
Ca' Maria Adele. See p61.
Locanda Novecento. See p50.
Locanda Orseolo. See p50.

For star-gazing
Ca' Maria Adele. See p61.
Cipriani. See p64.
Excelsior – during the film festival. See p64.

For getting away from it all
Boat & Breakfast. See p46.
Locanda Cipriani. See p64.

For good old-fashioned luxury
Cipriani. See p64.
Gritti Palace. See p49.
Il Palazzo at the Bauer. See p49.

For overall value for money
Al Ponte Mocenigo. See p59.
La Calcina. See p63.
Oltre il Giardino – in low season. See p60.
San Samuele. See p51.

For making your train
Ai Due Fanali. See p59.
Locanda Marinella. See p60.
Salieri. See p60.
Sofitel. See p58.

San Marco, 1490
30124 VENEZIA
Tel: 041.5222858
Fax: 041.5202668
E-mail: info@hotel-firenze.com
www.hotel-firenze.com

The Hotel lies thirty meters from Saint Mark's Square. The building was rebuilt at the end of the 19th century and the façade is a fine combination of marble and iron, enhancing the charm of the Art Nouveau style.

It boasts 25 bedrooms in the classic Venetian style all with bath/shower, hair dryer, summer winter air conditioning, mini bar, satellite TV, radio electronic safe, plug to connect to internet.

On the top floor there is a wonderful terrace which offers a breathtaking view of the city.

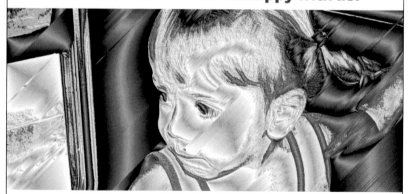

San Marco

Deluxe

Bauer, Il Palazzo & Casa Nova

San Marco 1459, campo San Moisè (041 520 7022/fax 041 520 7557/www.bauerhotels.com). Vaporetto Vallaresso. **Rooms** 191. **Rates** €370-€770. **Breakfast** €44. **Credit** AmEx, DC, MC, V. **Map** p326 B2 ❶

This is a hotel with many guises. The five-star hotel that stands on campo San Moisè occupies an ugly '40s extension of the original 18th-century hotel building; inside, the vast hall with its marble, gold and black has hints of one of those grand old ocean liners. More antique in style, and with Grand Canal frontage is Il Palazzo which is housed in the older building. Recently restored, it now offers even more luxurious accommodation than its younger sister. Adjacent to the Bauer, Casa Nova is a series of spacious, serviced apartments complete with kitchenette for guests who want more independence. The latest addition (from June 2006) is Il Palladio, a hotel and spa housed in an ex-church complex on the Giudecca; as we went to press the spa was not yet open. While the new hotel is impressive in position and dimensions, its style (a seriously awry attempt at mod-Venetian) lacks cohesion and atmosphere. For our money (and you'll need plenty of it), Il Palazzo's discreet, sober opulence is the best bet.
Bars. Business Centre. Concierge. Disabled-adapted rooms. Gym. Internet. Restaurant. Room service. TV.

Gritti Palace

San Marco 2467, campo Santa Maria del Giglio (041 794 611/fax 041 520 0942/www.luxurycollection.com/grittipalace). Vaporetto Giglio. **Rooms** 91. **Rates** €391-€515 single; €400-€913 double; €3,300-€4,390 suite. **Credit** AmEx, DC, MC, V. **Map** p326 A2 ❷

Expect few postmodern frills, just a studied air of old-world charm and nobility in this 15th-century palazzo, former home of Doge Andrea Gritti. Refined and opulent, adorned with antiques and fresh flowers, each room is uniquely decorated; one is entirely lined with antique floor-to-ceiling mirrors. If you want a canal or campo view, specify when booking: some rooms overlook a dingy courtyard. A courtesy boat ferries guests to the Starwood group's sports facilities on the Lido. An aperitivo on the vast canal terrace is an experience in itself.
Bar. Business centre. Concierge. Disabled-adapted rooms. Internet. Restaurant. Room service. TV.

Hotel Monaco & Grand Canal

San Marco 1332, calle Vallaresso (041 520 0211/ fax 041 520 0501/www.hotelmonaco.it). Vaporetto Vallaresso. **Rooms** 99 + 40. **Rates** €110-€290 single; €170-€590 double; €260-€725 suite. **Credit** AmEx, DC, MC, V. **Map** p326 B2 ❸

Now owned by the Benetton group, this Grand Canal classic just across the road from Harry's Bar (*see p171*) is a curious hybrid. The lobby and bar area is a fussy mix of classic and modern, but the rooms in the main building are untouched by the design revolution; those along the calle Vallaresso side have a slightly tacky 1980s feel, while those on the Grand Canal frontage are ultra-traditional Venetian. More *charmant* are the rooms in the Palazzo Selvadego residence: no lagoon views, but rooms are done out in a modern, ethnic Mediterranean style. Even if you are not staying here, pop in for a look at the extraordinary Teatro Ridotto (up the stairs off the reception hall), a 17th-century jewel that was Venice's first gambling hall; Giacomo Casanova and other young rakes would come to lose money and win hearts.
Bar. Business centre. Concierge. Disabled-adapted rooms (6). Internet. Restaurant. Room service. TV.

Luna Hotel Baglioni

San Marco 1243, calle larga dell'Ascensione (041 528 9840/fax 041 528 7160/www.baglionihotels. com). Vaporetto Vallaresso. **Rooms** 104. **Rates** €206-€373 single; €369-€600 double; €480-€2,300 suite. **Breakfast** €22. **Credit** AmEx, DC, MC, V. **Map** p326 B2 ❹

This 15th-century hotel is located near Harry's Bar (*see p171*), but with the exception of original frescoes and stucco decorations in the conference room, little of the period decor remains after refurbishment. Elsewhere, kilometres of shiny marble, swathes of rich fabric and lots of Murano glass provide the backdrop for luxurious bedrooms and communal areas. Views from the rooms are of the Giardinetti Reali, the lagoon and San Giorgio Maggiore.
Bar. Business centre. Concierge. Disabled-adapted rooms. Internet. Restaurant. Room service. Safe. TV.

Palazzo Sant'Angelo sul Canal Grande

San Marco 3878B, fondamenta del Teatro a Sant'Angelo (041 241 1452/fax 041 241 1557/ www.palazzosantangelo.com). Vaporetto Sant' Angelo. **Rooms** 26. **Rates** €396-€446 single; €492-€558 double; €773-€1,066 suite. **Credit** AmEx, DC, MC, V. **Map** p325 F1 ❺

While it enjoys a stunning location, with its own landing stage on the Grand Canal near San Marco, and its facilities are luxurious, Palazzo Sant' Angelo is rather lacking in soul. The red and gold bedrooms are traditional in style; all have whirlpool baths, fine bed linen, fluffy robes and slippers. You have to pay a hefty supplement for a room overlooking the Grand Canal, but you can watch the gondolas drift by from the ground floor sitting room and bar area.
Bar. Disabled-adapted rooms. Internet. Room service. TV.

Expensive

Saturnia & International

San Marco 2398, via XXII Marzo (041 520 8377/fax 041 520 7131/www.hotelsaturnia.it). Vaporetto Vallaresso. **Rooms** 93. **Rates** €180-€300 single; €300-€492 double.* **Credit** AmEx, DC, MC, V. **Map** p326 A2 ❻

An old-fashioned, friendly atmosphere pervades this bustling hotel. The 14th-century building's interior has been done up in a faux-Renaissance style. The bedrooms vary considerably: the majority are done out in fairly traditional Venetian style, but five have been given a more contemporary makeover in the retro style of sister hotel Ca' Pisani (*see p61*). A roof terrace has a view on to Santa Maria della Salute. *Bar. Business centre. Concierge. Disabled-adapted room. Internet. Restaurant. Room service. TV.*

Moderate

Casa de' Uscoli

San Marco 2818, campo Pisani (041 241 0669/fax 041 241 9659/www.casadeuscoli.com). Vaporetto Giglio or Accademia. **Rooms** 3. **Rates** €170 double; €400 suite. **Credit** AmEx, DC, MC, V. **Map** p325 F2 ⑦

Two of the bedrooms in Casa de' Uscoli, the eclectic home of Spanish nobleman Alejandro Suarez Diaz de Bethencourt, overlook the Grand Canal. Reached down a gloomy alleyway off campo Pisani and popular with an arty crowd, the palazzo is grand in size but laid-back in atmosphere. Slightly faded antiques rub shoulders with huge contemporary pieces and quirky modern art. *Internet.*

De l'Alboro

San Marco 3894B, corte dell'Alboro (041 522 9454/ fax 041 522 8404/www.alborohotel.it). Vaporetto Sant'Angelo. **Rooms** 16. **Rates** €80-€150 single; €120-€250 double. **Credit** AmEx, DC, MC, V. **Map** p326 A1 ⑧

Set on a peaceful little campo sandwiched between Palazzo Grassi and Palazzo Fortuny (for both, *see p90*), this small hotel lies off the main tourist route and yet is within easy reach of the Rialto bridge and campo Santo Stefano. The spacious bedrooms are plain but clean (about half have canal views), the management is friendly and prices are reasonable. *Bar. TV.*

Do Pozzi

San Marco 2373, via XXII Marzo (041 520 7855/ fax 041 522 9413/www.hoteldopozzi.it). Vaporetto Giglio. **Rooms** 29. **Rates** €75-€135 single; €130-€280 double. **Credit** AmEx, DC, MC, V. **Map** p326 A2 ⑨

This hotel has a homely, friendly feeling and is very appealing in spite of some rather cramped rooms and tiny bathrooms. Although it's situated very near to piazza San Marco, it's down a little alleyway and off the main tourist track. In front of the hotel is a lovely courtyard with an ancient well in the middle where guests can eat breakfast or relax with a book. *Room service. TV.*

Flora

San Marco 2283A, calle Bergamaschi (041 520 5844/fax 041 522 8217/www.hotelflora.it). Vaporetto Vallaresso. **Rooms** 43. **Rates** €110-€190 single; €140-€300 double. **Credit** AmEx, DC, MC, V. **Map** p326 A2 ⑩

Book well in advance if you want to stay at the perennially popular Flora. Situated at the bottom of a cul-de-sac near piazza San Marco, it offers a dreamy, tranquil stay in the palazzo adjacent to what's known as Desdemona's house. The decor in the bedrooms is classic Venetian, varying significantly from quite opulent to relatively spartan; some are tiny. There's a cosy bar and a delightful garden with wrought-iron tables and a fountain. *Bar. Internet. TV.*

Locanda Art Deco

San Marco 2966, calle delle Botteghe (041 277 0558/fax 041 270 2891/www.locandaartdeco.com). Vaporetto San Samuele or Sant'Angelo. **Rooms** 10. **Rates** €70-130 single; €80-€170 double. **Credit** AmEx, DC, MC, V. **Map** p325 F1 ⑪

This friendly little hotel is situated off campo Santo Stefano on a busy street known for its antique shops. The welcoming entrance hall and the simple but stylish bedrooms are dotted with original pieces of 1930s and '40s furniture, and other deco details. There's a tiny breakfast area on a mezzanine floor. *Internet. TV.*

Locanda Fiorita

San Marco 3457, campiello Nuovo (041 523 4754/ fax 041 522 0843/www.locandafiorita.com). Vaporetto Sant'Angelo. **Rooms** 9. **Rates** €60-€125 single; €85-€155 double. **Credit** AmEx, DC, MC, V. **Map** p325 F1 ⑫

This cosy, family-run hotel between *campi* Santo Stefano and Sant'Angelo has nine smartly refurbished rooms with beamed ceilings; a couple have wonderful views through the hotel's vine-covered entrance. The reception and breakfast room have been smartened up and enlarged and an annexe houses more upmarket (and pricier) rooms. *Internet. Room service. TV.*

Locanda Novecento

San Marco 2683-4, calle del Dose (041 241 3765/ fax 041 521 2145/www.novecento.biz). Vaporetto Giglio. **Rooms** 9. **Credit** AmEx, DC, MC, V. **Map** p326 A2 ⑬

This home-from-home is a real pleasure to come back to after a hard day's sightseeing, especially when it's warm enough to chill out in the delightful little garden. The cosy Novecento is owned by the same family as the Flora (*see above*) and, with its friendly, helpful staff, reading and sitting rooms and mellow background sounds, is a very special place to stay. Wooden floors, ethnic textiles, oriental rugs, Indonesian furniture, duvets and individually decorated rooms make a refreshing change from the pan-Venetian style found in most of the city's hotels. Art shows are regularly mounted in the public rooms. *Internet. TV.*

Locanda Orseolo

San Marco 1083, corte Zorzi (041 520 4827/fax 041 523 5586/www.locandaorseolo.com). Vaporetto Vallaresso or Rialto. **Rooms** 15. **Rates** €150-€250 double. **Credit** AmEx, DC, MC, V. **Map** p326 B1 ⑭

Home from home: **B&B San Marco**. *See p54*.

This *locanda* is an old Venetian house in miniature with beamed ceilings, painted wood panelling, leaded windows and rich colours. There's even a tiny water entrance. An exceptionally generous breakfast (home-made cakes, eggs, fresh fruit) is served in the ground floor breakfast room, while upstairs the immaculate bedrooms (on three floors; no lift) are carefully furnished in a fairly restrained Venetian style. You can choose between a canal view (which can be noisy) or quieter rooms overlooking the campo. The young, enthusiastic team who run the place bend over backwards to ensure their guests are happy. To find this delightful doll's house of a hotel, go through the low iron gate almost opposite the church in campo San Gallo; bear left into a smaller campo and you'll see the sign.
Internet. Room service. TV.

Budget

San Samuele

San Marco 3358, salizada San Samuele (tel/fax 041 522 8045/www.albergosansamuele.it). Vaporetto San Samuele or Sant'Angelo. **Rooms** 10. **Rates** €26-€70 single; €46-€120 double; €60-€150 triple. **No credit cards. Map** p325 F1 ⓯
Bright flowers cascade from the window boxes of this delightful and friendly little hotel. New owners have given the place a lick of paint and a general smarten-up, but the spotlessly clean rooms have retained their simple, sunny aspect and you will still get a warm welcome. Great prices and an excellent location raise the San Samuele several notches above most of its fellow one-star establishments, although both the single rooms and one of the doubles have bathrooms in the corridor. Breakfast (extra) is

served in the nearby Locanda Art Déco (*see p50*) which is under the same ownership. It's popular: book well in advance.

Castello

Deluxe

Danieli

Castello 4196, riva degli Schiavoni (041 522 6480/ fax 041 520 0208/www.starwoodhotels.com/italy). Vaporetto San Zaccaria. **Rooms** 220. **Rates** €393-€426 single; €658-€1090 double; €856-€3,300 suite. **Breakfast** €30-€50 extra. **Credit** AmEx, DC, MC, V. **Map** p326 C2 ⓰
Even if you can't afford the prices at this Venetian classic, twirl through the lovely old revolving door to gawp at the magnificent reception hall. The Danieli (which numbers Balzac, Dickens, Wagner and Proust among past guests) is split between an unprepossessing 1940s building and 14th-century Palazzo Dandolo: a room in the latter is definitely preferable if it's atmosphere and grandeur you're after but those on the top floors of the newer wing have terraces with watery vistas. The rooms are sumptuously decorated with Rubelli and Fortuny fabrics, antique furnishings and (rather dated) marble bathrooms, but some are quite small and looking frayed around the edges. Views from the roof-top restaurant (where breakfast is served) are spectacular. Guests can use the Starwood Group's sports facilities and beach on the Lido.
Bar. Business centre. Concierge. Disabled-adapted rooms. Internet. Restaurant. Room service. TV.

Londra Palace

Castello 4171, riva degli Schiavoni (041 520 0533/ fax 041 522 5032/www.hotelondra.it). Vaporetto San Zaccaria. **Rooms** 53. **Rates** €295-€645 double; €495-€690 suite. **Credit** AmEx, DC, MC, V. **Map** p327 D1 ⓱
It's no wonder that Tchaikovsky found this hotel – with no fewer than 100 of its bedroom windows facing San Giorgio Maggiore across the lagoon – a congenial spot in which to write his fourth symphony in 1877. Today the Londra Palace is elegant but restrained, offering traditional-style rooms furnished with antiques and paintings. You can sunbathe on the roof terrace or enjoy a romantic dinner at the Do Leoni restaurant where, in good weather, tables are laid out on the riva.
Bar. Concierge. Internet. Restaurant. Room service. TV.

Metropole

Castello 4149, riva degli Schiavoni (041 520 5044/ fax 041 522 3679/www.hotelmetropole.com). Vaporetto San Zaccaria. **Rooms** 72. **Rates** €210-€580 double; €390-€1,000 suite. **Credit** AmEx, DC, MC, V. **Map** p327 D1 ⓲
Of all the grand hotels that crowd this part of the riva, the Metropole is arguably the most characterful and interesting. Owner-manager signor Beggiato

Relax in comfort on Venice's doorstep

A refined Villa immersed in the silence of a large park.
Just ten minutes from Venice but without paying the price of Venice.

Park Hotel Ai Pini attracts and satisfies even the most demanding guests, tourists, families and business people. It combines a pleasant stay with the advantage of free private parking and a strategic position which allows you to reach Venice easily (*local bus stop just in front of the premise*), the train station, Marco Polo Airport and all the main cities in the region such as Padua, Verona, Vicenza and Treviso.

Rooms: Suites, junior suites, business rooms, deluxe, superior, standard, with all **comforts**.
Meeting: 6 modular **conference rooms** equipped with the latest in technology, ideal for small meetings or congresses of up to 240 persons.
Restaurant: choose from renowned **international cuisine** or taste traditional **dishes from the Veneto** with a direct view over the park.

Ai Pini

Park Hotel | Dependance
★★★★ ★★★
Restaurant | Conference

Venezia, Mestre via Miranese, 176 **tel. +39 041 91 77 22 www.aipini.it** info@aipini.it

is a passionate collector and his antiques and curios (fans, corkscrews, church pews, cigarette cases and much more) are dotted throughout, both in the elegant and varied bedrooms and the sumptuous and spacious public rooms. The velvet-draped *salone* comes into its own in winter when tea and cakes are laid out, while in summer guests relax in the gorgeous garden, where the only sounds are the occasional church bells and water trickling in the fountain. There are views over the lagoon (for a hefty supplement), the canal, or on to the garden. Excellent meals are served at the Met restaurant.
Bar. Concierge. Internet. Restaurant. Room service. TV.

Expensive

Ca' dei Conti
Castello 4429, fondamenta del Remedio (041 277 0500/fax 041 277 0727/www.cadeiconti.com). Vaporetto San Zaccaria. **Rooms** 34. **Rates** €155-€310 single; €200-€413 double; €310-€620 suite. **Credit** AmEx, DC, MC, V. **Map** p326 C1 ⑲
In a historic palazzo situated on a quiet canal between Santa Maria Formosa and San Marco, this small, elegant hotel has all the comforts you'd expect from a four-star place. The rooms are tastefully decorated in Venetian style with particular attention paid to fabrics. There's a wonderful little terrace from which to survey the surrounding rooftops too.
Internet. Room service. TV.

Locanda Vivaldi
Castello 4150-2, riva degli Schiavoni (041 277 0477/fax 041 277 0489/www.locandavivaldi.it). Vaporetto San Zaccaria. **Rooms** 27. **Rates** €130-€336 single; €180-€440 double; €340-€645 suite. **Credit** AmEx, DC, MC, V. **Map** p327 D1 ⑳
Don't let the term *'locanda'* mislead you; this is a luxurious hotel offering tasteful rooms with lashings of modern comforts. Located partly in the house where composer Antonio Vivaldi lived, and next to the church now devoted to his music, La Pietà (*see p100*), there are views of the island of San Giorgio from the magnificent roof terrace where breakfast is served in summer and, of course, from the front bedrooms.
Bar. Business centre. Disabled-adapted room. Internet. Room service. TV.

Palazzo Soderini
Castello 3611, campo Bandiera e Moro (041 296 0823/fax 041 241 7989/www.palazzosoderini.it). Vaporetto San Zaccaria or Arsenale. **Rooms** 3. **Rates** €120-€200 double. **Credit** AmEx, DC, MC, V. **Map** p327 D1 ㉑
Standing on the same charming campo as La Residenza (*see p54*), Palazzo Soderini's blinding white minimalism is broken only by the bright blue sofa in the living room – the ultimate relief from Venetian glitz or reminiscent of a doctor's waiting room, depending on your point of view. Its biggest asset is the delightful walled garden complete with

lily pond and a pretty patio area for al fresco breakfasts. Two of the three bedrooms have garden views.
Disabled-adapted rooms. Internet. TV.

Savoia & Jolanda
Castello 4187, riva degli Schiavoni (041 520 6644/041 522 4130/fax 041 520 7494/www.hotel savoiajolanda.com). Vaporetto San Zaccaria. **Rooms** 51. **Rates** €130-€207 single; €190-€398 double; €320-€590 suite. **Credit** AmEx, DC, MC, V. **Map** p326 C1 ㉒
A hotel of two different but equally lovely halves, the Savoia offers rooms with balconies and views across the watery expanse of the Bacino di San Marco to Palladio's church of San Giorgio Maggiore (*see p140*) in one direction, or, on the landward side, facing back towards the glorious façade of San Zaccaria (*see p96*). Decor manages to be pleasantly luxurious without going over the top.
Bar. Concierge. Internet. Restaurant. Room service. TV.

Moderate

Casa Fontana
Castello 4701, campo San Provolo (041 522 0579/fax 041 523 1040/www.hotelfontana.it). Vaporetto San Zaccaria. **Rooms** 15. **Rates** €60-€120 single; €90-€180 double. **Credit** AmEx, DC, MC, V. **Map** p326 C1 ㉓
It's all very well being in the thick of things, but it's a relief to leave the confusion of campo San Provolo behind you and enter this family-run hotel with its rather olde worlde decor. Some rooms have balconies and some at the top have a view over the romanesque *campanile* of San Zaccaria.
Bar. TV.

Casa Querini
Castello 4388, campo San Giovanni Novo (041 241 1294/fax 041 241 4231/www.locanda querini.com). Vaporetto San Zaccaria. **Closed** 3wks Jan. **Rooms** 11. **Rates** €50-€100 single; €80-€160 double. **Credit** DC, MC, V. **Map** p326 C1 ㉔
This friendly hotel has a pretty little terrace area shaded by big umbrellas on a quiet campo between bustling campo Santa Maria Formosa and St Mark's. From a tiny reception area, stairs lead up to the six comfortable bedrooms pleasantly decorated in sober Venetian style; all are spacious, but try to secure one with a view of the square rather than the side alley.
Internet. Room service. TV.

Casa Verardo
Castello 4765, calle della Sacrestia (041 528 6138/fax 041 523 2765/www.casaverardo.it). Vaporetto San Zaccaria. **Rooms** 25. **Rates** €60-150 single; €90-€275 double. **Credit** AmEx, DC, MC, V. **Map** p326 C1 ㉕
Tucked away as it is at the end of a narrow calle, and across its own little bridge only a few minutes from piazza San Marco, the first impression of Casa Verardo is of cool and calm. Walls in the public areas are white

Aristocratic **Palazzo Abadessa**. *See p57.*

and pale lemon while bedrooms are decorated in elegant, tasteful fabrics. There is a pretty courtyard at the back of the building and another terrace off the elegant salon where tables are laid for breakfast. The level of comfort and facilities is above what one would expect at these prices, and staff are helpful.
Bar. Internet. Room service. TV.

Locanda La Corte

Castello 6317, calle Bressana (041 241 1300/fax 041 241 5982/www.locandalacorte.it). Vaporetto Fondamente Nove. **Rooms** 18. **Rates** €90-€150 single; €99-€210 double. **Credit** AmEx, DC, MC, V. **Map** p322 C5 ㉖
Housed by a narrow canal in a small 16th-century palazzo down the side of the church of Santi Giovanni e Paolo, La Corte is far from the noisy tourist trails. Bedrooms are decorated in restful greens and there is a lovely little courtyard where breakfast is served in summer. There's now a little bar too, so you can wind down after a hard day's sightseeing with an *alfresco aperitivo*.
Bar. Disabled-adapted room. Internet. TV.

La Residenza

Castello 3608, campo Bandiera e Moro (041 528 5315/fax 041 523 8859/www.venicelaresidenza.com). Vaporetto Arsenale. **Rooms** 14. **Rates** €50-€100 single; €80-€160 double. **Credit** MC, V. **Map** p327 D1 ㉗
Occupying the first and second floors of a grand if rather faded Gothic palazzo, La Residenza possesses

a genteel old-fashioned air and offers great value for money. The interior has been spruced up and the splendid stucco work in the vast salon is positively gleaming. Bedrooms have all been pleasantly refurbished (albeit at the cost of their rather quirky character); numbers 221 and 228 overlook the pretty campo. The hotel has the feeling of being far from the crowds, but it is actually within easy walking distance of San Marco.
TV.

Budget

B&B San Marco

Castello 3385L, fondamenta San Giorgio degli Schiavoni (041 522 7589/335 756 6555/www. realvenice.it/smarco). Vaporetto San Zaccaria. **Closed** Jan; 2wks Aug. **Rooms** 3 + 1 apartment for 4. **Rates** €75-€115 double; €100-€160 apartment. **Credit** MC, V. **Map** p327 D1 ㉘
One of the few Venetian B&Bs that come close to the British concept of the genre, Marco Scurati's homely apartment lies just behind San Giorgio degli Schiavoni. Three cosy, antique-filled bedrooms share a bathroom; there's also an apartment which sleeps four. Breakfast is served in Marco's own kitchen and guests are treated as part of the family. **Photo** *p51.* *Internet.*

Ca' del Dose

Castello 3801, calle del Dose (tel & fax 041 520 9887/www.cadeldose.com). Vaporetto San Zaccaria or Arsenale. **Rooms** 5. **Rates** €70-€130 double. **Credit** AmEx, MC, V. **Map** p327 D1 ㉙
This friendly guesthouse, on a quiet calle off the busy riva degli Schiavoni, has simple, stylish rooms on three floors. If you're lucky (or book ahead), you can secure the one at the top with a fabulous little roof terrace; there is no extra charge. In the morning, the means for a simple breakfast are supplied in the rooms and you can order fresh croissants.
TV.

Casa Linger

Castello 3541, salizada Sant'Antonin (041 528 5920/fax 041 528 4851/www.hotelcasalinger.com). Vaporetto Arsenale. **Rooms** 11. **Rates** €80-€120 double. **Credit** MC, V. **Map** p327 D1 ㉚
A steep, narrow flight of stairs leads up to this unassuming little hotel with its clutch of spacious and airy bedrooms; the two at the top of the house have great views. The bathrooms have recently been refurbished, though four rooms are still not en suite. The busy street outside has true down-home Venetian atmosphere but it's quite a hike from the nearest vaporetto stop. Rates don't include breakfast; you'll have to stop in at the local bar for that.

Casa per Ferie

Castello 3701, calle della Pietà (041 2443639/ fax 041 241 1561/www.pietavenezia.org). Vaporetto San Zaccaria. **Rooms** 15. **Rates** €47 single; €94 double; €36 per person in dorm. **No credit cards.** **Map** p327 D1 ㉛

Small and chic

There's no stopping the rise and rise of the chic boutique-type hotel in Venice. The trend began in 2000 when the retro-chic **Ca' Pisani** (*see p61*) flew in the face of Venetian hotel tradition, ditching the damasks, the gilt and the Murano glass in favour of something much more *alla moda*. Nowadays, if you eschew the large and the lamentably predictable in favour of something more stylish and personal, your choice is far wider.

Top of the pile is **Ca' Maria Adele** (*see p61; pictured*), situated in the shadow of the great basilica of Santa Maria della Salute. Here, 18th-century Venetian meets modern design with some ethnic elements and a host of quirky tongue-in-cheek details thrown in. Brothers Alessio and Nicola Campa preside attentively over 12 luxurious bedrooms, five of which are themed; there's the sumptuous red and gold Doge's Room, the romantic white Sala del Camino and the ultra-sexy Sala Noire. There's an intimate little sitting room on the ground floor with chocolate brown faux-fur on the walls and black pony-skin sofas, plus a Moroccan-style roof terrace for sultry evenings.

Just west of Ca' Maria Adele, off a gated cul-de-sac (there is a sign, but it's so high up there's every chance you'll miss it), **DD 724** (*see p61*) is a design hotel in miniature. The bedrooms are stylishly understated in pale shades and dark wood, with contemporary art works from the owner's collection dotted around; several overlook the garden of the Guggenheim Foundation (*see p133*), and one has a little terrace. Bathrooms in pale travertine stone are tiny but super-modern with walk-in showers. Public spaces (and some bedrooms) are cramped, though, and the atmosphere isn't exactly warm.

Far away in terms of design ethic (though not in distance) is **Oltre il Giardino** (*see p60*). If you can imagine a country retreat inside Venice, this is it. Tucked away at the end of a narrow fondamenta north-east of the Frari (*see p123*) and accessed through the pretty *giardino* (garden) which gives it its name, this attractive brick-fronted

villa was once owned by Alma Mahler, widow of the composer Gustav. Today mother and son Alessandra Zambelli and Lorenzo Muner welcome guests to their stylish yet homely hotel where neutral shades and wood floors provide the backdrop for a very personalised mix of antique furniture, contemporary *objets* and unexpected splashes. Subtly colour-themed bedrooms vary considerably in terms of size (and price). All are equipped with LCD TVs, robes, slippers and Bulgari bath goodies.

Down a notch in price terms is **Al Ponte Mocenigo** (*see p59*), a delightful hotel across its own little bridge on a quiet canal near campo San Stae. This has to be one of Venice's best value accommodation options; it's officially a two-star, but could easily pass for something grander. It boasts tastefully decorated mod-Venetian rooms – some in a luscious shade of deep red, others in rich gold – and well-appointed bathrooms, not to mention wi-fi access throughout, a bar, a Turkish bath, a pretty courtyard garden and genuinely charming owners – Walter and Sandro – who manage to be warm and laid-back in just the right proportions.

Service and kindness in the city center of Venice – couples and family friendly!

Locanda Art Deco ★★★

Completely remodelled and tastefully furnished 3 star inn in San Marco – the very city center of Venice. Double and triple rooms and Junior Suite.

www.locandaartdeco.com

Locanda Salieri ★

Just off the Piazzale Roma car rental/Bus/taxi terminal. Completely remodelled hotel with charming rooms with views on the Tolentini canal and garden.

www.locandasalieri.com

Albergo San Samuele ★

In San Marco just a stone throw from the famous Piazza, rooms with private and shared facilities. Double, triple, and more… low budget.

www.albergosansamuele.it

Hotel Florida ★★

Just next to the railway station and Ghetto district, this completely remodelled hotel offers single, double, triple and quadruple rooms.

www.hotel-florida.com

The building which houses this clean, bright hostel is part of the sprawling Pietà complex which once housed the part of the girls' school where Vivaldi taught. It's spacious, sunny and spotlessly clean with around 40 beds; there are couple of singles and six doubles while the rest are multi-bedded rooms. None have private baths. The rooms occupy the top two floors of the building so there are some great views, especially from the terrace at the top. *Lift.*

Hotel Rio

Castello 4356, campo Santi Filippo e Giacomo (041 523 4810/fax 041 520 8222/www.aciugheta-hotelrio.it). Vaporetto San Zaccaria. **Rooms** 28. **Rates** €50-€130 single; €60-€170 double. **Credit** MC, V. **Map** p326 C1. 🕸

Under the same ownership as, and situated next door to, the Aciugheta restaurant, this hotel offers pleasant, modern rooms done out with a touch of originality; about half of them also have private bathrooms. If you want to pay a bit less, the hotel has simpler rooms in various adjacent buildings. Breakfast is served in the bar in the campo. *Internet. TV.*

Cannaregio

Expensive

Giorgione

Cannaregio 4587, calle larga dei Proverbi (041 522 5810/fax 041 523 9092/www.hotelgiorgione.com). Vaporetto Ca' d'Oro. **Rooms** 72. **Rates** €105-€173 single; €150-€265 double; €185-€400 suite. **Credit** AmEx, DC, MC, V. **Map** p322 B4 🕸

Just off the busy campo Santi Apostoli, the Giorgione exudes warmth. A 15th-century palazzo joins the newer extension around a flower-filled courtyard with a lily pond. Some split-level rooms have terraces overlooking the rooftops. *Bar. Concierge. Disabled-adapted room. Internet. Room service. TV.*

Locanda ai Santi Apostoli

Cannaregio 4391A, strada Nuova (041 521 2612/fax 041 521 2611/www.locandasantiapostoli.com). Vaporetto Ca' d'Oro. **Closed** mid Dec-Carnevale. **Rooms** 11. **Rates** €150-€280 double. **Credit** AmEx, DC, MC, V. **Map** p322 B4 🕸

A pair of handsome dark green doors on the busy strada Nuova lead through the courtyard of this palazzo (situated on the Grand Canal), where a lift will sweep you up to the third floor. The atmosphere in the hotel is discreet and understated. It feels like an elegant private apartment and the bedrooms are individually decorated. The two best rooms overlook the canal; they are a bargain compared with what some hotels charge for the same view, so it's essential to book well in advance (and be prepared to pay extra). A comfortable sitting room, filled with antiques, books and magazines, overlooks the water. *Bar. Internet. Room service. TV.*

Palazzo Abadessa

Cannaregio 4011, calle Priuli (041 241 3784/fax 041 521 2236/www.abadessa.com). Vaporetto Ca' d'Oro. **Rooms** 12. **Rates** €150-€230 single; €150-€295 double; €275-€550 suite. **Credit** AmEx, DC, MC, V. **Map** p322 B4 🕸

A beautiful shady walled garden is laid out in front of this privately owned 16th-century palazzo, which is filled with family antiques, paintings and silver and where the prevailing atmosphere is that of an aristocratic private home (which it is), restored and opened to guests. A magnificent double stone staircase leads to the 12 impressive rooms, some of which are truly vast. Beware, however; the low-ceilinged doubles on the mezzanine floor are rather cramped. **Photo** *p54. Internet. Room service. TV.*

Moderate

Ca' Dogaressa

Cannaregio 1018, calle del Sotoportego Scuro (041 275 9441/fax 041 275 7771/www.cadogaressa.com). Vaporetto Guglie or Tre Archi. **Rooms** 9. **Rates** €80-€180 doubles. **Credit** AmEx, DC, MC, V. **Map** p321 E2 🕸

This family-run hotel overlooking the Cannaregio canal offers a squeaky-clean modern take on 'traditional' Venetian accommodation decor: the Murano glass light fittings and brocade-covered walls (all colour co-ordinated) are there, but so are modern marble bathrooms, very comfortable beds and air conditioning. The pleasant owners serve breakfast on tables along the canalside on fine days and there is also a roof terrace with wonderful open views. *Internet. Room service. TV.*

Eden

Cannaregio 2357, campiello Volto Santo (041 524 4003/fax 041 720 228/www.htleden.com). Vaporetto San Marcuola. **Rooms** 11. **Rates** €65-€110 single; €95-€170 double. **Credit** AmEx, DC, MC, V. **Map** p322 A3 🕸

Situated on a tiny *campiello* just off busy rio Terà della Maddalena and not far from the station, the Eden offers a friendly welcome, quiet, pretty rooms (all with orthopaedic mattresses) and good value for money. One double has a (private) bathroom in the corridor. There is a cheerful breakfast room, but you can order breakfast in your room free of charge. *Internet. TV.*

Locanda del Ghetto

Cannaregio 2892-3, campo del Ghetto Nuovo (041 275 9292/fax 041 275 7987/www.locanda delghetto.net). Vaporetto San Marcuola or Guglie. **Rooms** 9. **Rates** €85-€220 double. **Credit** AmEx, DC, MC, V. **Map** p321 F2 🕸

The quiet campo del Ghetto Nuovo is only five minutes' walk from heaving lista di Spagna yet within easy reach of the peaceful Cannaregio backwaters. The building that houses this stylish guesthouse dates from the 15th century and several rooms have original decorated wooden ceilings. A small ground floor

Locanda del Ghetto.

breakfast room overlooks the canal while upstairs the light and airy bedrooms are all done out with pale cream walls, honey-coloured parquet floors and pale gold bedcovers. Two have small terraces on the campo side. *Internet. Room service. TV.*

Guerrini

Cannaregio 265, calle delle Procuratie (041 715 333/ fax 041 715 114/www.hotelguerrini.it). Vaporetto Ferrovia. **Rooms** 30. **Rates** €65-€100 single; €90-€150 double. **Credit** AmEx, DC, MC, V. **Map** p321 E3 ⓷⓽

Set in a quiet alley, this two-star hotel is handy for the station without being too close to the noisy, crowded lista di Spagna. All but four of the rooms now have private bathrooms, and while the decor is very simple, some effort has been made to cheer these bright, clean rooms up. *Internet. TV (in some rooms).*

Rossi

Cannaregio 262, calle delle Procuratie (041 715 164/ fax 041 717 784/www.hotelrossi.ve.it). Vaporetto Ferrovia. **Closed** Jan-Carnevale. **Rooms** 14. **Rates** €53-€69 single; €75-€92 double. **Credit** MC, V. **Map** p321 E3 ⓸⓪

Located at the end of the same quiet alley as the Guerrini (*see above*), this one-star hotel offers a cheaper option and is quite a find for the area around the railway station which, as a rule, is best avoided. The basic rooms are acceptably clean and all have air con. New bathrooms have been added recently; only four rooms are now without.

Budget

Ostello Santa Fosca

Cannaregio 2372, fondamenta Daniele Canal (tel/ fax 041 715 775/www.santafosca.it). Vaporetto San Marcuola. **Rooms** June-Sept 100 beds; Oct-May 20 beds. **Rates** €19 per person in dorm; €22 per person in double. **Credit** MC, V. **Map** p322 A3 ⓸⓵

This is a student hostel, so during the academic year (roughly mid June-mid September), there are only 20 beds (including one double room) available. During the summer holidays, however, all 100 beds are vacated and students take over the running of the place, not always very efficiently as far as bookings are concerned; make sure you confirm before arriving at midnight. There are a handful of doubles; the remaining rooms are multi-bedded sleeping a maximum of six. There are no private bathrooms. During the summer there is a kitchen for guests' use.

San Polo & Santa Croce

Deluxe

Sofitel

Santa Croce 245, Giardini Papadopoli (041 710 400/ fax 041 710 394/www.sofitel-venezia.com). Vaporetto Piazzale Roma. **Rooms** 97. **Rates** €178-€400 single; €225-€490 double; €300-€600 suite. **Credit** AmEx, DC, MC, V. **Map** p321 D5 ⓸⓶

Well placed for arrivals and departures both at piazzale Roma and the station, the Sofitel somehow avoids the total anonymity of hotels of this international-chain type. Rooms at the front of the modern building overlook a canal and bustling campo Tolentini; there are five floors, so those at the top have stunning views. There is an elegant cocktail bar and a restaurant housed in a lofty, plant-lined winter garden where breakfast is also served. *Bar. Concierge. Internet. Parking. Restaurant. Room service. TV.*

Expensive

Ca' Nigra Lagoon Resort

Santa Croce 927, campo San Simeon Grande (041 275 0047/fax 041 244 8721/www.hotelcanigra. com). **Rooms** 22. **Rates** €190-€750 double. **Credit** AmEx, DC, MC, V. **Map** p321 E4 ⓸⓷

Don't let the slightly misleading name (suggestive of rows of beach umbrellas) put you off; Ca' Nigra is a classy little hotel with a fantastic position on the Grand Canal, the nearest of the new generation of Venetian boutique hotels to the station. Reached through the same quiet campo as the Due Fanali (*see p59*) and under the same ownership, it occupies a striking 17th-century villa, painted deep red and set in a beautiful walled waterside garden. Public spaces and the spacious 'junior suite' bedrooms are done out with an interesting collection of antique oriental pieces dotted throughout; the super-modern

reception area has lots of glass, chrome and down lighting while the piano nobile has partially retained the period decor and furnishings. Ultra-contemporary bathrooms are particularly impressive; three are built in glass boxes in the rooms. Pick of the bedrooms is the Loggia Suite at the front with its private terrace: lie in bed and look over the canal through bottle-glass windows. Guests arriving by water disembark in the hotel's private covered dock.
Bar. Internet. Disabled-adapted rooms. TV.

La Villeggiatura
San Polo 1569, calle dei Botteri (338 853 1264/ tel & fax 041 524 4673/www.lavilleggiatura.it). Vaporetto San Silvestro or Rialto. **Rooms** 6. **Rates** €120-€220 double. **Credit** MC, V. **Map** p322 A4 ㊹
A rather scruffy entrance way and a steep climb will take you up to Francesca Adilardi's comfortable third-floor apartment which has six beautifully decorated bedrooms, each with its own character but all spacious and bright. Thai silks are draped over the generous-sized beds and at the windows of the subtly themed rooms, two of which have lovely old parquet floors. There's lots of attention to detail here: electric kettles with tea and coffee, bathroom goodies made in the women's prison on the Giudecca, and fairy lights draped over the bedhead in the 'Casanova' room. Breakfast is served round a big table in the sunny dining area.
Internet. TV.

Marconi
San Polo 729, riva del Vin (041 522 2068/fax 041 522 9700/www.hotelmarconi.it). Vaporetto Rialto. **Rooms** 25. **Rates** €91-€450 single; €85-€390 double. **Credit** AmEx, DC, MC, V. **Map** p322 B5 ㊺
If you don't mind the crowds, the Marconi enjoys an enviable location right by the Rialto bridge. You arrive into a sumptuous, olde worlde reception hall with dark wood panelling, velvet hangings and an impressive gold-embossed ceiling. The bedrooms are simpler, but still old-fashioned; two of them look out on to the Grand Canal, but the others are much quieter. There are some outdoor tables for morning coffee before a stroll through the Rialto market.
Bar. Room service. TV.

San Cassiano – Ca' Favretto
Santa Croce 2232, calle de la Rosa (041 524 1768/ fax 041 721 033/www.sancassiano.it). Vaporetto San Stae. **Rooms** 36. **Rates** €70-€265 single; €91-€450 double. **Credit** AmEx, MC, V. **Map** p322 A4 ㊻
A 14th-century Gothic building standing on the Grand Canal and facing the glorious Ca' d'Oro (*see p103*), the San Cassiano has its own private jetty, but if you're arriving on foot, get good directions as the hotel is difficult to find. The fustiness that we noted a couple of years ago seems to have evaporated (a lick of paint works wonders) and rooms are, on the whole, quite elegant. The airy breakfast room has huge windows overlooking the canal and there is a tiny but charming veranda right on the water, a great spot for an early evening *spritz*.
Bar. Disabled-adapted room. Room service. TV.

Moderate

Ai Due Fanali
Santa Croce 946, campo San Simeon Grande (041 718 490/fax 041 244 8721/www.aiduefanali.com). Vaporetto Riva di Biasio or Ferrovia. **Rooms** 16. **Rates** €78-€170 single; €93-€210 double. **Credit** AmEx, DC, MC, V. **Map** p321 E4 ㊸
Housed in what was once the annexe of the church of San Simeon Grande next door, this immaculate (if somewhat dingy) little hotel faces the Grand Canal across a pretty, quiet campo. One immediately appealing feature is the smart little terrace at the front where tables are set out under big white umbrellas; another is the rooftop breakfast room and *altana* (roof terrace). The reception area has classy antiques, oriental rugs and fresh flowers, and the 16 smallish bedrooms have painted bedheads, a refreshing lack of brocade and good, modern bathrooms. If the owners are not there to greet you on arrival, chances are they'll be just across the campo in their new, much more upmarket hotel, Ca' Nigra (*see p58*).
Bar. Internet. Room service. TV.

Al Ponte Mocenigo
Santa Croce 2063, fondamenta Rimpetto Mocenigo (041 524 4797/fax 041 275 9420/www.alponte mocenigo.com). Vaporetto San Stae. **Rooms** 10. **Rates** €70-€110 single; €90-€180 double. **Credit** AmEx, DC, MC, V. **Map** p321 F4 ㊼
See p55 **Small & chic**. **Photo** *p60.*
Bar. Internet. Room service. TV.

Al Ponte Mocenigo.

Oltre Il Giardino.

Falier

*Santa Croce 130, salizada San Pantalon (041
710 882/fax 041 520 6554/www.hotelfalier.com).
Vaporetto Piazzale Roma or San Tomà.* **Rooms** 19.
Rates €70-€150 single; €90-€180 double. **Credit**
MC, V. **Map** p321 E5 ⑭

This smart little two-star place is well located on busy
salizada San Pantalon, ten minutes' walk from the station. Rooms are done out in fairly restrained Venetian
style and are surprisingly upmarket considering the
reasonable price; those on the second floor are newer.
There is a comfy sitting area in the reception hall and
a cosily beamed breakfast room.
Internet. Room service. TV.

Locanda Marinella

*Santa Croce 345, rio terà dei Pensieri (041 275
9457/fax 041 710 386/www.locandamarinella.com).
Vaporetto Piazzale Roma.* **Rooms** 6. **Rates** €60-€90
single; €85-€135 double. **Credit** AmEx, DC, MC, V.
Map p321 D5 ⑩

On a tree-lined street near piazzale Roma, the
Marinella offers stylish, comfortable rooms done out
in pale yellow and blue. A tiny garden at the back is
shaded by white umbrellas. This is a good choice for
those with late arrivals or early departures. There are
now two smart little apartments available for rent.

Locanda Sturion

*San Polo 679, calle dello Sturion (041 523 6243/
fax 041 522 8378/www.locandasturion.com).
Vaporetto Rialto.* **Rooms** 11. **Rates** €70-€180 single;
€120-€310 double. **Credit** MC, V. **Map** p322 A5 ⑪

Established in the late 13th century by the doge as
an inn for visiting merchants, this hotel is still
thriving – not surprising, given its Grand Canal
location. Only two of the rooms overlook the canal
(the others give on to a quiet calle), but even if you
decide you can't afford the view, you can enjoy it
from the breakfast room. It's a long haul up steep
stairs, however, and there's no lift. Staff can be terse.
Internet. Room service. TV.

Oltre il Giardino

*San Polo 2542, fondamenta Contarini (041 275
0015/ fax 041 795 452/www.oltreilgiardino-
venezia.com). Vaporetto San Tomà.* **Rooms**
6. **Rates** €150-€250 double; €200-€280 suite.
Credit AmEx, DC, MC, V. **Map** p321 F5 ⑫
See p55 **Small & chic.** **Photo** *p59.*
Internet. Room service. TV.

Budget

Casa Peron

*Santa Croce 84, salizada San Pantalon (041
710 021/fax 041 711 038/www.casaperon.com).
Vaporetto San Tomà.* **Closed** Jan. **Rooms** 11.
Rates €45-€85 single; €70-€95 double. **Credit**
MC, V. **Map** p321 E5 ⑬

Prices have not gone up at Casa Peron since our last
edition: it makes an excellent budget choice. The
friendly Scarpa family and their vociferous parrot
Pierino preside over the simple, clean hotel, conveniently located in the bustling university area with
the shops, restaurants and bars of campo Santa
Margherita nearby. Two rooms at the top of the
house have private terraces; all have showers,
though three are without toilets.

Salieri

*Santa Croce 160, fondamenta Minotto (041
710 035/fax 041 721 246/www.hotelsalieri.com).
Vaporetto Ferrovia or Piazzale Roma.* **Rooms** 10.
Rates €43-€85 single; €55-€145 double. **Credit**
AmEx, MC, V. **Map** p321 D5 ⑭

This simple one-star located between the railway
station and piazzale Roma offers ten bedrooms on
three floors that have been recently smartened up.
Unusually for a hotel of this category, all have bathrooms and air-con. Some rooms look over the canal
leading to the architecture university; others have
garden or rooftop views. Guests won't have to go far
for a meal; Ribò, the restaurant and wine bar next
door, is under the same ownership.

Dorsoduro

Expensive

Accademia – Villa Maravege

*Dorsoduro 1058, fondamenta Bollani (041 521
0188/fax 041 523 9152/www.pensioneaccademia.it).
Vaporetto Accademia.* **Rooms** 29. **Rates** €80-€130
single; €135-€285 double. **Credit** AmEx, DC, MC, V.
Map p325 E2 ⑮

This wonderful secluded 17th-century villa used to be the Russian embassy; in spite of the not-always-friendly staff, it's perennially popular with visitors seeking comfortable pensione-style accommodation. Located at the junction of the Toletta and Trovaso canals with the Canal Grande, it has a wonderful waterside patio (where breakfast is served) as well as a grassy rear garden. The rooms are stylish, if fairly traditional, with antiques and marble or wood floors. *Bar. Concierge. Internet. Room service. TV.*

American

Dorsoduro 628, fondamenta Bragadin (041 520 4733/fax 041 520 4048/www.hotelamerican.com). Vaporetto Accademia. **Rooms** 30. **Rates** €75-€200 single; €90-€300 double. **Credit** AmEx, MC, V. **Map** p325 F3

Situated in the peaceful area of Dorsoduro, the pleasant American is a well-run and popular hotel offering friendly service. Set on the delightful rio di San Vio its generally spacious rooms are decorated in antique Venetian style; some have verandas adorned with bright geraniums and look over the canal. Try to secure one of the corner rooms where multiple French windows make for wonderful light. There's a tiny terrace where breakfast is served under a pergola in summer. *Bar. Concierge. Internet. Room service. TV.*

Ca' Maria Adele

Dorsoduro 111, rio terà dei Catecumeni (041 520 3078/fax 041 528 9013/www.camariaadele.it). Vaporetto Salute. **Rooms** 12. **Rates** €280-425 double; €420-€630 suite. **Credit** AmEx, DC, MC, V. **Map** p326 A3
See p55 **Small & chic**.
Internet. Room service. TV.

Ca' Pisani

Dorsoduro 979A, rio Terà Foscarini (041 277 1478/fax 041 277 1061/www.capisanihotel.it). Vaporetto Accademia. **Rooms** 29. **Rates** €210-€345 double; €290-€400 suite. **Credit** AmEx, DC, MC, V. **Map** p325 F3

Ca' Pisani's luxurious, designer-chic rooms in 1930s and 1940s style make a refreshing change from the usual fare of glitz, gilt and Murano glass; this was the first hotel to throw off the yawn-making pan-Venetian style, and though it's no longer the only one, it's still one of the most effective. The striking pink-painted 16th-century palazzo is conveniently located behind the Accademia (*see p132*). Bedrooms are all generously sized and there's a restaurant with tables outside in the summer, a sauna, a roof terrace and a discount at the gym round the corner. *Bar. Concierge. Disabled-adapted rooms. Internet. Restaurant. Room service. Spa. TV .*

DD 724

Dorsoduro 724, ramo da Mula (041 277 0262/fax 041 296 0633/ww.dd724.com). Vaporetto Accademia. **Rooms** 7. **Rates** €260-€300 double, €380-€480 suite. **Credit** AmEx, DC, MC, V. **Map** p325 F3

See p55 **Small & chic**.
Room service. TV.

Moderate

Agli Alboretti

Dorsoduro 884, rio terà Foscarini (041 523 0058/fax 041 521 0158/www.aglialboretti.com). Vaporetto Accademia. **Closed** 3wks Jan. **Rooms** 23. **Rates** €90-€115 single; €150-€200 double. **Credit** AmEx, MC, V. **Map** p325 F3

The model ship in the window of the tiny, wood-panelled reception area of this friendly hotel lends a vaguely nautical air to the place. The simply decorated rooms are comfortable and well equipped, though some are truly tiny. Unusually for Italy, each has an electric kettle and the makings for tea and coffee. There is a pretty, pergola-covered terrace at the back of the hotel where meals are served in summer; in cooler weather, the restaurant next door comes into its own. Staff are exceptionally helpful. *Bar. Internet. Restaurant. Room service. TV.*

Alla Salute da Cici

Dorsoduro 222, fondamenta Ca' Balà (041 523 5404/fax 041 522 2271/www.hotelsalute.com). Vaporetto Salute. **Closed** mid Nov-Carnevale. **Rooms** 56. **Rates** €60-€115 single; €70-€150 double. **Credit** MC, V. **Map** p326 A3

This pleasant hotel has a pretty terrace garden and is just a stone's throw from most of the major sights, but also well away from the worst of the hubbub. It's perfectly situated for lovely, languid strolls along

La Calcina. *See p63.*

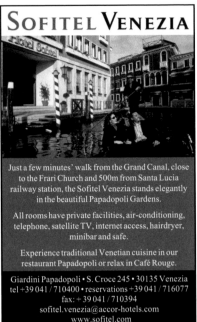

the Zattere. The design of rooms varies enormously between some pretty dull ones with dated bathrooms in the main house and the much smarter doubles in the new annexe; not all are en suite. Plans are afoot to upgrade the place to four stars; this will involve a period of closure, so check before booking. *Bar.*

Ca' Zose

Dorsoduro 193B, calle del Bastion (041 522 6635/ fax 041 522 6624/www.hotelcazose.com). Vaporetto Salute. **Rooms** 12. **Rates** €65-€160 single; €80-€260 double. **Credit** AmEx, DC, MC, V. **Map** p326 A3 ⑥²
The enthusiastic Campanati sisters run this immaculate little guesthouse, situated on a corner near the Guggenheim Collection (*see p133*). There's a tiny, neat breakfast room off the cool white reception area; upstairs, bedrooms are done out in a fairly restrained traditional Venetian style with painted furniture. *TV.*

La Calcina

Dorsoduro 780, fondamenta delle Zattere (041 520 6466/fax 041 522 7045/www.lacalcina.com). Vaporetto Zattere or Accademia. **Rooms** 27. **Rates** €70-€106 single; €99-€201 double. **Credit** AmEx, DC, MC, V. **Map** p325 F3 ⑥³
The Redentore church and open vistas of the Giudecca canal provide the backdrop for meals taken on the terrace of this hotel, a view shared by the bedrooms at the front of the building. John Ruskin stayed at La Calcina in 1877 while writing *St Mark's Rest*. Today it's one of the best value hotels in this category. There is an air of civilised calm about the place, starting with classical music in the reception area. Rooms have dark parquet floors, classic 19th-century furniture and a refreshingly uncluttered feel; one single is without private bath. There is an *altana* on the roof which can be booked for private use and a number of suites and self-catering apartments are available in adjacent buildings. **Photo** p61.
Bar. Internet. Restaurant. Room service. TV.

Locanda San Barnaba

Dorsoduro 2785-6, calle del Traghetto (041 241 1233/fax 041 241 3812/www.locanda-san barnaba.com). Vaporetto Ca' Rezzonico. **Rooms** 13. **Rates** €70-€110 single; €120-€180 double; €160-€210 suite. **Credit** AmEx, MC, V. **Map** p325 E2 ⑥⁴
Situated at the end of a quiet alleyway with a welcoming atmosphere and 13 comfortable, individually decorated rooms (featuring a mix of antique furniture and elegant fabrics), the San Barnaba is one of the better hotels in this price range and area. There's a small courtyard and roof terrace, and no bridges to cross to get to the nearest vaporetto. *Bar. Internet. TV.*

Messner

Dorsoduro 216, fondamenta Ca' Balà (041 522 7443/fax 041 522 7266/www.hotelmessner.it). Vaporetto Salute. **Closed** 3wks Dec. **Rooms** 40. **Rates** €70-€110 single; €90-€160 double. **Credit** AmEx, DC, MC, V. **Map** p326 A3 ⑥⁵

The Messner's rather dull, modern rooms may not be very inspiring, but the location, the shady garden and the warm staff more than compensate. Between the main building and two annexes, there is a choice of rooms from fairly basic standards to 'de luxe junior suites'; prices vary accordingly. The hotel also manages some apartments in the area.
Bar. Disabled-adapted rooms. Internet. Restaurant. TV (in some rooms).

Palazzo dal Carlo

Dorsoduro 1163, fondamenta di Borgo (tel & fax 041 522 6863/www.palazzodalcarlo.com). Vaporetto Ca' Rezzonico or Zattere. **Rooms** 3. **Rates** €145-€160 double. **No credit cards. Map** p325 E2 ⑥⁶
Roberta dal Carlo's elegant palazzo-home on a quiet Dorsoduro backwater is filled with gorgeous heirloom-antiques and pictures, but in spite of the grandeur this is a thoroughly laid-back place to stay thanks to Roberta's genuinely warm welcome. She has three bedrooms available for guests, one of which has direct access to the roof terrace. To round it all off, a generous breakfast is served off white linen in the pastel-coloured dining room with gorgeous stucco mouldings.

Budget

Antica Locanda Montin

Dorsoduro 1147, fondamenta delle Eremite (041 522 7151/fax 041 520 0255/www.locanda montin.com). Vaporetto Accademia or Zattere. **Rooms** 12. **Rates** €50-€70 single; €110-€140 double. **Credit** AmEx, DC, MC, V. **Map** p325 E2 ⑥⁷
It's difficult to get a booking in this charming *locanda*, which overlooks a delightful canal. It owes its popularity to the fact that it is also home to one of Venice's most famous – though very overrated – restaurants. Rooms house an eccentric mix of old and new furniture, but the overall feeling is homely and cosy. Only half have private bathrooms.
Bar. Restaurant.

Ca' Foscari

Dorsoduro 3887B, calle della Frescada (041 710 401/fax 041 710 817/www.locandacafoscari.com). Vaporetto San Tomà. **Rooms** 11. **Rates** €67 single; €77-€97 double. **Credit** MC, V. **Map** p325 E1 ⑥⁸
The delightful Scarpas have been offering a friendly welcome to guests at this wonderful little *locanda* since the 1960s. The simple but cosy and homely rooms are on the second and third floors of the building (it's a bit of a climb); they are done out in cheerful colours and are spotlessly clean. The quietest of them have views over neighbouring gardens while others face the street; not all have private bathrooms.

La Giudecca

Deluxe

See also p49 **Il Palladio**.

Cipriani

Giudecca 10, fondamenta San Giovanni (041 520 7744/fax 041 520 3930/www.hotelcipriani.com). Hotel launch from Vallaresso vaporetto stop. **Closed** end Oct-mid Mar. **Rooms** 104. **Rates** €499-€755 single; €625-€1,330 double; €1,110-€4,030 suite; €4,700-€8,330 Palladio Suite. **Credit** AmEx, DC, MC, V. **Map** p326 C4 ⑥⑨

Set in a verdant paradise on the eastern tip of the Giudecca island, the Cipriani has great facilities as well as a private harbour for your yacht and a higher-than-average chance of rubbing shoulders with a film star. Rooms are exquisitely decorated, many with marble bathrooms. If this seems too humdrum, take an apartment in the neighbouring 15th-century Palazzo Vendramin, complete with butler service and private garden. Leisure facilities include tennis courts, a pool, a sauna, a spa and a gym. There's a motorboat to San Marco, but many guests choose not to leave the premises, inviting the question: do they come here for Venice or for the Cipriani itself?

Bars (3). Concierge. Conference facilities. Gym. Internet. Restaurants (4). Pool. Room service. Spa. TV.

Budget

Ostello di Venezia (Youth Hostel)

Giudecca 86, fondamenta delle Zitelle (041 523 8211/fax 041 523 5689/www.hihostel.com). Vaporetto Zitelle. **Closed** 2wks Dec. **Rates** €19.50 per person; €9 dinner. **Credit** MC, V. **Map** p326 B4 ⑦⓪

A vaporetto ride away from the main island, this large youth hostel (there are 260 beds) offers stunning and unique views across the lagoon towards the church of Santa Maria della Salute and San Marco. You should book in advance (through the web site), especially during the summer months. Unadventurous but very cheap meals are served.

Lido & Lagoon

Deluxe

Des Bains

Lungomare Marconi 17, Lido (041 526 5921/fax 041 526 0113/www.starwood.com/italy). Vaporetto Lido. **Closed** early Nov-mid Mar. **Rooms** 191. **Rates** € 375 single; € 690-€ 820 double; € 1,170-€ 2,035 suite. **Credit** AmEx, DC, MC, V. **Map** p317 B4 ⑦①

Thomas Mann wrote, and Luchino Visconti filmed, *Death in Venice* in this glorious art deco hotel set in its own park. Des Bains has a private beach just across the street and access to tennis courts, a golf course and riding facilities. A courtesy boat ferries guests to San Marco every half-hour.

Bar. Concierge. Conference facilities. Gym. Internet. Parking (free). Pool (outdoor). Restaurant. Room service. TV. Private beach and facilities. Tennis courts. Free shuttle bus from/to The Westin Excelsior from Apr to late Oct.

Excelsior

Lungomare Marconi 41, Lido (041 526 0201/fax 041 526 7276 /www.starwood.com/italy). Vaporetto Lido. **Closed** early Nov-late Mar. **Rooms** 197. **Rates** € 745 double € 830-€ 950; € 1,980-€ 3,530 suite. **Credit** AmEx, DC, MC, V. **Map** p317 B5 ⑦②

The early-1900s pseudo-Moorish Excelsior hosts hordes of celebrities when the Venice Film Festival (*see p210*) swings into action each September (the festival headquarters is just over the road). Demand a sea-facing room for a view of beach happenings and the Adriatic beyond. The Excelsior's beach huts are the last word in luxury. There are tennis courts and a water taxi to San Marco.

Bar. Conference facilities. Internet (in-room high-speed Internet). Parking (daily fee). Pool (outdoor). Private beach and facilities. Restaurant. Room service. TV. Tennis courts. Free shuttle boat from/to other Starwood hotels in central Venice, from Apr to late Oct.

San Clemente Palace

Isola di San Clemente (041 244 5001/fax 041 244 5800/www.sanclemente.thi.it). Hotel launch shuttle service from jetty at piazza San Marco. **Rooms** 200. **Rates** €240-€410 single; €270-€530 double; €475-€1700 suite; €1,100-€3,000 residential suite. **Credit** AmEx, DC, MC, V.

Over time the island of San Clemente has hosted a hospice for pilgrims, a powder store, an ecclesiastical prison for unruly priests and, more recently, a mental hospital. Today the restored buildings of the hospital house this luxurious hotel set in extensive, landscaped grounds with 200-odd rooms (done out in traditional Venetian style), four restaurants, a business centre, a beauty farm and all the attendant facilities; there's even a three-hole practice golf course. Shuttle service to piazza San Marco.

Bars (2). Concierge. Conference facilities. Disabled-adapted rooms. Gym. Internet. Pool. Restaurants (3). Room service. Spa. TV.

Expensive

Locanda Cipriani

Torcello, piazza Santa Fosca (041 730 150/fax 041 735 433/www.locandacipriani.com. Vaporetto Torcello. **Rooms** 6. **Rates** €130 single; €260 double. **Credit** AmEx, DC, MC, V.

Some people might argue that there's no point in going to Venice and staying on the island of Torcello, but this famous green-shuttered inn (owned by a branch of the Cipriani family) is special enough to justify the remoteness of the setting, at least for a couple of nights. Some of the six rooms (done out in understated, elegant country style) look over the hotel's gorgeous garden; you might end up in the one where Ernest Hemingway wrote *Across the River and into the Trees*, apparently standing up because of haemorrhoids. The (expensive) restaurant (*see p170*) enjoys a blissful setting under a vine-clad terrace; half board costs an extra €50 per head.

Bar. Internet. Restaurant. Room service.

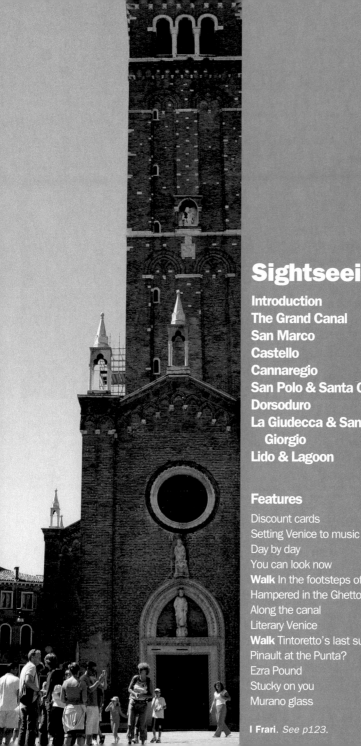

Sightseeing

I Frari. *See p123.*

Introduction

Surprisingly, it's just like you thought it would be.

Venice's watery high street.

First encountered at a distance, mediated through the beautifying camera lens, many of the world's great cities are a let-down when you get there. But not Venice. Nobody can come here without some idea of what to expect. The surprise is that it's true. The streets really are full of water – everywhere. The *palazzi* really do have a fairy-tale quality. And it's not just a matter of a carefully preserved little tourist centre surrounded by the usual high-rise flats and car parks; the *whole* of Venice is the centre.

Then there are highlights. The **basilica di San Marco** (*see p78*) is one of Christendom's greatest churches; the **Gallerie dell'Accademia** (*see p132*) contain an unparalleled selection of Renaissance art; and the **Rialto** is a powerful symbol of mercantile energy as well as a fine bridge. But Venice is much more than this and the best way to get an impression of its full diversity is to leave the main routes.

With its double topography of streets and canals, Venice provides a challenge even to the most skilled map-readers. But when you do lose your bearings, don't be alarmed: the *calli* will close in around you; you'll come to innumerable dead ends and find yourself returning inexplicably to the same (wrong) spot over and over. But eventually you'll hit a busy

thoroughfare or the Grand Canal and a vaporetto stop. Until that happens, enjoy the feel of village Venice – or, more appropriately, island Venice. The city is made up of over 100 islands, and every one has something – magnificent or quaint, historic or charming – to offer.

Venice is divided into six *sestieri*. They are worth getting to grips with, first and foremost because all addresses include the *sestiere* name. Cradled by the great lower bend of the Grand Canal is the *sestiere* of **San Marco**, the heart of the city; east of here is **Castello**, one of the most lived-in areas; extending to the west and north is **Cannaregio**, whose western stretches are among the most peaceful parts of Venice. To the west of the Rialto bridge is **San Polo**, bristling with churches; north of that is **Santa Croce**, short on sights but not on atmosphere; while further to the south is **Dorsoduro**, one of the city's most elegant and artsy districts, with its wide Zattere promenade looking across to the long residential island of the **Giudecca** – the honorary seventh *sestiere*.

CHURCHES

Venice began life as a host of separate island communities, each clustered around its own parish church. The bridges came later. Like many later visitors to the city, Napoleon thought that there were far too many churches; during his brief rule (*see p23*) he cleared away a good 40 or so, but there are still well over 100 of them left, containing inestimable artistic treasures.

Most of the major churches have reliable opening times; hours in minor churches depend on the goodwill or whim of the priest or sacristan. It's well worth exploring these too, since there is not a single one that does not contain some item of interest, whether it be a shrivelled relic or a glowing Madonna with *bambino*. In general, early morning and late afternoon are the best times for church-crawling. But it's best never to pass an opportunity by: if you see one open without a service under way, go in and poke around. No Sunday opening times are given in listings for churches that open only for Mass.

MUSEUMS, GALLERIES AND *SCUOLE*
On the whole, Venice's museums and galleries adhere to the basic pre-modern requirement that they should be passive containers for beautiful and/or instructive things. But some of those things are very beautiful indeed, especially in treasure troves such as the Gallerie dell'Accademia. Instruction can be fun too. The **Museo Storico Navale** (*see p100*) provides a colourful introduction to Venice's maritime past, while a grasp of the elaborate mechanisms of Venetian government will turn the slog around the **Palazzo Ducale** (Doge's Palace; *see p84*) into a voyage of discovery.

Then there are the curiosities – **Ca' d'Oro** (*see p103*), where a patchy gallery with the occasional gem is housed inside one of the city's most extraordinary architectural frames; **Ca' Rezzonico** (*see p129*), where 18th-century Venice is recreated in all its finery and foppery and the smaller but eclectic **Museo della Fondazione Scientifica Querini Stampalia** (*see p93*), a private foundation with a fascinating collection of scenes of 18th-century Venetian life and a glorious Bellini (the painter, not the cocktail).

Among the museums must also be included the *scuole*, uniquely Venetian establishments which were a kind of blend of art-treasure house and social institution. Essentially, they were devotional lay brotherhoods, subject to the state rather than the Church. The earliest were founded in the 13th century; by the 15th century there were six *scuole grandi* and as many as 400 minor *scuole*. The *scuole grandi* had annually elected officers drawn from the 'citizen' class (those sandwiched between the governing patriciate and the unenfranchised *popolani*). While members of the *scuole grandi* (such as **Scuola di San Rocco**, *see p125*, and

Scuola di San Giovanni Evangelista, *see p120*) were mainly drawn from the wealthier professional classes, the humbler *scuole piccole* were exclusively devotional groups, trade guilds or confraternities of foreign communities (such as **Scuola di San Giorgio degli Schiavoni**, *see p101*). The wealthier confraternities devoted a great deal of time and expense to beautifying their meeting houses (the *scuole* themselves), sometimes hiring one major painter to decorate the whole building; this was the case of Tintoretto in the Scuola di San Rocco and Carpaccio in the Scuola di San Giorgio degli Schiavoni, so that these buildings are essential viewing for anyone interested in their art.

Admission & tickets
In high season expect to queue to enter St Mark's, the Accademia and the Palazzo Ducale. Other sights rarely present any overcrowding problems except during special exhibitions. April and May are traditional months for Italian school trips: this can mean sharing your Titians and Tintorettos with gangs of bored teenagers.

Entry to all state-owned museums is, theoretically, free (or at least reduced) for citizens under 18 and over 65. Charges and concessions at city-run and privately owned museums vary; it pays to carry whatever ID cards you can muster (student card, press card, motoring association card and so on).

For one week each spring – designated the *Settimana dei Beni Culturali* (Cultural Heritage week) – most state-owned (but not city-owned) galleries and museums are free. See www.beniculturali.it for details.

Multi-entrance tickets
See also p68 **Discount cards**.

Many of Venice's landmarks offer multi-entrance tickets, which cut costs if you are planning to visit all the sights covered by any given ticket. Schemes include:

Musei Civici Veneziani
Venice's city-owned museums offer two multi-entrance options, both of which can be bought at participating establishments. The major museums (Musei di Piazza San Marco, Ca' Rezzonico and Ca' Pesaro) accept credit cards (MC, V).

Note that the Musei di Piazza San Marco can **only** be entered on a cumulative ticket.

For the others (Ca' Rezzonico, Carlo Goldoni's House, Museo di Palazzo Mocenigo, Ca' Pesaro, Museo Fortuny, the Glass Museum and Lace Museum), individual tickets are available. Information on www.museiciviciveneziani.it.

• **Musei di Piazza San Marco** (Palazzo Ducale, Biblioteca Marciana, Museo Correr, Museo Archeologico) €12; €6.50 concessions.
• **Museum Pass** (all the Musei Civici) €18; €12 concessions.

State Museums

The state-owned Gallerie dell'Accademia (*see p132*), Ca' d'Oro (*see p103*) and Museo Orientale (*see p118*) can be visited on a multi-entrance ticket costing €11 (€5.50 concessions) from participating sights. No credit cards except for online advance bookings. Information on www.artive.arti.beniculturali.it.

Chorus

The following churches belong to the Chorus scheme (041 275 0462/www.chorusvenezia.org), which funds upkeep by charging for entry:

San Marco: Santa Maria del Giglio (*see p91*), Santo Stefano (*see p90*).
Castello: Santa Maria Formosa (*see p96*), San Pietro di Castello (*see p101*).
Cannaregio: Santa Maria dei Miracoli (*see p111*), Sant'Alvise (*see p109*), Madonna dell'Orto (*see p109*).
San Polo & Santa Croce: San Polo (*see p115*), San Stae (*see p120*), I Frari (*see p123*), San Giacomo dell'Orio (*see p119*), San Giovanni Elemosinario (*see p115*).
Dorsoduro: Gesuati (*see p136*), San Sebastiano (*see p127*).
Giudecca: Il Redentore (*see p139*).

There's a fee of €2.50 for each church or you can get a multi-entrance ticket (€8; €5 concessions). Tickets can be bought in churches and VeLa shops (*see p286*). No credit cards.

Discount cards

Even if you only plan to spend a day in Venice, a discount card may be the remedy for extortionate transport costs and multiple museum entrance fees. Remember that ICOM members (with ID), children under five, disabled people with escorts, authorised guides, journalists (with ID), interpreters accompanying groups and group leaders receive free admission to many churches and museums; be sure to check policies before you invest in one of the following cards.

Other multi-entrance cards for Venice's museums and churches include the **Museum Pass**, various themed multi-entrance tickets to Venice's city-owned museums, and the **Chorus** pass for churches. For all, *see p68*.

Venice Card

www.venicecard.it
Produced by the city council, this is a one-, three- or seven-day card that gives an impressive array of discounts to services around the city. Its primary selling point is that it allows unlimited use of the city's extortionately expensive public transport, in addition to other benefits including a 20% reduction at the main car parks in Venice. Venicecards are non-transferable.

There are two types of cards, blue and orange. The blue card allows you to use public transport, toilets and baby-changing facilities while the orange card also includes admission to the Musei Civici (*see p67*) circuit and, on the 3 and 7 day cards, free access to all the Chorus Pass (*see p68*) churches. For a surcharge of €20 you can opt

to include a return Alilaguna journey to and from the airport. You must book your ticket at least 48 hours in advance on-line or by calling 041 24 24 (8am-7.30pm daily) and collect it on arrival in Venice at any VeLa office (*see p286*), from Alilaguna or from the ATVO office in the airport (*see p286*). Venicecard can also be purchased at VeLa ticket offices, APT tourist information offices and VTP Information points in the city (*see p302*).

There is a small discount for booking online. Note that children of four and under travel free with a Venicecard-holding guardian. 'Junior' rates are for five- to 29-year-olds, 'senior' for 30+.

Blue One-day €17 Senior; €15 Junior. Three-day €34 Senior; €30 Junior. Seven-day €52 Senior; €47 Junior.
Orange One-day €29 Senior; €22 Junior. Three-day €54 Senior; €45 Junior. Seven-day €76 Senior; €67 Junior.

Rolling Venice

www.venicecard.com/rolling_eng.jsp
Visitors aged between 14 and 29 can sign up for the **Rolling Venice** programme; this €4 card is valid until 31 December of the year of issue. Holders of a Rolling Venice card are eligible for discounts at selected hotels, museums (up to 50%), restaurants and shops (10-15%) around the city, as well as cut-price (€15) three-day vaporetto passes and 50% off tickets for concerts (not operas) at La Fenice. On sale, with a valid ID document at any VeLa (*see p286*) or APT office (*see p302*), or call 04 24 24.

The Grand Canal

The world's most unusual high street.

GRAND CANAL

It's the one trip you can't omit. Whether you take a leisurely (and budget-breaking) gondola trip, squeeze on to a packed vaporetto, or, like Lord Byron, swim all the way down it, you can't go home and say you haven't seen Venice's high street. The three-and-a-half kilometer trip also provides a superb introduction to the city, for this magnificent palace-lined waterway will tell you more about the way the city works – and has always worked – than any historical tome.

The **Grand Canal** may no longer be teeming with merchandise-laden cargo boats, but it is still the main thoroughfare of Venice, and only a little imagination is needed to understand its historical importance. Every family of note had to have a palazzo here – and this was not just for reasons of social snobbery. The *palazzi* are undeniably splendid but they were first and foremost solid commercial enterprises, and their designs are as practical as they are eye-catching.

Most of the notable buildings were built between the 12th and 18th centuries. When a family decided to rebuild a palazzo, they usually maintained the same basic structure – for the good reason that they could build on the same foundations. This resulted in some interesting style hybrids: the Grand Canal offers many examples of *palazzi* in which Veneto-Byzantine or Gothic features are incorporated into the Renaissance or baroque. Each palazzo typically had a main water entrance opening on to a large hall with storage space on either side; a *mezzanino* with offices; a *piano nobile* (the main floor – sometimes two in grander buildings) consisting of a spacious reception hall lit by large central windows and flanked on both sides by residential rooms; and a land entrance at the back. Over the centuries architectural frills and trimmings were added, but the underlying form was stable – and, as always in Venice, it is form that follows function.

In the following description of the most notable *palazzi*, many names recur, for the simple reason that families expanded, younger sons inheriting as well as older ones. Compound names indicate that the palazzo passed through various hands over time. Originally the term 'palazzo' was reserved for the Doge's Palace. Other *palazzi* were known as *Casa* ('house') or *Ca'* for short: this is still true of some of the older ones, such as Ca' d'Oro (*see p103*).

This chapter deals mainly with canal-side *palazzi*. Churches and museums facing on to the canal are covered elsewhere in the guide: in these cases, cross references are given. For information on the *vaporetti* that ply the Grand Canal, *see p287*.

▶ The itinerary on pages 70-75 is best followed from the rear deck of a *vaporetto*, looking backwards as you make your way from the station towards St Mark's square.

Sightseeing

Right bank

From the railway station to the Salute

Before the Scalzi bridge is the church of **San Simeone Piccolo**, with its high green dome and Corinthian portico. For those arriving in Venice it's a picturesque introduction to the city. The **Ponte degli Scalzi**, which leads across to the station, was built in stone by Eugenio Miozzi in 1934.

Ponte degli Scalzi

②

Vaporetto stop Riva di Biasio

Just before the rio del Megio stands the **Fontego dei Turchi**, a 19th-century reconstruction of the original Veneto-Byzantine building, which was leased to Turkish traders in the 17th century as a residence and warehouse. Some of the original material was used but the effect as a whole is one of pastiche. Once lived in by the poet Torquato Tasso, it's now the **Museo di Storia Naturale** (*see p118*).

The **Depositi del Megio** (state granaries) have a battlemented, plain-brick façade. The sculpted lion is a modern replacement of the original, destroyed at the fall of the Republic. The church of **San Stae** (*see p120*) has a baroque façade by Domenico Rossi, with exuberant sculpture.

Left bank

From the railway station to San Marco

① ▶ **Vaporetto stop Ferrovia**

At the foot of the Ponte degli Scalzi is the fine Baroque façade of the **Scalzi** church (*see p105*).

Scalzi bridge

Unusually narrow **Palazzo Flangini** is a 17th-century building by Giuseppe Sardi. Despite picturesque stories of quarrelling brothers, it owes its shape to the simple fact that the family's money ran out. Just before the wide Cannaregio Canal is the church of **San Geremia**; from the Grand Canal, the apse of the chapel of Santa Lucia is visible.

Standing with its main façade on the Cannaregio Canal is **Palazzo Labia**, the 18th-century home of the seriously rich Labia family. The story goes that parties ended with the host throwing his gold dinner plates into the canal to demonstrate his wealth; the servants would then be ordered to fish them out again. A famous fancy-dress ball thrown here in 1951 by Mexican millionaire Don Carlos de Beistegui continued this tradition of conspicuous consumption. The building is now the regional headquarters of the RAI (the Italian state broadcaster). It contains suitably sumptuous frescoes by Tiepolo.

Vaporetto stop San Marcuola

The next building of note is Palazzo Vendramin Calergi, an impressive Renaissance palazzo designed by Mauro Codussi in the first decade of the 16th century. It uses his characteristic arched windows incorporating twin smaller arches. Porphyry insets decorate the façade. Wagner died here in 1883. It now houses the Venice Casinò.

A fairly uneventful stretch ends at the Ca' d'Oro (see p103), the most gorgeously ornate Gothic building on the Grand Canal. For all its ornaments, it is sober in comparison with its original appearance; when its decorative features were gilded or painted in ultramarine blue and cinnabar red. It has an open loggia on the piano nobile, like the Doge's Palace, but unlike any other palazzo after the Byzantine period.

Vaporetto stop Ca' d'Oro

Just before the rio dei Santi Apostoli stands Palazzo Mangilli Valmarana, built in 1751 for Joseph Smith, the British consul, who amassed the huge collection of Canaletto paintings that now belongs to the Queen. The building is now the Argentinian Consulate.

Beyond the rio dei Santissimi Apostoli stands the Ca' da Mosto, once the site of the Leon Bianco (white lion) Hotel, and currently being returned to its original vocation as a luxury hotel. This is one of the earliest Veneto-Byzantine palazzi on the Grand Canal. It still has three of the original five arches of its water-entrance and a long array of Byzantine arches on the first floor.

At the foot of the Rialto bridge is the Fondaco dei Tedeschi, a huge residence-cum-warehouse leased to the German community from the 13th century onwards. The present building was designed by Spavento and Scarpagnino in 1505-8 after a fire. The façade once included glorious frescoes by Titian and Giorgione; these now lie in a sad state of repair in the Ca' d'Oro gallery (see p103). The Fondaco is now the main post office.

Vaporetto stop San Stae

On the rio di Ca' Pesaro, and with a magnificent side wall curving along the canal in gleaming marble, is Ca' Pesaro (see p118), a splendid example of Venetian baroque by Longhena.

After two smaller palazzi stands the Palazzo Corner della Regina, with a rusticated ground floor featuring grotesque masks, some just above water level. It was built for a branch of the Corner family, who were descended from Caterina Cornaro, Queen of Cyprus; Caterina was born in an earlier house on the site. The present palazzo dates from the 1720s.

The covered fish market or Pescaria has occupied a site here since the 14th century. The current neo-Gothic construction, however, was only built in 1907, replacing an iron one. Beyond this is a building with an endless parade of arches; this is the longest façade on the Grand Canal and belongs to Sansovino's Fabbriche Nuove, built in 1554-6 for Venice's financial judiciary; it now houses the Court of Assizes.

Just beyond this stands the Fabbriche Vecchie designed by Scarpagnino in the early 16th century.

Before the Rialto bridge, the Palazzo dei Camerlenghi (1523-5) is built around the curve of the canal; the walls lean noticeably. It was the headquarters of the Venetian Exchequer, with a debtors' prison on the ground floor.

Rialto bridge

The **Ponte di Rialto** was built in 1588-92 by the aptly named Antonio Da Ponte. Until the 19th century it was the only bridge over the Grand Canal. It replaced a wooden one, which can be seen in Carpaccio's painting of *The Miracle of the True Cross* in the *Accademia* (*see p132*). After the decision was taken to build it, 60 years passed, during the course of which designs by Michelangelo, Vignola, Sansovino and Palladio were rejected. Da Ponte's simple but effective project eventually got the green light, probably because it maintained the utilitarian features of the previous wooden structure, with its double row of shops. The bridge thus acts as a logical continuation of the market at its foot. Palladio's design was far more beautiful, but made no provision for the sale of counterfeit trainers and plastic gondolas.

Vaporetto stop San Silvestro

Beyond the San Silvestro vaporetto stop are a few houses with Veneto-Byzantine windows and decorations, including **Ca' Barzizza**, one of the earliest Byzantine houses in Venice.

Before the rio San Polo is the 16th-century **Palazzo Cappello Layard**, once the home of Sir Henry Austen Layard, archaeologist and British ambassador to Constantinople.

A little way before the San Tomà stop is the **Palazzo Pisani Moretta**, a large Gothic palazzo of the 15th century, often hired out for Hollywood-style parties.

Between the Rialto bridge and the Rialto vaporetto stop is **Palazzo Manin Dolfin**, with a portico straddling the *fondamenta*. The façade is by Sansovino (late 1530s); the rest was rebuilt by Ludovico Manin, the forlorn last doge of Venice (*see p23*). It now belongs to the Bank of Italy.

⑥ ▶ Vaporetto stop Rialto

Palazzetto Dandolo is a Gothic building that appears to have been squeezed tight by its neighbours. Enrico Dandolo, the blind doge who led the ferocious assault on Constantinople in 1204 (*see p17*) was born in an earlier palazzo that stood on this site.

Palazzo Farsetti and **Palazzo Loredan** are Veneto-Byzantine buildings that now house the city hall and various municipal offices. Though heavily restored, these two adjoining *palazzi* are among the few surviving examples of the 12th-century Venetian house, with its first-floor polyforate window.

Austerely classical **Palazzo Grimani** is one of the largest *palazzi* on the Grand Canal. Its creator, Michele Sanmicheli from Verona, was famous for his military architecture, and this building is characteristically massive and assertive. The Grimani family were nouveaux riches, and the story goes that they wanted each one of their windows to be larger than the front door of the palazzo that used to stand opposite.

Seven *palazzi* further on, before the rio Michiel, stands the pink Palazzo Benzon, home of Countess Marina Querini-Benzon, a great society figure at the end of the 18th century. Byron was charmed by her when she was already in her 60s. She inspired a popular song, '*La biondina in gondoleta*', which the gondoliers used to sing before international tourism imposed the unfittingly Neapolitan '*O' Sole Mio*'.

Before the Sant'Angelo vaporetto stop is the small-scale **Palazzo Corner**, built in the last decade of the 15th century by Mauro Codussi. It is one of the most beautiful early Renaissance buildings in Venice, with a rusticated ground floor, elegant balconies and the characteristic double-arched windows seen in Palazzo Vendramin Calergi (*see above*).

⑦

Vaporetto stop Sant'Angelo

A little beyond the traghetto stop (see p287) for San Tomà stand the four **Palazzi Mocenigo**, with blue and white poles in the water. The central double palazzo (16th century) was where Byron and his menagerie of foxes, monkeys and dogs lived in 1818-9; he wrote to a friend: 'Venice is not an expensive residence… I have my gondola and about 14 servants… and I reside in one of the Mocenigo palaces on the Grand Canal; the rent… is two hundred a year (and I give more than I need have done).'

Just before the San Samuele vaporetto stop is heavy, grey-white **Palazzo Grassi** (see p90), designed by Giorgio Massari. This was the last of the great patrician palazzi, built in grand style in 1748-72 when the city was already in terminal decline. Acquired in the 1980s by Fiat, it was sold again in 2005 as the car maker went into financial crisis; it now belongs to French billionaire François Pinault, who inaugurated his reign with a much-hyped exhibition of contemporary art.

Vaporetto stop San Tomà

Palazzo Balbi (1582-90) – with obelisks, indicating that an admiral lived here – is the seat of the Veneto Regional Council.

The rio Ca' Foscari becomes the rio Novo, dug in the 1930s to provide a short-cut to the station; traffic rocked the foundations of the buildings along the canal, so public transport stopped using the rio in the 1980s. Along it, you can see the archways of the fire station. Between here and **Palazzo Balbi** is a minor building, on a site once scheduled to hold a building by Frank Lloyd Wright; his designs were judged too radical for so conspicuous a spot.

Immediately beyond the rio Ca' Foscari come three mid 15th-century Gothic palazzi. The first and largest is **Ca' Foscari**. It was here that Henry III of France was entertained in 1574, so lavishly that his reason seems to have been knocked permanently askew. Doge Francesco Foscari died here of a broken heart after being ousted from office. The palazzo is now the HQ of the Università Ca' Foscari; after restoration (completed in 2005) the building no longer contains only administrative offices. The next two are the **Palazzi Giustinian**; Wagner stayed in one of them in the winter of 1858-9, composing part of *Tristan und Isolde*. The horn prelude to the third act was inspired by the mournful cries of the gondoliers.

Ca' Rezzonico (see p129) is a baroque masterpiece by Longhena, begun in 1667. Robert Browning died here, staying with his profitably married but otherwise talentless son Pen, who bought the palazzo with his wife's money. Later guests included Whistler and Cole Porter. It now houses the museum of 18th-century Venice.

Vaporetto stop Ca' Rezzonico

Next to the vaporetto stop is the quaint little neo-Gothic Palazzetto Stern, from the end of the 19th century; it has often featured in films, most recently the 2003 remake of the *The Italian Job*. The next building but one is the 15th-century **Palazzo Loredan**. The last palazzo before the Accademia Bridge housed the British vice-consulate until 2003.

Once the church and monastery of Santa Maria della Carità, the **Gallerie dell'Accademia** now boasts an unrivalled collection of Venetian paintings (see p132).

Vaporetto stop San Samuele

The **Ca' del Duca** incorporates in one corner a part of the aggressively rusticated base and columns of a palace that Bartolomeo Bon was going to build for the Cornaro family; in 1461 the site was bought by Francesco Sforza, Duke of Milan; Bon's project, which was clearly on a massive scale, was never completed.

Accademia bridge

In 1932 the iron **Ponte dell'Accademia** built by the Austrians was replaced by a 'temporary' wooden one. When this was discovered to be on the point of collapse in 1984, the Venetians had grown too fond of it to imagine anything else spanning the canal, so it was rebuilt exactly as before.

At the foot of the bridge is **Palazzo Franchetti**, built in the 15th century but much restored and altered in the 19th; it's now used as a conference centre and for exhibitions.

Immediately beyond this are two **Palazzi Barbaro**, which have literary associations. The first one – 15th-century Gothic, with a fine but battered Renaissance water entrance – still partly belongs to the Curtis family, who played host to Henry James at intervals between 1870 and 1875. The building was the model for Milly Theale's palazzo in *The Wings of the Dove*; for information on the present owners, see John Berendt's gossipy *City of Falling Angels*.

Just before one of the few Grand Canal gardens comes the bashful **Casetta delle Rose**, set back behind its own small trellised garden. Canova had a studio here; and controversial novelist Gabriele D'Annunzio, who set one of his most sensuous novels *Il Fuoco (Fire)* in Venice, stayed in the house.

The massive rusticated ground floor of the **Palazzo Corner della Ca' Grande** (now the Prefecture) influenced Longhena's baroque *palazzi*. The highest of High Renaissance, the imposing pile was commissioned in 1537 from Sansovino for Giacomo Cornaro, and built after 1545. Never one to mince words, Ruskin called it 'one of the worst and coldest buildings of the central Renaissance'.

Ponte dell'Accademia

⑫ ▼

Vaporetto stop Accademia

Once under the bridge, after four fine Renaissance *palazzi* comes campo San Vio, one of the few *campi* on the Grand Canal. In the corner is the Anglican church of **St George** (see p298). To one side of the campo is the 16th-century **Palazzo Barbarigo**, with eye-catching but tacky 19th-century mosaics. Next is the pretty Gothic **Palazzo da' Mula**.

A little beyond that is the single-storey **Palazzo Venier dei Leoni**. Work ground to a halt in 1749 when the family opposite objected to their light being blocked by such a huge pile. At the beginning of the 20th century the palazzo was lived in by the extravagant Marchesa Luisa Casati, who used to stroll around the city with a pair of leashed cheetahs and who famously declared 'I want to be a living work of art'. It was later acquired by the only slightly less flamboyant Peggy Guggenheim, who lived here from 1949-79; she was the last person in Venice to have her own private gondola. The building now contains the **Peggy Guggenheim Collection** (see p133).

Next but one comes the pure, lopsided charm of the Renaissance **Ca' Dario**, built in the 1470s, perhaps by Pietro Lombardo, with decorative use of coloured marbles and chimney pots. Venetians say the palazzo is cursed; certainly the list of former owners who have met sticky ends is impressive. It is the setting for a particularly gruesome crime in David Hewson's novel, *Lucifer's Shadow* (2001).

Palazzo Salviati is a 19th-century building with gaudy mosaics advertising the products of the Salviati glass works.

Towards the very end of the parade of *palazzi* is the large neo-Gothic **Palazzo Genovese**, built in 1892 on the site of the abbey of **San Gregorio**; as this guide went to press, the palazzo was being transformed into yet another luxury hotel. Just beyond it are the last remains of the abbey, with a fine 14th-century relief of St Gregory over a Gothic doorway. The former church of the same name can be seen just beyond the apse.

13 ▶ Vaporetto stop Giglio

After campo Santa Maria del Giglio comes the long, 15th-century Gothic facade of **Palazzo Gritti**, now one of Venice's poshest hotels (*see p49*).

Three *palazzi* further on is the narrow Gothic **Palazzo Contarini Fasan**, traditionally, but quite arbitrarily, known as Desdemona's house. It has beautiful balconies with wheel tracery.

The **Europa & Regina** hotel was once the home of Kay Bronson, an American society hostess whose hospitality was much appreciated by Henry James.

The last notable building is **Ca' Giustinian**, built in the late Gothic style of the 1470s, and once a hotel where Verdi, Gautier, Ruskin and Proust stayed. George Eliot's honeymoon here was ruined when her husband fell off the balcony into the Grand Canal and nearly died. At the corner of calle Vallaresso is the legendary **Harry's Bar** (*see p171*).

15 ▶ Vaporetto stop Vallaresso

Just beyond the vaporetto stop lie the pretty **Giardinetti reali** (*see p78*) and **piazza San Marco**.

14 ▶ Vaporetto stop Salute

In a triumphant position, at the very opening of the Grand Canal, stands the wonderfully curvy church of **Santa Maria della Salute** (*see p134*). Baldassare Longhena's audacious baroque creation (1671) took 50 years to build. Every year on 21 November (*see p204*) a procession from the basilica di San Marco makes its way across a specially erected bridge of boats to the church.

Beyond the church is the Patriarchal Seminary. The left bank ends with the **Dogana di Mare** (Customs House, 1677), with its tower, gilded ball, weathervane figure of Fortune and spectacular view out across the Bacino di San Marco towards the Lido. (Eastward-facing, the view is best savoured at sunrise, if you can manage it.) Ships wanting to enter Venice would have their cargoes examined by customs officials, who were based here. The warehouses before the Punta della Dogana date from the 19th century. Negotiations are currently under way between the town council and billionaire François Pinault (*see p131* **Pinault at the Punta?**) to transform these buildings into another exhibition space, after an unsuccessful bid by the Guggenheim Foundation for the property.

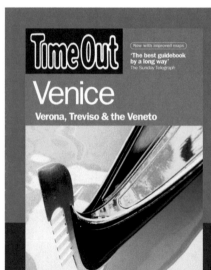

San Marco

The drawing room of Europe in the heart of Venice.

SAN MARCO

This *sestiere* is, of course, the heart of the city and at the very heart's core is the great square with the splendid church that gives the area its name. However, this is by no means all that the area has to offer. A stroll round this central part of the city reveals many other major sights.

The geography is not as difficult as it may first seem; there are essentially three main thoroughfares which link the key points of this neighbourhood, forming a rough triangle: one runs from piazza San Marco to the Rialto bridge, one from the Rialto to the Accademia bridge, and one from the Accademia to piazza San Marco. If you want a brief respite from the jostling crowds, it is always possible to wander off these routes; even in this most tourist-packed *sestiere* you can always find little havens of purely Venetian calm.

Piazza San Marco

Napoleon referred to piazza San Marco as the 'drawing room of Europe', a description that catches some of the quality of the place: it may not be homely, but it is a supremely civilised meeting place. Byzantine rubs shoulders with Gothic, late Renaissance and neo-classical. Napoleon intended to embellish this open-air salon with a statue of himself in the centre of the western wing. The work (acquired in 2002 by the **Museo Correr**, *see p83*) remained in front of the Palazzo Ducale for a few years but never made it into the piazza: the Venetians have always kept the square clear of public monuments (on occasions stooping to mendacity to do so – *see p93* **Monument to Bartolomeo Colleoni**). This is typical of Venice, where individual glory was always kept firmly in second place to communal progress.

The north side of the square dates from the early 16th century. Its 'troops of ordered arches' (to quote Victorian critic John Ruskin) take up a motif suggested by an earlier Byzantine building that can be seen in Gentile Bellini's painting *Translation of the Relics of the Cross* in the **Accademia** gallery (*see p132*). Here resided the procurators of St Mark's, who were in charge of maintaining the basilica – hence the name of this whole wing, the Procuratie Vecchie. At its eastern end is the **Torre dell'Orologio** (*see p87*).

Construction of the Procuratie Nuove on the other side of the square went on for most of the first half of the 17th century; it was built to designs by Vincenzo Scamozzi on the model of the Biblioteca Marciana around the corner. Napoleon, of course, had to join the two wings at the far end – not for the sake of symmetry, but in order to create the ballroom that was lacking in the Procuratie Nuove, which had become the imperial residence. So, in 1807, down came Sansovino's church of San Geminiano and up went the Ala Napoleonica, which now houses the Museo Correr. The cafés under the arches have their history too; but before you take the weight off your feet, bear in mind that a cup of coffee at an outside table may double your day's expenses.

The **Campanile** (*see p82*) and **Basilica di San Marco** (*see p78*) close off the square in all its splendour to the east.

PIAZZETTA DEI LEONCINI

On the north side of the basilica is this small square, named after two small marble lions rubbed smooth by generations of children's bottoms. The large palazzo at the far end of the square is the 19th-century residence of the patriarch (cardinal) of Venice which, at the time of writing, was under wraps for restoration.

LA PIAZZETTA

Between the basilica and the lagoon, the Piazzetta, as it is so economically known, is the real entrance to Venice, defined by two free-standing columns of granite. Generations of foreign visitors disembarked here, to be immediately struck by all that pomp and magnificence. The area directly in front of the **Palazzo Ducale** (Doge's Palace, *see p84*) corresponded to the modern-day parliamentary lobby. Known as the *broglio*, it was the place

The **Piazzetta** (*see p77*) is the real entrance to Venice.

where councillors conferred and connived (hence the term 'imbroglio'). Opposite the palace stands the **Biblioteca Marciana** (*see p83*), now the main city library.

The man who erected the two columns in the 12th century supposedly asked for the right to set up gambling tables between them. The authorities agreed, but soon put a damper on the jollity by using the pillars to string up criminals – which is why superstitious locals still avoid walking between them. What appears to be a winged lion on top of the eastern column is in fact a chimera from Persia, Syria or maybe China; the wings and book are Venetian additions. St Theodore, who tops the other one, was Venice's first patron saint.

BY THE LAGOON
West of the Piazzetta are the **Giardinetti Reali** (Royal Gardens), created by the French, who had the old granaries pulled down to provide a view for the royal residence they had set up in the Procuratie Nuove. The dainty neo-classical coffee house by Gustavo Selva is now a tourist information office (*see p302*).

By the Vallaresso vaporetto stop is Harry's Bar (*see p171*), the most famous watering hole in the city, founded in the 1920s. Ernest Hemingway, Orson Welles and many other famous drinkers have contributed to the legend of the place and the price of the food.

Going the opposite way from the Piazzetta, you cross the **ponte della Paglia** (Bridge of Straw). If you can elbow your way to the side of the bridge, there is a photo-op view of the **ponte dei Sospiri** (**Bridge of Sighs**), famous in legend and poetry linking the Palazzo Ducale to the prisons and thus, supposedly, offering a last glimpse of the outside to the condemned wretches. From the Bridge of Straw there is also a superb view of the Renaissance façade of the Palazzo Ducale, by Antonio Rizzo, which even Ruskin – a fan of the Byzantine and Gothic – was forced to admire against his will.

TICKETS
The museums around piazza San Marco (but not the paying parts of the basilica) must be visited on a multi-entrance ticket or with the Venice Card. *See p67* **Musei Civici Veneziani**, **Musei di piazza San Marco** and *p68* **Discount cards**.

Basilica di San Marco
San Marco, piazza San Marco (041 522 5205). Vaporetto San Zaccaria or Vallaresso. Basilica, Chancel & Pala d'Oro, Treasury **Open** *May-Sept* 9.45am-5.30pm Mon-Sat; 2-4pm Sun. *Oct-Apr* 9.45am-4.30pm Mon-Sat; 2-4pm Sun. **Admission** *Basilica* free. *Chancel & Pala d'Oro* €1.50; €1 concessions. *Treasury* €2; €1 concessions. *Loggia & Museo Marciano.* **Open** *Apr-Oct* 9.45am-5pm daily. *Nov-Mar* 9.45am-4pm daily. **Admission** €3; €1.50 concessions. **No credit cards**. **Map** p326 C1.
Note that large bags or rucksacks must be deposited at no charge in a building in calle San Basso, off the piazzetta dei Leoncini. The basilica is open for mass and private prayer from 7-9.45am, with entrance from the piazzetta dei Leoncini door.

Throughout history, the basilica di San Marco has provoked extreme reactions. Some, like John Ruskin, pitch head first into purple prose: 'The crests of the arches break into a marble foam, and toss themselves far into the blue sky in flashes and wreaths of sculpted spray.' Others, resentful of its opulence, take the dissenting view. Mark Twain described it as a 'vast and warty bug taking a meditative walk'.

Often seen as the living testimony of Venice's links with Byzantium, the basilica is also an expression of the city's independence. In the Middle Ages any self-respecting city state had to have a truly important holy relic. So when two Venetian merchants swiped the body of St Mark (though some historians believe they got Alexander the Great's remains by mistake) from Alexandria in 828, concealed from prying Muslim eyes under a protective layer of pork, they were going for the very best – an Evangelist, and an entire body at that. Fortunately, there was a legend (or one was quickly cooked up) that the saint had once been caught in the lagoon in a storm, and so it was fitting that this should be his final resting place.

The Venetians were traders, but they never looked askance at a bit of straightforward looting as well. The basilica – like the city as a whole – is encrusted with trophies brought back from Venice's greatest spoliatory exploit, the Sack of Constantinople in 1204, during the free-for-all that went under the name of the Fourth Crusade.

The present basilica is the third on the site. It was built mainly between 1063 and 1094, although the work of decoration continued all the way through to the 16th century. The church only became Venice's cathedral in 1807, ten years after the fall of the Republic; until then the bishop exerted his authority from San Pietro in Castello (see p101).

Next door to the Palazzo Ducale, Venice's most important church was associated with political as much as spiritual power. Venetians who came to worship here were very aware that they were guests of the doge, not the pope, and the basilica was an integral part of the city's self-glorifying mythology.

Exterior

The first view of the basilica from the western end of the square is an unforgettable experience. It is particularly impressive in the evening, when the mosaics on the façade glow in the light of the setting sun (as they are mostly 17th- and 18th-century replacements, the distance improves them). The façade consists of two orders of five arches, with clusters of columns in the lower order; the upper arches are topped by the fantastic Gothic tracery that inspired Ruskin to reach for those metaphors.

The only original mosaic is the one over the north door, *The Translation of the Body of St Mark to the Basilica*, which contains the earliest known representation of the church; it dates from around 1260. Of curiosity value is the 17th-century mosaic over the south door, which shows the body of St Mark being filched from Alexandria and the Muslims reeling back in disgust from its pork wrapping.

The real treasures, though, are the sculptures, particularly the group of three carved arches around the central portal, a masterpiece of Romanesque work. The inner curve of the outer arch is the liveliest, with its detailed portrayals of Venetian trades, arts, crafts and pastimes such as shipbuilding, hunting and fishing. The upper order, with its fine 14th-century Gothic sculpture by the Dalle Masegne brothers and later Tuscan and Lombard sculptors, can be seen from the Loggia.

The south façade, towards the Palazzo Ducale, was the first side seen by visitors from the sea and is thus richly encrusted with trophies proclaiming Venice's might. There was a ceremonial entrance to the basilica here as well, but this was blocked by the construction of the Zen Chapel (see p81) in the 16th century. At the corner stand the Tetrarchs, a fourth-century porphyry group of four conspiratorial-looking kings. These come from Constantinople and are usually accepted as representing Diocletian and his Imperial colleagues. However, popular lore has it that they are four Saracens turned to stone after an attempt to burgle the Treasury.

The two free-standing pillars in front of the Baptistry door, with Syrian carvings from the fifth century, come from Acre, as does the stumpy porphyry column on the corner, known as the Pietra del Bando, where official decrees were read. It bore the brunt of the fall of the Campanile (see p82) in 1902, hence its rather battered appearance.

The north façade, facing piazzetta dei Leoncini, is also studded with loot. One example is the carving of 12 sheep on either side of a throne bearing a cross, a Byzantine work of the seventh century. Note the beautiful 13th-century Moorish arches of the Porta dei Fiori, which enclose a Nativity scene.

The narthex (porch) has an opus sectile marble floor; a small lozenge of porphyry by the central door is said to mark the spot where the Emperor Barbarossa paid homage to Pope Alexander III in 1177. The influence of Islamic art comes through in the few remaining grilles that cover the wall niches where early doges were buried. Above, a series of 13th-century mosaics by Venetian craftsmen in the Byzantine style shows Old Testament scenes.

Interior

A lifetime would hardly suffice to see everything contained in this cave of wonders. But you'll probably have to make do with a couple of stopovers, preferably at different times of day, to appreciate the varying effects of light on the mosaics. The lambent interior exudes splendour and mystery, even when bursting with tourists. It is in many ways an exercise in obsession: for centuries the Venetians continued to add to its treasures, leaving nothing uncovered.

The basilica is Greek in form, surmounted by five great 11th-century domes. The surfaces – all the surfaces – are covered by more than four square kilometres (1.5 square miles) of mosaics, the result of 600 years of labour. The finest pieces, dating from the 12th and 13th centuries, are the work of Venetian craftsmen influenced by Byzantine art but developing their own independent style. The chapels and Baptistry were decorated in the 14th and 15th centuries; a century later, replacements of earlier mosaics were made using cartoons by such artists

Setting Venice to music

Venice has always had a close connection with opera. It's not just that its opera houses have seen numerous important premières, from Verdi to Stravinsky to Britten; the city itself has been literally set to music.

Few other places have provided the backdrop for so many major works. Opera composers have seized upon its theatrical quality to create some splendid music, evoking all the mysterious slipperiness of this watery city.

Not surprisingly, some of the first Venetian operas have libretti by Venice's greatest dramatist, Carlo Goldoni (*see p116* **Literary Venice**). A dramatic all-rounder, Goldoni inevitably ended up writing for Vivaldi and Galuppi. Even the 12-year-old Mozart attempted to set one of his works to music. However, few of these have the familiar Venetian settings of Goldoni's plays. It is not until the Romantic period that we find any major operas actually set in Venice – and, as with the best literature set here, it was non-Venetians who reacted most keenly to the city's magic.

It was the most famous poet-in-exile of all who really set the ball rolling. Byron's Venetian dramas proved particularly alluring to Italian composers. Donizetti turned *Marino Faliero* (1835) into an opera; Verdi did the same for his sombre drama *The Two Foscari* (1844), a particularly claustrophobic piece set almost entirely between the Doge's Palace and the prisons, with just one unconvincing barcarolle in piazza San Marco in an attempt to lighten the atmosphere.

Verdi put the lagoon at the centre of another opera, *Attila*, which, like *Ernani*, *Rigoletto* and *La Traviata*, premiered in Venice (1846); the second scene opens with the fleeing citizens of Aquileia bemoaning their homelessness amid the unpromising mud-flats. In his much later and decidedly less romantic opera *Otello* (1887), Verdi resists the temptation of

La Serenissima, confining the action to Cyprus – unlike an earlier version by Rossini (1816) which is set entirely on the lagoon.

Wagner, who loved Venice and paid it the ultimate tribute of dying there, set none of his determinedly Teutonic operas there. However, the city made its musical contribution to *Tristan und Isolde* (1865): the shepherd's mournful pipe-tune in Act III was inspired by the cries of gondoliers beneath Palazzo Giustinian (*see p73*) where he composed the work.

The most unabashedly melodramatic portrait of the city is to be found in an enjoyable work by a lesser-known composer, Amilcare Ponchielli. *La Gioconda* (1876) is based on a play by Victor Hugo and presents all the clichés of the Venetian anti-myth: spies, secret denunciations, the Inquisition and the sinister Council of Ten. As it calls for six first-rate principals and has a large-scale ballet, it is rarely staged.

A more enchanting, if still unsettling, vision of the city is to be found in Act III of Offenbach's *The Tales of Hoffmann* (1881), in which it acts as backdrop to one of Hoffmann's fantastic stories; the opera includes the most haunting and famous of all barcarolles. Johann Strauss adopted an 18th-century setting for his purely escapist operetta *Eine nacht in Venedig* (1883), which includes a polka celebrating the pigeons of San Marco.

In the 20th century Venetian Ermanno Wolf-Ferrari turned a number of Goldoni's locally set comedies into light operas, the most successful being *I quattro rusteghi* (1906) and *Il campiello* (1935), which are often revived in the composer's home-town.

With Benjamin Britten's last opera, *Death in Venice* (1973), we return to Venice as the city of melancholy brooding. Britten, a composer always inspired by the sea, reacts strongly to the mysteriously amphibious quality of the city.

as Titian and Tintoretto. However, most of these later mosaics are fundamentally flawed by the attempt to achieve the three-dimensional effects of Renaissance painting.

In the apse, Christ Pantocrator is a 16th-century reproduction of a Byzantine original. Beneath, in what may be the oldest mosaics in the church, are four saint-protectors of Venice: Nicholas, Peter, Mark and Hermagoras. The central dome of the

Ascension, with its splendidly poised angels and apostles, dates from the early 13th century. It is said to have influenced fresco painting in the area as well as the sculptures on the façade. The Passion scenes on the west vault (12th century) are a striking blend of Romanesque and Byzantine styles. The Pentecost dome (near the entrance) was probably the first to be decorated; it shows the *Descent of the Holy Spirit*. Four magnificent angels hover in the pendentives.

Worth seeking out is the scene of the *Miraculous Rediscovery of the Body of St Mark* in the right transept. This refers to an episode that occurred after the second basilica was destroyed by fire, when the secret of the whereabouts of the body was lost. The Evangelist obligingly opened up the pillar where his sarcophagus had been hidden (it's just opposite and is marked by an inlaid marble panel). Notice too the spectacular 12th-century marble, porphyry and glass mosaics on the floor, which have been much restored.

Baptistry & Zen Chapel

The Baptistry contains the Gothic tomb of Doge Andrea Dandolo and some interesting mosaics such as an image of Salome dancing. It is open for private prayer; enter discreetly if you must. The adjoining Zen Chapel, with its bronze 16th-century tomb of Cardinal Zen (a common Venetian surname), was closed for restoration as this guide went to press.

Chancel & Pala d'Oro

The Chancel is separated from the body of the church by the iconostasis – a red marble rood screen by the Gothic sculptors Jacobello and Pier Paolo Dalle Masegne, with fine naturalistic statues of the Madonna, the apostles and St George. Access to the Chancel is via the San Clemente chapel to the right, with a mosaic showing merchants Rustico di Torcello and Buono di Malamocco, apparently about to Fed-Ex the body of St Mark to Venice. St Mark's sarcophagus is visible through the grate underneath the altar. It was moved here from the 11th-century crypt in 1835; the crypt remains a popular venue for society weddings, though it's closed to the rest of us.

The indigestibly opulent Pala d'Oro (Gold Altarpiece) is a Byzantine work and, for a change, was acquired honestly. It was made in Constantinople in 976 on the orders of Doge Pietro Orseolo I and further enriched in later years with amethysts, emeralds, pearls, rubies, sapphires and topaz, topped off with a Gothic frame and resetting in 1345. It's a worldly corner of the church, this. Set in the frame of the curving sacristy door are bronze busts of its maker, Sansovino, and his friends, Titian and Aretino, who helped to get him out of prison in 1545. Aretino was a poet and playwright who moved to Venice in 1527 after scandalising Rome with his 'Lewd Sonnets'. A great satirist and hedonist, he is said to have died laughing at a filthy joke about his sister.

The left transept contains the chapel of the Madonna Nicopeia (the Victory Bringer), named after the tenth-century icon on the altar – another Fourth Crusade acquisition. She is still much revered: early in the morning praying Venetians can often be seen here confiding in her. The St Isidore chapel beyond, with its 14th-century mosaics of the life of the saint, is reserved for private prayer and confessions; as with the Baptistry, visitors are asked to show discretion if entering. The same goes for the adjacent Mascoli chapel. The altarpiece in this chapel, featuring Saints Mark and John the Evangelist, with the Virgin between them (in this

Piazza San Marco
See p77.

Sightseeing

unusual representation the Virgin has a graceful bend round about her midriff), is a striking piece of Gothic statuary. The chapel's mosaics, dating from 1430-50, have a definite Renaissance look to them, with classical architecture featuring in their backgrounds. They are mostly by Michele Giambono, although some of the figures have been attributed to Jacopo Bellini and to the Florentine Andrea del Castagno, who was in Venice in 1432, working in San Zaccaria, *see p96*.

Loggia & Museo Marciano

Of all the pay-to-enter sections of the basilica, this is definitely the most worthwhile – and moreover it's the only part of the church that can be visited on a Sunday morning. Up a narrow stairway from the narthex are the bronze horses that vie with the book-bearing lion of St Mark as the city's symbol; here too is Paolo Veneziano's exquisite Pala Feriale, a painted panel that was used to cover the Pala d'Oro on weekdays. The Loggia also provides a marvellous view over the square.

The original bronze horses are now kept indoors. They are the greatest piece of loot – apart from the body of St Mark – in the whole city. They were among the many treasures that Venice brought back from the Sack of Constantinople, where they had stood above the Hippodrome. The horses' origins are uncertain. For many years they were attributed to a Greek sculptor of the fourth century BC, but the idea that they may be an original Roman work of the second century AD has recently come into favour: the half-moon shape of their eyes is said to have been a

Roman characteristic. They were at first placed in front of the Arsenale (*see p88*), but around 1250 they found their place of honour on the terrace of the basilica, supreme expressions of Venetian pride.

In 1797 it was Napoleon's turn to play looter; the horses did not return to Venice from Paris until after his defeat at Waterloo. Apart from the parentheses of the two World Wars, when they were put away in safe storage, they remained on the terrace until 1974, when they were removed for restoration. Since 1982 they have been on display in a room inside the basilica, with exact but soulless copies replacing them on the terrace.

Treasury

This contains a hoard of exquisite Byzantine gold and silver plunder – reliquaries, chalices, candelabras. If you can stand the glitter, the highlights are a silver perfume censer in the form of a church and two 11th-century icons of the Archangel Michael.

Campanile

San Marco, piazza San Marco.
Vaporetto San Zaccaria or Vallaresso.
Open *Apr-June,*
Sept-Oct 9.30am-7pm daily. *July-Aug* 9am-9pm daily. *Nov-Mar* 9.30am-4.15pm daily. **Admission** €6; €3 concessions. **No credit cards. Map** p326 C1.

Venice's most protuberant landmark – at almost 99m (325ft) it's the tallest building in the city – was originally built between 888 and 912. Its present appearance, with the stone spire and the gilded angel on top, dates from 1514.

The Campanile served both as a watchtower and a bell tower. It provided a site for public humiliations: people of 'scandalous behaviour' were hung in a cage from the top. More wholesome fun was provided by the *volo dell'anzolo*, when an *arsenalotto* (shipwright) would slide down a rope strung between the Campanile and the Palazzo Ducale at the end of Carnevale.

In July 1902 it fell down. Some blamed old age and weak foundations; others, such as crusty old travel writer Augustus Hare, put it down to 'gross neglect and criminal misusage'. The Campanile was tidy in its collapse, imploding in a neat pyramid of rubble; the only victim was the custodian's cat.

Torre dell'Orologio. *See p87.*

It was rebuilt exactly 'as it was, where it was', as the town council of the day promised. Holy Roman Emperor Frederick III rode a horse to the top of the old version in 1451; these days visitors take the lift. The view through the anti-suicide grate is superb, taking in the Lido, the whole lagoon and (on a clear day) the Dolomites in the distance. Sansovino's little Loggetta at the foot of the tower, which echoes the shape of a Roman triumphal arch, was also rebuilt, jigsaw-fashion, using bits and pieces found in the rubble. In the 18th century the Loggetta was where the state lottery was drawn.

Museo Correr, Biblioteca Marciana & Museo Archeologico

San Marco 52, piazza San Marco/sottoportego San Geminian (041 240 5211/www.museicivici veneziani.it). Vaporetto Vallaresso. **Open** *Apr-Oct* 9am-7pm daily (ticket office closes 6pm). *Nov-Mar* 9am-5pm daily (ticket office closes 4pm). **Admission** by multi-entrance ticket (*see p68* **Musei di Piazza San Marco**). **Map** p326 B2.

These three adjoining museums are all entered on the same ticket and by the same doorway, which is situated beneath the Ala Napoleonica at the western end of piazza San Marco.

Museo Correr

The Museo Correr is Venice's civic museum, dedicated to the history of the Republic – which means that it acts as a storeroom for all the bits and pieces that didn't fit in elsewhere. Based on the private collection of Venetian nobleman Teodoro Correr (1750-1830), it is elevated beyond mere curiosity value by the second-floor gallery, which is essential viewing for anyone interested in Venetian early Renaissance painting. The museum is housed in the Ala Napoleonica, the wing that closes off the narrow western end of the piazza, and in the Procuratie Nuove. Napoleon demolished the church of San Geminiano to make way for this exercise in neo-classical regularity, complete with that essential imperial accessory, a ballroom. The spirit of these years is conserved in the first part of the collection, dedicated to the beautiful if icy sculpture of Antonio Canova, whose first Venetian commission – the statue of Daedalus and Icarus, displayed here – brought him immediate acclaim. Some of the works on display are Canova's plaster models rather than his finished marble statues.

The historical collection, which occupies most of the first floor of the Procuratie Vecchie building, documents Venetian history and social life in the 16th and 17th centuries. Among the globes, lutes, coins and robes, interesting light is thrown on various aspects of life in the Republic. Room 6, devoted to the figure of the doge, features Lazzaro Bastiani's famous portrait of Doge Francesco Foscari (c1460). Room 11 has a collection of Venetian coins, plus Tintoretto's fine *St Justine and the Treasurers*. Beyond are rooms dedicated to the Arsenale (*see p88*): a display of weaponry and some occasionally charming miniature bronzes.

The bulk of one's critical energy should be saved, however, for the Quadreria picture gallery upstairs – perhaps the best place in the city to get a grip on the development of Venetian painting between the Byzantine stirrings of Paolo Veneziano and the full-blown Renaissance story-telling of Carpaccio. Rooms 24 to 29 are dedicated to Byzantine and Gothic painters – note Paolo Veneziano's fine *St John the Baptist* and the rare allegorical fresco fragments from a 14th-century private house in Room 27. Room 30 fast-forwards abruptly with the macabre, proto-Mannerist *Pietà* of Cosme Turà.

Room 32, the Sala delle Quattro Porte, is one of the only rooms in the museum that still preserves its 16th-century structure; it contains the famous aerial view of Venice by Jacopo de' Barbari, dated 1500. This extraordinary woodcut is so finely detailed that the architectural details of every single church, palazzo and well head in the city seem to have been diligently copied; also on display are the original matrices in pear wood. Beyond here, the Renaissance gets into full swing with Antonello da Messina's *Pietà with Three Angels*, haunting despite the fact that the faces have nearly been erased by cack-handed restoration. The Bellinis get Room 36 to themselves – note the rubicund portrait of Doge Giovanni Mocenigo by Gentile Bellini (1475).

The gallery's most fascinating work, though, must be Vittore Carpaccio's *Two Venetian Noblewomen* – long known erroneously as *The Courtesans* – in Room 38. These two bored women are not angling for trade: they're waiting for their husbands to return from a hunt. This was confirmed when *A Hunt in the Valley* in the Getty Museum in Los Angeles was shown to be this painting's other half. Downstairs, the collection continues with rooms dedicated to the Bucintoro (state barge), festivities and trade guilds. The last two rooms have paintings of fairground trials of strength.

Museo Archeologico

This collection of Greek and Roman art and artefacts is interesting not so much for the quality of the individual pieces as for the light they cast on the history of collecting. Assembled mainly by Cardinal Domenico Grimani and his nephew Giovanni, mainly from Roman finds, the collection is a discerning 16th-century humanist's attempt to surround himself with the classical ideal of beauty; as such these statues were much copied by Venetian artists. Among the highlights are the original fifth-century BC Greek statues of goddesses in Room 4, which are among the few such works known to the Italian Renaissance, the Grimani Altar in Room 6, and the intricate cameos and intaglios in Room 7 or Room 12 (depending on temporary exhibitions).

There are free guided tours in English (11am Sat & 10.30am Sun); it's best to book (041 522 5978). **Biblioteca Marciana/Libreria Sansoviniana** For information on use of the library, *see p285*.

In 1468 the great humanist scholar Cardinal Bessarion of Trebizond left his collection of Greek and Latin manuscripts to the state. This time the

Venetians didn't lose them, as they seem to have done with Petrarch's library, although they didn't get round to constructing a proper home for them – a splendid building right opposite the Palazzo Ducale – until 1537. Jacopo Sansovino, a Florentine architect who had settled in Venice after fleeing from the Sack of Rome in 1527, was appointed to create the library. Palladio described it as the 'richest and most ornate building since antiquity'.

With this building, Sansovino brought the ambitious new ideas of the Roman Renaissance of Donato Bramante and Michelangelo into Venice. He also appealed to the Venetian love of surface decoration by endowing his creation with an abundance of statuary. His original plan included a barrel-vault ceiling. This collapsed shortly after construction, however, and the architect was immediately clapped into prison. His rowdy friends Titian and Aretino had to lobby hard to have him released.

The working part of Venice's main library is now housed in La Zecca (see p87) and contains some 750,000 volumes and around 13,500 manuscripts, most of them Greek.

The main room has a magnificent ceiling, with seven rows of allegorical medallion paintings, produced by a number of Venetian Mannerist artists as part of a competition. Veronese's *Music* (sixth row from entrance), perhaps the least Mannerist in style, was awarded the gold chain by Titian. Beyond this is the ante-room, in which a partial reconstruction has been made of Cardinal Grimani's collection of classical statues, as arranged by Scamozzi (1596). On the ceiling is *Wisdom*, a late work by Titian.

In a room off the staircase landing is Fra Mauro's map of the world (1459), a fascinating testimony to the great precision of Venice's geographical knowledge, with extraordinarily accurate depictions of such places as China and India.

There are free guided tours (10am, noon, 2pm, 3pm Sat & Sun; to be sure of a tour in English phone tel. 041 240 7241); tours can be booked on Thursdays.

Palazzo Ducale (Doge's Palace)

San Marco 1, piazzetta San Marco (041 271 5911/bookings 041 520 9070/www.museicivici veneziani.it). Vaporetto San Zaccaria. **Open** *Apr-Oct* 9am-7pm daily (ticket office closes 6pm). *Nov-Mar* 9am-5pm daily (ticket office closes 4pm). **Admission** with multi-entrance ticket (*see p68* **Musei di Piazza San Marco**). **No credit cards. Map** p326 C1.

There are frequent guided tours (€6) of the palace from November to March; call 041 520 9038 for information and bookings.

An unobtrusive side door halfway down the right wall of the nave in San Marco leads straight into the courtyard of the Palazzo Ducale (Doge's Palace). Today's visitors take a more roundabout route, but that door is a potent symbol of the entwinement of Church and state in the glory days of *La Serenissima*. If the basilica was the Venetian Republic's spiritual nerve centre, the Doge's Palace was its political and judicial hub. The present site

was the seat of ducal power from the ninth century onwards, though most of what we see today dates from the mid 15th century. Devastating fires in 1574 and 1577 took their toll, but after much debate it was decided to restore rather than replace – an enlightened policy for the time.

The architectural form of the building testifies to Venetian confidence in the impossibility of invasion or attack: whereas Renaissance seats of government in other Italian towns look like castles, this is very definitely a palace. It is the great Gothic building of the city, but is also curiously eastern in style, achieving a marvellous combination of lightness and strength. The ground floor was open to the public; the work of government went on in the more closed part above. This arrangement resulted in a curious reversal of the natural order. The building gets heavier as it rises: the first level has an open arcade of simple Gothic arches, the second a closed loggia of rich, ornate arcading. The top floor is a solid wall broken by a sequence of Gothic windows. And yet somehow it doesn't seem awkward.

The Piazzetta façade was built in the 15th century as a continuation of the 14th-century waterfront façade. On the corner by the ponte di Paglia (Bridge of Straw) is an exquisite marble relief carving, the *Drunkenness of Noah* from the early 15th century, while on the Piazzetta corner is a statue of Adam and Eve from the late 14th century. The capitals of the pillars below date from the 14th to the 15th centuries, although many of them are 19th-century copies (some of the originals are on display inside). On the waterfront side (ninth pillar from the left) is what appears to be a boy eating an ice-cream cone; don't disappoint your kids by telling them it's really a chicken leg.

The Porta della carta (or Paper Gate – so called because this was where permits were checked), between the palace and the basilica, is a grand piece of florid Gothic architecture and sculpture (1438-42) by Bartolomeo and Giovanni Bon. The statue of Doge Francesco Foscari and the lion is a copy dating from 1885; French troops smashed the original when they occupied the city in 1797.

Behind the palace's fairy-tale exterior the machinery of empire whirred away with the same kind of assembly-line efficiency that went into the building of ships over at the Arsenale (*see p88*). Anyone really interested in the inner workings of the Venetian state should take the 90-minute *Itinerari segreti* tour (book at least two days in advance, 041 520 9070 or on-line on the www.museicivicveneziani.it website; tours in English depart 9.55am, 10.45am, 11.35am daily, €16, €10 concessions). This takes you into those parts of the palace that the official route does not touch: the cramped wooden administrative offices; the stark chambers of the *Cancelleria segreta* where all official documents were written up in triplicate by a team of 24 clerks; the chamber of the three heads of the Council of Ten, connected by a secret door in the wooden panelling to the *Sala del Consiglio dei Dieci*, and the torture chambers beyond.

Campo Santo Stefano. *See p89.*

The tour ends up in the leads – the sweltering prison cells beneath the roof from which Casanova staged his famous escape (probably by bribing the guard, though his own account was far more action hero) – and among the extraordinary beams and rafters above the Sala del Maggior Consiglio (*see below*).

Following reorganisation, the main visit – for which an audio guide (€5) is recommended – now begins at the Porta del Frumento on the lagoon side of the palace, rather than at the main Piazzetta entrance. At peak times it is worth pre-booking tickets (on 041 520 9070, or online via the www.museicivicivenezianiit website) to bypass the queue.

The Museo dell'Opera, just to the left of the ticket barrier, has the best of the 14th-century capitals from the external loggia; the ones you see outside are mostly copies.

In the main courtyard stands the Arco dei Foscari – another fine late Gothic work, commissioned by Doge Francesco Foscari in 1438, when Venice was at the height of its territorial influence. It was built by Antonio Bregno and Antonio Rizzo. Rizzo also sculpted the figures of Adam and Eve (these too are copies; the originals are in the first-floor *liagò*), which earned him gushing accolades and led to his appointment as official architect in 1483, after one of those disastrous fires. Rizzo had time to oversee the building of the overblown Scala dei Giganti (where doges were crowned) and some of the interior before he was found to have embezzled 12,000 ducats; he promptly fled, and died soon after.

The official route now leads up the ornate Scala d'Oro staircase by Jacopo Sansovino, with stuccoes by Vittoria outlined in 24-carat gold leaf.

First floor: Doge's apartments

And to think this is supposed to be the domestic side of the operation. In reality, the doge's private life was entirely at the service of *La Serenissima*, and even his bedroom had to keep up the PR effort. These rooms are occasionally closed or used for temporary

exhibitions; when open, the Sala delle Mappe (also known as the Sala dello Scudo) merits scrutiny. Here, in a series of 16th-century maps, is the known world as it radiated from Venice. Just to the right of the entrance is a detailed map of the New World with Bofton (Boston) and Isola Longa (Long Island) clearly marked. Further on, it's worth seeking out Titian's well-hidden fresco of St Christopher (above a doorway giving on to a staircase), which, astonishingly, took the artist a mere three days to complete.

Second floor: State rooms

This grandiose series of halls provided steady work for all the great 16th-century Venetian artists. Titian, Tintoretto, Veronese, Palma il Vecchio and Jacopo Bassano all left their mark, though the sheer acreage that had to be covered, and the subjects of the canvases – either allegories or documentary records of the city's pomp and glory – did not always spur them to artistic heights.

The Sala delle Quattro Porte was where the Collegio – the inner cabinet of the Republic – met before the 1574 fire. After substantial renovation it became an ambassadorial waiting room, where humble envoys could gaze enviously at Andrea Vicentino's portrayal of the magnificent reception given to the young King Henry III of France in 1574 (the triumphal arch that you can see in the picture was put up overnight). The Anticollegio, restored in part by Palladio, has a spectacular gilded stucco ceiling, four Tintorettos and Veronese's blowsy *Rape of Europa* (much loved by the novelist Henry James).

Beyond here is the Sala del Collegio, where the inner cabinet convened. The propaganda paintings on the ceiling are by Veronese; note the equal scale of the civic and divine players, and the way that both Justice and Peace are mere handmaidens to Venice herself. But for real hubris you have to stroll into the next room, the Sala del Senato, where Tintoretto's ceiling centrepiece shows *The Triumph of Venice*. Here the Senate, which by 1450 had grown from 60 to an unwieldy 300 members, met to debate questions of foreign policy, war and commerce, and to hear the reports of returning Venetian ambassadors. Beyond again are the Sala del Consiglio dei Dieci and the Sala della Bussola, where the arcane body set up specifically to act as a check on the doge considered matters of national security. In the former, note Veronese's ceiling panel, *Juno Offering Gifts to Venice*. By the time this was painted in 1553, the classical gods had started to replace St Mark in Venice's self-aggrandising pantheon.

Here the itinerary heads through a bristling armoury, whose ingenious instruments of war impressed early visitors. But, as one 17th-century tourist pointed out, the collection was established so that 'if the People should conspire against the Nobles, and make any Attempt against them while they are sitting, they might be furnished with Arms upon the Spot to defend themselves'.

First floor: State rooms

The Sala dei Censori now leads down to a *liagò* (covered, L-shaped loggia), which gives on to the Sala della Quarantia Civil Vecchia (the civil court) and the Sala del Guariento. The latter's faded 14th-century fresco of *The Coronation of the Virgin* by Guariento (for centuries hidden behind Tintoretto's *Paradiso* in the Sala del Maggior Consiglio) looks strangely innocent amid all this worldly propaganda. The shorter arm of the *liagò* has the originals of Antonio Rizzo's stylised marble sculptures of Adam and Eve from the Arco dei Foscari.

Next comes the Sala del Maggior Consiglio – the largest room in the palace. It had to be big, as by 1512, according to historian Marin Sanudo, 2,622 patrician men were entitled to sit on the *maggior consiglio* (Greater Council). This was in effect the Republic's lower house – though with the top-heavy Venetian system of government, this council of noblemen had fairly limited powers. Before the fire of 1577 the hall had been decorated with paintings by Bellini, Titian, Carpaccio and Veronese – a choice collection that was so costly to commission that in

1515 a group of patricians complained about the expense. When these works went up in smoke, they were replaced by less exalted works – with one or two exceptions. Tintoretto's *Paradise* on the far wall, sketched out by the 70-year-old artist but completed after his death in 1594 by his son Domenico, is liable to induce vertigo, as much for its theological complexity as its huge scale. In the ceiling panels are works by Veronese and Palma il Giovane; note too the frieze of ducal portraits carried out by Domenico Tintoretto and assistants, with the black veil marking the place where Marin Falier's face would have appeared had he not unwisely conspired against the state in 1356.

On the left side of the hall, a balcony gives a fine view over the southern side of the lagoon. A door leads from the back of the hall into the Sala della Quarantia Civil Nuova and the large Sala dello Scrutinio, where the votes of the *maggior consiglio* were counted; the latter is flanked by vast paintings of victorious naval battles, including a dramatic *Conquest of Zara* by Jacopo Tintoretto and *Battle of Lepanto* by Andrea Vicentino.

Criminal courts & *prigioni*

Backtracking through the Sala del Maggior Consiglio, a small door on the left leads past the Scala dei Censori to the Sala della Quarantia Criminale – the criminal court. The room next door retains some of the original red and gold leather wall coverings. Beyond this is a small room that has been arranged as a gallery, with Flemish paintings from Cardinal Grimani's collection, originally hidden from public view. The hysterical religious mysticism of Bosch's *Inferno* strikes an odd note here: though rational, Venice was not always immune to religious fanaticism.

The route now leads over the Bridge of Sighs to the Prigioni Nuove, where petty criminals were kept. Lifers were sent down to the waterlogged *pozzi* (wells) in the basement of the palazzo itself. By the

Palazzo Grassi. See p90.

19th century most visitors were falling for the tour guide legend that, once over the Bridge of Sighs, prisoners would 'descend into the dungeon which none entered and hoped to see the sun again', as Mark Twain put it. But when this new prison wing was built in 1589, it was acclaimed as a paragon of comfort; in 1608 the English traveller Thomas Coryat remarked, 'I think there is not a fairer prison in all Christendom'.

Some of the cells have their number and capacity painted over the door; one has a *trompe l'œil* window, drawn in charcoal by a bored inmate. On the lowest level is a small exercise yard, where an unofficial tavern used to operate. Up the stairs beyond is a display of Venetian ceramics found during excavations, and more cells, one with a fascinating display of cartoons and caricatures left by 19th-century internees. Back across the Bridge of Sighs, the tour ends on the lower floor in the Avogaria – the offices of the clerks of court. Next to this a bookshop has been set up, with a good selection of works on Venice. On the ground floor is a welcome (though not particularly cheap) cafeteria.

Torre dell'Orologio

San Marco 147, piazza San Marco (041 522 4951/ www.museicivicivivenezi.it). Vaporetto San Zaccaria. **Open** closed to the public at the time of writing; due to reopen Sept 2006. **Map** p326 C1.

The clock tower, designed by Maurizio Codussi, was built between 1496 and 1506; the wings were an addition, perhaps by Pietro Lombardo. Above the clock face is the Madonna. During Ascension week and at Epiphany, the Magi come out and bow to her every hour, in an angel-led procession. At other times of year the burly Moors on the roof, made of gunmetal and cast in 1497, strike the hour. Another Moore – Roger – sent a villain flying through the clock face in the film *Moonraker*.

In 1999 the tower went under wraps and the whole building, along with the elaborate clock mechanism was restored with the assistance of Maison Piaget. As the guide goes to press, it has not yet been reopened to visitors; when it does so, it will only admit small groups with prior bookings. **Photo** *p82*.

La Zecca

San Marco 7, piazzetta San Marco (041 520 8788). Vaporetto Vallaresso. **Open** 8.10am-7pm Mon-Fri; 8.10am-1.30pm Sat. **Admission** free. **Map** p326 C2.

The Mint, designed by Sansovino, was completed by 1547. It coined Venice's famous gold ducats – later referred to as *zecchini*, whence the English 'sequins'. It is more impregnable in appearance than the neighbouring Biblioteca Marciana (*see p83*), though the façade had to accommodate large windows on the *piano nobile* (for relief from heat) and open arches on the ground floor, where the procurators of St Mark's owned a number of cheese shops. The architect's son, author of the first famous guidebook to the city, described the building as 'a worthy prison for all that precious gold'. It now houses most of the contents of the civic library.

Piazza San Marco to the Rialto

Piazza San Marco is linked to the Rialto by the busiest, richest and narrowest of shopping streets: the Mercerie. The name is plural, since it is divided into five parts: the Merceria dell'Orologio, di **San Zulian** (on which stands the church of the same name, *see p88*), del Capitello, di **San Salvador** (with its homonymous church, *see p87*, in the beautiful cloisters of which is the **Telecom Italia Future Centre** visitors' installation, *see p88*) and del 2 Aprile.

Mercerie mean 'haberdashers', but we know from John Evelyn's 1645 account of 'one of the most delicious streets in the world' that in among the luxury textile emporia were shops selling perfumes and medicines too.

Most of the big-name fashion designers are to be found here now, and most of Venice's short-stay tourists too. The ponte dei Baretteri (the Hatmakers' Bridge), in the middle of the Mercerie, is, by the way, a minor record holder in Venice: there are six different roads and alleys leading directly off the bridge.

The Mercerie emerge near campo San Bartolomeo, the square at the foot of the Rialto, with the statue of playwright Carlo Goldoni looking amusedly down at the milling crowds. This square, together with the nearby campo San Luca, has long been a standard meeting-place for Venetians, although younger Venetians now seem to prefer the bars on the other side of the Rialto Bridge (*see p177* **In the market**).

Calle dei Stagneri leads out of the campo to the 18th-century church of **Santa Maria della Fava** (technically in the *sestiere* of Castello).

Roughly parallel to the Mercerie, from Sotoportego dei Dai halfway down the same side of piazza San Marco, the calle dei Fabbri also leads in the direction of the Rialto; just before the first bridge is the new and mildly controversial **Museo d'Arte Erotica** (*see p88*), with four floors devoted to the rich story of Venice's erotic past.

San Salvador

San Marco, campo San Salvador (041 270 2464). Vaporetto Rialto. **Open** 9am-noon, 4-6.30pm Mon-Sat; 4-6pm Sun. **Map** p322 B5.

If you can't make it to Florence on this trip, come to San Salvador instead, which has one of Venice's most Brunelleschi-esque interiors: a pass-the-baton effort begun by Giorgio Spavento in 1506, continued by Tullio Lombardo and completed by Sansovino in 1534. But even though the geometrical sense of space and the use of soft-toned greys and whites exude Tuscan elegance, the key to the church's structure is in fact a combination of three domed

Greek crosses, which look back to the Byzantine tradition of St Mark's. The church contains two great Titians, the *Annunciation* at the end of the right-hand aisle (with the signature '*Tizianus fecit, fecit*'; the repetition was intended either to emphasise the wonder of his unflagging creativity, or is a simple absent-minded mistake – take your pick) and the *Transfiguration* on the high altar; the latter painting conceals a silver reredos, revealed at Christmas, Easter and 6 August (the feast of San Salvador).

There's also some splendid Veneto-Tuscan sculpture, including Sansovino's monument to Doge Francesco Venier, situated between the second and third altar on the right. Here too, at the end of the right transept, is the tomb of Cristina Cornaro, the hapless Queen of Cyprus (d.1510), a pawn in a game of Mediterranean strategy that ended with her being forced into abdicating the island to Venetian rule. By way of compensation she was palmed off with the town of Asolo (*see p276*) and the title 'Daughter of the Republic'. In the left aisle, the third altar belonged to the school of the Luganagheri (sausage makers), and has vibrant figures of San Rocco and San Sebastiano by Alessandro Vittoria, influenced by Michelangelo's *Slaves*. The sacristy contains delightful 16th-century frescoes of birds and leafage, discovered in the 1920s and restored in 2003.

Santa Maria della Fava

San Marco, campo della Fava (041 522 4601). *Vaporetto Rialto*. **Open** 8.30-11.30am, 4.30-7pm Mon-Sat. **Map** p322 B5.
St Mary of the Bean – the name refers to a popular bean cake that was turned out by a bakery that used to stand nearby – is on one of the quieter routes between the Rialto and San Marco. This 18th-century church is worth visiting for two paintings by the city's greatest artists of that period, which neatly illustrate their contrasting temperaments. Tiepolo's *Education of the Virgin* (first altar on the right) is an early work, painted when he was still under the influence of Giovanni Battista Piazzetta; but the bright colours and touchingly human relationships of the figures are nonetheless in great contrast with the sombre browns and reds of the latter's *Virgin and Child with St Philip Neri* (second altar on the left). In Piazzetta's more earnest painting, which still bears traces of Counter-Reformation gravity, the lily, bishop's mitre and cardinals' hats show the worldly honours rejected by the saint.

San Zulian

San Marco, mercerie San Zulian (041 523 5383). *Vaporetto Vallaresso or San Zaccaria*. **Open** 8.30am-7pm daily. Mass in English 11.30am & 7pm Sun. **Map** p326 B1.
The classical simplicity of Sansovino's façade (1553-55) is offset by a grand monument to Tommaso Rangone, a wealthy and far from self-effacing showman-scholar from Ravenna, whose fortune was made by a treatment for syphilis, and who wrote a book on how to live to 120 (he only made it to 80 himself). He unilaterally declared his library to be one of the seven wonders of the world, and had himself prominently portrayed in all three of Tintoretto's paintings for the Scuola di San Marco (now in the Accademia, *see p88*). The interior has a ceiling painting of *The Apotheosis of St Julian* by Palma il Giovane, here in Tintoretto mode, and a more Titianesque *Assumption* by the same painter on the second altar on the right, which also has good statues of St Catherine of Alexandria and Daniel by Alessandro Vittoria. The first altar on the right has a *Pietà* by Veronese. San Giuliano (Zulian to Venetians) is one of only two churches in Venice that you can walk all the way around. (The other is the Angelo Raffaele in Dorsoduro, *see p126*.)

Museo d'Arte Erotica

San Marco 834, calle dei Fabbri (041 520 3900/ *www.museodarteerotica.it*). *Vaporetto Vallaresso or San Zaccaria*. **Open** 10am-11pm daily. **Admission** €10; €6-€8 concessions. **Credit** AmEx, DC, MC, V. **Map** p326 B1.
This museum (accessible to over-18s only) opened in spring 2006 to inevitable protests from the religious authorities of Venice and other local worthies. The museum itself was perhaps equally inevitable, in the city of Casanova and Veronica Franco (*see p21* **La più onorata cortigiana**). It occupies four floors of Palazzo Rota in the busy calle dei Fabbri and hosts a number of rotating exhibitions of local and international artists devoted to erotic themes. The permanent exhibition, entitled *Venezia di piacere* (Venice of pleasure), occupies a number of rooms on the first floor devoted to such figures as Pietro Aretino, Veronica Franco, Giorgio Baffo and Casanova, often with explicit illustrations. The temporary exhibitions generally range from the intriguing to the mildly titillating and the frankly kitsch.

Telecom Italia Future Centre

San Marco 4826, campo San Salvador (041 521 3272/*www.futurecentre.telecomitalia.it*). *Vaporetto Rialto*. **Open** 10am-6pm Tue-Sun. **Admission** free. **Map** p322 B5.
Though the Italian telephone company acquired the 16th-century cloisters of the monastery of San Salvador after World War I, it was not until the 1980s that it embarked upon a thorough restoration of the buildings to provide a prestigious showcase for its latest offerings. The Future Centre offers a tour through the latest innovations in information technology. The first cloister contains numerous computers with cutely playful lessons on various aspects of Venetian art and history, in Italian and English. Don't miss the splendid refectory with a 16th-century frescoed ceiling.

From the Rialto to the Accademia Bridge

The route from the Rialto to the Accademia passes through a series of ever-larger squares. From cosily cramped campo San Bartolomeo,

Day by day

If you're in Venice for a limited time, treat it as a taster. The 'must-see' sights are also 'must-queue' sights: plan your stay accordingly.

One day

Of the marvels around **piazza San Marco**, limit yourself to the **basilica** itself. Then escape the hordes and explore one glorious *sestiere*: **Castello**. The basilica remains open all day (unlike many of the lesser sights), so begin with a walk-about. Make your way along the riva degli Schiavoni to campo **San Zaccaria**, where the splendid Gothic-cum-Renaissance church (*see p96*) offers you a stunning Bellini. From there proceed to the **Scuola di San Giorgio degli Schiavoni** (*see p101*), which contains a superb cycle of paintings by Carpaccio. Head north to San Francesco della Vigna (*see p94*) in one of the city's quieter corners; there's another small Bellini and peaceful Franciscan cloisters.

From here, the long straight street called Barbaria delle Tole leads to campo **Santi Giovanni e Paolo**. Here you can wonder at the great Gothic church (*see p95*), the Renaissance façade of the **Scuola di San Marco** and the equestrian statue of **Bartolomeo Colleoni** (*see p93*). Leave the interior of the church, with its statues of dead doges, for your next visit and instead head to the jewel-like perfection of nearby **Santa Maria dei Miracoli** (*see p111*) – another church which offers plenty of aesthetic satisfaction from the outside.

From here it's a short walk to the **Rialto** (*see p87*): climb the bridge for a superb view of the Grand Canal. There are restaurants and snack-bars galore nearby in which to refuel before heading back to piazza San Marco: either to take the five-minute stroll down the **Merceria**, Venice's chic-est (and most crowded) shopping street, or a 25-minute ride on a vaporetto, marvelling at the world's most splendid high street. Once in the piazza join the queue for the one sight you can't omit on this unforgettable day: the glorious interior of San Marco.

Two days

Devote day two to the other side of the Grand Canal. An early start from the north-west foot of the Rialto bridge allows you to experience the colourful bustle of the market. Then strike out through the oldest and most tightly-packed part of the city for your morning coffee in campo **San Polo**. Beyond, the **Frari** (*see p123*) has two fine Titians, a splendid Bellini and a host of other treasures. Behind the church is the **Scuola di San Rocco** (*see p126*) with its works by Tintoretto. A full appreciation of both church and scuola will take you through to lunch time.

Campo **Santa Margherita** has a choice of cafés in which to take coffee before heading out of the square past the **Carmini** church (*see p130*) and on to **San Sebastiano** (*see p127*); what San Rocco was to Tintoretto, this church is to his contemporary Paolo Veronese.

From here continue for a view of the **Giudecca canal** from the **Zattere**. Stroll along until you reach the bridge over the rio di San Trovaso, home to the city's most picturesque *squero* (boat-yard). At the end of the *fondamenta* along the rio, a right turn will bring you to the Grand Canal at the **Accademia bridge** (*see p74*).

If you're thirsting for still more Venetian painting, visit the **Accademia** gallery (*see p132*) here. Or for a contrast, head east into the quiet reaches which harbour the **Peggy Guggenheim Foundation** (*see p133*) with its Miròs and Pollocks. But these two – plus the great church of the **Salute** (*see p134*) – would make a good third day's sightseeing.

the well-marked path leads to campo San Luca with its bars and cakeshops. Beyond this is campo Manin with its 19th-century statue of Daniele Manin, leader of the 1848 uprising against the Austrians (*see p23*). An alley to the left of this campo will lead you to the **Scala del Bòvolo** (*see p80*), a striking Renaissance spiral staircase. Back on the main drag, the calle della Mandola leads to broad campo Sant'Angelo with its dramatic view of **Santo Stefano**'s leaning tower (*see p90*); off calle della Mandola to the right is the Gothic

Palazzo Fortuny (*see p90*), once home to the Spanish fashion designer Mariano Fortuny.

Just before the Accademia bridge, campo Santo Stefano is second in size only to piazza San Marco in the *sestiere*. Until 1802, when part of a stand collapsed, this was where *corse al toro* (bullfights) took place. Nowadays the tables of several bars scarcely encroach on the space where children play on their bikes or kick balls around the statue of Risorgimento ideologue Nicolò Tommaseo, known locally as *Cagalibri* (bookshitter) for reasons that are obvious when the monument is viewed from the rear. In December the square hosts a market of products from the various regions of Italy. At the Accademia bridge end of the square is the 18th-century church of **San Vidal** (*see p90*), now mainly used for concerts. For information on the bridge, *see p74*.

On the Grand Canal to the north-west of campo Santo Stefano is campo San Samuele, with a deconsecrated 11th-century church and the massive **Palazzo Grassi** (*see p90*), an exhibition centre recently re-opened amid great hype. Nearby, in calle Malipiero, the 18th-century love machine, Giacomo Casanova, was born (though in which house exactly is not known). The neighbourhood is full of Casanova associations, including the site of the theatre where his mother performed (corte Teatro).

Palazzo Fortuny

San Marco 3780, campo San Benedetto (041 520 0995). Vaporetto Sant'Angelo. **Open** during exhibitions only 10am-6pm Tue-Sun (hours subject to change). **Admission** varies, usually €4; €2.50 concessions. **No credit cards. Map** p326 A1.

This charming 15th-century palazzo, which belonged to Spanish fashion designer Mariano Fortuny (1871-1949), has been undergoing restoration and reorganisation for several years now. However, the *piano nobile*, where Fortuny had his studio, is generally open for temporary exhibitions. These are usually photographic, photography being one of Fortuny's interests, alongside theatrical set design, cloth dyes and elegant silk dresses. Also on display are some of Fortuny's paintings of Middle Eastern views.

Palazzo Grassi

San Marco 3231, campo San Samuele (041 523 1680/www.palazzograssi.it). Vaporetto San Samuele. **Open** during exhibitions 10am-7pm daily (hours subject to change). **Admission** €10; €6 concessions (subject to change depending on exhibition). **Credit** MC, V. **Map** p325 F1.

This superbly – though boringly – regular 18th-century palazzo on the Grand Canal was bought in 2005 from the Italian car maker Fiat by the French billionaire businessman François-Henri Pinault. When Fiat bought it in 1984 they hired architect Gae Aulenti to transform it into a high-profile exhibition space; Pinault looked further afield, and called upon Japanese architect Tadao Ando for another expensive overhaul, which increased the exhibition space by 2,000 square metres. This new phase in the life of the palazzo was inaugurated by a much publicised (and, in the tradition of the palazzo, much inflated) exhibition of contemporary art, featuring a selection of post-war works from Pinault's own collection, with the somewhat pretentious title, 'Where Are We Going?' Pinault's Venetian ambitions did not end with the acquisition of this palazzo; *see p131* **Pinault at the Punta?**. **Photo** *p86*.

Santo Stefano

San Marco, campo Santo Stefano (041 522 5061/ www.chorusvenezia.org). Vaporetto San Samuele or Accademia. **Open** 10am-5pm Mon-Sat. **Admission** *Church* free. *Sacristy* €2.50 (*see also p68* **Chorus**). **Map** p325 F1.

Santo Stefano is an Augustinian church, built in the 14th century and altered in the 15th. The façade has a magnificent portal in the florid Gothic style. The large interior, with its splendid ship's keel roof, is a multicoloured treat, with different marbles used for the columns, capitals, altars and intarsia, and diamond-patterned walls, as on the Palazzo Ducale. On the floor is a huge plaque to Doge Morosini (best known for blowing up the Parthenon) and a more modest one to composer Giovanni Gabrielli. On the interior façade to the left of the door is a Renaissance monument to Giacomo Surian by Pietro Lombardo and his sons, decorated with skulls and festoons. In the sacristy are two tenebrous late works by Tintoretto: *The Washing of the Feet* and *The Agony in the Garden* (*The Last Supper* is by the great man's assistants) and three imaginative works by Gaspare Diziani (*Adoration of the Magi, Flight into Egypt, Massacre of the Innocents*). From the first bridge on the calle that leads from the campo towards piazza San Marco, there's a good view of the apse of Santo Stefano with a canal passing underneath it.

San Vidal

San Marco, campo San Vidal (041 522 2362). Vaporetto Accademia. **Open** 9.30am-6pm daily. **Map** p325 F2.

This early 18th-century church, with a façade derived from Palladio, was for years used as an art gallery. It has now been restored and hosts concerts. Over the high altar is a splendid Carpaccio painting (1514) of St Vitalis riding what appears to be one of the bronze horses of San Marco. The third altar on the right has a painting by Piazzetta (*Archangel Raphael and Saints Anthony and Louis*).

Scala Contarini del Bòvolo

San Marco 4299, corte dei Risi (041 532 2920). Vaporetto Rialto. **Closed** for restoration, due to reopen 2009. **Map** p326 A1.

Follow the signs for the Scala del Bòvolo from campo Manin and you will emerge in a narrow courtyard entirely dominated by this elegant Renaissance spiral staircase, built c1499 by Giovanni Candi. Spiral staircases are called *scale a chiocciola* (snail staircases) in Italian; *bòvolo* is Venetian dialect for snail. It was beautifully restored in 1986 but further work began recently – a shame, as the view from the top is charming.

The Accademia Bridge to piazza San Marco

The route from Santo Stefano back to piazza San Marco zigzags at first, passing through small squares, including campo San Maurizio, with its 19th-century church now transformed into the **Museo della Musica** (*see below*) and campo **Santa Maria del Giglio** (aka Santa Maria Zobenigo, *see below*) with the most boastful church façade in Venice. It winds past banks and hotels, along with a few top-dollar antique shops, to end in wide via XXII Marzo, with an intimidating view of the baroque statuary of **San Moisè** (*see below*). To the left is the opera house, **La Fenice** (*see below*), rebuilt after a fire in 1996.

Press on and you are ready for arguably the greatest view in the world: piazza San Marco from the west side.

Museo della Musica

San Marco 2601, campo San Maurizio (041 2411 840). Vaporetto Giglio. **Open** 9.30am-7.30pm daily. **Admission** free. Map p326 A2.
This small museum, set up in the ex-church of San Maurizio, is run by the Rivoalto recording company. Serving partly as a sales and promotion outlet, the museum also contains an interesting collection of period instruments. The free visit to the building offers a chance to appreciate the neo-classical interior of the church, designed by Giannantonio Selva, the architect of the Fenice theatre (*see below*).

Santa Maria del Giglio

San Marco, campo Santa Maria Zobenigo (041 275 0462/www.chorusvenezia.org). Vaporetto Giglio. **Open** 10am-5pm Mon-Sat. **Admission** €2.50 (*see also p68* **Chorus**). **No credit cards**. Map p326 A2.
This church's façade drew the censure of Ruskin for its total lack of any Christian symbols (give or take a token angel or two). Built between 1678 and 1683, it's really a huge exercise in defiant self-glorification by Admiral Antonio Barbaro, who was dismissed by Doge Francesco Morosini for incompetence in the War of Candia (Crete). On the plinths of the columns are relief plans of towns where he served, including Candia; his own statue (in the centre) is flanked by representations of Honour, Virtue, Fame and Wisdom. The interior is more devotional. You may not have heard of the painter Antonio Zanchi (1631-1722), but this is definitely his church. Particularly interesting is *Abraham Teaching the Egyptians Astrology* in the sacristy, while the Cappella Molin has *Ulysses Recognised by his Dog* (an odd subject for a church). The chapel also contains a *Madonna and Child*, which is proudly but probably erroneously attributed to Rubens. Behind the altar there are two paintings of the Evangelists by Tintoretto, formerly organ doors.

San Moisè

San Marco, campo San Moisè (041 528 5840). Vaporetto Vallaresso. **Open** 9.30am-12.30pm daily. **Map** p326 B2.
The baroque façade of San Moisè has been lambasted by Ruskin ('one of the basest examples of the basest school of the Renaissance') and just about everybody else as one of Venice's truly ugly pieces of architecture. Inside, an extravagant piece of baroque sculpture occupies the high altar, representing not only Moses receiving the stone tablets but Mount Sinai itself. Near the entrance is the grave of John Law, author of the disastrous Mississippi Bubble scheme that almost sank the French central bank in 1720.

Teatro La Fenice

San Marco 1983, campo San Fantin (041 2424/ 041 786 511/www.teatrolafenice.it). Vaporetto Giglio. **Open** for guided tours only; times vary depending on performances and rehearsals. **Admission** €7; €5 concessions. **Map** p326 A1.
Guided tours must be pre-booked at the number given above. For performance information, *see p227.*
Venice's principal opera house, with its highly appropriate name of La Fenice ('the phoenix'), has a long history of fiery destruction and miraculous rebirth. The original theatre designed by Giannantonio Selva (1792) replaced the Teatro San Benedetto, which had burnt down in 1774. Selva's building was destroyed in 1836, and was rebuilt by the Meduna brothers, recreating the style of Selva. Roughly a century and a half later, in 1996, while restoration work was being carried out on the building, a massive blaze broke out, courtesy of two electricians (for the full crime story see John Berendt's book, *City of Falling Angels*). After many years of legal wrangling, the theatre was rebuilt 'as it was, where it was' (a slogan first coined after the collapse of the campanile of San Marco, *see p82*), and inaugurated in December 2003. Hidden away from view behind the born-again ornate gilding and baroque plush of the original are state-of-the-art technological innovations. The guided tour, including the foyers, stalls and royal box, lasts 45 minutes.

Teatro La Fenice.

Castello

From industrial powerhouse to picturesque abandonment.

CASTELLO

Castello takes its name from a defensive fortress that once stood at the eastern end of the city, protecting it from invasion by sea. The *sestiere* still contains the great expanse of the Arsenale, which was once the city's great military powerhouse, but most of this now lies in desolate, if picturesque, abandonment.

But Castello contains a great deal more than just relics of former military splendour. It's the largest *sestiere* in the city and probably the most varied in character. The western end, around San Zaccaria and Santi Giovanni e Paolo, is second only to piazza San Marco in pomp and grandeur, but head eastwards, beyond the Arsenale, and the tone becomes more homely in the bustling areas around via Garibaldi or the leafy calm of Sant'Elena.

Northern & western Castello

The canal dividing the Doge's Palace (*see p84*) from the prison marks the end of the *sestiere* of San Marco. This means that the **Museo Diocesano di Arte Sacra** (*see p93*) and stately **San Zaccaria** (*see p96*), although closely associated with San Marco, actually belong to Castello. But the heart of northern and western Castello lies inland: campo **Santa Maria Formosa** (literally 'Shapely St Mary', *see p96*), a large, bustling, irregular-shaped square on the road to just about everywhere.

This square has all you could possibly need: a fine church, a market, a couple of bars and an undertaker's. Nearby is the museum-cum-library of the **Fondazione Querini Stampalia** (*see p93*). Buzzing with locals and tourists, the campo is surrounded by *palazzi* that range in style from the very grand to the very homely. It is, in fact, Castello in miniature.

Southward from the campo runs the busy shopping street ruga Giuffa (named after either a community of Armenian merchants from Julfa, or a band of thugs – *gagiuffos* in 13th-century dialect – who terrorised the area). The first turning to the left off this street leads to **Palazzo Grimani**, the grandiose 16th-century home of Cardinal Grimani, whose collection of Greek and Roman antiquities formed the basis of the **Museo Archeologico** (*see p83*). The palazzo has been under very slow restoration since the 1980s and is to be opened as a museum, offering an example of a splendid patrician residence, in the not too distant future… or so the powers-that-be continue to promise (see www.museicivicveneziani.it for details). When it does finally open its doors to the public, film buffs will recognise it as the setting for the final gory scenes of Nicolas Roeg's film, *Don't Look Now*.

For more grandeur, head north from here to campo **Santi Giovanni e Paolo** (*see p95*). This square is second only to piazza San Marco in monumental magnificence. The Gothic red brick of the Dominican church is beautifully set off by the glistening marble on the *trompe l'œil* façade of the **Scuola Grande di San Marco** (*see p97*) – now a hospital – and the freshly restored bronze of the equestrian **monument to Bartolomeo Colleoni** (*see p93*) gazing contemptuously down.

It's a short walk through narrow *calli* from Santi Giovanni e Paolo to the fondamenta Nuove, where the northern lagoon comes into view. Murano (*see p143*) and further flung Burano (*see p145*) and Torcello (*see p148*) are visible on clear days, as are the foothills of the Dolomites. The cemetery island San Michele is always in sight, acting as a grim *memento mori* for patients in the hospital.

Eastwards from Santi Giovanni e Paolo runs a road called Barbaria delle Tole. *Tole* are planks (*tavole* in Italian); various explanations are offered for *barbaria*: the wild appearance of the area, the presence of numerous barbers' shops, the barbaric behaviour of the carpenters, the fact that the planks were destined mainly for 'Barbaria' (the Barbary Coast). The road passes the baroque church of **Santa Maria dei Derelitti** (commonly known as Ospedaletto, *see p85*) by Baldassare Longhena, with its alarmingly teetering façade adorned by leering faces. The church now belongs to an old people's home, which contains an exquisite 18th-century music room. Barbaria delle Tole leads into one of the least touristy areas of the city. Here, beyond the old gasworks, is **San Francesco della Vigna** (*see p94*), an austere church whose remoteness is part of its charm.

Monument to Bartolomeo Colleoni

Campo Santi Giovanni e Paolo. Vaporetto Fondamente Nove. **Map** p322 C5.
Colleoni was a famous *condottiere* (mercenary soldier), who left a legacy to the Republic on the condition that a statue be erected to him in front of St Mark's. Not wishing to clutter up St Mark's square with the statue, but loath to miss out on the money, Venice's wily rulers found a solution to their conundrum in 1479 when they hit upon the idea of giving him a space in front of the Scuola di San Marco. Geddit? In order, perhaps, to make up for this flagrant deception, the Republic did Colleoni proud, commissioning the Florentine artist Andrea Verrocchio to create an equestrian statue that is widely agreed to be one of the world's finest. On Verrocchio's death it was completed, together with the pedestal, by Alessandro Leopardi (1488-96). It is not a portrait, since Verrocchio never saw Colleoni, but a stylised representation of military pride and might. Colleoni's coat of arms (on the pedestal) includes three fig-like objects, a reference to his name, which in Italian sounds very similar to *coglioni* – testicles, of which this soldier was said to possess three. The statue has just undergone a lengthy and elaborate restoration (completed June 2006).

Museo Diocesano di Arte Sacra

Castello 4312, ponte della Canonica (041 522 9166). Vaporetto San Zaccaria. **Open** depends on exhibition. **Admission** free (donations accepted). **Map** p326 C1.
In theory, this museum tucked in a hard-to-find corner behind the palace of Venice's patriarch (cardinal) contains a hotchpotch of a collection, but it can seem haphazard until you realise its purpose: to act as a storeroom and restoration clinic for works of art from local churches and monasteries. But in recent months the curiosities have been removed and the space has been given over to temporary exhibitions, the first of which was a rare glimpse of artworks by Tintoretto usually kept in the patriarch's palace but moved here while the prelate had the builders in. As this guide went to press, not even the museum staff were able to say whether the museum will return to its original vocation or continue to host shows.

Museo della Fondazione Querini Stampalia

Castello 5252, campo Santa Maria Formosa (041 271 1411/www.querinistampalia.it). Vaporetto Rialto. **Open** *Museum* 10am-6pm Tue-Thur, Sun; 10am-10pm Fri, Sat. **Admission** *Museum* €8; €6 concessions. *Library* free. **Credit** AmEx, DC, MC, V. **Map** p322 C5.
For library opening times, *see p295*.
This Renaissance palazzo and its art collection were bequeathed to Venice by Giovanni Querini, a 19th-century scientist, man of letters and silk producer. He came from one of the city's most ancient families, which was permanently excluded from running for

Museo Querini Stampalia: library, gallery and concert space.

You can look now

Following in the footsteps of Donald Sutherland and Julie Christie in *Don't Look Now* will probably disappoint any fan hoping to have his spine tingled. It was part of Nicolas Roeg's skill that he succeeded in making this most placid of cities seem chillingly creepy, even if puzzling camera cutaways and unexplained eerie superimpositions were part of the trick.

The church Sutherland is restoring in the film is San Nicolò dei Mendicoli (*see p126*), at the dockland end of Le Zattere (which was being restored at the time of shooting). The first murdered corpse is pulled from the canal just round the corner, by the church of Angelo Raffaele (*see p126*).

Most of the rest of the film is shot on the other side of the Grand Canal, with the exception of two short scenes in campo Castelforte, behind the Scuola di San Rocco (*see p125*), where Sutherland muses over a doll floating in the canal.

Although the hotel Sutherland and Christie are staying at is referred to as the Europa, it is clearly the Gabrielli Sandwirth, at the Arsenale end of the riva degli Schiavoni (map p327 E2).

The church where Christie lights a candle (which mysteriously self-extinguishes) is Santi Giovanni e Paolo (*see p95*). The adjacent hospital is used in a few shots as an imposing police station. The various dimly lit bridges and archways affording flitting glimpses of a sinister red-coated figure can be found behind the Fondazione Querini Stampalia museum (*see p93*).

The final shocking sequence, where Sutherland meets his red-hooded nemesis, was shot outside and inside Palazzo Grimani, on rio San Severo (map p322 C5), also near Santa Maria Formosa. One of the finest baroque palaces in the city, it was in a state of highly filmable abandonment at the time but has been under slow but steady restoration since.

Sutherland's funeral is celebrated in the church of San Stae (*see p120*), on the Grand Canal.

the dogeship due to involvement in the 1310 Bajamonte Tiepolo plot (*see p18*). Giovanni Querini specified in his will that a library should be created here that would open 'particularly in the evenings for the convenience of scholars', and that the foundation should promote 'evening assemblies of scholars and scientists'. The Querini Stampalia still exudes something of its founder's spirit: the first-floor library is a great place to study, and the Foundation organises conferences and concerts (5pm, 8.30pm Fri, Sat; included in admission price). The ground floor and gardens, redesigned in the 1960s by Carlo Scarpa, offer one of Venice's few successful examples of modern architecture. On the second floor, the gallery contains some important paintings, including Palma il Vecchio's portraits of Francesco and Paola Querini, for whom the palace was built in the 16th century, a marvellous *Presentation in the Temple* by Giovanni Bellini and a striking *Judith and Holofernes* by Vincenzo Catena. It also has a fascinating series of minor works, such as Gabriele Bella's 67 paintings of Venetian festivals, and a selection of Pietro Longhi's scenes of bourgeois life in 18th-century Venice. On the top floor is a gallery designed by Mario Botta, which hosts exhibitions of contemporary art.

San Francesco della Vigna

Campo San Francesco della Vigna (041 520 6102). Vaporetto Celestia. **Open** 8am-12.30pm, 3-7pm Mon-Sat; 3-6.30pm Sun. **Map** p323 E5.

San Francesco may be off the beaten track, but the long trek over to the down-at-heel area beyond the gasworks, where the church's Palladian façade is half-concealed by the surrounding buildings, is well worth it. In 1534 Jacopo Sansovino was asked by his friend Doge Andrea Gritti to design this church for the Observant Franciscan order. The Tuscan architect opted for a deliberately simple style to match the monastic rule adopted by its inhabitants. The façade (1568-72) was a later addition by Andrea Palladio; it is the first example of his system of superimposed temple fronts.

The dignified, solemn interior consists of a single broad nave with side chapels, which are named after the families who paid for them – and who held no truck with Franciscan notions of modesty and self-effacement. The Cappella Giustiniani on the left of the chancel holds a marvellous cycle of bas-reliefs by Pietro Lombardo and school, moved here from an earlier church on the same site. In the nave, the fourth chapel on the right has a *Resurrection* attributed to Paolo Veronese. In the right transept is a fruity, flowery *Madonna and Child Enthroned* (c1450), a signed work by the Greek artist Antonio da Negroponte. From the left transept a door leads into the Cappella Santa, which contains a *Madonna and Saints* (1507) by Giovanni Bellini (perhaps assisted by Girolamo da Santacroce). From here it is possible to visit two of the church's peaceful Renaissance cloisters (another, generally closed to the public, has a magnificent vegetable garden).

Back in the church, the fifth chapel on the left is home to Paolo Veronese's first Venetian commission, the stunning *Holy Family with Saints John the Baptist, Anthony the Abbot and Catherine* (c1551). The third chapel has *trompe l'œil* frescoes in chiaroscuro by GB Tiepolo (1743, recently restored). The second chapel has three powerful statues of saints Roch, Anthony the Abbot and Sebastian (1565) by Alessandro Vittoria.

Santi Giovanni e Paolo (San Zanipolo)

Campo Santi Giovanni e Paolo (041 523 5913). Vaporetto Fondamente Nove. **Open** 9.30am-6pm Mon-Sat; 1-6pm Sun. **Admission** €2.50. **No credit cards. Map** p322 C5.

Santi Giovanni e Paolo was founded by the Dominican order in 1246 but not finished until 1430. Twenty-five doges were buried here between 1248 and 1778; from the 15th century onwards all ducal funerals were held here. The vast interior – 101m (331ft) long – is a single spatial unit; the simple columns serve to enhance the unity of the whole, rather than dividing the body of the church into separate aisles. The monks' choir was removed in the 17th century, leaving nothing to impede the view. Santi Giovanni e Paolo is packed with monuments not only to doges but also to Venetian heroes. The entrance wall is entirely dedicated to a series of funerary tributes to the Mocenigo family. The grandest – a masterpiece by Pietro, Tullio and Antonio Lombardo – belongs to Pietro Mocenigo, who died in 1476: the doge stands on his own sarcophagus, supported by three warriors representing the three ages of man. The religious reference above – the three Marys at the sepulchre – seems almost an afterthought. Renaissance elegance continues in the second altar on the right, which features an early

polyptych by Giovanni Bellini (1465) in its original frame. Continuing down the right side of the church, the huge baroque mausoleum by Andrea Tirali (1708) has two Valier doges and a *dogaressa* taking a bow before a marble curtain. Tirali also designed the Chapel of St Dominic, notable for its splendid ceiling painting by Giovani Battista Piazzetta of *St Dominic in Glory* (c1727).

The right transept has a painting of *St Antonine Distributing Alms* (1542) by the mystically minded Lorenzo Lotto, who asked only for a decent funeral as payment – but then died far away in Loreto. Above are splendid stained-glass windows, to designs by such Renaissance artists as Bartolomeo Vivarini and Cima da Conegliano (1470-1520).

On the right of the chancel, with its baroque high altar, is the Gothic tomb of Michele Morosini, which Ruskin loved. Opposite is the tomb of Doge Andrea Vendramin, by the Lombardo family, which the architectural arbiter just as predictably hated. Just to confirm his prejudice, he climbed a ladder and was shocked to discover that the sculptor had not bothered to carve the unseen side of the face.

The rosary chapel, off the left transept, was gutted by fire in 1867, just after two masterpieces by Titian and Bellini had been placed here for safe keeping. It now contains paintings and furnishings from suppressed churches. The ceiling paintings, *The Annunciation, Assumption* and *Adoration of the Shepherds*, are by Paolo Veronese, as is another *Adoration* to the left of the door.

Santa Maria dei Derelitti (Ospedaletto)

Barbarie delle Tole 6691 (041 271 9012). Vaporetto Fondamente Nove. **Open** 3.30-6.30pm Thur-Sat. **Admission** (incl guided tour) €2. **No credit cards. Map** p323 D5.

San Francesco della Vigna. *See p94.*

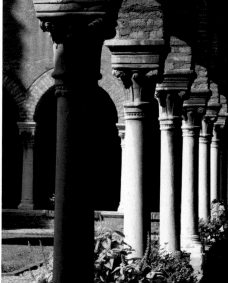

Real Venetian life on **via Garibaldi**. *See p98.*

The church was built in 1575 within the complex of the Ospedaletto, a hospice for the poor and aged. There is still an old people's home here. Between 1668 and 1674 Baldassare Longhena gave the church its staggering façade, complete with bulging telamons (architectural supports in the shape of male figures) and leering faces. The interior contains interesting 18th-century paintings, including one of Giambattista Tiepolo's earliest works, *The Sacrifice of Isaac* (fourth on the right). The hospice contains an elegant music room with charming frescoes by Jacopo Guarana (1776), depicting the girl musicians performing for Apollo; the scene is stolen by a dog in the foreground being tempted with a doughnut. There is also a fascinating spiral staircase, apparently unsupported, designed by Sardi and completed by Longhena; the stairs are wide and shallow, to aid the aged inhabitants of the building.

Santa Maria Formosa

Campo Santa Maria Formosa (041 275 0462/ www.chorusvenezia.org). Vaporetto San Zaccaria or Rialto. **Open** 10am-5pm Mon-Sat. **Admission** €2.50 (*see also p68* **Chorus**). **No credit cards**. **Map** p322 C5.

In the pre-Freudian seventh century, St Magnus, Bishop of Oderzo, had a rather pleasant vision in which the Virgin appeared as a buxom (*formosa*) matron, and a church was built in this bustling square to commemorate the fact. The present church was designed by Mauro Codussi in 1492 and has

something fittingly bulgy about it. It has two façades, one on the canal (1542), the other on the campo (1604). The baroque *campanile* has a grotesque mask, memorably reviled by Ruskin but now recognised as a portrait of a victim of the hideously disfiguring Von Recklinghausen's disease. Codussi retained the Greek cross plan of the original church in his own Renaissance design; the spatial effects reveal how strong the Byzantine tradition remained in Venice. The first chapel in the right aisle has a triptych by Bartolomeo Vivarini, *Madonna of the Misericordia* (1473), which includes a realistic *Birth of the Virgin.*

The altar in the right transept was the chapel of the Scuola dei Bombardieri, with an altarpiece of St Barbara, patron saint of gunners (a heaven-sent stun gun in the shape of a lightning bolt saved Barbara's life when it struck her father as he prepared to kill her), by Palma il Vecchio. The model was apparently the artist's daughter. George Eliot described it as 'an almost unique presentation of a hero-woman'. Half-hidden by the elaborate high altar is one of the few works on show in Venice by a woman artist: an 18th-century *Allegory of the Foundation of the Church, with Venice, St Magnus and St Maria Formosa* by Giulia Lama. She has been described as a pupil of Giovani Battista Piazzetta, but Piazzetta's only known portrait from life (in the Thyssen-Bornemisza collection in Madrid) is of Giulia Lama: its tenderness suggests she was more than a pupil.

San Zaccaria

Campo San Zaccaria (041 522 1257). Vaporetto San Zaccaria. **Open** 10am-noon, 4-6pm Mon-Sat; 4-6pm Sun. **Map** p327 D1.

Founded in the ninth century, this church has always had close ties with the Doge's Palace. Eight Venetian rulers were buried in the first church on the site, one was killed outside and another died while seeking sanctuary inside. This is a holy booty church: the body of St Zacharias, the father of John the Baptist, was brought to Venice in the ninth century, at the same time as that of St Mark; it still lies under the second altar on the right. The current church was begun in 1444 but took decades to complete, making it a curious combination of Gothic and Renaissance. The interior is built on a Gothic plan – the apse, with its ambulatory and radiating cluster of tall-windowed chapels, is unique in Venice – but the architectural decoration is predominantly Renaissance. Similarly, the façade is a happy mixture of the two styles. Inside, every inch is covered with paintings of varying quality. Giovanni Bellini's magnificently calm *Madonna and Four Saints* (1505), on the second altar on the left, leaps out of the confusion. In the right aisle is the entrance to the Chapel of St Athanasius (open same hours as the church, admission €1), which contains carved 15th-century wooden stalls and *The Birth of St John the Baptist*, an early work by Tintoretto and a striking *Flight into Egypt* by Giandomenico Tiepolo. The adjoining Chapel of St Tarasius was the apse of an earlier church on the site; it has three altarpieces (1443) by Antonio Vivarini and Giovanni d'Alemagna – stiff, iconic works in elaborate Gothic frames that are in keeping with the architecture of the chapel. Definitely not in keeping are the frescoed saints in the fan vault by the Florentine artist Andrea del Castagno. Though painted a year before the altarpieces, they have a realistic vitality that is wholly Renaissance in spirit. In front of the altar there are remains of the mosaic floor from the early Romanesque church. It is possible to descend into the 10th-century crypt, which is usually flooded.

Attached to the church was a convent, where aristocrats with more titles than cash dumped female offspring to avoid having to rake together a dowry. The nuns were not best known for their piety. While tales of rampant licentiousness may have been exaggerated, a painting in Ca' Rezzonico (*see p129*) shows that such convents were more worldly salon than place of contemplation.

Scuola Grande di San Marco (Ospedale Civile)

Campo Santi Giovanni e Paolo (041 529 4111). Vaporetto Fondamente Nove. **Open** 24hrs daily. **Map** p322 C4.

This is one of the six *scuole grandi*, the confraternities of Venice (*see p67*). It's now occupied by the city hospital, which extends all the way back to the lagoon. The façade by Pietro Lombardo and Giovanni Buora (1487-90) was completed by Mauro Codussi (1495). It has magnificent *trompe l'œil* panels by Tullio and Antonio Lombardo representing two episodes from the life of St Mark and his faithful lion. Over the doorway is a lunette of *St Mark with the Brethren of the School* attributed to Bartolomeo Bon.

Southern & eastern Castello

The low-rise, clustered buildings of working-class eastern Castello housed the employees of the **Arsenale** (*see p88*) – Venice's dockland – much of which now lies poignantly derelict.

Like London's East End or New York's Brooklyn, eastern Castello had its foreign communities, as local churches testify. There's **San Giorgio dei Greci** (Greeks, *see p101*), with its adjoining **Museo dell'Istituto Ellenico** (*see p99*) icon museum. (Fans of Donna Leon will naturally recognise the bar at the foot of the Ponte dei Greci as the one where her detective Commissario Brunetti often stops in for a quick cappuccino; the Questura – police headquarters – is further down the canal on the left.)

And there's the **Scuola di San Giorgio degli Schiavoni** (Slavs, *see p101*), with its captivating cycle of paintings by Vittorio Carpaccio. Indeed, the great promenade along the lagoon – the riva degli Schiavoni – was named after the small community.

Inland from the *riva* is the quaint Gothic church of **San Giovanni in Bragora** (*see p101*) and, further back in the warren of streets, the church of Sant'Antonin undoubtedly the only church in Venice in which an elephant has been shot. The unfortunate animal escaped from a circus on the *riva* in 1819 and took refuge in the church, only to be finished off by gunners summoned from the Arsenale (a lively dialect poem commemorates the event).

Sightseeing

Museo Storico Navale. *See p100.*

Back on the riva degli Schiavoni is the church of **La Pietà** (*see p101*), where Vivaldi was choir master. In calle della Pietà, alongside the church, is the **Piccolo Museo della Pietà** (*see p100*), a small museum dedicated to the Pietà (a foundling home) and the composer.

Head on eastwards past the Ca' di Dio, once a hostel for pilgrims setting out for the Holy Land and now an old people's home, and the *Forni pubblici* (public bakeries), where the biscuit (*bis-cotto*, literally 'twice-cooked') – that favourite, scurvy-encouraging staple of ancient mariners – was reputedly invented.

Crossing the bridge over the rio dell'Arsenale, you can see the grand Renaissance entrance to the huge **Arsenale** shipyard (*see p88*), once a hive of empire-building industry and closely guarded secrets, now an expanse of crumbling warehouses and empty docks, parts of which are regularly brought to life by temporary exhibitions.

Just beyond the rio dell'Arsenale, the model-packed **Museo Storico Navale** (*see p100*) lovingly charts Venice's shipbuilding history. A little further on, the wide via Garibaldi forks off to the left. This road, like the nearby *Giardini pubblici*, is a legacy of French occupation in the early 19th century. For proof that Venice is not a dead city, head here in the morning (Mon-Sat) to catch the bustle at the market. Otherwise, take an evening stroll and join Venetians *en masse*, from kiddies on tricycles to old men propping up bars.

Via Garibaldi leads eventually to the island of **San Pietro** (*see p101*), where the former cathedral stands among modest, washing-garlanded houses. For centuries before relocating to St Mark's, the bishop (later patriarch) of Venice was relegated here, at a safe distance from the decision-making centre. Nowadays the island has a pleasant backwoods feel to it; on the feast of Saints Peter and Paul (29 June), locals spill on to the patchy grass in front of the church for the nearest thing Venice offers to a village fête, complete with *alfresco* dining, dancing, music and gallons of wine. Bring your clogs.

Back on the lagoon, the riva degli Schiavoni changes its name after the rio dell'Arsenale to become the riva dei Sette Martiri, named after seven partisans executed here in 1944 (a striking recumbent statue by the Giardini vaporetto stop recalls the event; it is currently awaiting restoration). Created in 1936, this long, wide section is often dwarfed by moored cruise ships. By the vaporetto stop of the same name, you'll find the shady *Giardini pubblici*, public gardens that took the place of four suppressed convents. A Renaissance archway from one has been reconstructed in a corner.

In another corner lies the entrance to the **Biennale**; the international pavilions, ranging in style from the seedy to the pompous, used to remain locked up except for those few weeks every two years when a major contemporary art bonanza (*see p215* **La Biennale**) would be set up; other more recently created events such as the Biennale dell'Architettura mean the pavilions get more frequent airings.

The riva ends in the sedately residential district of Sant'Elena. This, in Venetian terms, is a 'modern' district. In 1872 work began to fill in the *barene* (marshes) that lay between the edge of the city and the ancient island of **Sant' Elena** (*see p100*), with its charming Gothic church, which now stands just the other side of the football stadium (*see p233*). Sant'Elena has a distinctly suburban feel to it: children play and dogs are walked in grassy expanses dotted with holm oak and pine trees. It's the ideal spot for an evening drink as the sun sets dramatically over the lagoon.

Arsenale

Campo dell'Arsenale. Vaporetto Arsenale.
Map p327 E1.

The word *arsenale* derives from the Arabic *dar sina'a*, meaning 'house of industry': the industry, and efficiency, of Venice's Arsenale was legendary: the *arsenalotti* could assemble a galley in just a few hours. Shipbuilding activities began here in the 12th century, and before long all Venice's galleys were constructed within its confines. At the height of the city's power, 16,000 men were employed. Production expanded until the 16th century, when Venice entered its slow but inexorable economic decline.

The imposing land gateway by Antonio Gambello (1460) in campo dell'Arsenale is the first example of Renaissance classical architecture in Venice, although the capitals of the columns are 11th-century Veneto-Byzantine. The gateway was modelled on a Roman arch in the Istrian city of Pola. The winged lion gazing down from above holds a book devoid of the traditional words *Pax tibi Marce* (Peace to you, Mark), clearly unsuitable in this military context. Outside the gate, four Greek lions keep guard. Those immediately flanking the terrace were looted from Athens by Doge Francesco Morosini in 1687; the larger one stood at the entrance to the port of Piraeus and bears runic inscriptions on its side, hacked there in the 11th century by Norse mercenary soldiers in Byzantine service. The third lion, whose head is clearly less ancient than its body, came from Delos and was placed here to commemorate the recapture of Corfu in 1716.

Shipbuilding activity ceased in 1917, but the Arsenale has remained navy property. Officers in smart white uniforms cut fine figures against the red brickwork, but appear to put the decaying facilities to no practical use. Exhibitions and performances are now occasionally held in the cavernous spaces

Walk: in the footsteps of Vivaldi

Antonio Vivaldi's music disappeared from public sight and hearing for over a century after his death, but there's no getting away from it nowadays in Venice, with his top hits a fixture on concert programmes.

But apart from a hotel named after him and a small museum dedicated to his memory, the city of Venice hasn't gone out of its way to exploit its most famous son. Houses he lived in are without plaques, either because the exact location is uncertain or because present inhabitants want to discourage gawpers.

The best starting point for a Vivaldi pilgrimage is campo San Giovanni in Bragora (aka campo Bandiera e Moro). The composer was born in this square on 4 March 1678, although the exact house is not known. Two months later he was baptised in the church of **San Giovanni in Bragora** (*see p101*); there's a copy of the baptism certificate next to the font.

Leave the square by calle del Dose and turn right along the riva degli Schiavoni. After the first bridge stands the church of **Santa Maria della Pietà** (*see p100, pictured*). The current church was built after Vivaldi's death but it was on this site that he spent most of his working life. He began here as *maestro di violino* in 1703, teaching the orphan girls in the institute attached to the church to play the violin, and writing music for them. He was to work here, with occasional intervals of travel, until 1740, when he left for Vienna.

To the right of the church is calle della Pietà, which leads to the small **museum** (*see p100*) dedicated to him. From the museum continue along the street, which becomes calle dei Greci. At the end turn left towards the ponte dei Greci and proceed along fondamenta dell'Osmarin to campo Santi Filippo e Giacomo. The **Hotel Rio** in this square (number 4536) is where the composer lived in 1705-8 and 1711-22.

Retrace your steps to fondamenta dell'Osmarin and take the first bridge. From here the ruga Giuffa will lead you to campo Santa Maria Formosa. Make your way round the church to **ponte del Paradiso**, a fine bridge with an archway surmounted by a sculpture of the Madonna. The house at the foot of the bridge (number 4850) is where the composer lived from 1722-30.

At the end of calle del Paradiso, turn right into salizada San Lio, which leads to campo San Bartolomeo. Head towards the Rialto bridge; instead of crossing it, turn left along the fondamenta and cross the first bridge to the **riva del Carbon**. Vivaldi lived in a house on the riva from 1730-40, when he left Venice for Vienna, where he died the following year.

within its walls: the *Artiglierie* and the grandiose *Gaggiandre*, dockyards designed by Sansovino. In campo della Tana, on the other side of the rio dell'Arsenale, is the entrance to the *Corderia* (rope factory), an extraordinary building 316m (1,038 ft) long. This vast space is used to house the overflow from the Biennale and for other temporary exhibitions.

Museo dell'Istituto Ellenico

Castello 3412, ponte dei Greci (041 522 6581). Vaporetto San Zaccaria. **Open** 9am-5pm daily. **Admission** €4; €2 concessions. **No credit cards.** Map p327 D1.

The Byzantine side of Venice is played up in this temple of icons. The adjacent church of San Giorgio dei Greci was a focal point for the Greek community, which was swollen by refugees after the Turkish capture of Constantinople in 1453. There have been a Greek church, college and school on this site since the end of the 15th century, and the museum is an essential adjunct to the centre for Byzantine studies next door. The oldest piece in the collection is the 14th-century altar cross behind the ticket desk. The icons on display mainly follow the dictates of the Cretan school, with no descent into naturalism, though some

San Giovanni in Bragora. *See p101.*

of the 17th- and 18th-century pieces make jarring and often kitsch compromises with Western art. The best pieces are those that are resolute in their hieratic (traditional-style Greek) flatness, such as *Christ in Glory among the Apostles* and the Great Deesis from the first half of the 14th century. St George is a popular subject (see also in the adjoining church) and there is one splendid painting of him dating from the late 15th century. Also on display are priestly robes and other Greek-rite paraphernalia.

Museo Storico Navale

Castello 2148, campo San Biagio (041 520 0276).
Vaporetto Arsenale. **Open** 8.45am-1.30pm Mon-Fri;
8.45am-1pm Sat. **Admission** €1.55. **No credit cards.** **Map** p327 E2.

Housed in an old granary, this museum dedicated to ships and shipbuilding is a treasure trove. It continues an old tradition: under the Republic, the models made for shipbuilders in the final design stages were kept in the Arsenale. Some of the models on display are survivors from that collection. The ground floor has warships, cannons, explosive speedboats and dodgy-looking manned torpedoes, plus a display of ships through the ages. On the walls are relief models in wood and papier mâché, dating from the 16th to the 18th century, of Venetian fortresses and possessions, including a massive model of the entire island of Crete. On the first floor are ornamental trimmings and naval instruments, plus a series of impressive models of Venetian ships, including a huge 16th-century galleass. Here, too, is a richly gilded model of the Bucintoro, the doges' state barge. The second floor has uniforms, more up-to-date sextants and astrolabes, and models of modern Italian navy vessels. On the third floor there are models of Chinese and Korean junks, cruise ships and liners, and a series of fascinating naïve votive paintings, giving thanks for shipwrecks averted or survived. A room at the back has a display of gondolas, including a 19th-century example with a cabin, and the last privately owned covered gondola in Venice, which belonged to Peggy Guggenheim (*see p133*). The Swedish Gallery on the top floor

testifies to links between Venice and Sweden, and also contains a collection of sea shells donated by the designer Roberta di Camerino. **Photo** *p97.*

Piccolo Museo della Pietà 'Antonio Vivaldi'

Calle della Pietà 3701 (041 523 9079).
Vaporetto San Zaccaria or Arsenale. **Open** 11am-4pm Mon, Wed. **Admission** €3. **No credit cards.** **Map** p327 D1.

This small museum was opened in May 2004 and chronicles the activities of the Ospedale della Pietà, the orphanage where Antonio Vivaldi was violin teacher and choir master. Numerous documents recount such details as the rules for admission of children to the Ospedale and the rations of food allotted them; the 'Daughters of the Choir' received more generous portions of food and wine. Other documents testify to Vivaldi's activities. There is also a selection of period instruments.

La Pietà (Santa Maria della Visitazione)

Riva degli Schiavoni (041 523 1096). *Vaporetto San Zaccaria.* **Open** 10am-noon, 4-6pm Mon-Fri. 10am-noon, 4-5.30pm Sat, Sun. **Map** p327 D2.

By the girls' orphanage of the same name, the church of La Pietà was famous for its music. Antonio Vivaldi, violin and choir master in the 18th century, wrote some of his finest music for his young charges. The present building by Giorgio Massari was begun in 1745, four years after Vivaldi's death. Music inspired its architecture: the interior, reached through a vestibule resembling a foyer, has the oval shape of a concert hall. The ceiling has a *Coronation of the Virgin* (1755) by Giambattista Tiepolo.

Sant'Elena

Servi di Maria 3, campo Chiesa Sant'Elena (041 520 5144). *Vaporetto Sant'Elena.* **Open** 5-7pm Mon-Sat. **Map** p328 C4.

The red-brick Gothic church of Sant'Elena is reached by a long avenue alongside Venice's football ground (*see p233*). Though it contains no great works of art (the church was deconsecrated in 1807, turned into an iron foundry, and not opened again until 1928), its austere Gothic nakedness is a relief after all that Venetian ornament. In a chapel to the right of the entrance lies the body of St Helen, the irascible mother of the Emperor Constantine and finder of the True Cross. (Curiously enough, her body is also to be found in the Aracoeli church in Rome.) To the left are the charming cloisters and rose garden, tended by the three monks left in the monastery buildings.

San Giorgio dei Greci

Fondamenta dei Greci (041 523 9569). Vaporetto San Zaccaria. **Open** 9am-1pm, 3-5pm Mon, Wed-Sat. **Map** p327 D1.

By the time the church of San Giorgio was begun in 1539, the Greeks were well established in Venice and held a major stake in the city's numerous scholarly printing presses. Designed by Sante Lombardo, the church's interior is fully Orthodox in layout, with its women's gallery, and high altar behind the iconostasis. A heady smell of incense lends the church an Eastern mystique, enhanced by dark-bearded priests in flowing robes. The *campanile* is decidely lopsided. Next to the church are the Scuola di San Nicolò (now the Museo dell'Istituto Ellenico, *see p99*) and the Collegio Flangini (now seat of the Istituto Ellenico di Studi Bizantini e post-Bizantini), both by Baldassare Longhena.

San Giovanni in Bragora

Campo Bandiera e Moro (041 270 2464). Vaporetto Arsenale. **Open** 9-11am, 3.30-5.30pm Mon-Sat. **Map** p327 D1.

San Giovanni in Bragora (the meaning of *bragora* is as obscure as the date of the foundation of the first church here) is an intimate Gothic structure. The church where composer Antonio Vivaldi was baptised (a copy of the entry in the register is on show), San Giovanni also contains some very fine paintings. Above the high altar is the recently restored *Baptism of Christ* (1492-5) by Cima da Conegliano (which can 'only properly be seen by standing on the altar', according to Victorian traveller Augustus Hare), with a landscape recalling the countryside around the painter's home town of Conegliano. A smaller Cima, on the right of the sacristy door, shows *Constantine Holding the Cross and St Helen* (1502). On the same wall, just before the second altar, is a triptych by Bartolomeo Vivarini, *Madonna and Child and Two Saints*, dated 1478. The church also contains a splendidly heroic *Resurrection* (1498) by his nephew, Alvise Vivarini, in which the figure of Christ is based on a statue of Apollo, now in the Museo Archeologico (*see p83*); this painting is currently being held in the sacristy. **Photo** *p100*.

San Pietro in Castello

Campo San Pietro (041 275 0462/www. chorusvenezia.org). Vaporetto San Pietro. **Open** 10am-5pm Mon-Sat. **Admission** €2.50 (*see also p68* **Chorus**). **No credit cards. Map** p328 B2.

Until 1807 San Pietro in Castello was the cathedral of Venice, and its remote position testifies to the determination of the Venetian government to keep the clerical authorities well away from the centres of temporal power. The island of San Pietro is connected to the rest of Venice by two long bridges, but even today it has a distinctly insular feel to it. There has probably been a church here since the 7th century, but the present building was constructed in 1557 to a design by Andrea Palladio. San Pietro's lofty interior looks as if it has seen better days, but it contains some minor gems. The body of the first patriarch of Venice, San Lorenzo Giustiniani, is preserved in an urn elaborately supported by angels above the high altar: a magnificent piece of Baroque theatricality designed by Baldassare Longhena (1649). In the right-hand aisle is perhaps the church's most interesting artefact, the so-called 'St Peter's Throne', a delicately carved marble work from Antioch containing a Muslim funerary stele and verses from the Koran. The baroque Vendramin Chapel in the left transept was again designed by Longhena, and contains a *Virgin and Child* by the prolific Neapolitan Luca Giordano. Outside the entrance to the chapel is a late work by Paolo Veronese, *Saints John the Evangelist, Peter and Paul*. San Pietro's canal-side 'church green' of scrappy grass under towering trees and a punch-drunk *campanile* in white marble is a charming place to relax and have a picnic.

Scuola di San Giorgio degli Schiavoni

Castello 3259A, calle dei Furlani (041 522 8828). Vaporetto San Zaccaria or Arsenale. **Open** 9.30am-12.30pm, 3.30-6.30pm Tue-Sat; 9.30am-12.30pm Sun. **Admission** €3; €2 concessions. **No credit cards. Map** p327 D1.

The Schiavoni were Venice's Slav inhabitants, who had become so numerous and influential by the end of the 15th century that they could afford to build this *scuola* or meeting house by the side of their church, San Giovanni di Malta. The *scuola* houses one of Vittore Carpaccio's two great Venetian picture cycles. In 1502, eight years after completing his St Ursula cycle (now in the Accademia, *see p132*), Carpaccio was commissioned to paint a series of canvases illustrating the lives of the Dalmatian saints George, Tryphone and Jerome. In the tradition of the early Renaissance *istoria* (narrative painting cycle), there is a wealth of incidental detail, such as the decomposing virgins in *St George and the Dragon*, or the little dog in the painting of *St Augustine in his Study* (receiving the news of the death of St Jerome in a vision) – with its paraphernalia of humanism (astrolabe, shells, sheet music, archaeological fragments). It's worth venturing upstairs to see what the meeting hall of a working *scuola* looks like. The upstairs room provided the setting for a scene in Vikram Seth's 1999 novel, *An Equal Music*. San Giorgio degli Schiavoni still provides scholarships, distributes charity and acts as a focal point for the local Slav community. The opening hours are notoriously changeable.

Cannaregio

Kitsch, atmosphere and the original Ghetto.

CANNAREGIO

Cannaregio is the second largest *sestiere* in the city, extending from the station almost to the Rialto. It was always the first part of Venice to greet travellers from the mainland; while present-day tourists walk out of the station into a seedy sprawl of bars, hotels and tacky souvenir shops, earlier travellers would make their stately way down the wide Cannaregio Canal towards the Grand Canal.

It has been suggested that the name of the *sestiere* is a contraction of 'Canal Regio' (Regal Canal), but others attribute it to the *canne* (reeds) that grew along the banks here.

The first places to be settled (pre-AD1000) were the islands close to the Rialto area: the parishes of Santi Apostoli and San Giovanni Crisostomo in particular. The zones alongside the Grand Canal were the next to be built up. Urbanisation proceeded northwards, gradually spreading around the convents and monasteries that had been set up earlier in remote areas (the Misericordia, the Madonna dell'Orto, the Servi and Sant'Alvise). The construction of the railway bridge in the 19th century changed the configuration of the *sestiere*.

Large slaughterhouses (recently converted to university buildings, but the animal-skull friezes are a reminder; *see p110* **Along the canal**) were set up at the north end of the Cannaregio Canal, while several abandoned churches and convents were given over to civic and industrial purposes. (Ruskin writes memorably of the smoke rising from the chimney *campanile* of San Girolamo.) Roughly parallel to the Grand Canal, a wide pedestrian route – the strada Nuova – was carved, linking the Rialto to the station. But despite these changes, much of Cannaregio remains pleasingly calm and quiet.

From the station to the Rialto

Few other cities offer newly arrived tourists such a feast for the eyes as they step out of the railway station. You're greeted not by a dingy carpark or snarling flurry of buses and taxis but by the Grand Canal itself. What comes next, if you decide to walk to the centre, is a bit of a let-down: beyond the magnificent Baroque façade of the **Scalzi** church (*see p106*) lies a jostling array of souvenir stalls, grotty bars and downmarket hotels on and around the thronging lista di Spagna.

The squalor is, mercifully, circumscribed. Heading away from the station towards the Rialto, the *lista* leads to the large campo San Geremia, overlooked by the church of the same name (containing the shrivelled body of St Lucy) and Palazzo Labia, currently occupied by the RAI (Italian state television). The palazzo contains frescoes by Tiepolo, visible by appointment (041 781 111; being restored as this guide went to press).

Once over the Cannaregio Canal (*see p110* **Along the canal**) – by way of a grandiose bridge with obelisks – the route assumes more character, taking in lively street markets with Venetians going about their daily business. Off to the right, in a square giving on to the Grand Canal, is the church of **San Marcuola** (*see p104*), with an unfinished façade. A bit further on, the more picturesque church of **La Maddalena**, inspired by the Pantheon in Rome, stands in the small campo della Maddalena with a large assortment of fantastic chimney pots.

Beyond this, the wide strada Nuova begins. Off to the left is the church of **San Marziale**, with whimsical ceiling paintings; on the strada Nuova itself stands the church of **Santa Fosca**, another mainly 18th-century creation. In front of the church stands a statue of Paolo Sarpi, one of Venice's finer heroes, who helped Venice to resist a Papal Interdict in the 17th century and underwent an assassination attempt as a result. Down a calle to the right is the entrance to the **Ca' d'Oro** (*see p103*), Venice's most splendid Gothic palazzo.

The strada Nuova ends by the church of **Santi Apostoli** (*see p105*); the route to the Rialto soon becomes reassuringly narrow and crooked, passing the church of **San Giovanni Crisostomo** (*see p104*) and the adjacent courtyard of the Corte Seconda del Milion, where **Marco Polo** was born. Some of the Veneto-Byzantine-style houses in the courtyard would have been there when he was born in 1256. It was to this courtyard that we have to imagine Marco Polo returning with his father and uncle in 1295 after 24 years travelling the Far East.

As the story goes, the three men turned up in the old Polo home dressed in shabby Tartar costume. Nobody recognised them until they threw back their hoods. Then, to general amazement, Marco slit open the lining of their rough clothes and out poured a glittering shower of diamonds and precious stones. The name of the courtyard derives from the title of his own account of his adventures; it was said that he was unable to describe what he had seen using any figure lower than a million.

The *corte* also has a splendidly carved horseshoe arch. It was on the wellhead in the centre of the *corte* that Dirk Bogarde collapsed in Visconti's *Death in Venice*, his hair dye and mascara trickling down his face in the rain.

There's a plaque commemorating Marco Polo on the rear of the **Teatro Malibran** (*see p227*), formerly the Teatro di San Giovanni Crisostomo, one of Venice's earliest theatres and opera houses. The theatre was reopened in 2001, its slow-moving restoration fast-tracked after the city's main opera house, **La Fenice** (*see p91*), was destroyed by fire.

Ca' d'Oro (Galleria Franchetti)

Cannaregio 3932, calle Ca' d'Oro (041 523 8790/ www.artive.arti.beniculturali.it). Vaporetto Ca' d'Oro. **Open** 8.15am-2pm Mon; 8.15am-7.15pm Tue-Sun. *Courtyard* Apr-Oct 8.15am-6.45pm Tue-Sun. **Admission** €5; €2.50 concessions. **No credit cards. Map** p322 A4.

In its 15th-century heyday, the façade of this pretty townhouse on the Grand Canal must have looked a psychedelic treat: the colour scheme was light blue and burgundy, with 24-carat gold highlights. Though the colour has worn off, the Grand Canal frontage of Ca' d'Oro – built for merchant Marin Contarini between 1421 and 1431 – is still the most elaborate example of the florid Venetian Gothic style besides the Doge's Palace. Inside, little of the original structure and decor has survived the depredations of successive owners. The pretty courtyard was reconstructed with its original 15th-century staircase and well head a century ago by Baron Franchetti; the mosaic floor is a 19th-century imitation of the floors in Torcello and San Marco. The Baron also assembled the collection of paintings, sculptures and coins that is exhibited on the first and second floors. The highlight of the collection is Mantegna's *St Sebastian*, one of the painter's most powerful late works; the Palladian frame contrasts oddly with the saint's existential anguish. The rest is good in parts, though not necessarily the parts you would expect. A small medal of Sultan Mohammed II by Gentile Bellini (a souvenir of his years in Constantinople) is more impressive than the worse-than-faded frescoes by Titian and Giorgione removed from the Fondaco dei Tedeschi, now the post office. There are some good Renaissance bronzes from deconsecrated churches in the city and

Campo del Ghetto Nuovo. *See p105.*

small but vigorous plaster models by Bernini for the statues on the fountains in Rome's piazza Navona. A recent intriguing addition is a series of small Dutch paintings on copper from the 16th century depicting the *Four Seasons* and Dutch landscapes and gardens; they provide early testimony of the Dutch tulip-mania.

San Giovanni Crisostomo

Cannaregio, campo San Giovanni Crisostomo (041 522 7155). Vaporetto Rialto. **Open** 8.30am-noon, 3.30-7pm Mon-Sat; 3.30-7pm Sun. **Map** p322 B5.

This small church by Mauro Codussi is dedicated to St John Chrysostomos, archbishop of Constantinople, and shows a fittingly Byzantine influence in its Greek cross form. It contains two great paintings. On the right-hand altar is *Saints Jerome, Christopher and Louis of Toulouse*, signed by Giovanni Bellini and dated 1513. This late work is one of his few Madonna-less altarpieces and shows the Old Master ready to experiment with the atmospheric colouring techniques of such younger artists as Giorgione. On the high altar hangs *Saints John the Baptist, Liberale, Mary Magdalene and Catherine* (c1509) by Sebastiano del Piombo, who trained under Bellini but was also influenced by Giorgione. Henry James was deeply impressed by the figure of Mary Magdalene: she looked, he said, like a 'dangerous, but most valuable acquaintance'. On the left-hand altar is *Coronation of the Virgin*, a fine relief (1500-02) by Tullio Lombardo.

San Marcuola

Cannaregio, campo San Marcuola (041 713 872). Vaporetto San Marcuola. **Open** 10am-noon, 5-6pm Mon-Sat. **Map** p321 F3.

There was no such person as St Marcuola; the name is a local mangling of the over-complicated *santi Ermagora e Fortunato*, two early martyrs. The church, designed by 18th-century architect Giorgio Massari – he of the Palazzo Grassi on the Grand Canal, *see p80*) has been beautifully restored and its gleaming interior comes as a surprise after the unfinished brick façade.

It contains some vigorous statues by Gianmaria Morleiter and, in the chancel, a *Last Supper* (1547) by Tintoretto, his first treatment of what was later to become one of his favourite subjects; the layout is uncharacteristically symmetrical but indications of the later Tintoretto can be seen in the restless movements of the disciples and the background figures. Opposite is a 17th-century copy of another Tintoretto (*Christ Washing the Feet of His Disciples*); the original can be found in Newcastle.

San Marziale

Cannaregio, campo San Marziale (041 719 933). Vaporetto San Marcuola or Ca' d'Oro. **Open** 4-6.30pm Mon-Sat; 8.30-10am Sun. **Map** p322 A3.

The real joy of this church is its ceiling, with its four luminous paintings (1700-05) by the vivacious colourist Sebastiano Ricci. Two of them depict *God the Father with Angels* and *St Martial in Glory*; the other two recount the miraculous story of the wooden statue of the Madonna and Child that resides on the second altar on the left – apparently, it made its own way here by boat from Rimini. The high altar has an equally fantastic baroque extravaganza: a massive marble group of Christ, the world and some angels looms over the altar while St Jerome and companions crouch awkwardly beneath.

View from the fondamenta Nuove. *See p107.*

Santi Apostoli

Cannaregio, campo Santi Apostoli (041 523 8297).
Vaporetto Ca' d'Oro. **Open** 8.30am-noon, 5-7pm
Mon-Sat; 4-7pm Sun. **Map** p322 B4.
According to tradition, the 12 apostles appeared to
the seventh-century Bishop of Oderzo, St Magnus,
telling him to build a church where he saw 12 cranes
together – a not uncommon sight when Venice was
little more than a series of uninhabited islands poking out of marshes. Magnus followed orders, but the
ancient church was rebuilt in the 17th century. Its
campanile (1672), crowned by an onion dome added
50 years later, is a Venetian landmark.

The Cappella Corner, off the right side of the nave,
is a century older than the rest of the structure. It
was built by Mauro Codussi for the dispossessed
Queen Caterina Cornaro of Cyprus; she was buried
here in 1510 alongside her father and brother but
subsequently removed to San Salvador (*see p87*). On
the altar is a splendidly theatrical *Communion of St
Lucy* by Giambattista Tiepolo; the young saint,
whose gouged eyes are in a dish on the floor, is
bathed in a heavenly light. The chapel to the right
of the high altar has remnants of 14th-century frescoes while the one to the left has a dramatically
stormy painting of *The Guardian Angel* by
Francesco Maffei. As this guide went to press the
chancel was being restored.

Gli Scalzi

*Cannaregio, fondamenta degli Scalzi (041 715
115). Vaporetto Ferrovia.* **Open** 7-11.45am,
4-6.45pm Mon-Sat; 4-7pm Sun. **Map** p321 D3.
Officially Santa Maria di Nazareth, this church
is universally known as Gli Scalzi after the order
of *Carmelitani scalzi* (Barefoot Carmelites) to whom
it belongs. They bought the plot in 1645 and
subsequentlycommissioned Baldassare Longhena
to design the church.

The fine façade (1672-80) is the work of Giuseppe
Sardi; it was paid for by a newcomer to Venice's
ruling patrician class, Gerolamo Cavazza, determined to make his marble mark on the landscape.
The interior is striking for its coloured marble ('a
perfect type of the vulgar abuse of marble in every
possible way,' wrote Ruskin sniffily) and massively
elaborate baldachin over the high altar. There are
many fine baroque statues, including the St John of
the Cross by Giovanni Marchiori in the first chapel
on the right and the anonymous marble crucifix and
wax effigy of Christ in the chapel opposite. An
Austrian shell that plummeted through the roof in
1915 destroyed the church's greatest work of art,
Tiepolo's fresco, *The Transport of the House of
Loreto,* but spared some of the artist's lesser frescoes, *Angels of the Passion* and *Agony in the Garden,*
in the first chapel on the left, and *St Theresa in Glory,*
which hovers gracefully above a ham-fisted imitation of Bernini's sculpture, *Ecstasy of St Theresa,* in
the second on the right. In the second chapel on the
left lie the remains of the last doge of Venice,
Lodovico Manin.

Il Ghetto

The word ghetto (like arsenal and ciao) is one
that Venice has given to the world. It originally
meant an iron foundry, a place where iron was
gettato (cast). Until 1390, when the foundry was
transferred to the Arsenale, casting was done
on a small island in Cannaregio. In 1516 it was
decided to confine the city's Jewish population
to this island; here they remained until 1797.

Venetian treatment of the Jews was by no
means as harsh as in many European countries,
but neither was it a model of open-minded
benevolence. The Republic's attitude was
governed by practical considerations, and
business was done with Jewish merchants at
least as early as the tenth century. It was not
until 1385, however, that Jewish moneylenders
were given permission to reside in the city
itself. Twelve years later, permission was
revoked amid allegations of irregularities in
their banking practices. For a century after that,
residence in Venice was limited to two-week
stretches.

In 1509, when the Venetian mainland
territories were overrun by foreign troops, great
numbers of Jews took refuge in the city. The
clergy seized the opportunity to stir up anti-
Jewish feeling and demanded their expulsion.
Venice's rulers, however, had begun to see the
economic advantages of letting them stay, and
in 1516 a compromise was reached. In a
decision that was to mark the course of Jewish
history in Europe, the refugees were given
residence permits but confined to the Ghetto.

Restrictions were many and tough. Gates
across the bridges to the island were closed an
hour after sunset in summer (two hours after in
winter), reopening at dawn. During the day,
Jews had to wear distinctive badges or
headgear. Most trades other than moneylending
were barred to them. One exception was
medicine, for which they were famous: Venetian
practicality allowed Jewish doctors to leave the
Ghetto at night for professional calls. Another
was music: Jewish singers and fiddlers were
hired for private parties.

The Ghetto became a stop on the tourist
trail. In 1608 traveller Thomas Coryat came
to gaze at the Jews – never having seen any in
England – and marvelled at the 'sweet-featured
persons' and the 'apparel, jewels, chains of
gold' of the women.

The original inhabitants were mostly
Ashkenazim from Germany; they were joined
by Sephardim escaping from persecution in
Spain and Portugal and then, increasingly,
by Levantine Jews from the Ottoman Empire.
These latter proved key figures in trade
between Venice and the East, particularly

Hampered in the Ghetto

In 1492 Jews were expelled from Spain and from the Spanish-controlled territories of southern Italy. As these refugees – many of them highly educated, talented professionals – poured into the city-states of northern Italy to swell the existing communities there, they were not only imbued with the extraordinary energy of the Renaissance which was in full swing – they contributed to it.

Jewish money-lenders financed it, Jewish doctors ministered to its, and Jewish musicians played, and composed, the soundtrack. Nowhere was this truer than in Venice, with one of Italy's largest, most venerable Jewish communities; hemmed in by gates and limitations in their Ghetto, Jews were allowed out with few limitations if they were exiting in order to strum or sing.

The most famous Jewish musician of the Italian Renaissance was singer, composer and violinist Salamone Rossi. Based in Mantua, he was chief musician at the court there from 1587 until 1628. His visits to Venice were frequent, however, both for professional engagements – many of them involving his sister Ester, known as Madama Europa, and a fine soprano – and to oversee the publication of his music in Venice's renowned printing presses.

La Serenissima's own leading Jewish musician was Leon Modena, a contemporary of Rossi's and the man brought in to solve the problem of how to print Rossi's new musical settings (written left to right) of Hebrew liturgical pieces (written right to left; in the end, he printed it all left to right, presuming that the words of Jewish ceremonies were so well known that no one would read them anyway).

Modena's aspirations to become a rabbi were hamstrung by his passion for gambling. He dedicated himself instead to alchemy… and teaching, printing and encouraging the new music of the northern Italian Jewish communities – music that broke with centuries of tradition, brought him closer to Rossi, and put him on a collision course with some community elders.

In 1628 Modena asserted his leadership of the Venetian Jewish musical community when he set up the Accademia degli Impediti – the Academy of the Hampered; motto, *Cum recordaremur Sion*, when we remembered Zion – and taking on the role of choirmaster. The ranks of musicians who joined the academy were swollen by Jews fleeing from dynastic struggles between branches of Mantua's ruling family, and may have included Rossi. But the great plague of 1629-31 decimated the academy, and put an end to the great age of musical innovation in the Ghetto.

after Venice lost so many of her trading posts in the eastern Mediterranean. By the mid 16th century the Levantine Jews, the richest community, were given permission to move from the Ghetto Nuovo to the confusingly named Ghetto Vecchio (the 'old Ghetto', the site of an earlier foundry); in 1633 they expanded into the Ghetto Nuovissimo. Nonetheless, conditions remained cramped, and the height of the buildings in the campo del Ghetto Nuovo shows how the inhabitants, unable to expand in a horizontal direction, did so vertically, creating the first high-rise blocks in Europe. A recent study has calculated that at certain periods overcrowding was such that the inhabitants must have had to take it in turns to sleep.

Despite this, room was found for five magnificent synagogues, however, each new influx of immigrants wanting its own place of worship. The German, Levantine and Spanish synagogues can be visited as part of the **Museo Ebraico** tour (*see below*).

With the arrival of Napoleon in 1797, Jews gained full rights of citizenship; many chose to remain in the Ghetto. In the deportations during the Nazi occupation of Italy in 1943, 202 Venetian Jews were sent to the death camps, including the chief rabbi and 20 inmates of an old people's home. The Jewish population of Venice and Mestre now stands at about 500, though only around a dozen Jewish families still live in the Ghetto. The Ghetto remains, however, the centre of spiritual, cultural and social life for the Jewish community: you'll also find a museum, a library, a kosher restaurant, bakeries and a nursery school. Orthodox religious services are held in the Scuola Spagnola in the summer and in the Scuola Levantina in winter.

Museo Ebraico

Cannaregio 2902B, campo del Ghetto Nuovo (041 715 359/www.museoebraico.it). Vaporetto Guglie or San Marcuola. **Open** *June-Sept* 10am-7pm Mon-Fri, Sun; guided tours hourly 10.30am-5.30pm. *Oct-May* 10am-6pm Mon-Fri, Sun; guided tours hourly

Sightseeing

10.30am-3.30pm Mon-Thur, Sun; 10.30am-2.30pm Fri. **Admission** *Museum only* €3; €2 concessions. *Museum & synagogues* €8.50; €7 concessions. **Credit** MC, V. **Map** p321 F2

Venice's Jewish community has been enjoying a renaissance recently, and this well-run museum and cultural centre – founded in 1953 – has been spruced up accordingly, with the addition of a bookshop. In the small museum itself there are ritual objects in silver – Trah finials, Purim and Pesach cases, menorahs – sacred vestments and hangings, and a series of marriage contracts. To get the most out of the experience, the museum should be visited as part of the guided tours in English and Italian. These take in three synagogues – the Scuola canton (Ashkenazi rite), the Scuola italiana (Italian rite) and the Scuola levantina (Sephardic rite).

North-western Cannaregio

If you're tired of the crowds, there's no better place to get away from it all than the north-western areas of Cannaregio. Built around three long parallel canals, it has no large animated squares and (with the exception of the Ghetto; *see p105*) no sudden surprises – just occasional views over the northern lagoon.

That's not to say it doesn't have its landmarks, including the *vecchia* (old; 14th-century) and *nuova* (new; 16th-century) Scuole della Misericordia, the 'new' one being a huge building by Sansovino, its façade never completed. Long used as a gym, it now awaits conversion into a new cultural institution of some kind. Plans so far have included an auditorium, a multimedia archive and a music museum. The latest rumour is of a 'House of Fashion', under the aegis of Prada… but don't hold your breath.

Behind the *scuole*, the picturesque campo dell'Abbazia, overlooked by the baroque façade of the **Abbazia della Misericordia** and the Gothic façade of the *Scuola vecchia*, is one of the most peaceful retreats in Venice; on the façade of the latter you can still see the outlines of sculptures (now in London's Victoria & Albert Museum) by Gothic master Bartolomeo Bon. Since 1983 the building has been used as an art restoration workshop.

On the northernmost canal (rio della Madonna dell'Orto) are the churches of the **Madonna dell'Orto** (*see p109*) and **Sant'Alvise** (*see p109*), as well as many fine *palazzi*. At the eastern end of the *fondamente* along this canal, Palazzo Contarini dal Zaffo, was built for Gaspare Contarini, a 16th-century scholar, diplomat and cardinal. Behind, a large garden stretches down to the lagoon; in its far corner stands the Casinò degli Spiriti (best seen from fondamenta Nuove). It was designed as a meeting place for the 'spirits' (wits) of the

day, though the name and the lonely position of the construction have given rise to numerous ghost stories over the years.

The Madonna dell'Orto area may have been the home of an Islamic merchant community in the 12th and 13th centuries, centring on a since-destroyed Fondaco (meeting place and storehouse) degli arabi. Opposite the church of Santa Maria dell'Orto is the 15th-century Palazzo Mastelli, also known as Palazzo del Camello because of its relief of a turbaned figure with a camel. The Arabic theme continues in the campo dei Mori ('of the Moors') across the bridge, named after the three stone figures set into the façade of a building, all wearing turbans. The one with the comically prominent iron nose – dubbed 'Sior Antonio Rioba' – was the Venetian equivalent of Rome's Pasquino: disgruntled citizens or local wits would hang their rhyming complaints on him under cover of darkness, or use him as a pseudonym for published satires. The three figures are believed to be the Mastelli brothers, owners of the adjacent palazzo, who came to Venice as merchants from the Greek

Madonna dell'Orto.
See p109.

I Gesuiti. *See p110.*

Peloponnese (then known as Morea – which, of course, offers another possible explanation of the campo's name).

Madonna dell'Orto

Cannaregio, campo Madonna dell'Orto (041 275 0462/www.chorusvenezia.org). Vaporetto Orto. **Open** 10am-5pm Mon-Sat. **Admission** €2.50 (*see also p68* **Chorus**). **No credit cards.** **Map** p322 A2.

The 'Tintoretto church' was originally dedicated to St Christopher (a magnificent statue of whom stands over the main door), the patron saint of the gondoliers who ran the ferry service to the islands from a nearby jetty. However, a cult developed around a large, unfinished and supposedly miraculous statue of the Madonna and Child that stood in the nearby garden of sculptor Giovanni de Santi. In 1377 the sculpture was solemnly transferred into the church (it's now in the chapel of San Mauro), and the church's name was changed to the Madonna dell'Orto – of the Garden.

It was rebuilt between 1399 and 1473, and a monastery was constructed alongside. The beautiful Gothic façade is similar to those of the Frari (*see p123*) and Santi Giovanni e Paolo (*see p95*), although the false gallery at the top is unique. The sculptures are all fine 15th-century works. But it is the numerous works by Tintoretto that have made the Madonna dell'Orto famous. Tradition has it that the artist began decorating the church as penance for insulting a doge: in fact, it took very little to persuade Tintoretto to get his palette out, and the urgent sincerity of his work here speaks for itself.

Two colossal paintings dominate the side walls of the chancel. On the left is *The Israelites at Mount Sinai*; some have seen portraits of Venice's artistic top four (Giorgione, Titian, Veronese and Tintoretto himself) in the bearers of the Golden Calf, although there is no actual documentary evidence for this, nor for the identification of the lady dressed in blue as Mrs Tintoretto.

Opposite is a gruesome *Last Judgment*. Like Dante and Michelangelo, Tintoretto had no qualms about mixing religion and myth: note the classical figure of Charon ferrying the souls of the dead. Tintoretto's paintings in the apse include *St Peter's Vision of the Cross* and *The Beheading of St Paul* (or Christopher, according to some), both maelstroms of swirling angelic movement. On the wall of the right aisle is the *Presentation of the Virgin in the Temple*, a calmer, more reverential work. It was painted as a deliberate response to Titian's masterpiece on the same theme in the Accademia, and is more characteristically mystical in tone.

The Contarini Chapel, off the left aisle, contains the artist's beautiful *St Agnes Reviving the Son of a Roman Prefect*. Once again, it is the swooping angels that steal the show in their dazzling blue vestments. Tintoretto, his son Domenico and his artistically gifted daughter Marietta are buried in a chapel off the right aisle. When the Tintorettos get too

much for you, take a look at Cima da Conegliano's freshly restored masterpiece *Saints John the Baptist, Mark, Jerome and Paul* (1494-5) over the first altar on the right. The saints stand under a ruined portico against a sharp, wintry light. There used to be a small *Madonna and Child* by Giovanni Bellini in the chapel opposite, but it was stolen in 1993. The second chapel on the left contains on the left-hand wall a painting by Titian of *The Archangel Raphael and Tobias* (and dog) that has been moved here from the church of San Marziale (*see p104*).

In a room beneath the bell tower, a small treasury contains reliquaries and other precious objects. The room is dedicated to the memory of Sir Ashley Clarke, a former British ambassador to Italy and chairman of Venice in Peril which was responsible for the church's restoration. **Photo** *p107*.

Sant'Alvise

Cannaregio, campo Sant'Alvise (041 275 0462/ www.chorusvenezia.org). Vaporetto Sant'Alvise. **Open** 10am-5pm Mon-Sat. **Admission** €2.50 (*see also p68* **Chorus**). **No credit cards.** **Map** p321 F1.

A pleasingly simple Gothic building of the 14th century, Sant'Alvise's interior was remodelled in the 1600s with extravagant, if not wholly convincing, *trompe l'oeil* effects on the ceiling. On the inner façade is a barco, a hanging choir of the 15th century with elegant wrought-iron gratings, formerly used by the nuns of the adjacent convent. Beneath the barco are eight charmingly naïve biblical paintings in tempera, fancifully attributed by Ruskin to the ten-year-old Carpaccio; they have been more realistically attributed to Lazzaro Bastiani. On the right wall of the church are two paintings by Tiepolo, *The Crowning of Thorns* and *The Flagellation*. A larger and livelier work by the same painter, *Road to Calvary*, hangs on the right wall of the chancel, with rather ill-suited circus pageantry, complete with trumpets and prancing horses.

Anyone looking for a picnic spot will find a garden nearby, complete with picturesque classical 'ruins'; walk westwards along the fondamenta and take calle del Capitelo to the right.

North-eastern Cannaregio

North-eastern Cannaregio is more intriguingly closed in, with many narrow alleys (including the Venetian record holder: calle Varisco which is 52 centimetres (20 inches) wide at its narrowest point), charming courtyards and well heads, but no major sights, with the exception of the spectacularly ornate church of **I Gesuiti** (*see p110*), the **Oratorio dei Crociferi** (*see p110*) and, further east, the miniature marvel of **Santa Maria dei Miracoli** (*see p111*). Titian had a house here, with a garden extending to the lagoon; the courtyard where the house was located is raised to the dignity of a 'campo' and named after the artist.

Along the canal

Apart from the Grand Canal and the Giudecca there is only one waterway in the city that is dignified by the name of canal, and that is the Cannaregio Canal. It is still the only canal in residential Venice other than the Grand Canal and the Giudecca to host *vaporetti*.

For centuries this waterway was the main route into Venice from the mainland and it is suitably impressive, with wide *fondamente* on each side and several imposing *palazzi*. It's spanned by two stately bridges, the ponte delle Guglie (Bridge of the Obelisks, 1823), and the ponte dei Tre Archi, the only three-arch stone bridge in Venice, built by Andrea Tirali in 1688. Heading towards the lagoon from the ponte delle Guglie on the right-hand fondamenta, you pass the *sottoportico* leading to the Jewish Ghetto (*see p105*).

Beyond this stands the Palazzo Nani (No.1105), a fine Renaissance building dating from the 16th century. Two hundred metres (700 feet) further on is the Palazzo Surian-Bellotto (No.968): in the 18th century this was the French embassy, where Jean Jacques Rousseau worked – reluctantly – as a secretary. Beyond, Santa Maria delle Penitenti, with its unfinished façade, was formerly a home for the city's fallen women.

On the left bank is the Palazzo Priuli-Manfrin (Nos.342-3), another Tirali creation dating from 1735, in a neo-classical style of such severe plainness that it prefigures 20th-century purist art.

The imposing 17th-century Palazzo Savorgan (No.349) – now a school – has huge coats of arms and reliefs of helmets; the owners were descended from Federigo Savorgnan who, in 1385, became the first non-Venetian to be admitted to Venice's patrician ruling clique. Behind it is the Parco Savorgnan, a charming public garden that is one of Venice's better-kept

I Gesuiti

Cannaregio, campo dei Gesuiti (041 528 6579). Vaporetto Fondamente Nove. **Open** 10am-noon, 4-6pm daily. **Map** p322 C3.

The Jesuits were never very popular in Venice and it wasn't until 1715 that they felt secure enough to build a church here. Even then they chose a comparatively remote plot on the edge of town. But once they made up their mind to go ahead, they went all out: local architect Domenico Rossi was given explicit instructions to dazzle the Venetians.

The result leaves no room for half measures: you love it or you hate it, and most people do the latter, considering the result the ultimate in church kitsch. The exterior, with a façade by Gian Battista Fattoretto, is conventional enough; the interior is any-thing but. All that tassled, bunched, overpowering drapery is not the work of a rococo set designer gone berserk with luxurious brocades: it's plain old green and white marble. Bernini's altar in St Peter's in Rome

was the model for the baldachin over the altar, by Fra Giuseppe Pozzo. The statues above the baldachin are by Giuseppe Torretti, as are the rococo archangels at the corners of the crossing. Titian's *Martyrdom of St Lawrence* (1558-9), over the first altar on the left side, came from an earlier church on this site, and was one of the first successful night scenes ever painted. According to writer WD Howells – who labelled the church 'indescribably table-clothy' – the saint seems to be the only person in the building not suffering from the cold. **Photo** *p108*.

Oratorio dei Crociferi

Cannaregio 4905, campo dei Gesuiti (041 270 2464). Vaporetto Fondamente Nove. **Open** *Apr-Oct* 3.30-6.30pm Fri, Sat. *Nov-Mar* by appointment. **Admission** €2. **No credit cards**. **Map** p322 C3.

Founded in the 13th century by Doge Renier Zeno, the oratory is a sort of primitive *scuola* (*see p67*), with the familiar square central meeting hall but secrets. A little further on, the ponte della Crea spans a canal that was covered over for centuries, only to be re-excavated in 1997.

After passing the ponte dei Tre Archi (with the Renaissance church of San Giobbe off to the left) the fondamenta continues to the ex-slaughterhouse, built in the 19th century by the Austrians. Long used by a rowing club, it has recently been taken over and revamped by Venice University's economics faculty.

Two fairly recent housing projects are easily reachable from the canal. From the left bank calle delle due Corti leads to the Area Saffa, a complex built to designs by Vittorio Gregotti between 1981 and 1994; the complex is surprisingly large but owing to the enclosed nature of the site and the use of high dividing walls, the overall effect is claustrophobic. More successful is the housing project of sacca San Gerolamo, at the end of the right bank, to designs by Franco Bortoluzzi (1987-1990); the complex makes picturesque use of traditional elements, such as slabs of Istrian marble framing green-shuttered windows and large archways giving on to the lagoon.

San Giobbe

Campo San Giobbe (041 524 1889). Vaporetto Crea or Ponte Tre Archi. **Open** 10am-noon, 3-6pm Mon-Sat; 3.30-6pm Sun. **Map** p321 D2.
Job (Giobbe) has given saint status by Venice, despite his Old Testament pedigree. The church named after him was built to celebrate the visit in 1463 of St Bernardino of Siena, a high-profile Francescan evangelist. The first Venetian creation of Pietro Lombardo, it introduced a new classical style, immediately visible in the doorway (three statues by Pietro Lombardo that once adorned it are now in the sacristy). The interior of what was probably the first single-naved church in Venice is unashamedly Renaissance. Members of the Lombardo family are responsible for the carvings in the domed sanctuary, all around the triumphal arch separating the sanctuary from the nave, and on the tombstone of San Giobbe's founder Cristoforo Moro, in the centre of the sanctuary floor. This doge's name has given rise to associations with Othello, the Moor of Venice; some have seen the mulberry symbol in his tombstone (*moro* means mulberry tree as well as Moor) as the origin of Desdemona's handkerchief, 'spotted with strawberries'. The church's treasures – altarpieces by Giovanni Bellini and Vittore Carpaccio – are now in the Accademia (*see p132*). An atmospheric *Nativity* by Gerolamo Savoldo remains, as does an *Annunciation with Saints Michael and Anthony* triptych by Antonio Vivarini. The Martini Chapel, the second on the left, is a little bit of Tuscany in Venice. Built for a family of silk-weavers from Lucca, it is attributed to the Florentine Bernardo Rossellino. The terracotta medallions of Christ and the Four Evangelists are by the Della Robbia studio – the only examples of its work in Venice.

without the quasi-masonic ceremonial trappings. Palma il Giovane's colourful cycle of paintings shows Pope Anacletus instituting the order of the Crociferi (cross-bearers), and dwells on the pious life of Doge Pasquale Cicogna, who was a fervent supporter of the order.

Santa Maria dei Miracoli

Cannaregio, campo Santa Maria dei Miracoli (041 275 0462/www.chorusvenezia.org). Vaporetto Rialto or Fondamente Nove. **Open** 10am-5pm Mon-Sat. **Admission** €2.50 (*see also p68* **Chorus**). **No credit cards**. **Map** p322 C5.
Arguably one of the most exquisite churches in the world, Santa Maria dei Miracoli was built in the 1480s to house a miraculous image of the Madonna, reputed to have revived a man who had spent half an hour underwater in the Giudecca Canal, and to have cancelled all traces of a knife attack on a woman. The building is the work of the Lombardo family, early Renaissance masons who fused architecture, surface detail and sculpture into a unique whole. Pietro Lombardo may have been a Lombard by birth but he soon got into the Venetian way of doing things, employing Byzantine spoils left over from work on St Mark's to create a work of art displaying an entirely Venetian sensitivity to texture and colour. There is an almost painterly approach to the use of multicoloured marble in the four sides of the church, each of which is of a slightly different shade. The sides have more pilasters than are strictly necessary, making the church appear longer than it really is. Inside, 50 painted ceiling panels by Pier Maria Pennacchi (1528) are almost impossible to distinguish without binoculars. Instead, turn your attention to the church's true treasures: the delicate carvings by the Lombardi on the columns, steps and balustrade. The details are so exquisite and life-like that even Renaissance-resisting Ruskin couldn't help admiring them.

MUSEUM HOURS:
From October 1 to May 31, 10 am / 6 pm
From June 1 to September 30, 10am / 7 pm
Closed on Saturdays and Jewish holidays

SYNAGOGUE'S TOURS:
In Italian and English, every hour
from 10.30 am until 4.30 pm
(from October 1 to May 31)
From June 1 to September 30,
(from 10.30 am until 5.30 pm)
Also available:
private thematic tours,
tours in German, French,
Spanish and Hebrew

Information and reservations:
T. +39 041 715 359
F. +39 041 723 007

IN THE WORLD'S FIRST GHETTO
THE ANCIENT SYNAGOGUES AND
THE MUSEUM OF THE JEWISH
COMMUNITY OF VENICE

THE ANCIENT JEWISH CEMETERY ON THE LID
GUIDED TOURS:
From June 1 to September 30
Sunday 2.30

Information and reservations
T. +39 041 715 359
F. +39 041 723 007

M U S E O
E B R A I C O
di VENEZIA

Cannaregio 2902/B - 30121 Venezia
T. +39 041 715359 F. +39 041 723007
museoebraico@codesscultura.it
www.museoebraico.it

www.studiolanza.com

San Polo & Santa Croce

Bustling markets, art-packed churches.

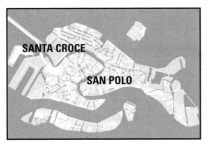

SANTA CROCE

SAN POLO

It is probably only the postman who can distinguish between these two *sestieri*, which nestle within the pear-shaped bulge of the upper loop of the Grand Canal. The area is perhaps more usefully divided into east and west, with the rio San Polo – which slices through from north to south (changing its name three times en route) – acting as boundary between the two halves. The eastern portion, tightly clustered around the Rialto market, is the city's ancient heart and despite the invasion of trashy tourist-trinkets one can still feel its steady throb here. The western part was settled later and has a slightly more spacious feel; its fulcrum is the great religious complex of the **Frari** (*see p123*) and the *scuole* of **San Rocco** (*see p125*) and **San Giovanni Evangelista**.

The Rialto Markets

This is where the city began. *Rialto*, most experts agree, derives from *Rivoaltus* (high bank), and it was on this point of higher ground at the mid-point along the Grand Canal that one of the earliest settlements was founded in the fifth century. The district has been the commercial centre of the city since the market was moved here from campo San Bartolomeo (*see p87*) in 1097. The present layout of the market and adjacent buildings is the result of a reconstruction project by Scarpagnino after a vast fire in 1514 that destroyed the whole area.

As usual in Venice, the project made use of the previous foundations, so the present street-plan probably reflects quite faithfully the earliest urban arrangement, with long, narrow parallel blocks running behind the grand *palazzi* along the riva del Vin, and smaller, squarer blocks further inland for the market workers.

At the foot of the Rialto bridge, where the tourist stalls are thick on the ground, stand (to the south) the **Palazzo dei Dieci Savi**, which housed the city's tax inspectors but is now used by the ancient but extant lagoon water authority, *Il magistrato alle acque*, and (to the north) the **Palazzo dei Camerlenghi**, which housed the finance department.

Beyond, the small church of **San Giacomo di Rialto** (*see p114*, known affectionately as San Giacometto) is generally agreed to be the first of the city's churches – tradition has it that it was founded in 421. All around it stretch the markets, around which commercial and administrative buildings and areas of low-cost housing mushroomed after trade was shifted from across the canal. Despite an over-abundance of souvenir stalls, the Rialto market remains the best place to buy your fruit, veg and seafood. In recent years this area has taken on a new lease of life as one of the centres of that rare phenomenon, Venetian night-life, with a number of bars having been opened under the porticos of the Renaissance *Fabbriche Vecchie* (Scarpagnino, 1520-22); several of them give onto the open space of the *Erberia* on the Grand Canal. See *p177* **In the market**.

The name *Erberia* denotes the fact that vegetables are sold here; there are other examples of such names in the streets and squares nearby (*Naranzeria* – oranges; *Casaria* – cheese; *Speziali* – spices), while the narrower alleys mostly bear the names of ancient inns and taverns – some still in operation – such as 'The Monkey', 'The Two Swords', 'The Two Moors' (fans of Donna Leon's novels will recognise this as one of her detective's favourite bars), 'The Ox', 'The Bell'. Then as now, market traders hated to be too far from liquid refreshment.

On the other side of campo San Giacomo, behind the fruit stalls, is a 16th-century statue of a kneeling figure supporting a staircase leading up to a small column of Egyptian granite, from which laws and sentences were pronounced. It was to this figure – the *Gobbo di Rialto* (the Hunchback of the Rialto, although he is, in fact, merely crouching) – that naked malefactors clung in desperate and bloody relief, since the statue marked the end of the gauntlet they were condemned to run from piazza San Marco as an alternative to gaol.

The **Rialto markets** buzz by day and night. *See p113.*

The ruga degli Speziali leads to the **Pescaria** (fishmarket; open Tue-Sat morning). The present neo-Gothic arcade (1907) replaced the iron structure of the previous century. Beyond the market extends a warren-like zone of medieval low-rent housing interspersed with proud *palazzi*. This area is traversed by two main pedestrian routes from the Rialto bridge, one running westward, more or less parallel to the Grand Canal, towards campo San Polo, and the other zigzagging north-westwards via a series of small squares towards campo **San Giacomo dell'Orio** (*see p119*) and the station.

San Giacomo di Rialto

San Polo, campo San Giacomo (041 522 4745). Vaporetto Rialto. **Open** 9.30am-noon, 4-6pm Mon-Sat. **Map** p322 B5.
The traditional foundation date for this church is that of the city itself: 25 March 421. It has undergone several radical reconstructions since its foundation, the last in 1601. Nonetheless, out of respect for the history of the building, the original Greek cross plan was always preserved, as were its minuscule dimensions. The interior has columns of ancient marble with 11th-century Corinthian capitals. According to Francesco Sansovino (son of the architect and author of the first guide to the city in 1581), the brick dome may have been a model for the domes of St Mark's. In 1177 Pope Alexander III granted plenary indulgence to all those who visited the church on Maundy Thursday; among the eager visitors every year was the doge. The special role of this church in Venetian history was given official recognition after 1532, when Pope Clement VII bestowed the patronage of the church on the doge, effectively annexing it to the Ducal Chapel of St Mark's.

West from the Rialto

The route to campo San Polo traverses a series of straight, busy shopping streets, passing the church of **San Giovanni Elemosinario** (*see p115*) and the deconsecrated church of Sant'Aponal, which has fine Gothic sculpture on its façade. To the south of this route, towards the Grand Canal, stands **San Silvestro** (*see p115*), with a good Tintoretto, while to the north is a fascinating network of quiet, little-visited alleys and courtyards.

Curiosities worth seeking out (take calle Bianca Cappello from campo Sant'Aponal) include **Palazzo Molin-Cappello**, birthplace of Bianca Cappello, who in 1563 was sentenced to death *in absentia* for eloping with a bank clerk but managed to right things between herself and the Most Serene Republic by later marrying Francesco de' Medici, Grand Duke of Tuscany. North-westwards from here is campiello Albrizzi, overlooked by Palazzo Albrizzi, with its sumptuous baroque interior (closed to the public).

Nearby is one of Venice's early red-light zones; the district of **Ca' Rampana** was notorious enough to have passed on its own name (*carampana* means 'slut') to the Italian language. Just round the corner is the **ponte delle Tette** (Tits Bridge), where prostitutes were allowed to display their wares with the aim of saving Venetian men from less 'acceptable' vices.

After the shadowy closeness of these *calli*, the open expanse of campo **San Polo** – home to the church (*see p115*) of the same name – comes as a sudden sunlit surprise. This is the largest square on this side of the Grand Canal and in the past was used for popular occasions such as bull-baiting, religious ceremonies, parades and theatrical spectacles as well as weekly markets. Venue of an open-air film season in the summer, its main day-to-day function is that of a vast children's playground.

The curving line of *palazzi* on the east side of the square is explained by the fact that these buildings once gave on to a canal, which was subsequently filled in. They still have a water entrance, on the other side, which means that when they were first built, access was by boat or bridge only. The two *palazzi* Soranzo (Nos.2169 and 2170-1) are particularly attractive Gothic buildings with marble facing and good capitals. In the 18th century these houses had three bridges leading to them. It was while playing the violin at an aristocratic wedding feast in one of the *palazzi* that Casanova first met Senator Bragadin. The aged senator offered Casanova a ride in his gondola, and on the way home suffered a stroke; showing great coolness Casanova had the gondoliers stop and called a surgeon, saving the man's life. The senator ended up by adopting Casanova.

In the north-west corner is a view of Palazzo Corner (the main façade is on the rio di San Polo), a 16th-century design by Sanmicheli. Novelist Frederick Rolfe stayed here – until his English hosts read the manuscript of his work, *The Desire and Pursuit of the Whole* (1909), which contained vitriolic portraits of their friends. They turned him out of the house, thus earning a place for themselves in this grudge novel.

San Giovanni Elemosinario

San Polo, ruga vecchia San Giovanni (041 275 0462/www.chorusvenezia.org). Vaporetto San Silvestro or Rialto. **Open** 10am-5pm Mon-Sat. **Admission** €2.50 (*see also p68* **Chorus**). **No credit cards. Map** p322 B5.
This small Renaissance church – a Greek cross within a square – was reopened in 2002 after remaining closed for an unexplained 20 years. It was founded in the ninth or tenth century but rebuilt after a fire in 1514, probably by Scarpagnino. On the high altar is a painting by Titian of the titular saint, *St John the Alms Giver.* (The saint's body is preserved in the church of San Giovanni in Bragora, *see p101.*) In the left aisle is a medieval fragment of sculptural relief (12th or 13th century) of the Nativity, which shows an ox and donkey reverently licking the face of the Christ child.

San Polo

Campo San Polo (041 275 0462/www. chorusvenezia.org). Vaporetto San Silvestro or San Tomà. **Open** 10am-5pm Mon-Sat. **Admission** €2.50 (*see also p68* **Chorus**). **No credit cards. Map** p321 F5.

The church of San Polo faces away from the square, towards the canal, although later buildings have deprived it of its façade and water entrance. The *campanile* (1362) has two 12th-century lions at the base, one brooding over a snake and the other toying with a human head, which Venetians like to think of as that of Count Carmagnola, who was beheaded for treachery in 1402. This Gothic church was extensively altered in the 19th century, when a neo-classical look was imposed on it. Some of this was removed in 1930, but the interior remains an awkward hybrid. Paintings include a *Last Supper* by Tintoretto to the left of the entrance, and a Tiepolo: *The Virgin Appearing to St John of Nepomuk*. Giambattista Tiepolo's son, Giandomenico, is the author of a brilliant cycle of Stations of the Cross in the Oratory of the Crucifix (entrance under the organ), freshly restored. He painted these, and the ceiling paintings, at the age of 20.

San Silvestro

San Polo, campo San Silvestro (041 523 8090). Vaporetto San Silvestro. **Open** 7.30-11.30am, 4-6pm Mon-Sat. **Map** p322 A5.
This church was rebuilt in the neo-classical style between 1837 and 1843. It contains a *Baptism of Christ* (c1580) by Tintoretto over the first altar on

Palazzo Mocenigo. *See p118.*

Literary Venice

Venice produced great painters, sculptors and musicians but few great writers. However, the city was always very pleased to welcome writers from elsewhere, particularly if their writings would help to promote the city's image. And so there is a long tradition of foreign writing on the city, even if not all the writers have been pleased with what they saw. English writers in particular have been torn between romantic admiration and puritan disapproval, ever since Venice first became a major tourist attraction.

The city enters English literature with **William Shakespeare**. The Bard never actually set foot here, but nonetheless the city of *The Merchant of Venice* and *Othello* is a more fully realised place than, say, the Sicily of *Much Ado About Nothing*. Clearly, Venice was already as powerful an icon as New York is today; the Rialto and gondolas are mentioned as casually as Wall Street and yellow cabs. Shakespeare's Venice is very much a mercantile city, a place of deals, exchanges and bonds. But it is also a place of licentiousness and scheming, where people aren't always what they seem. Desdemona, according to Iago, is a 'super-subtle Venetian'.

The first detailed description by an English visitor was that of insatiable literary traveller **Thomas Coryat**, who set out on foot from Odcombe in Devon in 1608. *Coryat's Crudities* is one of the first gobsmacked-tourist descriptions of Venice: 'Such is the rarenesse of the situation of Venice, that it doth even amaze and drive into admiration all strangers that upon their first arrival behold the same.'

In the more cynical 18th century, wariness predominated over bedazzlement. Venice was viewed less as a real place and more as a metaphor – usually a negative one. English travellers set their burgeoning sense of national self-importance against Venice's decline. **Edward Gibbon** is strikingly dismissive: 'The spectacle of Venice afforded some hours of astonishment and some days of disgust… stinking ditches dignified with the pompous denomination of Canals; a fine bridge spoilt by two rows of houses upon it, and a large square decorated with the worst Architecture I ever yet saw.'

Then suddenly, with the Romantics, decadence was the whole point. Writers such as **William Beckford**, **Lord Byron** and **Percy Bysshe Shelley** thrilled. They sought shudders by visiting the prisons of the Palazzo Ducale; they saw romance in the mix of decay and splendour.

Byron's twofold reaction to Venice makes him the most interesting expatriate writer of the period. In his immensely fashionable poem *Childe Harold's Pilgrimage*, he draws Venice as a dream; the city is seen at 'airy distance'. Its past is melodramatic: dungeons, the Council of Ten, vendettas. It's a purely literary creation, based more on a writerly tradition than on observation.

But in *Beppo* Byron draws a very different picture, describing Venice at Carnevale time: a menacing Turk turns out to be a lost husband; and when this husband finds his wife has taken a lover, no knives are pulled; instead they discuss the situation over coffee and all three settle down to live together happily ever after.

---

the right, with the River Jordan represented as a mountain brook. Opposite is *St Thomas à Becket Enthroned* (1520) by Girolamo da Santacroce, with the saint in startling white robes against a mountain landscape; the other two saints are 19th-century additions. Off the right aisle (ask the sacristan to let you in) is the former School of the Wine Merchants; on the upper floor there's a chapel with 18th-century frescoes by Gaspare Diziani. Opposite the church is the house (No.1022) where Giorgione died in 1510.

North-west from the Rialto

Yellow signs pointing to 'Ferrovia' mark the zigzagging north-western route from the Rialto past the fishmarket, through campo **San Cassiano**. The uninspiring plain exterior of the church (*see p118*) here gives no clue to its heavily decorated interior.

Across the bridge is campo **Santa Maria Mater Domini** with its Renaissance church (*see p120*). Before entering the campo, stop to admire the view from the bridge of the curving Grand Canal-facing marble flank of **Ca' Pesaro** (*see p118*): this is seat of the **Museo Orientale** and **Galleria d'Arte Moderna** . On the far side of the square, which contains a number of fine Byzantine and Gothic buildings, the yellow road sign, in true Venetian fashion, indicates that the way to the station is to the left *and* to the right. Take your pick.

Byron enjoyed the contrast with England, the 'tight little island', and the tolerance of Venetian society, where 'a woman is virtuous (according to the code) who limits herself to her husband and one lover – those who have two, three or more are a little wild.'

Throughout the 19th century travellers drifted through Venice in their closed gondolas. In their accounts of their visits, they fall into swoons or trances; the city mesmerises them. It's Turner's Venice they describe: a dreamscape where buildings seem less substantial than the dazzling light and shimmering water. In *Pictures From Italy*, **Charles Dickens** recounts the experience of floating through the city, even through St Mark's, which is described purely in terms of colour and perfumes.

The strongest reaction to all this came from **John Ruskin**. He can be prejudiced, inconsistent and sometimes plain barmy. But the greatest contribution he made to Venetian studies was his continual emphasis on the physical reality of the place. In an age when most visitors saw it through a romantic haze, Ruskin focused his attention on the stones of Venice – the crumbling bricks and marble.

Every major writer on Venice thereafter – **Marcel Proust**, **WD Howells**, **Henry James** – had to break free from Ruskin: it took courage to like the baroque with Ruskin's fulminations ringing in one's ears. Gradually a new taste arose, in which the ambivalence of Venice played a key role, attracting writers such as **John Addington Symonds** and **Frederick Rolfe** – the self-styled 'Baron Corvo' who described an androgynous city. The mysterious secrecy of the city was perfect

for **Henry James**, who wrote: 'Venice is the refuge of endless strange secrets, broken fortunes and wounded hearts.'

Modernist authors seemed torn between disgust and admiration. **DH Lawrence** and **TS Eliot** saw the city as irredeemably commercial and sordid. Lawrence pictures it as the 'Abhorrent green, slippery city'. Eliot describes a city where 'the rats are underneath the piles'. In **Ezra Pound**'s *Cantos*, on the other hand, the Golden Age of Venice appears as one of the positive poles, an image of luminous splendour to set against the corruption of contemporary society based on usury. Perhaps the finest summation of the two contrasting visions of the city can be found in the narrative poem *The Venetian Vespers* (1979), by the American poet **Anthony Hecht**, whose disturbed protagonist seems to have chosen the city as his place of residence precisely because its internal contrasts so perfectly match his own inner lacerations.

Recent literature and cinema have mostly remained faithful to the *Childe Harold* version of Venice: sex, lies and dirty canals. The city is murky, treacherous and damp in novels by **Ian McEwan**, **Barry Unsworth** and **Lisa St Aubin de Téran**. Romance returns in two more recent novels with Venetian settings. In *An Equal Music* **Vikram Seth** revives the dream vision, tempering it with Carpaccio-esque humour. The bestseller by **Sally Vickers**, *Miss Garnett's Angel*, gives us a refreshingly ungloomy Venice; awe prevails for the protagonist of this novel, who finds her rigid atheism shaken by the almost paradisiacal qualities of what appears to be a city of angels.

The quieter route to the right curls parallel to the Grand Canal. The road towards Ca' Pesaro passes Palazzo Agnusdio, a small 14th-century house with an ogival five-light window decorated with bas-reliefs of the Annunciation and symbols of the evangelists; the house used to belong to a family of sausage makers who were given patrician status in the 17th century.

Many of the most important sights face on to the Grand Canal, including the 18th-century church of **San Stae** (*see p120*) and the Fondaco dei Turchi (the Warehouse of the Turks), home to the city's **Museo di Storia Naturale** (*see p118*), which has been undergoing restoration for several years now and has just two rooms open to the public.

On the wide road leading towards San Stae is **Palazzo Mocenigo** (*see p118*), with its collection of textiles and costumes. Nearby is the quiet square of San Zan Degolà (**San Giovanni Decollato**), with its well-preserved 11th-century church (*see p120*). From here, a series of narrow roads leads past the church of **San Simeone Profeta** (*see p120*) to the foot of the Scalzi bridge across the Grand Canal.

Leave campo Santa Maria Mater Domini by the route to the left, on the other hand, and you'll make your way past the near-legendary Da Fiore eaterie (*see p163*) to the house (No. 2311) where Aldo Manuzio (Aldus Manutius) set up the Aldine Press in 1490, and where the humanist Erasmus came to stay in 1508. To the right, by a building with a 14th-century relief of Faith and Justice above its doorway, the rio terà del Parrucchetta (reportedly named after a seller of animal fodder who used to wear a ridiculous wig, or *parrucca*) leads to the large leafy campo **San Giacomo dell'Orio** (*see p119*). The church has its back and sides to the square; the main entrance was from the water.

Ca' Pesaro – Galleria Internazionale d'Arte Moderna

Santa Croce 2076, fondamenta Ca' Pesaro (041 524 0695/www.museiciviciveneziani.it). Vaporetto San Stae. **Open** *Apr-Oct* 10am-6pm Tue-Sun. *Nov-Mar* 10am-5pm Tue-Sun. Box office closed one hour earlier. **Admission** €5.50; €3 concessions; includes Museo Orientale (*see also p67* **Musei Civici Veneziani**). **No credit cards**. **Map** p322 A4.

This grandiose *palazzo* was built in the second half of the 17th century for the Pesaro family (celebrated in Titian's great painting *La Madonna di Ca' Pesaro* in the Frari), to a project by Baldassare Longhena. When Longhena died in 1682, the family entrusted the completion of the project to Gian Antonio Gaspari, who concluded it in 1710, sticking largely to the original blueprint. The interior of the palazzo still contains some of the original fresco and oil decorations, although the family's great collection of Renaissance paintings was auctioned off in London by the last Pesaro before he died in 1830. The palazzo passed through many hands until its last owner, Felicita Bevilacqua La Masa, bequeathed it to the city. Into it went the city's collection of modern art, gleaned from the Biennale (*see p215*). Between 1908 and 1924 its mezzanine floor played host to the renowned Bevilacqua La Masa exhibitions (*see p213*), which gave hanging space to young Italian artists, as well as providing healthy competition for the Biennale. The museum now covers a century of mainly Italian art, from the mid 19th century to the 1950s. On the stately ground floor are a number of 20th-century Italian sculptures, including a monumental *Eve* by Francesco Messina and a bronze *Cardinal* by Giacomo Manzù.

The first rooms on the *piano nobile* contain atmospheric works by 19th-century painters such as Ippolito Caffi and Guglielmo Ciardi and some striking sculptures by Medardo Rosso. In the central hall are works from the early *Biennali* up to the 1930s, including pieces by Gustav Klimt and Vassily Kandinsky, alongside more conventional vast-scale 'salon' paintings. Room 4 holds works by Giorgio Morandi, Joan Mirò and Giorgio De Chirico. After rooms devoted to international art from the 1940s and '50s, the collection winds up with works by post-war Venetian experimentalists such as Armando Pizzinato, Giuseppe Santomaso and Emilio Vedova.

Ca' Pesaro – Museo Orientale

Santa Croce 2070, fondamenta Ca' Pesaro (041 524 1173/www.museiciviciveneziani.it). Vaporetto San Stae. **Open** *Apr-Oct* 10am-6pm Tue-Sun. *Nov-Mar* 10am-5pm Tue-Sun. Box office closed one hour earlier. **Admission** €5.50; €3 concessions; includes Galleria d'Arte Moderna (*see also p67* **Musei Civici Veneziani**). **Map** p322 A4.

If Japanese art and weaponry of the Edo period (1600-1868) are your thing, you'll love this eclectic collection, put together by Count Enrico di Borbone – a nephew of Louis XVIII – in the course of a round-the-world voyage between 1887 and 1890. After the count's death the collection was sold off to an Austrian antique merchant; it bounced back to Venice after World War I as reparations. The Museo Orientale might seem an odd attraction for such a monocultural city as Venice, but if you come here after the Palazzo Ducale and the Museo Correr, all this ceremonial paraphernalia will seem oddly familiar. The collection features parade armour, dolls, decorative saddles and case upon case of curved samurai swords forged by smiths who had to perform a ritual act of purification before putting their irons in the fire. There is a dwarf-sized lady's gilded litter, and lacquered picnic cases that prove that the Japanese obsession with compactness pre-dates Sony. The final rooms have musical instruments and eastern miscellanea, including Chinese crockery and Indonesian shadow puppets.

Museo di Storia Naturale

Santa Croce 1730, salizada del Fondaco dei Turchi (041 275 0206). Vaporetto San Stae. **Open** 9am-1pm Tue-Fri; 10am-4pm Sat, Sun. **Admission** free. **Map** p321 F3.

This museum has long been closed, undergoing very leisurely restoration. For the last two years just two rooms have been open to the public.

The museum is housed in the Fontego dei Turchi, a Venetian-Byzantine building leased to the Turks in the 17th century as a residence and warehouse. The present building is essentially a 19th-century reconstruction of the original. Before restoration the museum displays were the fruit either of Victorian enthusiasm (numerous stuffed animals and varied ethnographic material collected between 1859-60) or of 20th-century-focused research (erudite displays on the lagoon flora and fauna). At present visitors can see the *Acquario delle tegnue*, devoted to aquatic life of the northern Adriatic, and the *Sala dei dinosauri*, a state-of-the-art exhibition chronicling the Ligabue expedition to Niger (1973), which unearthed a fossil of the previously unknown *Auronosaurus nigeriensis* and a giant crocodile.

Palazzo Mocenigo

Santa Croce 1992, salizada San Stae (041 721 798/www.museiciviciveneziani.it). Vaporetto San Stae. **Open** *Apr-Oct* 10am-5pm Tue-Sun. *Nov-Mar* 10am-4pm Tue-Sun. **Admission** €4; €2.50 concessions (*see also p67* **Musei Civici Veneziani**). **No credit cards**. **Map** p321 F4.

The Palazzo Mocenigo will not come top of anyone's museum list, but it is a good place to while away half an hour. The museum serves a double purpose. The interior gives a fine illustration of the sort of furniture and fittings an 18th-century Venetian noble family liked to surround itself with. The Mocenigo family (which also owned a complex of *palazzi* on the Grand Canal) provided the Republic with seven doges, and the paintings, friezes and frescoes by late 18th-century artists such as Jacopo Guarana and Gian Battista Canal glorify their achievements. In the rooms off the main *salone* the neo-classical influence already makes itself felt. Here too are the dusty display cases that serve the museum's other function: to chronicle 18th-century Venetian dress. An andrienne dress with bustles so horizontal you could rest a cup and saucer on them, antique lace and silk stockings, a whalebone corset – it's a patchy but charming collection. **Photo** *p118*.

San Cassiano

San Polo, campo San Cassiano (041 721 408).
Vaporetto San Stae. **Open** 9am-noon Tue-Sat.
Map p322 A4.
This church has a singularly dull exterior and a heavily decorated interior, with a striking ceiling (freshly restored) by the tiepolesque painter Constantino Cedini. The chancel contains three major Tintorettos: *Crucifixion, Resurrection* and *Descent into Limbo*. The *Crucifixion* is particularly interesting for its viewpoint. As Ruskin puts it, 'The

San Giovanni Decollato. *See p120.*

horizon is so low, that the spectator must fancy himself lying full length on the grass, or rather among the brambles and luxuriant weeds, of which the foreground is entirely composed'. In the background the soldiers' spears make a menacing forest against a dramatic stormy sky.

Off the left aisle is a small chapel with coloured marbles and inlays of semi-precious stones. On the wall opposite the altar is a painting by Antonio Balestra, which at first glance looks like a dying saint surrounded by *putti*. On closer inspection it transpires that the chubby children are, in fact, hacking the man to death: the painting represents *The Martyrdom of St Cassian*, a teacher who was murdered by his pupils with their pens. This, of course, makes him the patron saint of schoolteachers. The painting features in David Hewson's 2001 novel, *Lucifer's Shadow*.

San Giacomo dell'Orio

Santa Croce, campo San Giacomo dell'Orio (041 275 0462, www.chorusvenezia.org). Vaporetto Riva di Biasio. **Open** 10am-5pm Mon-Sat. **Admission** €2.50 (*see also p68* **Chorus**). **No credit cards**.
Map p321 F4.
Campo San Giacomo dell'Orio (St James of the wolf, the laurel tree, the rio or the Orio family – take your pick) has a pleasantly downbeat feel, with its trees, bars and children. It's dominated by the church with its plump apses and stocky 13th-century campanile. As with most older Venetian churches, the main entrance faces the canal rather than the campo.

The interior is a fascinating mix of architectural and decorative styles. Most of the columns have 12th- or 13th-century Veneto-Byzantine capitals; one has a sixth-century flowered capital and one is a solid piece of smooth verd-antique marble, perhaps from a Roman temple sacked during the Fourth Crusade. Note, too, the fine 14th-century ship's-keel roof. The *Sacrestia nuova*, in the right transept, was built in 1903 on the site of the Scuola del Sacramento. This was the original home of the five gilded compartments on the ceiling with paintings by Veronese: an *Allegory of the Faith* surrounded by four Doctors of the Church. Among the paintings in the room is *St John the Baptist Preaching* by Francesco Bassano, which includes a portrait of Titian (in the red hat).

Behind the high altar is a *Madonna and Four Saints* by Lorenzo Lotto, one of his last Venetian paintings. There is a good work by Giovanni Bonconsiglio at the end of the left aisle, *St Lawrence, St Sebastian and St Roch*; St Sebastian is conventionally untroubled by his arrow, but St Roch's plague sore has an anatomical precision that is really rather unsettling. The third of these saints, St Lawrence, also has a chapel all to himself in the left transept, with a central altarpiece by Veronese and two fine early works by Palma il Giovane. As you leave, have a look at the curious painting to the left of the main door, a naïve 18th-century work by Gaetano Zompini, showing a propaganda miracle involving a Jewish scribe who attempted to profane the body of the Virgin on its way to the sepulchre (which made its way into David Hewson's novel, *Lucifer's Shadow*).

San Giovanni Decollato (San Zan Degolà)

Santa Croce, campo San Giovanni Decollato (041 524 0672). Vaporetto Riva di Biasio. **Open** 10am-noon Mon-Sat. **Map** p321 F4.

The church of Headless Saint John, or San Zan Degolà in Venetian dialect, stands in a quiet campo near the Fondaco dei Turchi; it's a good building to visit if you want a relief from baroque excesses and ecclesiastic clutter. It was restored and reopened in 1994 after being closed for nearly 20 years, and preserves much of its original 11th-century appearance. The interior has Greek columns with Byzantine capitals supporting ogival arches, and an attractive ship's-keel roof. During the restoration a splendidly heroic 14th-century fresco of St Michael the Archangel came to light in the right apse. The left apse has some of the earliest frescoes in Venice, Veneto-Byzantine works of the early 13th century. The church is used for Russian Orthodox services. **Photo** *p120*.

San Simeone Profeta

Santa Croce, campo San Simeone Profeta (041 718 921). Vaporetto Ferrovia. **Open** 8am-noon, 5-6.30pm Mon-Sat. **Map** p321 E4.

More commonly known as San Simeone Grande, this small church of possibly tenth-century foundation underwent numerous alterations in the 18th century. The interior preserves its ancient columns with Byzantine capitals. To the left of the entrance is Tintoretto's *Last Supper*, with the priest who commissioned the painting standing to one side, a spectral figure in glowing white robes. The other major work is the stark, powerful statue of a recumbent St Simeon, with an inscription dated 1317 attributing it to an otherwise unknown Marco Romano. The prophet has a 'face full of quietness and majesty, though very ghastly', as Ruskin puts it. Outside, beneath the portico flanking the church, is a fine 15th-century relief of a bishop praying.

San Stae

Santa Croce, campo San Stae (041 275 0462, www.chorusvenezia.org). Vaporetto San Stae. **Open** 10am-5pm Mon-Sat. **Admission** €2.50 (*see also p68* **Chorus**). **No credit cards**. **Map** p321 F4.

Stae is the Venetian version of Eustachio or Eustace, a martyred saint who was converted to Christianity by the vision of a stag with a crucifix between his antlers. This church on the Grand Canal has a dramatic late baroque façade (1709) by Swiss-born architect Domenico Rossi. The form is essentially Palladian but enlivened by a number of vibrant sculptures, some apparently on the point of leaping straight out of the façade. Venice's last great blaze of artistic glory came in the 18th century, and the interior is a temple to this swansong. On the side walls of the chancel, all the leading painters operating in Venice in 1722 were asked to pick an apostle,

any apostle. The finest of these are: Tiepolo's *Martyrdom of St Bartholomew* (left wall, lower row); Sebastiano Ricci's *Liberation of St Peter*, perhaps his best work (right wall, lower row); Pellegrini's *Martyrdom of St Andrew*; and Piazzetta's *Martyrdom of St James*, a disturbingly realistic work showing the saint as a confused old man in the hands of a loutish youth. The church is often used for temporary exhibitions; Chorus pass holders can see these for free.

Santa Maria Mater Domini

Santa Croce, calle della Chiesa (041 721 408). Vaporetto San Stae. **Open** 10am-12.30pm, 3.30-6pm Tue, Fri; 10am-noon, 3.30-6pm Wed; 10am-noon Thur. **Map** p321 F4.

This church, which was restored by the Venice in Peril fund in the 1980s, is set just off the campo of the same name, which has a number of fine *palazzi*. It was built in the first half of the 16th century to a project by either Giovanni Buora or Maurizio Codussi; the façade is attributed to Jacopo Sansovino; the harmonious Renaissance interior alternates grey stone with white marble. The *Vision of St Christine* on the second altar on the right is by Vincenzo Catena, a spice merchant who seems to have painted in his spare time. St Christine was rescued by angels after being thrown into Lake Bolsena with a millstone tied round her neck; in the painting she adores the Risen Christ, while angels hold up the millstone for her. In the left transept hangs *The Invention of the Cross*, a youthful work by Tintoretto.

From the Frari to Piazzale Roma

At the heart of the western side of the two *sestieri* lies the great gothic bulk of Santa Maria Gloriosa dei Frari (aka **I Frari**, *see p123*), with its 70-metre (230-foot) *campanile*, matched by the Renaissance magnificence of the *scuola* and church of San Rocco. These buildings contain perhaps the greatest concentration of influential works of art in the city outside piazza San Marco and the **Accademia** (*see p132*).

The monastery buildings of the Frari contain the State Archives, a monument to Venetian reluctance ever to throw anything away. In 300 rooms, about 15 million volumes and files are conserved, relating to all aspects of Venetian history, starting from the year 883. Faced with this daunting wealth of information, ranging from ambassadors' dispatches on foreign courts to spies' reports on noblemen's non-regulation cloaks, grown historians have been reduced to quivering wrecks.

Beyond the archives is the **Scuola di San Giovanni Evangelista**, one of the six *scuole grandi* (*see p67*) which played such an important part in the complex Venetian system of social checks and balances. The courtyard is protected by a screen with a magnificent eagle pediment and a frieze of leaf-sprays by Pietro Lombardo, while the building itself contains a magnificent double staircase by Maurizio Codussi.

North of here runs rio Marin, a canal with *fondamente* on both sides, lined by some fine buildings; these include the late 16th-century Palazzo Soranzo Capello (No.770) with a small garden (to the rear) that figures in D'Annunzio's torrid novel *ll Fuoco* and Henry James' more restrained *The Aspern Papers*, and the 17th-century Palazzo Gradenigo, (768, although the number is half-concealed by foliage) the garden of which was once large enough to host bullfights.

South-west of the Frari is the quiet square of **San Tomà**, with a church on one side and the *Scuola dei Calegheri* (cobblers) opposite; the *scuola* (now a library) has a protective mantle-spreading Madonna over the door and above it a relief by Pietro Lombardo of *St Mark Healing the Cobbler Annanius*, who became bishop of Alexandria and subsequently the patron saint of shoemakers. Directly south of here is campo **San Pantalon** (*see p125*, technically in Dorsoduro); its church has an extraordinary Hollywood-rococo interior. If you walk out of the church towards the canal, an alley to the left will take you into little campiello d'Angaran, where there is a carved roundel of a Byzantine emperor, which experts believe possibly dates from the tenth century.

Returning to the campo, you'll see a slab in the wall by the canal, which indicates the minimum lengths allowed for the sale of various types of fish.

Just off the square of San Tomà is Palazzo Centani, the birthplace of Carlo Goldoni, the prolific Venetian playwright. The house, which has an attractive Gothic courtyard with a fine well head and staircase, contains a small museum and library (**Casa di Carlo Goldoni**, *see p123*) devoted to the writer and to Venetian theatre in general.

Nearby are the curiously named fondamenta and ponte della Donna Onesta (honest woman). Explanations for the name abound: the tiny sculptured face of a woman in a house over the bridge was once pointed out as being Venice's only 'honest woman'; a local prostitute was famous for carrying on her trade with singular honesty; the wife of a local sword maker, raped by a client of her husband, stabbed herself in desperation with one of her husband's daggers.

Heading west from the Frari, the route leads past the **church** and *scuola* of **San Rocco** (*see p125*), treasure troves for Tintoretto lovers, and ends up in a fairly bland area of 19th-century housing, which replaced medieval gardens and orchards. At the edge of this stands the baroque church of **San Nicolò dei Tolentini** (*see p124*); the adjoining former monastery houses part of the Venice University Architecture Institute.

The rather forlorn Giardino Papadopoli, a small park with Grand Canal views, stands

Casa di Carlo Goldoni. *See p123.*

Walk Tintoretto's last suppers

No-one ever accused Tintoretto of being a slacker. His paintings, nearly all on a huge scale, are to be found in almost every major church in Venice. And while other big producers – such as the depressingly ubiquitous Palma il Giovane – tended to repeat themselves unashamedly, Tintoretto never ceases to astonish by the fertility of his imagination.

This is even more apparent if you study his variations on one theme. One subject in particular seemed to hold an unending fascination for him: the Last Supper. There are seven paintings of these by Tintoretto in Venice, and they give a good idea of the development of his techniques and style.

The earliest is in the church of San Marcuola (*see p104*) by the vaporetto stop of that name. In this early work Tintoretto still organises the mainly horizontal composition in terms of symmetry and narrative clarity.

From here, head towards the station and cross the bridge; take the *calle* directly at the foot of the bridge, turn left at the end and cross a canal. Here, in the church of San Simeone Profeta (*see p120*; aka San Simeone Grande), hangs a comparatively small *Last Supper*, tentatively dated 1560. Probably done with the help of assistants, the most striking element is the spectral figure of the man who commissioned the work in the background on the left.

Some deft map-reading will be needed to get to campo San Polo. The *Last Supper* (1568) in the church of the same name (*see p115*) has a foreshortened beggar on the floor, accepting a crust of bread from one of the apostles, pulling the viewer into the painting.

It's a short hop west from here past the great bulk of the Frari to the Scuola di San Rocco (*see p125*), where the *Last Supper* (1578-81) has an elevated stage-setting used in an earlier painting in the church of Santo

Stefano (*see below*); the same dog seems to stand quivering on the steps in both pictures. The table is set low, with the apostles almost squatting around it. Around the table and in the background everyday life goes on, with servants in the kitchen baking bread and clearing dishes. This only adds to the visionary quality of what is happening in the foreground.

Follow the flow southwards to San Trovaso (*see p131*) which contains a *Last Supper* dated 1556. Though this is an early version, it's original in concept, with a greater emphasis on realism; the setting seems to be a tavern and the apostles sit in unceremonious poses around a table set at an angle to the viewer.

Make your way to across the nearby Accademia bridge into campo Santo Stefano. Hanging in the sacristy of the eponymous church (*see p90*) is Tintoretto's first truly large-scale version of the Last Supper theme (1576). Although it contains a good deal of studio work, the design is clearly by the *maestro* and paves the way for the great painting in the Scuola di San Rocco. The setting is more grandiose than in the earlier versions but the details of the serving women and the begging dogs are as earthy as ever, combining curiously with the increasingly visionary atmosphere.

For Tintoretto's final version, go through St Mark's square to the riva degli Schiavoni, and take a vaporetto to the island of San Giorgio Maggiore. The vast painting (1591) that hangs to the right of the high altar in the church there (*see p140*) is a magnificent work intended to dazzle the viewer, with its bewildering mixture of lights and shadows, movement and stillness; the long table occupies one half of the painting and angels appear mysteriously in the swirling smoke from the oil-lamps above. The combination of earthy realism and visionary mysticism is here taken to startling new levels.

on the site of the church and convent of Santa Croce. The name survives as that of the *sestiere*, but the church is one of many suppressed by the French at the beginning of the 19th century. All that remains of Santa Croce is a crenellated wall next to a hotel on the Grand Canal. The garden was much larger until the rio Novo was cut in 1932 and 1933 to provide faster access from the new car park to the St Mark's area. The decision was much contested at the

time; as the canal had to be closed to regular waterborne traffic in the early 1990s owing to subsidence in the adjacent buildings, it would seem that the protesters had a point.

Beyond the garden there is little but the carbon-monoxide kingdom of piazzale Roma and the multi-storey car parks. One last curiosity is the complex of bridges across the rio Novo known as Tre Ponti (three bridges); there are, in fact, five interlocking bridges.

Casa di Carlo Goldoni

San Polo 2794, calle dei Nomboli (041 275 9325).
Vaporetto San Tomà. **Open** *Apr-Oct* 10am-5pm
Mon-Sat. *Nov-Mar* 10am-4pm Mon-Sat.
Admission €2.50; €1.50 concessions (*see also*
p67 **Musei Civici Veneziani**). **No credit**
cards. **Map** p321 F5.

Officially the Casa di Goldoni e Biblioteca di studi
teatrali (Goldoni's house and library of theatre studies) this museum is really only for specialists,
although the attractive Gothic courtyard, with its
carved well head and staircase, is worth seeing. It is
the birthplace of Venice's greatest writer, the playwright Carlo Goldoni, who over the course of his
long career, transformed Italian theatre, moving it
away from the stultified clichés of the *Commedia del-*
l'arte tradition and introducing a comedy based on
realistic observation. Inevitably, he also made a
number of enemies – including, at first, some of the
actors, who weren't happy with the idea of having
to learn lines rather than simply improvise around
a skeleton plot. On the first floor there are reproductions of prints based on Goldoni's works and a
few 18th-century paintings; the best item is a splendid 18th-century miniature theatre complete with
puppets of *Commedia dell'arte* figures. The library
on the upper floor has theatrical texts, studies and
original manuscripts. **Photo** *p122*.

I Frari

San Polo, campo dei Frari (041 522 2637,
www.chorusvenezia.org). Vaporetto San Tomà.
Open 9am-6pm Mon-Sat; 1-6pm Sun. **Admission**
€2.50 (*see also p68* **Chorus**). **No credit cards**.
Map p321 E5.

A gloomy Gothic barn, the brick house of God
known officially as Santa Maria Gloriosa dei Frari
may not be the most elegant church in Venice, but
it is certainly one of the city's most significant artistic storehouses. The Franciscans were granted the
land in about 1250 and they completed a first church
in 1338. At this point they changed their minds and
started work on a larger building which was finally
completed just over a century later. The church is
98m (320ft) long, 48m (158ft) wide at the transept
and 28m (92ft) high – just slightly smaller than the
Dominicans' Santi Giovanni e Paolo (see *p95*) – and
has the second highest *campanile* in the city. And
while the Frari may not have as many dead doges
as its Dominican rival, it undoubtedly has the artistic edge. This is one church where the entrance fee
is not a recent imposition; tourists have been paying
to get into the Frari for over a century. At the
entrance you are brought face to face with the long
sweep of church with Titian's glorious *Assumption*
above the high altar.

Right aisle

In the second bay, on the spot where Titian is
believed to be buried (the only victim of the 1575-6
plague who was allowed a city burial), is a loud monument to the artist, commissioned nearly 300 years
after his death by the Emperor of Austria. On the
third altar is a finer memorial, Alessandro Vittoria's

statue of St Jerome, generally believed to be a
portrait of his painter friend.

Right transept

To the right of the sacristy door is the tomb of the
Blessed Pacifico (a companion of St Francis) attributed to Nanni di Bartolo and Michele da Firenze
(1437); the sarcophagus is surrounded by a splendidly carved canopy in the florid Gothic style. The
door itself is framed by Lorenzo Bregno's tomb of
Benedetto Pesaro, a Venetian general who died in
Corfu. To the left of the door is the first equestrian
statue in Venice, the monument to Paolo Savelli
(d.1405). The third chapel on the right side of this
transept has an altarpiece by Bartolomeo Vivarini,
in its original frame, while the Florentine Chapel,
next to the chancel, contains the only work by
Donatello in the city: a striking wooden statue of a
stark, emaciated St John the Baptist.

Sacristy

Commissioned by the Pesaro family, this contains
one of Giovanni Bellini's greatest paintings: the
Madonna and Child with Saints Nicholas, Peter,
Benedict and Mark (1488), still in its original frame.
'It seems painted with molten gems, which have
been clarified by time,' wrote Henry James, his eye,
as ever, firmly on the prose structure, 'and it is as
solemn as it is gorgeous and as simple as it is deep.'
Also in the sacristy is a fine Renaissance tabernacle,
possibly by Tullio Lombardo, for a reliquary
holding Christ's blood.

Chancel

The high altar is dominated by Titian's *Assumption*,
a visionary work that seems to open the church up
to the heavens. In the golden haze encircling God the
Father, there may be a reminiscence of the mosaic
tradition of Venice. The upward-soaring movement
of the painting may owe something to the Gothic
architecture of the building, but the drama and
grandeur of the work essentially herald the baroque.

On the right wall of the chancel is the monument
to Francesco Foscari, the saddest doge of all. The
story of his forced resignation and death from heart-
break (1547) after the exile of his son Jacopo is
recounted in Byron's *The Two Foscari*, which was
turned into a particularly gloomy opera by Verdi
(*see p226* **Viva Verdi!**). The left wall boasts one of
the finest Renaissance tombs in Venice, the monument to Doge Niccolò Tron, by Antonio Rizzo (1473).
This is the first ducal tomb in which the subject is
upright; he sports a magnificent bushy beard grown
as a sign of perpetual mourning after the death of
his favourite son.

Monks' choir

In the centre of the nave stands the choir, with wood-
en stalls carved by Marco Cozzi (1468), inlaid with
superb intarsia decoration. The choir screen is a
mixture of Gothic work by Bartolomeo Bon and
Renaissance elements by the Lombardi.

Left transept

In the third chapel, with an altarpiece by Bartolomeo
Vivarini and Marco Basaiti, a slab on the floor marks
the grave of composer Claudio Monteverdi. The

Corner chapel, at the end, contains a mannered statue of St John the Baptist by Sansovino; this sensitively wistful figure could hardly be more different from Donatello's work of a century earlier.

Left aisle

Another magnificent Titian hangs to the right of the side door: the *Madonna di Ca' Pesaro*. This work was commissioned by Bishop Jacopo Pesaro in 1519 and celebrates victory in a naval expedition against the Turks, led by the bellicose cleric in 1502. The bishop is kneeling and waiting for St Peter to introduce him and his family to the Madonna. Behind, an armoured warrior bearing a banner has Turkish prisoners in tow. This work revolutionised altar paintings in Venice. It wasn't just that Titian dared to move the Virgin from the centre of the composition to one side, using the splendid banner as a counterbalance; the real innovation was the rich humanity of the whole work, from the beautifully portrayed family (with the boy turning to stare straight at us) to the Christ child, so naturally active and alive, twisting away from his mother (said to be a portrait of Titian's wife) to gaze curiously at the saints clustered around him. The timeless 'sacred conversation' of Bellini's paintings here becomes animated, losing some of its sacredness but gaining in drama and realism.

The whole of the next bay, around the side door, is occupied by another piece of Pesaro propaganda – the mastodontic mausoleum of Doge Pesaro (died 1659), attributed to Longhena, with sculptures by Melchior Barthel of Dresden. Even the most ardent fans of the baroque have trouble defending this one, with its 'blackamoor' caryatids, bronze skeletons and posturing allegories.

The penultimate bay harbours a monument to Canova, carried out by his pupils in 1827, five years after his death, using a design of his own that was intended for the tomb of Titian. His body is buried in his native town of Possagno (*see p275*), but his heart is conserved in an urn inside the monument. The despondent winged lion has a distinct resemblance to the one in *The Wizard of Oz*.

San Nicolò da Tolentino

Santa Croce, campo dei Tolentini (041 710 806). Vaporetto Piazzale Roma. **Open** 8.30am-noon, 4.30-6.30pm Mon-Sat; 4.30-6.30pm Sun. **Map** p321 D5.

This church (1591-5), usually known as I Tolentini, was planned by Vincenzo Scamozzi. Its unfinished façade has a massive Corinthian portico (1706-14) added by Andrea Tirali.

The interior (most of which has been recently restored) is a riot of baroque decoration, with lavish use of stucco and sprawling frescoes. The most interesting paintings – as so often in the 17th century – are by out-of-towners. On the wall outside the chancel to the left is *St Jerome Succoured by an Angel* by Flemish artist Johann Liss. Outside the chapel in the left transept is *The Charity of St Lawrence* by the Genoese Bernardo Strozzi, in which

Not very elegant, but artistically significant: **I Frari**. *See p123.*

the magnificently hoary old beggar in the fore-ground easily upstages the rather wimpish figure of the saint. In the chancel hangs an *Annunciation* by Neapolitan Luca Giordano and opposite is a splendidly theatrical monument to Francesco Morosini (a 17th-century patriarch of that name, not the doge) by Filippo Parodi (1678), with swirling angels drawing aside a marble curtain to reveal the patriarch lounging at ease on his tomb.

In 1780 the priests of this church handed over all their silverware to a certain 'Romano', who claimed to have a secret new method for cleaning silver and jewellery. He was never seen again.

San Pantalon

Santa Croce, campo San Pantalon (041 523 5893). Vaporetto San Tomà. **Open** 8-10am, 4-6pm Mon-Sat. **Map** p325 E1.

The dedicatee of this church is St Pantaleon, a court physician to Emperor Galerius, who was arrested, tortured and finally beheaded during Diocletian's persecution of the Christians in the late 3rd century. The saint's story is depicted inside the church in one of the most extraordinary ceiling paintings in Italy – a huge illusionistic work, painted on 40 canvases, by the Cecil B De Mille of the 17th century, Gian Antonio Fumiani. It took him 24 years to complete the task (1680-1704) and at the end of it all he fell with choreographic grace from the scaffolding to his death. Veronese depicts the saint in less melodramatic fashion in the second chapel on the right, in what is possibly his last work, *St Pantaleon Healing a Child.*

To the left of the chancel is the Chapel of the Holy Nail. The nail in question, supposedly from the Crucifixion, is preserved in a small but richly decorated Gothic altar. On the right wall is a fine *Coronation of the Virgin* by Antonio Vivarini and Giovanni d'Alemagna.

San Rocco

San Polo, campo San Rocco (041 523 4864). Vaporetto San Tomà. **Open** Apr-Oct 8am-12.30pm, 3-5pm daily. *Nov-Mar* 8am-12.30pm Mon-Fri; 8am-12.30pm, 2-4pm Sat, Sun. **Map** p321 E5.

If you have toured the school of San Rocco (*see below*) and are in the mood for more Tintorettos (perhaps after a stiff drink or a lie down), look no further. Built in Venetian Renaissance style by Bartolomeo Bon from 1489 to 1508, but radically altered by Giovanni Scalfarotto in 1725, the church has paintings by Tintoretto, or his school, on either side of the entrance door, between the first and second altar on the right, and on either side of the chancel. Nearly all are connected with the life of St Roch; the best is probably *St Roch Cures the Plague Victims* (chancel, lower right). The altar paintings are all rather difficult to see; they're high up and not very well lit. Even if you could get a good view, you might not be much the wiser: even Ruskin, Tintoretto's greatest fan, was completely baffled as to their subject matter.

Scuola Grande di San Rocco

San Polo 3054, campo San Rocco (041 523 4864/www.sanrocco.it). Vaporetto San Tomà. **Open** Apr-Oct 9am-5.30pm daily. Nov-Mar 10am-5pm daily. **Admission** €5.50; €4 concessions. **Credit** AmEx, DC, MC, V. **Map** p321E5.

The Archbrotherhood of St Roch was the richest of the six *scuole grandi* (*see p67*) in 15th-century Venice. Its members came from the top end of mercantile and professional classes. It was dedicated to Venice's other patron saint, the French plague protector and dog lover St Roch/Rock/Rocco, whose body was brought here in 1485.

The *scuola* operated out of rented accommodation for many years, but at the beginning of the 16th century a permanent base was commissioned. The architecture, by Bartolomeo Bon and Scarpagnino, is far less impressive than the interior decoration, which was entrusted to Tintoretto in 1564 after a competition in which he stole a march on rivals Salviati, Zuccari and Veronese by presenting a finished painting rather than the required sketch. In three intensive sessions over the following 23 years, Tintoretto went on to make San Rocco his epic masterpiece. Fans and doubters alike should start here; the former will no doubt agree with John Ruskin that paintings such as the *Crucifixion* are 'beyond all analysis and above all praise', while the latter may well find their prejudices crumbling. True, the devotional intensity of his works can shade a touch too much into kitsch for the post-modern, 21st-century soul; but his feel for narrative structure is timeless.

To follow the development of Tintoretto's style, pick up the free explanatory leaflet and the audio guide and begin in the smaller upstairs hall – the Albergo. Here, filling up the whole of the far wall, is the *Crucifixion* (1565), of which Henry James commented: 'It is one of the greatest things of art… there is everything in it.' More than anything it is the perfect integration of main plot and sub-plots that strikes the viewer; whereas most paintings are short stories, this is a novel. Tintoretto began work on the larger upstairs room in 1575, with Old Testament stories on the ceiling and a Life of Christ cycle around the walls, in which the man who possessed what Vasari referred to as 'the most extraordinary mind that the art of painting has produced' experimented relentlessly with form, lighting and colour. Below the canvases is a characterful series of late 17th-century wooden carvings, including a caricature of Tintoretto himself, just below and to the left of *The Agony in the Garden.* Finally, in the ground-floor hall – which the artist decorated between 1583 and 1587, when he was in his 60s – the paintings reach a visionary pitch that has to do with Tintoretto's audacious handling of light and the impressionistic economy of his brush strokes. The *Annunciation*, with its domestic Mary surprised while sewing, and *Flight into Egypt*, with its verdant landscape, are among the painter's masterpieces. Admission is free on 16 August, the feast of St Roch.

Dorsoduro

From beggars to billionaire art collectors.

Dorsoduro – literally 'hard back' – is Venice's southern *sestiere*, stretching from the western docks to the magnificent church of the Salute. It is home to a varied social mix; the eastern areas around the Salute, with their quiet *campielli* and well-restored *palazzi*, exude international affluence, while Santa Marta in the west is home-grown working class. In between these geographical and social extremes is the wholly democratic campo Santa Margherita, Dorsoduro's largest square. Here the full range of Venice's shifting population can be seen at all hours: tourists, workers, loafers, tourists, shoppers, students and, of course, tourists.

Western Dorsoduro

This was one of the first areas in the lagoon to be settled. The church of San Nicolò was founded as early as the seventh century. The full name of the church is **San Nicolò dei Mendicoli** (*see below*) – 'of the beggars'. The locals have never been in the top income bracket and in the past were mostly fishermen or salt-pan workers. The area gave its name to one of two factions into which the proletariat was divided: the *nicolotti*. The *nicolotti* were proud enough to maintain a certain form of local autonomy under a figure known as the *gastaldo*, who, after his election, would be received with honours by the doge.

The area is still noticeably less sleek than the centre, although fishing was superseded as a source of employment by the port long ago and subsequently by the Santa Marta cotton mill – now stunningly converted into the **Istituto Universitario di Architettura di Venezia** (*see p300*). Massive redevelopment schemes have been talked about for much of

this downbeat district, with plans to revitalise it in a vast university-meets-London-Docklands-style project, to a design by the late Catalan architect Enric Miralles. The plans include an auditorium, conference hall, restaurant and huge centralised university library, thus providing Venice university with something approaching a genuine campus. For the moment, everything seems to be on hold.

Moving eastwards, the atmosphere remains unpretentious around the churches of **Angelo Raffaele** (*see below*) and **San Sebastiano** (*see p127*), with its splendid decoration by Paolo Veronese. Northwards from here, on the rio di Santa Margherita, are some grander *palazzi*, including Palazzo Ariani, with Gothic tracery that is almost oriental in its intricacy, and, further up, the grand Palazzo Zenobio, now an Armenian school and institute, containing early Tiepolo frescoes (not accessible to the public) and giving on to an elaborate garden where plays are sometimes performed in the summer.

Angelo Raffaele

Dorsoduro, campo Angelo Raffaele (041 522 8548). Vaporetto San Basilio. **Open** 8am-noon, 3-5pm Mon-Sat; 9am-noon Sun. **Map** p324 C2.

This is one of eight churches in Venice that, tradition has it, were founded by St Magnus in the eighth century, although the present free-standing building – one of only two churches in the city that you can walk right around – dates from the 17th century. The very high ceiling has a lively fresco by Gaspare Diziani of *St Michael Driving out Lucifer*, with Lucifer apparently tumbling out of the heavy stucco frame into the church.

There are matching *Last Supper*s on either side of the organ (by Bonifacio de' Pitati on the left and a follower of Titian on the right). But the real jewels of the church are on the organ loft, where five compartments, painted by Giovanni Antonio Guardi (or perhaps his brother Francesco), recount the story of *Tobias and the Angel* (1750-3). They are works of dazzling luminosity, quite unlike anything else done in Venice at the time and with something pre-Impressionist about them. The paintings and the story they recount play a significant role in Sally Vickers' novel *Miss Garnet's Angel* (2000). Mass is said daily at 10am.

San Nicolò dei Mendicoli

Dorsoduro, campo San Nicolò (041 275 0382). Vaporetto San Basilio or Santa Marta. **Open** 10am-noon, 4-6pm Mon-Sat; 4-6pm Sun. **Map** p324 C2.

San Nicolò is one of the few Venetian churches to have maintained its 13th-century Veneto-Byzantine structure, despite numerous refurbishings. Between 1971 and 1977 the church underwent a thorough restoration by the Venice in Peril Fund, and traces of the original foundations were uncovered, confirming the church's seventh-century origins. Film buffs will recognise this as the church from Nicolas Roeg's dwarf-in-Venice movie *Don't Look Now*. The 15th-century loggia at the front is one of only two extant examples of a once-common architectural feature (the other is on the equally ancient San Giacomo di Rialto, *see p114*); it originally served as a shelter for the homeless. The interior contains a marvellous mish-mash of architectural and decorative styles combines to create an effect of cluttered charm. The structure is that of a 12th-century basilica, with two colonnades of stocky columns topped by 14th-century capitals. Above are gilded 16th-century statues of the Apostles. The paintings are mainly 17th century. There are also some fine wooden sculptures, including a large statue of San Nicolò made in the 15th century in the workshop of sculptor Bartolomeo Bon. In the small campo outside the church is a column with a diminutive winged lion.

San Sebastiano.

San Sebastiano

Dorsoduro, fondamenta di San Sebastiano (041 275 0642/www.chorusvenezia.org). Vaporetto San Basilio. **Open** 10am-5pm Mon-Sat. **Admission** €2.50 (*see also p68* **Chorus**). **No credit cards. Map** p325 D2. This contains perhaps the most brilliantly colourful church interior in Venice – all the work of one man, Paolo Veronese. One of Veronese's earliest commissions in Venice (in 1555) was *The Coronation of the Virgin* and the four panels of the Evangelists in the sacristy (open 10am-5pm Sat, 1-5pm Sun). From then on there was just no stopping him: between 1556 and 1565 he did three large ceiling paintings for the nave of the church, frescoes along the upper parts of the walls, organ shutters, huge narrative canvases for the chancel, and the painting on the high altar. The ceiling paintings depict scenes from the life of Esther (*Esther Taken to Ahasuerus, Esther Crowned Queen by Ahasuerus* and *The Triumph of Mordecai*). Esther was considered a forerunner of the Virgin, interceding for Jews in the same way that the Virgin interceded for Christians – or (more pertinently) for Venice. These works are full of sumptuous pageantry: no painter gets more splendidly shimmering effects out of clothing, which is probably why Veronese's nude St Sebastians are the least striking figures in the compositions. These huge canvases on the side walls of the chancel depict, on the right, *The Martyrdom of St Sebastian* (who was in fact cudgelled to death – the arrows were just one of a number of attempts) and, on the left, *St Sebastian Encouraging St Mark and St Marcellan*. Other paintings in the church include *St Nicholas*, a late painting by Titian, in the first altar on the right. Paolo Veronese and his brother Benedetto are buried here. In 2004 restoration work was completed on the sacristy; the ceiling paintings of the *Coronation of the Virgin* and *The Evangelists* are Veronese's earliest recorded works in Venice (1555). Around the walls are works by Bonifacio de' Pitati and others.

Campo Santa Margherita to the Accademia

A long, irregular-shaped campo with churches at both ends, **campo Santa Margherita** is full of life by day and night. The morning market (Mon-Sat) is a non-stop bustle of shopping housewives, hurrying students and scavenging pigeons. In the evening the bars and cafés are invaded by hordes of Venice's under-30s, much to the irritation of local residents. As a nightlife hub in Venice, this square is only rivalled by the bars around the **Rialto market** (*see p177* **In the market**).

There are several ancient *palazzi* around the square, with Byzantine and Gothic features.

In the middle is the isolated Scuola dei Varoteri, the School of the Tanners. At the north end is the former church of Santa

Margherita, long used as a cinema and now beautifully restored as a conference hall for the university; the interior (sneak in the back for a quick gawp if there's a meeting going on) is so unashamedly theatrical it's difficult to imagine how it was ever used for religious purposes. St Margaret's dragon features on the *campanile*, and the sculpted saint also stands triumphant on the beast between the windows of a house at the north end of the square. A miraculous escape from the dragon's guts for some reason makes her the patron saint of pregnant women. At the other end of the square are the **scuola** and **church of the Carmini** (*see p130*).

Leaving the campo by the southern end you reach the picturesque rio di San Barnaba. At the eastern end of the fondamenta is the entrance to the swaggering **Ca' Rezzonico** (*see below*), designed by Longhena and now home to the museum of 18th-century Venice.

The middle of the three bridges across the canal is ponte dei Pugni, with white marble footprints indicating that this was one of the bridges where punch-ups were held between the rival factions of the *nicolotti*, from the western quarters of the city, and the *castellani*, from the east. These brawls, often extremely violent, were tolerated by the authorities, who saw them as a chance for the working classes to let off steam in a way that was not disruptive to the state. However, after a particularly bloody fray, the Council of Ten banned them in 1705.

Past the most photographed greengrocer's in the world (a barge moored in the canal), is campo San Barnaba. The church of **San Barnaba** has nothing special about it except a picturesque 14th-century *campanile*; however, the campo is a good place in which to sit outside a bar and watch the world go by. San Barnaba has never been grand. In the final years of the Republic it was where penniless patricians used to end up, since apartments were provided here by the state for their use. The *barnabotti*, as they were known, could make a few *zecchini* by peddling their votes in the Maggior Consiglio ; otherwise they hung around in their tattered silk, muttering (after 1789) subversive comments about Liberty, Fraternity and Equality. Katharine Hepburn fell into a nearby canal in the film *Summertime*, causing permanent damage to her eyesight. In *Indiana Jones and the Last Crusade*, on the other hand, Harrison Ford entered the church (a library in the film) and after contending with most of Venice's rat population, emerged from a manhole on to the pavement outside.

From the campo the busy route towards the **Accademia** (*see p132*) passes alongside the rio della Toletta (where a small plank or *tola – tavola* in Italian – once served as a bridge)

towards rio San Trovaso. This handsome canal has twin *fondamente* lined by fine Gothic and Renaissance palaces housing secondary schools and university buildings. One of the most hectic chases in the 2003 film *The Italian Job* took place along this canal. Off to the right is the church of **San Trovaso** (*see p130*), with two identical façades, one on to the canal and one on to its own campo. Backing on to the campo is a picturesque *squero*, one of the few remaining yards where gondolas are made.

The Accademia, Venice's most important picture gallery, is just a short walk from here, situated at the foot of the reconstructed wooden bridge of the same name over the Grand Canal.

Ca' Rezzonico (Museo del Settecento Veneziano)

Dorsoduro 3136, fondamenta Rezzonico (041 2410 100/www.museicivaveneziani.it). Vaporetto Ca' Rezzonico. **Open** *Apr-Oct* 10am-6pm Mon, Wed-Sun. *Nov-Mar* 10am-5pm Mon, Wed-Sun. **Admission** €6.50; €4-€4.50 concessions (*see also p67* Musei Civici Veneziani). **No credit cards. Map** p325 E1.

The museum of 18th-century Venice was reopened in July 2001 after careful restoration and is now a gleaming (if somewhat chilly) showcase, complete with bookshop and café, dedicated to the art of the Republic's twilight years. For most visitors the paintings on display here will appear less impressive than the palazzo itself, an imposing Grand Canal affair designed by Baldassare Longhena for the Bon family in 1667. Bon ambitions exceeded Bon means, and the unfinished palace was sold on to the Rezzonico family – rich Genoese bankers who bought their way into Venice's register of nobility. The Rezzonicos' bid for stardom was crowned in 1758 by two events: the election of Carlo Rezzonico as Pope Clement XIII, and the marriage of Ludovico Rezzonico into one of Venice's most ancient noble families, the Savorgnan. Giambattista Tiepolo was called upon to celebrate the marriage on the ceiling of the *sala del trono* and he replied with a composition so tumbling and playful that it's easy to forget that this is all about purchasing rank and power. Giovanni Battista Crosato's over-the-top ceiling frescoes in the ballroom have aged less well but, together with the Murano chandeliers and the intricately carved furniture by Andrea Brustolon, they provide an accurate record of the lifestyles of the rich and famous at the time. There are historical canvases by Giovanni Battista Piazzetta and Antonio Diziani, plus other gems; detached frescoes, recently restored, of *pulcinellas* (characters from Italian folk theatre, ancestors of the English Punch) by Giandomenico Tiepolo from the Tiepolo family villa capture the leisured melancholy of the moneyed classes as *La Serenissima* went into terminal decline. There are some good genre paintings by Pietro Longhi, whom Michael Levey calls 'the Jane Austen of Venetian art', and a series of smooth pastel portraits by Rosalba Carriera, a female 'prodigy' who was kept busy by English travellers eager to bring back a souvenir of their Grand Tour. On the third floor is the Egidio Martini gallery, a large collection of mainly Venetian works assembled by a scholar and donated to the city, and a reconstruction of an 18th-century pharmacy, with fine majolica vases.

A staircase at the far end of the entrance hall leads to the 'Mezzanino Browning', where the poet Robert Browning died in 1889. This contains the Mestrovich Collection of Veneto paintings, donated to the city by Ferruccio Mestrovich as a sign of gratitude for the hospitality afforded to his family after they had been expelled from their Dalmatia in 1945.

Santa Maria dei Carmini

Dorsoduro, campo dei Carmini (041 522 6553). **Open** 8am-noon, 2.30-6.30pm Mon-Sat; 2.30-6.30pm Sun. **Map** p325 D1.

The church officially called Santa Maria del Carmelo has a tall *campanile* topped by a statue of the Virgin, a frequent target for lightning. It is richly decorated inside, with 17th-century gilt wooden statues over the arcades of the nave and, above, a series of baroque paintings illustrating the history of the Carmelite order. However, the best paintings in the church are a *Nativity* by Cima da Conegliano on the second altar on the right and *St Nicholas of Bari* by Lorenzo Lotto opposite; the latter has a dreamy land-

San Trovaso.

scape – one of the most beautiful in Italian art, according to art historian Bernard Berenson – containing tiny figures of St George and the dragon. To the right of the Lotto painting is a Veronese *Holy Family*, recently moved here from the church of San Barnaba. In the chapel to the right of the high altar is a graceful bronze relief of *The Lamentation over the Dead Christ*, including portraits of Federico da Montefeltro and Battista Sforza, by the Sienese sculptor, painter, inventor, military architect and all-round Renaissance man Francesco di Giorgio.

San Trovaso

Dorsoduro, campo San Trovaso (041 522 2133). *Vaporetto Zattere.* **Open** 8-11am, 3-6pm Mon-Sat. **Map** p325 E2.

This church overlooking its quiet campo has two almost identical façades, both modelled on the sub-Palladian church of Le Zitelle (*see p138*) on the Giudecca. The story goes that San Trovaso was built on the very border of the two areas of the city belonging to the rival factions of the *nicolotti* and *castellani*; in the event of a wedding between members of the two factions, each party could make its own sweeping entrance and exit. There was no saint called Trovaso: the name is a Venetian telescoping of martyrs San Protasio and San Gervasio. There are five works by the Tintoretto family in the church; three are probably by the son, Domenico, including the two on either side of the high altar, which are rich in detail but poor in focus. In the left transept is a smaller-than-usual version of one of Tintoretto's favourite subjects, *The Last Supper*; the tavern setting is strikingly realistic. In the chapel to the left of the high altar is *The Temptations of St Anthony the Abbot*, featuring enough vices to tempt a saint – note the harlot with 'flames playing around her loins', as John Ruskin so coyly put it.

On the side wall of this latter chapel is a charming painting in the international Gothic style by Michele Giambono, *St Chrisogonus on Horseback* (c1450); the saint is a boyish figure on a gold background, with a shyly hesitant expression and a gorgeously fluttering cloak and banner. In the right transept, in the Clary Chapel, is a set of Renaissance marble reliefs (c1470) showing angels playing musical instruments or holding instruments of the Passion. The only attribution scholars will risk is to the conveniently named 'Master of San Trovaso'.

Scuola dei Carmini

Dorsoduro 2617, campo dei Carmini (041 528 9420). Vaporetto Ca' Rezzonico or San Basilio. **Open** *Apr-Oct* 10am-5pm daily. *Nov-Mar* 10am-4pm daily. **Admission** €5; €4 students; €2 children under 14. **No credit cards. Map** p325 D1.

Begun in 1670 to plans by Baldassare Longhena, the building housing this *scuola* (*see p67*) run by the Carmelite order was spared the Napoleonic lootings that dispersed the fittings of most of the other *scuole*. As a result, we have a good idea of what an early 18th-century Venetian confraternity HQ must have looked like, from the elaborate Sante Piatti altarpiece

Pinault at the Punta?

François Pinault owns Yves Saint Laurent, FNAC and Christie's. He owns a collection of modern and contemporary art believed to amount to over 2500 pieces. But until he bought Palazzo Grassi (*see p80*), he owned nowhere suitable for displaying his treasures.

A small selection of Pinault's possessions – some Rothkos, Damian Hirst's dissections and a couple of Koons among others – appeared in the inaugural display at Palazzo Grassi in April 2006. But even that hulking Grand Canal pile, now pared back inside to a stark white shell by Japanese architect Tadao Ando, is far too small to house all the French magnate's goodies.

Pinault had been planning to create his own gallery – to an Ando design, with an estimated $195 million budget – on the Ile Seguin near Paris, but bureaucratic hurdles left him wondering, as he approached his 70s, whether he'd live to see the place built. When Fiat put Palazzo Grassi up for sale, he grabbed it as a handy place for one-off shows; the problem of where to install a more permanent selection of his pictures now seems to have been solved by a Venice city council apparently bending over backwards to accommodate this free-spending collector and his pet architect.

The question of what to do with the huge, decaying warehouses on the Punta della Dogana, east of the Salute church, has been open for decades. The Peggy

Guggenheim Foundation (*see p133*) tried hard to get its hands on it. But an invitation for tenders to redevelop the Punta issued in 2006 might have been dictated by Pinault himself, so closely did its terms match what the Frenchman had to offer.

The Ile Seguin saga well behind him, Pinault has shown his no-heel-dragging approach to getting his artworks on show: the overhaul of Palazzo Grassi, for example, was carried out between October 2005 and April 2006. Ando has already been spotted lurking in the scaffolded-off area beyond the Salute church, and a blueprint no doubt already exists for the new exhibition space. If (cynics say 'when') Pinault wins the Punta contract, it surely won't be long before this quiet, prosperous corner of the lagoon city that already houses the Guggenheim collection becomes a world-class mecca for fans of modern and contemporary art.

downstairs to the staircase with its excrescence of gilded cherubs. On the upper floor is one of the most impressive of Giambattista Tiepolo's Venetian ceilings. The airy ceiling panels, in the main first-floor hall, were painted from 1740 to 1743 and are best viewed with one of the mirrors provided. Don't even try to unravel the story – a celestial donation that supposedly took place in Cambridge, when Simon Stock received the scapular (the badge of the Carmelite order) from the Virgin. What counts, as always with Tiepolo, is the audacity of his off-centre composition. If the atmosphere were not so ultra-refined, there would be something disturbing in the Virgin's sneer of cold contempt and those swirling Turneresque clouds. The central painting fell from the woodworm-ridden ceiling in August

2000 but has been beautifully restored. In the two adjoining rooms are wooden sculptures by Giacomo Piazzetta and a dramatic *Judith and Holofernes* by his more gifted son Giovanni Battista Piazzetta.

Eastern Dorsoduro

The eastern reaches of Dorsoduro, between the **Accademia** and the **Salute**, is an area of elegant, artsy prosperity, home to many artists and would-be artists, writers and wealthy foreigners. Ezra Pound spent his last years in a small house near the Zattere; Peggy Guggenheim hosted her collection of modern artists in her truncated palazzo on the Grand Canal (now the **Peggy Guggenheim**

Collection, *see p133*); artists use the vast spaces of the old warehouses on the Zattere as studios. On Sunday mornings, campo San Vio is some corner of a foreign land, as British expats home in on the Anglican church of St George. Overlooking the campo, the **Galleria Cini** has a collection of Ferrarese and Tuscan art.

It is a district of quiet canals and cosy *campielli*, perhaps the most picturesque being campiello Barbaro, behind pretty, lopsided Ca' Dario (rumoured, after the sudden deaths of owners over the centuries, to be cursed). But all that money has certainly driven out the locals: nowhere in Venice are you further from a simple *alimentari* (grocer's).

The colossal magnificence of Longhena's church of **Santa Maria della Salute** brings the residential area to an end. You can stroll on past the church to the old *Dogana di mare* (Customs House) on the tip of Dorsoduro. Debate about redeploying this empty space has been raging for years. For a while it seemed likely that the Peggy Guggenheim Collection would take it over. More recently, the town council has stipulated conditions for the development of the site that seem to point to just one candidate: the big new name on the Venetian scene, French billionaire Francois Pinault (*see p131* **Pinault at the Punta?**).

Crowning the corner tower of the Dogana, a 17th-century weathercock figure of Fortune perches daintily on top of a golden ball. For the last few years access to this spot, with its spectacular view across the water towards St Mark's, has been blocked by apparently non-existent restoration work.

Gallerie dell'Accademia

Dorsoduro 1050, campo Carità (041 522 2247/www.artive.arti.beniculturali.it). Vaporetto Accademia. **Open** 8.15am-2pm Mon; 8.15am-7.15pm Tue-Sun. **Admission** €6.50; concessions €3.25 (*see also p68* **State Museums**). Audio guides: single €4, double €6. Video-guides €6. **No credit cards. Map** p325 F2.

The Accademia is the essential one-stop shop for Venetian painting, and one of the world's greatest art treasure houses. At the time of writing – and until late 2007 at the very earliest – it is also a hive of construction and restoration work; though the gallery will remain open throughout its grand makeover, visitors should be prepared to find hanging arrangements changed and some rooms closed completely from time to time.

It is located inside three former religious buildings: the Scuola Grande di Santa Maria della Carità (the oldest of the Venetian *scuole*, founded in the 13th century), the adjacent church of the Carità, and the Monastery of the Lateran Canons, a 12th-century structure radically remodelled by Andrea Palladio. It was Napoleon who made the collection possible,

first by suppressing hundreds of churches, convents and religious guilds, confiscating their artworks for the greater good of the state; and second by moving the city's Accademia di Belle Arti art school here, with the mandate both to train students and to act as a gallery and storeroom for all the evicted artworks, which were originally displayed as models for pupils to aspire to. The art school moved to a new site on the nearby Zattere in September 2004; the premises formerly occupied by students are now being restored and will eventually provide new exhibition space, with the number of works on show expected to rise from the current 400 to around 650; there are also plans to equip the museum with a cafeteria and new bookshop.

In its current layout, the collection is arranged chronologically, with the exception of the 15th- and 16th-century works in rooms 19-24 at the end. It opens with 14th- and 15th-century devotional works by Paolo Veneziano and others – stiff figures against gold backdrops, still firmly in the Byzantine tradition. This room was the main hall of the *scuola grande*: note the original ceiling of gilded cherubim, whose faces are all subtly different. Rooms 2 and 3 have devotional paintings and altarpieces by Carpaccio, Cima da Conegliano and Giovanni Bellini (a fine *Enthroned Madonna with Six Saints*).

Rooms 4 and 5 bring us to the Renaissance heart of the collection: here are Mantegna's *St George* and Giorgione's mysterious *Tempest*, which has had art historians reaching for symbolic interpretations for centuries. In Room 6 the three greats of 16th-century Venetian painting, Titian, Tintoretto and Veronese, are first encountered. But the battle of the giants gets under way in earnest in Room 10, where Tintoretto's ghostly chiaroscuro *Transport of the Body of St Mark* vies for attention with Titian's moving *Pietà* – his last painting – and Veronese's huge *Christ in the House of Levi*. Originally commissioned as a *Last Supper*, this painting emerged so full of anachronistic and irreverent detail ('buffoons, drunkards, Germans, dwarfs, and similar indecencies' according to the Inquisition investigation) that the artist was accused of heresy and ordered to alter the painting; instead – and with admirable chutzpah – he simply changed its name.

Room 11 covers two centuries, with canvases by Tintoretto (the exquisite *Madonna dei Camerlenghi*), Bernardo Strozzi and Tiepolo. The series of rooms beyond brings the plot up to the 18th century, with all the old favourites: Canaletto, Guardi, Longhi and soft-focus, bewigged portraits by female superstar Rosalba Carriera.

Rooms 19 and 20 take us back to the 15th century; the latter has the rich *Miracle of the Relic of the Cross* cycle, a collaborative effort by Gentile Bellini, Carpaccio and others, which is packed with telling social details; there's even a black gondolier in Carpaccio's *Miracle of the Cross at the Rialto*.

An even more satisfying cycle has Room 21 to itself. Carpaccio's *Life of St Ursula* (1490-5) tells the story of the legendary Breton princess who embarked on a pilgrimage to Rome with her betrothed so that he could be baptised into the true faith. All went swimmingly until Ursula and all the 11,000 virgins accompanying her were massacred by the Huns in Cologne (the initial 'M' for martyr used in one account of the affair caused the multiplication of the number of accompanying maidens from 11 to 11,000, M being the Roman numeral for 1000). More than the ropey legend, it's the architecture, the ships and the pageantry in these meticulous paintings that grab the attention. Perhaps most striking, amid all the closely thronged, action-packed scenes, is the rapt stillness and solitude of *The Dream of St Ursula*, a painting much loved by Ruskin.

Room 23 is the former church of Santa Maria della Carità: here are devotional works by Vivarini, the Bellinis and others. Room 24 – the Albergo Room (or secretariat) of the former *scuola* – contains the only work in the whole gallery that is in its original site: Titian's magnificent *Presentation of the Virgin*.

Until the refurbished gallery is ready, a free guided tour of the *Quadreria* (which is essentially the museum's storeroom, containing paintings – including some very major works – otherwise not on show) can be taken on Friday at 11am and noon; pre-booking is essential (041 522 2247).

Galleria Cini

Dorsoduro 864, piscina del Forner (041 521 0755/ www.cini.it). Vaporetto Accademia. **Open** during exhibitions only 10.30am-1pm, 3-6.30pm. **Admission** €6.50; €5.50 concessions. **No credit cards. Map** p325 F3.
This collection of Ferrarese and Tuscan art was put together by industrialist Vittorio Cini, who created the Fondazione Cini on the island of San Giorgio Maggiore (*see p139*). It's small but there are one or two gems, such as the unfinished Pontormo double *Portrait of Two Friends*, on the first floor, and Dosso Dossi's *Allegorical Scene* on the second, a vivacious character study from the D'Este Palace in Ferrara. There are also some delicate, late-medieval ivories and a rare, 14th-century wedding chest decorated with chivalric scenes.

Peggy Guggenheim Collection

Dorsoduro 701, fondamenta Venier dei Leoni (041 520 6288/www.guggenheim-venice.it). Vaporetto Accademia or Salute. **Open** 10am-6pm Wed-Mon. **Admission** €10; €8 over-65s; €5 students. **Credit** AmEx, MC, V. **Map** p325 F3.
This remarkable establishment, tucked behind a high wall off a quiet street, is the third most visited museum in the city. It was founded by one of the most colourful of Venice's expat residents, Peggy Guggenheim, whose father went down in the Titanic, leaving her with $460,000. The money came in useful as she set out busily to satisfy her ravenous appetite for men and art. Peggy may have hated her bulbous nose – the result of a botched job by a Cincinnati plastic surgeon – but that didn't stop her running up a list of lovers that reads like a who's who of contemporary culture, including Samuel Beckett, Yves Tanguy, Roland Penrose (who liked to tie her up) and Max Ernst, to whom she was briefly married. When asked how many husbands she had had, Peggy replied: 'Do you mean mine, or other people's?' Ms Guggenheim took the same voracious approach to art as to men.

She turned up in Venice in 1949 looking for a home for her already sizable collection. A short-sighted curator at London's Tate Gallery had described her

Le Zattere. *See p135.*

Sightseeing

growing pile of surrealist and modernist works as 'non-art'. Venice, still struggling to win back the tourists after World War II, was less finicky, and Peggy found a perfect, eccentric base in Palazzo Venier dei Leoni, a truncated 18th-century Grand Canal palazzo; the building had from 1910-24 been the home of another lady determined to make her mark on the city, the Marchesa Luisa Casati, who liked to parade through piazza San Marco with a pair of cheetahs on diamond-studded leashes.

There are big European names in the collection, including Picasso, Duchamp, Brancusi, Giacometti and Max Ernst, plus a few Americans such as Calder and Jackson Pollock, whose career was jump-started by Peggy. Highlights include the beautifully enigmatic *Empire of Light* by Magritte and Giacometti's disturbing *Woman with Her Throat Cut*. The flamboyant *Attirement of the Bride*, by Peggy's husband, Max Ernst, often turns up as a Carnevale costume. But perhaps the most startling exhibit of all is the rider of Marino Marini's *Angel of the City* out on the Grand Canal terrace, who thrusts his manhood towards passing *vaporetti*. Never the shrinking wallflower, Peggy took delight in unscrewing the member and pressing it on young men she fancied.

Another wing has been given over to Futurist works on long-term loan from the collection of Gianni Mattioli. The gallery also has a charming garden, best surveyed from the terrace of the café-restaurant.

Santa Maria della Salute

Dorsoduro, campo della Salute (041 522 5558).
Vaporetto Salute. **Open** *Apr-Sept* 9am-noon,
3-5.30pm daily. *Oct-Mar* 9am-noon, 3-5.30pm
daily. **Map** p326 A3.

This magnificent baroque church, queening it over the entrance of the Grand Canal, is almost as recognisable an image of Venice as St Mark's or the Rialto bridge. It was built between 1631 and 1681 in thanksgiving for the end of Venice's last bout of plague, which had wiped out at least a third of the population in 1630. The church is dedicated to the Madonna, as protector of the city.

The terms of the competition won by 26-year-old architect Baldassare Longhena represented a serious challenge, which beat some of the best architects of the day. The church was to be colossal but inexpensive; the whole structure was to be visually clear on entrance, with an unimpeded view of the high altar, the ambulatory and side altars coming into sight only as one approached the chancel; the light was to be evenly distributed; and the whole building should *creare una bella figura* – show itself off to good effect.

Longhena succeeded brilliantly in satisfying all these requisites – particularly the last and most Venetian one. The church takes superb advantage of its dominant position and pays homage to both the Byzantine form of San Marco across the Grand Canal and the classical form of Palladio's Redentore, across the Giudecca Canal. Longhena said he chose the circular shape with the reverent aim of offering a crown to the Madonna. She stands on the lantern above the cupola as described in the Book of Revelations: 'Clothed in the sun, and the moon under her feet, and upon her head a crown of twelve stars.' Beneath her, on the great scroll-brackets around the cupola, stand statues of the apostles – the 12 stars in her crown. This Marian symbolism continues inside the church, where in the centre of the mosaic

floor, amid a circle of roses, is an inscription, *Unde origo inde salus* (from the origin comes salvation) – a reference to the legendary birth of Venice under the Virgin's protection.

Longhena's intention was for the visitor to approach the high altar ceremoniously through the main door. If visitors were able to take this route, the six side altars would only come into view upon reaching the very centre of the church, where they appear framed theatrically in their separate archways. However, the main door is rarely open and often the central area of the church is roped off, so you have no choice but to walk round the ambulatory and visit the chapels separately.

The three on the right have paintings by Luca Giordano, a prolific Neapolitan painter who brought a little southern brio into the art of the city at a time (the mid 17th century) when most painting had become limply derivative.

On the opposite side is a clumsily restored *Pentecost*, by Titian, transferred here from the island monastery of Santo Spirito (demolished in 1656). The high altar has a splendidly dynamic sculptural group by Giusto Le Corte, the artist responsible (with assistants) for most of the statues inside and outside the church. This group represents *Venice Kneeling before the Virgin and Child*, while the plague, in the shape of a hideous old hag, scurries off to the right, prodded by a tough-looking *putto* with a flaming torch. In the midst of all this marble hubbub is a serene Byzantine icon of the *Madonna and Child*, brought from Crete in 1669 by Francesco Morosini, the Venetian commander responsible for blowing up the Parthenon. The best paintings are in the sacristy (open same hours as church; admission

€1.50). Tintoretto's *Marriage at Cana* (1551) was described by Ruskin as 'perhaps the most perfect example which human art has produced of the utmost possible force and sharpness of shadow united with richness of local colour'. He also points out how curiously difficult it is to spot the bride and groom in the painting.

On the altar is a very early Titian of *Saints Mark, Sebastian, Roch, Cosmas and Damian*, saints who were all invoked for protection against the plague; the painting was done during the outbreak of 1509-14. Three later works by Titian (c1540-9) hang on the ceiling, violent Old Testament scenes also brought here from the church of Santo Spirito: *the Sacrifice of Abraham, David Killing Goliath* and *Cain and Abel*. These works established the conventions for all subsequent ceiling paintings in Venice; Titian decided not to go for the worm's-eye view adopted by Mantegna and Correggio, which sacrificed clarity for surprise, and instead chose an oblique viewpoint, as if observing the action from the bottom of a hill. More Old Testament turbulence can be seen in works by Salviati (*Saul Hurling a Spear at David*) and Palma il Giovane (*Samson and Jonah* – in which the whale is represented mainly by a vast lolling rubbery tongue).

Le Zattere

From Punta della Dogana, the mile-long stretch of **Le Zattere**, Venice's finest promenade after the riva degli Schiavoni, leads back westwards past the churches of **I Gesuati** (*see p136*) and **Santa Maria della Visitazione** (*see p137*) to the San Nicolò zone.

Santa Maria della Salute.

This long promenade bordering the Giudecca Canal is named after the *zattere* (rafts) that used to moor here, bringing wood and other materials across from the mainland. The paved quayside was created by decree in 1519. It now provides a favourite strolling ground, punctuated by some spectacularly situated (if somewhat shadeless) benches for a picnic, and several bars and *gelaterie*. The eastern end is usually quiet with the occasional flurry of activity around the vast 14th-century salt warehouses, now used by rowing clubs.

Westward from these is the church of **Spirito Santo** and the long 16th-century façade of the grimly named **Ospedale degli Incurabili** (the main incurable disease of the time was syphilis), long used as a juvenile court but now serving as the new premises of the Accademia di Belle Arti (art school, **photo** *p133*), recently evicted from the Accademia. In Ben Jonson's play *Volpone*, the title character's property is confiscated and he himself sent to this hospital at the end of the play.

The liveliest part of the Zattere is around the church of **I Gesuati**. Venetians flock here at weekends and on warm evenings to savour ice-cream or sip drinks at canal-side tables.

The final and widest stretch of the Zattere passes several notable *palazzi*, including the 16th-century Palazzo Clary – until recently the French consulate – and the Gothic Palazzo Molin, which is now used by the Società

Adriatica di Navigazione. Towards the end is the 17th-century façade of the Scuola dei Luganegheri (sausage makers' school), with a statue of the sausage makers' protector, St Anthony Abbot, whose symbol was a hog.

I Gesuati

Dorsoduro, fondamenta Zattere ai Gesuati (041 275 0642/www.chorusvenezia.org). Vaporetto Gesuati. **Open** 10am-5pm Mon-Sat. **Admission** €2.50 (*see also p68* **Chorus**). **No credit cards. Map** p325 E3.
The official name of this church is Santa Maria del Rosario, but it is always known as the Gesuati, after the minor religious order that owned the previous church on the site. The order merged with the Dominicans – the present owners of the church – in 1668. I Gesuati is a great piece of teamwork by a trio of remarkable rococo artists: architect Giorgio Massari (he of Palazzo Grassi on the Grand Canal, *see p80*), painter Giambattista Tiepolo and sculptor Giovanni Morlaiter.

The façade deliberately reflects the Palladian church of the Redentore opposite, but the splendidly posturing statues give it that typically 18th-century touch of histrionic flamboyance. Plenty more theatrical sculpture is to be found inside the church, all by Morlaiter. Above is a magnificent ceiling by Tiepolo, with three frescoes on obscure Dominican themes (a mirror is provided for the relief of stiff necks). These works reintroduced frescoes to Venetian art after two centuries of canvas ceiling paintings. The central panel shows St Dominic passing on to a crowd of supplicants the rosary he has

Le Zattere, Venice's favourite strolling ground.

Ezra Pound

'Venice is an excellent place to come to from Crawfordsville, Indiana,' wrote Ezra Pound in an essay in 1920. He was to return many times, and lived out the last 14 years of his life here. He died in 1972 and is buried on the island of San Michele (*see p143*).

Pound was a central figure in Modernism. Yet such effusions as 'San Vio June' and 'Alma Sol Veneziae' show the influence of Provençal and early Italian poetry, and the quaint medievalising language of English Pre-Raphaelitism. Pound was later to reject these early poems but never the sentiments behind them; they are still a moving testimony to the effect that Venice's beauty had upon the earnest young poet from the Mid-West:

Old powers rise and do return to me
Grace to thy bounty, O Venetian sun.

Pound clearly does not share his contemporaries' vision of Venice as a place of moral, material and spiritual decadence. While his friend TS Eliot describes a city of crumbling *palazzi*, where 'the rats are underneath the piles', Pound celebrates a city of spring-like beauty and promise.

In his magnum opus, the rambling, fragmentary and frustrating *Cantos*, Venice recurs frequently and always in positive terms, as a place where art, history and society formed a miraculous and redemptive whole. Certain buildings have a particular resonance for him: the Palazzo Ducale is an image of Venetian power, beauty and wise government; the mosaics of San Marco prefigure his own artistic methods, with their 'gold' against the 'gloom' providing a recurring image of desire; Santa Maria dei Miracoli, with its clean, stern lines and its jewel-like decorations, almost stands as a symbol of his own poetry.

But Venice had more than just a symbolic significance for him. After World War II Pound was imprisoned in an American detention camp outside Pisa for having broadcast anti-Semitic propaganda on Fascist radio; in the camp he wrote the harrowing *Pisan Cantos* in which he recalls the places he loved: 'Will I ever see the Giudecca again? / or the lights against it, Ca' Foscari, Ca' Giustinian…' In particular, he recalls his early days in Dorsoduro: 'well, my window / looked out on the Squero where Ogni Santi / meets San Trovaso…'

Pound was saved from execution by being declared insane, and spent 12 years in an asylum in the US. Upon being released he returned to Venice (notoriously giving a Fascist salute as he descended from the plane) and settled with his mistress Olga Rudge back in Dorsoduro; they lived in a small house near the Salute (calle Querini), which still belongs to their daughter. Here he became one of the sights of Venice, strolling along the Zattere or reading at cafés; he was visited by such writers as Allan Ginsberg, but for the most part remained in quiet seclusion, with a close circle of Venetian and foreign friends. In the end Venice gave him a certain peace.

just received from the cloud-enthroned Madonna. Tiepolo also painted the surrounding grisailles, which, at first sight, look like stucco reliefs.

There is another brightly coloured Tiepolo on the first altar on the right, *The Virgin and Child with Saints Rosa, Catherine and Agnes*. Tiepolo here plays with optical effects, allowing St Rosa's habit to tumble out of the frame. In his painting of three Dominican saints on the third altar on the right, Giovanni Battista Piazzetta makes use of a narrower and more sober range of colours, going for a more sculptural effect.

Santa Maria della Visitazione

Dorsoduro, fondamenta Zattere ai Gesuati (041 522 4077). Vaporetto Zattere. **Open** *Apr-Sept* 8am-12.30pm, 2.30-7pm Mon-Sat. *Oct-Mar* 8am-12.30pm, 2.30-6pm Mon-Sat. **Map** p325 E3.

Confusingly, this has the same name as the Vivaldi church on the riva degli Schiavoni – though the lat-ter is usually known as La Pietà (*see p100*). Santa Maria della Visitazione stands on the Zattere just a few yards from the larger church of I Gesuati (*see p136*); it is now the chapel of the Istituto Don Orione, which has taken over the vast complex of the monastery of the Gesuati next door.

Designed by Tullio Lombardo or Mauro Codussi and built in 1423, the church has an attractive early Renaissance façade. It was suppressed (that rascal Napoleon again) at the beginning of the 19th century and stripped of all its works of art with the exception of the original coffered ceiling, an unexpected delight that contains 58 compartments with portraits of saints and prophets by an Umbrian painter of Luca Signorelli's school (mirrors are provided), one of the few examples of central Italian art in Venice. To the right of the façade is a lion's mouth for secret denunciations: the ones posted here went to the *Magistrati della sanità*, who dealt with matters of public health.

La Giudecca & San Giorgio

Convents, industry and a wonderful view south.

LA GIUDECCA

SAN GIORGIO

The **Giudecca** lies south of Venice proper, a gondola-shaped strand of eight islands. It has its own distinct character, owing to its anomalous status, being a part of and apart from Venice. Although it has a reputation as one of the poorer areas in the city, it manages to attract more than its fair share of celebrities.

It was once known as 'Spinalonga', from an imagined resemblance to a fish-skeleton (*spina* means fish bone). Some claim that the present name derives from an early community of Jews, and others to the fact that the island was a place of exile for troublesome nobles, who had been *giudicati*, 'judged'. But the exile was sometimes self-chosen, as people used the islands as a place of rural retreat. Michelangelo, when exiled from Florence in 1529, chose it as a place to mope; three centuries later, during his steamy and highly public love affair with George Sand, Alfred de Musset wrote in praise of the flowery meadows of 'la Zuecca'.

During the 19th century the city authorities began to make use of the numerous abandoned convents and monasteries, converting them into factories and prisons. The factories have almost all closed down, while the prisons (one for drug offenders, one for women) remain in use. A great deal of low-rent housing has been created, much of it on Sacca Fisola at the western end, an island created from mud dredged from the lagoon.

Some of the factories remain abandoned, contributing to the run-down appearance of the south side of the Giudecca, but a few have been converted into new residential complexes. Much hope is pinned on the transformation of the

most conspicuous one: the Molino Stucky (*see p140* **Stucky on you**), the largest building on the lagoon. The work was nearing completion as this guide went to press.

The Giudecca still has a reputation as one of the city's rougher areas, but the *palazzi* along the northern *fondamenta* enjoy a splendid view of Venice and continue to attract well-heeled outsiders (Elton John and Giorgio Armani, for example) in search of picturesque holiday homes. There are also a number of major hotels, including Venice's most expensive, the Cipriani (*see p64*) at the eastern end, and the Bauer Palladio (*see p49*) in the former convent of Le Zitelle. A number of artists have chosen to live here, many using some of the island's disused warehouses as studios.

The main sights of the Giudecca are all on this *fondamenta*: **Santa Eufemia** (*see p139*), the Palladian churches of Le Zitelle ('the spinsters': the convent ran a hospice for poor girls who were trained as lace makers; the church is nearly always closed) and **Il Redentore** (*see p139*), as well as several fine *palazzi*.

Near Le Zitelle is the neo-Gothic Casa De Maria, with its three large inverted-shield windows. The Bolognese painter Mario De Maria built it for himself from 1910 to 1913. It is the only private palazzo to have the same patterned brickwork as the Doge's Palace.

On the fondamenta Rio della Croce (No.149, close to the Redentore) stands Palazzo Munster, a former infirmary for English sailors. The vitriolic Anglo-Catholic writer Frederick Rolfe received the last sacraments here in 1910, after slagging the hospital off in his novel *The Desire and Pursuit of the Whole*. (He then proceeded to live for two more vituperative years.)

Opposite is another expat landmark, the 'Garden of Eden', pleasure ground of Frederic Eden, a disabled Englishman who, like Byron, discovered that Venice was the perfect city for those with disabilities – particularly if they could afford their own gondola and steam launch. After a period in which it belonged to the ex-Queen of Yugoslavia, the garden passed into the hands of the Austrian artist, Fritz Hundertwasser and since his death in 2000 it has belonged to a Foundation in his name, which has, reportedly, allowed it to remain verdant but totally unkempt.

It is not particularly easy to get to the southern side of the island, but worth the effort. Take calle San Giacomo, west of the Redentore; just before the end turn left along calle degli Orti, and then right. At the end is a small public garden with benches looking out over the quiet southern lagoon and its lonely islands.

Il Redentore

Giudecca, campo del Redentore (041 275 0462/ www.chorusvenezia.org). Vaporetto Redentore. **Open** 10am-5pm Mon-Sat. **Admission** €2.50 (*see also p68* **Chorus**). **No credit cards. Map** p326 A5.

Venice's first great plague church was built to celebrate deliverance from the bout of 1575-7. An especially conspicuous site was chosen, one that could be approached in ceremonial fashion. The ceremony continues today, on every third Sunday of July, when a bridge of boats is built across the canal. Palladio (*see p266*) designed an eye-catching building whose prominent dome appears to rise directly behind the Greek-temple façade, giving the illusion that the church is centrally planned, as was traditional with sanctuaries and votive temples outside Venice. A broad flight of steps leads to the entrance. The solemn, harmonious interior, with its single nave lit by large 'thermal' windows, testifies to Palladio's study of Roman baths. But the Capuchin monks, the austere order to whom the building was entrusted, were not pleased by its grandeur; Palladio attempted to mollify them by designing their choir stalls in a plain style. The best paintings are in the sacristy, which is rarely open; they include a *Virgin and Child* by Alvise Vivarini and a *Baptism* by Veronese.

Santa Eufemia

Giudecca, fondamenta Santa Eufemia (041 522 5848). Vaporetto Santa Eufemia. **Open** 8am-noon, 3-5pm Mon-Sat; 3-7pm Sun. **Map** p325 E4.

This church is a 16th-century Doric portico along its flank (currently *in restauro*). The interior owes its charm to its mix of styles. The nave and aisles are essentially 11th century, with Veneto-Byzantine columns and capitals, while the decoration consists mainly of 18th-century stucco (freshly restored) and paintings. Over the first altar on the right is *St Roch and an Angel* by Bartolomeo Vivarini (1480; under restoration as the guide went to press).

Isola di San Giorgio

The island of **San Giorgio**, which sits in such a strategic position opposite the **Piazzetta** (*see p77*), realised its true potential under set designer extraordinaire Andrea Palladio, whose church of **San Giorgio Maggiore** (*see p140*) is one of Venice's most recognisable landmarks. Known in the early days of the city as the *Isola dei cipressi* (Cypress Island), it soon became an

important Benedictine monastery and centre of learning – a tradition that is carried on today by the **Fondazione Giorgio Cini** (*see below*), which runs a research centre and craft school on the island.

Fondazione Giorgio Cini & Benedictine monastery

(041 524 0119/www.cini.it). Vaporetto San Giorgio. **Open** *Monastery* 10am-4.30pm Sat, Sun with guided tours every hour. **Admission** €12; €10 concessions. **No credit cards. Map** 326 C3.

There has been a Benedictine monastery on the island since 982, when Doge Tribuno Memmo donated the island to the order. The monastery continued to benefit from ducal donations, acquiring large tracts of land both in and around Venice and abroad. After the church acquired the remains of St Stephen (1109), it was visited yearly by the doge on 26 December, the feast day of the saint. The city authorities often used the island as a luxury hotel for particularly prestigious visitors, such as Cosimo de' Medici in 1433. Cosimo had a magnificent library built here; it was destroyed in 1614, to make way for a more elaborate affair by Longhena (now open only to bona fide scholars with references to prove it; for opening times, *see p295*).

In 1800 the island hosted the conclave of cardinals that elected Pope Pius VII, after they had been expelled from Rome by Napoleon. In 1806 the French got their own back, supressing the monastery and sending its chief artistic treasure – Veronese's *Marriage Feast at Cana* – off to the Louvre, where it still hangs. For the rest of the century the monastery did ignominious service as a barracks and ammunition store. In 1951 industrialist Vittorio Cini bought the island to set up a foundation in memory of his son, Giorgio, killed in a plane crash in 1949. The Fondazione Giorgio Cini uses the monastery buildings for its activities, including artistic and musical research (it holds a collection of Vivaldi manuscripts, plus illuminated manuscripts), and a naval college. A portion of the complex was given

The view over the southern lagoon.

back to the Benedictines; there are currently eight monks in the monastery. The foundation is now open to the public at weekends for guided tours (in Italian, English, French and German). There are two beautiful cloisters – one by Giovanni Buora (1516-40), the other by Palladio (1579) – an elegant library and staircase by Longhena (1641-53), and a magnificent refectory (where Veronese's painting hung) by Palladio (1561). The tour includes the splendid garden behind the monastery.

San Giorgio Maggiore

(041 522 7827). Vaporetto San Giorgio. **Open** 9.30am-12.30pm, 2.30-6pm Mon-Sat; 2-6.30pm Sun. **Admission** *Church* free. *Campanile* €3, concessions €2. **No credit cards. Map** p326 C3.

This unique spot cried out for a masterpiece. Palladio provided it. This was his first complete solo church; it demonstrates how confident he was in his techniques and objectives. With no hint of influence from the city's Byzantine tradition, Palladio here develops the system of superimposed temple fronts with which he had experimented in the façade of San Francesco della Vigna *(see p94)*. The interior maintains the same relations between the orders as the outside, with composite half-columns supporting the gallery and lower Corinthian pilasters supporting the arches. The effect is of luminosity and harmony, decoration being confined to the altars. Palladio believed that white was the colour most pleasing to God, a credo that happily matched the demand from the Council of Trent for greater lucidity in church services.

There are several good works of art. Over the first altar is an *Adoration of the Shepherds* by Jacopo Bassano, with startling lighting effects. The altar to the right of the high altar has a *Madonna and Child with Nine Saints* by Sebastiano Ricci.

On the side walls of the chancel hang two vast compositions by Tintoretto, a *Last Supper* and the *Gathering of Manna*, painted in the last years of his life. The perspective of each work makes it clear that they were intended to be viewed from the altar rails. Tintoretto combines almost surreal visionary effects (angels swirling out from a lamp's eddying smoke) with touches of superb domestic realism (a cat prying into a basket, a woman stooping over her laundry). Tintoretto's last painting, a moving *Entombment*, hangs in the Cappella dei Morti (usually closed; the painting was being restored as this guide went to press). It's possible that Tintoretto included himself among the mourners: he has been identified as the bearded man gazing intensely at Christ's face. In the left transept is a painting by Jacopo and Domenico Tintoretto of the *Martyrdom of St Stephen*, placed above the altar containing the saint's remains (brought from Constantinople in 1109).

From the left transept follow the signs to the campanile. Just in front of the ticket-office stands the huge statue of an angel that crowned the bell tower until it was struck by lightning in 1993. To the left of the statue a corridor gives access to the lift which takes you up to the bell tower. The view from the top of the tower is extraordinary: the best possible panorama across Venice itself and the lagoon.

Stucky on you

The largest building in the lagoon, the Molino Stucky was also, for decades, the most desolate. A symbol first of industrial clout, then of decline, it's now hyped as a sign of refound confidence.

Italo-Swiss Giovanni Stucky was convinced that Venice with its cargo facilities had great potential. His first factory, built on the Giudecca in 1883, soon proved too small. German architect Ernst Wullekopf's design for a much larger, very un-Venetian one was controversial from the start. The town council demanded that points and pinnacles be removed. Stucky threatened to sack 187 workers. The council capitulated. By 1896 the crenellated Teutonic mass that became a beloved part of the Venetian cityscape had been completed.

The new mill employed 1500 workers and could grind 125 tonnes of flour a day. In 1908 Stucky purchased Palazzo Grassi (*see p90*) on the Grand Canal – not the last tycoon to do so. In 1910 Giovanni was murdered; production

plummetted after his son Giancarlo took over the business. An overhaul in the 1920s did nothing to improve the situation and in 1955, activity ceased.

In the 1990s the Acqua Marcia company obtained permission to restore the abandoned pile. Plans included a 2000-seater conference centre, a 400-room luxury hotel and 138 private flats. The outward appearance was to be preserved intact. Fire destroyed the east wing in 2003 (the single 42-year-old helicopter that had been available for fighting the fire at the Fenice, *see p91*, in 1996 was off being repaired at the time). But restoration hadn't even begun in that part of the building, and soon went on apace.

The Hilton group hotel/conference centre was slated to open here in the first half of 2007. Like it or not, this is probably the destiny of Venice: conference centre of the world. After all, who would refuse an invitation to talk shop while downing *aperitivi* and gazing across to the Zattere?

Lido & Lagoon

A watery paradise between the island and the sea.

A brief session with Google Earth focusing on this north-eastern corner of Italy will reveal just how improbable the situation of Venice is. It lies more or less in the middle of a salt-water lagoon, protected from the open sea by the two slender barriers of the Lido and Pellestrina. While other Italian towns defended themselves with monumental bastions and circling walls, Venice relied on her lagoon for protection.

For Venetians the greatest threat has always been the open sea, and their efforts have been devoted over the centuries to strengthening the natural defences offered by the Lido and Pellestrina; in the 18th century the *murazzi* were created: an impressive barrier of great stone and marble blocks all the way down both islands. Nowadays the threat is seen as coming from the three *bocche di porto* (the lagoon's openings to the sea) between the Lido and Cavallino, between the Lido and Pellestrina and between Pellestrina and Chioggia. Work has started on creating the highly controversial mobile dyke system known as MoSE.

Google Earth will also reveal that Venice is by no means the only island (or island-cluster) in the lagoon. If the jostling crowds in piazza San Marco get too much for you, a day out on the lagoon to one or more of these other islands may prove the ideal antidote. Such destinations as Murano and Burano can, in high season, seem only marginally less crowded, but the views from the vaporetto of the lagoon's empty reaches are enough to soothe even the most frayed of nerves. And other destinations, such as Sant'Erasmo, are always bucolically tranquil and almost entirely tourist-free.

There are 34 islands on the salt-water lagoon, most of them uninhabited, containing only crumbling masonry, home to seagulls and lazy lizards. The lagoon itself covers some 520 square kilometres (200 square miles) – the world's biggest wetland. Painters and photographers are just as well served out here as in the city itself, especially on clear autumn and winter days when the snow-capped peaks of the Dolomites stand starkly out on the horizon.

The wetlands of the lagoon are a wild, fragile environment; this is where Venetians take refuge from the tourist hordes, escaping by boat for picnics on deserted islands, or fishing for bass and bream. Others set off to dig up clams at low tide (most without the requisite

licence), or organise hunting expeditions for duck, using the makeshift hides known as *botte* ('barrels', which is what they were originally, sunk into the floor of the lagoon). Many just head out after work, at sunset, to row.

From the lagoon, the precarious position and the unique urban development of Venice come sharply into focus. Exploring some of the quieter corners of this waterscape is like being wafted back to the sixth century.

EXPLORING THE LAGOON

To learn more about the lagoon's ecostructure and bird life, catch the blue bus for Chioggia or Sottomarina from piazzale Roma and ask to get off at the WWF's **Oasi Valle Averto** (041 518 5068, open 9am-4pm Mon-Fri & Sun, admission €5, €3 concessions, free under-6s, guided tours at 10am & 2pm Sun, weekdays by appointment, minimum 10 people). Or contact **Limosa** (041 932 003/fax 041 538 4743, www.limosa.it), a group of dedicated environmentalists who will organise day trips by boat or bike, or entire holidays for individuals and groups.

For information on boat hire, *see p232*.

The Lido

Map p317

The **Lido** is the northernmost of the two strips of land that separate the lagoon from the open sea. It is no longer the 'bare strand / Of hillocks heaped from ever-shifting sand' that Shelley described in *Julian and Maddalo*, and nor is it the playground for wealthy aesthetes that fans of *Death in Venice* might come in fruitless search of. These days Venice-by-the-sea is a placidly residential suburb, where pale young boys in sailor-suits are in very short supply. On the whole the Lido is an escape from the strangeness of Venice to a normality of supermarkets and cars.

Things perk up in summer when buses are full of city sunbathers and tourists staying in the Lido's overspill hotels. However, the days of all-night partying and gambling are long gone. In January 2001 the Lido Casinò closed. Now the only moment when the place stirs to anything like its former vivacity is at the beginning of September when the film festival rolls into town for two weeks, with its bandwagon of stars, directors, PR people and sleep-deprived, caffeine-driven journalists and the two big hotels, Des Bains and the Excelsior, do their best to keep the legend of lazy luxury flickeringly alive (*for both, see p64*).

The Lido has few tourist sights as such. Only the church of San Nicolò on the riviera San Nicolò – founded in 1044 – can claim any great antiquity. It was here that the doge would come on Ascension Day after marrying Venice to the sea in the ceremony known as *lo sposalizio del mare* (*see p202* **Festa della Sensa**). Inside is the tomb of Nicola Giustiniani, a Benedictine monk who was forced to leave holy orders in 1172 to assure the future of his illustrious family, of which he was the sole heir. He married the doge's daughter, had lots of kids, then went back to being a monk. After his death he was beatified for his spirit of self-sacrifice.

Fans of art nouveau and deco have plenty to look at on the Lido. On the Gran Viale there are two gems: the tiled façade of the Hungaria Hotel (No.28), formerly the Ausonia Palace, with its Beardsley-esque nymphs; and Villa Monplaisir at No.14, an art deco design from 1906. There are other smaller-scale examples in and around via Lepanto, though, it's hard to beat the Hotel Excelsior on lungomare Marconi, a neo-Moorish party piece, complete with minaret.

The coloured houses of **Burano**. *See p145.*

At the eastern end of the Gran Viale is one of the city's more controversial new architectural offerings, Giancarlo De Carlo's Blue Moon complex, an elaborate building with curious domes, which, to the annoyance of locals, deprives the Gran Viale of its sea view.

The bus ride south along the lagoon-side promenade of the Lido is uneventful but passes some submerged history. The old town of Malamocco, near the southern end of the island, was engulfed by a tidal wave in 1107; it had been a flourishing port controlled by Padua. The new town, built further inland, never really amounted to much; today its sights consist of a few picturesque streets and a pretty bridge.

Offshore from Malamocco is the tiny island of Poveglia, once inhabited by 200 families, descendants of the servants of Pietro Tradonico, a ninth-century doge murdered by his rivals. His servants barricaded themselves inside the Palazzo Ducale and only agreed to leave when safe conduct to this new home was promised.

GETTING AROUND

The main Santa Maria Elisabetta stop on the Lido is served by frequent boats from Venice and the mainland. For details of routes, *see p287.* The San Nicolò stop to the north is served by the No.17 car ferry from Tronchetto.

Bus routes are confusing. The A (*arancione*, orange) and the B (*blu*) each have two routes, one going south and one north. The southward route of both (marked 'Alberoni') is the same, along the lagoon to Alberoni at the southern tip of the island, via Malamocco. The northward route of each (marked 'San Nicolò' or 'Ospedale') is circular: the A travels clockwise along the lagoon-front and then turns right towards the sea and the Ospedale al Mare and makes its way back to Santa Maria Elisabetta; the B does more or less the same route anticlockwise. In the summer the routes are extended to include popular beaches. The V (*verde*, green) does a shorter route, travelling to the Palazzo del Cinema on the seafront and ending up at via Parri. In summer there's another circular line, the C (*celeste*, light blue), which also travels to the Palazzo del Cinema and back again.

Finally, the No.11, which departs from the Gran Viale opposite the main vaporetto stop also heads down to Alberoni but then continues on to the car ferry across to Pellestrina island. Bike is a good way of getting around the pancake-flat Lido; for bike hire, *see p286.*

TOURIST INFORMATION

From June to September there's a tourist information office at Gran Viale 6A, Lido (041 526 5721/fax 041 529 8720), open 9.30am-1pm, 3-6.30pm daily. **Map** p317 A3.

The Northern Lagoon

San Michele

Halfway between Venice and Murano, this is the island where tourists begin their lagoon visit. For many Venetians, it's the last stop: **San Michele** is the city's cemetery (open Apr-Sept 7.30am-6pm daily, Oct-Mar 7.30am-4pm daily). Early in the morning, *vaporetti* (41 or 42) are packed with Venetians coming over to lay flowers. This is not a morbid spot, though: like Père Lachaise in Paris, it is an elegant city of the dead, with more than one famous resident.

An orderly red-brick wall runs round the whole of the island, with a line of tall cypress trees rising high behind it – the inspiration for Böcklin's famously lugubrious painting *Island of the Dead*. The island was originally just a Franciscan monastery, but during the Napoleonic period the grounds that used to extend behind the church were seconded for burials in an effort to stop unhygienic Venetians digging graves in the *campi* around parish churches. Soon it was the only place to be seen dead in. Most Venetians still want to make that last journey to San Michele, though these days it's more a temporary parking lot than a final resting place: the island reached saturation point long ago, and even after paying through the nose for a plot, families know that after a suitable period – generally around ten years – the bones of their loved ones will be dug up and transferred to an ossuary elsewhere.

Before visiting the cemetery, take a look at the church of **San Michele in Isola** (open 7.30am-12.15pm, 3-4pm daily); turn left after entering the cemetery and pass through the fine cloisters. The view of the façade is particularly striking. Designed by Mauro Codussi in the 1460s, this white building of Istrian stone was Venice's first Renaissance church.

Next to the church is a dignified archway marked by a 15th-century bas-relief of St Michael slaying a dragon with one hand and holding a pair of scales in the other. In the cloisters, staff hand out maps of the cemetery, which are indispensable for celebrity hunts. In the Greek and Russian Orthodox section of the cemetery are the elaborate tomb of Sergei Pavlovich Diaghilev, who introduced the Ballets Russes to Europe, and a simpler monument to the composer Igor Stravinsky and his wife. The Protestant section has a selection of ships' captains and passengers who ended their days in *La Serenissima*, plus the simple graves of Ezra Pound and Joseph Brodsky.

There's a rather sad children's section and a corner dedicated to the city's gondoliers, their tombs decorated with carvings and statues of gondolas. Visit the cemetery on the *Festa dei morti* – All Souls' Day, 2 November – and the vaporetto is free, but seriously packed.

Murano

Map p319

After San Michele, the number 42 or 41 vaporetto continues to **Murano**, one of the larger and more populous islands (lines LN and 13 also put in here, but only at the Faro stop). In the 16th and 17th centuries, when it was a world centre of glass production and a decadent resort for pleasure-seeking Venetians, Murano had a population of more than 30,000. These days fewer than 5,000 people live here, and many of the glass workers commute from the mainland.

Murano owes its fame to the decision taken in 1291 to transfer all of Venice's glass furnaces to the island because of a fear of fire in the main city. Their products were soon sold all over Europe. The secrets of glass were jealously guarded within the island: any glass maker leaving Murano was proclaimed a traitor. Even today there is no official glass school and the delicate skills of blowing and flamework are only learned by apprenticeship to one of the glass masters. At first sight Murano looks close to being ruined by glass tourism. Dozens of 'guides' swoop on visitors as they pile off the ferry, to whisk them off on tours of furnaces. Even if you head off on your own, you'll find yourself on fondamenta dei Vetrai, a snipers' alley of shops selling glass knick-knacks, most of which are made far from Murano. But there *are* some serious glass makers on the island and even the tackiest showroom usually has one or two gems. *See p144* **Murano glass**.

There's more to Murano, however, than glass. At the far end of fondamenta dei Vetrai is the nondescript façade of the 14th-century parish church of **San Pietro Martire** (*see p144*), which holds important works of art including Bellini's impressive altarpiece triptych.

Beyond the church, Murano's Canal Grande is spanned by Ponte Vivarini, an unattractive, 19th-century iron bridge. Before crossing, it is worth looking at the Gothic Palazzo Da Mula, just to the left of the bridge; this splendid, 15th-century building has been recently restored and transformed into council offices. In the morning you can stroll through its courtyard, which contains a monumental carved Byzantine arch from an earlier (12th- or 13th-century) building.

On the other side of the bridge, a right turn takes you along fondamenta Cavour; 200 metres further along, it veers sharply to the left,

Sightseeing

becoming fondamenta Giustinian. The 17th-century Palazzo Giustinian, situated far from tacky chandeliers and fluorescent clowns, is the **Museo dell'Arte Vetrario** (*see below*), the best place to learn about the history of glass. Just beyond this is Murano's greatest architectural treasure: the 12th-century basilica of **Santi Maria e Donato** (*see p145*), with its apse towards the canal.

Return to Ponte Vivarini and walk to the end of fondamenta Sebastiano Venier. Here, the church of Santa Maria degli Angeli (open Sun 11am) backs on to the convent where Casanova conducted one of his most torrid affairs, with a libertine nun named Maria Morosoni.

Museo dell'Arte Vetrario

Fondamenta Giustinian 8 (041 739 586). Vaporetto Museo. **Open** *Apr-Oct* 10am-5pm Mon, Tue, Thur-Sun. *Nov-Mar* 10am-4pm Mon, Tue, Thur-Sun. **Admission** €4; €2.50 concessions (*see also p67* **Musei Civici Veneziani**). **No credit cards.** **Map** p319 C2.

Housed in beautiful Palazzo Giustinian, built in the late 17th century for the bishop of Torcello, the museum has a huge collection of Murano glass. As well as the famed chandeliers, which only made their appearance in the 18th century, there are ruby-red beakers, opaque lamps and delicate Venetian *perle* – glass beads that were used in trade and commerce all over the world from the time of Marco Polo. One of the earliest pieces is the 15th-century Barovier marriage cup, decorated with portraits of the bride and groom. In one room is a collection of 17th-century oil lamps in the shapes of animals, some of which are uncannily Disney-like. On the ground floor is a good collection of Roman glass ware from near Zara on the Istrian peninsula.

San Pietro Martire

Fondamenta dei Vetrai (041 739 704). Vaporetto Colonna or Faro. **Open** 9am-noon, 3-6pm Mon-Sat; 3-6pm Sun. **Map** p319 B2.

Behind its unspectacular façade, San Pietro Martire conceals an important work by Giovanni Bellini, backed by a marvellous landscape: *The Virgin and

Murano glass

Murano has been the capital of glass since 1291. In that year Venice's rulers banished all glass furnaces to this island to avert the kind of conflagrations that would regularly devastate swathes of what was then a largely wooden city. Over the following centuries the island refining its particular traditional craft. Its vases, chandeliers, mirrors and drinking vessels were shipped over the known world by Venice's great merchant fleet.

Nowadays the assault of glass-blowing hustlers coupled with shop windows packed with glass *objets* of dubious taste and even more dubious origin make it hard to see the island's speciality as a noble art. But behind the tack, Murano remains a special place where glass-making techniques handed down over the centuries are still jealously preserved.

Murano glass can be divided into medium-to-large furnace-made pieces (blown glass, sculpture and lamps) and smaller pieces (beads and animals) fashioned from sticks of coloured glass in the heat of a gas jet. Once made, these objects may be engraved or patterned with silver; multi-piece objects need assembling... all of which keeps a healthy proportion of Murano's population employed.

But unless you have your wits about you, you may never get beyond shops and warehouses packed with glass freshly shipped from the Far East. Most hotel porters and concierges in central Venice have agreements of some kind with these emporia: don't expect disinterested advice on where to go. Tourist-trade Murano outlets with 'authentic' furnaces being used by 'authentic' glass-blowers rarely sell the few articles you'll see produced, whatever the salesmen tell you. Glass shops range from the excellent to the downright rip-off: labels proclaiming '*vetro di Murano*' mean very little ('*vetro artistico di Murano*' is meant to offer a firmer guarantee, though some of the best producers refuse to bow to this, believing that their reputation is all the guarantee they need to offer).

So, how do you go about making sure you get the real thing? One thing to remember: real Murano glass is fiendishly expensive. There's no such thing as a real €30 vase, or a genuine €5 wine glass... at those prices you can be sure you're taking home something 'authentically' Chinese. If you want genuine without paying much for it, you'll have to resort to the odd glass bead. Moreover, the best workplaces don't allow tourists to gawp, though in some cases you will be able to peer through an open front gate. And, occasionally, they'll invite you in if you really intend to purchase. If you're after a true Murano glass experience, just be brave: ring that doorbell and see if they'll humour you and allow you a peek.

Child Enthroned with St Mark, St Augustine and Doge Agostino Barbarigo. There is also a Tintoretto *Baptism*, two works by Veronese and assistants (mainly the latter) and an ornate altarpiece (*Deposition*) by Salviati that is lit up by the early morning sun. Opening hours are very fluid. The sacristy (offering of €1.50) contains remarkable wood-carvings from the 17th century and a small museum of reliquaries and other ornaments.

Santi Maria e Donato

Campo San Donato (041 739 056). Vaporetto Museo. **Open** 8.30am-noon, 4-6pm Mon-Sat; 4-6pm Sun. **Map** p319 C1.

Though altered by over-enthusiastic 19th-century restorers, the exterior of this church is a classic of the Veneto-Byzantine style, with an ornate blind portico on the rear of the apse. Inside is a richly coloured mosaic floor, laid down in 1140 at the same time as the floor of the basilica di San Marco, with floral and animal motifs. Above, a Byzantine apse mosaic of the Virgin looms out of the darkness surrounded by a field of gold.

Burano & Mazzorbo

Map p319

Mazzorbo, the long island before Burano, is a haven of peace, rarely visited by tourists. It is worth getting off here just for the sake of the quiet walk along the canal and then across the long wooden bridge that connects Mazzorbo to Burano. The view from the bridge across the lagoon to Venice is stunning, and there's always a chance you'll have it to yourself.

Mazzorbo was settled around the tenth century. When it became clear that Venice itself had got the upper hand, most of the population simply dismantled their houses brick by brick, transported them by boat to Venice, and rebuilt them there. Today Mazzorbo is a lazy place of small farms with a pleasant walk to the 14th-century Gothic church of Santa Caterina (opening times vary), whose wonky tower still has its original bell dating from 1318 – one of the oldest in Europe. Winston Churchill, a keen

Alfredo Barbini

Fondamenta Venier 44-8 (041 739 270). Vaporetto Venier or Museo. **Open** 8am-noon, 2-6pm Mon-Fri; by appointment Sat, Sun. **Credit** AmEx, MC, V. **Map** p319 B1.

If you get lucky, you'll find master glass-maker Alfredo (now in his 90s) himself holding court in this showroom where many of his classic designs are still on show, alongside more modern ones by his son Flavio. The showroom is situated inside glorious Palazzo Correr.

Berengo Fine Arts

Fondamenta dei Vetrai 109A (041 739 453/ www.berengo.com). Vaporetto Colonna or Faro. **Open** 10am-5.50pm daily. **Credit** AmEx, DC, MC, V. **Map** p319 B2.

Adriano Berengo commissions international artists to design brilliantly coloured scuptures – in glass, of course.

Cesare Toffolo

Fondamenta Vetrai 67A (041 736 460/ www.toffolo.com). Vaporetto Colonna. **Open** 10am-6pm daily. Closed Jan. **Credit** AmEx, DC, MC, V. **Map** p319 B2.

In this shop along thronging fondamenta Vetrai, Cesare Toffolo uses glass sticks and a gas flame to create intricate miniatures of Venetian classic designs: cups, vases and even chandeliers.

Davide Penso

Shop and workshop: riva Longa 48; gallery riva Longa 4 (041 527 4634/www.artstudio murano.com). Vaporetto Museo. **Open** 9.30am-1.30pm, 2.30-5.30pm daily. Closed Jan. **Credit** AmEx, DC, MC, V. **Map** p319 B2.

The Vetro Artistico® Murano trademark, a safeguard for *Made in Italy*.

Set up by the Veneto Region in 1994, the Vetro Artistico® Murano trademark, administered by the Promovetro Consortium, certifies the origin of glass products produced on Murano and guarantees the consumer's purchase as authentic. The mark is an essential safeguard of one of the symbols of *Made in Italy*.

Since 2002, the trademark has been present on artistic glass that respects the specific characteristics of the Murano tradition and can only be used by affiliated companies who affix it directly to the object. The mark represents the *borsella*, a traditional tool for shaping glass, and includes the code of the manufacturing company. It prevents counterfeiting as it cannot be removed without breaking into fragments.

Today there are more than 50 affiliated companies and their products can be bought in all sales outlets displaying the trademark sticker.

Always ask for goods bearing the original trademark. It's the only way to be certain that you're buying genuine Murano glass.

▶

amateur painter, set up his easel here more than once after World War II. Facing Burano is an area of attractive, modern, low-cost housing, in shades of lilac, grey and green, designed by the architect Giancarlo De Carlo.

One could almost believe that they invented the adjective picturesque to describe **Burano**. Together with its lace, its multicoloured houses make it a magnet for tourists armed with cameras. The locals are traditionally either fishermen or lace makers, though there are fewer and fewer of the latter, despite the best efforts of the island's **Scuola di Merletti** (Lace School, *see p147*) to pass on the skills to the younger generations.

The street leading from the main quay throbs with souvenir shops selling lace, lace and more lace – much of it machine-made in Taiwan. But Burano is big enough for the visitor to meander through its quiet backstreets and avoid a lace overload. It was in Burano that **Carnevale** (*see p202*) was revived in the 1970s; the modest

celebrations here are still far more authentically joyful than the antics of masked tourists cramming piazza San Marco.

Fishermen have lived on Burano since the seventh century. According to local lore they painted their houses different colours so that they could recognise them when fishing out on the lagoon – though in fact only a tiny proportion of the island's houses can actually be seen from the lagoon. Whatever the reason, the *buranelli* still go to great efforts to decorate their houses, and social life centres on the *fondamente* where the men repair nets or tend to their boats moored in the canal below, while their wives – at least in theory – make lace.

Lace was first produced in Burano in the 15th century, originally by nuns, but was quickly picked up by fishermen's wives and daughters. So skilful were the local lace makers that in the 17th century many were paid handsomely to work in the Alençon lace ateliers in Normandy. Today most work is

▶ Murano glass (continued)

Davide Penso makes and shows exquisite glass jewellery. His own creations are all one-off or limited edition pieces with designs drawn from nature: zebra-striped, mother-of-pearl or crocodile-skinned.

Fratelli Barbini
Calle Bertolini 36 (041 739 777). Vaporetto Colonna or Faro. **Open** *8am-6pm Mon-Fri.* **Credit** *AmEx, DC, MC, V.* **Map** *p319 A2.*
There's only one *fratello* (brother), Guido, left to carry on his family craft: mirror-making. In this workshop he silvers, engraves and mounts them according to long-running traditions.

Galleria Regina
Riva Longa 25A (041 739 202/ www.galleriaregina.com). Vaporetto Museo. **Open** *9.30am-5.30pm daily.* **Credit** *AmEx, MC, V.* **Map** *p319 B2.*
Not a glass shop, but a gallery... but this being Murano, the Regina shows mostly art in glass: sculptures, mosaics and stained glass windows mix with vases and glasses by contemporary designers.

Galliano Ferro
Fondamenta Colleoni 6 (041 739 477/www.gallianoferro.it). Vaporetto Faro. **Open** *by appointment only.* **No credit cards. Map** *p319 B2.*

Inspired by 18th-century Venetian classics, Ferro's rich, vibrant and intricate works are some of Murano's most sought-after models. There are early 20th-century designs too.

Luigi Camozzo
Fondamenta Venier 3 (041 736 875). Vaporetto Venier or Museo. **Open** *10am-6pm Mon-Fri; by appointment Sat, Sun.* **Credit** *AmEx, DC, MC, V.* **Map** *p319 B1.*
It would be over-simplifying things to describe Luigi Camozzo as a glass-engraver. Using a variety of different tools, he carves, sculpts and inscribes wonderfully soft, natural bas-

done on commission, though interested parties will have to get to know one of the lace makers in person, as the co-operative that used to represent the old ladies closed down in 1995.

The busy main square of Burano is named after the island's most famous son, Baldassare Galuppi, a 17th-century composer who collaborated with Carlo Goldoni on a number of operas and who was the subject of a poem by Robert Browning. The square is a good place for sipping a glass of prosecco. Across from the lace museum is the church of San Martino (open 8am-noon, 3-7pm daily), containing an early Tiepolo *Crucifixion* and, in the chapel to the right of the chancel, three small paintings by the 15th-century painter Giovanni Mansueti; the *Flight into Egypt* presents the Holy Family amid an imaginative menagerie of beasts and birds. There's a lively morning fish market (Tue-Sat) on the fondamenta della Pescheria.

Scuola di Merletti

Piazza B Galuppi 187 (041 730 034). Vaporetto LN. **Open** *Apr-Oct* 10am-5pm Mon, Wed-Sun. *Nov-Mar* 10am-4pm Mon, Wed-Sun. **Admission** €4; €2.50 concessions (*see also p67* **Musei Civici Veneziani**). **No credit cards. Map** p319 C2.
In a series of rooms with painted wooden beams are cases full of elaborate examples of lace work from the 17th century onwards; aficionados will have fun spotting the various stitches, such as the famous *punto burano*. Many of the older exhibits change every few months for conservation reasons, but if it's on display look out for the devout intricacy of the 17th-century altar cloth decorated with the Mysteries of the Rosary.

There are fans, collars and parasols, and some of the paper pattern-sheets that lace makers use. Unfortunately, the school that gives the museum its name is now virtually defunct, although occasional courses are offered by some of the older generation of Burano lace makers, who can often be seen at work in a corner of the museum. You can buy items of handmade lace at the scuola, too.

reliefs into glass. Drop by and you may even catch him in action.

Manin 56

Fondamenta Manin 56 (041 527 5392). Vaporetto Faro. **Open** 10am-6pm daily. Closed Jan. **Credit** AmEx, DC, MC, V. **Map** p319 B2.
This shop sells modern (though slightly staid) lines in glassware and vases from prestigious houses such as Salviati and Vivarini.

Marina e Susanna Sent

Fondamenta Serenella 20 (041 527 4665). Vaporetto Colonna. **Open** 10am-5pm Mon-Fri. **Credit** AmEx, DC, MC, V. **Map** p319 A2.
In the Sent sisters' Murano workshop you'll find clean, modern jewellery in glass in interesting counterpoise with innovative jewellery in other materials, including wood, coral, paper and rubber. It's always best to call ahead and make an appointment.

Murano collezioni

Fondamenta Manin 1C-D (041 736 272). Vaporetto Colonna or Faro. **Open** 10.30am-5.30pm Mon-Sat. Closed 1wk Jan. **Credit** AmEx, DC, MC, V. **Map** p319 B2.
This shop sells pieces by some of the lagoon's most respected producers, including Carlo Moretti, Barovier e Toso, and Venini. Room to move about and good lighting will help you make your choice.

Rossana e Rossana

Riva Lunga 11 (041 527 4076/www.ro-e-ro. com). Vaporetto Museo. **Open** 10am-6pm daily. **Credit** AmEx, MC, V. **Map** p319 B2.
The place to come for traditional Venetian glass, from filigree pieces to Veronese vases and elegant goblets from models popular in the early years of last century – all produced by master glass-maker Davide Fuin.

Seguso Viro

Fondamenta Venier 29 (041 527 5353/ www.segusoviro.com). Vaporetto Venier or Museo. **Open** *May-Oct* 10.30am-5.30pm Mon-Sat. *Nov-Apr* 11am-4pm Mon-Sat. **Credit** AmEx, MC, V. **Map** p319 B1.
Giampaolo Seguso comes from a long line of Venetian glass-makers. His modern blown glass is enhanced by experiments working around Murano traditions.

Venini

Fondamenta Vetrai 47-50 (041 273 7204/ www.venini.com). Vaporetto Colonna. **Open** 9.30am-5.30pm Mon-Sat. Closed 2wks Aug. **Credit** AmEx, DC, MC, V. **Map** p319 B2.
Venini was the biggest name in Murano glass for much of the 20th century, and remains in the forefront. Classic designs are joined by more innovative pieces, including a selection designed by major international glass artists.

San Francesco del Deserto

From behind the church of San Martino on Burano there is a view across the lagoon to the idyllic monastery island of **San Franceso del Deserto**. The island, with its 4,000 cypress trees, is inhabited by a small community of Franciscan monks. Getting there can be quite a challenge. If you take the water taxi from Burano, expect to pay at least €50 for the return ride. A better, and perhaps cheaper, option is to ask one of the local fishermen to give you a lift. They are usually willing to do so for a smallish fee – perhaps €25 for the return trip.

The other-worldly monk who shepherds visitors around will tell the story (only in Italian) of how the island was St Francis's first stop in Europe on his journey back from the Holy Land in 1220. He planted his stick, it grew into a pine and birds flew in to sing for him; there are certainly plenty of them in evidence in the cypress-packed gardens today. The medieval monastery – all warm stone and cloistered calm – is about as far as you can get from the worldly bustle of the Rialto.

Convento di San Francesco del Deserto

041 528 6863/www.isola-sanfrancescodeldeserto.it.
Open 9-11am, 3-5pm Tue-Sat; 3-5pm Sun.
Admission by voluntary donation.

Torcello

This sprawling, marshy island is where the history of Venice began. At low tide, you could well imagine yourself in the Fens, and there are certainly as many mosquitoes.

Torcello today is a rural backwater with a resident population of less than 20; each time an inhabitant moves away for the bright lights of Burano or Mazzorbo, it is headline news in the Venice press. It's difficult to believe that in the 14th century more than 20,000 people lived here. This was the first settlement in the lagoon, founded in the fifth century by the citizens of the Roman town of Altino on the mainland. Successive waves of emigration from Altino were sparked off by barbarian invasions, first by Attila and his Huns, and, in the seventh century, by the Lombards. But Torcello's dominance of the lagoon did not last: Venice itself was found to be more salubrious (malaria was rife on Torcello) and more easily defendable. Even the bishop of Torcello chose to live on Murano, in the palace that now houses the glass museum (*see p143*). But past decline is present charm, and rural Torcello is a great antidote to the pedestrian traffic jams around San Marco.

From the ferry jetty the *campanile* (*see below*) can already be made out; to get there, simply follow the main canal through the island. Halfway down the canal is the ponte del Diavolo (one of only two ancient bridges in the lagoon without a parapet), where there is a simple *osteria* called Al Ponte del Diavolo (041 730 401; lunch only except Fri and Sat; closed Mon and Dec-Jan) which is known for its reliable cooking; however, the prices are a little higher than the rustic simplicity of the *osteria* might suggest.

Across the bridge a path leads to a private palazzo in a well-tended garden where extravagant parties are occasionally held.

Torcello's main square has some desultory souvenir stalls, a small but interesting **Museo dell'Estuario** (*see p149*) with archaeological finds from around the lagoon, a battered stone seat known somewhat arbitrarily as Attila's throne, and two extraordinary churches.

The 11th-century church of Santa Fosca (open Apr-Oct 10.30am-5.30pm daily, Nov-Mar 10am-5pm daily, free) looks somewhat like a miniature version of Istanbul's Santa Sophia, more Byzantine than European with its Greek-cross plan and external colonnade; its bare interior allows the perfect geometry of the space to come to the fore. Next door to Santa Fosca is the imposing cathedral of **Santa Maria Assunta** (*see p149*).

By the churches, the Locanda Cipriani (*see p169*) is rated as one of Venice's top restaurants, with prices to match. The three big Cipriani concerns in Venice – the Hotel Cipriani (*see p64*), Harry's Bar (run by Arrigo Cipriani, son of the founder; *see p171*) and the Locanda Cipriani (run by Arrigo's sister Carla) have no business links; in fact, all have been involved in a long-running legal battle for the right to use the name 'Cipriani'.

A cumulative ticket for the basilica, *campanile* and Museo dell'Estuario is available at the sights themselves and costs €8 (€5.50 groups) or €5.50 (€3 groups) for the basilica and museum. No credit cards are accepted.

The ferry (line T) from Burano to Torcello leaves every half-hour during the day; the crossing takes five minutes.

Campanile di Torcello

041 730 119. **Open** *Apr-Oct* 10.30am-5pm daily. *Nov-Mar* 10am-4.15pm daily. **Admission** €3. **No credit cards.**
The view of the lagoon from the top of the *campanile* was memorably described by Ruskin: 'Far as the eye can reach, a waste of wild sea moor, of a lurid ashen grey.' And he concluded with the elegaic words: 'Mother and daughter, you behold them both in their widowhood, Torcello and Venice.' There is no lift, just a stiff walk up steep ramps.

Museo dell'Estuario

Palazzo del Consiglio (041 730 761). **Open** *Apr-Oct* 10.30am-5pm Tue-Sun. *Nov-Mar* 10am-4.30pm Tue-Sun. **Admission** €3. **No credit cards**.

A small but worthwhile collection of sculptures and archaeological finds from the cathedral and elsewhere in Torcello. Among the exhibits on the ground floor are late 12th-century fragments of mosaic from the apse of Santa Maria dell'Assunta, and two of the *bocche di leone* (lions' mouths) where citizens with grudges could post their denunciations. Upstairs are Greco-Byzantine icons, painted panels, bronze seals and pottery fragments, and an exquisite carved ivory statuette of an embracing couple from the beginning of the 15th century.

Santa Maria Assunta

041 270 2464. **Open** *Apr-Oct* 10.30am-5.30pm daily. *Nov-Mar* 10am-4.30pm daily. **Admission** €3 (€1 for audioguide). **No credit cards**.

Dating from 638, the basilica is the oldest building on the lagoon. The interior has an elaborate 11th-century mosaic floor,.but the main draws are the vivid mosaics on the vault and walls, which range in date from the ninth century to the end of the 12th. The apse has a simple but stunning mosaic of a *Madonna and Child* on a plain gold background, while the other end of the cathedral is dominated by a huge mosaic of the *Last Judgement.* The theological rigour and narrative complexity of this huge composition suggest comparisons with the *Divine Comedy,* which Dante was writing at about the same time, but the anonymous mosaicists of Torcello were even more concerned than him with striking fear into the hearts of their audience.

Sant'Erasmo & Vignole

Sant'Erasmo (served by vaporetto 13) is the best-kept secret of the lagoon: larger than Venice, but with a tiny population that contents itself with growing most of the vegetables eaten in *La Serenissima* – on Rialto market stalls the sign '*San Rasmo*' is a mark of quality. Venetians refer to the islanders of Sant'Erasmo as *i matti* ('the crazies') because of their shallow gene pool – everybody seems to be called Vignotto or Zanella. There are cars on this island, but as they are only used to drive the few miles from house to boat and back, few are in top-notch condition, a state of affairs favoured by the fact that the island does not have a single policeman. It also lacks a doctor, pharmacy and high school, but there is a supermarket and a primary school (14 pupils this year). There are also two restaurants: Ca' Vignotto (via Forti 71, 041 528 5329, average €25-€30, closed Tue and mid Dec to mid Jan), where bookings are essential, and a fishermen's bar-trattoria – Ai Tedeschi (open 9am-11pm all year around) – hidden away on a small sandy beach by the

Forte Massimiliano. This latter is a moat-surrounded Austrian fort that has recently been restored. Before restoration it was used by a local farmer to store his tools; it now has a brand-new metal gate barring access and is only open at weekends (Apr-Sept 10.30am-5.30 Sat & Sun; Oct, Feb-Mar 11am-4pm Sat & Sun; Nov-Jan 11am-3pm Sat & Sun). It occasionally hosts exhibitions by local painters.

The main attraction of the island lies in the beautiful country landscapes and lovely walks past traditional Veneto farmhouses, through vineyards and fields of artichokes and asparagus – a breath of fresh air after all the urban crowding of Venice. For those wanting to get around more swiftly, bicycles can be hired from the guesthouse Lato Azzurro, a ten-minute walk southwards from the vaporetto stop Capannone (041 523 0642): €3 for an hour, €5 for half a day, €8 for the whole day; no credit cards. By the main vaporetto stop (Chiesa) is the 20th-century church (on the site of an earlier one founded before 1000; opening hours vary). Over the entrance door is a gruesome painting, attributed to Domenico Tintoretto, of the martyrdom of St Erasmus, who had his intestines wound out of his body on a windlass. The resemblance of a windlass to a capstan resulted in St Erasmus becoming the patron saint of sailors.

If you're around on the first Sunday in October, don't miss the *Festa del mosto,* held to inaugurate the first pressing of new wine. This is perhaps the only chance you'll ever get to witness – or even participate in – *gara del bisato*: a game in which an eel is dropped into

Museo del Mancomio – the asylum museum. *See p150.*

a tub of water blackened by squid ink. Contestants have to plunge their heads into the tub and attempt to catch the eel with their teeth.

Opposite the Capannone vaporetto stop is the tiny island of Lazzaretto Nuovo. Get off here at the weekend, shout across, and with luck a boat might row over to get you. In the 15th century the island was fortified as a customs deposit and military prison; during the 1576 plague outbreak it became a quarantine centre. It is now a research centre for the archaeologists of the Archeo Club di Venezia, who are excavating its ancient remains, including a church that may date back to the sixth century.

The number 13 vaporetto also stops at the smaller island of **Vignole**, where there is a medieval chapel dedicated to St Erosia.

The Southern Lagoon

The southern part of the lagoon between Venice, the Lido and the mainland has 14 small islands, a few of which are still inhabited, though most are out of bounds to tourists. **La Grazia** was for years a quarantine hospital but the structure has now been closed. The huge **San Clemente**, originally a lunatic asylum and later a home for abandoned cats, has been turned into one of the lagoon's plushest hotels.

San Servolo and **San Lazzaro** (*for both see below*) are both served by the same vaporetto (number 20) and both are well worth visiting. From the 18th century until 1978 San Servolo was Venice's mental hospital (in his poem *Julian and Maddalo* Shelley describes a visit that he paid there with Byron); it is now home to Venice International University (*see p300*). In May 2006 the **Museo del Manicomio di San Servolo** (San Servolo Asylum museum; **photo** p139) was inaugurated and can be visited on a guided tour. The museum reveals the different ways in which mental diseases have been treated over the years; there are not only examples of the more or less brutal methods of restraint (chains, strait-jackets, handcuffs) but early examples of such treatment as hydro-massage and electrotherapy. One wall is devoted entirely to a series of 19th- and early 20th-century photographs of patients. The tour ends in the reconstructed 18th-century pharmacy, which relied partly on medicines obtained from some of the exotic plants grown on the island. After the tour it is possible to visit the extensive and charming gardens of the island.

A further five minutes on the number 20 will take you to the island of **San Lazzaro degli**

Armeni. Guided tours of this island are given every afternoon for visitors arriving on the 3.10pm boat from San Zaccaria.

A black-cloaked Armenian priest meets the boat and takes visitors on a detailed tour of the **Monastero Mechitarista**. This tiny island is a global point of reference for Armenia's Catholic minority, visited and supported by Armenians from Italy and abroad. Near the entrance stand the printing presses that helped to distribute Armenian literature all over the world for 200 years. They are now silent, with the monastery's retro line in dictionaries and liturgical texts farmed out to a modern press.

Originally a leper colony, in 1717 the island was presented by the doge to an Armenian abbot called Mekhitar, who was on the run from the Turkish invasion of the Peloponnese. There had been an Armenian community in Venice since the 11th century, centring on the tiny Santa Croce degli Armeni church, just round the corner from the piazza San Marco, but the construction of this church and monastery on the former leper colony made Venice a world centre of Armenian culture. The monastery was the only one in the whole of Venice to be spared the Napoleonic axe that did away with so many convents and monasteries: the emperor had a soft spot for Armenians and claimed this was an academic rather than a religious institute.

The tour takes in the cloisters and the church, rebuilt after a fire in 1883. The museum and the modern library contain 40,000 priceless books and manuscripts, and a bizarre collection of gifts donated over the years by visiting Armenians, ranging from Burmese prayer books to an Egyptian mummy.

The island's most famous student was Lord Byron, who used to take a break from his more earthly pleasures in Venice and row over three times a week to learn Armenian (as he found that his 'mind wanted something craggy to break upon') with the monks. He helped the monks to publish an Armenian-English grammar, although by his own confession he never got beyond the basics of the language. You can buy a completed version of this, plus a number of period maps and an illustrated children's Armenian grammar, in the shop just inside the monastery gate.

San Lazzaro degli Armeni – Monastero Mechitarista
041 526 0104. **Open** 3.20-5pm daily for guided visits. **Admission** €6; €3 concessions. **No credit cards.**

San Servolo – Museo del Manicomio
041 524 0119. **Open** weekends for guided visits; pre-booking essential. **Admission** free.

Eat, Drink, Shop

Un Mondo diVino. *See p175.*

Eating Out

An influx of foodies is pushing Venice's restaurant standards higher.

More and more it's the humble neighbourhood *bacaro* (a sort of wine-oriented trattoria) that's the salvation of the Venetian dining scene. With a few exceptions, proper restaurants charge more than the Italian average for less quality; there's little incentive to shoot for culinary excellence when you know that 95 per cent of your guests will drop in once and once only. At the lower end of the market, however, a faithful clientele of locals keeps standards high. There may be only 65,000 Venetian residents left in the *centro storico*, but both they and the small army of day workers who come across from the mainland are demanding gourmets.

With their blackened beams and rickety wooden tables, *bacari* (accent on the first syllable) are often hidden down backstreets or in quiet *campielli*. Here locals crowd the bar, swiftly downing a glass of wine (*un'ombra*) between work and home, and taking the edge off their appetites with one of the *cicheti* (snacks) that line the counter. The etiquette of *cicheti* is fairly straightforward. Once you've taken up your position at the bar and ordered a glass, just reach for the snacks and start eating. Keep tabs on how many you've consumed – though the barman should keep an accurate count. If you sit down at a table and order from the menu – which will include more abundant portions of those *cicheti*, plus a few hot dishes – expect prices to be more in line with the norm.

The lagoon city has a long and glorious culinary tradition based on fresh seafood, game and vegetables, backed up by northern Italy's three main carbohydrate fixes: pasta, risotto rice and polenta. Outside of a handful of top-notch (and top-dollar) hotel restaurants, you will invariably eat better here if you go with the flow of *la cucina veneta*. This requires a certain spirit of open-minded experimentation. Not everybody has eaten *granseola* (spider crab) before, or *garusoli* (sea snails) or *canoce* (mantis shrimps), but Venice is definitely the place to try these marine curios – plus market garden rarities like *castraure* (baby artichokes) and *fiori di zucca* (courgette flowers).

❶ Purple numbers given in this chapter correspond to the location of each restaurant as marked on the street maps. *See pp317-328.*

La Maison de Laurent. *See p156.*

Unfortunately, eating locally does not necessarily mean eating cheaply. A double pricing policy applies in many local places, with one tariff for Venetians and another (the one given on the menu, if it exists) for tourists. There is not much you can do about this unofficial congestion charge, but if you are careful, and don't require the full three-course experience, it's still possible to eat very well on the lagoon for €25 a head, including house wine, especially at lunchtime.

RULES OF ENGAGEMENT

In more rustic eateries, menus are often recited out loud, with off-the-cuff English translations, though these can be approximate. If you are unsure of the price of something, just ask. If there is a printed menu, note that fish is often quoted by weight – generally by the *etto* (100g).

Steer well clear of those restaurants – mainly around San Marco – that employ sharply dressed waiters to stand outside and persuade passing tourists to come in: an immediate recipe for rip-off prices and mediocre fare. Always ask for a written *conto* (bill) at the end of the meal, as it is, in theory, illegal to leave without one.

Finally, bear in mind that there are two timescales for eating in Venice. The more upmarket restaurants follow standard Italian practice, serving lunch from around 1pm to 3pm and dinner from 7.30pm until at least 10pm. But *bacari* and neighbourhood *trattorie* tend to follow Venetian workers' rhythms, with lunch running from noon to 2pm and dinner from 6.30pm to 9pm. In other words, if you want to eat cheaply, eat early.

WHAT'S ON THE PLATE (AND IN THE GLASS)

A writhing, glistening variety of seafood swims from the stalls of the Rialto and Chioggia markets into local kitchens it's not always cheap, but tfor dedicated pescivores, there are few better stamping grounds in the whole of Italy. To make sense of the bewildering variety of sea creatures, *see p160* **The menu**.

The once-strong local tradition of creative ways with meat is kept alive in a handful of restaurants (among them **Ai Gondolieri**, *see p165* and **Vini da Arturo**, *see p155*) and one marvellous trattoria, **Dalla Marisa** (*see p161*); it can also be found in bar-counter *cicheti* like *nervetti* (veal cartilage) and *cotechino* (spicy pig's intestine parcels filled with cuts of pork).

Vegetarians may be horrified to find that there is not a single veggie restaurant in the city. But Venetian cuisine relies heavily on seasonal vegetables (including aubergine, courgette, tomato, radicchio and exquisite little artichokes known as *castrauri*), so it is quite easy to eat a meat-free meal.

There is something of the Spanish tapas mentality about the Venetian approach to meals: not only in the tasty *cicheti* lined up on *bacaro* counters, but in the way the *antipasti* (hors d'oeuvres) often engulf the whole meal. If you nodded vigorously when the waiter suggested 'one or two' seafood *antipasti*, you may start to regret it when the fifth plate arrives – but it is perfectly OK to just eat a plate of pasta afterwards, or to skip to the *secondo*, or dessert: flexibility is the keyword.

Except in the more upmarket restaurants and one or two born-again *bacari*, wines will mostly be local. Luckily, the wine-growing area that stretches from the Veneto north-east to Friuli is, after Tuscany and Piedmont, one of Italy's strongest, with good whites like Tocai and Soave backed up by solid reds like Valpolicella and cabernet franc (*see p166* **Wines of the North-East**). This means that even in humbler establishments the house wine is usually drinkable and often surprisingly refined.

PIZZERIE
Venice has its fair share of pizza joints, though the standard's not particularly high; still, prices in *pizzerie* remain reasonably low, so they are a good standby between more expensive meals.

In the rest of Italy, *pizzerie* are generally open only in the evening; tourist demand, though, means that most Venetian pizza emporia serve the doughy discs at lunch too. Beer, rather than wine, is the traditional accompaniment to pizza.

READING THE LISTINGS
Average restaurant prices are based on a three-course meal for one person, with cover charge and house wine; these may seem high, but remember that it is perfectly OK just to order a pasta course, a salad and a coffee – which may halve the quoted price. For *pizzerie*, average prices are for one pizza, a medium beer and cover charge; a separate average is given if they also do restaurant meals. In the case of *bacari* that

Restaurants

For vegetarians
Alla Zucca (*see p162*); **Bancogiro** (*see p162*); **Cavatappi** (*see p155*); **L'Avogaria** (*see p166*).

For carnivores
Algiubagiò (*see p159*); **Dalla Marisa** (*see p161*); **La Bitta** (*see p166*); **Onigo** (*see p167*); **Vini da Arturo** (*see p155*).

For wine
Alle Testiere (*see p156*); **Cavatappi** (*see p155*); **Muro Vino e Cucina** (*see p163*); **Vini da Gigio** (*see p161*); **Vino Vino** (*see p155*).

For a cheap meal
Alla Palanca (*see p168*); **Alla Zucca** (*see p162*); **Al Diporto** (*see p156*).

For traditional Venetian
Antica Adelaide (*see p159*); **Ca d'Oro – Alla Vedova** (*see p160*); **Vini da Gigio** (*see p161*).

For creative cuisine
Ai Gondolieri (*see p165*); **Alle Testiere** (*see p156*); **Bea Vita** (*see p159*); **Boccadoro** (*see p159*); **Muro Vino e Cucina** (*see p163*); **Vecio Fritolin** (*see p165*).

For parents with small children
Birraria La Corte – outside tables (*165*); **Dai Tosi** (*see p157*).

Eat, Drink, Shop

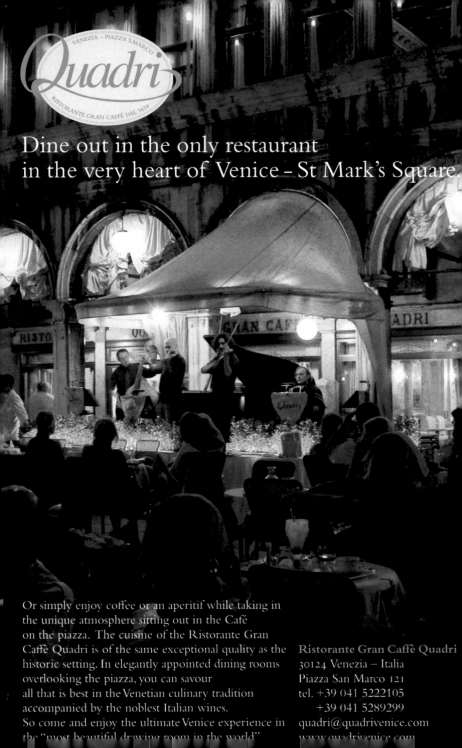

offer both bar snacks and full meals with waiter service, averages are for full sit-down meals; a plate of nibbles at the bar is a whole lot cheaper. For advice on tipping, *see p.302*.

Times given in the listings below refer to the kitchen's opening hours – ie, when it's possible to order food; establishments may keep their doors open well after this.

Bacari that are mainly drinking dens are listed in the **Cafés, Bars & Pasticcerie** chapter (*see pp170-9*). Where food is as much the point as wine, they are listed below.

San Marco

Restaurants & *bacari*

Cavatappi
San Marco 525, campo della Guerra (041 296 0252). Vaporetto Vallaresso. **Meals served** 11am-9pm Tue-Sat; 11am-3pm Sun. Closed Jan. **Average** €25. **Credit** DC, MC, V. **Map** p326 B1 ❶
One of Venice's brightest new wine bars, the clean-cut, modern Cavatappi ('corkscrew') has more than 30 high-quality wines available by the glass from 8.30am to 9pm. Owners Marco and Francesca also offer a small lunch and early dinner menu. The daily changing menu features three pasta dishes (ragù, tomato, and seafood are recurrent toppings) and two *secondi* (eg veal scallops in white wine). After 6pm hot dishes give way to gourmet bar snacks, creative salads and sandwiches – which are also available during the day. The *spritz* (*see p173* **Bar talk**) served here is one of the best in Venice. A 9-11am breakfast menu featuring brunch classics like scrambled eggs with bacon is a recent innovation.

Leon Bianco
San Marco 4153, salizada San Luca (041 522 1180). Vaporetto Rialto. **Open** 8am-10pm Mon-Sat. **Meals served** noon-3pm, 6-9.30pm Mon-Sat. **Average** €16. **No credit cards. Map** p326 B1 ❷
The 'White Lion' has long been one of the few places within pigeon-kicking distance of St Mark's where you can get a decent plate of pasta or risotto for €5, and the brand-new management promises it will stay that way. If you're looking for a snack on the run, they also do great toasted sandwiches.

Osteria San Marco
San Marco 1610, Frezzeria (041 528 5242). Vaporetto Vallaresso. **Meals served** 12.30-11pm Mon-Sat. Closed 2wks Jan, 2wks Aug. **Average** €55. **Credit** MC, V. **Map** p326 B1 ❹
This smart, modern osteria-wine bar on a busy shopping street is a breath of fresh air in the tourist-oriented San Marco area. The four young guys behind the operation are sometimes run off their feet, but they're serious about food and wine and their attention to detail shows through both in the bar-counter selection of snacks and wines by the glass, and in the sit-down menu, which changes regularly

and is based on the freshest local produce. Among the dishes that can be sampled in the long, rustic-minimalist dining area are *capesante con porcini su letto di polenta* (scallops within porcini mushrooms on a bed of polenta), *maialino da latte al mirto* (suckling pig aromatised with myrtle) and *scampi al forno con timo e zucchine* (baked scampi with thyme and courgettes). Prices are on the high side, but you're paying for the area as well as the quality and the mark-up on bottles is commendably low. Note too that this is one of the few places in Venice where you can eat a proper meal in the middle of the afternoon.

Vini da Arturo
San Marco 3656, calle dei Assassini (041 528 6974). Vaporetto Rialto or Sant'Angelo. **Meals served** 12.30-2.30pm, 7.30-11pm Mon-Sat. Closed 2wks after Carnevale; Aug. **Average** €75. **No credit cards. Map** p326 A1 ❺
This tiny place just north of La Fenice has a narrow, panelled interior that has earned it the nickname *il vagone* (the railway carriage). There's not a whiff of fish on the menu, which features the best fillet steak on the lagoon, as well as a few less carnivorous (the owner describes them as 'vegetarian') options – including some creative salad tasters, served as an *antipasto*. For dessert, try the creamy tiramisù, or the chocolate mousse. Service is affable and the quality of food is high, but so it should be at these prices – and note that they don't take credit cards.

Vino Vino
San Marco 2007A, ponte delle Veste (041 241 7688/ www.vinovino.co.it). Vaporetto Vallaresso or Giglio. **Open** 10.30am-2.30am Mon, Wed-Fri, Sun; 10.30am-12.30am Sat. **Average** €50. **No credit cards. Map** p326 A2 ❻
Overlooking a canal near La Fenice, Vino Vino was the city's first authentic wine bar, and it still has one of the best-stocked wine cellars. You can sample vintages from Australia, California and Spain, as well as local crus from the Veneto and Friuli regions. You used to be able to snack at the bar for a reasonable price, but now the menu – which includes the likes of quail with polenta, sautéd veal kidneys and *baccalà alla vicentina* – is only served for sit-down customers.

Castello

Restaurants & *bacari*

Al Covo
Castello 3968, campiello della Pescaria (041 522 3812). Vaporetto Arsenale. **Meals served** 12.45-2.15pm, 7.30-10pm Mon, Tue, Fri-Sun. Closed mid Dec-mid Jan, 2wks Aug. **Average** €80. **Credit** AmEx, MC, V. **Map** p327 E1 ❼
Al Covo is hidden away in a quiet alley behind the riva degli Schiavoni – though it's very much on the international gourmet map. Its high reputation is based on a single-minded dedication to serving the best and freshest seafood – sometimes it's not even cooked, as in the delicious sashimi of Adriatic fish

and crustaceans, served with a splash of Alex Nember's tangy olive oil. Other specialities include *lasagnetta* with mussels and aubergines, and pretty much any of their risottos (they change daily according to what's looked good at the market that morning). The restaurant's charming decor should make it ideal for a romantic dinner, but they take their cuisine so seriously here that it's more for foodies than lovers, and service can be prickly – especially if you commit the cardinal sin of turning up late. Chef/owner Cesare Benelli's American wife, Diane, talks non-Italian-speakers through the daily-changing menu; she is also responsible for the delicious desserts, including a knockout bitter cocoa cake drenched in chilli-spiked chocolate sauce.

Al Diporto

Sant'Elena 25, calle Cengio (041 528 5978). Vaporetto Sant'Elena. **Meals served** noon-2pm, 7.30-10pm Tue-Sun. Average €30. **Credit** MC, V. **Map** p328 B4 ❽

We were in two minds about whether to put Al Diporto in this guide, as there are few places left in Venice that are quite so authentic. But as long as you go in very small groups and only speak Italian we won't regret sharing our secret. Actually, its out-of-the-way location helps to limit the tourist hordes: best advice is to get off the boat at Sant'Elena – the leafy residential neighbourhood beyond Giardini – and ask. Once there, grab an outside table or dive into the basic but cheerful interior and order the spaghetti al Diporto (with seafood), *schie* (grey shrimps) with polenta, and their *pièce de resistance*, a magnificent *fritto misto* (mixed seafood fry-up). Come early, and don't tell your friends.

Alle Testiere

Castello 5801, calle del Mondo Novo (041 522 7220). Vaporetto Rialto. **Meals served** noon-2pm, 7-10.30pm Tue-Sat. Closed last wk Dec; 2wks Jan; last wk July; 3wks Aug. **Average** €60. **Credit** MC, V. **Map** p322 C5 ❾

One of the great success stories of recent years, this tiny restaurant is today one of the hottest culinary tickets in Venice. There are so few seats (22, to be precise) that they do two sittings each evening; booking for the later one (at 9pm) will ensure a more relaxed meal. Bruno, the cook, offers creative variations on Venetian seafood; the *caparossoli* (local clams) sautéed in ginger and the John Dory fillet sprinkled with aromatic herbs in citrus sauce are two mouth-watering examples. Sommelier Luca guides diners around a small but well-chosen wine list and a marvellously recherché cheeseboard. The desserts too are spectacular: don't miss the chocolate, pear and ricotta tart.

Al Portego

Castello 6015, calle Malvasia (041 522 9038/ www.alportego.it). Vaporetto Rialto. **Meals served** noon-2.30pm, 7-9.30pm Mon-Sat. Closed 2wks June. **Average** €25. **No credit cards**. **Map** p322 B5 ❿

With its wooden decor, this rustic osteria smacks of the mountain chalet. Alongside a big barrel of wine, the bar is loaded down with a selection of *cicheti*, from meatballs and tuna balls to fried courgette flowers and *nervetti* stewed with onions. There are also simple but honest pasta dishes, risottos and *secondi*, such as *fegato alla veneziana*, served up for early lunch (noon-2.30pm) and early dinner (7-9.30pm). Eat at the bar or queue for one of the tiny tables, as no reservations are taken.

Antica Trattoria Bandierette

Castello 6671, barbaria de le Tole (041 522 0619/ www.elmoro.com/bandierette.htm). Vaporetto Ospedale. **Meals served** noon-2pm Mon; noon-2pm, 7-10pm Wed-Sun. Closed 2wks Dec-Jan; 2wks Aug. **Average** €35. **Credit** DC, MC, V. **Map** p323 D5 ⓫

With its bland *tavola calda* decor and garish lighting, this busy trattoria between Santi Giovanni e Paolo and San Francesco is not the place to eat after that romantic gondola ride. But locals don't come for the decor: they're here for the good, reasonably priced seafood and the friendly service. The tagliatelle with scampi and spinach, and the spaghetti with prawns and asparagus are especially good.

Corte Sconta

Castello 3886, calle del Pestrin (041 522 7024). Vaporetto Arsenale. **Meals served** Feb-Dec 12.30-2.30pm, 7-10pm Tue-Sat. Closed Jan; mid July-mid Aug. **Average** €55. **Credit** MC, V. **Map** p327 E1 ⓬

This trailblazing seafood restaurant is now in the capable hands of Marco, son of founder Claudio Proietto. It's such a firm favourite on the well-informed tourist circuit that it is usually a good idea to book several days in advance. The main act is an endless procession of seafood *antipasti*; the day's catch might include *garusoli*, *schie* and *moscardini* (baby curled octopus). The pasta is home-made and the warm *zabaione* dessert is a delight. Decor is of the modern Bohemian trattoria variety, the ambience loud and friendly. In summer, try to secure one of the tables in the pretty, vine-covered courtyard.

Maison de Laurent

Castello 4509, campo Santi Filippo e Giacomo (041 520 8280). Vaporetto San Zaccaria. **Meals served** noon-2pm, 7-10pm Mon, Tue, Fri-Sun; 7-10pm Thur. **Average** €100. **Credit** AmEx, DC, MC, V. **Map** p326 C1 ❸

High-end restaurant openings are rare things in quick-bite, tourist-oriented Venice, so this elegantly modern gourmet eaterie is one to watch. The place is tiny: just 12 table settings in a flower-filled room with contemporary decor and a mirrored back wall which does its best to create an illusion of space. Based on a mix of fresh market produce and globally-sourced fine foods, the daily-changing, Gallic-tinged menu might take in such delights as risotto with pumpkin, grape-must and foie gras, or fresh Sicilian tuna with rock salt or a reduction of anise. The wine list offers a challenging selection of Italian and international crus. Maison de Laurent

Boccadoro. *See p159.*

sets itself lofty ambitions which it doesn't always quite fulfil – but it's early days yet, and at least they're trying to stir up the sluggish Venetian dining scene. **Photo** *p152*.

Osteria di Santa Marina

Castello 5911, campo Santa Marina (041 528 5239/ www.osteriadisantamarina.it). Vaporetto Rialto. **Meals served** 7.30-9.30pm Mon; 12.30-2.30pm, 7.30-9.30pm Tue-Sat. Closed 2 wks Jan; 2 wks Aug. **Average** €60. **Credit** MC, V. **Map** p322 C5 ⑬
A novelty that looks like its been around for ages, this upmarket osteria in pretty campo Santa Marina, not far from the Miracoli church (*see p111*), is a welcome addition to the fold. It has the kind of professional service and standards that are too often lacking in Venice, and the ambience and the high level of the seafood-oriented cuisine justify the price tag. Raw fish feature strongly among the *antipasti*; *primi* give local tradition a creative twist in dishes such as the turbot-and-mussel-filled ravioli in celery sauce, or the risotto with scallops and *bruscandoli* (hop shoots). The joy of this place is in the detail: the bread is all home-made, a taster course turns up just when you were about to ask what happened to the *branzino*… The secret is out, though, so book ahead.

Pizzerie

Dai Tosi

Castello 738, secco Marina (041 523 7102). Vaporetto Giardini. **Meals served** noon-2pm Mon, Tue, Thur; noon-2pm, 7-9.30pm Fri-Sun. Closed 2wks Aug. **Average** €15 pizzeria; €30 full meal. **Credit** MC, V. **Map** p328 A3 ⑭

In one of Venice's most working-class areas, in a street festooned with washing strung out to dry, this pizzeria is a big hit with local families and a welcome retreat to normality for visitors to the nearby Biennale dell'Arte (*see p215*). But beware of the restaurant of the same name on the street: this place (at No.738) is the better of the two establishments. The cuisine is humble but filling, the pizzas are tasty (try the Gregory Speck – *speck* is Tyrolean ham), and you can round the meal off nicely with a killer *sgropin* (a post-prandial refresher made with lemon sorbet, vodka and prosecco). In summer, angle for a garden table.

Cannaregio

Restaurants & *bacari*

Al Fontego dei Pescaori

Cannaregio 3711, sottoportego del Tagliapietra (041 520 0538). Vaporetto Ca' d'Oro. **Meals served** 12.30-2pm, 7.30-10pm Tue-Sun. **Average** €45. **Credit** AmEx, DC, MC, V. **Map** p322 A3 ⑮
This soberly elegant restaurant, housed in a former *fondaco* or *fontego* (Venetian merchants' warehouse) directly opposite Vini da Gigio (*see p161*), is spacious and welcoming. The seafood menu insists on fish and fresh veg or herb combos – as in the salad of shrimps and artichokes, or the spider crab with asparagus tips. There are also quite a few meaty *secondi*, including *tagliata di manza* (beef tenderloin) and *costicine di agnello* (baby rack of lamb). The excellent wine list has several by-the-glass options, and there's a pretty outside garden courtyard.

Eat, Drink, Shop

Algiubagiò

*Cannaregio 5039, Fondamenta Nuove (041 523
6084), Vaporetto Fondamente Nove.* **Open** 6.30am-
11.30pm Mon, Wed-Sun. **Meals served** noon-3pm,
7-10.30pm Mon, Wed-Sun. Closed Jan. **Average** €45.
Credit MC, V. **Map** p322 C3 **16**
Over the last few years this busy spot right by the
Fondamente Nove ferry wharf has morphed from
bar-pizzeria to full-on restaurant. Choose between the
lofty, wood-beamed interior with its urban design
details or the waterside terrace with views over the
northern lagoon. There's no seafood on the eclectic
menu, which ranges from meat, salad and cheese
antipasti (reindeer carpaccio, crudités with Alpine
goat cheese) through pasta dishes like tagliolini with
duck and autumn greens to the restaurant's real speciality, Angus steak, prepared every which way
(with chocolate and apple, anyone?). Vegetarians are
also well served with a dozen or so options; and
there's an extensive cheese board and a small but
well-chosen wine list. A long pizza menu and decent
spread of comfort-desserts like tiramisù round off the
restaurant's something-for-everyone selection.

Alla Fontana

*Cannaregio 1102, fondamenta Cannaregio (041
715 077). Vaporetto Guglie.* **Meals served** *Apr-Oct*
6.30-11pm Mon, Wed-Sat. *Nov-Mar* 7-10pm Mon-Sat.
Closed 3wks Jan-Feb. **Average** €45. **Credit** AmEx,
MC, V. **Map** p321 E2 **17**
This traditional osteria just five minutes from the
station has recently completed its move from wine-
and-snack *bacaro* to bona fide, evening-only restaurant. 'The Fountain' now offers a range of filling
trattoria dishes with a creative twist: tagliatelle with
eel, gnocchi with turbot and courgettes, *spezzatino*
(braised strips of veal) with polenta. In summer
tables line the busy canal pavement outside.

Alla Frasca

*Cannaregio 5176, campiello della Carità (041 528
5433). Vaporetto Fondamente Nove.* **Meals served**
July-Sept noon-2.30pm, 6.30-10pm Mon-Sat. *Oct-June*
noon-2.30pm, 6.30-9pm Mon, Wed-Sun. Closed 1wk
Aug, 2wks Dec-Jan. **Average** €40. **No credit
cards**. **Map** p322 C4 **18**
It's not on the cutting edge, gastronomically speaking, but this pleasant trattoria with outside tables
on a tiny square just south of fondamenta Nuove
must be one of the most picturesque places to eat in
Venice. Primi are based on homemade pasta, while
main courses range from grilled fish to some more
meaty options (like lamb cutlet) that betray the
Abruzzese origins of the young chef-owner. The
good-value €12 lunch menu includes first course,
second course, side dish, water and coffee.

Anice Stellato

*Cannaregio 3272, fondamenta della Sensa
(041 720 744). Vaporetto Guglie or Sant'Alvise.*
Meals served 12.30-2pm, 7.30-10pm Wed-Fri;
12.30-2pm, 7.30-10pm Sat, Sun. Closed 1wk Jan;
3wks Aug. **Average** €38. **Credit** MC, V.
Map p321 F2 **19**

This nouveau *bacaro* is a favourite with budget-conscious gourmets: the ambience is friendly and the
food good and reasonably priced. A walk-around bar
at the entrance fills up with *cichetari* (snacking locals)
in the hour before lunch and evening meals. Tables
take up two simply decorated rooms, and spill out on
to the canalside walk in summer. The name means
'star anise', and spices do play a role in the kitchen,
but there are also Venetian classics such as *bigoli in
salsa*, plus more creative outings like tagliatelle with
scampi and courgette flowers. It's hugely popular –
so avoid Saturdays and always book ahead.

Antica Adelaide

*Cannaregio 3728, calle larga Doge Priuli (041
523 2629). Vaporetto Ca d'Oro.* **Open** 7am-
midnight daily. **Meals served** noon-2.30pm,
7.30-10.30pm daily. **Average** €35. **Credit** DC,
MC, V. **Map** p322 A3 **20**
This historic bar-osteria just behind the busy, tack-
filled Strada Nuova dates back to the 18th century.
Abandoned for years, it was reopened in September
2006, after painstaking restoration, by dynamic
restaurateur and wine buff Alvise Ceccato.
Venetians love novelties, and within days it was
heaving around *aperitivo* time; but it looks set to
make a splash on the culinary front as well, with its
unusual menu of revisited traditional dishes from
the Veneto – like *oca in onto* (goose preserved in its
own fat) or freshwater lagoon fish done *in saor*,
rather than the more common sardines. There is a
large selection of cheeses and cured meats, and a
good pan-Italian wine list

Bea Vita

*Cannaregio 3082, fondamenta delle Cappuccine
(041 275 9347). Vaporetto Tre Archi or Sant'Alvise.*
Meals served noon-2.30pm, 7.30-10.30pm Mon-Sat.
Average €35. **Credit** DC, MC, V. **Map** p321 E2 **21**
On the long canalside promenade just north of the
Ghetto, this new place with rustic decor was a hit
from day one with hungry locals, who come for the
ample portions and decent prices. After a single
antipasto you're likely to feel full – but it's worth
pushing on through a creative menu that includes
red mullet on a bed of papaya purée with mint vinai-
grette; or herb tagliatelle with lamb ragù and cherry tomatoes. Leave room for themouth-watering
range of desserts. The small wine list includes a
decent by-the-glass wine selection. At lunch there's
a good-value €11 two-course *menu fisso*, while on
alternate Fridays they do special menus centring on
seasonal ingredients like *radicchio di Treviso*.

Boccadoro

*Cannaregio 5405A, campiello Widman (041
521 1021/www.osteriaboccadorove.org). Vaporetto
Fondamente Nove.* **Meals served** 12.30-2.30pm,
8-11pm Tue-Sun. **Average** €60. **Credit** AmEx, DC,
MC, V. **Map** p322 C4 **22**
Now under new management, this creative seafood
restaurant with pleasantly modern decor has slowly
picked up business and plaudits in the years since

Eat, Drink, Shop

The menu

Antipasti (starters)

The dozens of *cicheti* – tapas-style snacks – served from the counters of the traditional *bacaro* (*see p152*) are essentially *antipasti*; the choice may include: **baccalà mantecato** stockfish beaten into a cream with oil and milk, often served on grilled polenta; **bovoleti** tiny snails cooked in olive oil, parsley and garlic; **carciofi** artichokes, even better if they are **castrauri** – baby artichokes; **canoce** (or **cicale di mare**) mantis shrimps; **folpi/folpeti** baby octopus; **garusoli** sea snails; **moleche** soft-shelled crabs, usually deep-fried; **museo** a boiled brawn sausage, generally served on a slice of bread with mustard; **nervetti** boiled veal cartilage; **polpetta** deep-fried spicy meatball; **polenta** yellow or white cornmeal mush, served either runny or in firm sliceable slabs; **sarde in saor** sardines marinated in onion, vinegar, pine nuts and raisins; **schie** tiny grey shrimps, usually served on a bed of soft white polenta; **seppie in nero** cuttlefish in its own ink; **spienza** veal spleen usually served on a skewer; **trippa e rissa** tripe cooked in broth.

Primi (first courses)

Bigoli in salsa fat spaghetti in an anchovy and onion sauce; **gnocchi con granseola** potato gnocchi in spider-crab sauce; **pasta... e ceci** pasta and chickpea soup; **...e fagioli** pasta and borlotti bean soup; **spaghetti... alla busara** in anchovy sauce; **...al nero di seppia** in squid-ink sauce; **...con caparossoli/vongole veraci** with clams; **risotto... di zucca** pumpkin risotto.

Secondi (main courses)

In addition to the *antipasti* mentioned above you may find: **anguilla** eel; **aragosta/astice** spiny lobster/lobster; **branzino** sea bass; **cape longhe** razor clams; **cape sante** scallops; **cernia** grouper; **coda di rospo** anglerfish; **cozze** mussels; **granchio** crab; **granseola** spider crab; **orata** gilt-headed bream; **rombo** turbot; **pesce San Pietro** John Dory; **pesce spada** swordfish; **sogliola** sole; **tonno** tuna; **vongole/caparossoli** clams. Meat eaters are less well catered for in Venice; local specialities include: **fegato alla veneziana** veal liver cooked in onions; **castradina** a lamb and cabbage broth.

Dolci

Venice's restaurants are not the best place to feed a sweet habit – with a few exceptions, there are far more tempting pastries to be found on the shelves of the city's *pasticcerie*. The classic end to a meal here is a plate of **buranei** – sweet egg biscuits – served with a dessert wine such as Fragolino. Then it's quickly on to the more important matter of which grappa to order.

---

its uncertain 2001 debut. The cuisine is excellent, with a focus on fresh fish – tuna tartare, *cozze pepate* (peppery mussels), *tagliolini con alici e finochietto selvaggio* (thin pasta strips with anchovies and wild fennel). *Secondi* range from simple grilled fish to more adventurous seafood and vegetable pairings like fillet of turbot with courgettes. In summer, there are tables outside on a small neighbourhood *campo* – a great playspace for easily bored kids. **Photo** *p157*.

Ca' D'Oro (Alla Vedova)

Cannaregio 3912, ramo Ca' d'Oro (041 528 5324). Vaporetto Ca' d'Oro. **Meals served** 11.30am-2.30pm, 6.30-10.30pm Mon-Wed, Fri, Sat; 6.30-11pm Sun. Closed Aug. **Average** €35. **No credit cards**. **Map** p322 B4 ㉓
Deservedly famous, this is one of the best-preserved traditional *bacari* in town. Its official name is the Ca' d'Oro, but most Venetians know it as Alla Vedova – the Widow's Place. The widow has now, alas, joined her *marito*, but her family still runs the show and her spirit marches on in the traditional brass-pan and wooden-table decor and the warm, intimate atmosphere. Tourists head for the tables (it's best to book), where tasty pasta dishes (like spaghetti in cuttlefish ink) and *secondi* are served, while locals tend to stay at the bar snacking on a range of classic *cicheti*, from *folpeti* to fried artichokes to the best *polpette* (meatballs) in Venice.

Da Alberto

Cannaregio 5401, calle Giacinto Gallina (041 523 8153). Vaporetto Fondamente Nove. **Meals served** noon-3pm, 6.30-9.30pm Mon-Sat. Closed mid July-early Aug. **Average** €35. **Credit** MC, V. **Map** p322 C4 ㉔
This *bacaro* with charming trad decor, not far from campo Santi Giovanni e Paolo, has been through a couple of changes of ownership since the eponymous Alberto left to set up the Irish-style Inishark pub (*see p219*), but it still maintains a good standard and a well-stocked bar counter. The wide, sit-down menu centres on Venetian specialities such as *granseola* and *seppie in umido* (stewed cuttlefish), along with plenty of seafood pastas and risottos. A favourite with young Venetians, Alberto's is always buzzing and packed – so book ahead if you want to sit down and eat, rather than just snack at the bar.

Dalla Marisa

Cannaregio 652B, fondamenta San Giobbe (041 720 211). Vaporetto Tre Archi or Crea. **Meals served** noon-2.30pm Mon, Wed, Sun; noon-2.30pm, 8-9.15pm Tue, Thur-Sat. Closed Aug. **Average** €35. **No credit cards. Map** p321 D2 ㉕

Signora Marisa, the proud descendant of a dynasty of butchers, is a culinary legend in Venice, with locals calling up days in advance to ask her to prepare ancient recipes such as *risotto con le secoe* (risotto made with a special cut of beef from around the spine). Pasta dishes include the excellent *tagliatelle con sugo di masaro* (in duck sauce), while *secondi* range from tripe to roast stuffed pheasant. In summer tables spill out from the tiny interior on to the fondamenta overlooking the busy Cannaregio canal. Book well ahead – this place is not just *popolare* (proletarian), but popular too. Serving times are rigid: turn up late and you'll go hungry.

Da Rioba

Cannaregio 2553, fondamenta della Misericordia (041 524 4379). Vaporetto Orto. **Meals served** noon-2.30pm, 7.30-10.30pm Tue-Sun. Closed 3wks Jan. **Average** €35. **Credit** AmEx, DC, MC, V. **Map** p322 A2 ㉖

Taking its name from the iron-nosed stone figure of a turbaned merchant – known as Sior Rioba – which is set into a wall in nearby campo dei Mori, Da Rioba is a nice place for lunch on warm days, when tables are laid out along the edge of the Misericordia canal. A good fall back when nearby Anice Stellato (*see p159*) is full, this nouveau-rustic *bacaro* attracts a predominantly Venetian clientele – always a good sign. The menu ranges from local standards like *schie con polenta* and *spaghetti alla busara* forays like halibut fillet in pistachio crust on a bed of artichokes and asparagus tips.

Fiaschetteria Toscana

Cannaregio 5719, salizada San Giovanni Grisostomo (041 528 5281/www.fiaschetteria toscana.it). Vaporetto Rialto. **Meals served** 7.30-10.30pm Tue, Wed; 12.30-2.30pm, 7.30-10.30pm Mon, Thur-Sun. Closed mid July-mid Aug. **Average** €65. **Credit** DC, MC, V. **Map** p322 B5 ㉗

Though this was once a depot for wine and olive oil from Tuscany, today only a good selection of steaks and big Tuscan red wines betray its origins. Otherwise, the cuisine, which runs the gamut from meat to fish to game, is true to Venetian tradition, with favourites such as *schie con polenta* and *fegato alla veneziana*. Pasta is not a strong point; better to leap from the fine *antipasti* – which, when the market allows, include squeaky-fresh oysters – to delicious *secondi* like grilled John Dory, or a renowned *fritto misto*. The decor is a little tired and the service can be peremptory, but this place is a reliable, though hardly cheap, gourmet standby. Take the sting out of the bill with one of Mamma Mariuccia's fabulous desserts, and a bottle from one of the most extensive wine lists in town. In the evening they do two sittings; book for the later one (9-9.30pm) for a more relaxed meal.

Vini da Gigio

Cannaregio 3628A, fondamenta San Felice (041 528 5140/www.vinidagigio.com). Vaporetto Ca' d'Oro. **Meals served** noon-2.30pm, 7.30-10.30pm Wed-Sun. Closed 3wks Jan-Feb; 3wks Aug-Sept. **Average** €50. **Credit** DC, MC, V. **Map** p322 A3 ㉘

It's no longer any secret that this is one of the best-value restaurants in Venice, so make sure you book well in advance. Gigio is strong on Venetian *antipasti* such as *crocchette di baccalà* (breaded stockfish) and *canestrelli all griglia* (grilled razor clams); there are also a number of good meat and game options, like *masorini alla buranella* (roasted Burano-style duck). As the name suggests, wine is another forte – there are even bottles from Australia and South Africa, and there is always a good by-the-glass selection. The only drawback in this highly recommended restaurant is the decidedly unhurried service. Allow at least two hours for a complete meal, and don't go in a large group: this is a place that works best with tables of five or six maximum.

International

Mirai

Cannaregio 227, lista di Spagna (041 220 6517). Vaporetto Ferrovia. **Meals served** 7.30-11.30pm Tue-Sun. Closed 3wks Jan. **Average** €60. **Credit** AmEx, DC, MC, V. **Map** p321 E3 ㉙

One of the few interesting international options in Venice, this newish Japanese restaurant, run by a Japanese-Brazilian chef who moved here from Milan, has already built up a steady local following. It does all the classics – sushi, sashimi of salmon, tuna and bream, tempura – and it does them well. The classy modern decor makes for a cool refuge from the tacky lista di Spagna souvenir hell outside, and they've recently added a garden out back.

San Polo & Santa Croce

Restaurants & *bacari*

Al Garanghelo

San Polo 1570, Calle dei Botteri (041 721 721). Vaporetto Rialto or San Stae. **Meals served** noon-2.30pm, 6.30-9pm Mon-Sat. **Average** €30. **Credit** AmEx, MC, V. **Map** p322 A5 ㉚

Good, cheap food and friendly service? In Venice? Doubt not: this new (but authentic) osteria-*bacaro* not far from the church of San Cassiano offers both of these rare commodities. The place is dominated by the long wooden bar counter, where you can perch and tuck into a cornucopia of *cicheti* that range from the most obvious (meatballs and tunaballs) to more refined treats like halibut in spicy tomato sauce. These are on offer from eight in the morning until ten in the evening, but at mealtimes you can sit at one of the tables that are crammed into the tiny space and order from a small range of *primi* and *secondi* that might include risotto with *funghi porcini* and langostines, or a sapid *fegato alla veneziana*; don't miss the *budino del doge*, a creamy almond liqueur-flavoured dessert. Chef Renato and his front-of-house partner Annalisa practically adopt the few tourists that stumble in here.

Alla Madonna
San Polo 594, calle della Madonna (041 522 3824/ www.ristoranteallamadonna.com). Vaporetto Rialto or San Silvestro. **Meals served** noon-3pm, 7-10pm Mon, Tue, Thur-Sun. Closed Christmas-Jan. **Average** €45. **Credit** AmEx, MC, V. **Map** p322 B5 ③①
A sort of high-class canteen, this big, bustling fish trattoria with its friendly (though brisk) service and fair (though rising) prices has been piling in loyal locals and clued-up tourists for generations. It's a minute's walk from the Rialto, and while the cooking will win no prizes, it offers competent versions of old Venetian favourites such as *granseola* and *anguilla fritta*. The restaurant also turns out pan-Italian faves like *cotolette alla milanese* (breaded veal cutlets). Bookings are not taken; simply join the queue outside, which moves pretty fast.

Alla Zucca
Santa Croce 1762, ponte del Megio (041 524 1570/ www.lazucca.it). Vaporetto San Stae. **Meals served** 12.30-2.30pm, 7-10.30pm Mon-Sat. **Average** €35. **Credit** AmEx, MC, V. **Map** p321 F4 ③②
This is one of the first of Venice's 'alternative' trattorias and it's still one of the best – not to mention one of the best-value. By a pretty skewed bridge, the vegetarian-friendly Pumpkin offers a break from all that seafood. The menu is equally divided between meat (lamb roasted with fennel and pecorino cheese, ginger pork with pilau rice) and vegetables (*penne* with aubergine and feta, pumpkin and seasoned ricotta quiche). Women dining alone will feel at home in this mainly female-staffed eaterie. In summer book ahead for one of the few outside tables.

Antiche Carampane
San Polo 1911, rio terà delle Carampane (041 524 0165/www.antichecarampane.com). Vaporetto San Silvestro. **Meals served** 12.30-2.30pm, 7.30-10.30pm. Closed 1wk Jan, Aug. **Average** €55. **Credit** AmEx, DC, MC, V. **Map** p322 A5 ③③
This compact trattoria between campo San Polo and San Cassiano – in what was once the red-light district – could win the prize for the hardest-to-find restaurant in Venice. The inaccessibility is reinforced by a prickly attitude towards non-Venetians – who nevertheless constitute the majority of the clientele. But if you manage to break the ice, the Carampane will deliver a fine (though not cheap) seafood meal which goes beyond the ubiquitous standards to offer recherché local specialities like *spaghetti in cassopipa* (a piccante sauce of shellfish and crustaceans). Leave room for an unbeatable *fritto misto* (mixed seafood fry-up) and their delicious desserts (mousse, *bavarese*). Inside is cosy, but outside is better for balmy summer evenings.

Bancogiro
San Polo 122, campo San Giacomo di Rialto (041 523 2061). Vaporetto Rialto. **Meals served** *Sept-May* noon-2.30pm, 7.30-10.30pm Tue-Sun. *June-Aug* noon-10.30pm Tue-Sun. **Average** €35. **No credit cards. Map** p322 B5 ③④
The location of this updated *bacaro* is splendid: the main entrance gives on to the busy Rialto square of San Giacomo, while the back door gives access to a prime bit of Grand Canal frontage that until a few years ago was open only to market traders. Downstairs, hirsute player-manager Andrea dispenses excellent wines to an appreciative crowd of locals; above, at a few well-spaced tables squeezed in under the brick ceiling vaults, a light, creative, almost pasta-less menu is served, which might include turbot fillets with pumpkin and rosemary, squid with radicchio and cinnamon, and sweet ricotta dessert with fresh figs and chestnut honey. Not every dish lives up to its ambitions, but it's certainly a change from *bacalà mantecato*. Allow plenty of time, though, as service can be sluggish. In summer the ringside view of the Grand Canal from the outside tables makes up for the wait.

Al Garanghelo. *See p161.*

Birraria La Corte. *See p165.*

Da Fiore

San Polo 2202, calle del Scaleter (041 721 308).
Vaporetto San Stae. **Meals served** 12.30-2.30pm,
7.30-10.30pm Tue-Sat. Closed Christmas to mid Jan;
Aug. **Average** €100. **Credit** AmEx, DC, MC, V.
Map p321 F5 ③

Restaurant critics and local gourmets are almost
unanimous in considering the Michelin-starred Da
Fiore to be Venice's best restaurant. The façade and
the bar at the entrance hark back to its *bacaro* origins;
but the elegant, barge-like dining room inside is in
quite a different class. Owner Maurizio Martin treats
his guests – many of whom are visiting celebrities
or local big shots – with egalitarian courtesy, while
his wife Mara concentrates on getting the food right
(between writing cookbooks and running courses).
Raw fish and seafood is a key feature of the *antipasti*;
primi are equally divided between pasta dishes like
the classic *pennette* with scallops and broccoli and
a series of faultless risottos. *Secondi* are all about
bringing out the flavour of the fish without smoth-
ering it in sauce: the *tagliata di tonno al rosmarino*
is a case in point. There is also an exceptional selection of regional cheeses and a collection of decent
desserts. You pays your money, certainly, for what
is in the end a good, rather than a superlative, dining experience; but that's Venice for you.

Da Ignazio

San Polo 2749, calle dei Saoneri (041 523 4852).
Vaporetto San Tomà. **Meals served** noon-3pm,
7-10pm Mon-Fri, Sun. Closed 2wks Dec-Jan; 3wks
July-Aug. **Average** €48. **Credit** AmEx, DC, MC,
V. **Map** p321 F5 ③

The big attraction of this tranquil neighbourhood
restaurant between campo San Polo and the Frari is
its pretty, pergola-shaded courtyard. The cooking is
safe, traditional Venetian: mixed seafood *antipasti*
might be followed by a good rendition of *spaghetti
con caparossoli* or *risi e bisi* (risotto with peas), and
grilled fish; desserts include a decent tiramisù. Don't
expect any frills: just down home Venetian cooking
in pleasant surroundings.

Muro Vino e Cucina

*San Polo 222, campo Cesare Battisti (041 523
7495). Vaporetto Rialto.* **Meals served** noon-3pm,
7.30-11pm Mon-Sat. **Average** €45. **Credit** AmEx,
DC, MC, V. **Map** p322 B5 ③

Designed by Iranian-American architect Michael
Foroutan and his Venetian colleague Stefano Miatto,
Muro hosts not only a buzzing bar (*see p177*) but
one of the city's most interesting new restaurants.
German chef Jozef 'Beppe' Klostermaier plays fast
and loose with the local tradition in dishes like
caserecce (homemade pasta) with radicchio di
Treviso and pear in gorgonzola sauce, or chamoix
meatballs in Barbera d'Asti sauce with puréed
potatoes and red cabbage; but though these are risky
combos for conservative Venice, they (usually)
work. There's a serious grill for barbecued fish or
steak and a select wine list that is strong on the
Veneto, Friuli and Alto Adige. Another thing that
sets Muro apart from the pack is the fact that all dinner guests are offered a glass of prosecco, a small
starter and water free of charge. The lunch menu –
aimed at local workers and the staff of the nearby
magistrates' court – is simpler and cheaper.

Naranzaria

*San Polo 130, Erbaria (041 724 1035/www.
naranzaria.it). Vaporetto Rialto.* **Open** Apr-mid
Nov noon-2am Tue-Sun; mid Nov-Mar noon-3pm,
6pm-2am Tue-Sun. **Meals served** noon-3pm, 7-
11pm Tue-Sun. Closed 10 days Jan. **Average** €35.
Credit MC, V. **Map** p322 B5 ③

A touch snootier than its neighbour Bancogiro (*see
p162*), this relative newcomer on the eating and
drinking scene offers fine wines, many of them
produced in the neighbouring Friuli region by
Narazaria's co-owner Brandino Brandolini, plus a
small but interesting menu which ranges from local
specialities to coucous and sushi and sashimi
prepared by the restaurant's Japanese chef. There
are a few tables upstairs beneath the brick-arched
ceiling, but it's the handful of tables out in the
Naranzaria – the area of the Rialto markets where

Eat, Drink, Shop

citrus fruits were stored and, until recently, closed to the public – that make this place truly special: there can be few such wonderful places to dine in the whole city.

Vecio Fritolin
Santa Croce 2262, calle della Regina (041 522 2881/www.veciofritolin.com). Vaporetto San Stae. **Meals served** noon-2.30pm, 7-10.30pm Tue-Sun. **Average** €50. **Credit** AmEx, DC, MC, V. **Map** p322 A4 ㊴
This old-style *bacaro* hit a low patch a few years ago but has been nursed back to health as a full-on restaurant by the charming present owner. Wooden beams, sturdy tables and the long bar at the back of the main dining room set the mood; but the menu is more creative than the decor might lead you to expect, with a scallop and courgette flower risotto, or a main course of wild (not farmed) *branzino* with *funghi porcini*. There are evenings when the service can be a little uncertain, but all in all this is a pleasant enough south-bank option, with prices that are reasonably contained for Venice.

Pizzerie

Al Nono Risorto
Santa Croce 2338, sottoportico di Siora Bettina (041 524 1169). Vaporetto San Stae. **Meals served** noon-2.30pm, 7-11pm Mon, Tue, Fri-Sun; 7-11pm Thur. Closed 2wks Jan, 1wk Aug. **Average** €14 pizzeria; €30 full meal. **No credit cards**. **Map** p322 A4 ㊵
There's plenty of attitude in this lively spot. If you want to hang out over a tasty pizza margherita in a shady garden courtyard with Venice's bright young things, this is the place to come. It also does traditional Venetian trattoria fare, at traditional Venetian trattoria prices. The service is generally efficient even at peak times (ie almost always).

Birraria La Corte
San Polo 2168, campo San Polo (041 275 0570/ www.birrarialacorte.it). Vaporetto San Tomà or San Silvestro. **Meals served** noon-2.30pm, 7-10.30pm daily. **Closed** 2wks Nov. **Average** €15 pizza; €32 full meal. **Credit** AmEx, DC, MC, V. **Map** p321 F5 ㊶
The biggest square in Venice outside of St Mark's, campo San Polo is always busling with life. The outside tables of this huge, no-nonsense pizzeria are a great place to observe it – and a boon for parents with small children, who can chase pigeons while mum and dad tuck into a decent margherita or a more gourmet pizza like the *scoazzera*, whose ingredients include wild boar salami, peppers and spicy sausage. The restaurant occupies a former brewery (hence the name) – which has been revamped in an industrial-modern style – and beer still takes pride of place over wine on the drinks list. If pizza's not your thing there is also a regular menu that takes in some decent pasta options and some good grilled-meat *secondi*. Service can be slow and uncertain at peak times. **Photo** *p163*.

Il Refolo
Santa Croce 1459, campiello del Piovan (041 524 0016/www.dafiore.net). Vaporetto Riva di Biasio or San Stae. **Meals served** Apr-Oct 7-11pm Tue; noon-3.30pm, 7-11pm Wed-Sun. Closed Nov-Mar. **Average** €20 pizzeria; €35 full meal. **Credit** MC, V. **Map** p321 F4 ㊷
The 'Sea Breeze' has tables outside (and only outside) in one of Venice's prettiest squares, by a canal, with a good view of the church of San Giacomo dell'Orio. Set up by a scion of the **Da Fiore** dynasty (*see p163*), it is Venice's most luxurious pizzeria – a status that is reflected in the prices. There is also a small international-style restaurant menu featuring high-class deli fare such as marinated salmon, curried chicken and creative salads; the house white is an above-average Tocai. Note the four-month winter closure, and be sure to book ahead, even for lunch.

International

Frary's
San Polo 2559, fondamenta dei Frari (041 720 050). Vaporetto San Tomà. **Meals served** noon-3.30pm, 6.30-10.30pm Mon, Wed-Sun. Closed 10 days Aug. **Average** €28. **Credit** AmEx, DC, MC, V. **Map** p321 F5 ㊸
A friendly, reasonably-priced spot specialising in Arab cuisine, though there are some Greek and Kurdish dishes too. Couscous comes with a variety of sauces: vegetarian, mutton, chicken or seafood. The *mansaf* (Bedouin rice with chicken, almonds and yoghurt) is good, as are the falafel, tsatsiki and tara-masalata. The naïve Arabian Nights murals on the wall make a change from all that Tintoretto. At lunch there's a good value two-course menu for just €10.

Dorsoduro

Restaurants & *bacari*

Ai Gondolieri
Dorsoduro 336, fondamenta Ospedaletto (041 528 6396/www.aigondolieri.com). Vaporetto Accademia or Salute. **Meals served** noon-3pm, 7-10pm Mon, Wed-Sun. **Average** €75. **Credit** AmEx, DC, MC, V. **Map** p326 A3 ㊹
Not a bad alternative to Da Fiore if you're looking to splash out, Ai Gondolieri offers a creative menu that belies its ultra-traditional decor and service. It's also, unusually for Venice, fish-free. Rooted in the culinary traditions of north-east Italy, the attractively presented dishes include a warm salad of venison with blueberries, *panzerotti* (pasta parcels) filled with *topinambur* (Jerusalem artichokes) in Montasio cheese sauce, rack of lamb with Barolo and radicchio, pork fillet in pear sauce with wild fennel. Truffles invade the menu in autumn – but don't order these expensive delicacies without first enquiring about the price. Owner Giovanni Trevisan also runs the bar-restaurant inside the nearby Peggy Guggenheim Collection.

Wines of the north-east

Italy's north-east does not have the same brand recognition as Tuscany or Piedmont on the international wine circuit. But insiders know that this is one of Italy's most varied wine-making areas – not least because its whites are at least as important as its reds.

The area is divided into two regions, the Veneto and Friuli-Venezia Giulia. It's the latter which has the strongest reputation, mostly centred on the Collio and Colli Orientali appellations, a long range of rolling, vine-covered hills that nestle up against Italy's border with Slovenia. These two appellations can be confusing: unlike, say, Chianti, the names Collio and Colli Orientali don't tell you what you're getting in the glass: they're umbrella affairs, each hosting an impressive roster of wines, most distinguishable by grape variety: so you might order a Colli Orientali Tocai Friuliano, or refosco; or a Collio merlot, or sauvignon.

The Veneto is coming on too. Long considered good only for a couple of full-bodied reds, Amarone and Valpolicella, the region is now in the middle of an image makeover, thanks to a small, energetic cluster of winemakers who use local grape varieties like corvina and garganega to turn out some fine and complex wines. True, the region's whites still stand in the shadow of their Friulian cousins. But things are changing rapidly: even Soave, that two-litre party standby, has shown itself to be capable of greatness in the hands of producers like Pieropan or Inama. The Veneto is also home to Italy's favourite fizz, prosecco.

The following are the wines you are most likely to come across in wine bars and *bacari*:

RED

Cabernet: When Venetians ask for a glass of cabernet, they generally mean cabernet franc rather than its more famous cousin, cabernet sauvignon. A staple of the Veneto's upland wine enclaves, the grape yields an honest, more-ish red with an unmistakeable grassy aroma. Some of the best Cabernets in the Veneto come from the up-and-coming Colli Berici area – Mattiello, Costozza and Cavazza are producers to look out for. In Friuli, both cabernet sauvignon and cabernet franc have a foothold. Russiz Superiore and La Boatina make some of the best.

Raboso: The classic Venetian winter-warming red, raboso is like the Venetian character – rough, acidic, tannic and entirely lacking in pretension. The best kind is the stuff served from a huge demijohn in your local *bacaro*.

Refosco: A ruby-red wine with hints of grass and cherries, refosco is one of those varieties that locals like to keep to themselves. Until recently this need not have bothered us, but in last few years this Friulian grape has proved that it can do good things in the hands of the right producer. Check out the meaty version turned out by Dorigo.

Valpolicella, Recioto della Valpolicella & Amarone: An often disappointing red from

L'Avogaria

Dorsoduro 1629, calle dell'Avogaria (041 296 0491/www.avogaria.com). Vaporetto San Basilio. **Meals served** 12.30am-3pm, 7.30-midnight Mon, Wed-Sun. Closed 2wks Jan; 2wks Aug. **Average** €40. **Credit** AmEx, DC, MC, V. **Map** p325 D2 **45**

One of the first sharp design eateries to open on the lagoon, L'Avogaria is neither as pretentious nor as expensive as its appearance might suggest. At lunch you can eat a light two-course meal with wine for around €15 a head; the pricier dinner menu is a little more elaborate. The cuisine is *pugliese*, from the heel of Italy – so the usual Venetian fishy *antipasti* are replaced by vegetable nibbles like stuffed tomatoes or peppers in olive oil. Pasta courses include home-made *cavatelli* pasta with carpet shells and beans, followed by baked lamb and potatoes, or *burrata* (a sort of buttery, half-liquid mozzarella) with grilled vegetables. If you're tired of trad and bored of *baccalà*, L'Avogaria will come as a breath of fresh air – especially if you sit at one of the outside tables.

La Bitta

Dorsoduro 2753A, calle lunga San Barnaba (041 523 0531). Vaporetto Ca' Rezzonico. **Meals served** 6.30-11pm Mon-Sat. Closed Aug. **Average** €40. **No credit cards. Map** p325 E2 **46**

One of the few genuinely lively neighbourhoods left in Venice, with a happy mix of lounging students, and trolley-pushing old ladies, the area around San Barnaba has a number of reasonably priced eateries. One of the best is La Bitta, a warm and rustic osteria which stands out from the crowd by having virtually no fish on the menu, and which has the bonus of a small courtyard out back. The cuisine has more in common with the Veneto mainland than island Venice: dishes like *straccetti di pollo ai finferli* (chicken strips with chanterelle mushrooms) or *oca in umido* (stewed goose) make a welcome change from all that seafood risotto. They also have a good selection of cheeses, served with honey or chutney, and an intelligent by-the-glass wine option.

the hills north and west of Verona, standard Valpolicella suffers from overstretched DOC boundaries and overgenerous yields. But the best, bottled as Valpolicella classico or Valpolicella superiore, can be very good. Amarone and Recioto, the area's two famous *passito* wines, are made from partially dried Valpolicella grapes. Recioto is the sweet version, Amarone the dry. In the right hands, the latter can be explosive: powerful, smoky and concentrated, with bags of ripe fruit. The best producers include Allegrini (Recioto), Bussola, Cantina Sociale Valpolicella, Corte Sant'Alda, Dal Forno, Masi (Amarone), Quintarelli (Amarone), Viviani and Zenato.

WHITE AND SPARKLING

Soave & Recioto di Soave: In the Soave classico area, a handful of dynamic winemakers is showing that this blend of garganega and trebbiano is capable of greater things than its party-lubricant reputation would suggest: look out in particular for Pieropan's La Rocca or Calvarino selections. In the 1980s a few producers revived the tradition of Recioto di Soave, a delicious dessert wine made from raisinised garganega grapes. Best producers include Anselmi, Ca' Rugate, Gini, Inama, Pieropan and Suavia.
Friulian whites: The Collio and Colli Orientali appellations (there's little to choose between them) turn out some of Italy's most graceful white wines. Four varietals dominate: sauvignon (the Ronco delle Mele cru

produced by Venica & Venica is to die for); pinot bianco; pinot grigio; and Tocai Friuliano – a dry summery white, not to be confused with the Hungarian dessert wine, Tokay. Producers who do great things with two or more of these varietals include Dorigo, Miani, Russiz Superiore, Schioppetto, Castello di Spessa, Villa Russiz, Rodaro, Livio Felluga, Marco Felluga, Keber, Polencic, Princic, Ronco dei Tassi, Ronco del Gelso, Toros, Collavini, Venica & Venica, Kante, Jermann, Gravner, Primosic, Le Vigne di Zamò, Scubla, Ascevi, Humar, Ronco del Gnemiz, Puiatti, Pecorari, and Volpe Pasini. Other white varieties grown in these areas include chardonnay and ribolla gialla, a local grape that makes for fresh and lemony wines. Finally there is Picolit, the hugely expensive Italian take on Sauternes, made from partially-dried grapes.
Prosecco di Conegliano & Valdobbiadene: The classic Veneto dry white fizz, prosecco comes from vineyards around Valdobbiadene and Conegliano in the rolling hills north of Treviso. The grape is subjected to a double fermentation, using the Charmat method; the result is a light, dry, sparkling wine with a bitter finish. The most highly prized (and expensive) version of prosecco is known as Cartizze. A more rustic, unfizzy version – known as *prosecco spento* or simply *spento* – is served by the glass in *bacari*. Best producers include Bisol, Bortolomiol, Col Vetoraz, Le Colture, Nino Franco and Ruggeri & Co.

Oniga

Dorsoduro 2852, campo San Barnaba (041 522 4410/www.oniga.it). Vaporetto Ca' Rezzonico. **Meals served** noon-2.30pm, 7-10.30pm Mon, Wed-Sun. Closed 3wks Jan; 1wk Aug. **Average** €35. **Credit** AmEx, DC, MC, V. **Map** p325 E2 ㊼
A recent arrival with tables outside on bustling campo San Barnaba, Oniga has a friendly, local feel. The menu is downhome Venetian – though Hungarian chef Annika also does an excellent goulash, which sometimes makes an appearance on the menu in colder months. The pasta is really excellent: try the pumpkin gnocchi with prawns and *broccoletti*, or the spaghetti with veal and chicken ragù. Secondi mostly have a meaty slant: the pork chop with potatoes and figs is particularly good. Annika's husband Marino, who works the front of the house, is a real wine expert, and will guide you through the select list. At lunchtime a meat or fish two-course menu (including side salad and coffee, but not water or wine) is offered for €15 a head. We've had reports

that by the second dinner sitting (from 8.30pm on) the menu can be severely reduced as ingredients are used up – so come early if you want the full choice.

Pane, Vino e San Daniele

Dorsoduro 1722, campo dell'Angelo Raffaele (041 523 7456). Vaporetto San Basilio. **Meals served** noon-2.30pm, 7-10.15pm Mon, Tue, Thur-Sun. **Closed** 2wks Jan. **Average** €35. **Credit** DC, MC, V. **Map** p325 D2 ㊸
In the 1960s this campo in the western reaches of Dorsoduro was an artists' hangout. The bar that once stood here has been replaced by this *nouvelle osteria* belonging to an Italian chain specialising in the wine and ham of the Friuli region. But the place has a character of its own, determined partly by its high proportion of university patrons, partly by the fact that the Friulian imprint of dishes like gnocchetti alla San Daniele in *cestino di frico croccante* (little gnocchi in white sauce with San Daniele ham, served in a crunchy cheese basket) is varied by

Eat, Drink, Shop

Pane, Vino e San Daniele. *See p167.*

others that reflect the chef's Sardinian roots, including *coniglio al mirto* (rabbit baked with myrtle) or *porcheddu* (roasted piglet). A good place to escape the tourist hordes – and it functions as a bar all day (from 9am to 11pm) if you just want a drink in the pretty square. The single table tucked away down in the cellar is a romantic hideaway that you'll need to book well in advance.

Pizzerie

Casin dei Nobili

Dorsoduro 2765, sottoportego del Casin dei Nobili (041 241 1841). Vaporetto Ca' Rezzonico. **Meals served** noon-11pm Tue-Sun. **Average** €15 pizzeria; €35 full meal. **Credit** AmEx, DC, MC, V. **Map** p325 E2 ㊾

Just off campo San Barnaba, this large pizzeria-restaurant with artsy-rustic decor serves up tasty pizzas to a mainly student clientele. There is the usual range of Venetian *primi* and *secondi* on offer as well, but you'll eat better, and certainly more cheaply, if you stick to the pizzas. A garden out the back is a summer bonus.

Giudecca

Restaurants & *bacari*

Alla Palanca

Giudecca 448, fondamenta del Ponte Piccolo (041 528 7719). Vaporetto Palanca. **Open** 7am-8.30pm Mon-Sat. **Meals served** noon-2.30pm Mon-Sat. **Average** €30. **No credit cards. Map** p325 E4 ㊿

One of the cheapest meals-with-a-view in Venice is on offer at this humble, friendly bar-trattoria on the main Giudecca quay. It's a lunch-only place – the rest of the day it operates as a bar/magnet for local boatyard workers and assorted characters. Sit at one of the outside tables and order from a good-value menu that includes some surprisingly gourmet options like tagliatelle with *funghi porcini* or swordfish in orange and lemon marinade; finish up with a delicious chocolate mousse with candied fruit.

Harry's Dolci

Giudecca 773, fondamenta San Biagio (041 522 4844/www.cipriani.com). Vaporetto Sant'Eufemia. **Meals served** *Apr-Oct* noon-3pm, 7-10.30pm Mon, Wed-Sun. Closed Nov-Mar. **Average** €75. **Credit** AmEx, DC, MC, V. **Map** p325 D4 (51)

Arrigo Cipriani's second Venetian stronghold (his first is Harry's Bar, *see p171*), towards the western end of the Giudecca, is only open from April to October, when the weather allows outdoor diners to enjoy the stupendous views across the Giudecca Canal. The cuisine is supposedly lighter and more summery than *chez* Harry, but in practice many dishes – such as the flagship risottos – are identical and just as competently – if somewhat blandly – prepared. What changes is the cost: prices at Harry II are less than two-thirds of those at the mother ship (though that's still a big dent in the average wallet). Outside of mealtimes (or during, if they're not full) you can also order just a coffee and one of the delectable pastries that they make on the premises: the bar-pasticceria is open 10.30am-11pm. Come prepared for mosquitoes when the weather is hot.

Mistrà

Giudecca 212A, fondamenta del Ponte Lungo (041 522 0743). Vaporetto Redentore or Palanca. **Meals served** noon-3.30pm Mon; noon-3.30pm, 7.30-10.30pm Wed-Sun. **Closed** 3wks Jan; 3wks Aug. **Average** €45. **Credit** AmEx, DC, MC, V. **Map** p325 F5 (52)

The unvisited southern side of the Giudecca is about as far as you can get from tourist Venice, and it conceals one of the city's most unlikely gourmet treats. Amid a sprawl of boatyards, a fire-escape staircase leads up to this trattoria on the first floor of a warehouse with spectacular views over the southern lagoon. Once patronised exclusively by local shipwrights and gondola makers, Mistrà has become a word-of-mouth success among local foodies for its excellent fish menu (octopus and potato salad, baked fish with potatoes, cherry tomatoes and olives) and range of Ligurian specialities; they also do good steaks, if you're all fished out. Lunch is cheap and worker-oriented, dinner more ambitious and more expensive. To get there turn right along the quay from the Redentore vaporetto stop, continue past campo San Giacomo, then duck under the first covered passageway on the left – where there should be a sign to the restaurant.

Lido & Lagoon

Restaurants & *bacari*

Alla Maddalena
Mazzorbo 7B (041 730 151). Vaporetto Mazzorbo.
Meals served noon-3pm Mon-Wed, Fri-Sun.
Closed 20 Dec-10 Jan. **Average** €35. **Credit**
AmEx, DC, MC, V.
The ferry (line LN) from Fondamente Nove takes a
very pleasant 45 minutes to chug across the lagoon
to the island of Mazzorbo. Right opposite the jetty is
this lunch-only trattoria, which serves filling lagoon
cuisine. During the autumn hunting season, there's
no better place for wild duck, sourced directly from
local hunters; the rest of the year, seafood dominates.
Book ahead for Sunday lunch in summer, when the
waterside tables and those in the quiet garden behind
fill up with Venetian families. The house wine comes
from the family's own island vineyards.

Antica Trattoria Valmarana
Murano, fondamenta Navagero 31 (041 739 313).
Vaporetto Navagero. **Meals served** noon-3pm
daily. Closed 3wks Jan. **Average** €45. **Credit**
AmEx, DC, MC, V. **Map** p319 C2 🟠
A touch of class on the isle of glass, this elegant
restaurant with its Murano chandeliers and stuccoed
interior is a good lunch option even on a rainy day.
The kitchen does refined versions of seafood
classics like *risotto alla pescatora* as well as more
creative fare (tagliloini with wild boar ragù, or with
scallops and radicchio). Grilled fish star among the
secondi, but there are also a number of meat and
vegetarian dishes. In summer there are two *alfresco*
options: outside by the canal, or in the quiet garden
out the back. They also do bar-snacks, from
mozzarelle in carrozza (sort of like Scotch eggs
except with mozzarella where the egg should be)
to toasted sandwiches.

Busa alla Torre
Murano, campo Santo Stefano 3 (041 739 662).
Vaporetto Faro. **Meals served** noon-3.30pm daily.
Average €45. **Credit** AmEx, MC, V. **Map** p319 B2 🟠
This is Murano's ultimate gastronomic stop-off and
a perfect place for refuelling after resisting the hard
sell at the island's many glass workshops. In summer tables spill out into a pretty square opposite the
church of San Pietro Martire. The service is deft and
professional; the cuisine is reliable, no-frills seafood
cooking, with excellent *primi*, which might include
ravioli filled with *branzino* (bream) in a spider-crab
sauce, or tagliatelle with *canoce* (mantis shrimps).
The jovial owner, Lele, is a giant of a man and a real
character. Note the lunch-only opening.

La Favorita
Via Francesco Duodo 33, Lido (041 526 1626).
Vaporetto Lido. **Meals served** 7.30-10.30pm
Tue; 12.30-2.30pm, 7.30-10.30pm Wed-Sun.
Closed Jan. **Average** €55. **Credit** AmEx,
DC, MC, V. **Map** p317 B2 🟠

If you need to clinch a big deal with some industry
maven at the Venice Film Festival, you'll improve
your chances by inviting them to La Favorita. This
is the best restaurant on the Lido, and has a lovely
vine-shaded pergola for summer dining. It's an old-
fashioned and reassuring sort of place that does text-
book exemplars of Venetian seafood classics like
spaghetti ai caparossoli or *scampi in saor* (sweet-and-
sour sauce), plus a few more audacious dishes like
pumpkin gnocchi with scorpion fish and radicchio.
Service is professional, and the wine list has a fine
selection of bottles from the north-east.

Locanda Cipriani
Torcello, piazza Santa Fosca 29 (041 730 150/
www.locandacipriani.com). Vaporetto LN to Torcello.
Meals served noon-3pm, 7-9pm Mon, Wed-Sun.
Closed Jan. **Average** €80. **Credit** AmEx, DC, MC, V.
There is a lot to like about the high-class Locanda
Cipriani, which was one of Hemingway's haunts.
The setting, just off Torcello's pretty square, is
idyllic; tables spread over a large vine-shaded
terrace during the summer. And although there is
nothing remotely adventurous about the cuisine, it's
good in an old-fashioned way – as are the waiters.
Specialities such as *risotto alla torcellana* (with
seasonal vegetables) or *filetti di San Pietro alla
Carlina* (John Dory fillets with capers and tomatoes)
are done to perfection, and the desserts – including
a calorific giant meringue – are tasty treats for rich
kids. If the budget doesn't stretch to lunch or dinner,
stop off here for a hot chocolate and a *millefoglie*
pastry in mid-afternoon.

Busa alla Torre.

Cafés, Bars & Gelaterie

Eschew the €10 coffee – sweet treats and *spritz* is the Venetian way.

You'll be wanting to soak in art and culture on your Venetian trip, but don't forget to leave time to absorb Venetian life, too. And the best vantage point for this important pastime is a café table – preferably a pavement one, with just the right relaxation-to-entertainment ratio.

Italian bars and cafés (the terms are pretty much interchangeable) are multi-purpose establishments, and Venice's watering holes are no exception. In fact, to the usual Italian breakfast, light snacks, pastries and alcoholic beverages routine, Venice contributes its own specialities: the *ombra* (a small glass of wine), the *spritz* (see *p173* **Bar talk**) and the *cicheti* (tapas-like bar snacks). Time of day doesn't dictate what's on offer. Coffee is an all-day pick-me-up; a *spritz* can be sipped at any hour; and far from being a mere post-prandial *digestivo*, grappa is what many north-eastern Italian workers use to take the chill off the morning.

If a pre-breakfast grappa doesn't float your boat, then your first daily café-stop will be for coffee. Venice's relationship with this beverage is a long and significant one. The city's first *bottega del caffè* opened in 1683 in piazza San Marco. By the late 18th century as many as 24 coffee shops graced this square alone. San Marco continues to function as the city's most prestigious (and expensive) coffee-sipping drawing room. There's little to match enjoying a cup of java in that beautifully preserved historic **Caffè Florian** (see *p171*), the centre of 19th-century café culture. But unless you have a generous credit limit, take your *caffè* standing at the bar, rather than sitting in the square.

Venice is awash with good wine, and the next glass is as easy to find as the next bridge. The best bars offer an enormous choice of top-quality wines by the glass; bars specialising in wine are called *enoteche* or *bacari* (with the accent on the first a). *Bacari* are typically Venetian wine bars, usually with a range of *cicheti* on the counter. In some, food and seated meals have become the whole point: these are included in the **Eating Out** chapter, *see pp152-69*. Where drinking remains the *raison d'être*, they are listed here.

> ❶ Green numbers in this chapter correspond to the location of each café or bar as marked on the street maps. See *pp317-328*.

PASTICCERIE AND GELATERIE

Many of Venice's cake and ice-cream emporia double up as bars, with freshly prepared cakes and pastries for sale in addition to the usual coffee and liquor offerings. You'll find pastry shops everywhere; it will soon become very clear that Venetians don't like having to go too far for a sweet fix.

The Venetian day begins with a cappuccino and *brioche* (pronounced the French way), preferably one baked on the premises and kept warm until it is ready to be consumed. Any important meal invitation – and that includes Sunday with family or friends – involves investing in a big tray of sweet things to be shared. But in the lagoon city, cakes also take centrestage at *aperitivo* time: some of the best *spritz* in town are actually served at Venice's *pasticcerie*. Each *pasticceria* bakes its own specialities, so no two bakeries are ever alike and, consequently, no two pastries ever taste the same. These fact constitutes more than enough reason to do your own comparison taste testing.

Gelato was probably brought down to Venice by the settlers from the icy Dolomite mountains when they fled to the lagoon in ages past. Nowadays ice-cream shops are almost as numerous in Venice as mask shops. And as with mask shops, the quality of product varies greatly from place to place. A quick, foolproof, test of any shop is to eyeball the tub of banana ice-cream – if it's grey in colour, you know it's the real deal: bright yellow screams that it's been made from a mix.

ETIQUETTE

The usual practice in Italian bars is to decide what you want, pay at the till in advance, then order at the counter. If you return to the same establishment sufficiently often to be considered a regular, you can pay afterwards. Remember that anything ordered at the counter must then be consumed at the counter. If you want to sit at a café table, you should order from there (or at the very least indicate that you are planning to sit down); the privilege of occupying a table will push your bill up – a little in smaller, more hidden-away places but jaw-droppingly in, say, piazza San Marco, especially in the evening when a surcharge is added for the palm orchestras – don't expect much (if any) change from a €10 note.

Many bars that stay open late and/or have live music are listed in the **Music & Nightlife** chapter; see p218-223.

San Marco

Cafés & bars

See also p219 **Aurora**, p219 **Bacaro Jazz**, p219 **Centrale Restaurant Lounge**, p219 **Torino** and p219 **Vitae**.

Bar all'Angolo

San Marco 3464, campo Santo Stefano (041 522 0710). Vaporetto Sant'Angelo. **Open** 6.30am-9pm Mon-Sat. Closed Jan. **No credit cards. Map** p325 F1 ➊

If you're lucky enough to secure a table outside, you'll be well placed to watch the locals saunter through the campo as you enjoy a coffee or spritz. Inside you have your choice of standing at the usually crowded bar or relaxing in one of the comfy seats in the back where you'll find a mixed bag of locals and tourists being served good tramezzini, fresh salads and panini by friendly, if hurried, staff. There are certainly bigger bars in this busy campo, but none match the quality on offer here.

Caffè Florian

San Marco 56, piazza San Marco (041 520 5641/ www.caffeflorian.com). Vaporetto Vallaresso. **Open** May-Oct 10am-midnight daily. Nov-Apr 10am-midnight Mon, Tue, Thur-Sun. Closed early Dec-Christmas, 2wks Jan. **Credit** AmEx, DC, MC, V. **Map** p326 B1/2 ➋

Stepping into Florian sweeps you back to 18th-century Venice as you're swallowed into this mirrored, stuccoed and frescoed jewel of a café. Founded by a certain Floriano Francesconi in 1720 as 'Venezia Trionfante', its present appearance, complete with dozens of intimate wooden séparés, dates from an 1859 remodelling. Rousseau, Goethe and Byron hung out here – the last in sympathy, no doubt, with those loyal Venetians who boycotted the Quadri (see below) across the square, where Austrian officers used to meet. Times have changed and these days having a drink at Florian is not so much a political statement as a bank statement – especially if you sit at one of the outside tables, where nothing – not even a humble caffè – comes in at less than €10.

Gran Caffè Quadri

San Marco 121, piazza San Marco (041 522 2105/ fax 041 500 8041/www.quadrivenice.com). Vaporetto Vallaresso or San Zaccaria. **Open** Apr-Oct 9am-11pm daily. Nov-Mar 9am-11pm Tue-Sun. **Credit** AmEx, DC, MC, V. **Map** p326 B1 ➌

With its ornate stucco mouldings, 18th-century murals, huge mirrors and polished wooden furniture, Quadri is every inch the caffè storico. People have been drinking here since 1638, when it was called Il Rimedio. Giorgio Quadri was among the first to bring Turkish-style coffee to Venice when he

took the place over in the late 18th century. Stendhal, Wagner and Balzac were habitués. In the evening a palm orchestra competes out in the square with the one at Florian's (see above) opposite, and romantics pay small fortunes to sip cocktails under the stars. In neo-classical rooms upstairs, the Quadri has a restaurant that is as expensive as it is elegant. Gran Caffè literary trivia: Marcel Proust used to bring his mother to lunch here.

Harry's Bar

San Marco 1323, calle Vallaresso (041 528 5777/ www.cipriani.com). Vaporetto Vallaresso. **Open** 10.30am-11pm daily. **Credit** AmEx, DC, MC, V. **Map** p326 B2 ➍

This historic watering hole, founded by Giuseppe Cipriani in 1931, has changed little since the days when Ernest Hemingway came here to work on his next hangover… except for the prices and the numbers of tourists. But despite the pre-dinner crush and some offhand service, a Bellini (fresh peach juice and sparkling wine) at the bar is as much a part of the Venetian experience as a gondola ride (and at €14 far cheaper). At mealtimes the tables upstairs and down are reserved for diners who enjoy the Venetian-themed international comfort food and are prepared to pay very steep prices (€120-plus for three courses) to be seen chez Harry. Stick with a Bellini, and don't even think of coming in here wearing shorts or ordering a spritz.

The best Cafés

… for grand café ambience
Caffè Florian, **Gran Caffè Quadri** (for both, see above).

… for waterside views
Hotel Monaco & Gran Café (see p172), **Angiò** (see p172), **Al Chioschetto** (see p179).

… for a light lunch
La Cantina (see p175), **Bar ai Nomboli** (see p176), **Cantinone** (see p179).

… for coffee 'n' cakes
Andrea Zanin (see p172), **Rizzardini** (see p178), **Gobbetti** (see p179).

… for fine wines
Un Mondo diVino (see p175), **Al Prosecco** (see p178), **Do Mori** (see p178).

… for the evening in-crowd
Muro (see p177), **Al Mercà** (see p177), **Naranzaria** (see p165), **Vitae** (see p219), **Paradiso Perduto** (see p220), **Orange** and **Impronta Café** (for both, see p221).

Eat, Drink, Shop

Boutique del Gelato. *See p173.*

Hotel Monaco & Grand Canal Bar

San Marco 1332, calle Vallaresso (041 520 0211/ www.hotelmonaco.it). Vaporetto Vallaresso. **Open** 10am-midnight daily. **Credit** AmEx, DC, MC, V. **Map** p326 B2. ③

A short walk from piazza San Marco, the elegant Hotel Monaco & Grand Canal Bar is truly a special place to sit back and savour *La Serenissima*. There's a cosy, compact bar inside (it's just a pity they didn't use the stunning Ridotto theatre – available only for private functions – as an additional bar space) and a divine terrace overlooking the punta della Dogana and the Salute church: it really is just like floating along the Grand Canal. Granted, it's an expensive pleasure (a *spritz* will set you back the not insignificant sum of €9) but you're paying for sipping in one of the most enchanting points in the city. The restaurant looks enticing, but you'll be lucky to get a table without booking well ahead.

Enoteche & bacari

Alla Botte

San Marco 5482, calle della Bissa (041 520 9775). Vaporetto Rialto. **Open** 10am-3pm, 5.30-11pm Mon-Wed, Fri-Sat; 10am-3pm Sun. **Credit** DC, MC, V. **Map** p322 B5 ⑤

Though it's tucked away in a hidden calle close to campo San Bartolomeo, you won't have trouble finding Alla Botte: just follow the crowds of Venetians, both young and old, heading there. Don't let the packed-to-the-gills bar discourage you from making

your way up to the counter where 25 wines by the glass are available, in addition to an assortment of some of the city's best *cicheti*, including the most delicious *polpette* (meatballs) in the area. In warmer months the surrounding streets become a natural extension of the bar; the atmosphere inside becomes cosier (and more crowded) during cooler times. Dinner is also served in the adjacent dining room, but the bar is where the action is.

Gelaterie

Igloo

San Marco 3651, calle della Mandola (041 522 3003). Vaporetto Sant'Angelo. **Open** *Feb-Apr, Oct, Nov* 11.30am-7.30pm. *May-Sept* 11am-8pm daily. Closed mid Nov-Carnevale. **No credit cards.** **Map** p326 A1 ⑥

Generous portions of handmade, creamy *gelato* in a wide range of varieties to please everyone is what Igloo is all about. In the summer months fruit flavours such as fig or blackberry are made from the nearby market's freshest produce. In an area where *gelato* is found around any and every corner, Igloo is a tried and true favourite and easily found by spotting the crowd of happy ice cream-eaters spilling out into the compact street.

Pasticcerie

Andrea Zanin

San Marco 4589, campo San Luca (041 522 4803). Vaporetto Rialto. **Open** 7.30am-8pm Mon-Sat; 10.30am-7.30pm Sun. **No credit cards.** **Map** p326 B1 ⑦

This long-established cake shop has been refurbished and reinvented by master patisseur Andrea Zanin who has stocked it full of his delicious, award-winning goodies. His miniature pastries just beg to be tasted, each one a delectable morsel of whatever filling you've chosen – meringue, pistachio, tiramisu or coffee, to name just a few. At €2.50 a pop, it's more expensive than other *pasticcerie*, but for the privilege of sampling works of art like this, it really is worth splashing out.

Castello

Cafés & bars

See also p219 **Inishark Pub**.

Angiò

Castello 2142, ponte della Veneta Marina (041 277 8555). Vaporetto Arsenale. **Open** *Feb-May, Oct-Dec* 7am-9pm Mon, Wed-Sun. *June-Sept* 7am-midnight Mon, Wed-Sun. **Credit** MC, V. **Map** p327 E2 ⑧

Owned by siblings Andrea and Giorgia, Angiò is the finest stopping point along one of Venice's most tourist-trafficked spots – the lagoon-front riva degli Schiavoni. Tables line the water's edge; ultra-friendly staff serve up pints of Guinness, freshly made sandwiches and interesting selections of cheese and wine. Take in the stunning view of San Giorgio with either a morning coffee or an early evening *aperitivo* and enquire about the regular music events that are held here during the summer months on Saturday evenings.

Vincent Bar

Sant'Elena, viale IV novembre 36 (041 520 4493). Vaporetto Sant'Elena. **Open** 7am-10pm Tue-Sun. **No credit cards. Map** p328 B5 ⑨

Sant'Elena must be one of Venice's best-kept secrets – it's surely the only place you'll find more trees and grassy expanses than throngs of tourists. So, when you've had your fill of museums, churches and crowded squares, venture over to the eastern edge of the city and experience a real Venetian neighbourhood. Grab a seat – and a drink – outside this bar and join the locals gazing lazily across the lagoon at passing boats or keeping a watchful eye on their *bambini* as they play in the park. The bar's ice-cream is made on the premises. There are also several computers inside with high-speed internet connections (€4.50 per hour).

Enoteche & bacari

See also p219 **La Mascareta**.

Da Dante

Castello 2877, corte Nova (041 528 5163). Vaporetto Celestia or San Zaccaria. **Open** 8am-9pm Mon-Sat. Closed Aug. **No credit cards. Map** p323 D5 ⑩

Tourists? Here? Not likely. If you want to hang with the locals in a place that is as Venetian as it is possible to get, head for this out-of-the-way *bacaro* in the depths of Castello, proudly serving its loyal clientele since 1957. To accompany the banter of the local card-playing Venetians, there's white and red wine straight from the demijohn, and Dante's wife serves up specialities such as *bovoleti* (tiny snails in garlic) and *folpeti* (baby octopus).

Gelaterie

Boutique del Gelato

Castello 5727, salizzada San Lio (041 522 3283). Vaporetto Rialto. **Open** *Feb-May, Oct, Nov* 10am-8.30pm daily. *June-Sept* 10am-11.30pm daily. Closed Dec, Jan. **No credit cards. Map** p322 C5 ⑪

Most Venetians agree that some of the city's best *gelato* is served in this tiny outlet on the busy salizzada San Lio. You will have to learn to be patient, though, because there's always a huge crowd waiting to be served. See it as quality assurance – it's worth the wait.

Pasticcerie

Da Bonifacio

Castello 4237, calle degli Albanesi (041 522 7507). Vaporetto San Zaccaria. **Open** 7am-8.30pm Mon-Wed, Fri-Sun. Closed 3wks Aug, 1wk Christmas. **No credit cards. Map** p326 C1 ⑫

Tucked away in a narrow calle behind the Danieli Hotel, this is a firm favourite with Venetians, whom you'll find milling around outside the entrance in great numbers, waiting to squeeze inside for a coffee, drink and something from the cake cabinet. As well as offering a tempting array of snacks and traditional cakes such as *mammalucchi* (deep-fried batter cakes with candied fruit), Da Bonifacio is famous for its creative *fritelle* (wild berry, chocolate, almond and apple fillings are sold, in addition to the traditional *fritelle* found around the city), which start to appear on the scene in January and remain until Carnevale has come to a close. Each season brings a new pastry to their line-up, so don't be shy, ask what's special when you're visiting.

Pasticceria Melita

Castello 1000-4, fondamenta Sant'Anna (no phone). Vaporetto Giardini. **Open** 8am-2pm, 3.30-8.30pm Tue-Sun. **No credit cards. Map** p328 A2 ⑬

Eat, Drink, Shop

Bar talk

A selection of useful terms to help you with ordering, any time of the day:

Drinking...

bicchiere glass; **caffè americano** espresso diluted with hot water, served in a larger cup; **caffè** espresso; **caffè corretto** espresso with a shot of alcohol (usually grappa); **caffè doppio** double espresso; **caffè lungo** espresso made with slightly more water; **caffè macchiato** espresso with a dash of milk; **decaffeinato** decaf – can be **caffè decaffeinato** (decaf espresso) or **cappuccino decaffeinato** (decaf cappuccino); **enoteca**

wine bar and/or bottle shop; **fragolino** sweet white or red wine made from a particular strawberry-scented grape; **a mescita** (wine) by the glass; **ombra** small glass of wine; **prosecco** light, sparkling white wine; **prosecco spento** prosecco with no bubbles; **spritz** classic Venetian aperitivo of white wine, Campari and a shot of selzer or sparkling water; a sweeter version is made with low-alcohol Aperol.

Paying...

scontrino receipt; **conto** cheque; **cassa** cash desk.

Your senses will reel at the dizzying assortment of pastries on offer here. Don't let the brusqueness of the pastry chef put you off: he made pastries for the Hotel Danieli for 20 years before opening his own piece of sweet paradise here in the 1980s. There's no sitting down for a languorous coffee and cake session here: it's a stand-up or takeaway only kind of place, but is a local favourite.

Rosa Salva

Castello 6779, campo Santi Giovanni e Paolo (041 522 7949). Vaporetto Fondamente Nove. **Open** 7.30am-8.30pm Mon, Tue, Thur-Sun. **No credit cards. Map** p322 C5 ⑭
Take the time and pay the higher prices to sit down and savour the history that surrounds you in campo Santi Giovanni e Paolo – widely considered the most striking after piazza San Marco – while nursing one of the smoothest *cappuccini* in town and trying one of Rosa Salva's delicious cakes. If it's ice-cream you fancy, all their flavours are made on the premises. The Bartolomeo Colleoni equestrian monument (*see p93*) has just been restored and is back on view, set in front of the glorious façade of the Scuola Grande di San Marco (*see p88*).

Cannaregio

Cafés & bars

See also p159 **Algiubagiò**, *p219* **Do Fradei**, *p219* **Fiddler's Elbow Irish Pub**, *p220* **Iguana**, *p220* **Paradiso Perduto** and *p220* **Santo Bevitore**.

Do Colonne

Cannaregio 1814C, rio terà San Leonardo (041 524 0453). Vaporetto San Marcuola. **Open** 10am-8.30pm Mon-Fri, Sun. **No credit cards. Map** p321 F3 ⑮

On the bustling rio terà San Leonardo – one of the main arteries connecting the station to the city centre – this is a welcome stopping point with abundant choices for snacking. The large bar hosts a variety of offerings from innovative *tramezzini* on rye bread, *polpette* (meatballs), miniature sandwiches stuffed with cured meats and cheeses, overflowing crostini and a few hot plates which change daily. Wash everything back with a glass of wine, prosecco or beer before hitting the crowds and touring more sites around town.

Enoteche & bacari

La Cantina

Cannaregio 3689, campo San Felice (041 522 8258). Vaporetto Ca' d'Oro. **Open** 11am-10pm Tue-Sat. Closed 2wks July-Aug; 2wks Jan. **Credit** MC, V. **Map** p322 A3/4 ⑯
This is a wonderful place in which to enjoy your *aperitivo*, yet the snack offerings are so substantial that a quick drink can easily turn into a full meal. The ambience indoors is warm and cosy. Outside, tables set back from the packed strada Nuova are the perfect place for watching the world bustle by, assuming you can take your eyes off the creative nibbles. The friendly staff will help you to order a plate (or two or three) piled high with mouth-watering *crostini*, made on the spot with whatever's in season at the local fish and produce markets by food 'artist' Francesco: your plate is his canvas. Some 30 wines are available by the glass and they now sell Gaston, a beer brewed specially for the bar.

Un Mondo diVino

Cannaregio 5984A, salizada San Canciano (041 521 1093). Vaporetto Rialto or Ca' d'Oro. **Open** 10am-3pm; 5.30-10pm Tue-Sun. **Credit** MC, V. **Map** p322 B4 ⑰

Eat, Drink, Shop

Un Mondo diVino: divine wines.

Try the extra strong *spritz al bitter* at **Boscolo**.

Cora and Raffaele have recently opened what has fast become one of the most popular *bacari* in the city, a wonderful meeting-spot full of Venetians and visitors throughout the day. The intimate interior, with its low, wooden-beamed ceiling, begs passers-by to stop inside, where everyone is warmly welcomed by the owners and their staff. Over 40 fine wines are offered by the glass and the large bar has a bewilderingly large selection of *cicheti*, including wonderful artichokes, *bacalà*, meatballs and *melanzane alla parmigiana* (aubergines with mozzarella). In warm weather, enjoy your *aperitivo* and snacks outside under an awning thoughtfully provided to avert pigeon-damage.

Gelaterie

Il Gelatone

Cannaregio 2063, rio terà Maddalena (041 720 631). Vaporetto San Marcuola. **Open** *Mid Jan-Apr, Oct-mid Dec* 11am-8pm daily. *May-Sept* 11am-10.30pm daily. **No credit cards. Map** p322 A3 ⑱
Follow the trail of overflowing ice-cream cones between the railway station and the end of strada Nuova and you'll easily find Il Gelatone, just as hungry ice-cream seekers have been doing for the last 17 years. The luscious *gelato* comes in a number of gorgeous flavours and satisfying generous portions: the yoghurt-flavoured variety with sesame seeds and honey is especially suited to those with a sweet tooth.

Pasticcerie

Boscolo

Cannaregio 1818, campiello de l'Anconeta (041 720 731). Vaporetto San Marcuola. **Open** 6.40am-8.40pm Tue-Sun. Closed July; 2wks Feb. **No credit cards. Map** p321 F3 ⑲

The bar at Maria Boscolo's *pasticceria* is always packed; locals flock to enjoy an extra-strong *spritz al bitter* with one of her home-made *pizzette*. There is also an excellent assortment of Venetian sweets: *frittelle* during Carnevale, as well as *zaleti* and *pincia* (a sweet bread made with cornflour and raisins). Boscolo's range of chocolates in the form of interesting (and graphic) Kama Sutra positions have made this confectioner's famous.

San Polo & Santa Croce

Cafés & bars

See also p221 **Ai Postali,** p162 **Bancogiro,** p221 **Da Baffo,** p163 **Muro Vino e Cucina** and p163 **Naranzaria.**

Bar Ai Nomboli

San Polo 2717C, rio terà dei Nomboli (041 523 0995). Vaporetto San Tomà. **Open** 7am-9pm Mon-Fri. Closed 1wk Christmas; 3wks Aug. **No credit cards. Map** p321 F5 ⑳
This bar, much loved by Venice's student population, has expanded its already impressive repertoire of sandwich combinations. You'll need to summon all of your decision-making skills when faced with a choice of more than 100 sandwiches and almost 50 *tramezzini*: try the 'Serenissima' with tuna, peppers, peas and onions or perhaps the 'Appennino' with roast beef, broccoli and pecorino – or ask them to build your own creation, using any of their fresh ingredients. Take a seat outside, if one is available: even in inclement weather the wide awning will keep you nice and dry.

Caffè dei Frari

San Polo 2564, fondamenta dei Frari (041 524 1877). Vaporetto San Tomà. **Open** 8am-9pm daily. Closed 2wks Aug. **No credit cards. Map** p321 F5 ㉑

A cosy bar with an even cosier mezzanine, which is often packed with students and lawyers. The walls feature art nouveau interpretations of 18th-century Venice. This is the logical place to frequent after a morning or afternoon spent visiting the nearby Frari church or the Scuola Grande di San Rocco. Sit back and relax in one of their comfortable booths and enjoy a tasty spread of snacks, which accompany all of the *aperitivi* and drinks.

Caffè del Doge
San Polo 609, calle dei Cinque (041 522 7787/ www.caffedeldoge.com). Vaporetto San Silvestro. **Open** 7am-7pm Mon-Sat; 7am-1pm Sun. **No credit cards. Map** p322 A/B5 ㉒
Italians scoff at the idea of drinking cappuccino after 11am, but rules like this go by the board at the Caffè del Doge, a bright, minimalist space, where any time is good for indulging in the richest, creamiest and most luscious cup of coffee you'll taste in Venice. Two signature blends and ten single-origin coffees, imported exclusively from places such as Guatemala, Brazil, Venezuela, Cuba and Australia, are available in various preparations from espresso to filtered. Each is also available for purchase. Don't overlook the freshly made pastries, sweets and natural juices, and watch out for the speciality coffees, for which a portion of each sale goes to their own *bambini del caffè* (The Children of Coffee), a non-profit organisation that assists children who work on coffee plantations worldwide.

Muro Vino e Cucina
San Polo 222, campo Cesare Battisti già Bella Vienna (041 523 7495). Vaporetto Rialto. **Open** 9am-3.30pm, 5pm-1am Mon-Sat. **Credit** MC, V. **Map** p322 B5. ㊸
In an area where it's easier to find an *ombra* than a *spritz*, the stylish Muro Vino e Cucina – or Muro as it's more commonly known – is often packed with throngs of sophisticated-but-thirsty *spritz*-seekers. There's something for pretty much everyone here – from *aperitivi* and *cicheti* at their spacious downstairs bar and outside tables, to eclectic fine dining on the first floor (*see p165*). In the colourful area around the historic Rialto markets, Muro's sleek, modern design is complemented by the exceptionally friendly and warm staff.

Enoteche & bacari

Al Mercà
San Polo 213, campo Cesare Battisti già Bella Vienna (393 992 4781). Vaporetto Rialto. **Open** 9am-3pm, 6-9pm Mon-Sat; 6-9pm Sun. Closed 1wk Christmas. **No credit cards. Map** p322 B5 ㉓
With standing room only in the campo, Al Mercà has been serving Rialto market goers with their victuals since 1918. A recent change in ownership has brought young business partners Gabriele, Marco and Giuseppe together behind the counter. It's a wonder they all fit back there at the same time. Neatly packed into this tiny space is a snack-filled

In the market

Campo Santa Margherita (*see p127*), long Venice's drinking hub, continues to hum. But for real buzz nowadays, you'll need to head for the markets.

The high-density retail zone at the northwestern foot of the Rialto bridge used to be 'early to rise, early to bed' in the extreme: market traders would begin piling their stalls high with fruit, vegetables and fish well before sun-up, bustling through until around 2pm, after which campo Cesare Battisti (aka campo Bella Vienna), campo della Pescaria and the Naranzeria were eerily quiet... when not fenced off altogether.

There have always, of course, been bars and *bacari* here to slake the thirst of hungry market workers, but the last few years has seen an influx of hip new eateries and drinking dens, making this area an all-day (not to mention late-night) magnet.

The situation is ideal: there's hardly a single private house for streets around, allowing high decibel levels; and the setting is impossibly romantic, with unexpected vistas of the Grand Canal around each mysteriously shuttered-up corner.

It's a mixed crowd of mainly young(-ish), mainly professional locals, plus visitors in the know, who congregate here. The nearby law courts (soon to move to new premises in piazzale Roma) contribute a significant proportion of the crowd.

Tipplers in a hurry – or those who don't mind about niceties such as somewhere to sit – grab a glass at **Al Mercà** (*see p177*) and stand in campo Bella Venezia in the happy, noisy mêlée of *ombra* and *spritz* imbibers. **Muro**'s minimalist ground-floor bar (*see p177*) attracts a designy clientele, including a large student contingent, while serious foodies frequent the upstairs restaurant (*see p165*). You can segue from *aperitivi-and-cicheti* to fully fledged meals in **Naranzeria** (*see p165*) and **Bancagiro** (*see p162*) too; the latter attracts a more mature crowd, the former is more upscale. But both have a clutch of hotly contended tables looking out towards the Grand Canal in all its grandiose glory.

Eat, Drink, Shop

Caffè del Doge. See p177.

case with meatballs, artichoke hearts and mini-sandwiches in addition to more than 34 different options for *panini* toppings and a generous selection of wines by the glass. You can now purchase wines by the bottle here and have them delivered.

Al Prosecco
Santa Croce 1503, campo San Giacomo dell'Orio (041 524 0222). Vaporetto San Stae. **Open** *Feb-July, Sept-Dec* 8am-10pm Mon-Sat. Closed Jan, Aug. **No credit cards**. **Map** p321 F4
Prosecco – whether sparkling or still – is second only to *spritz* in terms of daily Venetian consumption, and this bar is a good place for consuming it. The shaded outside tables are a fantastic vantage point for observing daily life in a lively campo, but the interior is just as convivial on cooler days. Exceptional wines are served by the glass, with a first-rate choice of cheeses, cold meats, marinated fish and oysters to accompany any selection from the bar.

Da Lele
Santa Croce 183, campo dei Tolentini (no phone). Vaporetto Piazzale Roma. **Open** 6am-2pm, 4-8pm Mon-Fri; 6am-2pm Sat. **No credit cards**. **Map** p321 D5
There are plenty of bars around the bus station at piazzale Roma, but most of them are either sleazy or overpriced (or both). Gabriele's (Lele's) place is the first authentic *osteria* for those arriving in Venice – or the last for those leaving; look for the two barrels outside and you've found it. It's so small in here there isn't even room for a phone – but there are local

wines from Piave, Lison and Valdobbiadene on offer, as well as fresh rolls, which are made to order with meat and/or cheese fillings.

Do Mori
San Polo 429, calle dei Do Mori (041 522 5401). Vaporetto Rialto or San Silvestro. **Open** 8.30am-8.30pm Mon-Sat. **No credit cards**. **Map** p322 A5
The Do Mori – in a narrow alleyway in Rialto market territory – claims to be the oldest *bacaro* in Venice, dating back to 1462 when Jacopo Tintoretto was leaving his painted mark around town. Batteries of copper pans hang from the ceiling, and at peak times the narrow bar is a heaving mass of bodies, all lunging for the excellent *francobolli* (mini-sandwiches; literally, postage stamps) and the tremendous selection of fine wines. But don't point to a label at random, as prices can sometimes be in the connoisseur bracket. You won't go far wrong if you stick to a glass of the classic *spento* – prosecco minus the bubbles.

Gelaterie

Alaska Gelateria-Sorbetteria
Santa Croce 1159, calle larga dei Bari (041 715 211). Vaporetto Riva de Biasio. **Open** *Apr-Oct* 11am-midnight daily. *Nov, Feb-Mar* noon-9pm daily. Closed Dec, Jan. **No credit cards**. **Map** p321 E4
Carlo Pistacchi is passionate about making icecream and experimenting with new flavours using only the freshest natural ingredients. If you are feeling cautious, stick to tried and true choices such as hazelnut or yoghurt; braver types should branch out to sample seasonally changing exotic flavours, such as artichoke, fennel, celery, asparagus or ginger. Multiple visits are in order, not only to experience a variety of flavours but also fully to enjoy the antics of AS Roma-supporter Carlo.

Pasticcerie

Gilda Vio
Santa Croce 784, rio Marin (041 718 523). Vaporetto Riva di Biasio. **Open** 6.30am-8.15pm Mon, Tue, Thu-Sun. Closed Aug. **No credit cards**. **Map** p321 E4
Just a short hop across the Grand Canal from the train station, Gilda Vio's delicious pastry shop is a rewarding stopover on arrival in or departure from Venice – or at any other time, for that matter. There's a world of choice here, and a selection of sizes. Individual portions can be consumed with a coffee or drink at one of the tables along the rio Marin. Alternatively, treats such as a wonderful creation with cream and fresh fruit can be purchased family-size to take away.

Rizzardini
San Polo 1415, campiello dei Meloni (041 522 3835). Vaporetto San Silvestro. **Open** 7am-8.30pm Mon, Wed-Sun. Closed Aug. **No credit cards**. **Map** p322 A5

An eye-catching *pasticceria* with pastries, cookies and snacks to match. When owner Paolo is behind the bar, there's never a dull moment. It's especially good for traditional Venetian pastries, cookies, coffee, *frittelle* during Carnevale… anything, if you can manoeuvre up to the counter and place your order.

Dorsoduro

Cafés & bars

See also p221 **Café Blue**, *p221* **Impronta**, *p221* **Café Noir**, *p221* **Il Caffè** and *p221* **Orange**.

Ai Do Draghi

Dorsoduro 3665, calle della Chiesa (041 528 9731). Vaporetto San Tomà. **Open** *Apr-Oct* 7.30am-2am daily. *Nov-Mar* 7.30am-11pm daily. **No credit cards. Map** p325 E1 ㉚
Throngs of cheerful *spritz* drinkers cram into the small calle off campo Santa Margherita where the entrance to Ai Do Draghi is located – and also on to its numerous tables on the square – to enjoy draught beers, strong *spritz al bitter* and approximately 40 wines by the glass. Not only are the staff friendly and courteous, but the outdoor seating provides one of the best vantage points from which to observe the energetic and bustling pace of campo Santa Margherita. The indoor seating, a well-kept secret, is intimate and snug.

Al Chioschetto

Dorsoduro 1406A, fondamenta delle Zattere (348 396 8466). Vaporetto Zattere. **Open** *June-Sept* 7.30am-2am daily. *Oct-May* 7.30am-6pm daily. **No credit cards. Map** p325 E3 ㉛
A much-loved spot not only for scrumptious *panini* and nibbles, but also for the tranquillity of sitting outside along the Giudecca Canal with a sweeping view from industrial Marghera to Palladian San Giorgio Maggiore. Inclement weather poses a problem as seating is strictly outside, so take advantage of any sunny day throughout the year and head over here for your daily bar needs.

Da Gino

Dorsoduro 853A, calle Nuova Sant'Agnese (041 528 5276). Vaporetto Accademia. **Open** 6am-7.30pm Mon-Sat. Closed Aug; 2wks Dec-Jan. **No credit cards. Map** p325 F2/3 ㉜
You'll always be greeted with a smile by the Scarpa family, whether it's your first or your 100th visit; they take customer service seriously in a city where so many tourists make for some cranky hosts. During the warmer months, tables outside along the calle make excellent viewpoints for watching the flow of gallery-goers making their way between the Accademia and the Guggenheim Collection. Stop inside for a visit where you'll find Inter-fan Emilio expertly manning the coffee machine. Gino's serves some of the best *tramezzini* and made-to-order *panini* around.

Enoteche & bacari

Cantinone (già Schiavi)

Dorsoduro 992, fondamenta Nani (041 523 0034). Vaporetto Accademia or Zattere. **Open** 8am-8.30pm Mon-Sat; 9am-1pm Sun. Closed 1wk Aug. **No credit cards. Map** p325 E2 ㉝
Two generations of the Gastaldi family work here, filling glasses, carting cases of wine, and preparing huge *panini* with mortadella or more delicate *crostini* with, for example, creamy tuna spread with leeks. If you're thinking about making this your lunch stop, give yourself ample opportunity to select from the day's offerings by coming before the crowds pour in at 1pm. When the bar itself is full, you'll be in good company on the steps of the nearby bridge outside which make a good background for the Venetian ritual of *spritz* and prosecco consumption.

Gelaterie

Gelateria Lo Squero

Dorsoduro 989-90, fondamenta Nani (347 269 7921). Vaporetto Accademia or Zattere. **Open** 11am-9pm daily. **No credit cards. Map** p325 E3 ㉞
Simone Sambo makes of some of the finest ice-cream in Venice. He's hard-pressed to pinpoint a favourite flavour, but can happily rattle off those in in his current repertoire – which always depends on the freshest Italian ingredients available. His mousse series (blueberry, strawberry, amaretto, chocolate and hazelnut, among others) is so light and creamy it's served in a waffle cone so it doesn't fly away.

Pasticcerie

Gobbetti

Dorsoduro 3108B, rio terà Canal (041 528 9014). Vaporetto Ca' Rezzonico. **Open** 7am-8pm daily. **No credit cards. Map** p325 E1 ㉟
Though this shop is tiny, Gobbetti produces some of Venice's most delicious cakes and sells them in various outlets throughout the city. The sought-after chocolate mousse is their best-known delight and soon disappears after the day's fresh batch is displayed. If the whole cakes are sold out, check the display case for single servings.

Tonolo

Dorsoduro 3764, calle San Pantalon (041 523 7209). Vaporetto San Tomà. **Open** 7.45am-8pm Tue-Sat; 7.45am-1pm Sun. Closed Aug. **No credit cards. Map** p325 E1 ㊱
This Venice institution has been operating in the same spot since 1953. The coffee is exceptional. On Sundays the place fills up with locals buying sweet offerings to take to lunch – don't be shy about asserting your rights or you may never get served. All the delectable pastries – which are candy for the eyes as well as the stomach – come in miniature sizes to make sampling a little bit easier.

Eat, Drink, Shop

Shops & Services

High fashion and exquisite handicrafts – if you buy authentic.

Venice was once the crossroads between East and West, and merchants from all over Europe met those from the Levant here to trade throughout the city. Exotic spices and raw silks were among the goods imported from distant lands and sold by shrewd Venetian merchants, though humble salt was also a major player in Venetian trade. One of the most important events in Renaissance Venice was La Sensa fair (*see p202*), which lasted a fortnight and was particularly popular for purchasing wedding trousseaux.

Traders of different nations each had their *fondaco* (alternatively spelt *fontaco* or *fondego*), a warehouse-cum-lodging. So successful in their business – and so desirous of making an impression – were the German traders in Venice that their Fondego dei Tedeschi (now the main post office, *see p297*) was bedecked with frescoes by Titian and Giorgione.

The sumptuous brocades and damasks, Burano lace and Murano glassware still produced and found in the city are all legacies of *La Serenissima*'s thriving commerce. Though the prices of such authentic Venetian-made goods can be prohibitive, a recent resurgence of local artisans – shoemakers, jewellers, carpenters, mask makers and blacksmiths – has led to slightly more competitive rates, and has helped to keep traditional techniques alive.

The **Mercerie** – the maze of crowded, narrow alleyways leading from piazza San Marco to the Rialto – and the streets known collectively as the Frezzeria, which wind between La Fenice (*see p91*) and piazza San Marco have been the main retail areas in this city for the past 600 years or so. The densest concentration of big-name fashion outlets can be found around the calle larga XXII Marzo, just west of the piazza, where the top names such as Prada, Fendi, Versace and Gucci have all staked their boutiques.

Devotees of kitsch should not miss the stalls and shops near the train station, where plastic gondolas, illuminated gondolas, flashing gondolas, musical gondolas and even gondola cigarette lighters reign supreme.

For more tasteful souvenirs, Venice's glass, lace, fabrics and handmade paper are legendary – as are the much cheaper made-in-Taiwan substitutes that are passed off as the genuine article by unscrupulous traders. Sticking to the outlets listed below will help you to avoid unpleasant surprises.

The steady demographic drop has led to the demise of 'everyday' shops: bread, fruit and veg, milk and meat are increasingly difficult to get hold of. And while new supermarkets have opened in various parts of the city and on the Giudecca, the flipside of this is the threat now posed to the livelihood of the few remaining greengrocers, bakers and butchers.

OPENING HOURS AND TAX REBATES

Most food shops are closed on Wednesday afternoons, while some non-food shops stay shut on Monday mornings. During high season (which in Venice includes Carnevale in February/March, Easter, the summer season from June to October and the four weeks leading up to Christmas) many shops abandon their lunchtime closing and stay open all day, even opening on Sundays.

It pays to be sceptical about the hours posted on the doors of smaller shops: opening times are often determined by volume of trade or personal whim. If you want to be sure of not finding the shutters drawn, call before you set out.

Incomprehensibly – given that summer is Venice's busiest season – some shops close for holidays in August, but the majority of these are smaller ones that cater more for residents than tourists, such as *tabacchi* (*see p301*), photocopying centres and dry-cleaners.

If you are not an EU citizen, remember to keep your official receipt (*scontrino*) as you are entitled to a rebate on IVA (sales tax) paid on purchases of personal goods costing more than €154, as long as they leave the country unused and are bought from a shop that provides this service. Make sure that there is a sign displayed in the window and also ask for the form that you'll need to show at customs upon departure. For more information about customs, see the Italian government website (www.agenziadogane.gov.it) for info in English.

For obvious reasons, which relate primarily to lack of space, Venice is not shopping-centre friendly. If you are looking for a mall to fill all your needs, you'll have to journey to the mainland. The Centro Barche in Mestre offers everything from H&M to the Feltrinelli international bookstore.

Cool kitchenware from **Kirei**. *See p185*.

Eat, Drink, Shop

Antiques

Antique shops can be found throughout the city, though the concentration is greatest around campo San Maurizio and calle delle Botteghe (near campo Santo Stefano). There is also a *mercatino dell'antiquariato* (antiques fair) twice a year, in the week before Easter and Christmas, in campo San Maurizio (map p326 A2). Flyers around town advertise markets in via Garibaldi (Castello) or in campo Santa Maria Nova (Cannaregio); though they are organised on the fly, they usually take place on Sundays.

Antiquus
San Marco 2973 & 3131, calle delle Botteghe (041 520 6395). Vaporetto Sant'Angelo. **Open** 10am-12.30pm, 3-7.30pm Mon-Sat. **Credit** AmEx, DC, MC, V. **Map** p325 F1.
This charming shop has a beautiful collection of Old Master paintings, furniture, silver and antique jewellery, including Moors' heads brooches and earrings.
Other locations: Dorsoduro 873A (041 241 3725).

Guarinoni
San Polo 2862, calle del Mandoler (041 522 4286). Vaporetto San Tomà. **Open** 7am-noon, 3-7pm Mon-Sat. **Credit** MC, V. **Map** p325 E1.
An assortment of antique furnishings from as early as the 16th century is sold here. The shop also has a workshop that restores gilded ceilings and the like.

Art supplies

Angeloni
Galleria Matteotti 2, Mestre (041 974 236/041 986 264). Bus 4 from piazzale Roma to piazza Ferretto. **Open** 9am-12.30pm, 3.30-7.30pm Mon-Fri; 9am-12.30pm Sat. **Credit** MC, V.
Pleasant service and a wide range of supplies, this is where *real* artists go. The prices here are much better than anything you'll find in island Venice.

Arcobaleno
San Marco 3457, calle delle Botteghe (041 523 6818). Vaporetto Sant'Angelo. **Open** 9am-12.30pm, 4-7.30pm Mon-Fri; 9am-12.30pm Sat. **No credit cards. Map** p325 F1.
Arcobaleno stocks a vast assortment of artists' pigments – a veritable rainbow of colours. As well as a variety of art supplies, they carry all the basics in hardware, light bulbs and detergents.

Cartoleria Accademia
Dorsoduro 1044, campiello Calbo (041 520 7086). Vaporetto Accademia. **Open** *Sept-July* 8am-1pm, 3.30-7pm Mon-Fri; 8am-1pm Sat. *Aug* 9am-1pm Mon-Sat. **No credit cards. Map** p325 F2.
This small but well-stocked store carries a wide range of artists' supplies and is conveniently located just behind the Accademia. Cartoleria Accademia has been in the business since 1810, so it must be doing something right.

Other locations: Dorsoduro 2928, campo Santa Margherita (041 528 5283).

Testolini
San Marco 1744-8, fondamenta Orseolo (041 522 9265/www.testolini.it). Vaporetto Vallaresso or Rialto. **Open** 9am-7pm Mon-Sat. **Credit** AmEx, DC, MC, V. **Map** p326 B1.
Testolini carries stationery, backpacks, briefcases, calendars and supplies for both art and office. Branch stores carry computers and accessories. The staff can be on the cool side but the choice is huge… by Venetian standards.

Bookshops

Alberto Bertoni – Libreria
San Marco 3637B, calle de la Mandola (041 522 9583/www.bertonilibri.it). Vaporetto Sant'Angelo. **Open** 9am-1pm, 3-7.30pm Mon-Sat. **Credit** MC, V. **Map** p326 A1.
Just off calle de la Mandola (look for the display case with sale offers marking the turn-off), this well-hidden cavern is home to art books of all kinds, exhibition catalogues and the like, all with significant reductions off cover prices.
Other locations San Marco 4718, calle dei Fabbri (041 522 4615).

Cafoscarina
Dorsoduro 3259, campiello degli Squellini (041 240 4801/www.cafoscarina.it). Vaporetto Ca' Rezzonico or San Tomà. **Open** 9am-1pm, 2.30-7pm Mon-Fri; 10am-1pm Sat. **Credit** MC, V. **Map** p325 E1.
This is the official bookstore of the Università Ca' Foscari. On the other side of the campiello (Dorsoduro 3224) is Cafoscarina 3, which stocks a good selection of books in English.

Fantoni Libri Arte
San Marco 4119, salizada San Luca (041 522 0700). Vaporetto Rialto. **Open** 10am-8pm Mon-Fri; 10am-1.30pm, 4.30-8pm Sat. **Credit** AmEx, DC, MC, V. **Map** p326 B1.
Beautifully illustrated art, architecture, design, photography and textile books, mostly in Italian. There's also a small selection of cookbooks and works on Venice in English.

Filippi Editore Venezia
Castello 5284, calle Casselaria (041 523 6916). Vaporetto San Zaccaria. **Open** 9am-12.30pm, 3-7.30pm Mon-Sat. **Credit** MC, V. **Map** p326 C1.
Venice's longest-running publishing house is a father-and-son operation with more than 400 titles on Venetian history and folklore – all limited editions in Italian. The evocatively dark and dusty flagship store (address below) is a landmark in Venice.
Other locations: Castello 5763, calle del Paradiso (041 523 5635).

Laboratorio Blu
Cannaregio 1224, campo del Ghetto Vecchio (041 715 819). Vaporetto Guglie. **Open** 4-7.30pm Mon; 9.30am-12.30pm, 4-7.30pm Tue-Sat. **Credit** AmEx, DC, MC, V. **Map** p321 E2.
The only children's bookshop in Venice. Laboratorio Blu carries a good selection of books in English and offers courses for kids – drawing, painting, weaving and story telling.

Libreria Marco Polo
Castello 5469, salizada San Lio (041 522 6343/www.libreriamarcopolo.com). Vaporetto Rialto. **Open** 9.30am-8pm Mon-Sat; 11am-7pm Sun. **Credit** AmEx, DC, MC, V. **Map** p322 C5.
This friendly bookstore specialises in travel, from guides and maps to works of fiction. On the ground floor is a good selection of books aimed at foreign visitors, including guidebooks and fiction in English. An ingenious book exchange service means you can trade in your used novel (as long as it's in mint condition) and receive a discount on a new purchase. The shop also holds meetings with authors and book presentations.

Libreria Mondadori
San Marco 1345, salizada San Moisè (041 522 2193/www.libreriamondadorivenezia.it). Vaporetto Vallaresso. **Open** *Mar-Nov* upper floors 10am-8pm Mon-Sat; 11am-7.30pm Sun; ground floor 10am-11pm Mon-Sat; 11am-7.30pm Sun. *Dec-Feb* 10am-8pm Mon-Sat; 11am-7.30pm Sun. **Credit** AmEx, MC, V. **Map** p326 B2.
Venice's only mega-sized bookshop sprawls over three floors. The ground floor is reserved for exhibits, book signings, events and courses of various kinds. Upstairs, there's a wide selection of books in English and other foreign languages.

Libreria Toletta & Toletta Studio
Dorsoduro 1214, calle Toletta (041 523 2034). Vaporetto Accademia or Ca' Rezzonico. **Open** *Sept-June* 9.30am-7.30pm Mon-Sat; 3.30-7.30pm Sun. *July, Aug* 9.30am-1pm, 3.30-7.30pm Mon-Sat. **Credit** AmEx, DC, MC, V. **Map** p325 E2.
A good source of cheap books, the Toletta offers 20-40% off its stock from usual retail prices. Italian classics, art, cookery, children's books and history (mostly in Italian) all feature, along with a vast assortment of dictionaries and reference books. Next door is the Toletta Studio, which specialises in books about architecture. Toletta Cube (address given below) is their newest shop, just across the calle, and it carries art and photography books as well as posters, cards and gadgets.
Other locations: Dorsoduro 1175, calle Toletta (041 241 5660).

Mare di Carta
Santa Croce 222, fondamenta dei Tolentini (041 716 304/www.maredicarta.com). Vaporetto Piazzale Roma. **Open** 9am-1pm, 3.30-7.30pm Mon-Sat. **Credit** AmEx, DC, MC, V. **Map** p321 D4.
A must for boat lovers, this nautical bookshop stocks publications in English as well as Italian. The bulletin board has boats for sale for anyone interested in purchasing a gondola.

Studium

San Marco 337C, calle Canonica (041 522 2382).
Vaporetto San Zaccaria. **Open** 9am-7.30pm Mon-
Sat; 10am-1.30pm Sun. **Credit** AmEx, DC, MC, V.
Map p326 C1.
Located just behind St Mark's basilica, this two-
room shop has a wide selection of works on Venice,
travel books and novels in English. The shop's
true speciality is revealed as you step into the
back room, which is filled with theology studies,
icons and prayer books.

Cosmetics & perfumes

Cosmetics and toiletries can be found in the one-
stop stores (*see p191*) or in *farmacie*, although
prices tend to be higher at chemists. For
designer names try smaller, more specialised
profumerie. For herbal products of any type,
such as aromatherapy oils, you're best to
head for an *erboristeria*.

Body Shop

Cannaregio 3894, strada Nuova (041 277 0333).
Vaporetto Ca' D'Oro. **Open** 9.30am-7.15pm Mon-Sat;
10am-7pm Sun. **Credit** DC, MC, V. **Map** p322 B4.
If you've forgotten to pack your ginger shampoo,
don't fret. Just pop into Body Shop, which, despite
its recent takeover by L'Oreal, is still going great
guns on animal rights. However, you can probably
pick up their products cheaper back at home.

Il Bottegon

San Polo 806, calle del Figher (041 522 3632).
Vaporetto San Silvestro. **Open** 9am-12.45pm,
4-7.30pm Mon-Sat. **Credit** AmEx, MC, DC, V.
Map p322 A5.
Make a list before you go because you'll be so over-
whelmed with how much stuff is crammed into such
a tiny space that you'll have forgotten what you
came for. As well as cosmetics and toiletries: you'll
find pots, pans, rugs and hardware goods.
Other locations: Castello 1311, via Garibaldi
(041 521 0780).

L'Erbania

San Polo 1735, calle dei Botteri (041 723 215).
Vaporetto San Silvestro or San Stae. **Open** 10am-
1.30pm, 3.30-7.30pm Tue-Sat. **Credit** AmEx, DC,
MC, V. **Map** p322 A4.
A quaint shop near the Rialto where a herbalist will
mix up concoctions for you. Alternatively, choose
from a variety of prepared creams and perfumes.

Lush

*San Polo 95, ruga Rialto (041 522 1549/www.
lush.it). Vaporetto Rialto.* **Open** 10am-7.30pm
daily. **Credit** AmEx, DC, MC, V. **Map** p322 B5.
You can smell this store before you see it. For home-
sick travellers, Lush offers a whiff of Blighty.
As with the Body Shop, though, prices here are
slightly higher than you would pay in the UK.
Other locations: Cannaregio 3822, strada Nuova
(041 241 1200).

Design & household

Ceramics & china

Ceramiche La Margherita

*Santa Croce 2345, sottoportico della Siora Bettina
(041 723 120/www.lamargheritavenezia.com).*
Vaporetto San Stae. **Open** 9.30am-1pm, 3.30-7pm
Mon-Sat. **Credit** AmEx, MC, V. **Map** p321 F4.
A wonderful collection of handpainted terracotta
designed by the English-speaking owner. Plates,
bowls, teapots, ornaments and mugs in a variety
of colours and patterns.

Fustat

*Dorsoduro 2904, campo Santa Margherita (041 523
8504). Vaporetto Ca' Rezzonico.* **Open** 9.30am-4pm
Mon-Fri. **Credit** MC, V. **Map** p325 E1.
The pottery is handmade by the owner in this small
workshop/outlet. Raku demonstrations and courses
are also offered periodically.

Madera

*Dorsoduro 2762, campo San Barnaba (041
522 4181/www.maderavenezia.it). Vaporetto Ca'
Rezzonico.* **Open** 10.30am-1pm, 3.30-7.30pm Tue-
Sat. **Credit** AmEx, DC, MC, V. **Map** p325 E2.
Fusing minimalist design with traditional techniques, the young architect and craftswoman behind
Madera creates unique objects in wood. She also
sells exceptional lamps, ceramics, jewellery and textiles by other European artists.

Sabbie e Nebbie

San Polo 2768A, calle dei Nomboli (041 719 073).
Vaporetto San Tomà. **Open** 10am-12.30pm, 4-7.30pm
Mon-Sat. **Credit** AmEx, MC, V. **Map** p321 F5.
A beautiful selection of Italian ceramic pieces as well
as refined Japanese works. Also sells handmade
objects (lamps, candlesticks) by Italian designers.

Fabrics & accessories

Antichità Marciana

*San Marco 1691, Frezzeria (041 523 5666/www.
antichitamarciano.it). Vaporetto Vallaresso.* **Open**
3.30-7.30pm Mon; 9.30am-1pm, 3.30-7pm Tue-Sat.
Credit AmEx, MC, V. **Map** p326 B1.
A tasteful selection of antique baubles can be found
in this jewel of a shop; its speciality, however, is the
richly painted velvets created by the owner in her
workshop. A favourite among interior designers.

Arras

*Dorsoduro 3235, campiello Squellini (041 522 6460/
www.arrastessuti.com). Vaporetto Ca' Rezzonico.*
Open 9am-1pm, 3.30-7.30pm Mon-Sat. **Credit**
AmEx, DC, MC, V. **Map** p325 E1.
Handwoven fabrics are created here in a vast range
of colours and textures using different fabrics such
as silk, wool and cotton. These unique textiles are
then worked into bags, clothing, scarves.
Customised designs can be ordered.

Eat, Drink, Shop

Bevilacqua

San Marco 337B, ponte della Canonica (041 528 7581/www.bevilacquatessuti.com). Vaporetto San Zaccaria. **Open** 10am-7pm Mon-Sat; 10am-5pm Sun. **Credit** AmEx, DC, MC, V. **Map** p326 C1.

This small shop behind St Mark's basilica offers exquisite examples of both hand- and machine-woven silk brocades, damasks and velvets. The Venetian textile tradition is kept alive by these weavers, who use original 17th-century looms. **Other locations**: San Marco 2520, campo Santa Maria del Giglio (041 241 0662).

Fortuny Tessuti Artistici

Giudecca 805, fondamenta San Biagio (041 522 4078). Vaporetto Palanca. **Open** 9am-noon, 2-5pm Mon-Fri. **Credit** AmEx, MC, V. **Map** p325 D3.

This pared-back factory showroom space almost glows with the exquisite colours and patterns of original Fortuny prints. At an across-the-board price of €300 a metre, you may not be tempted to buy, but it's worth the trip just to see it.

Gaggio

San Marco 3441-3451 calle delle Botteghe (041 522 8574/www.gaggio.it). Vaporetto San Samuele or Sant'Angelo. **Open** 10.30am-1pm, 4-6.30pm Mon-Fri; 10.30am-1pm Sat. **Credit** AmEx, DC, MC, V. **Map** p325 F1.

Emma Gaggio is a legend among dressmakers and her sumptuous handprinted silk velvets (from €195 a metre) are used to make cushions and wall hangings as well as bags, hats, scarves and jackets.

Il Milione

Castello 6025, campo Santa Marina (041 241 0722/www.ilmilionevenezia.com). Vaporetto Rialto. **Open** 10am-12.30pm, 3-7.30pm Mon-Sat. **Credit** MC, V. **Map** p322 C5.

Handmade lamps and designer-inspired knock-offs that are a little more affordable.

Trois

San Marco 2666, campo San Maurizio (041 522 2905). Vaporetto Giglio. **Open** 4-7.30pm Mon; 10am-1pm, 4-7.30pm Tue-Sat. **No credit cards. Map** p326 A2.

This is one of the best places in Venice to buy original Fortuny fabrics – and at considerable savings on UK/US prices (though this still doesn't make them particularly cheap). Made-to-order bead-work masks and accessories are also available.

Venetia Studium

San Marco 2403, calle larga XXII Marzo (041 522 9281/www.venetiastudium.com). Vaporetto Giglio. **Open** 9.30am-7.40pm Mon-Sat; 10.30am-6pm Sun. **Credit** AmEx, DC, MC, V. **Map** p326 A2.

Venetia Studium stocks beautiful, pleated silks, in elegant pillows, lamps, scarves, handbags and other accessories in a marvellous range of colours. They are certainly not cheap, but they do make perfect gifts for those who have it all. **Other locations**: San Marco 723, Mercerie San Zulian (041 522 9859).

Kitchen & hardware

Domus

San Marco 4746, calle dei Fabbri (041 522 6259). Vaporetto Rialto. **Open** 9.30am-7.30pm Mon-Sat. **Credit** AmEx, MC, V. **Map** p326 B1.

This shop sells classy kitchenware and porcelain tableware. Get your Alessi pepper grinder here.

Kirei

San Polo 219, campo Cesare Battisti (041 522 8158). Vaporetto San Silvestro. **Open** 10am-12.30pm, 4-7.30pm Mon-Sat. **Credit** AmEx, MC, V. **Map** p322 B5.

This elegant kitchenware shop sells exquisite accessories for the kitchen and dining room, from Versace dinner services to Riedel glassware. **Photo** p181.

Ratti

Castello 5825, calle delle Bande (041 240 4600). Vaporetto San Zaccaria or Rialto. **Open** 9.15am-12.30pm, 3.30-7.15pm Mon-Fri; 9.15am-12.30pm Sat. **Credit** AmEx, DC, MC, V. **Map** p322 C5.

If Ratti doesn't have what you're looking for, it's time to worry. There are kitchen utensils, locks and other security items, household goods, televisions, radios, adapters and all kinds of electronic gadgets. They also cut keys.

Lace & linens

Lace can be bought on the island of Burano (*see p145*) where you can watch the women at their lacework. Remember: if it's cheap, it's machine made, and if it's very cheap it almost certainly hails from Taiwan rather than from some Venetian back room. If you want reliable, top-quality (and exorbitant) lace without the hassle of going over to Burano, stick to big names such as Jesurum and Martinuzzi.

Annelie

Dorsoduro 2748, calle lunga San Barnaba (041 520 3277). Vaporetto Ca' Rezzonico. **Open** 9.30am-1pm, 4-7.30pm Mon-Sat. **Credit** AmEx, DC, MC, V. **Map** p325 E2.

A delightful shop run by a delightful woman who has a beautiful selection of sheets, tablecloths, curtains, shirts and baby clothes, either fully embroidered or with lace detailing. Antique lace can also be had at reasonable prices.

Cristina Linassi

San Marco 3537, campo Sant'Angelo (041 523 0578/www.cristinalinassi.it). Vaporetto Sant'Angelo. **Open** 9.30am-1pm, 2.30-7.30pm Mon-Sat; 9.30am-1pm, 2.30-7pm Sun. **Credit** AmEx, MC, V. **Map** p325 F1.

Slightly more affordable than Jesurum (*see p186*), this tiny boutique has its workshop on the opposite side of town. It produces hand-embroidered nightgowns, towels and sheets, as well as a catalogue full of designs for made-to-order items.

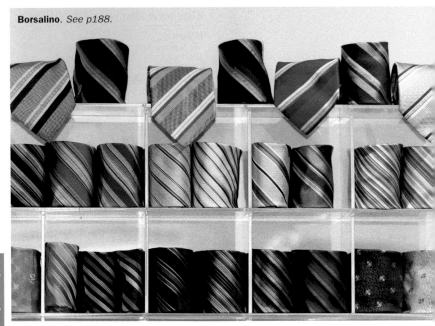

Borsalino. *See p188.*

Jesurum

Cannaregio 3219, fondamenta della Sensa (041 524 2540/www.jesurum.it). Vaporetto Guglie or San'Alvise. **Open** 10am-1pm, 1.30-5pm Tue-Sat. **Credit** AmEx, DC, MC, V. **Map** p321 F2.
Extremely elegant embroidered linens, towels and fabrics, from a lace company that has been going for more than 100 years (though in 2005 it was bought by a US-Swiss consortium). In the 19th century it was considered the only place to come for really good lace; it is still renowned for its sophisticated wares. Be warned: quality costs.

Martinuzzi

San Marco 67A, piazza San Marco (041 522 5068). Vaporetto Vallaresso. **Open** *Mar-Oct* 9am-7.30pm Mon-Sat; 9.30am-7pm Sun. *Nov-Feb* 9am-7pm Mon-Sat. **Credit** AmEx, DC, MC, V. **Map** p326 B1.
The oldest lace shop in Venice, Martinuzzi has exclusive designs for bobbin lace items such as place mats, tablecloths and linens. If you have an odd-sized bed, not to worry – Martinuzzi will create a sheet set especially for you.

Glass

Glass and Venice are well-nigh synonymous: the city was famous for its exquisite glassware even before the industry shifted to the island of Murano in 1291, when all glass furnaces except those faking gemstones were ordered to move

there in order to limit the fire hazard in Venice. While much of the glassblowing action takes place there, glittering glass can still be purchased in Venice itself.

The shops identified in this chapter are all reputable outlets. Always bear in mind, though, that good Venetian glass – like good Venetian lace, is not cheap; anything you find for under €10 is probably made in China.

For information about glass factories and shops in Murano, *see p144* **Murano glass.** For gallery information, *see p211-15.*

Beads

See also p193 **Beads.**

Antichità

Dorsoduro 1195, calle Toletta (041 522 3159). Vaporetto Accademia. **Open** 9.30am-1pm, 3.30-7pm Mon-Sat. **No credit cards. Map** p325 E2.
Beautiful, handpainted antique glass beads that can be purchased individually or made into jewellery. There's also a nice selection of antiques and lace.

Anticlea Antiquariato

Castello 4719A, calle San Provolo (041 528 6946). Vaporetto San Zaccaria. **Open** 10am-1.30pm, 2-7pm Mon-Sat. **Credit** AmEx, DC, MC, V. **Map** p326 C1.
Packed with curious antique treasures, as well as an outstanding selection of Venetian glass beads.

Perle e Dintorni

San Marco 3740, calle della Mandola (041 520 5068).
Vaporetto Sant'Angelo. **Open** 9.30am-7.30pm Mon-
Sat; noon-7pm Sun. **Credit** AmEx, DC, MC, V.
Map p326 A1.
Buy bead jewellery or assemble your own unique
pieces, choosing from a vast assortment of glass
beads, most of which are new versions based on
antique designs.
Other locations San Marco 5468, calle della Bissa
(041 522 5624).

Glassware

Zancopè

San Marco 2674, campo San Maurizio (041 523
4567/www.jurubeba.it). Vaporetto Giglio. **Open**
10.30am-1pm, 4-7.30pm Mon-Sat. **Credit** AmEx,
MC, V. **Map** p326 A2.
An eclectic collection of antique, old and contemporary glass at very good prices.

Canestrelli

Dorsoduro 1173, calle della Toletta (041 277 0617/
www.venicemirrors.com). Vaporetto Accademia.
Open 11am-1.30pm, 3.30-7.30pm Mon-Sat. **Credit**
MC, V. **Map** p325 E2.
Stefano Coluccio specialises in beautifully framed
convex mirrors.

Genninger Studio

Dorsoduro 2793A, calle del Traghetto (041 522
5565/www.genningerstudio.com). Vaporetto Ca'
Rezzonico. **Open** 10am-1.30pm, 2.30-7pm Mon-Sat.
Credit AmEx, MC, V. **Map** p325 E2.
Flame-worked and blown beads, custom jewellery,
knick-knacks, lighting and mirrors designed by
Leslie Ann Genninger. A contemporary take on
Venetian luxury and decadence in beautiful
surroundings on the Grand Canal.

L'Isola

San Marco 1468, campo San Moisè (041 523 1973/
www.lisola.com). Vaporetto Vallaresso. **Open** 9am-
7pm daily. **Credit** AmEx, DC, MC, V. **Map** p326 B2.
Carlo Moretti's showroom showcases his own elegant clear and coloured glass designs. Some unique
pieces and signed and numbered editions by Moretti
and a few selected artists working with his factory.

Marina & Susanna Sent

Dorsoduro 669, campo san Vio (041 520 8136).
Vaporetto Accademia. **Open** 10am-6pm daily.
Credit AmEx, MC, V. **Map** p325 F2.
Venice's best contemporary glass jewellery is created
by the Sent sisters. There's also a good selection of
the work of the contemporary design house Arcade.
See also p144 **Murano glass**.

Vittorio Costantini

Cannaregio 5311, calle del Fumo (041 522 2265/
www.vittoriocostantini.it). Vaporetto Fondamente
Nove. **Open** 9.15am-1pm, 2.15-6pm Mon-Fri.
Credit MC, V. **Map** p322 C4.

Vittorio Costantini was began his glasswork apprenticeship at the age of 11. Now internationally
renowned as one of the most original Venetian
lamp workers, his intricate animals, insects, fish
and birds are instantly recognisable for their fine
workmanship and great beauty.

Fashion

All the big-name fashion boutiques (Armani,
Prada, Gucci and so on) are clustered around
four streets in the vicinity of piazza San Marco:
calle Vallaresso; salizada San Moisè and its
continuation, calle larga XXII Marzo; calle
Goldoni; and the Mercerie. If you've seen it
all before, the shops listed below offer
something a little different.

Accessories

See also *p188* **Hibiscus**.

3856

Dorsoduro 3749, calle San Pantalon (041 720 595).
Vaporetto San Tomà. **Open** 10am-7.45pm Tue-Sat.
Credit AmEx, DC, MC, V. **Map** p321 E5.
This shop is particularly popular with fashion-
conscious students and, like Mary Poppins' bag,
fits a lot into a small space. Jewellery, scarves
and bags are tucked in alongside clothes and
Georgina Goodman shoes – the only Italian outlet
for this British designer.

L'Angolo

Dorsoduro 2755, calle lunga San Barnaba (041
277 7895). Vaporetto Ca' Rezzonico. **Open** 10am-
12.30pm, 4-7.30pm Mon-Sat. **Credit** DC, MC, V.
Map p325 E2.
L'Angolo has bags, hats and scarves in rich, colourful fabrics and unique styles. Jewellery and some
clothing are also available.

Monica Daniele

San Polo 2235, calle Scaleter (041 524 6242/www.
monicadaniele.com). Vaporetto San Stae or San
Silvestro. **Open** 9am-12.30pm, 3-6.30pm, 9.30pm-
midnight Mon-Sat. **Credit** AmEx, DC, MC, V.
Map p321 F5.
Hidden away behind campo San Polo, this odd little
shop specialises in *tabarri* (traditional Venetian
cloaks) and hats, from traditional panamas to stylish creations by the shop's owner. Monica Daniele's
boutique is one of the only shops in Venice you'll
find open until midnight.

ZaZú

San Polo 2750, calle dei Saoneri (041 715 426).
Vaporetto San Tomà. **Open** 9.30am-1.30pm, 2.30-
7.30pm Mon-Sat; 10am-1pm, 2.30-7pm Sun. **Credit**
AmEx, DC, MC, V. **Map** p321 F5.
Clothing and jewels from the East that are very
wearable in the West. There are handbags and other
accessories as well.

Eat, Drink, Shop

Hibiscus.

Boutiques & designers

Araba Fenice
San Marco 1822, Frezzeria (041 522 0664).
Vaporetto Giglio or Vallaresso. **Open** 9.30am-
7.30pm Mon-Sat. **Credit** AmEx, DC, MC, V.
Map p326 B1.
A classic yet original line of women's clothing made
exclusively for this boutique, plus jewellery in ebony
and mother-of-pearl.

Borsalino
*San Marco 4822, campo San Salvador (041 241
1945/www.borsalino.com). Vaporetto Rialto.* **Open**
10am-1pm, 2-7pm Mon-Sat; 10am-6pm Sun. **Credit**
AmEx, DC, MC, V. **Map** p326 B1.
This menswear store has an exemplary selection of
hats for both men and women. The clothing, often
inspired by Bertie Wooster, is all about casual elegance on the golf course and off. **Photo** *p186.*

Diesel
*San Marco 5315-5316, salizada Pio X (041 241
1937/www.diesel.com). Vaporetto Rialto.* **Open**
10am-7.30pm Mon-Sat; 11am-7pm Sun. **Credit**
AmEx, DC, MC, V. **Map** p326 B1.
'For successful living' is the motto of this Veneto-
based company – and they certainly seem to have
made a successful living from their brand. Their
kooky, club-wise, lifestyle-based styles and advertising campaigns have invaded Europe and North
America. This two-storey hipper than hip store has
become a landmark on the Venetian shopping scene.

Godi Fiorenza
*San Marco 4261, rio terà San Paternian (041 241
0866/www.fiorenzadesign.com). Vaporetto Rialto or
Vallaresso.* **Open** 9.30am-12.30pm, 3.30-7.30pm Mon-
Sat. **Credit** AmEx, DC, MC, V. **Map** p326 A1.
The London-trained Godi designer sisters sell
exquisite knitwear, stylish coats and chiffon evening
tops. All made on the premises, and complemented
with jewellery and shoes.

Hibiscus
*San Polo 1060-1061, ruga Rialto/calle dell'Olio
(041 520 8989). Vaporetto San Silvestro.* **Open**
9.30am-7.30pm Mon-Sat; 11am-7pm Sun. **Credit**
AmEx, DC, MC, V. **Map** p322 A5.
Viaggio nei colori – a voyage into colour – is the
Hibiscus motto; it is demonstrated on clothing, jewellery, handmade scarves, bags and ceramics with
an ethnic flair. Not cheap, but a refreshing change
from glass and mask shops.

Ottico Fabbricatore
*San Marco 4773, Calle dell'Ovo (041 522 5263/
www.otticofabbricatore.com). Vaporetto Rialto.*
Open 9am-12.30pm, 3.30-7.30pm Mon-Sat.
Credit AmEx, DC, MC, V. **Map** p322 B5.
As the name suggests, this ultra-modern shop spe-
cializes in designer eyewear you won't find anywhere
else in Venice, with frames varying from buffalo horn
to titanium. However, designers Francesco Lincetto
and Marianna Leardini also produce gossamer-like
cashmere and sensual silk apparel along with a range
of luxurious leather bags. **Photo** *p189.*

Pot-Pourri
*San Marco 1810, ramo dei Fuseri (041 241 0990/
www.potpourri.it). Vaporetto Vallaresso.* **Open** May-
July, Sept-Oct 10am-1pm, 3.30-7.30pm daily. Nov-Apr
Aug 10am-1pm, 3.30-7.30pm Mon-Sat. **Credit** AmEx,
DC, MC, V. **Map** p326 B1.
Walking into this shop is like stepping into an ele-
gant friend's bedroom. Clothes are draped over arm-
chairs or hang from wardrobe doors while charming
knick-knacks cover the dressing table. This faux-
boudoir houses designers such as Cristina Effe and
Marzi as well as homeware.

Leather goods & shoes

The big names in leather – Bruno Magli,
Fratelli Rossetti and Furla, to name but a few –
are all located around piazza San Marco. For a
more modest investment – or for something
completely different – you could try one of the
following places.

Daniela Ghezzo Segalin Venezia
*San Marco 4365, calle dei Fuseri (041 522 2115).
Vaporetto Rialto or Vallaresso.* **Open** 9.30am-
12.30pm, 3.30-7.30pm Mon-Fri; 9am-12.30pm Sat.
Credit AmEx, DC, MC, V. **Map** p326 B1.
The shoemaking tradition established by Rolando
Segalin, known as 'the Cobbler of Venice', continues
through his apprentice. Of the 250 or so models

handcrafted here a year, some of the most interesting creations are on display in the window, including an extraordinary pair of gondola shoes… there's no accounting for taste. A pair of Ghezzo's creations will set you back anything between €500 and €1,500. Repairs are done as well.

Francis Model
San Polo 773A, ruga Rialto/ruga del Ravano (041 521 2889). Vaporetto San Silvestro. **Open** 9.30am-7.30pm Mon-Sat; 10.30am-6.30pm Sun. **Credit** AmEx, DC, MC, V. **Map** p322 A5.
Handbags and briefcases are produced in this tiny *bottega* by a father-and-son team that has been in the business for more than 40 years.

Giovanna Zanella
Castello 5641, calle Carminati (041 523 5500). Vaporetto Rialto. **Open** 9.30am-1pm, 3-7pm Mon-Sat. **Credit** AmEx, DC, MC, V. **Map** p322 B5.
Venetian designer-cobbler Giovanna Zanella creates a fantastic line of handmade shoes in an extraordinary variety of styles and colours. A pair of shoes costs €350 to €500; clogs are slightly 'cheaper' at a bargain €280. There are bag, hats and a line of gloriously coloured clothes too.

Mori & Bozzi
Cannaregio 2367, rio terà Maddalena (041 715 261). Vaporetto San Marcuola. **Open** *Apr, May, Sept-Oct* 9.30am-7.30pm Mon-Sat; 11am-7pm Sun. *June-Aug, Nov-Mar* 9.30am-7.30pm Mon-Sat. **Credit** AmEx, DC, MC, V. **Map** p322 A3.
Shoes for the coolest of the cool: whatever the latest fad – pointy or square – it's here. Trendy names and the designer-inspired to please the Carrie Bradshaw in us all.

Pelletterie Silvia
San Marco 4466, calle dei Fuseri (041 523 5749). Vaporetto Vallaresso or San Zaccaria. **Open** 9am-7.30pm Mon-Sat. **Credit** AmEx, DC, MC, V. **Map** p326 B1.

This stylish shoe store stocks designers such as Lerre and Kalisté. Silvia also has a large range of bags and a smaller selection of clothing. **Photo** *p190*. **Other locations** Castello 5540, salizada San Lio (041 523 8568).

Second-hand clothes

Laura Crovato
San Marco 2995, calle delle Botteghe (041 520 4170). Vaporetto Sant'Angelo. **Open** 4-7.30pm Mon; 11am-1pm, 4-7.30pm Tue-Sat. **Credit** DC, MC, V. **Map** p325 F1.
Nestling between expensive galleries and antique shops, Laura Crovato offers a selection of used clothes and a sprinkling of new items, including raw-silk shirts and scarves, costume jewellery and sunglasses. This being Venice, the shop's not exactly giving it away – even though it's second-hand.

Food & drink

For the freshest fruit, vegetables, meat and fish at the most competitive prices – plus a slice of everyday Venetian life that should not be missed during your visit – the market that's held Monday to Saturday morning at the foot of the Rialto bridge is difficult to beat. For (slightly) less crowded market options, the market that sets up halfway along via Garibaldi in the eastern Castello every morning (except Sunday) is a more sedate affair; at the far end, make your purchases from one of Venice's few remaining boat-emporia.

Elsewhere, morning markets are once-weekly. Stalls are in operation by 7.30am and stallholders pack up by 1pm: the early bird definitely gets the best of the wares on offer. On Tuesdays head for the Lido's Venice-facing riviera B Marcello waterfront,

Eat, Drink, Shop

Ottico Fabbricatore. *See p188.*

Pelletterie Silvia. *See p189.*

while on Fridays there's also a small and endearingly unsophisticated market in campo della Chiesa on Sacca Fisola. Mestre on the mainland also has a huge market on Fridays, situated near piazza Barche. As well as groceries, you can pick up bargain shoes and clothing at all these markets.

Grocery shops (*alimentari*) offer all the usual staples from around Italy, as well as the odd Venetian speciality such as *baccalà mantecato* (a delectable spread made with dried cod) and *mostarda veneziana* (a sweet-and-sour sauce made with dried fruit).

Butchers and bakers are sadly becoming thin on the ground as the mushrooming supersize sell-everything malls across on the mainland steal their trade.

Venetians are famous for their sweet tooth. There is, therefore, an extraordinary variety of calorific delights to devour while strolling through the *calli; see also pp170-79* **Cafés, Bars & Pasticcerie.**

Alimentari

Aliani Gastronomia

San Polo 654, ruga Rialto/ruga vecchia San Giovanni (041 522 4913). Vaporetto San Silvestro. **Open** 8am-1pm, 5-7.30pm Tue-Sat. **Credit** MC, V. **Map** p322 A5.
A traditional grocery that stocks a selection of cold meats and cheeses hailing from every part of Italy. Also on offer is an assortment of prepared dishes and roast meats.

Drogheria Mascari

San Polo 381, ruga degli Spezieri (041 522 9762). Vaporetto San Silvestro. **Open** 8am-1pm, 4-7.30pm Mon-Sat. **No credit cards. Map** p322 A4.
Shops like this were quite common in Venice before the onslaught of commercial shopping centres on the mainland; now this is the only one left. It's the best place in the city to find exotic spices, nuts, dried fruit and mushrooms, as well as oils and wines from different regions in Italy.

Confectionery

See also p191 **Cioccolato**.

Marchini Pasticceria

San Marco 676, calle Spadaria (041 522 9109/ www.golosessi.com). Vaporetto Rialto or San Zaccaria. **Open** *June-Sept* 9am-8pm Mon, Wed-Sat. *Oct-May* 9am-10pm daily. **Credit** AmEx, DC, MC, V. **Map** p326 C1.
Probably Venice's most famous sweet shop, and certainly the most expensive, Marchini has recently moved to this newly remodelled location close to San Marco. Exquisite chocolate, including *Le Baute Veneziane* – small chocolates in the form of Carnevale masks. Cakes can be ordered.

Rizzo Regali

San Marco 4739, calle dei Fabbri (041 522 5811). Vaporetto Rialto. **Open** 9am-8pm Mon-Sat. **Credit** MC, V. **Map** p326 B1.
This old-fashioned shop sells traditional cakes, sweets and chocolates. For *pesce d'aprile* (April Fool's Day) you can buy bags of foil-wrapped chocolate goldfish and if you can't find the *torrone* (nougat) you're looking for here, then it doesn't exist.

Drink

See also pp170-79 **Cafés, Bars & Pasticcerie**.

Bottiglieria Colonna

Castello 5595, calle della Fava (041 528 5137). Vaporetto Rialto. **Open** 9am-1pm, 4-8pm Mon-Sat. **Credit** MC, V. **Map** p322 B5.
Extensive selection of local and regional wines. Helpful staff will give advice on which wines to try, and prepare travel boxes or arrange for shipping.

Vinaria Nave de Oro

Dorsoduro 3664, campo Santa Margherita (041 522 2693). Vaporetto Ca' Rezzonico. **Open** 9am-1pm, 5-8pm Mon, Tue, Thur-Sat; 9am-1pm Wed. **No credit cards. Map** p325 E1.
Bring your own bottles and staff will fill them with anything from Pinot Grigio to Merlot. For something different try Torbolino, a sweet and cloudy first-pressing white wine.
Other locations: Castello 5786B, calle del Mondo Nuovo (041 523 3056); Cannaregio 1370, rio terà San Leonardo (041 719 695); via Lepanto 24D, Lido (041 276 0055).

Vino e... Vini

Castello 3565-6, salizada Pignater (041 521 0184).
Vaporetto Arsenale. **Open** 9am-1pm, 5-8pm Mon-Sat.
Credit AmEx, MC, V. **Map** p327 E1.
A vast selection of major Italian wines, plus French,
Spanish, Californian and even Lebanese wines.

Health foods

Cibele

Cannaregio 1823, campiello dell'Anconetta (041
524 2113). Vaporetto San Marcuola. **Open**
8.30am-12.45pm, 4-7.45pm Mon-Sat. **Credit** MC,
V. **Map** p321 F3.
A full range of natural health foods, cosmetics and
medicines. Staff will also prepare blends of herbal
teas and remedies.

Rialto Bio Center

San Polo 366, campo Beccaria (041 523 9515).
Vaporetto San Silvestro. **Open** 8.30am-
1pm, 4.30-8pm Mon-Sat. **Credit** DC, MC, V.
Map p322 A4.
A little bit of just about everything can be found
in this small shop, located behind the Rialto fish
market, from wholewheat pasta, grains, honey and
freshly baked breads to natural cosmetics and
incense.

Supermarkets

Billa

Dorsoduro 1491, Zattere (041 522 6187). Vaporetto
San Basilio. **Open** 8.30am-8pm Mon-Sat; 9am-8pm
Sun. **Credit** AmEx, MC, V. **Map** p325 D2.

Cioccolato

Although culinary Venice is famous for all
things fishy, the sweet-toothed visitor needn't
despair. You can feed your cocoa habit at two
cioccolaterie that would put Vianne Rocher
to shame. The first, **Faggiotto**, is tucked
away between Accademia and the Zattere.
Giuseppe Fagiotto started out in Pordenone,
but recently opened this little shop of
wonders. Choc delights range from 100 per
cent cocoa chocolate slabs for
fundamentalists, to white chocolate novelty
football boots. If you can't make up your mind
which chocolate to try, try the mini-bar
selection: €19.90 gets you six tasters.
In colder weather, the hot chocolate made
following an old recipe using water rather than
milk is a must: get an
espresso-sized shot of
this dark gloopy delight to
boost your energy levels
after a deep midwinter
sightseeing session.

At San Tomà, **VizioVirtù**
serves up further
gluttonous pleasures.
Here you can witness
chocolate being made
before while sipping an
iced chocolate or nibbling
on a spicy praline. This
cornucopia of cocoa has
unusual delights such
as blocks of chocolate
Parmesan, and cocoa
tagliatelle (which the chef
recommends teamed with
game sauces). The shop

also caters to diabetic chocaholics. If you're
looking for something special, the Willy
Wonka of Venice will tailor-make it for you.

Faggiotto

Dorsoduro 1078, fondamenta Sangiatoffetti
(041 241 0386). Vaporetto Accademia.
Open 10.30am-1.30pm, 2.30-7.30pm
Tue-Fri; 9.30am-1pm, 3-7.30pm Sat-Sun.
Closed 2wks Aug. **Credit** MC, V. **Map** p325 E2.

VizioVirtù

San Polo 2898A, calle del Campaniel (041
275 0149/www.viziovirtu.com). Vaporetto
San Tomà. **Open** 10am-7.30pm daily (with
variations in July). Closed Aug. **Credit** MC,
V. **Map** p325 F1.

Open seven days a week, this supermarket on the Zattere stocks fruit, vegetables and other staples at lower prices than most *alimentari*.
Other locations: Cannaregio 3027M; calle delle Contiere (041 524 4786); Lido, Gran Viale (041 526 2898).

Coop
Santa Croce 506A, piazzale Roma (041 296 0621). Vaporetto Piazzale Roma. **Open** 8.30am-8pm daily. **Credit** MC, V. **Map** p320 C5.
The Coop offers goods at good prices. This branch caters to tourists, with a handy salad bar, snacks and Venetian specialities conveniently lumped together. The Coop also stocks organic produce and fair trade products. This main outlet is open seven days a week; the branches listed below close on Sunday.
Other locations: Santa Croce 1493, campo San Giacomo dell'Orio (041 275 0218); Giudecca 484, calle dell'Olio (041 241 3381).

Punto Sma
Dorsoduro 3017, campo Santa Margherita (041 522 6780). Vaporetto Ca'Rezzonico. **Open** 8.30am-8pm Mon-Sat. **Credit** DC, MC, V. **Map** p325 E1.
Prices may not be all that competitive in this small, fully stocked supermarket, but its central location certainly makes it handy.

Jewellery

Shops such as Nardi and Missiaglia in piazza San Marco have the most impressive and expensive jewellery, and Cartier (Mercerie San Zulian) and Bulgari (calle larga XXII Marzo) also have outlets in Venice. The smaller shops on the Rialto bridge offer more affordable silver and gold chains and bracelets sold by weight, and you will find handmade items in workshops far from the chi-chi areas of town.

For glass beads, *see p186*, and *below* **Beads**.

Beads

Underneath the arches at the north-western foot of the Rialto, jeweller-brothers Stefano and Daniele Attombri have been peddling their sumptuous wares since the early 1990s; their showroom across the Grand Canal in campo San Maurizio is a recent addition. These self-taught designers create intricate, unique pieces combining metal wire and delicate antique Venetian glass beads. Not only are the designs – ranging from minimalist bracelets to jaw-dropping necklaces – unique; branching out from their antiques-only creations, the brothers have taken to adding custom-made one-off blown glass cameos of their own design into their jewellery. The use of non-nickel metal means that even those with sensitive skin can indulge. Not content with confining themselves to trinkets and baubles, they also produce interior design pieces, including mirrors and lamps.

The showrooms may be small, but the brothers' stake in the market is expanding, their work being sold from New York to California, and their creations adorning the necks of Hollywood stars. In 2005 they made their British TV debut, appearing on a Trinny and Susannah *What Not to Wear* holiday special, with the two sartorial despots waxing lyrical about Attombri gems. However, it's not just the BBC fashion police who love their work: in 2006 they garnered the New Talents award at the Milan Design Fair, thanks to their 'irreverent and transgressive'

designs. Go to the store and let them drape their beady wonders around you.

Attombri
San Polo 74, sottoportego degli Orafi (041 521 2524/www.attombri.com). Vaporetto San Silvestro. **Open** 9.30am-1pm, 2.30-7pm Mon-Sat. **Credit** AmEx, DC, MC, V. **Map** p322 B5.
Other locations: San Marco 2668A, campo San Maurizio (041 521 0789).

Laberintho

*San Polo 2236, calle del Scaleter (041 710 017/
www.laberintho.it). Vaporetto San Stae or San
Tomà.* **Open** 9.30am-1pm, 2.30-7pm Tue-Sat.
Credit AmEx, DC, MC, V. **Map** p321 F5.
A group of young goldsmiths runs this tiny *bottega*
hidden away behind campo San Polo. They specialise in inlaid stones. In addition to the one-of-a-
kind rings, earrings and necklaces on display, they
will produce made-to-order pieces.

Sigfrido Cipolato

*Castello 5336, Casselleria (041 522 8437). Vaporetto
Rialto.* **Open** 11am-12.30pm Mon; 11am-7.30pm Tue-
Sat. **Credit** AmEx, DC, MC, V. **Map** p326 C1.
This jeweller painstakingly carves ebony to recre-
ate the famous Moors' heads brooches and earrings.

Masks

Ca' Macana

*Dorsoduro 3172, calle delle Botteghe (041 520 3229/
www.camacana.com). Vaporetto Ca' Rezzonico.* **Open**
10am-6pm daily. **Credit** AmEx, DC, MC, V. **Map**
p325 E1.
Easy to spot because of the masked statue of a little
boy standing at the entrance, this workshop is
packed with traditional papier-mâché masks from
the *Commedia dell'arte* theatre tradition. A careful
explanation of the mask-making process – from the
clay model to moulds – is enthusiastically given by
the artist in residence, who also organises courses.

Carta Alta

*Dorsoduro 2808, campo San Barnaba (041 523
8313/www.venicemaskshop.com). Vaporetto Ca'
Rezzonico.* **Open** 10.30am-2.30pm, 3.30-7.30pm
Mon-Sat. **Credit** MC, V. **Map** p325 E2.
Film buffs may recall seeing this shop in David
Lean's *Summertime*. Though essentially a mask
shop, you can also find handcrafted products and a
selection of accessories.

MondoNovo

*Dorsoduro 3063, rio terà Canal (041 528 7344/www.
mondonovomaschere.it). Vaporetto Ca' Rezzonico.*
Open 10am-6pm Mon-Sat. **Credit** MC, V. **Map**
p325 E1.
Venice's best-known *mascheraio* offers an enormous
variety of masks both traditional and modern. You
can also see his work at the recently restored Fenice
theatre where he worked on the sculptures.

Papier Mâché

*Castello 5175, calle lunga Santa Maria Formosa
(041 522 9995/www.papiermache.it). Vaporetto
Rialto.* **Open** 9am-7.30pm Mon-Sat; 10am-7pm Sun.
Credit AmEx, DC, MC, V. **Map** p322 C5.
Established for over 20 years, this workshop uses
traditional techniques to create contemporary
masks. The artists draw inspiration from the works
of Klimt, Kandinsky, Tiepolo and Carpaccio. The
decoration determines the price, with simple designs
starting at €40. Ceramics and painted mirrors too.

Tragicomica

*San Polo 2800, calle dei Nomboli (041 721 102/www.
tragicomica.it). Vaporetto San Tomà.* **Open** 10am-
7pm daily. **Credit** AmEx, MC, V. **Map** p321 F5.
A spellbinding collection of mythological masks,
Harlequins, Columbines and Pantaloons, as well as
18th-century dandies and ladies. All the masks sold
here are painted by an artist trained at Venice's
Accademia di Belle Arti. **Photo** *p194.*

Paper products

Carteria Tassotti

*San Marco 5472, calle de la Bissa (041 528 1881/
www.tassotti.it). Vaporetto Rialto.* **Open** 10am-1pm,
2-7pm daily. **Credit** AmEx, MC, V. **Map** p322 B5.
This Bassano-based family business has a charming selection of greeting cards, decorative paper,
diaries and notebooks. Wedding invitations and
business cards can also be ordered. **Photo** *p195.*

Ebrû

*San Marco 3471, campo Santo Stefano (041
523 8830/www.albertovallese-ebru.com). Vaporetto
Accademia or Sant'Angelo.* **Open** 10am-1.30pm,
2.30-7pm Mon-Wed; 10am-1pm, 2.30-7pm Thur-Sat;
11am-6pm Sun. **Credit** AmEx, MC, V. **Map** p325 F2.
Beautiful, marbled handcrafted paper, scarves and
ties. These are Venetian originals, whose imitators
can be found in other shops around town.

Legatoria Piazzesi

*San Marco 2511, campiello Feltrina (041 522 1202).
Vaporetto Giglio.* **Open** 10am-1pm, 3-7pm Mon-Sat.
Credit AmEx, DC, MC, V. **Map** p326 A2.
This Venetian paper maker uses the traditional
wooden-block method of printing to produce colour-
ful handpainted paper and cards.

Legatoria Polliero

*San Polo 2995, campo dei Frari (041 528 5130).
Vaporetto San Tomà.* **Open** 10.30am-1pm, 3.30-
7.30pm Mon-Sat; 10am-1pm Sun. **Credit** AmEx,
MC, V. **Map** p321 F5.
This bookbinding workshop, near the Frari church,
sells leather-bound diaries, frames and photograph
albums. It's not cheap but quality is assured.

Il Pavone

*Dorsoduro 721, fondamenta Venier dei Leoni
(041 523 4517). Vaporetto Accademia.* **Open**
9.30am-1.30pm, 2.30-6.30pm daily. **Credit** AmEx,
MC, V. **Map** p325 F3.
Handmade paper with floral motifs in a variety of
colours. Il Pavone also stocks boxes, picture frames,
key chains and other objects, all decorated in the
same style. Quality products at decent prices.

Records & music

Discoland

*Dorsoduro 2760, campo San Barnaba (041 528
7229). Vaporetto Ca' Rezzonico.* **Open** 10am-1pm,
3-7.30pm Mon-Sat. **Credit** MC, V. **Map** p325 E2.

Tragicomica. *See p195.*

Carteria Tassotti. *See p194.*

Don't get excited, this is not a nightclub. However, jazz aficionados should head here. The owner is knowledgeable and has a great range of CDs and DVDs with many imports hard to find elsewhere.

Il Tempio della Musica

San Marco 5368, ramo dei Tedeschi (041 523 4552). Vaporetto Rialto. **Open** 9am-7.30pm Mon-Sat. **Credit** AmEx, DC, MC, V. **Map** p322 B5.
A large selection of all musical genres, though classical, jazz and opera are its forte. Check the window display for the latest releases and special offers.

Nalesso

San Marco 5537, salizada fontego dei Tedeschi (041 522 1343). Vaporetto Rialto. **Open** 10am-7.30pm Mon-Sat; 11am-7pm Sun. **Credit** Am Ex, DC, MC, V. **Map** p322 B5.
You'll hear the music as you approach this small shop located across from the post office. Specialising in classical Venetian music, Nalesso also sells concert tickets for the Fenice and Malibran theatres as well as for concerts in various churches.

Wood, sculpture & frames

Cornici Trevisanello

Dorsoduro 662, campo San Vio (041 520 7779). Vaporetto Accademia. **Open** 9am-1pm, 3-7pm Mon-Fri; 9am-1pm Sat. **Credit** AmEx, MC, V. **Map** p325 F2.
Strategically located between the Accademia and the Guggenheim, this workshop is home to a father, son and daughter team that makes beautiful gilded frames, many with pearl, mirror and glass inlay. Custom orders and shipping are not a problem.

Dalla Venezia

Santa Croce 2074, calle Pesaro (041 721 276). Vaporetto San Stae. **Open** 8am-noon, 2.30-7pm Mon-Sat. **Credit** AmEx, DC, MC, V. **Map** p322 A4.
Employing the traditional technique of Venetian *tira-oro* (gold leaf decoration), Dalla Venezia creates exquisite gilded frames in his enchanting studio near Ca' Pesaro.

Gilberto Penzo

San Polo 2681, calle II dei Saoneri (041 719 372/ www.veniceboats.com). Vaporetto San Tomà. **Open** 9.30am-12.30pm, 3-6pm Mon-Sat. **Credit** MC, V. **Map** p321 F5.
This place is a truly fascinating workshop for anyone interested in Venetian boats. Gilberto Penzo creates astonishingly detailed models of gondolas, sandolos and topos as well as some remarkable reproductions of vaporettos. Inexpensive kits are also on sale if you would like to practise the fine art of shipbuilding.

Le Forcole di Saverio Pastor

Dorsoduro 341, fondamenta Soranzo de la Fornace (041 522 5699/www.forcole.com). Vaporetto Salute. **Open** 8.30am-12.30pm, 2-6pm Mon-Fri. **Credit** MC, V. **Map** p326 A3.
The place to come when you need a new *forcola* or pair of oars for your favourite gondola. Saverio Pastor is one of only three recognised *marangon* (oar makers) in all of Venice; he specialises in making the elaborate walnut-wood rests (*forcole*) that are the symbols of the gondolier's trade. Each gondolier has his very own, specially customised *forcola*, which he guards with his life. Non-rowing visitors may be more interested in purchasing the bookmarks, postcards and some books (in English) on Venetian boatworks.

Signor Blum

Dorsoduro 2840, campo San Barnaba (041 522 6367/www.signorblum.com). Vaporetto Ca' Rezzonico. **Open** 10am-7pm daily. **Credit** AmEx, DC, MC, V. **Map** p325 E2.

Mr Blum's colourful, handmade wooden puzzles of Venetian *palazzi*, gondolas and animals make great gifts for children and adults alike.

Services

Finding conveniences in a city such as Venice can be time consuming, but it's entirely possible. With the growing numbers of university students and tourists flocking to the city, internet access, photocopying and swift film-developing services are easy enough to find. You'll also find other useful services, such as post offices and couriers, listed in the Directory chapter (*see pp291-303*).

Beauticians

Beauty Care

San Marco 3564, calle Caotorta (041 241 0767). Vaporetto Sant Angelo. **Open** 10am-6.30pm Tue-Sat. **Credit** AmEx, MC, V. **Map** p326 A1.

This ultra-discreet beautician offers top-to-toe care, from pedicures to facials with a bikini wax in between. A manicure will set you back €15 and a bikini wax €8. The solarium costs €1 per minute.

Segreti di Donne

Santa Croce 2163-4, calle Longa (041 244 0123). Vaporetto San Stae. **Open** 9am-7pm Tue-Fri; 9am-3pm Sat. **Credit** AmEx, MC, V. **Map** p321 F4.

This beauty centre gives you the works, with a stone massage setting you back €70. A manicure is €12 and a well-earned pedicure costs €20. The girls are friendly and the parlour is clean and quietly elegant.

Clothing & shoe repairs

Daniela Ghezzo Segalin Venezia (*see p188*) and **Giovanna Zanella** (*see p189*) also do shoe repairs.

Calzolaio Pietro Rizzi

Dorsoduro 3799B, calle della Scuola (340 932 4268). Vaporetto San Tomà. **Open** 8am-1pm, 3-7.30pm Mon-Fri. **No credit cards**. **Map** p326 A3.

One of the few remaining shops that repairs shoes: a heel job will set you back €4.

Ricami Calle del Paradiso

Castello 5754, calle del Paradiso (no phone). Vaporetto Rialto. **Open** 10am-5.30pm Tue-Sat. **No credit cards**. **Map** p322 C5.

Two ladies carry out minor repairs and alterations, although embroidery is their speciality. A hem job starts at €10 and takes about a week. If the work is urgent, the price goes up.

Carnevale costume rentals

Atelier Pietro Longhi

San Polo 2604B, rio terà Frari (041 714 478/www. pietrolonghi.com) Vaporetto San Tomà. **Open** 10am-12.30pm, 3-7.30pm Mon-Fri; 10am-12.30pm Sat. **Credit** AmEx, DC, MC, V. **Map** p321 F5.

It costs between €160 and €600 to rent an outfit for the first day; each additional day is half-price. The shop offers discounts for groups.

Nicolao Atelier

Cannaregio 2590, fondamenta della Misericordia (041 520 7051/www.nicolao.com). Vaporetto Guglie. **Open** 9am-1pm, 2-6pm Mon-Fri. **Credit** MC, V. **Map** p322 A2.

A very simple costume rents for €80 a day; the more elaborate ones can go up to as much as €250 a day. There is, however, a reduction for each additional hire day thereafter.

Dry-cleaners & launderettes

In Venice, there are a growing number of self-service launderettes, but still only a small number of laundries that will do your wash, charging by the kilo. Small, family-run dry-cleaners, offering a more personal service, are more expensive than the chains that have opened up in recent years. Your hotel may also provide a laundry service, but compare prices with local establishments.

Centro Pulisecco

Cannaregio 6262D, calle della Testa (041 522 5011). Vaporetto Ca' d'Oro. **Open** 8.30am-12.30pm, 3-7pm Mon-Fri. **No credit cards**. **Map** p322 C4.

Centro Pulisecco offers dry-cleaning only. Trousers cost €2.90, jackets €3.90 and sweaters €2. An express service is available.

Other locations: Cannaregio 1749, rio terà del Cristo (041 718 020).

Speedy Wash

Cannaregio 1520, rio terà San Leonardo (347 359 3442/www.speedy-wash.it). Vaporetto San Marcuola. **Open** 8am-11pm daily. **No credit cards**. **Map** p321 F3.

This coin-op launderette charges €5 for 8kg, €7.50 for 16kg and €3 for the dryer.

Film & development

Bianconero

Cannaregio 4541, campo Santi Apostoli (shop 041 522 8781/darkroom 041 520 7535/www. bianconero-venezia.it). Vaporetto Ca' d'Oro. **Open** 9.30am-12.30pm, 3.30-7.30pm Tue-Sat. **Credit** MC, V. **Map** p322 B4.

Not only does this shop offer printing services, it also has a wonderful archive of photos (1947-1980), many of them depicting stars of the silver screen at the Venice Film Festival.

Eat, Drink, Shop

Talking shop

If price tags in the luxurious shops around St Mark's square are making you wince, and your credit card is melting, you can take comfort in the knowledge that retail therapy was just as painful for many a shopper in Renaissance Venice.

Just like today, keeping up with fashion was a problem for cash-strapped women in *über*-trendy 16th-century Venice. One way around this was recycling expensive fabrics and clothes, à la Scarlett O'Hara, to create more up-to-date pieces. Less talented needlewomen, on the other hand, could buy on credit: no threatening letters from Mastercard here, but creditors often lured women who couldn't keep up with repayments into prostitution to recoup their money.

Just as you might hire a snazzy outfit for Carnevale today, Renaissance women would rent spectacular outfits for special occasions. Men also rented sumptuous get-ups, but it didn't end with clothes. Sir Henry Wotton, English ambassador to Venice in the 17th century, rented everything from a billiards table to bed sheets.

Pawnbrokers and secondhand dealers did a roaring trade in Venice. And it was not only the poor who tried to pawn or sell goods, though they did so in more dramatic fashion: records show impoverished men pledging their wives and children against loans. Patrician families would furnish their servants' rooms with secondhand furniture, and sometimes their own living areas as well. They also pledged or re-mortgaged more valuable items, from fine linen to jewellery, in order to rustle up some ready cash.

The position of women in the marketplace was very different in Venice. Traveller Thomas Coryat noted in the early 17th century: 'I have observed a thing amongst Venetians that I have not a little wondered at, that their Gentlemen and greatest Senators... will come into the market, and buy their flesh, fish, fruites and other things.'

His wonderment was countered by a Venetian ambassador's astonishment when visiting London later that century: he remarked in particular on Englishwomen's 'great freedom to go out of the house without menfolk'.

Though Venetian women were often left out of the shopping experience, one woman whose shopping exploits would make a WAG weep was Isabella d'Este (1474-1539), marchioness of Mantua and a frequent visitor to Venice. As a young bride she asked a friend in Paris to purchase jewels and fabrics on her behalf – one of the first records of mail order shopping. She also had a personal shopper trawling the shops in Venice for her. One thing that caught her eye on a visit to the Sensa market in St Mark's Square was 'a magnificent show of beautiful glass'; other acquisitions included gems and luxurious fabrics. Although viewed as greedy and acquisitive, her purchasing power was a sign of political and financial clout, making her one of history's most remarkable and formidable shopaholics.

Cesana Photo

Dorsoduro 879, rio terà Antonio Foscarini (041 522 2020). Vaporetto Accademia. **Open** *Apr-Sept* 9am-1pm, 2.30-7pm Mon-Sat. *Oct-Mar* 9am-1pm, 2.30-7pm Mon-Fri. **Credit** MC, V. **Map** p325 F3.

You won't find low prices but you will find fast, good-quality service at this shop near the ponte dell'Accademia: colour developing can be done in just 25 minutes while slides only take an hour. There are services also for digital images, passport photos and photocopies.

Interpress Photo

San Polo 365, campo delle Beccarie (041 528 6978). Vaporetto San Silvestro. **Open** 9am-12.30pm, 3.30-7.30pm Mon-Sat. **Credit** DC, MC, V. **Map** p322 A4.

This is definitely one of the cheapest places in Venice for film development, and, happily, it's also probably one of the best: 24 exposures are a mere €6.50. The shop also provides one-hour service, passport photographs and photocopies. A small selection of authentic Murano glass is on sale alongside sunglasses.

Florists

Fioreia San Rocco

San Polo 3127, campo San Rocco (041 524 4271). Vaporetto San Tomà. **Open** 8.30am-12.30pm, 3.30-7.30pm Mon-Sat; 9am-12.30pm Sun. **Credit** AmEx, MC, V. **Map** p321 E5.

If you want to say it with flowers, head to Alessandra Gallenda's shop. She can provide you with anything from a single rose to a hothouse plant. The shop is affiliated to Interflora and will deliver to your hotel door or organize sending that special someone something abroad. Prices for a bouquet start at around €15.

Hairdressers

Prices are *à la carte*: each dab of styling foam or puff of hairspray pushes up the bill. Most salons are closed on Mondays.

Stefano e Claudia
San Polo 1098B, riva del Vin (041 520 1913). Vaporetto San Silvestro. **Open** 9am-5pm Tue-Sat. **Credit** AmEx, MC, V. **Map** p322 B5.
The Stefano e Claudia salon is easily the most contemporary on the lagoon. Prices are high and an appointment is a must. The real bonus is that as you're getting styled, you can enjoy a beautiful view of the Grand Canal.

Tocco di Gio'
Santa Croce 661A, campo della Lana (041 718 493). Vaporetto Ferrovia. **Open** 9am-6pm Tue-Sat. **No credit cards. Map** p321 E4.
For men and women. Get a good cut at a reasonable price in a friendly atmosphere.

Opticians

Most opticians will do minor running repairs on the spot and (usually) free of charge. See also **Ottico Fabbricatore,** *p188.*

Ottica Carraro Alessandro
San Marco 3706, calle della Mandola (041 520 4258/ www.otticacarraro.it). Vaporetto Sant'Angelo. **Open** 9am-1pm, 3-7.30pm Mon-Sat. **Credit** AmEx, DC, MC, V. **Map** p326 A1.
Get yourself some unique and funky eye wear – the frames are exclusively produced and guaranteed for life. Ottica Carraro Alessandro offers extraordinary quality at reasonable prices.

Punto Vista (Elvio Carraro)
Cannaregio 1982, campiello Anconeta (041 720 453). Vaporetto San Marcuola. **Open** 9am-7.30pm Mon-Sat. **Credit** MC, DC, V. **Map** p321 F3.
Eyeglasses, sunglasses, contact lenses and saline solution. Punto Vista also undertakes walk-in eye examinations and repairs.

Photocopies & faxes

Thanks to the Università Ca' Foscari and the University Institute of Architecture (both located centrally), finding a place to make a photocopy is neither difficult nor expensive (for more university information, *see p300*).

Also helpful are the many *tabacchi* (*see p301*) that send faxes; they usually announce the fact in their front windows, as do other service centres. (For couriers, *see p291*; internet points, *see p293*; *see also p198* **Cesana Photo.**)

Centro Copie Ca' Foscari
Dorsoduro 3253 fondamenta di Ca' Foscari (no phone). Vaporetto Ca' Rezzonico or San Tomà.
Open 9am-7pm Mon-Fri. **No credit cards. Map** p325 E1.
Photocopies, binding and laser printing are offered. Serves stressed-out students with thesis deadlines. It normally costs 7¢ per photocopy – but if you're copying from a book, it rises to 18¢, because you have to pay the copyright.

Micoud
San Marco 4581, campo San Luca (041 528 9275/ www.micoud.it). Vaporetto Rialto. **Open** 8.30am-12.30pm, 3-7.30pm Mon-Fri; 8.30am-12.30pm Sat. **Credit** AmEx, DC, MC, V. **Map** p326 B1
This tiny shop offers a variety of services: colour photocopies, fax, binding, digital images and much more. An A4 photocopy costs 15¢. Reliable, professional service.

Ticket agencies

VeLa-HelloVenezia *p286* has tickets for most major and many minor events taking place in Venice; see also **Nalesso** *p196.*

Bassani
Dorsoduro-Santa Marta, San Basilio Fabbricata 17 (041 520 3644/fax 041 520 4009/www.bassani.it). Vaporetto Santa Marta or San Basilio. **Open** 9am-1pm, 2-6pm Mon-Fri; 9.30am-12.30pm Sat. **Credit** AmEx, MC, V. **Map** p324 B2.
Inside the port authority complex at the western end of Dorsoduro, Bassani sells tickets for concerts held in churches around town and organises walking tours, gondola rides and visits to the islands of the lagoon. The company also functions as a regular travel agency.

Travel agencies

See also *above* **Bassani.**

CTS (Centro Turistico Studentesco)
Dorsoduro 3252, fondamenta del Tagliapietra (041 520 5660/www.cts.it). Vaporetto Ca' Rezzonico or San Tomà. **Open** 9.30am-1.30pm, 2.30-6pm Mon-Fri. **Credit** MC, V. **Map** p325 E1.
This agency caters to its own members (membership costs €30) and also to students in general, offering discount air fares, international train tickets and other useful information for student travellers. ISICs cost €10: bring a passport photo and a document proving you are a student. It also has tickets to concerts, exhibitions and the theatre at discounted prices for members.

Park View Viaggi
Dorsoduro 3944, calle San Pantalon (041 520 0988/www.parkviaggi.it). Vaporetto San Tomà. **Open** 9am-1pm, 3-7pm Mon-Fri. **Credit** AmEx, MC, DC, V. **Map** p321 E5.
The staff at this agency are not only friendly but extraordinarily efficient. Park View has a money-changing service too. You can purchase train tickets up to 6pm.

Eat, Drink, Shop

Arts & Entertainment

Festivals & Events

Don your mask and grab your oar – it's party time.

Many of Venice's best-known festivals –
Carnevale, for example, and the Regata Storica
– are late 20th-century reinventions of popular
revelries stamped out by the French when
they took control of the city in the early 19th
century. By that time Venice's celebrations
had become frantic and excessive, the tawdry
death-throes of a city in terminal decline.

Since the earliest days of the Republic,
festivals, processions and popular celebrations,
set against Venice's peerless backdrop, have
been an intrinsic part of the city's social fabric.
The government used pageantry both to assert
the hierarchical nature of society and to give
the lower orders the chance to let off steam.
The government declared official celebrations
in honour of anything from the end of plague
to a naval battle – and there was no shortage
of local saints' days to celebrate. For the
working classes, there were the *corse al toro*
(bullfights) in campo Santo Stefano, or bloody
battles between rival sections of the populace.

Nowadays you could be forgiven for thinking
that *feste* such as **Carnevale** (*see below*) are
merely media and tourism events. Yet Venetians
continue to take festivals seriously, especially
if they take place on the water. There are more
than 120 regattas in the lagoon each year.
The **Regata Storica** (*see p204*) may look
like it's funded by the tourist board, but
Venetians get seriously involved in the boat
races following the spectacle; the **Vogalonga**
(*see p203*) is a remarkable display of Venetian
love of messing about in boats. For public
holidays and religious days, *see p303*.

See also http://english.comune.venezia.it.

Spring

Carnevale

Date 10 days ending on Shrove Tuesday.
Though it had existed since the Middle Ages,
Venice's pre-Lenten Carnevale came into its own in
the 18th century: as the Venetian Republic went into
terminal decline, the city's pagan side began to
emerge. Carnevale became an outlet for all that had
been prohibited for centuries by the strong arm of
the doge. Elaborate structures would be set up in
piazza San Marco as stages for acrobats, tumblers,
wrestlers and other performers. Masks served not
only as an escape from the drabness of everyday life
but to conceal the wearer's identity – a useful ploy
for nuns on the lam or slumming patricians. The

Napoleonic invasion in 1797 brought an end to the
fun and games; Carnevale was not resuscitated until
the late 1970s. The city authorities and hoteliers'
association saw the earning potential, and today the
heavily subsidised celebrations draw revellers from
all over the world. The party starts ten days before
martedì grasso (Shrove Tuesday – literally 'Fat
Tuesday'), though plans were afoot to kick off the
festivities earlier. Tourist offices (*see p302*) provide
full Carnevale programmes.

Su e Zo per i Ponti

Information *041 590 4717/www.tgseurogroup.it/
suezo/index.htm.* **Date** 4th Sun of Lent.
Literally 'Up and Down the Bridges', this privately
organised excursion is inspired by the traditional
bacarada (bar crawl). It is an orienteering event in
which you are given a map and a list of checkpoints
to tick off in the city of Venice. Old hands take their
time checking out the *bacari* (*see chapter* **Cafés &
Bars**) along the way. Individuals can register at the
starting line in piazza San Marco on the morning of
the event, while groups should phone ahead.
Costumes, music and dancing liven up the route.

Benedizione del Fuoco

Basilica di San Marco (041 522 5205). *Vaporetto
Vallaresso or San Zaccaria.* **Date** Maundy Thursday.
Map p326 C1.
At around dusk all the lights are turned off inside
St Mark's basilica and a fire is lit in the narthex
(entrance porch). Communion is celebrated and
the four elements are blessed: earth represented by
the faithful masses, fire by the large altar candle,
water at the baptismal font and air from the
surrounding environment.

Festa di San Marco

Bacino di San Marco. *Vaporetto Vallaresso or
San Zaccaria.* **Date** 25 Apr. **Map** p326 C2.
The traditional feast day of Venice's patron saint is
a low-key affair. In the morning there is a solemn
Mass in the basilica, followed by a gondola regatta
between the island of Sant'Elena and the Punta della
Dogana at the entrance to the Grand Canal. The day
is also known as *La Festa del boccolo* ('bud'): red
rosebuds are given to wives and lovers.

Festa e Regata della Sensa

San Nicolò del Lido & Bacino di San Marco.
Information *041 529 8711/041 274 7737.*
Date Ascension Day (fifth Thursday after Easter).
Back in the days of the Venetian Republic, the doge
would board the glorious state barge, the Bucintoro,
and be rowed out to the island of Sant'Andrea, facing
the lagoon's main outlet to the Adriatic, followed by

a fleet of small boats. Here he would throw a gold ring overboard, to symbolise *lo sposalizio del mare* – Venice's marriage with the sea. Today the mayor takes the place of the doge, the Bucintoro looks like a glorified fruit boat and the ring has become a laurel wreath. The ceremony is now performed at San Nicolò, on the northernmost point of the Lido, and is followed by a regatta. If it rains, local lore says it'll tip down for the next 40 days. ('*Se piove il giorno della Sensa per quaranta giorni non semo sensa.*')

Vogalonga
Information *041 521 0544/www.vogalonga.it.*
Date one Sunday in May or early June.
Like San Francisco's 'critical mass'– during which bicycles clog downtown to demonstrate against congestion and pollution – Venetians (or at least those with strength enough to complete the 33km/20.5 mile route) protest against motorboats and the damage they do by boarding any kind of rowing craft and making their way through the lagoon and the city's two main canals in this annual free-for-all. They are joined by a host of out-of-towners and foreigners: in 2005, 5,165 people rowed, of which 1,121 were Venetians, 1,509 other Italians and 2,535 from further afield. Boats set off from in front of the lagoon façade of the Doge's Palace at 8.30am.

Venezia Suona
Information *041 275 0049/www.veneziasuona.it.*
Date weekend in late July.
The name means 'Venice plays'… and that it does, with hundreds of bands playing anything from rock to folk to reggae and jazz. Music can be heard from about 4pm onwards in *campi* all over the city.

Veneto Jazz Festival
Via Aldo Moro 29, Cavasagra di Vedelago (0423 452 069/fax 0423 451 327/www.venetojazz.com).
Box office at venues before performances. **Dates** Feb-Apr, June-Aug. **Credit** MC, V.
Giants of jazz perform alongside lesser known talents. Credit cards accepted for online bookings only.

Summer

Biennale d'Arte Contemporanea & Architettura
Giardini di Castello. Vaporetto Giardini.
Information *041 521 8711/www.labiennale.org.*
Date *Contemporary art* (odd years) June-Nov.
Architecture (even years) Sept-Nov. **Map** p328 A4.
The Biennale d'Arte, established in 1895, is the *Jeux sans Frontières* of the contemporary art world; its architectural counterpart draws a strong crowd.

Palio delle Antiche Repubbliche Marinare
Bacino di San Marco. Vaporetto Vallaresso or San Zaccaria. **Date** June or July.
This competition takes place in Venice once every four years (other times it's in Amalfi, Genova or Pisa) – 2007 being Venice's most recent turn. The 2000m race starts at the island of Sant'Elena and finishes at the Doge's palace. Before the race, 400-odd boats carrying costumed representatives of the four Marine Republics parade along the riva dei Sette Martiri and the riva degli Schiavoni. Venice's boat is the emerald green one with the lion of St Mark.

Festa di San Pietro
San Pietro in Castello. Vaporetto Giardini. **Date** week ending 29 June. **Map** p328 B2.
The most lively and villagey of Venice's many local festivals in celebration of San Pietro Martire. A week of events centres on the church green of San Pietro (*see p101*): there are competitions, concerts, food stands and bouncy castles.

Festa di San Giacomo dell'Orio
Campo San Giacomo dell'Orio. Vaporetto San Stae or Riva di Biasio. **Date** week ending 25 July. **Map** p321 F4.
Concerts, a barbecue and a charity raffle make up this local fair: a great occasion to 'do as the Venetians do' in a truly beautiful campo.

Cinema all'aperto

Campo San Polo. Vaporetto San Silvestro or San Tomà. **Information** *041 524 1320/www.comune. venezia.it/cinema.* **Date** 6wks late July-early Sept. **Map** p321 F5.

A huge outdoor theatre is set up in campo San Polo to show current films, usually dubbed into Italian, occasionally with English subtitles. *See p208.*

Festa del Redentore

Bacino di San Marco, Canale della Giudecca. **Date** 3rd weekend of July.

The Redentore is the oldest continuously celebrated date on the Venetian calendar. At the end of a plague epidemic in 1576 the city commissioned Andrea Palladio to build a church on the Giudecca – *Il Redentore* (the Redeemer). Every July a pontoon bridge is built across the canal that separates the Giudecca from Venice proper, so people can make the pilgrimage to the church. But, while the religious part of the festival falls on Sunday, what makes this weekend so special are the festivities on Saturday night. Boats of every shape and size gather in the lagoon between St Mark's, San Giorgio, the Punta della Dogana and the Giudecca, each holding merry-makers supplied with food and drink. This party culminates in an amazing fireworks display.

Ferragosto – Festa dell'Assunta

Date 15 Aug.

If you want Venice without Venetians, this is the time to come, as everyone who can leaves the city. Practically everything shuts down and people head to the beach. There is usually a free concert in the cathedral on the lagoon island of Torcello, Santa Maria Assunta (*see p149*), on the evening of the 15th. Tourist offices (*see p302*) have more information.

Regata Storica

Grand Canal. **Date** 1st Sun in Sept.

This event begins with a procession of ornate boats down the Grand Canal, rowed by locals in 16th-century costume. Once this is over, the races start – which is what most locals have come to see. There are four: one for young rowers, one for women, one for rowers of *caorline* – long canoe-like boats in which the prow and the stern are identical – and the last, the most eagerly awaited, featuring two-man sporting *gondolini*. The finish is at the sharp curve of the Grand Canal between Palazzo Barbi and Ca' Foscari: here the judges sit in an ornate raft known as the *machina*, where the prize-giving takes place.

Mostra Internazionale D'Arte Cinematografica (Film Festival)

One of the biggest events of the Venetian year. For further information, *see p210.*

Autumn

Sagra del Pesce

Island of Burano. Vaporetto 12. **Date** 3rd Sun in Sept. **Map** p319.

Fried fish and lots of white wine are consumed in this feast in the *calli* between Burano's brightly painted houses. Those rowers who are not legless then take part in the last regatta of the season.

Sagra del Mosto

Island of Sant'Erasmo. Vaporetto 13 to Chiesa. **Date** 1st weekend in Oct.

This festival is a great excuse for Venetians to spend a day 'in the country' at Sant'Erasmo (*see p149*), getting light-headed on the first pressing of wine. The salty soil does not lend itself to superior wine – which is why it's best to down a glass before the stuff has had much chance to ferment. Sideshows, grilled sausage aromas and red-faced locals abound.

Venice Marathon

Information *041 532 1871/www.venicemarathon.it.* **Date** last Sun in Oct.

This marathon starts in the town of Stra, east of Padua, follows the Brenta canal, and then winds through Venice to end on the riva Sette Martiri. The website is in Italian and English.

Winter

Festa di San Martino

Date 11 Nov.

Kids armed with mamma's pots and spoons raise a ruckus around the city centre, chanting the saint's praises and demanding trick-or-treat style tokens in return for taking their noise elsewhere. Horse-and-rider-shaped San Martino cakes, with coloured icing dotted with silver balls, proliferate in cake shops.

Festa della Madonna della Salute

Church of Madonna della Salute. Vaporetto Salute. **Date** 21 Nov. **Map** p326 A3.

In 1630-1 Venice was 'miraculously' delivered from plague, which claimed almost 100,000 lives – one in three Venetians. The Republic commissioned a church from Baldassare Longhena, and his Madonna della Salute (lit. 'good health', *see p134*) was completed in 1687. On this feast day a pontoon bridge is strung across the Grand Canal from campo Santa Maria del Giglio to La Salute so that a procession led by the patriarch (archbishop) of Venice can make its way on foot from San Marco. Along the way, stalls sell cakes and candyfloss, and candles that pilgrims light inside the church. Then everybody eats *castradina* – cabbage and mutton stew that tastes nicer than it sounds.

Christmas, New Year & Epiphany (La Befana)

Venice's Yuletide festivities are low-key affairs. There are two events: the New Year's Day swim off the Lido (www.lidovenezia.it) for hardy swimmers , and the *Regata delle Befane* (www.bucintoro.it) on 6 January, a rowing race along the Grand Canal in which the competitors, all aged over 50, are dressed up as *La Befana* – the ugly witch who gives sweets to good children and pieces of coal to bad ones.

Children

Wow them with this weird and wonderful world.

So long as you don't subject your kids to an unmitigated diet of Renaissance churches and overwhelming art galleries, it shouldn't be too difficult to keep their interest alive in a city as intrinsically weird and wonderful as Venice. With its labyrinthine geography, its hundreds of crooked bridges and its omnipresent winged lions, the city can be presented as a respectable rival to Hogwarts.

If you want to make sure that they see things this way, then you'll need to plan your day's activities with imaginative foresight. A good deal of walking is going to be necessary and few of the major sights are geared towards children. Little ones will be bedazzled by the sheer mechanics of the place: exploit it, and remember that hours hanging over bridges spotting fish-finger delivery boats is part of the Venetian experience too. Older kids may be inveigled into the right frame of mind with a pre-emptive gift of Cornelia Funke's *The Thief Lord*; if that intrigues them, a visit to campo Santa Margherita (*see p127*) will then be indispensable.

With strategies such as these, it should be possible to keep the kids interested enough not to be clamouring for the hotel's satellite TV. And if you're clamouring for a romantic dinner, you'll find larger hotels have childminders, while smaller ones can probably arrange them.

GETTING AROUND
The frequent absence of barriers between pavement and canal presents a problem for mobile toddlers: safety reins might not be a bad idea here. Pre-walkers present another dilemma. And after heaving a pushchair over the umpteenth bridge in a day, a baby backpack may seem like a gift from heaven.

Vaporetto travel is far from cheap. Children under five travel free; after that they pay full fare (*see also p68* **Discount cards**). But if you look on the means of transport as a Venetian experience in itself the cost will not seem so outrageous; it is perfectly acceptable to take your pram or pushchair onto the vaporetto at no extra cost – although it is probably better to avoid doing this on the smaller boats at rush-hour. A complete circle on line 82 (red) from the riva degli Schiavoni will take your fascinated offspring across to the Giudecca, then up to the station and port areas, giving them a glimpse of Venice's industrial underbelly as well as a triumphal march down the Grand Canal.

Most children will demand a gondola trip. Remember that this expensive experience (*see p289*) can be substituted by or supplemented with rides on the humbler but more useful *traghetti* (*see p287*) that ply across the Grand Canal at points distant from bridges. Let them stand up in the boat like real Venetians.

Sightseeing

Venice will leave all but the most cynical youngsters gobsmacked, so keeping them amused should not take too much effort. (Unless, of course, you bore them to death with a surfeit of churches and museums.)

Under-tens, especially, are a pushover. The city's 400-plus bridges are a joy: children love watching boats slipping under one side and emerging from the other. For a glimpse of illustrious craft of the past, head for the **Museo Storico Navale** (*see p100*), where Venice's maritime history is charted in scale models of ships built in the Arsenale over the centuries.

The well-heads of Venice

It's a while since anyone counted, but it's estimate the number of well-heads in Venice is around 2,500… a dramatic drop from the 6,782 counted by city authorities in 1858.

Look at the shape of squares with wells at their centre: you'll notice that the ground level is often raised, to keep salt water out during high tide. The paving is also angled towards drains where rain water would disappear, sink through filtering systems, and then find its way into cisterns beneath the well-heads.

But in 1882-4, pipes were laid to bring fresh water to the lagoon city from the mainland. With no practical purpose, monumental well-heads became just one more thing that poor Venetians could sell off to wealthy foreigners.

The most ancient
Corte Correra (between San Zaccaria and Santa Maria Formosa, map p326 C1, and not always accessible): a square well-head dating from the ninth or tenth century; the sculptured rosettes are 15th century.

Byzantine
Corte del Remer (near San Giovanni Crisostomo, map p322 B5): a fine example with elegant arches in red Verona marble.

Gothic
Corte Veniera (off campo Santi Giovanni e Paolo, map 322 C5): a fine specimen with ogival arches.
Ca' d'Oro (see p103): an elaborately carved late-Gothic well in the courtyard.

Renaissance
Campo Santi Giovanni e Paolo (map p322 C5): an elegant well-head with festoon-draped putti.
Campo San Zaccaria (map p327 D1), **campo San Giovanni Crisostomo** (map p322 B5), **campo della Maddalena** (map p322 A3): inspired by Corinthian capitals, these have delicate carvings of foliage and other decorative elements.

Campo Angelo Raffaele (map p324 C2): this cylindrical example has charming carvings of Tobias and the guardian angel.

Mannerist and baroque
Campo dei Frari (map p321 E5): a large cylindrical well with a swelling waist
Campo San Marcuola (map p321 F3): a lavish well with lion heads and scrolled shields amid ornate curlicues.

19th century
Campo San Polo (map p321 F5): this octagonal well-head is also the largest in the city (320cm in diameter).

The most monumental
Palazzo Ducale (Doge's palace, see p84): elaborate Renaissance works in bronze
I Frari (see p123): 18th-century, with pillars, a pediment and statuary in the cloister

The most intriguing
Corte Gregolin (off calle dei Fabbri, map p326 B1): completely unique, this 15th-century head has exquisite patterns, including two double-rope bindings and a 'wicker-work' base.

The most secret
Calle Bernardo (between campo San Barnaba and Ca' Foscari, map p325 E2): the only well-head in central Venice that still bears the lion of St Mark. In 1797 the French employed a sculptor to remove these symbols of Venetian independence, but he never found this one.

The most apologetic
Campo Do Pozzo (map p327 E1): though it's called 'Two Wells' this square only has one left; the survivor bears a carving of two.

The most forlorn
Calle del Aseo (near campo Santa Margherita, map p325 E1): this elegant well-head in Verona marble has had a garden-wall built through it.

Venetians have always devoted much time to games and sport; visit the **Museo Querini Stampalia** (see p93), where a collection of 18th-century scenes includes some very unlikely amusements: one painting, *La Guerra dei Pugni* by Antonio Strom, shows one of the mass boxing matches that occurred frequently on bridges. The initial four competitors – before proceedings degenerated into a free-for-all – started out with one foot on the white inlaid footprints on the corners of the top step: try it out for yourselves on ponte dei Pugni near campo San Barnaba, ponte della Guerra near campo San Zulian and ponte di Santa Fosca.

Don't forget to introduce your kids to the most famous Venetian game of all. With the lagoon behind you, and the lagoon-facing façade of the Doge's Palace in front of you, go to the third column from the left. Place your back firmly against it, then walk round it, all the way. Can you circumnavigate it without holding onto the pillar and without slipping off the shoe-worn marble pavement?

Subjects for I-Spy games are manifold: bell towers are good, as are lions. Piazza San Marco and its adjoining *piazzette* offer a pure pride, ranging from the ancient and exotic (Syrian, Persian or Chinese) to the pink and cuddly (the porphyry ones in piazzetta dei Leoncini).

Most of Venice's museums are singularly hands-off, but some may still appeal to kids. If the vast Tintorettos and echoing halls of the **Palazzo Ducale** (*see p84*) inspire only yawns, combine your visit there with a tour of the palace's secret corridors, the *Itinerari segreti* (*see p84*; not advisable for toddlers), which will take you into dungeons and torture rooms. Only two rooms are currently open at the **Museo di Storia Naturale** (*see p118*) but they house an aquarium, dinosaur and giant crocodile fossils.

Breaking your children into art with visits to less demanding exhibits, such as the **Scuola di San Giorgio degli Schiavoni** (*see p101*), where Vittorio Carpaccio's *St George* cycle is packed with fascinating detail. The grand Tintorettos in the **Madonna dell'Orto** (*see p109*), particularly *The Last Judgement*, are full of the kind of gruesome details – such as bodies with skulls for heads scrabbling their way out of the earth – likely to appeal to kids.

Don't be scared off from big galleries such as the **Accademia** (*see p132*): you may link up with one of the gallery's more child-friendly guides, who will bend over backwards to interest your offspring in the collection. The **Musei Civici** (*see p67*) organises family events, usually on Sunday afternoons (in Italian only at present); it's €10 for a family of four.

To win a little picture-viewing time in churches, try pointing out to your kids that the red marble used in so many church floors contains amazing fossils. While they embark on mini-palaeontological excursions, you can concentrate on the artworks.

When the culture all gets too much, take Junior up a campanile for a bird's-eye view of the city. The one in piazza San Marco (*see p82*) is the highest; **San Giorgio Maggiore**'s (*see p140*) affords a more detached vantage point. Time your ascent to coincide with the striking of an hour – midday is particularly deafening. As this guide went to press, the gracious, smaller-scale **Scala del Bòvolo** (*see p80*) was closed for restoration; but if it's open when you visit, this lift-less climb will give the kids the satisfaction of making their own panting way up to the top – as does the campanile at the basilica at **Torcello**, but via steep sloping ramps rather than stairs; a fine view over the lagoon is the reward.

Parks, beaches & entertainment

Most Venetian kids spend their free time in their local *campi*. Ball games are officially forbidden there, but you will find them going on in most of them, particularly the larger ones like campo Santa Maria Formosa and campo San Polo. Venetian kids are used to letting foreign visitors join in. In campo Santa Maria Formosa and campo Santo Stefano small play areas for toddlers have been set up next to the churches.

Although well hidden, there are public parks in the city too, and most of them – including the **Giardini pubblici** (*see p98*) and the **Parco Savorgnan** (*see p110*) – have been fitted up with swings and slides. At **Sant'Elena** (*see p100*) things improve with a grassy play area along the lagoon, and a roller skating/cycling rink. Sant'Elena is also where Venice's football team has its home ground (*see p233*).

On the mainland, the brand new Parco San Giuliano (bus 12 from piazzale Roma) is one of Italy's largest urban parks. The newly planted trees don't offer much shade on a blazing summer day, but there are play areas, football pitches a lake and a roller skating rink.

In summer break up the culture with a trip to the Lido and its beaches. Most of the main ones are sewn up by the big hotels, which will charge you for a small stretch of sand, sometimes with deckchair and umbrella, and always with huge numbers of near neighbours. Pleasant **Sant'Erasmo** (*see p149*), a large, rural island, can be cycled around in an hour or so. There's a small beach straight across the island from the ferry landing stage. Alternatively, head for the **Lido di Jesolo** (*see p222*).

Local feast days may also provide entertainment for your children, usually in the shape of puppet theatres. Watch walls around the city for posters announcing *feste*. Particularly picturesque is the feast of Saints Peter and Paul in the parish of San Pietro in **Castello** (*see p101*), culminating on 29 June.

See also p227 **Teatro Toniolo**.

Books

The excellent children's guide (in English) *Viva Venice* by Paolo Zoffoli and Paola Scibilia (Elzeviro, 2002) has games, informative illustrations and interesting facts. *Venice for Kids* by Elisabetta Pasqualin (Fratelli Palombi, 2004) belongs to a series of books on Italian cities. Cornelia Funke's *The Thief Lord* should stir their curiosity. Terry Jones's fantasy story *Nicobobinus* and Anthony Horowitz's *Scorpia* both begin with exciting scenes set in Venice.

Arts & Entertainment

Film

Don't expect much – unless you're here for the festival.

Venice has lured the likes of David Lean and Nicolas Roeg to its treacherous sand banks, but the city has greater difficulty enticing its populace into its cinemas. Many former picture palaces now house supermarkets. It is a pretty accurate reflection of local demand, with a diminishing population signifying decreasing numbers of moviegoers.

However, two crusaders help to save the cinematic day. The first is the annual **Film Festival** (*see p210*) at the beginning of September, when the Lido's bikini-clad hordes rub shoulders with journalists, photographers and a constellation of international stars.

The second is **Circuito Cinema** (*see p210*), a film promotion initiative established in 1981. A hive of film-related research and activity, it also runs and programmes a group of local arthouse cinemas, including the **Giorgione Movie d'Essai** (*see below*), Cannaregio's former porn palace. This has been joined by the **Multisala Astra** (*see below*) on the Lido and two other screens on the mainland: the **Mignon Arthouse** in Mestre and the **Aurora Movie d'Essai** in Marghera. The plush **Sala Perla** housed in the former Casinò on the Lido (lungomare Marconi, 041 524 1320) completes the set and now runs a Friday evening series of first-run films, as well as doubling as a Sunday afternoon theatre. The five cinemas show a selection of Festival films in September.

The dearth of original-language films infuriates expats and cinema buffs alike. Both the Giorgione and the Astra offer a limited selection of films in *versione originale*.

SCREENINGS AND TICKETS

Screening times in Venice are limited, and generally there are no performances before 5pm during the week: check local press for details. Tickets cost from €4.50 to €7.

Associations

Circuito Cinema

Palazzo Mocenigo, Santa Croce 1991, salizada San Stae (041 524 1320/www.comune.venezia.it/cinema). Vaporetto San Stae. **Map p321 F4.**
The Circuito Cinema operates as a publisher, a cine-club organising a series of themed seasons and workshops, and as a promoter. Its annual (July-June) *CinemaPiù* card gives discounts to all of Venice's cinemas as well as a number of theatres, restaurants,

shops and museums. It costs €25 (€20 for students) and can be bought from the Giorgione and Astra cinemas as well as the San Polo open-air cinema (*for all, see below*) in the summer.

Cinemas

Giorgione Movie D'Essai

Cannaregio 4612, rio terà dei Franceschi (041 522 6298). Vaporetto Ca' d'Oro. **No credit cards. Map p322 B4.**
This two-screener run by Circuito Cinema (*see p210*) combines the usual fare with themed seasons, kids' films (on Saturday and Sunday at 3pm) and English-language offerings on Tuesdays from October to May. English-language films and blockbusters are shown in the spacious Sala A; retrospectives and indie material are in living room-sized Sala B.

Multisala Astra

Via Corfù 9, Lido (041 526 5736). Vaporetto Lido. **No credit cards. Map p317 A3.**
Don't be fooled by the name: like its Venetian counterpart, the Giorgione (*see above*), the council-run Astra is a two-screener and has an identical programme to boot, usually offering the same fodder as the Giorgione a day later. During the Film Festival, the Astra is also home to the Venice Film Meeting, which promotes locally made films. Entrance is free.

Open-air

Arena di Campo San Polo

Campo San Polo (041 524 4347). Vaporetto San Silvestro or San Tomà. **Season** 6wks late July-early Sept. **Tickets** €5-€7; €24 for 6 (excluding special screenings and events). Ticket office opens at 7.30pm. **No credit cards. Map p321 F5.**
This vibrant square in the city centre is home to Venice's second most important cinematic event of the year. Around 1000 cinemagoers a night brave the mosquitoes to fill this open-air arena. Films are generally re runs of the previous season's blockbusters, plus the odd preview. Recent excursions into less mainstream delights include the *Emozioni forti* series in 2006, which offered classics such as Orson Welles' *Touch of Evil* in original sound. The programme *Un'estate al cinema* incorporates the Giorgione, Astra and San Polo venues and ticket prices are the same for each theatre. During the Film Festival (*see p210*) you can catch some original-language films a day or two after their Lido screening. Warning: many foreign-language films are only screened with Italian subtitles.

'Red wine with fish. Well, that should have told me something.'

Ah, Bond. Looking for those tell-tale clues everywhere. Even in Venice. The quote appears in *From Russia with Love* (1963), Bond's first foray in the labyrinthine city, and often considered the best of the Bonds, with Sean Connery as our hero. Appearing briefly at the beginning and the end of the film, Venice reprises her role as a link between East and West. However, filmed at the height of the Cold War, it was deemed inadvisable to portray Russians as the bad guys, though the SPECTRE criminal organization still contains many Soviet Secret Service defectors. And while we have often seen Bond tussling with babes in boudoirs, here we see him in combat with a woman in a Venetian hotel room. Bond may have a taste for women in spiked heels, but he is not so enamoured of the spike-toed variety, here in the guise of the deadly Rosa Klebb (Lotte Lenya).

Moonraker (1979), in which Venice plays a more visible role, is a complete rewrite of the Fleming novel, and this is probably its downfall. Visual gags such as gondolas being sliced in two, leaving hapless honeymooners sinking, or pigeons doing double takes, is hardly sophisticated film-making. To cite Bond's megalomaniac opponent, Hugo Drax: 'You must excuse me, gentlemen … I sometimes find your sense of humour rather difficult to follow.' Watching *Moonraker* – which stars the roguish Roger Moore – you may want to fraternise with the enemy.

The film is full of the excesses that we have come to associate with the 007 franchise: we see Bond enjoying a gondola ride when a speedboat appears full of men with machine guns, at which our hero simply flips a switch and puts the gondola into speedboat mode, allowing him to maintain a safe distance from his pursuers. When approaching St Mark's Square, Bond engages the hovercraft, a skirt inflates and the craft goes up a flight of steps and straight through the middle of the piazza. A fight sequence slightly more worthy of a macho Bond occurs when, neither shaken nor stirred, he takes on the bamboo-wielding martial arts killer Chang at the Venini glass factory (*see p147*).

After the mediocre *Moonraker*, Venice was not to be seen again until *Casino Royale* (2006), with Daniel Craig debuting as the first blond Bond. This movie is grittier than many of its predecessors, though excess is still the name of the game, with a Venetian palace disintegrating into the Grand Canal, causing the water to boil. St Mark's Square pops up again, this time acting as the backdrop to a bank heist and chase sequence. Less disturbing than the figure in red glimpsed in Nicolas Roeg's *Don't Look Now* (1973), the ubiquitous Bond girl – here played by Eva Green – also dons red as she lugs a silver briefcase through various parts of the city.

With the passion for celluloid Bond still seemingly unabated, it's possible that 007 and Venice may appear again together on screen in the future. As the villainous Drax wryly comments: 'You appear with the tedious inevitability of an unloved season.'

Videotheques

Videoteca Pasinetti
Palazzo Mocenigo, Santa Croce 1991, salizada San Stae (041 524 1320). Vaporetto San Stae. **Open** *Video archive* 8.30am-1.30pm Mon-Fri. *Video-projected cinema classics* 6pm, 9pm Tue, Fri. **Admission** by membership card (€25), valid for 9mths (Jan-Sept). **No credit cards. Map** p321 F4. This video archive, run the by city council, was founded in 1991 and given the task of collecting and conserving an incredible volume of audiovisual material concerning Venice, in all formats: feature film, TV documentary, newsreel, amateur video. More than 3,000 videos are kept here, with a screening room where brief film seasons are held. Members can make reservations for individual consultations.

Festivals

Asolo Art Film Festival
Information: Foresto Vecchio 8, Asolo (0423 199 5235/www.asolofilmfestival.it). **Dates** first wk Oct. **No credit cards.**
As well as being a leading protagonist in Liliana Cavani's *Ripley's Game*, Asolo also holds its own film festival, focusing on art and artists. Films are screened at the Teatro Duse (in piazzetta Eleonora Duse), and other sites around the town host events. Previous years have seen films on Venetian architect Carlo Scarpa and Caravaggio. The festival closed down during the '90s, but restarted in 2001. For information on accreditation and prices, contact the above number or email info@asolofilmfestival.it.

Circuito off – Venice International Short Film Festival

Information: Incubatore CNOMV, Giudecca 212, fondamenta delle Zitelle (041 244 6979/fax 041 244 6925/www.circuitooff.com). Vaporetto Redentore. **Dates** 1st wk Sep. **Admission** non-professional accreditation €10. **Map** p326 B4.

This short film festival, run by the Associazione Artecolica, includes competitions, retrospectives and videos. In 2006 it was held on the island of San Servolo. For information about submitting a film, see the website or email concorso@circuitooff.com

Le Giornate del Cinema Muto

Information: Cineteca del Friuli, Palazzo Gurisatti, via Bini 50, Gemona (0432 980 458/www. cinetecadelfriuli.org/gcm). **Dates** 2nd wk Oct. **No credit cards**.

Europe's most prestigious silent movie festival is being held at the Teatro Zancanaro (via P Zancanaro 26) in Sacile, while its traditional venue in nearby Pordenone is *in restauro*. Under director David Robinson, events include an international forum of musicians for silent movies, retrospectives and films such as the British documentary *The Battle of the Somme* (1916). Accreditation costs €30 and allows unlimited viewings except on the opening and closing nights when a silent movie with musical accompaniment costs €13. Non-accredited viewers pay €5 per screening. The website is in English too.

Mostra Internazionale d'Arte Cinematografica (Venice Film Festival)

Palazzo del Cinema, lungomare Marconi 90, Lido (041 521 8711/www.labiennale.org). Vaporetto Lido. **Date** 11 days from late Aug. **Tickets** *Season tickets for Sala Grande or Palabiennale* €130-€1100; *individual screenings* €10-€38. **Credit** AmEx, DC, MC, V. **Map** p317 B4.

The 11-day Venice Film Festival takes place along the main, sea-facing Lido esplanade, between the Hotel des Bains and the Excelsior (for both, *see p64*). Between these two grand hotels is the marble-and-glass Palazzo del Cinema, where official competition screenings take place in the Sala Grande; other festival screens can be found in the gargantuan PalaGalileo, inside the Casinò and at the Palabiennale marquee. 2006 saw big names such as Stephen Frears with *The Queen* and Brian De Palma's *The Black Dahlia* contending for the top Golden Lion award.

Press accreditation guarantees virtually unlimited access; the press pass costs €50 and permits priority entry to a number of special screenings, mostly in the morning and early evening. Arrange this at least two months in advance by contacting the Biennale press office (041 521 8857/fax 041 520 0569/ www.labiennale.org).

'Cultural' accreditation is another option; it allows access to a more restricted range of screenings. This should be arranged before the end of June. A special deal for people under 26/over 60 offers a six-day €100/11-day €130 festival pass. Film-makers wanting to submit a film for competition should contact cinema@labiennale.org.

Individual tickets are available on the day previous to screenings from the ticket office at piazzale Casinò (lungomare Marconi, Lido, open 8am-midnight daily); Palabiennale (via Sandro Gallo, open 8am-midnight); and at the offices of La Biennale (Palazzo Querini Dubois, San Polo 2004, campo San Polo, open 8am-1.30pm, 3.30-6pm). Same-day tickets are occasionally available. For further information, contact 041 272 8377/biglietteria.cinema@ labiennale.org. For season ticket requests send a fax to 041 272 6623. Note that these are 2006 prices; no information on possible increases was available as this guide went to press.

Galleries

Excellent exhibitions and the brilliant Biennale make for a pretty picture.

Museo Querini Stampalia: bequeathed by a 19th-century scientist-silkmaker. *See p93.*

On many fronts, 2006 was a key year for modern and contemporary art in Venice.

First and foremost, it saw the reopening of **Palazzo Grassi** (*see p90*), Venice's exhibition space *per eccellenza*. Managed in the 1960s by art patron Paolo Marinotti, and then from the mid-1980s by the Fiat car maker, the 18th-century palazzo on the Canal Grande in 2005 found a new owner and art patron in the French industrialist François Pinault. Although the first and – as this guide went to press – only exhibition can't be taken as a crystal ball, it looks likely that Monsieur Pinault will be concentrating more on exhibiting his own extensive private collection than in developing a community outreach programme.

In same year a pronouncement on the future of the bonded warehouses on the Punta della Dogana was expected (*see p131* **Pinault at the Punta?**). The majestic pile by the Salute church has been sitting empty for the most part, and in dire structural conditions, for over a decade, since it fell into the hands of the city on a century-long lease from the Italian state. Unexpectedly, the city put forward a call

for proposals and the chosen party – which will eventually manage the space following major restoration of the building – was expected to be announced before the end of the year. The two main bidders are Pinault and the Guggenheim Foundation (*see p133*), which has has the backing of the Veneto region. Whoever wins the commission, it will take a good six to eight years before the Dogana opens as an exhibition venue.

2006 was also the year that the massive Biennale exhibition (*see p215* **La Biennale**) reached long-term agreements for the use of its historical venue, the Giardini di Castello, and the more recently acquired venues inside the Arsenale for non-Biennale events. While everyone waits with bated breath for the Arsenale theatres to run year-round seasons or the Padiglione Italia (Italian pavilion) to function as a proper exhibition hall, the Biennale has announced the possibility of returning the ASAC (Archivio Storico delle Arti Contemporanee, *see p295*) to Venice from its new – but sadly dysfunctional – location in industrial Marghera.

Arts activity on the mainland continues to languish, though the Centro Culturale Candiani (*see p227*) is slowly learning how to create decent programming – an indication that Venice has not only kept afloat but is learning how to swim in the ever changing world of contemporary artistic practices.

Despite the Biennale's chronic lack of interaction with the city, plenty is being done to keep Venice on the international arts map by the arts and design department of the IUAV (*see p300*), which holds workshops run by internationally renowned artists, and the ever-green Bevilacqua La Masa with its restructured artists in residence.

These initiatives have also begun to revive 'local' artistic production at last. To make up for a slump in the Querini Stampalia foundation's (*see p93*) activities, and the Academy of Fine Arts' apparent inability to take advantage of its new headquarters in the former Ospedale degli Incurabili in Dorsoduro, a few interesting new galleries have opened recently.

San Marco

A+A
San Marco 3073, calle Malipiero (041 277 0466/www.aplusa.it). Vaporetto San Samuele. **Open** 11am-1pm, 2-6pm Tue-Sat. **No credit cards.** **Map** p325 F1.
A lively, and at times experimental, non-profit exhibition space sponsored by the Slovenian ministry of culture. It hosts numerous shows, events, conferences, and curatorial classes too, organized in collaboration with Slovenian-related or local institutions. It is home to the Slovenian Pavilion at the Biennale of Visual arts and/or architecture.

Bugno Art Gallery
San Marco 1996D, campo San Fantin (041 523 1305/www.bugnoartgallery.it). Vaporetto Vallaresso. **Open** 4-7.30pm Mon, Sun; 10.30am-12.30pm, 4-7.30pm Tue-Sat. **Credit** AmEx, DC, MC, V. **Map** p326 A1.
Large windows overlooking the Fenice opera house reveal a large space devoted to artists working in all medias. Well-known local artists are also included in the gallery's collection. So packed is the exhibition calendar that shows often spill over into a smaller exhibition space nearby.

Il Capricorno
San Marco 1994, calle dietro la Chiesa (041 520 6920). Vaporetto Vallaresso or Giglio. **Open** 11am-1pm, 5-8pm Mon-Sat. **No credit cards.** **Map** p326 A2.
Many artists who are now basking in the national or international limelight showed in this small, low profile gallery in the early stages of their careers. Various shows each year are dedicated to younger international artists.

Caterina Tognon Arte Contemporanea
San Marco 2671, campo San Maurizio (041 520 7859/www.caterinatognon.com). Vaporetto Giglio. **Open** 10am-1pm, 3-7pm Tue-Sat. **Credit** AmEx, MC, V. **Map** p326 A2.
Following the success of her first gallery in Bergamo, renowned curator Caterina Tognon opened this showcase for contemporary art in glass in 1998, and in 2004 expanded to the first floor of a nearby palazzo. Various shows take place each year by emerging and renowned artists.
Other locations: Caterina Tognon, San Marco 2746, calle del Dose da Ponte (041 522 3285).

Contini Galleria d'Arte
San Marco 2765, calle dello Spezier (041 520 4942/www.continiarte.com). Vaporetto Giglio or Accademia. **Open** 10am-1pm, 2.30-7pm daily. **Credit** AmEx, MC, V. **Map** p326 A2.
A very large space (certainly by Venetian standards) stretching along both sides of the street, the Contini is home to a large selection of 20th-century art. International masters are exhibited next to internationally renowned Italian artists. The Tuscan-born Continis have run sister galleries in Mestre and Cortina d'Ampezzo for years.
Other locations: via Ferro 11, Mestre (041 981 611).

Flora Bigai Arte Moderna e Contemporanea
San Marco 1652, piscina di Frezzeria (041 521 2208/041 241 3799/www.florabigai.com). Vaporetto Vallaresso. **Open** 3.30-7.30pm Mon; 10am-1pm, 3.30-7.30pm Tue-Sat. **Credit** AmEx, DC, MC, V. **Map** p326 B1.
Less active than its sister gallery in Tuscany, this large space presents a couple of exhibitions a year though with a rather irregular calendar. It tends to focus on international artists, and representatives of Pop Art in particular.

Fondazione Bevilacqua la Masa
Exhibition space *San Marco 71C, piazza San Marco (041 523 7819/www.bevilacqualamasa.it). Vaporetto Vallaresso.* **Open** during exhibitions only noon-6pm Mon, Wed-Sun. **Map** p326 B1.
Offices & exhibition space *Dorsoduro 2826, fondamenta Gerardini (041 520 7797). Vaporetto Ca' Rezzonico.* **Open** *Office* 9am-1pm Tue, Thur, Fri; 9am-1pm, 2-5pm Tue, Wed. *Exhibition space* varies. **Map** p325 E2.
The Fondazione Bevilacqua la Masa was founded more than a century ago by Duchess Felicita Bevilacqua La Masa, who left her palace of Ca' Pesaro (*see p118*) to the city in order to give local artists a space in which to explore new trends. This institution – now in separate headquarters – is very active in organizing exhibitions, collaborating with the Arts and Design departments of the IUAV (Architecture University), and with other organizations working to foster new art in Italy. There are talks, performances, an archive, an artist-in-residence programme on the Giudecca (041 520 7797,

Fondazione Bevilacqua la Masa – an artistic trendsetter. *See p213.*

open by appointment only). The annual *esposizione collettiva* is dedicated to artists based in the Veneto area under the age of 30.

Galerie Bordas
San Marco 1994B, calle dietro la Chiesa (041 522 4812/www.galeriebordas.com). Vaporetto Vallaresso. **Open** 11am-1pm, 4.30-7.30pm Mon-Sat. **Credit** AmEx, MC, V. **Map** p326 A2.
The only gallery dealing in serious graphics by internationally renowned masters such as Asger Jorn. The space is small but the collection of artists' books held here is huge.

Galleria Marina Barovier
San Marco 3216, salizada San Samuele (041 523 6748/www.barovier.it) Vaporetto San Samuele. **Open** 10am-12.30pm, 3.30-7.30pm Mon-Sat. **No credit cards**. **Map** p325 F1.
Marina Barovier hosts a collection of classic masterpieces of Venetian 20th-century works in glass and represents numerous renowned, local and international, artists working in glass. It stages a few shows a year.

Galleria Traghetto
San Marco 2543, campo Santa Maria del Giglio (041 522 1188/www.galleriatraghetto.it). Vaporetto Giglio. **Open** 3-7pm Mon-Sat. **Credit** AmEx, DC, MC, V. **Map** p326 A2.
This gallery with a 30-year history of dealing with Venetian 20th-century abstracts is a point of reference for established artists and for contemporary emerging artists working in all media. It has just opened a branch in Rome.

La Galleria
San Marco 2566, ramo Calegheri (041 520 7415/ www.galerie.vanderkoelen.de). Vaporetto Giglio. **Open** 10am-12.30pm, 3.30-7.30pm Mon-Sat. **Credit** AmEx, DC, MC, V. **Map** p326 A2.
A long standing reputation – owing partly to its German owner's scholarly publications and the sister gallery in Mainz which was founded almost 30 years ago – make this intimate space a must for viewing artworks and artists' books by well established artists.

Galleria Venice Design
San Marco 3146, salizada San Samuele (041 520 7915/www.venicedesignartgallery.com). Vaporetto San Samuele. **Open** 10am-1pm, 3-7pm daily. **Credit** AmEx, DC, MC, V. **Map** p325 F1.
As one of the historical landmarks of contemporary art in Venice, this gallery deals especially in sculpture by established artists both Italian and international. It also focuses on artists' jewels and interior design. This gallery's branch (*see below*) is open 10am-7.30pm Sat and Sun.
Other locations: San Marco 1310, calle Vallaresso (041 523 9082).

Jarach Gallery
San Marco 1997, campo San Fantin (041 522 1938/www.jarachgallery.com). Vaporetto Giglio. **Open** 2-8pm Tue-Sun; mornings by appointment only. **Credit** AmEx, DC, MC, V. **Map** p326 A1.
This large space tucked into a courtyard opposite the Fenice opera house is the latest addition to the Venetian gallery scene. It mainly deals with photography, but also hosts literary presentations.

Tornabuoni Arte
San Marco 2663, campo San Maurizio (041 523 1201/www.tornabuoniarte.it). Vaporetto Giglio. **Open** 10.30am-1pm, 2.30-7.30pm Tue-Sun. **No credit cards. Map** p326 A2.
The first Tornabuoni gallery opened a quarter of a century ago in chic via Tornabuoni in Florence. This is the latest, and a newcomer on the Venetian gallery scene. It organizes various shown dedicated to masters of Italian and international post-war art.

Castello

Galleria Michela Rizzo
Castello 4254, calle degli Albanesi (041 522 3186/ www.galleriamichelarizzo.net). Vaporetto San Zaccaria. **Open** 4am-12.30pm, 4.30-7.30pm Tue; 4.30-7.30pm Wed-Sat. **No credit cards. Map** p326 C1.
A recent addition and certainly a rising star on the Venetian scene, focusing on conceptual and more cutting-edge artists and performers. A packed though irregular exhibition programme which usually spills out of the small confines of this tiny space into the owner's apartment nearby.

Spiazzi
Castello 3865, campo San Martino (041 523 9711/ www.spiazzi.info). Vaporetto Arsenale. **Open** 2-6pm Mon-Fri. **No credit cards. Map** p327 E1.
This former carpenter's workshop has been transformed into a non-profit space organising exhibitions of very young, mainly local, artists. It offers a

dark-room facility and organises various craft workshops, and hosts sometimes hosts overspill from both the Art and Architecture Biennale.

Dorsoduro

See also p213 **Fondazione Bevilacqua la Masa**.

Galleria d'Arte l'Occhio
Dorsoduro 181, calle San Gregorio (041 522 6550/ www.gallerialocchio.net). Vaporetto Salute. **Open** 10am-6pm Mon, Wed-Sat. **Credit** AmEx, MC, V. **Map** p326 A3.
This intimate, friendly gallery has been around for 15 years but recently expanded its premises and can now stage 'true' exhibitions. It focuses on established younger artists, many of them local.

Giudecca

Nuova Icona
Giudecca 454, calle dell'Olio (041 521 0101/www. nuovaicona.org). Vaporetto Palanca. **Open** 4-8pm Thu-Sun during exhibitions; by appointment at other times. **No credit cards. Map** p325 E4.
Nuova Icona organises a packed calendar of shows, performances and other artistic events, often collaborating with national exhibits at the Art Biennale. It holds some events in the Oratorio San Ludovico near San Sebastiano (Dorsoduro 2552, corte dei Vecchi, contact gallery for opening times).

La Biennale

Officially known as the l'Esposizione Internazionale d'Arte della Biennale di Venezia, the Biennale was responsible for putting Venice on the map of international modern and contemporary art back in 1895. Since then this massive exhibition has been 'invading' Venice every odd year (the Architecture Biennale, on the other hand, is staged in even years and in 2006 celebrated its tenth birthday). It was the first (Sao Paolo didn't start until 1951) and remains one of the very few to include national exhibits as part of a wider-ranging collective event.

Artists are appointed to represent their countries, and it is one of the highest honours to be selected: Gilbert and George exhibited in 2005; Tracey Emin was Britain's choice for 2007 – only the second female solo artist to be selected. Another Brit, Rachel Whiteread was the other, in 1997.

The Biennale sprawls over the Giardini di Castello park, where the central Italian pavilion and 30 smaller national pavilions

are located. In recent years it has spilled over into the nearby Arsenale, with its immense, spectacular spaces once used for ship-building: the Corderie (rope factory), the Artiglierie (gun foundry), the Gaggiandre (dry docks), etc. The growing importance of being present at the Venice event has forced 'have-not' countries to rent exhibition spaces elsewhere in the city, prompting a welcome influx of funds and attention.

La Biennale di Venezia
Palazzo Giustinian Lolin, San Marco 2893, calle Giustinian (041 521 8711/ www.labiennale.org). Vaporetto Accademia. **Open** office 9am-6pm Mon-Fri. **Map** p325 F2. *Venues* Giardini di Castello, vaporetto Giardini (map p328 A4); Arsenale, vaporetto Arsenale (map p327 E1/2). **Open** 10am-6pm Tue-Sun. **Dates** mid June-early Nov in alternate years (odd for art; even for architecture). **Admission** (allowing access to all official shows) €13; €10 concessions. **No credit cards.**

Gay & Lesbian

A quiet, romantic break or canalside cruising – the choice is yours.

Venice would seem to provide the perfect backdrop for most gay fantasies – from the blissfully romantic to one-night stands. But, despite a massive population during spring and summer, the city offers little for gays and lesbians used to more fast-paced scenes.

To a certain extent this has led to two diametrically opposed realities. So we have the old city centre, with its laid-back, quiet gay scene tucked away in the private sphere, where dinner parties or quiet drinks at the local *bacaro* define the way the city's gay community go about their business. On the other hand, there is a much more keenly felt urban restlessness to Mestre and Marghera, the mainland part of Venice, where newer, flashier clubs and bars pull in the younger crowd from the province.

This neat division seems to define what's on offer. The old city centre and the islands in the lagoon tend to cater to those who are looking for a more peaceful, culture-laden break, with gay-friendly B&Bs seductively hidden away on islands such as Sant'Erasmo (*see below* **Il Lato Azzurro**) and Torcello (*see below* **Casa d'Artista Lucio Andrich Bed & Breakfast**), or in the city centre itself, just off the main tourist strip (such as Il Lato Azzurro's new B&B offerings near campo Santa Maria Nova). Formerly maligned Mestre, Marghera and, slightly further afield, Padua, however, are now offering what Venice has relinquished over the decades – *real* nightlife.

The twain meet over the summer in large numbers on the rather secluded **Alberoni Beach** (*see below*) and surrounding dunes, which indulge nude sunbathing and cruising. **Il Muro** (*see below*), one of the city's oldest cruising institutions, is no longer as popular as it once was, but still attracts a discrete number of post-midnight visitors.

The national gay rights group **ArciGay** sponsors activities, festivals, counselling and AIDS awareness. ArciGay membership is needed to enter several venues listed below: a one-month *tessera* (membership card) for non-Italian nationals costs €7 (annual membership is €14, and if you plan to be in Italy for more than a month it's worth it) and can be bought at the door of venues requiring it, or at the nearest ArciGay chapter, Tralaltro (corso Garibaldi 41, Padua, 049 876 2458, open 9-11.30pm Tue, 6-8pm Wed, 6.30-8pm Thur).

Venice

Open-air

Il Muro (The Wall)
Map p326 B2.
Behind the Procuratie Nuove, by the Giardinetti Reali (at the lagoon end of the piazzetta di San Marco, turn right and keep on walking), Il Muro has seen better days as the city's after-dark cruising area. Now rarely frequented from October to May, it can still pull a crowd during summer. But even with no one about the place has a romantic charm all its own, and is worth a visit just for the view it affords of San Giorgio Maggiore across the canal.

Alberoni Beach, Lido
Map off p317 B2.
Now an almost exclusively gay beach, Alberoni is *the* place to cruise in summer. The dunes and pine forest are where the action is. If the weather's good, cruising starts as early as April, but if you enjoy being spoilt for choice go for Saturdays and Sundays in July and August. Take Bus B/(Alberoni Spiaggia) from Santa Maria Elisabetta to the last stop, then turn right and walk about ten minutes.

Accommodation

Il Lato Azzurro
Via Forti 13, Sant'Erasmo (041 523 0642/ www.lato azzurro.it). Vaporetto 13 to Sant'Erasmo-Capannone. **Rates** €52 single; €78 double; €100 triple; €112 quadruple; €20 for each additional bed (dinner €20). **Credit** AmEx, MC, DC, V.
This gay-owned and operated guest house on the vegetable-garden island of Sant'Erasmo (*see p149*) is the ideal place to stay if you want a really quiet retreat. If you prefer something more urban, Il Lato Azzurro now has new B&B rooms in Venice itself (Cannaregio 6057, calle Widman, €65 for a single, €90 for a double and €110 for a triple) and two apartments (€750 a week each) at Santa Maria Nova (**map** p322 C4). All prices are high season maximums, and are slightly lower off season (from autumn to early spring, Christmas and Carnevale excluded).

Casa d'Artista Lucio Andrich Bed & Breakfast
Via Borgognoni 4L, Torcello (041 735 292/www. lucioandrich.com). Vaporetto LN to Burano, LT to Torcello. **Rates** €60 single (Stanza del Sottotetto, in main house); €80 double (Stanza Carciofi, in converted fisherman's cottage); €120 double (Stanza

Il Muro (see p216).

del Maestro, in main house); €160 quadruple (Stanza Palude della Rosa, in converted fisherman's cottage). **No credit cards**.

This bed and breakfast on Torcello caters to an exclusive clientele, and is just the thing if you need to get away from it all. The guest rooms, located in the main house and in the *cason* (fisherman's cottage), afford incredible views. The owner, Paolo, also rents boats (€50 for a three-hour tour with Paolo at the helm) if you're interested in exploring the lagoon.

Eating & drinking

Over the past few years, the entire campo Santa Margherita (**map p325 E1**) has become the focal point for the trendier young Venetian. Its bars and pizzerie are all extremely busy during summer. Not the cruisiest of places, but you never know. *See also p162* **Alla Zucca**, one of Venice's most gay-friendly restaurants.

PDM Bar Porto de Mar
Via delle Macchine 41-3, Marghera (041 921 247/ www.portodemar.com). Bus 2 or 7 from piazzale Roma/train to Mestre station, then a 10min walk. **Open** 10pm-2am Wed, Thur, Sun; 10pm-4am Sat. **Admission** with ArciGay membership (*see p216*) €5; €10 for special events. **Credit** MC, V.
The Venetian expression *porto de mar* loosely translates as hubbub, but literally means sea port. This new venue, with darkroom, bar and outside area used for cruising in summer, is worth the trip just for a glimpse of the old port before it is fully regenerated. The bar's popular with a younger crowd, but is very welcoming if you're the wrong side of 40.

Sauna

Metrò Venezia Club
Via Cappuccina 82B, Mestre (041 538 4299/ www. metroclub.it). Bus 2 or 7 from piazzale Roma/train to Mestre, then a 5min walk. **Open** 2pm-2am daily. **Admission** €15 (€12 after 8pm) with ArciGay membership (*see p216*); €12 under-26s. **Credit** MC, V.
The first gay venue to open in the Venice area, Metro has a bar, a dry sauna, steam sauna, private rooms, darkroom and solarium. Massage and hydro-massage are also available. Trade here is very brisk.

Tours

Venice à la Carte
041 277 0564/www.tourvenice.org. **Rates** vary according to tour. **Credit** AmEx, MC, V.
Tailor-made tours of Venice and the Veneto villas, catering for a wide variety of cultural interests and credit limits, organised by Alvise Zanchi, a native Venetian and expert tour guide. Member of IGLTA.

Padua

The following list contains only those gay places that are most easily accessible by public transport or taxi from Venice or Mestre (*see chapters* **Directory**: **Getting Around** and **The Veneto: Padua**). Cruising continues to be very risky, especially around Padua station, and should be avoided, even during the day.

Bars & entertainment

Flexo Club
Via Turazza 19, int. 3 (049 807 4707/www.flexo club.it). **Open** 9pm-2am Wed-Sun. **Admission** with ArciGay membership (*see p216*) €10; €13 Fri & Sat; 1 drink incl. **Credit** MC, V.
Flexo has just moved to larger premises and now offers a cocktail bar, disco, solarium, cruising area, darkrooms, gym, beauty centre, hydro-massage and a large cruising garden. It has also softened its no-women policy, though Saturdays are men-only. The first Saturday of every month is bears night, and Thursdays have been set aside for naked parties in a cordoned-off section of the club.

Sauna

Metrò Sauna
Via Turazza 19, int. 1 (049 807 5828/www.metro club.it). **Open** 2pm-2am daily. **Admission** with ArciGay membership (*see p216*) €15 before 8pm; €12 after 8pm; €12 Mon-Sat for under-26s. **Credit** MC, V.
Large, modern and well equipped, this place has a proper work-those-pores Finnish sauna. It also has well-earned rest and private massage facilities.

Music & Nightlife

Start with a *spritz*, then dance till dawn (on the mainland).

Glowing **Aurora**. *See p219.*

Venice – Byron's 'revel of the Earth' – was once notorious for its nightlife. Nowadays, with its ageing and shrinking population, it's notorious for the lack of it. Yet while the city can certainly not boast the status of Europe's party capital any longer, there's still a surprising amount of life after dark. A typical Venetian night out starts with a post-work and pre-prandial *spritz* in one of the bars around the Rialto market area, which might develop into a *giro de ombre*, a bar-crawl Venetian style. And for those still standing when the traditional *bacari* close, there's a network of late-opening bars hidden away all over town. Native night owls return to Rialto, make for northern Cannaregio's 'party' fondamenta della Misericordia or cluster around Venice's 'alternative' drawing room of campo Santa Margherita, in the heart of the city's southern Dorsoduro district.

MUSIC

Unfortunately, stringent noise pollution regulations and lack of adequate venues have effectively pulled the plug on large music events, **Carnevale**, **Venezia Suona** (for both,

see *pp202-203*) and the summer events (*see p202* **Summer Festivals**) being the exceptions. Rock 'n' roll royals who do dates in Venice are usually confined to the extremely formal setting of one of the local theatres. There's better news for serious jazz heads as regular series of high-quality jazz and experimental music are organised by local cultural organisations like Caligola (www. caligola.it) or Vortice (www.provincia.venezia. it/vortice), which has managed to pull such avant-jazzers as Larry Ochs, Dave Douglas and Elliot Sharp. Performances usually take place in the more intimate **Teatro Fondamenta Nuove**. And you can go crazy on the island of **San Servolo** (www.sanservolo.provincia. venezia.it) – former site of the insane asylum – which hosts an annual jazz meet in November.

Thanks to the tenacity of the few bar owners still willing to wrestle with red tape and persist in the face of party-pooper petitioning neighbours, it's still possible to play and hear live music in various *locali* around town. Venetian vibes tend to be laid-back and these small, free gigs are almost always reggae, jazz or blues with the occasional rock, Latino or world session. Clubs and venues on the nearby mainland draw bigger acts.

CLUBS

For serious club culture, make for the mainland. In the winter a short bus or train ride to Mestre or Marghera (just across the bridge and well served by night buses) is all it takes to dance until dawn. In the summer most of the dance action moves out to the seaside resort of **Lido di Jesolo** (*see p222*), the place to be for house and techno, with a smattering of Latino to swing your suntan to.

INFORMATION AND TICKETS

Day-to-day listings are carried by the two local papers, *Il Gazzettino* and *La Nuova Venezia*. For a more complete overview of concerts and festivals, with English translations, the monthly listings magazine *Venezia News* is indispensable. Also keep your eyes peeled around town for posters advertising upcoming gigs and events. Tickets are usually available at the venue but in some cases they can be bought in advance at the CD shop **Parole e Musica**, Castello 5673, salizada San Lio (041 521 2215) or via the national ticket agency www.boxoffice.it.

Unless specified, the bars listed below have no extra charge for music. Note that smoking is strictly forbidden in all indoor spaces – including clubs and bars – open to the public except in designated rooms with efficient extraction systems.

San Marco

Late bars & bars with music

Aurora
San Marco 49, piazza San Marco (041 528 6405/ info@aurora.st). Vaporetto Vallaresso. **Open** 7pm-2am Wed. **Credit** AmEx, DC, MC, V. **Map** p326 C1.
The evening management of this classic café right by the *campanile* in St Mark's square is trying to bring Venetians of all ages back to their *piazza* by organising 'Queer Wednesdays', art exhibitions, video projections and DJ sets to go with affordable cocktails and that favourite of Venetian tipples, *spritz* (€4 inside, €6 at a table in the square).

Bacaro Jazz
San Marco 5546, salizada del Fontego dei Tedeschi (041 528 5249/www.bacarojazz.com). Vaporetto Rialto. **Open** 4pm-3am daily. **Credit** AmEx, DC, MC, V. **Map** p322 B5.
Venice's most central late-night watering hole, Bacaro Jazz is a place to mingle with fellow tourists or foreign students rather than meet the locals. It hots up during happy hour (4-7pm) and the background jazz and wide range of killer cocktails keep the party going into the early hours.

Centrale Restaurant Lounge
San Marco 1659B, piscina Frezzeria (041 296 0664/ www.centrale-lounge.com). Vaporetto Vallaresso. **Open** 7pm-2am daily. **Credit** AmEx, DC, MC, V. **Map** p326 B1.
Only the exposed bricks of the original 16th-century palazzo's walls will remind you you're in Venice: this cool, contemporary restaurant and lounge bar is more New York or London. Owners Franco and Alfredo lay on events like live drum 'n' bass and jazz or a regular international gay night and serve a full, fresh à la carte menu until closing time. Thursday nights draw crowds of Venetian 30-somethings for the bounteous buffet served up free when you buy a glass of wine. Alternatively, go after dinner to sink into one of the designer armchairs, explore the cocktail menu and chill out to lounge and house sounds.

Torino@Notte
San Marco 4591, campo San Luca (041 522 3914). Vaporetto Rialto. **Open** 8pm-1am Tue-Sat. **No credit cards**. **Map** p326 B1.
This dreary daytime snack bar switches management after dark and transforms into a happening hotspot. DJ sets and live music on Wednesdays keep the mix of students and older mods grooving to acid jazz, fusion and funky tunes while Carnevale brings a week of live gigs in the campo outside.

Vitae
San Marco 4118, calle Sant'Antonio (041 520 5205). Vaporetto Rialto. **Open** 8pm-midnight Mon-Fri; 5pm-2am Sat. **No credit cards**. **Map** p326 B1.
Known as 'Il Muro' (the wall), this tiny bar behind campo San Luca is busy long into the night with a more mature, yuppie set who come for Mojitos, mouth-watering snacks and the background sounds of smooth soul and acid jazz.

Castello

Late bars & bars with music

Inishark
Castello 5787, calle del Mondo Novo (041 523 5300). Vaporetto Rialto. **Open** 6pm-1.30am Tue-Sun. **No credit cards**. **Map** p322 C5.
Tucked away in a small calle near Santa Maria Formosa, this Irish-style pub has the best Guinness on tap in town and great snacky food to soak up the black stuff – we recommend the roast suckling pig and mustard sandwiches. Satellite TV packs in the fans for Champions League football.

La Mascareta
Castello 5183, calle lunga Santa Maria Formosa (041 523 0744). **Open** 7pm-2am Mon, Tue, Fri-Sun. **Credit** DC, MC, V. **Map** p322 C5.
Genial, bow-tied Mauro Lorenzon keeps hundreds of wines – including some rare vintages – in his cellars, serving them up by the bottle or glass along with plates of cheeses, seafood, cold meats or crostini. There are also more filling options – hearty soups, for example – every evening.

Cannaregio

Late bars & bars with music

Do Fradei
Cannaregio 1974A, rio terà San Leonardo (338 944 6218). Vaporetto San Marcuola. **Open** 8am-2am Tues-Sun. **No credit cards**. **Map** p321 F3.
This tiny bar gets lively between April and November when it spills out into the square outside opposite Teatro Italia. A great place to stop off for salads and snacks during the day, in the evening it's busy till late with a mix of young Venetians and tourists – both groups come for the live music on Wednesdays and Fridays.

Fiddler's Elbow Irish Pub
Cannaregio 3847, corte dei Pali già Testori (041 523 9930). Vaporetto Ca' d'Oro. **Open** 5pm-1am daily. **Credit** AmEx, MC, V. **Map** p322 A4.
Expats, locals and tourists of all ages prop up the bar in Venice's oldest Irish pub. Party-pooping neighbours have put a stop to regular live music nights, but local bands still play on special occasions such as Hallowe'en and St Patrick's Day. Big sports events are screened in the campo outside.

Arts & Entertainment

Summer festivals

As winter loosens its grip, stages are set up in squares, parks and villas to host concerts in Venice, on the islands and in the surrounding mainland area. There is a wealth of other festivals in the region – look out for the posters around town. *See also chapter* **Festivals and Events**.

Festa di Liberazione
San Polo, campo dell'Erberia (www.rifond azionecomunistaveneto.it). Vaporetto Rialto. **Dates** late Aug-early Sept. **Map** p322 B5. Rally meets rave at Rialto for the Rifondazione comunista party's festival. Serious debates and films are followed by nightly concerts with salsa, rock, blues, reggae and world music.

Marghera Village Estate
Via Orsato 9, Panorama car park, Marghera (333 786 5622/www.villagestate.it). Bus 6/ from piazzale Roma. **Dates** June-Aug 6pm-2am daily; concerts 9.45pm. **Admission** free. The Village's setting – on a scrap of grass amid hypermarkets – may not be awe-inspiring, but this is where Venetians and *mestrini* of all ages spend their summer nights. Free nightly live music is followed by dancing and DJ sets as well as a host of bars and food stalls to keep the party going.

Venice Airport Festival
Forte Bazzera, via Bazzera, Tessera (333 973 4330/www.jamclubvenice.com). Bus 5 from piazzale Roma to Tessera church stop. **Dates** one week late July/early August; 7pm-2am daily; concerts 9pm. **Admission** free; €5 for special events. **No credit cards.**

Strictly no cover bands: this festival hosts nightly gigs by top quality Italian and international indie rock bands, drawing fans from all over the region. Concerts are followed by DJ sets and off-beat film screenings.

Villa Pisani Strà Festival
Via Alvise Pisani 1, Strà (049 502 074/ www.zedlive.com). Bus for Padua from piazzale Roma. **Dates** June-Sept; concerts 9.30pm. **Admission** €25-€50. **Credit** MC, V. Held in the beautiful grounds of 18th-century Villa Pisani, this annual festival organises several dates over the summer by stars – Dido, Bob Dylan and BB King in recent years.

Veneto Jazz Festival
Via Aldo Moro 29, Cavasagra di Vedelago (0423 452 069/www.venetojazz.com). **Box office** at venues before performances or www.boxofficeitalia.com. **Dates** Feb-Apr, June-Aug. **Credit** MC, V for online bookings only. Jazz giants such as Herbie Hancock, Keith Jarrett and Chick Corea perform alongside lesser-known talents against the spectacular backdrop of Verona's Teatro Romano (*see p260*), a castle in Bassano or in cloisters, parks and squares all over the Veneto.

Venezia Suona
Cannaregio 3546, fondamenta dell'Abbazia (041 275 0049/www.veneziasuona.it). **Venues** around the city. **Dates** 3rd or 4th Sun in June or last weekend in July. 'Venice Plays' with anything from a cappella choirs and jazz quartets to punk or Zappa revival bands who jam in *campi* and by canals all over the city. Events are free.

Iguana
Cannaregio 2515, fondamenta della Misericordia (041 713 561). Vaporetto San Marcuola. **Open** 6pm-2am daily. **Credit** MC, V. **Map** p322 A2. With tacos, tequila and tecate in addition to mescal and Margaritas, the Misericordia's Mexican swings to salsa sounds till late. The music comes live between 7 and 9pm, usually on Tuesdays and/or Thursdays, while a daily *spritz* hour (€1 a *spritz* 6-8pm) packs in the students.

Paradiso Perduto
Cannaregio 2540, fondamenta della Misericordia (041 720 581). Vaporetto San Marcuola. **Open** 7pm-1am Tue-Thur; 11am-2am Fri-Sun. **Credit** DC, MC, V. **Map** p322 A2. Probably the most famous Venetian haunt after Harry's Bar (*see p171*), this 'Paradise Lost' is well

worth finding. Arty types of all ages take their places at the long *osteria* tables for the mix of seafood and succulent sounds (mainly jazz and salsa), which go live on Fridays and Sundays.

Santo Bevitore
Cannaregio 2393A, campo Santa Fosca (041 717 560/www.ilsantobevitorepub.com). Vaporetto Ca' d'Oro or San Marcuola. **Open** 7am-midnight Mon-Fri; 9.30am-1am Sat. **No credit cards.** **Map** p322 A3. This friendly pub-café on campo Santa Fosca, just off strada Nova, has consistently proved popular with both Venetian locals and visitors, who drop in to munch *cicheti* during the day or come to while away the evening over a beer or a glass of wine. The Santo Bevitore experience is enlivened by live jazz acts on Mondays.

San Polo & Santa Croce

See also p163 **Muro Vino e Cucina.**

Late bars & bars with music

Al Pesador
San Polo 125-6, campo San Giacomo di Rialto (041 523 9492). Vaporetto Rialto. **Open** 10pm-2am Tue-Sun. **No credit cards. Map** p322 B5.
This beautiful bacaro-style bar was once the place where fruit and veg were weighed for the local market. These days crowds of students cram inside or hang out at the back, overlooking the Grand Canal.

Ai Postali
Santa Croce 821, fondamenta Rio Marin (no phone). Vaporetto Riva di Biasio or San Tomà. **Open** 7.30pm-2am Mon-Sat. Closed Aug. **No credit cards. Map** p321 E4.
This long-established *osteria* is a firm Venetian favourite. Locals moor their boats beneath the outside terrace to drop in for a drink.

Bagolo
Santa Croce 1584, campo San Giacomo dell'Orio (041 717 584). Vaporetto San Stae. **Open** 7.30am-1am Mon-Fri; 8am-1am Sat; 9am-1am Sun. **No credit cards. Map** p321 F4.
Laid-back Bagolo attracts a mature crowd who sit up at the high stools inside or sink into an armchair outside and explore the excellent Friulian grappas.

Da Baffo
San Polo 2346, campiello Sant'Agostin (041 520 8862). Vaporetto San Stae or San Tomà. **Open** 7.30am-2am Mon-Sat. **No credit cards. Map** p321 F5.
Named after the 18th-century erotic poet whose saucy sonnets are on display inside, this is one of the hippest hangouts in Venice. Locals, students and their profs all come to sample the Italian wines, international beers and single malts. Literary evenings and gastronomic nights replace live music.

Dorsoduro

Late bars & bars with music

Café Blue
Dorsoduro 3778, calle de la Scuola (041 710 227). Vaporetto San Tomà. **Open** 8pm-2am daily. **Credit** DC, MC, V. **Map** p321 E5.
This pub-style boozer bulges with students and an older international set well into the small hours. Enjoy a wee dram in the Whiskeria while chilling out to the occasional DJ set.

Café Noir
Dorsoduro 3805, crosera San Pantalon (041 710 925/www.cafenoirvenezia.it). Vaporetto San Tomà. **Open** 8am-2am Mon-Sat; 7pm-2am Sun. **No credit cards. Map** p325 E1.

Warm and intimate Café Noir is a winter favourite among the university and 20-something crowd, who while away their days over *panini* and hot chocolate. As it livens up later, crowd inside and out for *spritz* and alcopops.

Il Caffè
Dorsoduro 2963, campo Santa Margherita (041 528 7998). Vaporetto Ca' Rezzonico. **Open** 7am-1am Mon-Sat. **No credit cards. Map** p325 E1.
Whether for its red exterior, or for the political leanings of its core clientele, the campo's oldest bar is universally known as 'Caffè Rosso'. Relaxed and bohemian, it attracts a mixed crowd of all ages who spill out from its single room to sip a *spritz* in the campo or to choose from the impressive wine list. Excellent live music, usually on Thursdays.

Impronta Café
Dorsoduro 3815, crosera San Pantalon (041 275 0386). Vaporetto San Tomà. **Open** 7am-2am Mon-Sat. **Closed** 3wks Aug. **Credit** AmEx, DC, MC, V. **Map** p325 E1.
Modern and minimalist, Impronta is packed until the small hours with students during the winter, and is busy throughout the year with anyone looking for an affordable bite to eat, cool cocktails or a night cap.

Orange
Dorsoduro 3054A, campo Santa Margherita (041 523 4740). Vaporetto Ca' Rezzonico. **Open** 7.30am-2am Mon-Sat; 5pm-2am Sun. **No credit cards. Map** p325 E1.
The newest and coolest kid on the campo whose sleek and stylish design, creative cocktails and friendly staff have made it a roaring success with a hip mixture of young locals and students. In winter smokers huddle around heaters in the internal garden, while in summer everyone grabs a table outside in the campo, to see and be seen.

Clubs

Piccolo Mondo
Dorsoduro 1056/1, calle Contarini-Corfù (041 520 0371). Vaporetto Accademia. **Open** 10.30pm-4am daily. **Admission** €10. **Credit** MC, V. **Map** p325 F2.
Called 'El Souk' in better days, this 'small world' remains one of the few places to dance in Venice proper. You may, therefore, find yourself on its dancefloor. If you do, you'll be mixing with ageing medallion men, lost tourists and foreign students so desperate to dance, they'll go anywhere!

Round Midnight
Dorsoduro 3102, fondamenta dei Pugni (041 523 2056). Vaporetto Ca' Rezzonico. **Open** midnight-4am Wed-Sat. Closed July-Sept. **Admission** free. **No credit cards. Map** p325 E1
This absolutely tiny DJ bar behind campo Santa Margherita has no charge on the door and disco sounds that keep its minuscule dancefloor busy with bouncing students all night long.

Arts & Entertainment

Giudecca

Centro Zitelle Culturale Multimedialei CZ95

Giudecca 95, sottoportego della Croce (041 528 9833/www.cz95.org). Vaporetto Zitelle. **Open** 5.30-11pm Mon-Sat. **Admission** free. **No credit cards.** **Map** p326 B4.

This cultural centre behind the youth hostel on the Giudecca has a media library and internet point. It also hosts exhibitions, film and video projections, regular live music and occasional parties.

Further afield

Mestre & Marghera

Area Club

Via Don Tosatto 9, Mestre (041 958 000/www. areaclub.it). Bus 3 from Mestre. **Open** 11.30pm-4am Fri-Sun. **Admission** €15-€30. **Credit** DC, MC, V.

The first venue in the region to specialise in hardcore techno; big-name DJs and well-heeled clubbers.

Blu Paradise at The Blv Rooms

Via delle Industrie 29, Marghera (041 531 7357). Bus 2, 4, 4/, 6 or 6/ from piazzale Roma. **Open** *Sept-Apr* 12.30am-4am Sat. **Admission** €15-€19 (incl drink). **Credit** AmEx, MC, V.

Just over the bridge from piazzale Roma, this is Venice's nearest mainland dance club. A young 'n' trendy set don their posh togs and come for hardcore house and a mix of commercial and revival. During the week it hosts tango nights.

Molo 5

Via dell'Elettricità 8, Marghera (041 538 4983/www. blunotte.it). Bus 2, 4, 4/, 6 or 6/ from piazzale Roma. **Open** *May-Sept* 8pm-4am Thurs-Sun. **Admission** €13-€16 (incl 1 drink) **Credit** AmEx, MC, V.

The summer version of the Blv Rooms (*see above*). Attracts reality TV stars who come to dine and strut their designer tans to the house, commercial and Latino sounds. The restaurant is open all year.

T.A.G. Club

Via Giustizia 19, Mestre (334 824 5710). Train to Mestre. **Open** 10pm-8am Wed, Fri, Sat. **Admission** €8 (incl 1 drink). **No credit cards.**

A small but lively club just behind the train station in Mestre that puts on an eclectic range of concerts and exhibitions and pop/rock nights. 'Afterhours' parties follow, starting after 3am and featuring house music mixed by well-known DJs – among them local boy Spiller.

Al Vapore

Via Fratelli Bandiera 8, Marghera (041 930 796/ www.alvapore.it). Train to Mestre, or bus 6 or 6/ from piazzale Roma. **Open** 7am-3pm, 6pm-2am Tue-Sat. **Admission** Tue-Fri free; Sat €10 (incl 1 drink). **No credit cards.**

This music bar has been putting on jazz, blues, soul and rock gigs for years and is very active on the local scene. Popular Jazz Buffet nights take place in the week with funky DJ sets and a free buffet; at weekends well-known Italian and international musicians perform on the tiny stage. There's no charge on Fridays, but drinks cost more. Over summer, Al Vapore moves to Marghera Village (*see above*).

On the mainland

New Age Club

Via Tintoretto 14, Roncade (Treviso) (0422 841 052/www.newageclub.it). Venice Trieste motorway, exit Quarto d'Altino; follow signs for Roncade. **Open** 9.30pm-5am Fri; 11.30pm-5am Sat. Closed July-Aug. **Admission** *Disco* free after 12.30am for ARCI members Fri (annual membership €8 at the door); €8 (incl 1 drink) Sat. *Concerts* €8-€22. **No credit cards.**

You'll need a car to get to this spot but if you're a pop, rock or metal fan it can be well worth it for some of the big acts that pass through to play on its small stage. Interpol, the Veils, Supergrass and Black Rebel Motorcycle Club have been among recent guests. A rock disco follows the gigs.

Lido di Jesolo

Getting there

The Lido di Jesolo bus (information 0421 380 035) leaves from piazzale Roma, but it's more fun to get the double-decker *motonave* from San Zaccaria-Pietà, on the riva degli Schiavoni, to Punta Sabbioni and bus it from there. There are regular boats making the return journey, with a change at Lido between 1am and 6am. Note that if you drop before dawn you'll need a lift or taxi (call 0421 372 301, €40 approx) back to the boat stop at Punta Sabbioni as no buses link up with the boats between 12.30am and 5.10am.

Clubs

Most of Jesolo's clubs open at 11pm, but nobody who's anybody shows up until 1am. Save money (rather than face) by picking up flyers offering reduced entrance before 1am. The clubs listed below are perennial favourites.

Empire Music Hall

Via Fausta 279, Cavallino (338 875 2823/ www.soundgardencafe.com). **Open** May-Sept 10pm-4am daily. **Admission** €6-€8 (incl drink). **No credit cards.**

If you're tired of techno and you've had it with house, head for this club opposite the Union campsite in Cavallino, the closest to Punta Sabbioni. A mix of pop and rock are on the turntable during the week and it cranks up the guitars on Saturdays with punk, new wave and metal.

And the beat goes on ... (sort of)

'In every house someone plays a musical instrument, someone sings, someone accompanies. Everywhere someone makes music or rushes to hear it,' commented a French visitor to Venice in the 18th century. And the Serene Republic of Music was once renowned around the world for its composers and musicians, for its instrument makers and music printing. Such an illustrious musical tradition now lies firmly in the past.

In the 1960s Pino Donaggio – now a prolific film and TV soundtrack composer, teaming up with the likes of Brian De Palma – was Venice's Doge of Pop, writing '*Lo che non vivo*', which was translated into English as 'You Don't Have to Say You Love Me' for Dusty Springfield and later sung by Elvis; and sultry crooner Patty Pravo played the *dogaressa*. Since then, few of the lagoon city's productions have hit the world stage.

Cover bands abound today; best known are **La Mente di Tetsuya**, Lido lads who take their covers of Japanese cartoon theme tunes around Italy. Enough said. More fun to catch when they play in Venice are **Discofever** whose tongue-in-cheek renditions of '70s hits (with platforms and wigs) bring Chic and Co to the campo to make a great '70s night party.

Yet while the local music scene is small, it is by no means dormant. Internationally known home-grown talent includes Groove Jet producer and DJ **Spiller** and Treviso-born **Tolo Marton**, 'Italy's Hendrix'. The vast majority of Venetian vibes, however, have their roots in Kingston Town and local musicians and the music-going public love to 'Lively Up Themselves' to roots reggae. Venetians started skanking to **Pitura Freska**, whose

unlikely mix of Venetian dialect and reggae shot them to national fame and brought two rare platinum discs back to the Lagoon. Since the band split frontman **Sir Oliver Skardy** has gone solo, and gigs by **Gialloman** and **Caraibi Near** always draw droves of dread-nodding fans. Catering to a younger Jah-loving generation, ska band **Fahreheit 451**'s hit *Veleno* has made them a household name and the outstanding musicians forming the ubiquitous **Ska-J** have shared stages with the Wailers and the Skatalites.

A low-key but often high-calibre jazz scene has produced some fine musicians including **Pietro** and **Marcello Tonolo** and the genre's rising star, bassist **Andrea Lombardini**, while the various formations revolving around the *Suono Improvviso* project often play during local festivals such as Carnevale and the Rendentore. Smooth sounds are also the speciality of non-native but Venice-based **Nossa Alma Canta**, whose Brazilian beats often rouse their adopted hometown, while the island's indie rock ambassadors are **One Dimensional Man**.

The mainland has a far more varied scene, with bands like the highly talented **Good Morning Boy**, great indie rockers **Zabrisky** and the magnificent **Mastica** who, despite singing in Italian, managed to rock even London's Brixton Academy recently. The newest formation from the Mestre milieu, and one to look out for, is **Grimoon**, who make their own short films to accompany each song. Their haunting melodies blend pop, rock and folk with *chansons françaises* and have earned them success both locally and internationally. Catch them if you can!

Il Muretto

Via Roma Destra 120 (0421 371 310/www.ilmuretto. net). **Open** 11pm-4am Wed, Fri, Sat, Sun. Closed Oct-Mar. **Admission** €20-€50. **Credit** MC, V.
The home of Italian house and a Jesolo legend, Il Muretto has been going for over 40 years yet remains super-trendy. A mass of ecstatic youth floods the dancefloor for serious house music expertly spun by highly respected resident DJs and guests who are living legends in clubland: Rampling, Oakenfold, Kevorkian, Tenaglia and the Chemical Brothers to name just a few.

Terrazza Mare Teatro Bar

Vicolo Faro 1, Jesolo (0421 370 012/www.terrazza mare.com). **Open** 6pm-4am daily. Closed Oct-Mar. **Admission** free-€10. **No credit cards.**

This once humble beach bar by the lighthouse is more of a cultural space than a club, organising music, exhibitions and theatre and dance productions as well as club nights. With free entry, no heavy-handed bouncers or label-led dress code, the informal atmosphere attracts a mixed group of groovers, who flock here in their thousands.

Vanilla Club

Via Buonarroti 15, Jesolo (0421 371 648/www. vanillaclub.eu). **Open** *June-mid July, mid Aug-Sept* 11pm-4am Fri, Sat. *Mid July-mid Aug* 11pm-4am daily. Closed Oct-May. **Admission** €7-€10. **No credit cards.**
House, hip hop and R&B are the resident sounds in this club in the Acqualandia complex, with a dash of disco sounds to boogie to under the palm trees.

Performing Arts

You don't *have* to watch the *Four Seasons* on repeat, you know.

Night after night in the 17th and 18th centuries, Venetians flocked to their city's theatres, which once numbered as many as 18. Theatregoers demanded constant novelty, so houses renewed their repertoires freqently to compete for audiences. As a result, play production was prolific. The popular *Commedia dell'arte* offerings of playwrights Pietro Chiari and Carlo Gozzi – who went on to produce fairy tale works including the original *Turandot* – were ousted from centre stage when Carlo Goldoni came on the scene in the mid 18th century.

A law student who ran away from school to join a band of travelling players, Goldoni reformed the genre to bring to the stage his satirical observations, usually in dialect, of Venetians and their foibles; Gozzi accused him of creating 'an instrument of social subversion'. After being signed by the Teatro Sant'Angelo, Goldoni produced 16 major works in the 1750-51 season alone; he kept up his rate of productivity after moving to the Teatro San Luca, now called the Teatro Goldoni.

The same abundance also applied to operatic output with as many as 1,274 operas being produced in Venice in just over a generation. After the fall of the Republic, Venice's opera house established a European reputation, with composers such as Donizetti, Bellini and Rossini regularly providing it with new works. Verdi's *Rigoletto* and *La Traviata* both premiered here, as did Britten's *The Turn of the Screw* and *The Rake's Progress* by Stravinksy (who is buried on San Michele). The 20th century also saw Berio and Venice's greatest modern composer, Luigi Nono, being commissioned to write for the opera house.

Today's theatre-going public seems less demanding and there has been little dramatic departure in repertoires since Goldoni's time. But the growth and revamping in recent years of small theatres have finally given a little more space for experiments in the avant-garde.

The **Teatro Carlo Goldoni** (*see p226*) in Venice and the **Teatro Toniolo** (*see p227*) in Mestre tend to serve up standard theatrical fare, but you can find more cutting edge work in Venice's smaller theatres: the **Teatro Fondamenta Nuove** (*see p227*), which initially opened for contemporary dance productions but has now branched out into all forms of experimental expression; the

Teatrino Groggia (*see p225*) and the **Teatro Junghans** (*see p227*); or at Mestre's **Teatrino della Murata** (*see p227*). The **Teatro a l'Avogaria** (*see p225*) explores the outer reaches of Venetian and Italian theatre, often using theatre for didactic purposes, while the **Centro Culturale Candiani** (*see p227*) in Mestre puts on contemporary pieces.

The summer provides welcome relief in terms of contemporary theatre, dance and music when performances abound during the Biennale di Venezia, Danza-Musica-Teatro (*see p230*) which brings high-quality international productions and artists, with works often commissioned specifically for the festival, including, for example, underwater music performances – the audience don swimming costumes and dive into a pool to listen.

DANCE

The Teatro Fondamenta Nuove hosts an annual dance festival in the autumn, but most dance events are limited to the summer months when the Biennale provides contemporary performances. The Teatro Toniolo and Centro Culturale Candiani also have fairly mainstream contemporary dance offerings. The seasons at **La Fenice** and **Teatro Malibran** (*for both see p227*) always include classical ballet features. In the summer, tango aficionados can watch or even join in performances in campo San Giacomo dell'Orio, on the steps of the station, or in front of the the the Salute basilica (www.tangoaction.com). Dancers are mainly amateurs but the backdrop makes for a striking set and visiting professionals often drop in.

CLASSICAL MUSIC AND OPERA

Venice has become a victim of its own musical tradition, with Vivaldi still pouring out of its churches and *scuole*, more often than not performed by bewigged and costumed players. For many visitors, experiencing Vivaldi in Venice is, quite rightly, an absolute must. But with tourists far outnumbering the local music-going public, discerning music lovers looking for a daily dose of classical music might feel somewhat baroqued out by the predictable programmes performed by local groups, whose technical ability can range from average to good. Obvious exceptions are the Venice Baroque Orchestra, a global success story (*see p41* **Reviving Vivaldi**), and the orchestra of

La Fenice, one of the best in the country. As well as its opera and ballet seasons, La Fenice has at least two concert seasons a year and has recently shown a penchant for 20th-century music. The **Teatro Malibran** shares the Fenice's programmes and also has its own chamber music season, with performances by the (mercifully wigless) Società Veneziana dei Concerti, and Mestre's **Teatro Toniolo** also has a symphony and chamber music season. Most other musical events in Venice take place in churches or *scuole* (*see p67*).

St Mark's basilica only holds a smattering of ceremonial concerts throughout the year, with the patriarch deciding who is to attend. But lovers of sacred music should catch one of two regular Sunday appointments: the sung Mass at St Mark's (10.30am) and the Gregorian chant on the island of San Giorgio (11am).

Visiting foreign music groups often come to town to giving one-off, free performances in Venice's fabulous churches; look out for posters around town. The city has two resident gospel choirs, the Venice Gospel Ensemble (www.venicegospel.com) and the Joy Singers of Venice (www.joysingers.it), who perform frequently at various venues around town, and particularly during the Venice Gospel Festival (*see p230*).

THE SEASON

Venice's theatre and dance season stretches from November to June – though La Fenice keeps on going most of the year, closing only for August. Tourist-oriented classical music concerts are held all year. Smaller theatre groups take advantage of the summer temperatures from June and move into Venice's open spaces (*see chapter* **Festivals**).

But the colder months are not without their serious attractions: look out for concerts held throughout the city during late December to provide some Christmas sparkle.

INFORMATION AND TICKETS

Tickets for concerts and performances can usually be purchased at theatre box offices immediately prior to shows; the tourist information office near piazza San Marco (*see p302*), HelloVenezia offices (*see p286*) and the Vivaldi Store opposite the central post office (San Marco 5537, 041 5221343) sell tickets for 'serious' events; most travel agents and hotel receptions will obtain tickets for classical music concerts.

For high-profile or first-night productions at prestigious venues such as La Fenice, Teatro Carlo Goldoni, Teatro Malibran or the Teatro Toniolo, the limited number of seats not taken by season-ticket holders will sell out days or even weeks in advance: ideally, tickets should

Teatro Malibran. *See p227.*

be reserved at the theatres themselves or on their websites at least ten days before performances, and picked up – in most cases – no later than one hour before the show begins. Alternatively, you can always book for any concert through a ticket agency (*see p218*) or at some tourist information offices (*see p302*).

Local newspapers *Il Gazzettino* and *La Nuova Venezia* carry listings of theatrical events, as does the bilingual monthly *Venezia News*. Ticket prices vary according to productions.

Theatres

Teatrino Groggia

Cannaregio 3150, Parco di Villa Groggia (041 524 4665/www.comune.venezia.it/teatrinogroggia). *Vaporetto Sant Alvise or San Marcuola.* **Open** *Box office* 1hr before start. *Performances* 9pm, days vary. **No credit cards. Map** p321 F1.

Tucked away in the trees, this excellent little space in the northern part of Cannaregio has earned a firm following for its variety of multimedia performances, experimental music and drama, and shows for children in the beautiful garden.

Teatro a l'Avogaria

Dorsoduro 1607, corte Zappa (041 520 9270/ www.teatroavogaria.it). *Vaporetto San Basilio or Ca'Rezzonico.* **Open** *Performances* 8.30pm Mon-Sat; 5pm Sun. **Map** p325 D2.

Arts & Entertainment

This experimental theatre (entry to which is by voluntary donation) was founded in 1969 by renowned director Giovanni Poli. It was at the Teatro a l'Avrogia that he continued the experimental approach he developed in the 1950s. Since his death in 1979, Poli's disciples have pressed on with his experiments, staging works by lesser-known playwrights from the 15th to 19th centuries. Places must be booked at the number above between 2.30 and 4.30pm. The theatre opens its doors 15 minutes before performances.

Teatro Carlo Goldoni

San Marco 4650B, calle Goldoni (041 240 2011/ www.teatrostabileveneto.it/www.hellovenezia.it) Vaporetto Rialto. **Open** *Box office* 10am-1pm, 3-7pm Mon-Fri; Sat varies; 1hr before performances. *Performances* 8.30pm Tue, Wed, Fri, Sat; 4pm Thur, Sun. **Credit** MC, V. **Map** p326 B1.

The Goldoni regularly serves up Venetian classics by its namesake and 20th-century classics regularly feature on the programme, as do, more recently, more contemporary Italian pieces.

Viva Verdi!

When the curtain first went up in 1792 at **La Fenice** – today Venice's one and only opera house – it had seven or eight rivals in a city that boasted an opera tradition stretching back over a century and a half. It was built to replace the Teatro San Benedetto which burnt down in 1774 and, living up to its name (*fenice* means phoenix), it has burned to the ground twice since opening and twice risen from the ashes, most recently in 2003 after the devastating fire in 1996. Rebuilt 'where and as it was', it has been restored to its former glory, with the bonus of updated stage machinery and surtitles for the audience.

The 20th century saw significant musical milestones with Britten's *The Turn of the Screw* and Stravinsky's *The Rake's Progress* both opening here, but it was in the 19th century that the theatre's reputation glittered as brightly as its opulent gilded interior. The greatest composers of the age wrote for the theatre: Bellini, Donizetti and Rossini, whose *Tancredi* and *Semiramide* both premiered here. But from the 1840s on, Verdi stole the show. His *Attila* opened here and the theatre directly commissioned *Simon Boccanegra* (1857), *Rigoletto* (1851) and *La Traviata* (1853), though this last flopped miserably.

The *Traviata* 'fiasco', as the great man called it, was easily forgotten as La Fenice was also the focal point for revolutionary struggles for Italian unity and anti-Austrian protest in this period, and Verdi was their standard bearer. The Fenice audience would join in his operas' rallying, patriotic choruses and throw bouquets of red, white and green, the colours of Italy's tricolour, on to the stage with cries of '*Viva Verdi*' – the composer's name but also an acronym for *Vittorio Emanuele, Re d'Italia*, (Vittorio Emanuele, King of Italy). When the Austrians got wise to this, the Italian colours were banned and forcibly replaced by Austria's

black and yellow, which the performers left where they landed in disdain.

Verdi took centrestage again in 2006, this time as champion of the cultural nation; each night before the curtain rose in the reborn Fenice, his patriotic hymn from *Nabucco*, *Va' pensiero,* was begun but was interrupted half-way through as a protest against the Berlusconi government's crippling cuts to the arts which caused La Fenice to cancel part of its programme, unable to cover the costs of completing the season. Hopefully, La Fenice will survive its resurgence from this latest inferno of insolvency and will not have to lament for 'oh my country, so lonely and lost!' again.

Teatro Junghans

Giudecca 494, campo Junghans (041 241 1974/ www.teatrojunghans.it). Vaporetto Palanca. **Open** *Box office* 1hr before performances. *Performances* 8.30pm, days vary. **Tickets** €6; €4 concessions. **No credit cards. Map** p325 E5.

Opened in 2005 on the Giudecca, in what was once a storehouse for fuses for bombs produced in the factory of the same name during World War II, the intimate space of Venice's newest theatre is devoted to dance and experimental drama productions as well as *Commedia dell'arte* puppet shows.

Teatro Fondamenta Nuove

Cannaregio 5013, fondamenta Nuove (041 522 4498/www.teatrofondamentanuove.it). Vaporetto Fondamente Nove. **Open** *Box office* 1hr before performances. *Performances* 9pm, days vary. **No credit cards. Map** p322 C3.

Opened in 1993 in an old joiner's shop, the Teatro Fondamenta Nuove stages contemporary dance and avant-garde drama, including works by Crimp and Copi, and high-quality experimental music performances. It also organises film festivals, symposiums, exhibitions and workshops.

Teatro La Fenice

San Marco 1965, campo San Fantin (041 786 575/ www.teatrolafenice.it). Vaporetto Giglio. **Open** *Box office* Hello Venezia *(see p286). Performances* varies. **Credit** AmEx, MC, V. **Map** p326 A1.

Newly restored and positively gleaming, La Fenice is back in business offering opera, ballet and concert seasons. Performance times given above may vary. Rehearsals allowing, 40-minute tours (€7; €5 concessions) can be booked at the box office.

Teatro Malibran

Cannaregio 5873, calle dei Milion (041 786 603/ www.teatrolafenice.it). Vaporetto Rialto. **Open** *Box office* Hello Venezia *(see p286)*; 1hr before performances. **Performances** 7 or 8pm, days vary; 3.30pm Sat, Sun. **Credit** AmEx, MC, V. **Map** p322 B5.

Inaugurated in 1678 as Teatro San Giovanni Grisostomo, the 900-seater was built on the site where Marco Polo's family palazzo once stood; sections of this and even older buildings were uncovered during the theatre's recent restoration. In the 17th century this was the first of Venice's theatres to throw its doors open to anyone who could afford a ticket, rather than catering to the patrician class exclusively.

However, in the 17th and 18th centuries, when other theatres were bringing ticket prices down in order to fill seats, the San Giovanni Grisostomo remained resolutely and expensively elitist. In 1835 the theatre was renamed after Maria Garcia Malibran, the celebrated Spanish soprano who gave a free recital there (then later died in Manchester aged 28 after falling from a horse while hunting). The theatre now shares the classical music, ballet and opera season with La Fenice and has its own chamber music season. **Photo** *p225.*

Further afield

Centro Culturale Candiani

Piazzale Candiani 7, Mestre (041 238 6111/www. comune.venezia.it/candiani). Bus 2 from piazzale Roma, get off at piazza Ferretto. **Open** *Box office* 9am-7pm Tue-Fri. *Centre* 9am-10pm Tue-Sun. Ticket prices vary according to productions. **No credit cards.**

This 1970s arts centre contains an auditorium, video library, exhibition space and outdoor arena. Alfresco performances are held June-Sept. Entertainment ranges from Bach to *The Vagina Monologues*, plus mini film festivals.

Teatrino della Murata

Via Giordano Bruno 19, Mestre (041 989 879/ www.teatromurata.it). Bus 2 from piazzale Roma, get off in via Einaudi. **Open** *Box office* 30mins before performances. *Performances* 9pm Mon-Sat; 5pm, 9pm Sun. **No credit cards.**

The tiny Teatrino della Murata (which contains a mere 70 seats) is situated in a former warehouse under the remains of the ancient city walls. Funded by the city and regional councils, it specialises in showcasing multicultural theatre.

Teatro Toniolo

Piazzetta Battisti 1, Mestre (041 274 9070/box office 041 971 666/www.culturaspettacolovenezia.it). Bus 2 or 7 from piazzale Roma, get off at hospital in via Poerio. **Open** *Box office* 11am-12.30pm, 5-7.30pm Tue-Sun. *Performances* times and days vary. **Credit** MC, V.

Founded in 1913, the Teatro Toniolo in Mestre is now run by the local council. Serving up an assortment of performances, from vernacular favourites to contemporary plays, new stagings of Italian and foreign classics, musicals, cabaret, classical and pop music, and contemporary dance and ballet, there is definitely something to suit all tastes.

Churches, *scuole* & *palazzi*

For information on musical events in Venice's churches, check the local press *(see p296)*.

Ateneo San Basso

San Marco 315A, piazzetta dei Leoncini (041 528 2825/www.virtuosidivenezia.com). Vaporetto Vallaresso. **Open** *Box office* 10am-1pm, 2-8pm Mon-Sat. *Performances* 8.30pm Mon-Sat. **Tickets** €25; €20 concessions. **No credit cards. Map** p326 C1.

Just off St Mark's Square, the Ateneo puts on the *Four Seasons* and other Vivaldi works played by the St Mark's Chamber Orchestra.

Basilica dei Frari

San Polo, campo dei Frari (041 719 308/www.basilica deifrari.it). Vaporetto San Tomà. **Map** p321 E5.

The lofty Gothic Frari *(see also p123)* is one of the best venues in Venice for catching high-standard performances of sacred music. It has regular seasons in the autumn and spring; organ recitals and a

An open-air performance in **campo Pisani**. *See p230.*

number of free or low-cost afternoon concerts are held especially over Christmas and the New Year, and are sponsored by the local paper *Il Gazzettino*. A word of warning, though: if you go to one of the winter concerts, wrap up warm.

Palazzo Barbarigo Minotto

San Marco 2504, fondamenta Duodo o Barbarigo (340 971 7272/www.musicapalazzo.com). Vaporetto Giglio. **Open** *Box office from 8pm. Performances* 8.30pm **Tickets** €40. **No credit cards**. **Map** p325 F1.

In the beautiful surroundings of a 17th-century palazzo, performances include a variety of classic opera arias, Neapolitan songs and complete operas with few instruments and a piano to accompany the singers. During the evening, the small audience follows the performers around the salons of the palazzo, from the frescoed Sala Tiepolo to the bedroom for the more intimate 'love duets'.

Palazzo delle Prigioni

Castello 4209, ponte della Paglia (041 984 252/www. collegiumducale.com). Vaporetto San Zaccaria. **Open** *Box office* 10.30am-8.30pm on performance days. *Performances* 9pm. **Tickets** €25; €20 concessions. **No credit cards**. **Map** p326 C1.

Just over the Bridge of Sighs from the Doge's Palace, the prisons host concerts by the Collegium Ducale Orchestra – which performs its Venetian baroque and German romantic repertoires several times a week – and also jazz evenings courtesy of the Venice Jazz Quartet.

San Giacomo di Rialto

San Polo, campo di San Giacomo (041 426 6559/ www.ensembleantoniovivaldi.com). Vaporetto Rialto. **Open** *Box office* at venue from 10am-6pm; 10am-8.45pm on performance days. *Performances* 8.45pm Wed, Fri, Sun. **Tickets** €22; €17 concessions. **Credit** MC, V. **Map** p322 B5.

One of the oldest churches in Venice, affectionately known as San Giacometto, it hosts concerts by the Ensemble Antonio Vivaldi.

Santa Maria Formosa

Castello, campo Santa Maria Formosa (041 984 252/www.collegiumducale.com). Vaporetto Rialto. **Open** *Box office* 10.30am-8.30pm on performance days. *Performances* 9pm days vary. **Tickets** €25; €20 concessions. **No credit cards**. **Map** p322 C5.

This charming church is the alternative venue for performances by the Collegium Ducale Orchestra (*see also above,* Palazzo delle Prigioni) and also hosts free concerts by visiting foreign choirs.

Santa Maria della Salute

Dorsoduro, campo della Salute (041 274 3928/ www.marcianum.it/salute). Vaporetto Salute. Performances 4pm Sun. **Map** p326 A3.

Purpose-built to thank God for delivery from the 1630-31 plague, the Salute church hosts free Saturday afternoon organ recitals at 4pm.

San Vidal

San Marco 2862B, campo San Vidal (041 277 0561/ www.interpretiveneziani.com). Vaporetto Accademia. **Open** *Box office* 9.30am-8.30pm Mon-Sat; 10am-6pm Sun. *Performances* 9pm Mon-Sat (8.30pm in winter). **Tickets** €22; €17 concessions. **Credit** MC, V. **Map** p325 F2.

For highly professional renditions of Venice's favourite composer, Vivaldi, visit the church of San Vidal, where the no-frills *Interpreti veneziani* play to a backdrop of Carpaccio's San Vitale on a white horse over the high altar.

Scuola Grande di San Giovanni Evangelista

San Polo 2454, campiello della Scuola (041 718 234/information and bookings 340 546 6965/ www.musicainmaschera.it). Vaporetto San Tomà. **Open** *Box office* 6pm on performance days. *Performances* 9pm, days vary. **Tickets** €25-€40; €20-€30 concessions. **Credit** MC, V. **Map** p321 E5.

This 14th-century *scuola*, with an imposing marble staircase and paintings by Tintoretto and Tiepolo, hosts *Musica in maschera*, an orchestra and choir performing shrink-wrapped opera.

Scuola di San Teodoro

San Marco 4810, salizzada San Teodoro (041 521 0294/www.imusicveneziani.com). Vaporetto Rialto. **Open** *Box office at venue 10am-7pm daily. Performances 9pm Tue, Wed, Fri-Sun.* **Tickets** €22-€32; €17-€27 concessions. **No credit cards.** **Map** p322 B5.

If your heart is set on performers in wigs and silk acetate, head for the Scuola Grande di San Teodoro, where *I musici veneziani* dish up Vivaldi every Wednesday, Friday and Sunday and a medley of opera arias on Tuesday and Saturday.

Other music venues

Fondazione Querini Stampalia

Castello 5252, campo Santa Maria Formosa (041 271 1411/www.querinistampalia.it). Vaporetto Rialto. **Open** *Performances 5pm, 8.30pm Fri, Sat.*

Tickets €8; €6 concessions. **Credit** AmEx, DC, MC, V. **Map** p322 C5.

The soirées that are organised by this enterprising museum and cultural foundation take the form of a half-hour recital of lesser-known works – usually from the Renaissance or baroque periods. It's certainly a far cry from your costumed Vivaldi concert (for which, *see above*).

Fondazione Cini

Isola di San Giorgio (041 528 9900/www.cini.it). Vaporetto San Giorgio. **Map** p326 C3.

The foundation draws on its impressive archives to organise music seminars, workshops, masterclasses and concerts of rare or neglected music. Concerts are held at the Fondazione HQ or at Palazzo Cini (Dorsoduro 864, piscina del Forner, 041 521 0755). Just turn up at the venues in time for the concerts, which are free. For more information about the foundation, *see p139*.

Mozart's libertine librettist

Opera was the last thing on the mind of Mozart's future librettist while he lived in Venice. Born Emanuele Conegliano to a Jewish family in the Venetian city of Ceneda, on converting to Christianity he had taken the name of his godfather and patron, the Venetian noble and bishop of Ceneda, Lorenzo Da Ponte, whose family palazzo still stands by campo San Maurizio (San Marco 2476).

He studied in a seminary but six months after he was ordained as a priest, lured by excitement of life in the capital city and probably by a certain married woman, the young Abbé Da Ponte had thrown his cassock to the wind and made his way to the metropolis, where he would begin a series of fantastic adventures that make his life story read more like the plot of one of the *libretti* he would later pen.

When he wasn't gambling feverishly in dens like the Ridotto at San Moisè (now part of the Hotel Monaco), passing himself off as an alchemist or having a string of licentious liaisons, he spent his time in the salons of his more progressive noble patrons like Bernardo Memmo (whose mistress Da Ponte promptly seduced), and Pietro Zaguri for whom he worked as a secretary in the family home, just across campo San Maurizio (now San Marco 2631) from the original Da Ponte's, and where he also became friends with Giacomo Casanova.

Still celebrating mass at San Luca, until the vicar banned him from his church for his inappropriately trendy hairstyle and flirtatious

behaviour, Da Ponte also wrote poetry which was deemed dangerously revolutionary by the wobbly authorities. Eventually, he was secretly denounced for his lifestyle seen as scandalous even by Venetian standards, and, after a three-month show trial, was banished from the republic for 15 years. He didn't return to Venice until nearly 20 years later in 1798.

In that time he had travelled Europe, plagued by perpetual professional, political and romantic intrigue; and he had turned his hand to libretto-writing when penniless in Vienna, working with Mozart to produce three of his most popular and enduring operas – *The Marriage of Figaro, Don Giovanni* and *Così fan tutte.* The next stage in his itinerant life was to take him to the New World but first he stopped over back in Venice, where he was horrified at the state to which the Austrian occupiers had reduced the city, his friends and even his former enemies.

The Austrians expelled him after two days, but he must have had few regrets as he put the city behind him. This was no longer a place which could inspire anything like Da Ponte's *Catalogue* song, when Don Giovanni's servant lists the number of women his master has seduced:

In Italy six hundred and forty
In Germany, two hundred and thirty-one.
A hundred in France, in Turkey ninety-one,
But in Spain already a thousand three
… a list which must have had even his old pal Casanova wondering.

Arts & Entertainment

Festivals

For information on **Natale a Venezia** contact local tourist offices (*see p302*). For **Venezia Suona**, *see p203*.

Biennale di Venezia, Danza-Musica-Teatro

Palazzo Querini Dubois, San Polo 2004, fondamenta Erbe (041 521 8711/www.labiennale.org). Vaporetto San Silvestro or San Tomà. **Venues** various. **Tickets** Hello Venezia (*see p286*). **Dates** *dance* mid-end June; *theatre* July; *music* end Sept-mid Oct. **Map** p321 F5.

Venice's Biennale festival umbrella has recently allotted new funds to its dance, music and theatre department. The programme remains restricted to the summer months and is staged in newly restored venues inside the Arsenale (*see p98*): the Teatro Tese, the Tese alle Vergini and the smaller Teatro Piccolo Arsenale (all open for Biennale performances only), as well as squares and venues around the city.

Festival Galuppi

San Marco 3972, calle Sant'Andrea (041 522 1120/www.culturaspettacolovenezia.it) Vaporetto Sant'Angelo. **Venues** various. **Tickets** at venues 2hrs before performance; Hello Venezia (*see p286*). **Dates** late Aug-mid Oct. **Map** p326 A1.

This festival is dedicated to the Venetian composer Baldassarre Galuppi, affectionately known as *Il Buranello*. It's an opportunity to hear 18th-century classical music in otherwise inaccessible venues, such as the islands of San Francesco del Deserto and Lazzaretto Nuovo; Vivaldi doesn't get a look in.

Le Giornate Wagneriane

Associazione R Wagner, c/o Associazione Culturale Italo-Tedesca, Palazzo Albrizzi, Cannaregio 4118, fondamenta Sant' Andrea (041 523 2544/www.acitve.com). **Venues** Palazzo Albrizzi; Fondazione Cini (*see p229*); Fondazione Levi (San Marco 2893, calle Giustiniani). **Tickets** by invitation. **Dates** 16 Oct-26 Nov. **Map** p322 B3.

Wagner is the star of a series of world-class concerts organised by the Associazione R Wagner; the Giornate Wagneriane also includes conferences on the great man, and visits to the house he occupied while in Venice. Concerts are free, and by invite only, though these are easily obtainable: call 041 526 0407 between 9.30am and 12.30pm Mon-Fri from October or email arwv@libero.it.

Teatro in Campo

Pantakin da Venezia, Giudecca 620-2, campo San Cosmo (041 522 1740/bookings 340 844 4117/www.pantakin.it/www.destateincampo.it). **Venue** campo Pisani. **Tickets** at venue from 6pm on performance days; HelloVenezia (*see p286*). **Dates** late July-mid Aug. **Map** p325 F3.

The Teatro in Campo festival graces campo Pisani near the Accademia, with good drama and opera. The programme also includes free performances on the islands of the lagoon; see the website for details.

Venice Gospel Festival

Castello 2786A, campo San Francesco (041 296 0385/bookings 041 271 9090/www.veneziagospel festival.it). **Venues** around the city. **Tickets** www.boxofficeitalia.com. **Dates** late May **Map** p323 E5.

The three-day festival in late May hosts local and international choirs in a variety of venues, including St Mark's basilica and gondolas on the Grand Canal. Phone bookings are accepted from the beginning of May.

Venice Music Festival

1 East 53rd Street, 10th Floor, New York, NY (00 1 212 688 8788/www.venicemusicfestival.org); C/o AMO Srl, San Marco 4410, campiello della Regina d'Ungheria **Venues** around the city. **Tickets** online bookings only. **Dates** mid-Oct. **Map** p326 B1.

This US organisation organises a four-day festival showcasing both emerging and established musicians from around the world, including the Venice Baroque Orchestra (*see p41* **Reviving Vivaldi**). Its impressive programme is often performed in locations otherwise closed to the public. Designed for its patrons and subscribers, it also organises exhibition visits, tours and receptions but individual performances are open to the public.

Further afield

See also p203 **Veneto Jazz Festival**.

OperaEstate

(0424 217 819/fax 0424 524 214/www.opera estate.it). **Box office** IAT, largo Corona d'Italia 35, Bassano del Grappa. **Open** 9.30am-12.30pm, 4-6.30pm Mon-Sat. **Dates** June-Sept.

The Bassano town council organises this summer feast of dance, theatre, opera, music and cinema in Bassano and more than 30 other towns around the Veneto, including the breathtakingly beautiful Asolo (*see p230*), the chessboard town of Marostica and Montecchio Maggiore. Jazz and classical music are on offer through the summer, with international performers including Sarah Jane Morris. You can also catch dance performances with recent guests including Royal Ballet soloists, Israel's dance star Talia Paz and Moses Pendleton with Momix, and a bag of treats in the theatre.

Settimane Musicali al Teatro Olimpico

Contrà San Pietro 67, Vicenza (347 492 5005/www.olimpico.vicenza.it). **Box office** *April-June* at the Teatro Olimpico (*see pp262-72* **Vicenza**) 9am-4.30pm Tue-Sun; from 7pm on performance days. **Dates** first 2wks June.

In the sumptuous setting of Palladio's final masterpiece (*see p266* **Palladio**) Vicenza's annual music festival focuses on a theme or composer each year, with conferences and concerts as well as films. Tickets can be booked by phone on 0424 600 458 (operates 8am-8pm Mon-Fri; 8am-3pm Sat).

Sport & Fitness

Learn the best way to put your oar in.

No other Italian city puts its inhabitants through their paces like Venice. In return for tramping miles on foot each day and being compelled into step aerobics every ten paces, Venetians are amply rewarded with general good health into ripe old age.

However, watery pursuits are what web-footed Venetians really like best. Traditional water-borne competitions have stood the test of time, with the **Regata storica** (*see p204*) taking place since the 15th century and still going strong. Over 120 regattas are held throughout the year, clearly demonstrating Venice's love for all things aquatic.

SAILING THE SEVEN SEAS

Two activities dominate on the mosquito-infested lagoon: Venetian rowing (*voga alla veneta*) and three-sail sailing (*vela al terzo*).

In *voga alla veneta* the rower stands up, facing the direction of travel. There are various types of *voga alla veneta* – team rowing is one, and the impressive solo, cross-handed, two-oar method known as *voga alla valesana* is another. But the most famous type is *voga ad un solo remo* (one-oar rowing) – one of the most difficult rowing strokes of all – as practised

by Venetian gondoliers. The gondolier only ever puts his oar in the water on the right side of the boat. Pushing on the oar makes the craft turn to the left; the downstroke corrects the direction. In theory, a gondolier uses up no more energy rowing a half-tonne gondola with three passengers than the average person expends in walking, though that doesn't quite explain how they get those bodybuilder biceps.

Vela al terzo was once the means of transporting goods for trade throughout Venice's Adriatic dominions. But the city's traditional wooden flat-bottomed sailing craft is now found only in the lagoon, being used exclusively for pleasure and sport. Depending upon their length, these boats can hoist one or two square sails, plus the classic triangular jib. They can also be rowed in the traditional standing-up position. Courses in both are available from some of the clubs listed below.

ROWING RACES

The most sumptuous of all the Venetian regattas is the Regata Storica on the first Sunday in September. This isn't just a tourist-pleasing pageant: rowers of all ages in craft of various classes compete for glory and prizes.

Shipshape

Fishing is a time-honoured Venetian pastime, the Giardini embankment (*see p98*) and the Zattere (*see p135*) being two popular haunts. Angling requirements can be met at **Nautica & Pesca** (San Polo 3137, campiello San Rocco, 041 277 0919, www.ferramenta deluca.com), which sells everything from lugworms to wellies – but tackle isn't for hire.

Armed with your rod and worms, you may have a yen for a boat. **Cristiano Brussa** has two hire shops in Cannaregio (fondamenta di Cannaregio 1030, 041 275 0196, www. cristianobrussa.com, open 7.30am-5.30pm Mon-Fri) and Castello (fondamenta dei Greci 5030, 041 528 4333, open 7.30am-5.30pm daily) with boats available by the hour or the day. No licence is needed, but they'll take you on a test run. A six-person boat costs €20 per hour or €120 per day, petrol included. A valid document must be left at the hire shop while renting. No credit cards.

If you've had one too many at Hemingway's old watering hole (*see p171* **Harry's Bar**) and envisage yourself battling it out with the big boys on the high seas, contact **Big Game Fishing** (campo Stringari 13, Sant'Elena, 041 528 5123, www.biggames portfishing.it). Staff will rig you out and escort you to the Adriatic. Smaller catches like mackerel make up the normal fare but tuna, shark and other monsters of the deep are possible. Day trips cost €100 per person (min four/max ten people, novices welcome); staff prefer a week's notice. No credit cards.

If you fancy messing about on the water without having to expend energy, contact **Navigador** (fondamenta Terranova 15, Burano, 041 527 2253, www.navigador.com). This company offers a range of activities, such as a day cruise on a Turkish schooner, from April-Oct. As the crew hoists sail, you can lounge on the deck or lord it at the cocktail bar. A chartered day tour with captain and crew will set you back €700, but if you slum it with 16 fellow shipmates, prices are as low as €24 for a half-day tour. This sumptuous schooner also acts as a floating B&B (min two-night stay from €62). A three-day cruise with meals on board and a double cabin costs €288 per person, minimum six people. You can also brace the mainsail on the lagoon aboard a *bragozzo*, a traditional wooden sailboat. A guide can be arranged for more cerebral sailors. Per-person rates (minimum six people) range from €19 to €250.

Perhaps even more spectacular is the **Vogalonga**, which follows a 30-kilometre (18-mile) route around Venice and the northern lagoon. The race is held in June and is open to anyone with a boat and an oar. Rowers descend from all over the country and further afield: in fact, in the 31st Vogalonga, held in 2005, there were 1462 craft, which carried 1121 Venetian rowers – and 2531 rowers from outside Italy. For more information, and details of how to take part, *see p203*.

For a taste of history, catch the ceremonial wedding of Venice to the sea on Ascension Day (La Sensa, *see p202*). This is followed by a multicoloured gondola regatta.

Boating

Canottieri Giudecca

Giudecca 259, fondamenta Ponte Lungo (041 528 7409/www.canottierigiudecca.com). Vaporetto Palanca. **Open** *Office* 4-6pm Tue, Thur. *Lessons* 2.30-7.30pm Mon; 8.30am-12.30pm, 2.30-7.30pm Tue-Sat; 9am-12.30pm Sun. **Rates** €26 enrolment; €5 insurance; €156 yearly membership; €13 monthly membership; €6 per lesson. **No credit cards.** **Map** p325 F4.

Beginners can put their seamanship to the test in the tranquil waters of the southern lagoon behind the Giudecca. Options include Venetian rowing in *mascareta* (small, sporty, gondola-like craft), canoes and sailboats, plus use of the gym. Hours vary in winter depending on fog and daylight. All rowers must pay the enrolment and insurance fees; short-stay visitors will be charged the monthly membership fee. A free trial can be arranged at the discretion of the club.

Reale Società Canottieri Bucintoro

Dorsoduro 10, 15 & 261, Zattere (tel & fax 041 520 5630/041 523 7933/www.bucintoro.org). Vaporetto Zattere or Salute. **Open** *Office* 3.30-5.30pm Wed, 10.30am-12.30pm Sat. *Lessons* 9am-5pm Tue-Sat; 9am-1pm Sun. **Rates** €65 membership; €85 8 rowing lessons; €85 *vela al terzo* sailing course. **No credit cards. Map** p326 A3.

Founded in 1882, the Reale Società Canottieri Bucintoro is one of Italy's oldest sports clubs, and boasts a slew of Olympic rowing records. The club offers canoeing, kayaking and Venetian rowing, plus a well-equipped gym; they recommend a minimum of two weeks to complete a rowing or sailing course. Courses do not require membership fees.

Remiera Canottieri Cannaregio

Cannaregio 3161, campo Sant'Alvise (041 720 539). Vaporetto Sant'Alvise. **Open** 8.30am-12.30pm, 2.30-6pm Tue-Sun. **Rates** €30 enrolment; €10 monthly membership; individual lessons by arrangement. **No credit cards. Map** p321 F1.

This boat club does beginners' *voga alla veneta* courses by arrangement. There's a good gym, which remains open until 9pm.

Società Canottiere Francesco Querini

Castello 6576D, fondamenta Nuove (041 522 2039/www.canottieriquerini.it). Vaporetto Ospedale. **Open** 8am-7pm Tue-Sat; 8am-1pm Sun. **Rates** €26 enrolment fee; €80 8 lessons. **No credit cards. Map** p323 D4.

Venice's second-oldest boat club, the Querini now also boasts a good gym. The club offers rowing, canoeing and Venetian rowing.

Cycling

Though a recent decree allows kids to whizz around the *campi* to the peril of passers-by, cycling is prohibited for adults. However, it is possible – and enjoyable – to hire bikes on the (flat) Lido (for bike hire information, *see p286*) and the island of Sant'Erasmo (*see p149*).

Fencing

AS DLF Scherma

Cannaregio 47, Parco di Villa Groggia (041 717 960/www.dielleffescherma.it). Vaporetto Sant'Alvise. **Open** 5.30-7.30pm Mon-Fri. **Rates** on request. **No credit cards. Map** p321 F1.

With Italy cleaning up at the Olympics and gold medallist Aldo Montano rated as a national pin-up, fencing remains fighting fit in Italy. Head to the Dielleffe Fencing Club to battle it out.

Football

Football comes top of the league as far as *terra firma* sports go. Despite the dearth of anything resembling a grass pitch, Venetians are just as *calcio* crazed as their land-dwelling compatriots. On match days supporters sail to the football stadium at Sant'Elena – the only league ground in Europe entirely surrounded by water. The opposition's fans are herded on to their own steamer and shipped across like convicts.

A season of Serie A glory in 2000 still bolsters long-suffering Venezia fans, despite their subsequent wavering second and third division status in the Italian league. Home matches take place on alternate Saturdays or Sundays from September to June.

Tickets cost €8-€25 in the stands (concessions for under-18s/over-60s; under-10s pay €1 if accompanied by adult) and are on sale at the ground (follow the fans heading to the tiny island of Sant'Elena in the extreme west of Venice; vaporetto Sant'Elena, map p328 C4), at main ACTV and VeLa (*see p286*) ticket offices, and at the train station (8.30am-6.30pm). For further information check www.veneziacalcio.it.

Golf

Circolo Golf Venezia

Strada Vecchia 1, Alberoni-Lido (041 731 333/www.circologfvenezia.it). Vaporetto Lido, then bus B to Alberoni. **Open** *Apr-Sept* 8am-8pm Tue-Sun. *Oct-Mar* 8.30am-6pm Tue-Sun. **Rates** €65 Tue-Fri; €75 Sat, Sun. Children 50% reduction. **Credit** AmEx, DC, MC, V. **Map** off p317 B5.

One of Italy's top ten courses, the Lido links have three practice courses as well as an 18-hole one. Open to non-members, though only to those with proof of membership of golf clubs elsewhere.

Gyms

For rowing clubs equipped with gyms, *see above*.

Eutonia Club

Dorsoduro 3656, calle Renier (041 522 8618/www.eutoniaclub.it). Vaporetto San Tomà or Ca' Rezzonico. **Open** 8am-10.30pm Mon-Fri; 10am-1pm Sat. **Rates** €29.50 annual enrolment or €14 daily entrance fee for use of the gym; €48 8 sessions (1 month); €36 per hr with a personal trainer. **No credit cards. Map** p325 E1.

This gym has three well-lit rooms and friendly staff to put you through your paces. Courses range from boxing to belly dancing. Kids' courses available.

ASD Novafit

Cannaregio 5356, calle Stella (041 522 8636/www.paginegialle.it/novafit). Vaporetto Fondamente Nove. **Open** 8.30am-9.30pm Mon-Fri; 8.30am-12.30pm Sat. **Rates** €30 annual enrolment; €80 per month 'open' lessons and gym/€65 per month 'open' lessons; €250 for five sessions/€430 for 10 sessions with a personal trainer. **No credit cards. Map** p322 C4.

This gym, tucked away behind Palazzo Widman, has an air-conditioned fitness room, with equally breezy instructors. Courses include pilates and yoga and the monthly 'open' fee lets you choose from a huge range of pursuits and hours to suit you.

Running

The best time for '*footing*' along the Venetian streets is early morning. Popular spots include wider pavements on the Zattere, the fondamenta by the Giardini vaporetto stop, or further east under the shady *pineta* of Sant'Elena. For a less knee-crunching experience, head for the Lido's long stretches of beach and well-paved roads.

The 42-kilometre (26-mile) **Venice Marathon** (*see p204*) takes place in October, usually on the fourth Sunday of the month. The starting line is at the Villa Pisani at Strà (*see chapter* **Padua**); the race passes along the Brenta Canal, over the bridge to Venice, then by a specially erected pontoon over the lagoon to the finishing line on the riva degli Schiavoni.

The less competitive **Su e Zo per i Ponti** (*see p202*) takes place in March. There are three races in one (14km, 10km and 3km) so people of all ages and abilities can participate.

Swimming

See also below **Tennis Club Ca' del Moro.** Although often lukewarm and jellyfish infested, the Lido's Adriatic water draws locals in their thousands. For public beaches, *see pp142-149.*

There are three public pools in the city, though Byzantine timetables and lengthy holiday closures leave few windows for a spontaneous quick dip. Swimming caps in the water and poolside flip-flops are obligatory.

Piscina Comunale Sant'Alvise
Cannaregio 3163, calle del Capitello (041 715 650). Vaporetto Sant'Alvise. **Open** 9-9.45am, 1-2.30pm Mon, Wed, Fri; 1-4pm Tue, Thur; 9am-noon, 6-7.30pm Sat; 10am-noon Sun. **Rates** €5 per session; €48 10 sessions. **No credit cards. Map** p321 F1.
This peaceful pool (open daily from 9am to 10.30pm) offers courses for all, with a warm mini-pool for small fry. Non-course dips can be taken at the hours given above. Variations during summer hols.

Piscina Comunale Sacca Fisola
Giudecca, San Biagio-Sacca Fisola (041 528 5430). Vaporetto Sacca Fisola. **Open** 9.45am-noon, 1-2.30pm, 7.15-8.45pm Mon, Tue, Thur, Fri; 3.30-5pm, 6.30-7.15pm Wed; 3.30-6pm, Sat; 3-6pm Sun. **Rates** €5 per session; €43 10 sessions (valid 3mths). **No credit cards. Map** p324 B3.

Situated in a council estate where a waste dump once stood, this pool is for serious swimmers (no mini-pool here). Open daily from 9am to 10.30pm; hours given above are for non-taught swimming.

Piscina Ca' Bianca
Ca' Bianca, via Sandro Gallo, Lido (041 526 2222). Vaporetto Lido, then bus B towards Malamocco. **Open** 10.45-11.30am, 8.30-9.15pm Mon, Tue, Thur, Fri; 10am-noon, 4.45-5.30pm Sat. **Rates** €4.90 per session; €44 10 sessions. **No credit cards. Map** p317 B2.
The newest pool in town, very popular with the inhabitants of the Lido. No mini-pool. The above hours are for 'free' swimming.

Tai chi

Tai Chi in the Park
Information: Centro Ricerca Tai Chi Italia, campo del Grappa 4, Sant'Elena (041 716 045/349 777 4952/www.taichi.it). **Map** p328 B4.
This initiative offers free alfresco tai chi from mid June-mid September. Courses take place throughout Venice and Mestre in a different park each evening from 6.30pm; for venues, consult the website or posters all over the city. Venetian haunts include: Pineta Sant'Elena, Parco Savorgnan (vaporetto San Marcuola) and Lido's piazzale San Nicolò.

Tennis

Tennis Club Ca' Del Moro
Via Ferruccio Parri 6, Lido (041 770 965/tennisclub cadelmoro@tiscali.it). **Vaporetto** Lido, then bus V. **Open** 8.30am-9pm Mon-Fri; 8.30am-8pm Sat, Sun. **Rates** €9 per hr per person; €36 per court for 4 people for 90mins. **Pool** €8 half day; €16 full day. **No credit cards. Map** off p317 B5.
This sports centre is equipped with ten tennis courts. Other facilities at the Tennis Club Ca' del Moro include a gym, swimming pool and football pitches.

Yoga & shiatsu

Yoga Studio di Paola Venturini
San Polo 2006, campo San Polo (348 293 6522). Vaporetto San Tomà or San Silvestro. **Rates** €20 2hr session; private sessions by arrangement. **No credit cards. Map** p321 F5.
You'll find that more traditional iyengar yoga predominates in Venice. Though not as energetic-looking as ashtanga, a session with Paola Venturini will still put you through your paces.

Cristina Gemin Zanchi
Dorsoduro 3707, campo San Pantalon (041 528 6154). Vaporetto San Tomà. **Rates** €35 per hr. **No credit cards. Map** p325 E1.
If your energy channels are blocked after traipsing up and down bridges all day, Cristina Gemin, an experienced qualified shiatsu practitioner, will put you to rights after another cultural onslaught.

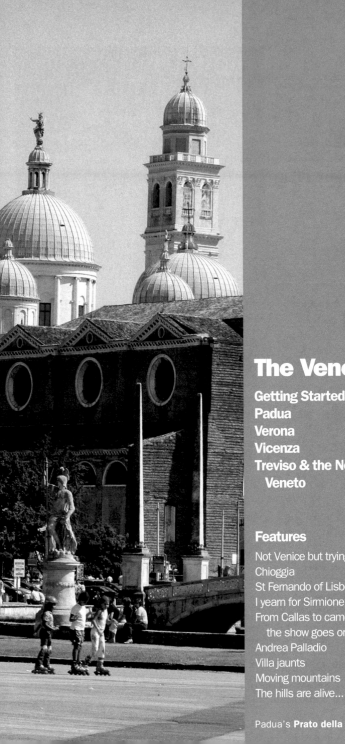

The Veneto

Padua's **Prato della Valle**. *See p242.*

Getting Started

The Veneto has the missing pieces of the cultural jigsaw.

The **Odeo Cornaro** is said to have inspired Palladio's designs. *See p245.*

Venice offers so much that it's easy to forget that there are pieces of the cultural jigsaw missing. But the Veneto – the region that extends inland from the shores of the lagoon – fills the gaps admirably. For Roman ruins, try **Verona** (*see p252*) with its magnificent Arena. Giotto's works in the Scrovegni chapel in **Padua** (*see p242*) are the *nec plus ultra* of the Renaissance fresco cycle by a maestro who hardly got a look-in in *La Serenissima*. And though Venice boasts some great Palladio churches, you'll have to visit his Basilica Palladiana in **Vicenza** (*see p262*) to experience the great architect's take on urban restyling, and the villas of the *vicentino* countryside (*see p271*) for his stately rural retreats.

Venice, moreover, is a little short on natural beauties. There is the misty, moody lagoon of course, but the mainland's the place to go for rolling greenery. If the Veneto region's landscape was never as striking as, say, Tuscany's, the environmental ravages of the economic miracle (*see pp24-26*) have, thankfully, spared some lovely, untouched and under-visited corners,

particularly in the hills and mountains: the Colli Euganei beyond Padua and the Colli Berici south of Vicenza roll pleasantly above the industrial sprawl.

Further north, mountains loom and the scene changes. Still on the plain, Treviso has frescoed *palazzi* and an economic vitality – of which the Benetton empire is the most famous flag-bearer – that gives the town a lively, dynamic feel. In the gentle foothills of the Dolomites are the wine-producing centres of **Conegliano** (*see p278*) and **Valdobbiadene** (*see p279*); **Asolo** (*see p276*) and **Possagno** (*see p275*), given up respectively to the leisured laziness of *il dolce far niente* and the cold neo-classical visions of Antonio Canova; and **Bassano del Grappa** (*see p276*), home of the fiery spirit that keeps the *veneti* going through those foggy winter evenings (and mornings, come to that).

Beyond **Belluno** (*see p279*) the mountains begin in earnest, bringing hordes of *beau monde* skiers to the elegant resort of **Cortina d'Ampezzo** (*see p279*) and queues of summer hikers to attempt one of the many *alte vie*

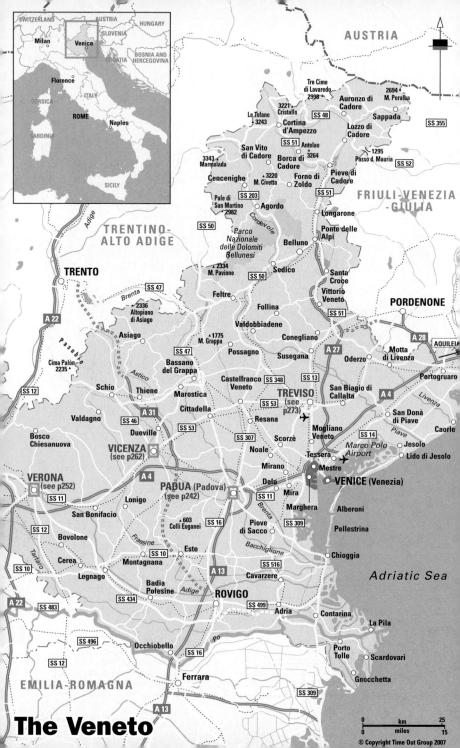

Not Venice but trying

Anyone familiar with even the most beautiful Italian cities (Rome, Florence, Arezzo…) knows that they become very ugly once you leave the *centro storico*. Venice is the exception: it is *all* historical centre. Its unsightly 1950s and '60s residential and industrial sprawl is on the other side of the lagoon. The sprawl is known as **Mestre**… and it's not happy with its role as ugly stepsister to the glamorous queen of the lagoon.

Mestre has no illustrious history to pride itself on. An insignificant walled town from the tenth century (the only notable remnant of these medieval fortifications is the tower in its main piazza), it did not begin to grow exponentially until the last century, with the creation of the industrial port of Marghera. Then the lure of jobs attracted thousands of workers from all over Italy. From the 1950s lagoon-dwelling Venetians began to move here too, fleeing high house prices in Venice itself, or simply seeking the convenience of mainland life, with all its luxurious trappings such as cars and supermarkets.

As Venice's population dwindled, Mestre's expanded, galloping outwards and upwards in grim concrete. Defined by what it is not (ie Venice), Mestre has only recently begun to strive for its own identity; the quest is helped by the fact that most younger *mestrini* have none of the sentimental ties that still bind many of their elders to *La Serenissima*. And the young in Mestre are a far more significant sector of the population than they are across the lagoon. One evening visit to piazza Ferretto – the attractive square at Mestre's heart – will suffice to get a sense of the extent to which this is a youth-oriented city. Indeed, anyone looking for some active nightlife should consider a trip here, once campo Santa Margherita's (*see p127*) attractions have been explored and exhausted. Mestre has more cinemas than Venice; both the centre and the environs are home to some great clubs, gay and straight (*see pp216-17 and p222*).

It is also fair to say that the ugliness of Mestre has been exaggerated. Piazza Ferretto is as attractive a central piazza as you will find in many small Italian towns, with lively bars and cafés. Around the square, a large pedestrian zone has been created, and there are attractive arcaded streets to the north (via Palazzo) and a pleasant market area to the east of the square. There are no major artistic or architectural sights: the churches of **San Rocco** (open Sept-June 10am-noon, 4-7pm Mon-Sat; 9am-noon Sun for mass in Romanian) with its 18th-century decorations, and **San Girolamo** (open 9am-noon, 4-6.30pm Mon-Sat), with its restored gothic interior are worth a look, and there are some fine classical villas, particularly in the greener areas northwards on the way towards Carpenedo (which an imaginative Mestre legend says is where Icarus fell to earth).

But, over recent years, Mestre has gone a long way towards establishing some cultural independence: its theatres (*see p227*) provide musical and theatrical seasons that rival anything Venice has to offer (with the exception of opera). There are lively historical societies and creative writing workshops. In 2001 a long-promised new cultural centre was finally opened: the **Centro Culturale Candiani** (*see p227*) is a five-storey building with spaces for exhibitions, workshops and multimedia events, not all of which have proved successful (*see pp211-15*).

In May 2004 dreary Mestre's desire for green space was answered by the opening of **Parco San Giuliano**, a 70-hectare (175-acre) area of former wasteland between the town and the lagoon, with bicycle tracks, woods, canals, play areas, a roller-skating rink and lake; over 3,000 trees and 10,000 shrubs were planted there. A 140m (380ft) pedestrian bridge crosses the busy ringroad to connect the park to the city. The walk across the park is worth it for the view over the lagoon to Venice – and that, of course, sums up Mestre's problem.

(high-altitude footpaths; for information see www.dolomiti-altevie.it or www.cai.it) that traverse the pink granite Dolomites.

Heading north-east from Venice, a straggle of seaside resorts with high-density beach umbrellas, campsites and discos stretches from **Lido di Jesolo** (*see p222*) to the border of the Veneto. Beyond here, in the region of Friuli-

Venezia Giulia, are the twin pulls of **Aquileia** (*see p281*) – a tiny village with a glorious Roman past – and Grado, one of the pleasantest of the northern Adriatic resorts, with a quiet, island-studded lagoon of its own.

But for many visitors – especially those who don't read the small print on their travel itinerary – the first experience of the Veneto is

The Veneto

The Adige river in **Verona**. *See p252.*

Mestre (*see p239* **Not Venice but trying**) or **Chioggia** (*see p241* **Chioggia**). Chioggia, at the southern end of the lagoon, is half lively fishing port complete with Venice-style canals, and half high-rise tourist resort. Industrial Mestre – with its plethora of cheaper, modern overspill hotels – is not as bleak a prospect as it first appears: it has nightlife, cinemas, theatre… and if all else fails, there's plenty of transport across the lagoon.

Getting around

By train

For general information on the Italian rail network, *see p290.*

Padua (30 minutes from Venice), Vicenza (55 minutes) and Verona (85 minutes) are all connected to Venice by frequent fast Intercity or Eurostar trains on the Venice–Milan–Turin line. Slower *interregionali* trains also stop at small towns such as Monselice (53 minutes).

From the latter, the branch line to Mantua (Mantova) serves the stations of Este (12 minutes from Monselice) and Montagnana (35 minutes from Monselice), though you should study the timetable carefully as these trains are infrequent.

Heading north from Venice is less straightforward. Treviso (20-30 minutes) and Conegliano (40-50 minutes) are on the main line from Venice to Udine, and are served mainly by *interregionale* trains. To the north-west, Castelfranco Veneto (40 minutes) and Bassano del Grappa (60 minutes)

are served by a local line with around 15 trains a day. Around seven local trains a day make the agonisingly slow but very pretty haul up the Piave valley from Padua to Feltre (90 minutes) and Belluno (two hours); some then proceed beyond to Calalzo-Pieve di Cadore (three hours), which is connected by bus to Cortina d'Ampezzo. Consult the skiiing website www.dolomitisuperski.it for further resort and travel information.

There are buses from Grado and Aquileia to the station of Cervignano (85 minutes) on the main Venice–Trieste line.

By bus

Italian long-distance buses are not as frequent, cheap nor relaxing as the train. An exception is on mountain routes, where they are often the only mode of public transport. The ski resort of Cortina d'Ampezzo, for example, is best reached by bus (*see p289*).

Many destinations can be reached by combining train and bus journeys. See individual chapters in the Veneto section for details of bus services to more out-of-the-way destinations. Note that in almost all cases, Sunday services are very limited.

By car

The larger towns in the Veneto are all connected to Venice by fast motorway links: note that tolls on Italian motorways (*autostrade*, prefix 'A' followed by number) are not cheap.

Surprisingly, northern Italy's A-roads (*strade nazionali* or *strade statali*, prefix 'N' or 'SS' followed

Chioggia

A small town of Roman origin, Chioggia spreads over a rectangular island split down the middle by the Canal Vena; to the east is the long arm of the beach resort of Sottomarina. The topography of Chioggia is linear: from piazzetta Vigo, where the ferry docks, the long, wide corso del Popolo extends the whole length of the island, parallel to the Canal Vena. On either side, narrow lanes lead off towards the lagoon.

The only sight not on the corso is the church of San Domenico (open 8am-noon, 2.30-5.30pm daily), on its very own island at the end of the street that begins across a balustraded bridge from piazzetta Vigo. A barn-like, 18th-century reconstruction, it has lost its greatest work, Vittore Carpaccio's *St Paul*, to the Museo Diocesano (*see below*; a copy now hangs in the church). What remains is a huge wooden crucifix – possibly a German work of the 14th century – and a Rubens-like Tintoretto. More charming is the collection of naïve ex-voto paintings placed by grateful fishermen in a side chapel.

Midway down the corso, the church of San Giacomo (open 7am-noon, 4-6.30pm daily), has a high altar in elaborate faux-baroque (1907) which contains the *Madonna della Navicella*, an image of the Virgin as she appeared to a Sottomarina peasant in 1508. Back on the corso is the Granaio, the former municipal granary, built in 1322 but heavily restored in the 19th century; it now hosts the fish market (open 8am-noon Tue-Sun).

Across the canal is the church of the Filippine, an 18th-century building (open for services only) with an extraordinary Chapel of Reliquaries (third on the right).

Near the end of the corso, two churches stand side by side on the right. The smaller one is San Martino (open for services only), a Venetian Gothic jewel built in 1393. Next door, the huge 17th-century **Duomo** was built to a design by Baldassare Longhena after a fire destroyed the original tenth-century church. Only the 14th-century 64-metre (210-foot) *campanile* across the road remains from the earlier structure. The chapel

to the left of the chancel contains a series of grisly 18th-century paintings depicting the torturously prolonged martyrdom of the two patron saints of Chioggia, Felix and Fortunatus (Happy and Lucky).

The road to the left of the Duomo leads to the new **Museo Diocesano**. It contains a collection of religious art, including two fine polyptychs by Paolo Veneziano and a series of wooden bas-reliefs of the *Mysteries of the Rosary* by the workshop of Andrea Brustolon. The most important work is Vittore Carpaccio's last painting, a graceful, poised *St Paul*, signed and dated 1520.

The Torre di Santa Maria marks the end of the old town; just beyond, in campo Marconi, is the deconsecrated church of San Francesco, which has been turned into the **Museo Civico della Laguna Sud.** Though patchy, the museum provides a good introduction to aspects of lagoon life. On the top floor is an exhaustive collection of model fishing boats, plus a small gallery, which contains an attractive triptych by Ercole del Fiore (1436), *Justice between Saints Felix and Fortunatus*.

When the museum is open, the front desk also functions as a tourist information office.

Duomo

Calle Duomo 77 (041 400 496). **Open** May-Sept 8.30am-noon, 3.30-6pm daily. *Oct-Apr* 8.30am-noon, 3.30-7pm daily.

Museo Civico della Laguna Sud

Campo Marconi 1 (041 550 0911). **Open** Sept-mid June 9am-1pm Tue, Wed; 9am-1pm, 3-6pm Thur-Sat; 3-6pm Sun. *Mid June-Aug* 9am-1pm Tue, Wed; 9am-1pm, 7.30-11.30pm Thur-Sat; 7.30-11.30pm Sun. **Admission** €3.50; €1.75 concessions. **No credit cards**.

Museo Diocesano

Via Sagrato (041 550 7477). **Open** Sept-May 9am-noon Thur; 3-6pm Fri, Sun. *June-Aug* 8.30-10.30pm Tue, Fri; 9am-noon Thur, 3.30-7.30pm Sun. **Admission** €3; €1.50 concessions. **No credit cards.**

by a number) are not always as good as their equivalent roads further south – and for some reason will often take a direct route right through the centre of towns (with a consequently high risk of encountering traffic confusion) rather than simply bypassing them.

For more out-of-the-way destinations and mountain roads, a good map is essential; those in the 1:200,000-scale series published by the Touring Club Italiano (TCI) have plenty of detail and are available in most bookshops and in motorway service stations. For car-hire information, *see p289.*

The Veneto

Padua

Giotto, the Ghetto and the Gran Caffè.

Padua (Padova; pop. c220,000) claims to be the oldest city in northern Italy: agricultural communities lived in the region since around 1200 BC. The Romans developed this fertile spot into the thriving town of Patavium; the ruins of their Arena lie just outside the Musei Civici complex. Little else survived the attacks of Attila and his Huns in 452. After becoming an independent republic in 1164, the city's political and cultural influence peaked under the Carrara family (1338-1405). Venice (from 1405-1797), Austria, Napoleon and again Austria had their turns ruling; however, Paduans played an active role in freeing northern Italy from foreign dominion, with Caffè Pedrocchi the scene of a student revolt in 1848. In 1866 the Austrians were banished, and Padua and the Veneto were annexed to the united Kingdom of Italy.

Sightseeing

If you only see one sight in Padua, make it the dazzling **Cappella degli Scrovegni** (Scrovegni Chapel, *see p243*), Giotto's masterpiece. The chapel forms part of Padua's **Complesso Eremitani**, also encompassing the Pinacoteca (picture gallery), Museo Archeologico, and a museum of applied arts. Nearby, the church of **Gli Eremitani** (*see p244*) has frescoes by Mantegna.

Towards the city centre, corso Garibaldi becomes pedestrianised and altogether more pleasant, arriving at **Caffè Pedrocchi** (*see p244*) with the university HQ at **Palazzo del Bò** (*see p246*) opposite. To the west lie Padua's three main *piazze*, which are surrounded and linked by attractive cobbled streets, boutiques and shady loggias. Between piazza della Frutta and piazza delle Erbe is the **Palazzo della Ragione**, which houses the enormous public chamber known to locals as **Il Salone.** Piazza dei Signori is dominated by **Palazzo del Capitanio**. The façade (1532) supports an elaborate mechanical clock, built in 1437 to a design by Maestro Novello – a reproduction of the first clock made in Italy (1344).

To the south lies the underwhelming **Duomo** (*see p244*), Padua's cathedral, and its fabulously frescoed 12th-century **baptistry**. Between piazza del Duomo and via VIII Febbraio are the tranquil alleys of the old **Ghetto** (*see p244*).

Continuing south along via Roma, the church of **Santa Maria dei Servi** (1393) is only open for mass, but look out for the beautifully carved wooden door (1511) by Bartolomeo Campologno.

Via Roma becomes via Umberto I before reaching the **Prato della Valle**. Immediatedly left on entering the Prato is the delightful **Museo del Precinema** (*see p245*). Further south towards the river is the beautiful medieval complex housing **La Specola** (*see p245*), the observatory. The extensive Prato della Valle claims to be the largest public square in Italy, its elliptical shape reflecting that of the Roman theatre which once stood on the site.

Facing the Prato to the south stands one of Christendom's biggest churches, **Santa Giustina** (*see p246*). Where via Belludi meets the Prato is the Drogheria Preti, a delightful former *spezzeria* (an apothocary selling herbs and spices for medicinal use) which has changed little in the past century. A stone's throw away is **Il Santo** (*see p246*), whose economic name belies an awe-inspiring interior; pilgrims flock to the reliquary containing St Anthony's tongue, and the prospect of touching his sarcophagus. The little **Scoletta del Santo** and **Oratorio di San Giorgio**, both in piazza del Santo, offer interesting frescoes on a smaller scale. Next door is the **Orto Botanico** (Botanical Garden, *see p245*) and on the other side another fine work by Falconetto, the **Loggia e Odeo Cornaro** (*see p245*).

TICKETS

The **Padovacard** (€14 for 48 hours) allows free access for one adult and one child (under 12) to virtually all Padua's attractions. It can be purchased at the sights covered by the ticket, and at the town's tourist offices (*see p248*). Further discounts are included, plus free travel on APS buses. For further information ring 049 876 7927 or visit www.turismopadova.it. The Padovacard cannot be purchased with credit cards, except when purchasing it at the same times as booking a visit to the Scrovegni chapel on www.cappelladegliscrovegni.it.

Complesso Eremitani: Scrovegni Chapel & Musei Civici

Piazza Eremitani 8 (049 820 4551/049 201 0020/ www.cappelladegliscrovegni.it). **Open** *Jan-Feb* 9am-7pm daily; *Mar-Jan* 9am-10pm daily. **Admission** NB add €1 booking fee to any ticket that includes the

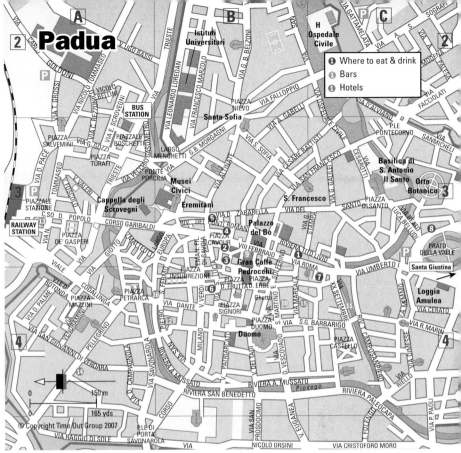

Scrovegni chapel. *Museum & chapel* €11; €8 and €5 concessions. *Museums only* €10; €8 and €5 concessions. *Chapel only* €7. **Credit** (online bookings only) MC, V. **Map** p243 A/B3.

The Complesso Eremitani includes the Cappella degli Scrovegni (Scrovegni chapel), the Musei Civici (city museums) the Pinacoteca (picture gallery), Museo Archeologico (archeological museum) and the Museo di Arti Applicate (museum of applied arts) housed in Palazzo Zuckermann.

Booking is obligatory for the Scrovegni Chapel and should be done two to three days in advance. Tickets must be collected at least one hour before allotted entry time. You can book online by credit card (at least 24hrs in advance) or directly at the Musei Civici. Although the chapel is included on the Padovacard (*see p242*), a reservation must still be made and the €1 booking fee be paid. In March 2006 the chapel began opening 7-10pm as well, charging €7 (plus booking fee) for a regular 20-minute evening visit or €11 (plus booking fee) for a 40-minute stay.

After this complicated procedure, you get a mere 15-20 minutes to admire the masterpiece. But one look and it will seem worth the hassle.

Cappella Scrovegni (Scrovegni Chapel)

This externally unassuming building was commissioned by Enrico Scrovegni, and construction began in 1303. Dante immortalized Enrico's father, Reginaldo, in his *Inferno*, accusing him of usury. It is said that Enrico commissioned the chapel in order not to secure himself the same fate. Enrico is pictured, dressed in violet – the colour of penitence – offering the chapel to Mary in the *Last Judgement* fresco at the far end. The chapel, consecrated in 1305, was originally connected to the Scrovegni palace, which stood inside the area of the Arena, but was demolished in 1827. Centuries of neglect left the frescoes in a state of disrepair, but in 2002, after extensive restoration work, the chapel reopened to the public looking more magnificent than ever.

The two sculptures on the altar, *Two Angels* and *The Virgin & Child*, are by Giovanni Pisano. But it's Giotto's magnificent fresco cycle that utterly dominates the interior. Painted c1304-13, it tells the story of mankind's salvation through the lives of the Virgin, Christ, and depictions of stories of Mary's parents Joachim and Anne. The story of Christ unfolds in the middle and lower rows, with the middle of the right-hand wall dominated by the scene of Judas's kiss.

The high dado at the base of the walls is decorated with fine grisaille paintings of the seven Virtues and Vices. Particularly striking are the figures of Envy blinded by her own serpentine tongue and Prudence equipped with pen and mirror. In the huge *Last Judgment*, covering the west wall of the Chapel, suffering souls are tortured by the kind of demonic beasts that Enrico hoped to avoid, still as hellishly captivating as they must have been 700 years ago.

Pinacoteca & Museo Archeologico

These moderately interesting civic collections are housed in the cloisters of the Eremitani church (*see below*). The archeological wing on the ground floor contains some fine pieces, including remains from Roman Padua in room 5. A fifth-century AD skeleton of a young man and his horse is unusual: the animal may have been sacrificed and buried alongside him to speed him on his voyage into the afterlife.

Upstairs, the Pinacoteca starts with Giovanni Bellini's intriguing *Portrait of a Young Senator*. Works by Titian, Palma il Vecchio, Domenico Tintoretto, Veronese and the collection's only female artist, Chiara Varotari (1584-1663) follow. Next up is a Giotto *Crucifixion* that originally hung in the Scrovegni Chapel. There are also fine works by the Bassano family, Pozzoserrato, Luca Giordano, altarpieces by Romanino and Tintoretto, and several sculptures by Canova. The final painting, by Giorgio Fossati (1706-85), is a birds'-eye view of the Prato della Valle (*see p242*), showing how the city looked in the 18th century when the area was used as a fair.

Museo di Arti Applicate

Housed since 2004 in Palazzo Zuckermann, with its entrance at corso Garibaldi 33, this section of the civic museums contains a small collection of ceramics, furniture, lace, clothes and jewellery. A set of 1781 printing plates show a map (in mirror-version of course) of Padua before the fall of *La Serenissima*.

Duomo

Piazza Duomo (church 049 662 814/baptistery 049 656 914). **Open** *Church* 7.30am-noon, 3.45-7.30pm Mon-Sat; 7.45am-1pm, 4-8.30pm Sun. *Baptistery* 10am-6pm daily. **Admission** *Church* free. *Baptistery* €2.50; €1.50 concessions. **No credit cards. Map** p243 B4.

The first church on this site was destroyed in 899 by rampaging Huns; its Romanesque replacement, consecrated in 1075, is pictured in the frescos of the baptistery next door. In 1552 Michelangelo was commissioned to design the current cathedral and construction was begun in 1547, though consecration wasn't until 1754. That Michelangelo's designs were not adhered to is obvious from the uninspiring final form. Inside are paintings by Stefano dell'Arzere, Tiepolo, Paris Bordone and a panel painting of a Byzantine style *Virgin and Child,* a copy of the original by Giotto. The real jewel is the 12th-century baptistry next door, frescoed from floor to ceiling by the 14th-century Florentine Giusto de Menabuoi.

Gli Eremitani

Piazza Eremitani 9 (049 875 6410). **Open** *Apr-Sept* 8.30am-12.30pm, 3.30-6.30pm Mon-Sat; 10am-12.30pm, 4-6pm Sun. *Oct-Mar* 8.30am-12.30pm, 3.30-6pm Mon-Sat; 10am-12.30pm, 4-6pm Sun. **Map** p243 B3.

The original building, dating from 1276, was bombed on 11 March 1944, then meticulously restored. The reconstructed wooden ceiling (finished at the start of the 14th century) was designed by Friar Giovanni degli Eremitani, who was also responsible for the imposing vaulted ceiling of il Salone (*see p242*). The church's most valuable treasures – frescoes by Mantegna who began the work in 1448 when he was just 17 years old – were almost totally destroyed. Fortunately the *Martyrdom of St Christopher*, the *Carrying of the Body of St Christopher* and *Our Lady of the Assumption* survived the bombing raids, having been removed some decades earlier; colour photographs taken just before the War have enabled the restoration of the *Martyrdom of St James* and *St Christopher Converts the Knights* from fragments found in the rubble. The tomb of Jacopo da Carrera (workshop of Andriolo de' Santi, 1345-50) features an inscription of Latin verses that the poet Francesco Petrarch dedicated to a friend. Bizarrely enough, the church was the original home of the tomb of the very Protestant Prince Frederick William of Orange, who died in Padua in 1799. It was removed to a more appropriate spot in Delft, Holland, in 1896, but a bronze copy of the marble *Pietà* (1806-8) by Antonio Canova which adorns the tomb, can still be seen in the vestibule opposite the chapel.

Il Ghetto

Map p243 B3/4.

Padua's Ghetto is now a beautifully renovated pedestrian zone with shops and bars lining the cobbled streets. The area was closed off in 1603 by four gates restricting its Jewish inhabitants' movements, and remained that way until 1797. One synagogue remains on via Solferino; beneath the 16th-century loggia in Nanto stone is a plaque commemorating the deaths of 46 Paduan and 8,000 Italian Jews during the Holocaust. All that is left of the Sinagoga Tedesca (German Synagogue) – the city's oldest synagogue, destroyed in 1943 by anti-Semitic *padovani* – is a plaque on via delle Piazze. **Photo** *p254.*

Gran Caffè Pedrocchi

Via VIII Febbraio 15, entrance from piazzetta Pedrocchi (049 878 1231/www.caffepedrocchi.it). **Open** *Architectural rooms and Museo del Risorgimento e dell'Età Contemporanea* 9.30am-12.30pm, 3.30-6pm Tue-Sun. **Admission** €4; €2.50 concessions. **No credit cards. Map** p243 B3. For café and restaurant opening times, *see p247.*

Antonio Pedrocchi's vision to build a café which was 'the most beautiful on the face of the Earth' lives on today in his Gran Caffè Pedrocchi, a unique combination of architectural styles and interior designs. Opened to the public in 1831, it soon became known as 'the café without doors' because it was open 24/7.

The **Ghetto**. *See p244.*

Other than the opening hours, which became somewhat less ambitious during World War I, little has changed in the café, despite extensive restorations from 1995-99. The great Venetian architect Giuseppe Jappelli was chosen by Pedrocchi to realize his vision and work commenced in 1826. When the upper floor, designed to serve as a Ridotto (a club for gambling and dancing), was opened in 1842, the frescoes were still wet. It contains a condensed tour of Western culture: the Etruscan, Greek, Roman, Herculaneum, Renaissance, Moorish and Egyptian rooms, all lavishly decorated, surround the ballroom, or Sala Grande. Also known as the Rossini Room, the ballroom is twice the height of the others and features a balcony where performances and recitals were staged. Pedrocchi liked to look down, unseen, on the gambling nobles from one of the windows situated high in the walls. The Caffè Pedrocchi's first-floor rooms also house the **Museo del Risorgimento e dell'Età Contemporanea**, with military memorabilia from 1797-1945.

Loggia e Odeo Cornaro

Via Cesarotti 37 (335 142 8861). **Open** *Feb-Oct* 10am-1pm Tue-Fri; 10am-1pm, 4-7pm Sat, Sun. *Nov-Jan* 10am-1pm Tue-Fri; 10am-1pm, 3-6pm Sat, Sun. **Admission** €3; €2 concessions. **No credit cards.** **Map** p243 C3.

This Renaissance gem was once the home of Alvise Cornaro, a wealthy Venetian and patron of the arts, who commissioned his friend the Veronese architect Giovanni Maria Falconetto (who stayed at the house as Cornaro's guest for 21 years) to design the loggia in the internal courtyard for theatrical performances. Completed in 1524, this was Falconetto's first architectural work, followed in 1530 by the Cornaro Odeum, a frescoed octagonal room. The house became popular as a theatre and intellectual salon; Palladio's villa designs are said to have been inspired by visits to the house. **Photo** *p237 and p248.*

Museo del Precinema (Collezione Minici Zotti)

Prato della Valle 1A (049 876 3838/www.minicizotti. it). **Open** *Mid June-mid Sept* 4-10pm Mon, Wed-Sun. *Mid Sept-mid June* 10am-4pm Mon, Wed-Sun. Closed 2wks Aug. **Admission** €3; €2 concessions; €5 guided tours. **No credit cards**. **Map** p243 C3.

This minute museum houses a collection of optical curiosities. The delightful display of magic lanterns, precursors to photo and film includes hand-painted glass slides, optical instruments, and a Javanese puppet theatre; some of which are in such good working order that they may be operated by visitors.

Orto Botanico (Botanical Garden)

Via Orto Botanico 15 (049 827 2119/www.orto botanico.unipd.it). **Open** *Apr-Oct* 9am-1pm, 3-6pm daily. *Nov-Mar* 9am-1pm Mon-Sat **Admission** €4; €1-€3 concessions. **No credit cards**. **Map** p243 C3.

This compact botanical garden founded in 1545 – the first of its kind in Europe – is home to an impressive 4,000 species. Originally a garden of *simples* (medicinal herbs) providing the raw materials for the university's medical faculty, it now provides a tranquil refuge from the surrounding bustle. It also contains exquisite freshwater habitats.

Osservatorio Astronomico – Museo La Specola

Vicolo dell'Osservatorio 5 (049 829 3469/www.pd. astro.it/museo-laspecola). **Open** (guided tours only) *Oct-Apr* 4pm Sat, Sun; *May-Sept* 6pm Sat, Sun. **Admission** €7; €5 concessions. **No credit cards**. **Map** p243 C4.

Tickets must be purchased in advance from the Oratorio di San Michele, opposite the Specola at piazzetta San Michele 1.

This beautifully situated medieval tower overlooking the river was made into an observatory by the city's Venetian overlords in 1761. A guided tour takes you up the tower to the observatory rooms and finally to the figures room, an octagonal chamber whose walls were frescoed in the 18th century with life-size portraits of eight eminent astronomers. There's also a collection of antique telescopes, quadrants, sextants and other heavenly paraphernalia.

Palazzo della Ragione

Via VIII Febbraio (049 820 5006). **Open** *Feb-Oct* 9am-7pm Tue-Sun. *Nov-Jan* 9am-6pm Tue-Sun. **Admission** €4; €2 concessions. **No credit cards**. **Map** p243 B3.

Entrance is via the staircase in piazza delle Erbe, or from via VIII Febbraio for wheelchair users.

Il Salone, as locals call it, was originally built in 1218-9 to provide the city with a prison and public offices. Between 1306-09 it was converted to accommodate the law courts, and the external loggia of the *piano nobile* was added. The impressive ship's-keel roof, said to have been painted with over 7,000 stars and planets by Giotto and assistants (1315-7), was destroyed by fire in 1420 and promptly rebuilt. But the doomed ceiling was again destroyed in 1756, this

The Veneto

time ripped off by a hurricane, and again reconstructed to the original design in 1759. Inside, the Salone is frescoed with representations of the zodiac, months and seasons, but is mostly empty apart from a huge wooden horse, created for a tournament in 1466. In the north-east corner of the hall sits the *Pietra del vituperio* (stone of shame) where, according to 1261 statutes, insolvent debtors had to sit in their underwear, repeating the words *cedo bonis* (I renounce my worldly goods) before being banished. Those who tried to return risked a repeat of the punishment – plus having three buckets of water poured over their heads. There is an extra (variable) charge for temporary exhibitions.

Santa Giustina

Prato della Valle (049 822 0411). **Open** *May-Oct* 7.30am-noon, 3-7.45pm Mon-Sat; 6.45am-1pm, 3-4.30pm Sun. *Nov-Apr* 7.30am-noon, 3-7pm daily. **Map** off p243 C3.

The sparse basilica of Santa Giustina, built 1532-79, is the 11th largest Christian church in the world. It houses paintings by Palma il Giovane, Luca Giordano, Carlo Loth and an altarpiece by Veronese depicting the martyrdom of St Justine. Among the relics in the corridor of the martyrs are bits of St Luke the Evangelist and St Matthias. To the right of the high altar is St Luke's Chapel, which contains the tomb of Elena Lucrezia Cornaro Piscopia (1646-84) the first woman in the world to get a university degree; ask one of the friendly monks if you want to go in.

Il Santo (Basilica di Sant'Antonio)

Piazza del Santo (049 878 9722/www.basilicadel santo.org). **Open** *Apr-Oct* 6.30am-7.45pm daily. *Nov-Mar* 6.20am-7pm Mon-Fri; 6.20am-7.45pm Sat, Sun. **Map** p243 C3.

Although St Anthony was a preacher who rejected worldly wealth, the *padovani* built one of Christendom's most lavish churches to house his remains. Popularly known as Il Santo, the basilica is one of Italy's most important pilgrimage churches. Work on the church began soon after the saint's death (1231) and canonisation (1232), although the main structure remained unfinished until around 1350, when his body was moved to its present tomb in the Cappella dell'Arca. This chapel also contains some of the basilica's great artistic treasures: a series of marble bas-reliefs of scenes from the life of the saint by Jacopo Sansovino, Tullio Lombardo and Giovanni Minello. The chapel's ceiling, by architect Giovanni Maria Falconetto, dates from 1533. Unfortunately, visitors are kept away from the high altar which supports Donatello's bronze panels and crucifix (1444-5); behind the altar, his stone bas-relief of the Deposition is more visible, as are two of the bronzes: a bull and a lion, representing the evangelists St Mark and St Luke. Other works of interest include Altichiero's late 14th-century frescoes in the Cappella di San Felice (on the south wall), Giusto de Menabuoi's frescoes in the Cappella del Beato Luca Belludi and two fine funeral monuments – to Alessandro Contarini (d.1553) and Cardinal Pietro

Bembo (d.1547) – both by Michele Sanmicheli. At the back of the apse is the florid Cappella del Tesoro, to which Anthony's 'miraculous' relics were transferred in 1745 for safe-keeping. Here you can inspect the reliquary containing the saint's tongue, his original coffin and fragments of his robes, all housed in their specially built, garish Baroque setting.

In the piazza in front of the church stands the great Renaissance masterpiece, Donatello's monument to the famous *condottiere* (mercenary soldier) Erasmo da Narni (d.1443), aka Gattamelata, who is buried inside the basilica. Commissioned by the *condottiere*'s family in 1453 and cast the same year, it was the first full-size equestrian bronze to be made since antiquity. Donatello is known to have inhabited the house at piazza del Santo 19, between 1444 and 1454.

Scuola del Santo & Oratorio di San Giorgio

Piazza del Santo 11 (049 875 5235). **Open** *Apr-Sept* 9am-12.30pm, 2.30-7pm daily. *Oct-Mar* 9am-12.30pm, 2.30-5pm daily. **Admission** €2; €1.50 concessions. **No credit cards**. **Map** p243 C3.

The Scuola del Santo contains 16th-century frescoes, some of which Titian is said to have had a hand in. The oratory, constructed in 1377 for the Lupi di Soragna family, contains a cycle of frescoes by Altichiero (1379-84) depicting scenes from the lives of Saints Catherine and George. Altichiero is at his best here, and this place is worth a visit even after the long hike around the basilica.

Università di Padova, Palazzo del Bò (University)

Via VIII Febbraio 2 (049 827 5111/049 827 3047 www.unipd.it). **Open** (guided tours only) *Mar-Oct* 3.15pm, 4.15pm, 5.15pm Mon, Wed, Fri; 9.15am, 10.15am, 11.15am Tue, Thur, Sat. *Nov-Feb* 3.15pm, 4.15pm Mon, Wed, Fri; 10.15am, 11.15am Tue, Thur, Sat. **Admission** €5; €3.50 groups; €2 concessions. Tickets on sale at office in the Atrium 15mins before tour. **No credit cards**. **Map** p243 B3.

Note that opening times are liable to change without warning.

The second-oldest university in Italy (after Bologna) was officially founded in 1222, but didn't move to its current location, Palazzo del Bò (bull) – named after the butchers' inn that used to stand on the site – until 1493. The Old Courtyard, designed by Andrea Moroni, is decorated with the coats of arms and family crests of illustrious rectors and students. Alumni include Copernicus, Sir Francis Walsingham and Oliver Goldsmith, all of whom are remembered in the Sala dei Quaranta, where you can also see Galileo's lectern (he taught here from 1592 to 1610). The university attracted students from all communities, and in the mid 14th century its medical faculty became the first in Europe to accept Jewish students (albeit on payment of double fees). In 1678 Elena Lucrezia Cornaro Piscopia became the first woman graduate (philosophy) in Europe; there is a statue dedicated to her on the stairway. The magnificent oval wooden-benched anatomy theatre, the first of its kind in the world, built by Girolamo Fabrizi Aquapendente in 1594, marked the beginnings of empirical modern medicine.

The university also has a gift shop offering such delights as notebooks adorned with Galileo and key rings bearing the university's coat of arms. The shop is open all year round (9am-12.30pm, 3-7pm Mon-Fri 9am-12.30pm Sat), barring the university's brief summer recess and public holidays.

Where to eat & drink

See also p247 **Gran Caffè Pedrocchi**, **Highlander Pub**.

If you're on a tight budget, the morning markets in piazza delle Erbe or piazza della Frutta and shops in the arcades around them offer a wide range of local produce for picnics. If DIY sandwiches are not your thing, head for the finest *panini* in Padua at **Bar Maximilian**, on the corner of corso del Popolo and via Nicolò Tommaseo (closed Sat and Sun). Or take a seat and watch the passing Paduans from one of the many reasonably priced cafés on via Roma, whose seating and umbrellas fill the street.

Bar Fuji
Via Roma 53 (049 875 9485). **Open** 9am-12.30am daily. **Average** €12. **Credit** MC, V. **Map** p243 B3 ❶
A great place to pop for lunch, this new café serves the usual *panini* and *tramezzini*, but the highlight is sushi. They serve an excellent value fixed menu plate for €6 (four pieces of sushi plus rice) or a ten-piece platter for €9.90.

Caffè Cavour
Piazza Cavour 10 (049 875 1224/www.caffe cavour.com). **Open** 7.30am-midnight Mon, Wed-Sun. **Average** €25. **Credit** AmEx, MC, V. **Map** p243 B3 ❷
This elegant patisserie is home to world-renowned pastry chef, Emanuele Saracino. Incredibly intricate – and unmissable – cakes and pastries are on offer on the ground floor, while upstairs you can savour a pleasant meal overlooking the square.

Le Calandre
Via Liguria 1, Sarmeola di Rubano (049 630 303/ www.calandre.com). **Meals served** noon-2pm, 8-10pm Tue-Sat. Closed 3wks Dec/Jan, 3wks Aug. **Average** €130. **Credit** AmEx, DC, MC, V.
This restaurant, 4km (2.5 miles) west of the city, boasts the youngest chef to have been awarded three Michelin stars. Local boys Massimiliano and Raffaele Alajmo serve up such delights as red in hazelnut and raspberry soup and cuttlefish *cappuccino* in its own ink. Though it may sound like hauling coals to Newcastle, try their fish and chips. After washing it all down with wine from a superlative list, a lime and celery sorbet with passion fruit *jus* is all you need to clean the palate. Break the bank (and your diet): Le Calandre is not to be missed. Booking is essential.

Graziati
Piazza della Frutta 40 (tel/fax 049 875 1014/www. graziati.com). **Meals served** noon-2.30pm Tue-Sun. **Average** €25. **Credit** MC, V. **Map** p243 B3 ❸
Graziati is essentially a *pasticceria* (open 7.30am-8.30pm Tue-Sun), specialising in a calorific range of tantalising millefeuille pastries. For something more substantial, the subterranean restaurant serves hearty lunches. On display is a beautiful 14th-century wooden door rediscovered during restoration.

PePen
Piazza Cavour 15 (049 875 9483/www.pepen.it). **Meals served** noon-2.45pm, 6.30pm-1am Mon-Sat. Closed 2wks Aug **Average** €45. **Credit** AmEx, DC, MC, V. **Map** p243 B3 ❹
This popular haunt for the young and lovely at lunchtime has great outdoor seating in summer. As well as pizza, the menu offers a selection of meat and fish dishes, along with an extensive wine list.

Pinguino Blu
Via Ponte Altinate 6 (049 876 4706). **Open** 11am-midnight daily. **No credit cards**. **Map** p243 B3 ❺
This friendly ice-cream parlour serves ice-cream and *granite* (crushed water-ice) made on the premises. No artificial preservatives or flavourings are used. Good for vegans and those with food allergies.

Rosso Pomodoro
Via Santa Lucia 68 (049 875 1645). **Meals served** 12.30-3pm, 7.30pm-midnight daily. **Average** €18. **Credit** AmEx, MC, V. **Map** p243 B4 ❻
Good, family-friendly Neapolitan pizzeria.

Shop & Coffee
Via Roma 96 (049 875 7975). **Open** 8am-2am daily. **Credit** AmEx, MC, V. **Map** p243 C4 ❼
A pleasant spot for a coffee break, light lunch, early evening *aperitivo* or late night liqueur.

Zairo
Prato della Valle 51 (tel/fax 049 663 803). **Meals served** noon-2.30pm, 7pm-1am Tue-Sun. **Average** €25. **Credit** AmEx, DC, MC, V. **Map** p243 C3 ❽
Its outdoor seating with views over the Prato (*see p242*) and its late-night opening make Zairo a popular meeting point.

Bars & nightlife

For gay and lesbian venues in Padua, *see p217.*

Gran Caffè Pedrocchi
Via VIII Febbraio 15/piazzetta Pedrocchi (049 878 1231/www.caffepedrocchi.it). **Open** *Bar* 9am-9pm Mon-Wed, Sun; 9am-midnight Thur-Sat. *Restaurant* 12.30-2pm Thur-Tue. **Average** €35. **Credit** AmEx, DC, MC, V. **Map** p243 B3 ❾
For centuries Padua's most elegant watering hole, and now restored to its former glory, Pedrocchi's is a landmark in its own right (*see p244*). Try the speciality, a cappuccino with a wicked twist. The restaurant plans to open in the evenings as of spring 2007.

Highlander Pub

Via Santi Martino e Solferino 69 (049 659 977).
Open 11am-3pm, 7pm-2am Mon-Fri, Sun; 11am-3pm, 6pm-2am Sat. **Average** €12. **Credit** AmEx, DC, MC, V. **Map** p243 B4 ⑩

With tables to seat over 400, this pub is not exactly your cosy local. But after a few pints (no litres allowed), the faux-Scottish decor becomes less abrasive and the vast selection of bar snacks (*panini*, salads and pastas) beats the genuine fare of crisps and pork-scratchings any day. Food is served both day and night and Erasmus students get a 10% discount on food and drink with a valid student card.

Sottosopra Bar Tea Room

Via XX Settembre 77 (049 664 898). **Open** *May-Sept* 11am-3pm, 7pm-1am Tue-Sun. *Oct-Apr* 11am-1am Tue-Sun. **Credit** MC, V. **Map** p243 C4 ⑪

A studenty café with a slightly hippy vibe to it. There's a good selection of herbal teas, and salads for around €8.

Villa Barbieri

Via Venezuela 11 (tel/fax 049 870 3223). **Open** 8.30pm-4am Wed, Fri, Sat. **Admission** €15 (men); €11 (women). **Credit** AmEx, MC, V.

This summer haunt for Paduan night owls is set in beautiful grounds buried within the industrial outskirts of the city. It's a fair hike to get there: follow signs for Padova Est to Sheraton roundabout, take the motorway towards Bologna, exiting at corso Stati Uniti, which leads to via Venezuela. Music is mainly house and revival, with live music some nights; you'll be turned away if you look scruffy.

Where to stay

Albergo Dante

Via San Polo 5 (049 876 0408). **Rates** €39 single; €45 double without bath; €55 double. **Credit** MC, V. **Map** p243 B4 ⑫

Seriously cheap, this hotel has rather bare rooms, several without their own bathroom, but nicely situated north of the Duomo, near the river. Breakfast is not included.

Grand'Italia

Corso del Popolo 81 (049 876 1111/fax 049 875 0850/www.hotelgranditalia.it). **Rates** €99-€180 single; €130-€210 double; €200-€290 suite. **Credit** AmEx, DC, MC, V. **Map** p243 A3 ⑬

This art nouveau hotel is ideally situated close to the train station and major sights of the city centre. The recently restored rooms are quiet and comfortable, and many have balconies.

Hotel Piccolo Vienna

Via Beato Pellegrino 133 (tel/fax 049 871 6331/www.hotelpiccolovienna.it). **Rates** €38-€40 single; €50-€66 double; *breakfast* €3 extra. **Credit** MC, V. **Map** p243 A4 ⑭

For the cash-strapped traveller, this hotel in the historic centre of the city provides clean – if cramped – rooms (some without WC).

Majestic Toscanelli

Via dell'Arco 2 (049 663 244/fax 049 876 0025/www.toscanelli.com). **Rates** €115 single; €172 double; €220 suite. **Credit** AmEx, DC, MC, V. **Map** p243 B4 ⑮

All the rooms in this quiet hotel offer attractive views over the quaint streets of the Ghetto, just one minute's walk away from the town's main squares.

Sant'Antonio

Via San Fermo 118 (049 875 1393/fax 049 875 2508/www.hotelsantantonio.it). **Rates** €42 single without bath; €60 single; €90 double. *Breakfast* €7.50 extra. **Credit** MC, V. **Map** p243 A4 ⑯

Sant'Antonio is centrally located and good value for money, unless you get one of the rooms looking out on to a busy street corner very early in the morning.

Resources

Tourist information

IAT *Padua railway station (049 875 2077/fax 049 875 5008/www.turismopadova.it).* **Open** 9.15am-6.30pm Mon-Sat; 9am-noon Sun. **Map** p243 A3.
IAT *Galleria Pedrocchi, next to Gran Caffè Pedrocchi (049 876 7927/fax 049 836 3316).* **Open** 9am-1.30pm, 3-7pm Mon-Sat. **Map** p243 B3.
IAT *Piazza del Santo, opposite the basilica (049 875 3087).* **Open** *Apr-Oct* 9am-1.30pm, 3-6pm daily. Closed Nov-Mar. **Map** p243 C3.

Getting around

Buses in Padua are operated by APS (049 20111/www.apsholding.it); tickets must be bought before boarding, cost €1 and are valid for an hour. Destinations outside the city covered in this chapter are served by blue SITA buses (049 820 6811), which depart from the bus station in piazzale Boschetti. Bicycle rental is available from a small kiosk at the station which is open 24/7 throughout the year (348 701 6373). It costs €3 for the first hour and €1 for each successive hour, or €6 per day. €50 deposit (cash only) required for each bike.

Getting there

By car

Padua is on the A4 *La Serenissima* motorway.

By train

All trains bound south-west from Venice stop at Padua. Journey time 25-35mins.

By bus

From Venice's piazzale Roma bus terminus, orange ACTV buses saunter slowly to Padua. Blue SITA buses (049 820 6811) speed along the motorway. In Padua, both stop at the bus station in piazzale Boschetti.

Around Padua

South of Padua

Arquà Petrarca is the tiny town where poet Francesco Petrarch (1304-73) spent the last years of his life. Still with a delightfully medieval air, the town offers the chance to make a pilgrimage to Petrarch's tomb in the local churchyard and to visit the 14th-century house that the poet built, **Casa di Petrarca** (*see below*), and where he lived with his daughter from 1370-3. It houses some portraits of the poet and several well-preserved friezes. One look at the views from the windows and you'll be waxing lyrical yourself.

Between Arquà Petrarca and Padua stand the spa resorts of **Abano Terme** and **Montegrotto** at the foot of the verdant Euganean Hills. Romans enjoyed the restorative powers of the area's volcanic springs and mud. Montegrotto is home to a butterfly farm: tiny tourists and budding lepidopterists will love **Butterfly Arc** (*see below*).

If you've packed walking boots, now is the time to use them: the Monte Grande pathway can be traversed by even the most urban hiker. Starting at **Passo Fiorine**, a two-hour trek along the Monte Grande takes you on a circuit of public footpaths. You'll be rewarded with a ruined castle and the lushest of panoramas. For information about trails and maps, ask at the IAT offices in either Padua or Abano Terme.

Six kilometres (four miles) west of Abano is the **Abbazia di Praglia** (*see below*). Though founded by Benedictine monks in the 12th century, the abbey's present buildings date from the 1400s. A friendly monk conducts guided tours every 40 minutes.

Abbazia di Praglia
Via Abbazia 16, Teolo (049 999 9300). **Open** *Last 2wks Jan* 2.30-4.30pm Sat, Sun. *Apr-Oct* 3.30-5.30pm Tue-Sun. *Nov-Mar* 2.30-4.30pm Tue-Sun. **Admission** free (donations welcome). Visit by guided tour only, every 40 mins. Group bookings possible in the mornings

Butterfly Arc
Via degli Scavi 21bis, Montegrotto Terme (049 891 0189/www.butterflyarc.it). **Open** *Feb-Nov* 9.30am-4.30pm daily. Closed Dec & Jan. **Admission** €7; €5 concessions. **Credit** AmEx, MC, V. Note that opening hours are subject to change.

Casa di Petrarca
Via Valleselle 4, Arquà Petrarca (0429 718 294). **Open** *Mar-Oct* 9am-noon, 3pm-18.30pm Tue-Sun. *Nov-Feb* 9am-noon, 2.30-5pm Tue-Sun. **Admission** (free with the Padovacard – see p242) €3; €1.50 concessions. **No credit cards**.

Tourist information

IAT
Terme Euganee Via P d'Abano 18, Abano Terme (049 866 9055/fax 049 866 9053/www.turismo termeeuganee.it). **Open** 8.30am-1pm, 2.30-7pm Mon-Sat; 10am-1pm, 3-6pm Sun.

Getting there

By car
Take the A13 Padua–Bologna motorway, turning off at Padova Sud for Abano, and 20km (12.5 miles) further south at the Terme Euganee exit for Arquà; Praglia is accessible by minor roads from Abano.

By train
Frequent services (approx every 20mins) to Terme Euganee and Montegrotto for Abano on the Padua–Bologna line.

By bus
ACAP city buses and SITA buses (*see p258*) run approximately every 15mins from Padua to Abano; SITA buses serve Montegrotto, Praglia and Arquà.

Monselice

Monselice is small and industrial; by far the most impressive site is the **Castello** (via del Santuario, 0429 72 931, guided tours only), a complex that includes the 13th-century Palazzo di Ezzelino, the Palazzo Marcello, an 18th-century chapel, and a crenellated structure built in the 15th century. Don't miss the **Santuario delle Sette Chiese** (open 10am-noon, 2-7pm daily), designed by Vincenzo Scamozzi, Palladio's brilliant pupil and erstwhile guide to Inigo Jones. Situated by the town's Porta Romana gate, the church was completed between 1592 and 1593, the chapels coming later in 1605.

Tourist information

IAT
Via del Santuario 6 (0429 783 026/www.comune. monselice.padova.it). **Open** 9.30am-12.30pm, 2.30pm-5.30pm Tues-Sun; 9.30am-12.30pm Mon.

Getting there

By car
Leave the A13 Padua–Bologna motorway at the Monselice exit.

By train
Direct services on the Padua–Bologna line.

By bus
SITA buses (*see p248*) run from Padua.

Este

The **Museo Nazionale Atestino**'s (Via Guido Negri 9, 0429 2085 open 9am-8pm daily; admission €2; €1 concessions) houses a rather lovely *Madonna and Child* by Cima da Conegliano. Turning west from the museum, you come to the **Duomo** (open 10am-noon, 4-6pm daily), which contains Giambattista Tiepolo's *St Thekla Interceding with God the Father to Free the City from the Plague* (1757).

Tourist information

Pro-Loco
Piazza Maggiore 9A (0429 3635). **Open** 9am-12.30pm Mon-Sat.

Getting there

By car
Take the A13 Padua–Bologna motorway, exiting at Monselice; take the SS10 from here to Este.

By train
Direct services on the Padua–Mantua line, or change at Monselice on the Padua–Bologna line.

By bus
By SITA (*see p248*) bus from Padua.

Montagnana

Montagnana is a picture postcard town. The preserved medieval walls were built between 1360 and 1362. Since 1996 the castle has housed the **Museo Antonio Giacomelli** with modest archeological, medieval and modern rooms.

The town boasts two other architectural gems. The first is Palladio's **Villa Pisani** (not open to the public but partly visible from outside). The second, inside the town walls, is the **Duomo** (open 8am-12.30pm, 4-7.30pm daily), a striking mix of Gothic and Renaissance. Begun in 1431, it was not consecrated until 1502. The present main portal, attributed to Jacopo Sansovino, was added in 1530. Above the main altar is a *Transfiguration* by Paolo Veronese, while on the second altar along the south wall is an altarpiece of the *Madonna and Child Enthroned*, considered one of the masterpieces of Giovanni Buonconsiglio.

However, the greatest curiosity is in the Rosary Chapel. In 1959 the baroque altar was removed to reveal original 15th-century frescoes, which form an esoteric astrological allegory, with two bears (ursa major and ursa minor) separated by the curls of a dragon (the draco constellation) alongside a representation of Pegasus and the ship of the Argonauts.

These astrological figures may represent a particular conjunction of the heavenly bodies relating to the Feast of the Annunciation. The iconography is similar to one at the Castle of Esztergom in Hungary; the 15th-century physician and astrologer Galeotto Marzio da Narni lived in both places for some time.

Museo Antonio Giacomelli
Castel San Zeno, piazza Trieste 15 (0429 804 128). **Open** (guided tours only) *Apr-Sept* 11am, noon, 4pm, 5pm, 6pm Wed-Fri; 10.30am, 11.30am, 1pm, 4pm, 5pm, 6pm Sat, Sun; *Oct-Mar* 11am Wed-Fri; 11am, noon, 3pm, 4pm, 5pm Sat, Sun. **Admission** €2.10; €1.60 concessions. **No credit cards**.

Tourist information

IAT Pro-Loco
Castel San Zeno, Piazza Trieste 15 (0429 81 320/ prolocomontagnana@tiscali.it). **Open** *Apr-Oct* 4-7pm Tue; 9.30am-12.30pm, 4-7pm Wed-Sun. *Nov-Mar* 3-6pm Tue; 9.30am-12.30pm, 3-6pm Wed-Sun.

Getting there

By car
Leave the A13 Padua–Bologna motorway at the Monselice exit, then take the SS10 to Montagnana.

By train
Services on the Padua–Mantua line.

By bus
SITA (*see p248*) buses run from Padua.

The Brenta canal

Stretching for 36km (22miles) between Venice and Padua, the Brenta was canalised in the 16th century. Goethe fondly enjoyed cruising down the Brenta canal in 1786, enjoying 'the banks studded with gardens and summer houses; small properties stretch down to the edge of the river and now and then the busy high road beside it'. Nowadays many of the formerly glorious gardens and summer houses have been replaced by housing estates and industrial sites.

A number of Palladian villas do still grace the canal, part of which can be navigated in a boat that chugs up the Brenta from Venice as far as Strà, where you are transferred on to a bus to Padua. The boat journey includes the *ville* Widmann, Pisani and **Foscari** (*see p251*). Villa Foscari, aka 'La Malcontenta', is one of the most acclaimed creations of Andrea Palladio. The origin of the villa's nickname is hotly disputed, but is said to refer to an unhappy ('*malcontenta*') woman who was housed there in isolation. Some say she was a disgraced Foscari

St Fernando of Lisbon?

St Anthony of Padua was not a local saint. He was born Fernando de Bulhões to noble parents near Lisbon in 1195. At 15 he joined the scholarly Augustinian order. But a visit from a group of Franciscan missionaries – subsequently martyred in Morocco – gave Fernando a yen for a more active life. In 1220 he switched to the Franciscan order, changed his name and set off for north Africa to preach the Faith to the Saracen hoards.

Poor health forced him back to Europe in 1221, when his ship was shipwrecked in Sicily. In a Franciscan convent near Forli he performed menial tasks until he was asked to preach to St Francis himself; amazed at the young man's previously undiscovered learning, wisdom and oratory skills, Francis dispatched him forthwith to stamp out the Albigensian and Cathar heresies rife in northern Italy and southern France. Anthony's fame spread not only

because of his fiery preaching, but through reports of miracles. In 1230 Anthony moved to Padua, where he preached passionately against heresy and usury. In 1231 he persuaded the city to pass a law in protecting debtors. Less than a year after his death in 1231 he was canonized.

Anthony is usually portrayed holding a lily or holding the infant Jesus. This latter refers to an incident in which someone putting the saint up during his travels noticed a celestial glow coming from his guest's room and peeked in to see Anthony chatting with a miraculous babe. He's the patron saint of sailors and travellers (having survived shipwreck to reach Italy) and of lost property and persons. The story supporting this one is feebler: a precious book of psalms belonging to the saint was purloined by a novice, who came penitently back to Anthony after some praying for the return of the tome.

wife; others that when the family abandoned the villa shortly after the fall of the Venetian Republic in 1797, rumours of a mysterious, outcast woman arose to keep undesirables away. With its double staircase and elegant Greek temple façade, the Villa Foscari has been the inspiration for thousands of buildings throughout Europe and America. The boat trip ends at the Villa Pisani in Strà, a remarkable design of the early to mid 18th century.

The more parsimonious traveller can enjoy a similar route at a fraction of the price by taking the ACTV No.53 bus (bound for Padua) from piazzale Roma, leaving at 25 and 55 minutes past the hour. From April-October, take advantage of the Pass Ville ticket, which costs €19 (€12 concessions) and allows entrance to the houses and gardens of Villa Pisani, Villa Widmann and the *barchesse* (large porticoed extensions) of Villa Valmarana, Villa Alessandri and Villa Foscarini Rossi. Buy it from these villas or at any APT tourist office in the area.

By car, take the SS11 from Mestre-Venezia to Padua, then the A4 motorway.

SITA – Divisione Navigazione 'il Burchiello'

Via Orlandini 3, Padua (049 820 6910/fax 049 820 6923/www.ilburchiello.it). **Services** *Mar-Oct* Venice–Padua departure from Pietà boat stop (near San Zaccaria, Venice) at 9am Tue, Thur, Sat; Padua–Venice departure from piazzale Boschetti at 8.15am on Wed, Fri, Sun. Closed Nov-Feb. **Rates**

€62, €31-€44 concessions (incl entrance to Villa Foscari and Barchessa Valmarana or Widmann and return SITA bus journey, but not Villa Pisani or return boat journey). **Lunch** three-course €24/light lunch €15. Booking online advisable, half-day programmes available upon request. **Credit** MC, V.

Villa Foscari 'La Malcontenta'

Via dei Turisti 9, Malcontenta (May-Oct 041 547 0012/Nov-Apr 041 520 3966/www.lamalcontenta. com). Bus 53 from piazzale Roma. **Open** *May-Oct* 9am-noon Tue, Sat; other times by appointment. **Admission** €7 Tue, Sat; other times €8; €6 concessions. **No credit cards**.

North of Padua

Located in the otherwise unremarkable little town of Piombino Dese, **Villa Cornaro** is one of the most satisfying and elegant of Palladio's free-standing, two-storey villas (as opposed to the elongated farmhouse style of the Villa Barbaro or Villa Emo, *for both see p277*). Constructed in 1552-3 for Giorgio Cornaro, it introduced to Western architecture the two-storey projecting portico-loggia motif and the aesthetically pleasing golden ratio.

Villa Cornaro

Via Roma 92, Piombino Dese (049 936 5017). SITA bus from Padua (piazzale Boschetto) for Trebaseleghe. 2 blocks from Piombino Dese train station, on the line between Venice and Padua **Open** May-Sept 3.30-6pm Sat; other times by appointment for groups only. **Admission** €5. **No credit cards**.

The Veneto

Verona

City of love, city of opera.

*'There is no world without Verona walls
But purgatory, torture, hell itself
Hence banished is banish'd from the world;
And world's exile is death.'*
Romeo and Juliet, Act III

Verona may conjure up tragic images of pubescent pining, but lovers' laments had rung out from the city long before the Bard made it his. Catullus, born in Verona in 84BC, longed to cover his Lesbia in so many kisses that he had to introduce a new word for kiss into Latin, borrowing *basium* from his native dialect. It was here that Dante completed *Paradiso*, where he finally meets his divine Beatrice; while Petrarch lamented the death of Laura 'while I was in Verona, alas ignorant of my fate'. Yet while undeniably romantic, Verona's citizens prefer to focus on their rich art, architecture and a history going back millennia.

After being colonised by the Romans in 89 BC, Verona became a frequent prize of conquest. By the 12th century, however, it had become an independent city-state. It reached its zenith in the 13th and 14th centuries when the home-grown Della Scala (or Scaligero) dynasty (hence the ladder in local coats-of-arms – *scala* in Italian means 'ladder'), brought a period of peace to the city, racked by Montague and Capulet-style family feuding. Patronage of the arts was the flip side of the Della Scala lust for power. The dynasty fell in 1387 and was replaced by Milan's Viscontis, superseded in turn by the Venetian Republic. Renaissance Verona lent its Venetian overlords its refined architect Sanmicheli and his protégé, Paolo Veronese. Only in 1866 did Verona rid itself of foreign rulers, when it joined the newly united Kingdom of Italy.

Sightseeing

Dominating the entrance to the old town in piazza Brà is the magnificent Roman **Arena** (*see p254*). Veronese architecture rests on its ancient Roman remains – literally. The streets were laid out to a grid plan decreed by Emperor Augustus; the Teatro Romano and ponte Pietra are further signs of the ancients. Many modern buildings stand on Roman foundations; some have fragments of Roman marble-work in their fabric, like the columns on the building opposite the Prada store in corso Borsari.

Verona's medieval architecture dates mostly from after the great north Italian earthquake of 1117. In the building boom that followed, the city was adorned with some of its finest buildings: the basilica of **San Zeno** (*see p257*), the **Duomo** (*see p256*) and the Gothic churches of **Sant'Anastasia** (*see p257*) and **San Fermo** (*see p256*). Ancient, medieval and modern are knitted together with the ever-present pink-tinged stone and marble.

The old town, nestling in the loops of the meandering **Adige River**, stretches out from piazza Brà. Overshadowed by the magnificent Arena, this large square is home to a number of cafés on the *Liston*, the Veronese promenade, and the **Museo Lapidario** (1.30-7.30pm Mon, 8.30am-7.30pm Tue-Sun), a small collection of Greek and Roman fragments and inscriptions. A short walk north-east from piazza Brà along via Mazzini takes you to the heart of the city in the adjoining squares, piazza delle Erbe and piazza dei Signori.

Once the site of the Roman forum, **piazza delle Erbe** is today the site of a somewhat tacky market (Mon-Sat), which nevertheless can't detract from the stunning surrounding buildings (all closed to the public). At the northern end is the huge 14th-century **Casa Mazzanti** with its splendid late Renaissance frescoes on the outer façade, the highly ornamented **Palazzo Maffei** and the medieval **Torre Gardello**, Verona's first clock tower, built in 1370. Dotted among the stalls are the gleaming 16th-century *Berlina*, under which public officials were invested with their office, and a fountain (1368), whose basin is of Roman origin, as is the body of the statue known as the 'Madonna Verona', which stands above it. The tall houses at the square's southern end once marked the edge of the Jewish ghetto.

A detour south-east out of piazza delle Erbe along via Cappello leads to **Casa di Giulietta** (Juliet's house, *see p256*). Further down via Cappello is the **Porta Leoni**, a fragment of a Roman city gate and now part of a medieval house; recent excavations have exposed the full extent of the towered and arched structure. Just over the bridge from here is the district where artist Paolo Veronese hailed from; the modern church of **San Paolo** (via XX Settembre 2, open 9-11.30am, 4.30-6pm daily) has one of his early works, the *Madonna and Saints*.

Verona

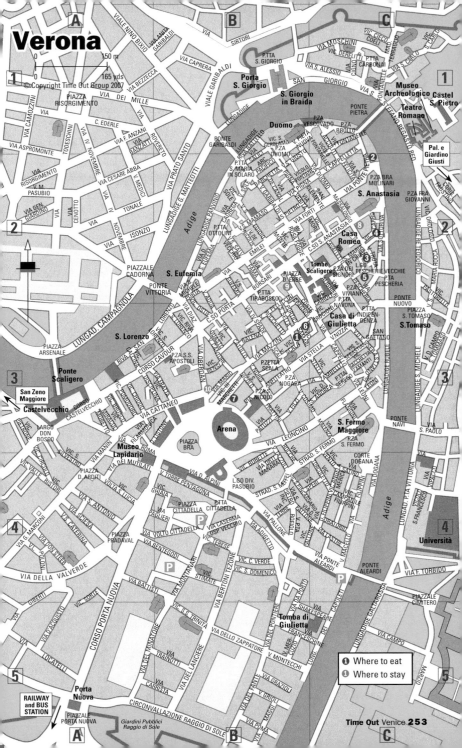

150 m
165 yds
© Copyright Time Out Group 2007

VIALE NINO BIXIO
VIA ANITA GARIBALDI
VIA SIRTORI
VIC. CIECO COEL
VIA MOSCHINI
VIC. DEREUTTI
P.TTA CARBONAI
VIC. S. CARLO
VIA S. FERRAIOLO

PIAZZA RISORGIMENTO
VIA BEZZECCA
VIA CAPRERA
VIALE GARIBALDI
VIA DEI MILLE
VIA DEL MILLE
P.TTA S. GIORGIO
VIA S. ALESSIO
VIA S. GIORGIO
SAN GIORGIO

Porta S. Giorgio

Museo Archeologico
Castel S. Pietro

C. EDERLE
VIA TODESCHINI
VIA IV NOVEMBRE
VIA F. ANZANI
VIA RANZANTI
VIA MEDICI

S. Giorgio in Braida

Teatro Romano

VIA ASPROMONTE
VIA CAMOZZINI

PONTE GARIBALDI
RIVA SAN LORENZO

Duomo
PZA VESCOVADO
PZA BROLO
PZA DUOMO
PONTE PIETRA
PONTE NUOVO

Pal. e Giardino Giusti

VIA RISORGIMENTO
VIA C. CESARE ABBA
VIA PRATO SANTO
LUNGADIGE G. MATTEOTTI

VIA GEN GIARDINO
VIA IV NOVEMBRE
ISONZO
TONALE
LUNGADIGE PALLONE

Adige

P.ZA BRA MOLINARI
PZA FRA GIOVANNI

S. Anastasia

PIAZZALE CADORNA
S. Eufemia
PONTE VITTORIA

Casa Romeo

PIAZZA D'ERBE
Tombe Scaligere
PZA DEI SIGNORI
PESCHERIE VECCHIE
P.TA PESCHERIA

PONTE NUOVO
PIAZZA S. TOMASO

S. Lorenzo
CORSO CAVOUR
PZA S.S. APOSTOLI

Casa di Giulietta
SAN GAETANO
S. Tomaso

PIAZZA ARSENALE
Ponte Scaligero

San Zeno Maggiore
Castelvecchio
CORSO CASTELVECCHIO
CORSO PORTA
VIA CATTANEO

PZETTA SCALA
PZA NOGARA
PZA S. NICOLO

S. Fermo Maggiore
PZA S. FERMO

PONTE NAVI
VIA S. PAOLO

LARGO DON BOSCO

Arena
Museo Lapidario
PIAZZA BRA

CORTE DOGANA
VIA DOGANA

PIAZZA D. ARDITI
PIAZZA CITTADELLA
P.TTA CITTADELLA

VIA D. ALPINI
L.GO DIV. PASUBIO

Adige

PIAZZA PRADAVAL

VIA CASERMA OSP. VECCHIO

Università

VIA VOLTO CITTADELLA
VIA BENTEGODI
VIC. TERESE
VIC. C. VERDE
VIC. S. DOMENICO

PONTE ALEARDI
VIA PONTE ALEARDI

VIA DELLA VALVERDE
VIA BATTISTI

VIA F. TORBIDO

PIAZZALE CIMITERO

VIC. SORTE
VIC. S.S. TRINITA

Tomba di Giulietta

VIA DELLO ZAPPATORE
VIA FRANCESCHINE

Porta Nuova

RAILWAY and BUS STATION
PIAZZALE PORTA NUOVA

CIRCONVALLAZIONE RAGGIO DI SOLE
Giardini Pubblici Raggio di Sole

❶ **Where to eat**
① **Where to stay**

Verona's **Arena**.

The heart of medieval Verona's governance and finance, piazza dei Signori, contains the 15th-century **Loggia del Consiglio** (closed to the public) topped by statues of illustrious Veronese gentlemen, including Catullus. From one of its eight elegant arches – Arco della Costa – hangs a whale bone, which local legend holds will fall if an adult virgin passes beneath.

The town is quietly boastful about the fact that Dante lived in exile at the court of the Della Scala family from 1304 and dedicated *Paradiso* to one of the city's 'top dogs', Cangrande I. Linking *piazze* delle Erbe and dei Signori is the 12th-century **Palazzo della Ragione**. Once the civic centre of the Veronese city state, as this guide went to press it was closed for renovation and conversion to an exhibition and museum space, due to be completed in spring 2007.

A gateway on the piazza dei Signori side of the palazzo leads into the **Mercato Vecchio** courtyard, with its huge Romanesque arches and magnificent outdoor Renaissance staircase. The palazzo is dominated by the medieval 83-metre-high **Torre dei Lamberti** (1462; also due to reopen in spring 2007). From the next courtyard on the right you can descend into the archeological site of the **Scavi Scaligeri** (*see p258*). At the eastern exit from piazza dei Signori are the Della Scala family tombs (**tombe** or **arche scaligere**, *see p258*).

Moving northwards, the peaceful, narrow streets are a captivating labyrinth dotted with medieval and Renaissance *palazzi*. In via Pigna, take a look at the carved marble Roman pine cone (*pigna*) before heading north down via San Giacomo alla Pigna towards the Duomo, or south towards the imposing church of Sant'Anastasia. Close by, ponte Pietra is Verona's oldest bridge and for centuries was the only link between the city centre and the suburbs beyond. The two stone arches on the left bank of the river are Roman and date back to before 50 BC. The other three brick arches date from between 1200 and 1500. The bridge was reconstructed using original stones in 1957 after being destroyed by retreating Germans.

The ponte Pietra leads across the river to some of Verona's most beautiful churches – including **San Giorgio in Braida** (*see p257*) and **Santa Maria in Organo** (*see p257*) – as well as the **Museo Archeologico** (*see p256*) and the remains of the **Teatro Romano** (*see p258*). The area around Castel San Pietro (closed to the public) – part of the city's medieval and Renaissance fortifications, heavily redesigned by Austrian occupiers in the mid 19th century – offers a bird's-eye view of the city. Head south-east from the bridge along regaste Redentore and its continuations for the pretty **Giardino Giusti** (*see p256*). Back towards the river is the church of San Tommaso, where Mozart, aged 13, played the organ on his visit to the city, birthplace of his future archrival, Salieri.

Corso Porta Borsari, Roman Verona's busy main street, leads out of the north end of piazza delle Erbe towards the **Porta Borsari**, the best-preserved of the city's Roman gates; it probably dates from the reign of Emperor Claudius (AD 41-54). In a small garden along corso Cavour is the **Arco dei Gavi**, a triumphal arch attributed to Vitruvius, dating from about 50 BC. The medieval fortress of **Castelvecchio** (*see p256*), adorned with swallow-tail battlements, hosts a museum and gives on to the ponte Scaligero, the other stone bridge crossing the Adige.

The stunning basilica di San Zeno, home to Verona's patron saint, is located outside the centre, to the west of piazza Brà.

TICKETS

An admission fee is charged by some churches and all museums in Verona. Cut costs by purchasing a Verona Card (€8 for one day, €12 for three days), valid for all the sights that charge. It can be bought at the exchange office in the station or ticket offices of any of the churches or museums participating in the scheme, and includes all bus fares around the city. No credit cards accepted.

A second scheme (the *itinerario completo*) offers entrance to five of Verona's churches (San Zeno, San Lorenzo, Sant'Anastasia, San Fermo and the Duomo) for €5, €4 concessions.

Arena

Piazza Brà (045 800 3204). **Open** 1.45-7.30pm Mon; 8.30am-7.30pm Tue-Sun (ticket office shuts one hour earlier; closes at 4.30pm during opera season).

The Veneto

Admission €4; €3 concessions. For opera booking details, *see p258*. **No credit cards. Map** p253 B3.
The largest Roman amphitheatre in northern Italy, Verona's Arena was capacious enough to seat the city's whole population of 20,000 when it was constructed in about AD 30. The 44 tiers of stone seats inside the 139m x 110m (456ft x 361ft) amphitheatre are virtually intact, as is the columned foyer. After the earthquake of 1117 destroyed most of the Arena's outer ring (the remaining four arches are known as the 'ala') the city repaired the damage almost immediately. Originally the site of gladiatorial games and – filled with water for the occasion – naval battles, it was used by post-Roman inhabitants as a shelter during fifth- and sixth-century Barbarian invasions. Medieval *veronesi* used it as a red-light district and home to the city's cut-throats. Later, city masters used the Arena as law court and site of the occasional execution. It functioned as theatre in the 17th and 18th centuries, hosted circuses and hot-air balloon launches in the 19th and was used as a football stadium in the early 20th century.

Casa di Giulietta (Juliet's house)
Via Cappello 23 (045 803 4303). **Open** 1.30-7.30pm Mon; 8.30am-7.30pm Tue-Sun. **Admission** €4; €3 concessions. **No credit cards. Map** p253 C3.
The *veronesi* may believe that San Zeno (*see p257*) is the city's symbol; millions of tourists think otherwise. Yes, the Montagues and Capulets were real enough, but no, the Capulets never lived in the so-called Casa di Giulietta. Nonetheless, tourists have long crowded the courtyard below for photo

I yearn for Sirmione…

Just 30 kilometres from Verona lie the shores of Italy's largest lake: **Garda**, 'beautiful as Paradise' according to DH Lawrence. The lake's jewel is the southern peninsula of **Sirmione**, with the 13th-century Scaligero castle standing guard. From here, narrow pedestrian streets lead past the Romanesque church of San Pietro in Mavino to the **Grotte di Catullo**, ruins of a well-to-do Roman resort (Catullus' family had a villa here). Behind this is the villa Maria Callas escaped to when the glam opera world became too oppressive.

From Sirmione, head through the fortress town of Peschiera and take the Gardesana Orientale road past Gardaland, Italy's biggest theme park, to the pretty port of **Lazise**; enclosed in swallow-tailed castle walls, this was once Venice's main lake port. *La Serenissima*'s customs house can still be seen by the harbour, next to the Romanesque church of San Nicolò, protector of fishermen.

An obligatory stop for oenophiles, especially during the annual 'grape cure' in September, is the next town up the coast, **Bardolino**. Visit the vineyards along the Bardolino wine road (SP31) out of Lazise via Calmasino and Cavaion, or follow the road hugging the lake, past the **Museo dell'Olio d'Oliva** (olive oil museum; 9am-12.30pm; 2.30-7pm Mon-Sat; 9am-12.30pm Sun), where you can taste the area's other main product, which gives this stretch its name, the *Riviera degli ulivi*.

In Bardolino, the eighth-century San Zeno and 12th-century frescoes at San Severo both merit a visit before stopping off at the stylish **Enoteca del Bardolino** (piazza Principe Amedeo 3-4, 045 721 1585, www.enoteca delbardolino.it, open 10am-1am daily) on the lakefront for lunch. Between the next resort towns of Garda and Torri del Benaco nestles the cypress-tipped promontory, **Punta di San Vigilio**, with its gorgeous Renaissance villa by Sanmicheli. Park at the top, and head for the lakeside park of **Baia delle Sirene** (mermaid bay, 045 725 6676, www.parcobaiadelle sirene.it). For €10 a day or €2 an hour you get a sunlounger to set up on the pebble beach or the shady olive terraces. A cobbled street leads down to a hotel and taverna (045 725 5190, www.punta-sanvigilio.it, closed Nov-Mar, average €70), probably the most romantic (if pricey) meal on the lake.

Further north, before the Mediterranean landscape gives way to the sheer cliffs of the Trentino region is **Malcesine**, where narrow medieval streets cling to the lakeside beneath a castle (closed Sun, admission €4). Climb to the top of the castle for breathtaking views over the lake. For even more dramatic views, a 10-minute cable car ride (045 740 0206, www.funiviedelbaldo.it, departs every 30mins, €16 return) takes you up to the 1783m peak of **Monte Baldo**, from which walkers, mountain bikers, parascenders (and skiers in winter) all make their way down. Malcesine's lakeside bars and eateries offer the perfect place to watch the sun set before heading home. Alternatively, rest up for the night and take the car ferry in the morning across to **Limone**, unsurprisingly famous for its lemons but also for the population's total lack of heart disease. From here you can take another day to explore the lake's western shore as you head back down south. Like Callas, you may already have begun to 'yearn for Sirmione'.

The Veneto

Scribbled love letters at **Juliet's house**. *See p255.*

opportunities, hoping that a quick grope of a bronze statue of Juliet will bring some luck in love. An admission fee allows you inside to pen and post your own letter to Juliet, before taking a quick bow on the balcony (a 1920s addition). Romeo's house – which at least may have actually belonged to the Montague family – is tastefully not open to the public just across from the Della Scala tombs (*see p258*) at Arche Scaligere 4 (map p253 C2).

Castelvecchio
Corso Castelvecchio 2 (045 806 2611/www.comune. verona.it/castelvecchio/cvsito). **Open** 1.30-7.30pm Mon; 8.30am-7.30pm Tue-Sun. **Admission** €4; €3 concessions. **No credit cards. Map** p253 A3.
The Della Scala family came to power in the 13th century as a result of the Guelf-Ghibelline conflicts that shaped so much of northern Italian politics in the Middle Ages. By the time Duke Cangrande II began building the castle in 1355, the family needed a fortress for waging war and a refuge from overtaxed Veronese citizens: ponte Scaligero, the magnificent fortified medieval bridge, was intended as an emergency escape route.

The castle is now a museum and exhibition venue, with interiors beautifully redesigned in the 1960s by Venetian architect Carlo Scarpa. The museum itself contains important works by Mantegna, Crivelli, Pisanello, Giovanni Bellini, Veronese, Tintoretto, Gianbattista Tiepolo, Canaletto and Guardi, plus a magnificent collection of 13th- and 14th-century Veronese religious statuary. An armoury and local jewellery complete the collection.

Duomo
Piazza Duomo (045 592 813/www.chieseverona.it). **Open** *Mar-Oct* 10am-5.30pm Mon-Sat; 1.30-5.30pm Sun. *Nov-Feb* 10am-1pm;1.30-4pm Tue-Sat; 1-5pm Sun. **Admission** €2.50. **No credit cards. Map** p253 B3.
Verona's cathedral, begun in 1139, is Romanesque downstairs, Gothic upstairs and Renaissance at the top half of the bell tower. The elegant front portico is decorated with Romanesque carvings of the finest quality, showing Charlemagne's paladins Oliver and Roland (feature players in the medieval epic *Chanson de Roland*). Inside, the first chapel on the left has a magnificent *Assumption* by Titian and an altar by Jacopo Sansovino. In the same complex is the ancient church of Sant'Elena, with the remains of an earlier Christian basilica and Roman baths. And, at the back of the cathedral, to the right of its graceful apse, is the chapel of San Giovanni in Fonte, with a large, carved, octagonal, Romanesque, baptismal font. On the right as you leave the church is the Biblioteca Capitolare, one of the oldest libraries in the world, where Petrarch discovered letters by Cicero.

Giardino Giusti
Via Giardino Giusti 2 (045 803 4029). **Open** *Apr-Sept* 9am-8pm daily. *Oct-Mar* 9am-7pm daily. **Admission** €5. **No credit cards. Map** off p253 2C.
The façades of one of Verona's most traffic-clogged streets hide one of the finest Renaissance gardens in Italy. Tucked behind the great Renaissance townhouse of the Giusti family – the Palazzo Giusti del Giardino – the statue-packed gardens with their tall cypresses were laid out in 1580. The wild upper level climbs the steep slopes of the hill behind, which offers superb viewing and picnic opportunities.

Museo Archeologico
Regaste Redentore 2 (045 800 0360/www. comune.verona.it/castelvecchio/cvsito/mcivici2.htm). **Open** 1.30-7.30pm Mon; 8.30am-7.30pm Tue-Sun. **Admission** €3; €2 concessions (includes Teatro Romano, *see p258*). **No credit cards. Map** p253 C1.
This small museum contains a fine collection of Roman remains. Situated in a former monastery, the museum offers incomparable views over Verona and the River Adige. **Photo** *p257.*

San Fermo Maggiore
Stradone San Fermo (045 592 813/www.chiese verona.it). **Open** *Mar-Oct* 10am-6pm Mon-Sat; 1-6pm Sun. *Nov-Feb* 10am-4pm Tue-Sat; 1.30-5pm Sun. **Admission** €2.50. **No credit cards. Map** p253 C3.

The Veneto

At San Fermo you get two churches for the price of one: the intimate and solemn lower church is romanesque and the upper church, towering and full of light, is Gothic. Its wooden ceiling resembles an upturned Venetian galleon. Among the important frescoes is an *Annunciation* by Antonio Pisanello to the left of the main entrance.

San Giorgio in Braida

Piazzetta San Giorgio 1 (045 834 0232). **Open** 8am-11am, 5-7pm Mon-Sat; 9.15am-10.30am; 5-7.30pm Sun. **Map** p253 B1.

This great domed Renaissance church, probably designed by the Veronese military architect Michele Sanmicheli between 1536 and 1543, contains some of the city's greatest treasures. Shining in this light-filled masterpiece are a *Baptism of Christ* by Tintoretto, above the entrance door, and a moving *Martyrdom of St George* by Paolo Veronese. But even these greats are put in the shade by a serene *Madonna and Child with Saints Zeno and Lawrence* by local dark horse Girolamo dai Libri.

Santa Maria in Organo

Piazzetta Santa Maria in Organo (045 591 440). **Open** 8am-noon, 2.30-6pm Mon, Tue, Thur, Sat, Sun; 8am-noon Wed, Fri. **Map** off p253 C2.

This Renaissance church has a host of frescoes by local painters. Pass them by and make your way to the apse and sacristy to see what Giorgio Vasari described as the most beautiful choir stalls in Italy. A humble monk, Fra Giovanni da Verona (d.1520), worked for 25 years cutting and assembling these infinitely complex, coloured, wooden images of animals, birds, landscapes, cityscapes, religious scenes and musical and scientific instruments in dozens of intricate intarsia panels.

Sant'Anastasia

Piazza Sant'Anastasia (045 592 813/www.chiese verona.it). **Open** *Mar-Oct* 9am-6pm Mon-Sat; 1-6pm Sun. *Nov-Feb* 10am-4pm Tue-Sat; 1-5pm Sun. **Admission** €2.50. **No credit cards**. **Map** p253 C2.

This imposing brick Gothic church is best visited early in the morning, when sunlight streams in to illuminate Antonio Pisanello's glorious fresco (1433-38; above the terracotta-clad Pelligrini chapel) of St George girding himself to set off in pursuit of the dragon that has been pestering the lovely princess of Trebizond. Carved scenes from the life of St Peter Martyr adorn the unfinished façade, while inside, two delightful *gobbi* (hunchbacks) crouch down to support the holy water font; the one on the left was carved by Paolo Veronese's father in 1495. On the left of the church stands the tiny, deconsecrated San Pietro in Martire (San Giorgetto dei Domenicani), with three Gothic funerary monuments on its exterior. It is sometimes opened by volunteers to let the public see the fragments of frescoes inside. **Photo** *p260.*

San Tomaso Cantuariense

Piazza San Tomaso 1 (045 803 356). **Open** 8am-noon; 4-7.30pm daily. **Map** p253 C3.

Dedicated to the martyred archbishop of Canterbury, this 16th-century church was designed by Sanmicheli, who is buried here. It contains works by local artists and the recently restored Bonatti organ, which the young Mozart played in 1770.

San Zeno Maggiore

Piazza San Zeno 2 (045 592 813/www.chieseverona. it). **Open** *Mar-Oct* 8.30am-6pm Mon-Sat; 1-6pm Sun. *Nov-Feb* 10am-4pm Tue-Sat; 1-5pm Sun. **Admission** €2.50. **No credit cards**. **Map** off p253 A3.

One of the most spectacularly ornate Romanesque churches in northern Italy, this was built between 1123 and 1138 to house the tomb and shrine of San Zeno, an African who became Verona's first bishop in 362 and is now the city's much-loved patron saint.

The façade, with its great rose window and porch, is covered with some of Italy's finest examples of Romanesque marble sculpture. Scenes from the Old Testament and the life of Christ mingle with hunting and jousting scenes, attributed to the 12th-century sculptors Nicolò and Guglielmo. The graceful porch is supported by columns resting on two carved marble lions; they serve as a frame for the great bronze doors of the basilica; nicknamed 'the poor man's bible', the 48 panels have scenes from the Bible and from the life of San Zeno, and a few that experts have been hard-pressed to pin down, including a woman suckling two crocodiles. The panels on the left-hand door date from about 1030 and came from an earlier church. Inside the lofty church (note the magnificent ceiling built in 1386), a staircase descends into the crypt, which contains the tomb of San Zeno. The magnificent Mantegna triptych which dominated the altar has alas, been packed off to Florence and isn't expected to return until 2010. The enduring love affair between San Zeno and the city that adopted him may have something to do with the huge early 12th-century marble

The view from the **Museo Archeologico**. *See p256.*

From Callas to camels... the show goes on

While the bloodshed and torment that filled Verona's **Arena** (*see p255*) over 2000 years ago are now purely theatrical, the spectacle has remained, with stagings of classics by Puccini, Bizet, Verdi and co every night from June to September. The best to see are the grand-scale productions with huge choruses and spectacular sets. The atmosphere is charged with excitement as music lovers start squeezing onto the (unnumbered) stone terraces (bottom price €10) a good two hours before the performance begins (9.15pm June and July; 9pm August.)

Some might have already eaten at the self-service restaurant **Brek** (*see p259*) right opposite in piazza Brà. Others stock up at the local supermarket and settle down with their picnics. All bring or rent (€2) a cushion as a night perched on a two-millenia-old piece of marble can seem long and painful. Occupants of the *poltronissime*, the red-cushioned stalls seats, can saunter in just before the show commences, perhaps after having tucked into one of the pre-opera menus in the courtyard of the baroque ristorante **Maffei** (*see p259*) nearby. Armani-clad industrialists show off their expensive seats (top price €157) and

their even more expensive consorts. Differences dissipate as darkness descends; a hush falls over the 15,000-capacity crowd as the overture is played to the flickering of *mocoleti*, the candles traditionally lit all around the amphitheatre for the prelude.

In the Arena's 80-plus-year operatic history, divas such as Renata Tebaldi, Angela Gheorghin and Maria Callas – who made her international debut here as La Gioconda in 1947 – have all trod the boards, together with tenors from Beniamino Gigli to José Carreras. Scenic extravaganzas have been staged, with designers such as Franco Zeffirelli called upon to recreate the River Nile or Sevillian mountains. Casts of hundreds have included horses, elephants and even camels, one of which managed to escape one year and lope off around town.

Centre stage drama once turned into a backstage fracas when director Roberto Rossellini conjured up over-realistic smoke effects during a performance of *Othello*, nearly choking the leading man, tenor Mario del Monaco. The fuming *divo* won the day and Rossellini was sent packing before the show would go on; while fully front stage tragedy

---

statue of the African bishop having a grand old chuckle, which is found in a niche to the left of the apse. His black face, with its distinctly African features, is unique in Italian religious statuary. When he wasn't converting Veronese souls to Christianity he is held to have spent his time fishing in the River Adige, seated on a rock in front of the (now closed) San Zeno Minore church nearby. Covering the inside walls of the basilica are frescoes dating from the 12th to the 14th centuries, but perhaps more interesting than the paintings themselves is the 15th- to 17th-century graffiti scratched into them.

To the right of the church is a massive bell tower, 72m (236ft) high, begun in 1045. To the left is a lower tower, which is all that remains of the Benedictine monastery that stood on the site before the basilica was built, and which, according to local lore, stands over the grave of Pepin, Charlemagne's disinherited hunchback son. Behind is a Romanesque cloister.

Scavi Scaligeri

Corte del Tribunale (piazza Viviani) (045 800 7490 www.comune.verona.it/scavi scaligeri). **Open** 10am-7pm Tues-Sun. **Admission** €4.10. **No credit cards.** **Map** p253 A2.

The excavations are a good place to get a feel for the city's historical layering as you move between Roman mosaics and roads, interspersed at random with medieval and Lombard remains.

Teatro Romano

Regaste Redentore 2 (045 800 0360/www.comune. verona.it/Castelvecchio/cvsito). **Open** 1.30-7.30pm Mon; 8.30am-7.30pm Tue-Sun. **Admission** €3; €2 concessions (includes Museo Archeologico, *see p256*). **No credit cards.** **Map** p253 C1.

The Roman theatre, dating from around the first century BC, was buried under medieval houses until the late 19th century. The theatre offers beautiful views over the city and is an evocative venue for an annual festival of theatre (Shakespeare is a perennial favourite), ballet and jazz. For programme and booking details contact Estate Teatrale Veronese (045 807 7201, www.estateteatraleveronese.it). Tickets cost €8-€28 and can also be purchased at the *teatro* immediately before performances.

Tombe or Arche Scaligere (Della Scala family tombs)

Via Santa Maria in Chiavica. (Closed though visible from outside). **Map** p253 C2.

turned to comedy more recently when a voluptuous 'calamity' Carmen fell out of her costume, taking the puff out of her dying gasp.

But even the rare glitches can't detract from the show; hours of magical music with natural acoustics and the stunning setting make a night in the world's largest open air opera house a matchless experience.

After the final curtain, the crowd go their separate ways with the final notes still ringing in their ears; some go off to star-spot at the **Liston** (see below), where cast and conductors are known to eat after the show. Others dive into the narrow street behind the Arena for dinner at the **Bacaro** on Tre Marchetti (see below), which has served meals since 1291, or to the simpler Bacaro dell'Arena. Those who've already booked at the **Bottega del Vino** (see below), have Veronese dishes awaiting them with a choice of over 3,000 wines to uncork as they discuss the show. Wherever they go, all will agree that the evening under the stars in a 2,000-year-old theatre can only be described as pure magic.

Fondazione Arena di Verona

Via Dietro l'Anfiteatro 6B (045 800 5151/ www.arena.it). **Performances** *June-Aug* 9pm Tue-Sun. **Tickets** €10-€157. **Credit** AmEx, DC, MC, V.

Seats are sometimes available on the day of the show, especially midweek.

Antica Bottega del Vino

Via Scudo di Francia 3 (045 800 4535/ www.bottegavini.it) **Open** 10.30am-3pm, 6pm-midnight (3am on opera nights) Mon, Wed-Sun. **Average** €50. **Credit** AmEx, DC, MC, V.

Brek

Piazza Brà 20 (045 800 4561). **Open** 10.30am-3pm, 6-10pm daily. **Average** €15; kids' menu €4.40 **Credit** AmEx, DC, MC, V.

Il Bacaro dell'Arena

Vicolo Tre Marchetti 1B (045 590 503). **Open** noon-3pm, 6.30pm-midnight Tue-Sun (2.30am on opera nights). **Average** €25. **Credit** MC, V.

Liston

Via Dietro Liston 19 (045 800 4515). **Open** noon-2.30pm, 6.30-11pm (later on opera nights) Mon, Tue, Thur-Sun. **Average** €30 **Credit** AmEx, MC, V.

PAM supermarket

Via dei Mutilati 3 (045 803 2822). **Open** 8am-8pm daily. **Credit** AmEx, DC, MC, V.

Ristorante Maffei

Piazza delle Erbe 38 (045 801 0015/www. ristorantemaffei.it). **Open** noon-2.30pm, 7-10.30pm Mon-Sat; pre-opera menus from 6.30pm (€40-45 without wine). **Closed** Sun in Oct-Mar. **Credit** AmEx, DC, MC, V.

The Gothic tombs of medieval Verona's 'top dogs', the Della Scala family, date from 1277 to the final years of the 14th century and give a good idea of the family's sense of its own importance. Carved by the most sought-after stonemasons of the era, the more lavish tombs are topped with spires. Note the family's odd taste in first names. The monument to Cangrande (Big Dog, d.1329) above the doorway to the church of Santa Maria Antica, shows the valiant duke smiling in the face of death, guarded by crowned dogs. (This is a copy; the original is in the Castelvecchio, see p256.). Poking out from above the fence are the spire-topped final resting places of Cansignorio (Lord Dog, d.1375) and Mastino II (Mastiff the Second, d.1351). Among the less flamboyant tombs is that of Mastino I (d.1277), founder of the doggy dynasty.

Next door, the intimate church of Santa Maria Antica (open 7.30am-noon, 3.30-7pm daily) was the Della Scala family chapel. Indirectly, the church has lent its name to Milan's famous opera house *La Scala;* when Beatrice Regina della Scala married and moved to Milan, she had her own prayer chapel built there in 1381, modelled on and named after this chapel, on the site of the future opera house.

Where to eat

Verona's cuisine is a mix of Middle European heft and Italian sensibility. Boiled and roasted meats are popular, served up with *cren*, the local take on horseradish sauce, and *peará*, made of bone marrow, bread and pepper. Braised horse meat (*pastissada de caval*) is another local speciality, as is donkey *ragù*. Vegetarians take heart: *bigoli*, a sort of thick spaghetti, is often served with meat-free sauces, and local farms yield excellent vegetables. Pumpkin-stuffed ravioli is a speciality.

The vineyards around Verona produce some of Italy's most recognisable wine exports: Soave, Bardolino and Valpolicella. These names are known more for their undiscerning Bridget Jones-type quaffing qualities than for their heft. In fact, the Veronese take their wine very seriously (the ultra-serious Vinitaly takes place in Verona's fairgrounds every spring; see www.veronafiere.it for information), keeping the lightweight export names for everyday use and the better-kept secrets like Amarone and Valpolicella Classico for special occasions.

The Veneto

Sant'Anastasia, *See p257.*

Ristorante Al Cristo

Piazzetta Pescheria 6 (045 594 287/www.ristorante alcristo.it). **Meals served** noon-2.30pm; 7-11pm Tues-Sun. **Average** €80. **Credit** AmEx, DC, MC, V. **Map** p253 C2 ❺
Fish fiends can feast on sushi and sashimi, oysters and Iranian caviar. Booking advisable at weekends.

Ristorante Greppia

Vicolo Samaritana 3 (045 800 4577/www.ristorante greppia.com). **Meals served** noon-2.30pm, 6.30-10.30pm Tue-Sun. Closed 2wks June. **Average** €35. **Credit** AmEx, DC, MC, V. **Map** p253 B3 ❻
Off via Mazzini, this Verona institution serves up some of the best renditions in town of local classics.

Trattoria Tre Marchetti

Vicolo Tre Marchetti 19B (045 803 0463). **Meals served** *June-Sept* noon-2.30pm, 6.30-10.30pm daily; *July, Aug* noon-2.30pm; 6.30-2am Tue-Sun. Closed 2wks June, 1wk Sept. **Average** €50. **Credit** MC, V. **Map** p253 B3 ❼
Meals have been served on these premises since 1291, making it one of the most ancient eateries in Europe. It has lost none of its allure over the centuries: informal and crowded, with specialities of *bigoli* with duck, *pastissada de caval* and *baccalà* (cod) *alla vicentina*. Booking is advisable.

Where to stay

Hotels fill up during the opera season, so it's best to book in advance. **CAV** (via Patuzzi 5, 045 800 9844, fax 045 800 9372, www.cav.vr.it, open 10am-7pm Mon-Sat) runs a free hotel-booking bureau.

Campeggio Castel San Pietro

Via Castel San Pietro 2 (045 592 037/www.camping castelsanpietro.com). Bus 41 or 95 from the station, get off at first stop in via Marsala. **Rates** €6-€8 per plot; €6.50 per person; €4.50 under-8s. Closed mid Oct- Apr. **No credit cards.**
This camp site is in a stunning position 15 minutes' walk from the centre.

Due Torri Hotel Baglioni

Piazza Sant'Anastasia 4 (045 595 044/fax 045 800 4130/www.baglionihotels.com). **Rates** €160-€430 single; €230-€550 double. **Credit** AmEx, DC, MC, V. **Map** p253 C2 ❽
This celebrated hotel (Beethoven, Mozart and Goethe have been among its guests) is widely considered to be the city's finest. Some of the rooms let guests go eyeball to eyeball with Gugliemo di Castelvarco, whose tomb tops the archway across from the hotel.

Hotel Aurora

Piazzetta XIV Novembre 2 (045 594 717/fax 045 801 0860/www.hotelaurora.biz). **Rates** €56-€120 single; €98-€140 double. **Credit** AmEx, DC, MC, V. **Map** p253 B2 ❾
This simple hotel is friendly and efficiently run and has a great terrace for people-watching.

Bottega del Vino

Via Scudo di Francia 3 (045 800 4535/www.bottega vini.it). **Meals served** 10.30am-3pm, 6pm-midnight Mon, Wed-Sun. **Average** €45. **Credit** AmEx, DC, MC, V. **Map** p253 B3 ❶
Open the heavy wooden door to find a bustling, flamboyantly decorated dining room which serves up excellent local dishes, including *pastissada de caval,* and an amazing selection of wines.

Cappa Caffè

Piazzetta Brà Molinari 1A (corner of via Ponte Pietra) (045 800 4516/www.cappacafe.it). **Open** 9am-2am daily. **Credit** AmEx, DC, MC, V. **Map** p253 C2 ❷
A great place for an early evening drink on its terrace, with views of the ponte Pietra and across the Adige to the Teatro Romano and cypress-clad hillside above. It livens up later on with a young crowd.

Hostaria La Vecchia Fontanina

Piazzetta Chiavica 5 (045 591 159). **Meals served** noon-2.30pm, 7-10.30pm Mon-Sat. **Average** €25. **Credit** AmEx, DC, MC, V. **Map** p253 C2 ❸
Popular with savvy locals and a good option for non-donkey-eating vegetarians, this eatery serves a varied menu of creative versions of local specialities, including *bigoli* with nettles.

Ostaria Sottoriva

Via Sottoriva 9A (045 801 4323). **Meals served** noon-2pm, 5-10.30pm Mon, Tue, Thur-Sun. **Average** €20. **Credit** MC, V. **Map** p253 C2 ❹
Under the porticos in a picturesque street, this traditional Veronese *osteria* is proud of its venerable status. The menu is simple and traditional and there's a good selection of wines, but they don't serve anything as newfangled as coffee.

The Veneto

Hotel Bologna
Piazzetta Scalette Rubiani 3 (045 800 6830/fax 045 801 0602/www.hotelbologna.vr.it). **Rates** €62-€125 single; €80-€185 double. **Credit** AmEx, DC, MC, V. **Map** p253 B3 ⑩
A comfortable hotel in a perfect spot for exploring.

Residence Antico San Zeno
Via Rosmini 15 (045 800 3463/www.residence anticosanzeno.it). **Rates** €80-€110 single; €90-€130 double. **Credit** AmEx, DC, MC, V. **Map** off p253 A3.
Just around the corner from the church of San Zeno, this quiet and beautifully restored hotel has enormous rooms and mini-apartments for up to five people, all with their own cooking facilities. During the opera season and important trade fairs, prices here almost double.

Resources

Tourist information

IAT *Via degli Alpini 9 (045 806 8680/fax 045 800 3638/www.tourism.verona.it).* **Open** 9am-7pm Mon-Sat; 9am-3pm Sun.
IAT *Railway station, piazza XXV Aprile (tel/fax 045 800 0861).* **Open** 9am-7pm Mon-Sat; 9am-3pm Sun.
IAT *Verona airport (tel/fax 045 861 9163).* **Open** 9am-6pm Mon-Sat.

Getting around

By bus
AMT (045 887 1111/www.amt.it) runs the city bus service (orange buses), most of which start and terminate at Porta Nuova. Tickets can be purchased at any tobacconist's. A €1 ticket is valid for one hour and should be punched on each bus boarded.
The **APT Verona bus company** (045 805 7911/www.aptv.it) runs services (blue coaches) to towns in the area around Verona, including Lake Garda and the Monti Lessini. Buses depart from the bus station, in front of Porta Nuova train station.

By bicycle
The tourist office at the station (*see above*) offers bikes for free. Leave a passport or another document and get the bike back before the office closes.

Getting there

By air
See p285.

By train
Regular services from Milan and Venice (75-90mins).

By car
Take the A4 La Serenissima motorway.

Around Verona

Verona is a splendid gateway to Lake Garda (*see p255* **I yearn for Sirmione**), the rich farmland (and culinary delights) of the Po Valley and the Soave, Valpolicella and Bardolino wine-growing regions.

Caldiero

Caldiero's ancient hot springs – the **Terme di Giunone** – have been joined by more modern pools to accommodate the crowds in this spa 18 kilometres (11 miles) east of Verona. Water bubbles up at a temperature of 28° centigrade (82° farenheit).

Terme di Giunone
Via delle Terme 2 (045 615 1288/www.termedi giunone.it). **Open** June-Sept 9am-8pm daily. Apr, May, Oct 11am-6pm daily. **Admission** €8 Mon-Fri; €9 Sat, Sun & public holidays. **No credit cards**.

Valeggio sul Mincio

Valeggio was once the centre of Italy's carriage-building industry. After the carriage business slumped, the area's womenfolk opened scores of tiny restaurants serving dishes like *tortelli di zucca* (pumpkin-stuffed pasta) and grilled fish. It's also home to the pretty **Sigurtà** garden.

Parco Giardino Sigurtà
Via Cavour, Valeggio (045 637 1033/www. sigurta.it). **Open** Mar-Nov 9am-6pm daily. Closed Dec-Feb. **Admission** €8.50; free-€7 concessions. **No credit cards**.

Where to eat

Alla Borsa
Via Goito 2, Valeggio (045 795 0093/www.ristorante borsa.it). **Meals served** 12.15-2pm, 7.15-10pm Mon, Thur-Sun; 12.15-2pm Tue. **Closed** mid July-mid Aug; 2wks Feb. **Average** €40. **Credit** MC, V.
Informal and noisy, Alla Borsa serves perhaps the most delicious pumpkin *tortelli* in existence, plus fish from nearby Lake Garda, plus stuffed guinea-fowl, roast pork shanks and duck.

Tourist information
See above.

Getting there
There are regular APTV bus services (045 805 7911/www.aptv.it) for Caldiero and Valeggio sul Mincio from Verona bus station, in front of Porta Nuova train station.

The Veneto

Vicenza

The golden city of Palladio.

Located 60km west of Venice, Vicenza (pop. 110,000) has two monikers, pinpointing two of its fundamental characteristics. The first, *Città di Palladio* (Palladio's city) is a tribute one of the most influential architects of all time, Andrea Palladio, whose buildings define the appearance of the town we see today. The second, *Città dell'oro* (City of gold), celebrates Vicenza's fame as a centre for precious metals. The city also hosts the world-famous VicenzaOro trade fair (www.vicenzaoro.org) three times a year.

Evidence exists that the city was settled in the third-second centuries BC, but it was the Romans, in 157 BC, who put 'Vicetia' on the map. Vicenza became an important Lombard and Frankish centre, but was destroyed by Magyar ravagers in 899. During the early Middle Ages when barbarians were looting and pillaging along the peninsula, astute locals took advantage of their position as a crossroads and the link between the city's two rivers.

In 1404 Vicenza came under the rule of Venice, and thus began a veritable building boom. Vicenza's leading families had been ennobled by various Holy Roman emperors, and yet suddenly their city was controlled by crass Venetian interlopers. One way to assuage their hurt feelings – and to proclaim their superiority – was to commission sumptuous townhouses and country *ville*. Additionally, Venetian nobles being encouraged to develop country estates in order to strengthen the Republic's grip on the surrounding territory.

It was into this cauldron of Renaissance resurgence that Andrea Palladio (*see p266* **Andrea Palladio**) fell in the 1540s. He and his contemporaries and followers have made Vicenza's main street a theme ride in Architectureland: palazzo after palazzo is adorned with gracious balconies, loggias, arches and columns. On their ground floors, upmarket stores glisten with world-class jewels, designer clothing and exorbitant geegaws.

Outside the city centre, the industrial boom of the 1970s has irreparably altered Vicenza. The surrounding countryside once compared favourably with the Tuscan hills for aesthetic appeal. Now it is a repository for factories and malls, although you still don't have to travel far to find some beautiful viewpoints, and *ville*, mercifully, tend to have their own well preserved parks and gardens – though most are private.

Sightseeing

Vicenza's character is very much medieval and Renaissance, although the town's Roman layout is still virtually intact. Just outside the town walls, to the west of the centre, is the statue-dotted **Giardino Salvi**. This pleasant public park houses Andrea Palladio's **Loggia Valmarana**, a Doric-style temple spanning the waters of a canal. Nearby is a baroque loggia by Baldassare Longhena.

Inside the walls, piazza del Castello takes its name from a castle built in 1337-8 by the Della Scala family, who ruled here from 1311 to 1404. The tower in the corner of the piazza is all that remains of the castle. The adjoining gate, **Porta Castello**, was constructed in 1343 on the site of the city's Roman gate. The piazza is home to the odd-looking **Palazzo Porto Breganze**, a tall awkward fragment in the southern corner, designed by Palladio but never finished.

Palladio had a hand in five of the grandiose *palazzi* lining corso Palladio (all are closed to the public). The first palazzo of note, on the left-hand side as you exit piazza del Castello, is the magnificent **Palazzo Thiene Bonin Longare**, begun in 1562. At No.45 is **Palazzo Capra** (now home to the department store Coin), almost certainly designed by the young Palladio between 1540 and 1545.

A quick turn right into contrà Battisti (streets in Vicenza's centre are called 'contrà' instead of 'via') leads to the **Duomo** (*see p265*), opposite which is the entrance to the **criptoportico romano** (*see p265*), the only surviving remnant of Roman Vicetia. Back on corso Palladio, |a detour to the left leads to the Gothic brick church of **San Lorenzo** (*see p265*), while at No.92 is **Palazzo Pojana** (1564-6), which consists of two separate buildings cunningly joined together by Palladio. **Palazzo Trissino Baston**, at No.98, was designed in 1592 by Palladio's student Vincenzo Scamozzi but not completed until 1667. Interior visits are by appointment only (0444 221 111).

In the vast and elegant piazza dei Signori, south of the corso is the spectacular 82-metre (269-foot) Torre di Piazza clock tower, which dates from the 12th century. Tacked gracefully onto the Gothic Palazzo della Ragione assembly hall (known as the **Basilica Palladiana**, *see p265*, in the Roman sense of the word '*basilica*'

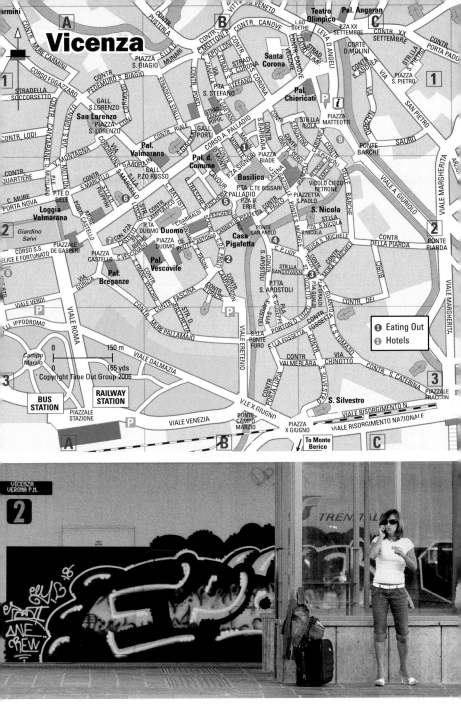

Vicenza

A **B** **C**

Teatro Olimpico
Pal. Angaran

Santa Corona

Pal. Chiericati

San Lorenzo

Pal. Valmarana

Pal. d. Comune

Basilica

Loggia Valmarana

Casa Pigafetta

S. Nicola

Duomo

Pal. Vescovile

Pal. Breganze

Giardino Salvi

Campo Marzio

Copyright Time Out Group 2006

❶ Eating Out
❶ Hotels

0   150 m
0   165 yds

BUS STATION

RAILWAY STATION

PIAZZALE STAZIONE

PIAZZALE FRACCON

S. Silvestro

To Monte Berico

A **B** **C**

– a public place where justice is dispensed) is Palladio's marvellous loggia. Opposite this is his Loggia del Capitanato, a fragment of a building, built to celebrate Venice's victory over the Turks in the Battle of Lepanto in 1571. On the same side is the complex of the Monte di Pietà, the city's 16th-century pawn shop.

Piazza delle Erbe is dominated by a medieval tower where wrongdoers were taken to be tortured. In the labyrinth of streets to the south of piazza delle Erbe is the **Casa Pigafetta** (contrà Pigafetta 9). Dating from 1444 and built in late Spanish Gothic style, this strange, highly decorated townhouse was the birthplace of Antonio Pigafetta, who was one of only 21 survivors of Magellan's epoch-making circumnavigation of the globe(1519-1522).

Coming off corso Palladio north of piazza Signori is contrà Porti, a real palazzo feast. The clannish Porto family all built their houses in one street. At No.11 is the **Palazzo Barbaran Da Porto**, designed and built by Palladio (1569-71), with an interior by Lorenzo Rubini. After a 20-year restoration, it is enjoying a renaissance, hosting such exhibitions as the **Museo Palladiano** (*see p265*).

Casa Porto (No.15) is an undistinguished 15th-century building that was badly restored in the 18th century but is of interest as the home of Luigi Da Porto (d.1529), writer of the first known account of the Romeo and Juliet story. At No.19 the exquisite, late Gothic **Palazzo Porto Colleoni** is a typical 15th-century attempt to beat the Venetians at their own game. **Palazzo Iseppo Da Porto**, at No.21, is one of Palladio's earliest creations, its interior decorated with frescoes by Tiepolo, but again it's not open to the public.

At the end of the street, over the Bacchiglione, river, contrà San Marco is a wide street lined with fine 16th- and 17th-century *palazzi*, including **Palazzo Da Schio**, an elegant townhouse designed by Palladio in the 1560s. Back on corso Palladio, **Palazzo Caldogno Da Schio** (No.147), a flamboyant 14th-century jewel, which once boasted gilded capitals – hence its other name, *Ca' d'Oro* – is still owned by the Da Schio family. Under the portico is a lapidarium of stone fragments collected by Giovanni da Schio (1798-1868).

The **Gallerie di Palazzo Leoni Montanari** (*see p265*), in contrà Santa Corona just off the corso, contains charming 18th-century genre paintings by Pietro Longhi. Also in contrà Santa Corona is the **Museo Naturalistico Archeologico**, whose entrance is included on the multiple admission ticket (*see p265*). On the corner of this street and the corso, the great Gothic church of **Santa Corona** (*see p266*) was completed in 1270

San Lorenzo. *See p265.*

and is Palladio's final resting place. Just a stone's throw away is the tiny **Casa Cogollo** (No.167), attributed to designs made by Palladio in 1560-70.

The main street ends in piazza Matteotti, where two of Vicenza's real artistic treats await: Palazzo Chiericati (1550), one of Palladio's finest townhouses, now the city's art gallery (**Museo Civico**, *see p265*); and the architect's final masterpiece, the **Teatro Olimpico** (*see p267*).

Perched on one of the hilltops that surround Vicenza to the south is the charming **Santuario di Monte Berico** (*see p266*). Fantastic views over the city and across to the Alps await those who make the 20-minute journey up the hill in the shade of the handy 18th-century loggia that lines Viale X Giugno. Further along the same road is the **Museo del Risorgimento e della Resistenza**, entrance to which is included on the multiple admission ticket (*see p265*).

To the south-east of the centre at the end of viale Risorgimento, Palladio's **Arco della Scalette** stands at the foot of 192 steps leading to **Villa Valmarana 'Ai Nani'** (*see p268*) – 'of the dwarves'. Further along the same path is the Villa Capra Valmarana, better known as **Villa Rotonda** (*see p268*), possibly the most famous of all Palladio's buildings. Even if the villa is closed, you can still admire the exterior from the garden.

TICKETS

Admission to the Museo Civico, Museo Naturalistico Archeologico, the Museo del Risorgimento e della Resistenza and the Teatro Olimpico is by *biglietto unico* only. Tickets, valid for three days, can only be bought at the Teatro Olimpico (*see p267*). No credit cards. **Biglietto unico**: €8, €5 concessions, €12 family (1-2 adults and 2-3 children), €15 season ticket (valid one year at all four museums plus one exhibition at the Basilica Palladiana).

Basilica Palladiana (Palazzo della Ragione)

Piazza dei Signori (0444 323 681). **Admission** during exhibitions only; prices & times vary. **Map** p263 B2.

'It is not possible to describe the impression made by Palladio's Basilica…' gushed Goethe, about Palladio's most famous piece of urban restyling. The original Palazzo della Regione, seat of city government, was built in the 1450s; but the loggia that surrounded it and helped to support it collapsed in 1496. The city fathers canvassed the leading architects of the day; luckily for Palladio (who was only 17 at the time – they dithered for 20 years before accepting the audacious solution he proposed in 1546 – a neat alternative to scaffolding. Palladio's double-tiered loggia, composed of serlian windows, encases the original Gothic palazzo in a unifying Renaissance shell. The basilica is now used as an exhibition space and it is only open for shows, many of which are free to enter. The space underneath is home to bars, jewellery shops and several art galleries.

Criptoportico Romano

Piazza Duomo (0444 226 626). **Open** (guided tours only) 10am-noon Sat. **Admission** free. **Map** p263 B2.

This incredibly preserved structure, all that remains of a large, first-century *domus* (Roman townhouse) is now substantially submerged after 2000 years of rising ground levels. Builders stumbled upon it in 1954. The 90m of vaulted tunnels formed part of the foundations supporting the walled internal garden. Well ventilated in summer, and possibly heated in winter, the space was most likely used for the storage of food and wine. Admission is by guided tour only. These take about 15 minutes and, though they're in Italian only, compensate somewhat for the lack of explanation *in situ*. If the guide is underground with a group, wait by the gate. The are also tours 10am-noon and 2.30-4pm (3.30-5pm in summer) on every second Sunday of the month.

Duomo

Piazza Duomo 8 (0444 320 996). **Open** 10.30am-noon, 3.30-5.30pm Mon-Fri; 10.30am-noon Sat. **Map** p263 B2.

The history of Vicenza's cathedral is perhaps more interesting than the building that stands today. The site is believed to have been occupied from around the fifth century by a Christian basilica which was modified in the ninth century, and again in the tenth and 11th centuries. Its present form is the result of reconstruction carried out between 1267 and 1290, but the Duomo suffered extensive damage during World War II. The Palladian dome has been painstakingly restored to its former splendour, as has the Gothic pink marble façade, attributed to Domenico da Venezia (1467). The banal brick interior contains an important polyptych by Lorenzo Veneziano, signed and dated 1366.

Gallerie di Palazzo Leoni Montanari

Contrà Santa Corona 25 (0444 991 291/www. palazzomontanari.com). **Open** 10am-6pm Tue-Sun. **Admission** €4; €3 concessions. **No credit cards.** **Map** p263 B1.

A curious collection of two completely different fields of art. On permanent display are 14 masterpieces by the 18th-century Venetian genre painter Pietro Longhi, plus several other paintings of Venice, including an interesting Canaletto, and an extraordinary collection of ancient Russian icons. The museum is worth a visit for the magnificent interiors alone, especially in the *Galleria della verità*. Temporary exhibitions rotate every few months.

Museo Civico

Palazzo Chiericati, piazza Matteotti 37-9 (0444 321 348/www.comune.vicenza.it/musei/civico/home.htm). **Open** Sept-June 9am-5pm Tue-Sun. *July, Aug* 10am-6pm Tue-Sun. **Admission** by *biglietto unico* only (*see above*). **Map** p263 C1.

The art gallery of this Palladian palazzo contains a fascinating collection of works by local painters, and Bartolomeo Montagna (1450-1523) in particular. The highlight is a 1489 Cima da Conegliano altarpiece, *Madonna Enthroned with Child between Saints Giacomo (James) and Girolamo (Jerome)*. It also houses works by the likes of Van Dyck, Tintoretto, Veronese, Tiepolo, and a *Crucifixion* by the Flemish master Hans Memling, the central part of a triptych whose side panels are in New York.

Museo Palladiano

Palazzo Barbaran Da Porto, contrà Porti 11 (0444 323 014/fax 0444 322 869/www.cisapalladio.org). **Open** 10am-6pm Tue-Sun. **Admission** €5; €3 concessions. **No credit cards.**

This palazzo houses the International Centre for the Study of the Architecture of Andrea Palladio, which hosts irregular temporary exhibitions on architectural themes. The main draw is the palazzo itself, although it's only open when exhibitions are on.

San Lorenzo

Piazza San Lorenzo (0444 321 960/ www.sanlorenzo. vi.it). **Open** *Apr-Sept* 7am-noon, 4-7pm daily. *Oct-Mar* 10.30am-noon, 3.30-6.30pm daily. **Map** p263 A1.

The exterior of this rather sparse Gothic church, built at the end of the 13th century, is the highlight; the magnificent marble portal encases an exquisite 14th-century lunette depicting the *Madonna and Child*. The Poiana altar in the right transept is a late Gothic assemblage of paintings and frescoes by various artists, including a 1500 frescoed lunette of the crucifixion by

The Veneto

Andrea Palladio

Arguably the most influential figure in Western architecture, Andrea Palladio owed his success not only to his peerless talent as a designer and his refined aesthetic judgement, but to a host of factors that conspired to create his momentous legacy.

Palladio had an unremarkable start. He was born in Padua on 30 November 1508 and baptised Andrea di Pietro della Gondola. His father apprenticed him at the age of 13 to Giovanni da Porlezza, a stonecarver in Vicenza. Recognising his talent, the workshop put up the money for Andrea's guild entrance fee. He learned to design and carve church altars, tombs and architectural elements, many commissioned by Vicenza's nobility.

Between 1530 and 1538, while working on a villa on the outskirts of Vicenza, he met its owner, Count Giangiorgio Trissino, the wealthy, influential leader of a group of Humanist intellectuals dedicated to reviving classical culture. This chance meeting was to change the course of Western architecture.

Trissino set about turning Andrea into a worthy heir to Vitruvius, the ancient architect whose treatise *De Architectura* underpinned the return to classical models in the Italian Renaissance. He also gave Andrea a more suitable name: 'Palladio' resonated with classical associations, and was the name of a helpful angel in Trissino's epic poem *Italia liberata dai goti* (*Italy Liberated from the Goths*). Trissino also gave Palladio time off

and funds to study Roman antiquities in Verona and Padua, and took him to Rome three times between 1540 and 1550. Palladio studied, measured and sketched all the major classical remains, as well as the buildings and plans of Renaissance greats throughout Italy, including Sanmicheli, Raphael and Giulio Romano. In 1554 he published *Le antichità di Roma*, a sort of predecessor to the guidebook.

Palladio's early patrons were part of the Trissino circle, who provided both work and intellectual stimulation after Trissino died in 1550. Among these enlightened Vicentine nobles were Pietro Godi – whose **Villa Godi Valmarana ora Malinverni** (*see p270*) was Palladio's first independent commission in 1537 – and the Barbaro brothers, whose encouragement generated one of Palladio's masterpieces, the **Villa Barbaro** (1550-7, *see p277*) at Maser. Another patron, Girolamo Chiericati helped give the architect his first big break in 1549, restructuring Vicenza's town hall (the **Basilica Palladiana**, *see p265*), which established Palladio as one of the leading architects of his day.

Like all great artists, Palladio also benefited from good timing. In the 16th century the Venetian government insisted that nobles build villas on the *terra firma* (mainland) to boost agricultural production and increase *La Serenissima*'s control over the countryside. Commissions for villas were thus plentiful

---

Bartolomeo Montagna. The peaceful 16th-century cloister contains a medieval wellhead. **Photo** *p264*.

Santa Corona

Contrà Santa Corona (0444 321 924). **Open** 4-6pm Mon; 8.30am-noon, 3-6pm Tue-Sat; 3-5pm Sun. **Map** p263 B1.

This magnificent Gothic brick church was built between 1260 and 1270, to house a stray thorn from Christ's crown. Its interior, consisting of three unequally sized naves, contains an *Adoration of the Magi* (1573) by Paolo Veronese in the third chapel on the right. In the crypt is the Valmarana Chapel, one of the few examples of religious architecture designed by Palladio. Another artistic treasure is the beautifully elaborate high altar by Francesco Antonio Corberelli, 1670, a masterpiece of intricate marble inlay. The church's highlight however, in the fifth chapel on the left of the nave, is a beautiful 1502 *Baptism of Christ* by Giovanni Bellini (under restoration at time of going to press).

Santuario di Monte Berico

Viale X Giugno 87 (0444 320 998/www.monte berico.it). **Open** 6am-12.30pm, 2.30-6pm Mon-Sat; 6am-7pm Sun.

This is a breathtakingly beautiful spot with fantastic views. The church itself was largely rebuilt in the 18th century; its interior contains Veronese's *Supper of St Gregory the Great* (1572) in the refectory, as well as a moving *Pietà* by Bartolomeo Montagna and a fine collection of fossils. The Virgin is said to have appeared twice here – in 1426 and 1428, making it a popular destination with pilgrims. An attractive 18th-century loggia built by Francesco Muttoni leads up Viale X Giugno to the church. A map available free from the Tourist Information Offices (*see p270*) indicates the route from the town centre. If you don't feel like making the 20-minute walk up hill on foot, take bus number 6 from the railway station. There's also a dedicated bus service (no number – ask at the stop) from the railway station Mon-Sat, though it is irregular. Bus 18 runs on Sunday.

throughout the Veneto; Palladio's soon became the most famous. In 1570 he moved to Venice, to become unofficial chief architect, with prominent churches like **San Giorgio Maggiore** (see p140) and the **Redentore** (see p139) reinforcing his fame. His fame spread beyond the Veneto thanks to his influential treatise, *I quattro libri dell'architettura* (*The Four Books of Architecture*, 1570).

The pared-back design for which Palladio became so famous was certainly inspired by Roman and Greek architecture, but was never copied; Palladio utilised classical motifs, creating a style that defined the essence of elegance. The most recognisable feature of his buildings is the use of the Greco-Roman temple front as a portico; equally innovative were the dramatic high-relief effects on façades. The floor plans usually emphasised a strong central axis and symmetrical wings, with the proportions of the rooms determined mathematically to create harmonic spaces, typically with high ceilings. Though always unmistakably his, each of Palladio's buildings is startlingly different from the stark simplicity of **Villa Pisani** (see p270) at Bagnolo di Lonigo, almost totally devoid of decorative elements, to the immense complexity of the statue-crowned **Palazzo Chiericati** in the centre of Vicenza (see p264-65).

In his day, it Palladio's domestic villa architecture largely overshadowed his other accomplishments. His country residences differed from their urban counterparts as they uniquely combined both a working farmhouse and elegant country retreat, with much of the decoration serving a function: the gracious entrance ramp at the **Villa Emo** (see p277) was also intended as a platform for threshing grain. Palladio's designs also encompassed other practical functions: stables, cellars, granaries and dovecotes were located within the compounds and were intrinsic to the villa as a whole. Never ostentatious, overbearing in size or using of costly materials, they make subtle statements through a dignified classical vocabulary (columns, cornices, pediments), harmony of proportions both external and internal, and a human scale. Palladio's inventiveness and sensitivity extended to the aspect and location of villas, which he regarded as highly important in their function as an antidote to the stresses of urban life. Building near a river or canal was recommended; as well as allowing easy access by boat, water guaranteed cool breezes during the hot summer months, irrigated the gardens and, not incidentally, 'will afford a beautiful prospect'.

Palladio's revival of ancient Greek and Roman architecture created a style that was to be copied throughout Europe. In the centuries after his death in 1580, architects and patrons across the world came to see Palladio's homes as a standard of excellence, exemplifying that less could indeed be more.

Teatro Olimpico

Piazza Matteotti 11 (0444 222 800/www.comune. vicenza.it/olimpico/teatro.htm). **Open** *Sept-June* 9am-5pm Tue-Sun. *July, Aug* 9am-7pm Tue-Sun. **Admission** by *biglietto unico* only (see p265). **Map** p263 C1.

Note that the theatre may close occasionally in spring and autumn for rehearsals.

The remarkable Teatro Olimpico was Palladio's final masterpiece. Designed in 1579-80, just a few months before the architect's death, it was the first permanent indoor theatre to be built in Europe since the fall of the Roman Empire. His son Silla and his star pupil Vincenzo Scamozzi took over, and the two took considerable liberties with the original blueprint. The decorative flamboyance of the wood-and-stucco interior contrasts notably with its modest entrance and severe external walls. Based on Roman theatres described by Vitruvius, it has 13 semicircular wooden steps, crowned by Corinthian columns holding up an elaborate balustrade topped with elegant 'antique' sculpted figures. The permanent stage set, designed by Scamozzi, with its seven *trompe l'œil* street scenes, represents the city of Thebes in Sophocles' *Oedipus Rex*, which was the theatre's first performance, on 3 March 1585.

The elaborately frescoed antechambers to the theatre were also designed by Scamozzi and were used for meetings and smaller concerts of the Accademia Olimpica, the learned society of humanists that commissioned the place. Don't miss the chiaroscuro fresco in the entrance hall depicting a delegation of Japanese noblemen who visited Vicenza in 1585.

Performances were brought to a halt by Counter-Reformation censorship. It wasn't until after World War II that the theatre once again realised its potential as a venue. A season of classical dramas in September and October usually includes a staging of *Oedipus Rex* (in Italian). Concerts tend to be concentrated in May and June. For information, contact the tourist office (see p270) or Vicenza's website (www.comune.vicenza.it).

The Veneto

Villa Rotonda

Via della Rotonda 45 (0444 321 793/fax 049 879 1380). Bus 8 or 13 from train station. **Open** *Gardens* Mar-Nov 10am-noon, 3-6pm Tue-Sun. *Interior* mid Apr-early Nov 10am-noon, 3-6pm Wed. **Admission** *Gardens* €5. *Interior* €10. **No credit cards**.

One of the most famous buildings in Western architecture, **La Rotonda** – designed between 1567 and 1570, but not completed until 1606 – is not strictly speaking a villa at all. It was planned as a pleasure pavilion for retired cleric Paolo Almerico. The Rotonda (the Villa Almerico-Capra Valmarana, officially) was the first to be given a dome, a form previously associated with ancient temples or Renaissance churches. Scholars may be granted permission to visit the lavish interior outside the limited opening times. Those left outside can behold the building's grandiose exterior, and the garden is 'one of the most agreeable and delightful sites that one could hope to find,' according to Palladio. It is possible to walk to the villa centre, passing Villa Valmarana ai Nani, and continuing on the unsurfaced via Valmarana. This route takes five minutes from Villa Valmarana ai Nani, but is only suitable for the sure-footed; maps are free from the tourist offices (*see p270*).

Villa Valmarana ai Nani

Via dei Nani 2-8 (0444 321 803/www.villavalmarana. com). Bus 8 from viale Roma. **Open** *Mid Mar-mid Nov* 10am-noon, 3-6pm Tue-Sun. *Mid Nov-mid Mar* 10am-noon, 2.30-4.30pm Sat, Sun. **Admission** €6. **No credit cards**.

This delightful villa was designed by Antonio Muttoni in 1688 and still belongs to the Valmarana family. For once it's the interior that is the main attraction, thanks to a remarkable series of frescoes painted by Giambattista Tiepolo and his son Giandomenico in 1757. The statues of dwarves (*nani*) lining the wall to the right of the main villa were added in 1785 by Elena Garzadori who redesigned the garden. Legend has it that the family built the statues in order to give their own dwarf daughter friendly familiars to gaze upon. The walk from the centre to this villa takes about 30 minutes. Climb the 192 steps from Palladio's Arco delle Scalette; then veer left and keep going along via dei Nani. A map available free from the tourist office (*see p270*) indicates the route from the town centre.

Where to eat & drink

The *vicentini* have been eating *baccalà alla vicentina* – dried cod stewed in milk and oil – since at least 1269. There are two ways of preserving cod: it can be salted and partially dried (salt cod; *baccalà*) or just dried (stockfish; *stoccafisso*). When stockfish was introduced to the *vicentini* in the 15th century they decided they preferred it to established *baccalà*. But *stoccafisso* is not an easy word to pronounce in Vicentine dialect, so they kept calling it *baccalà*.

Another firm favorite in the Veneto is *bollito misto* (mixed boiled meat), which is far more appetizing than it sounds. Expect to see some combination of sausage (*cotechino*), whole hen (*gallina*) or chicken (*pollo*), veal's tongue (*lingua*), calf's head (*testina*), and a cut of beef (*manzo*). This is served with boiled potatoes and sauces: *salsa verde* (parsley and capers), *mostarda* (spicy preserved fruit), *cren* (horseradish), and *peàra* (combination of bread crumbs and bone marrow) are considered the classic accompaniment to this favourite dish.

Antica Casa della Malvasia

Contrà delle Morette 5 (0444 543 704). **Meals served** 12.30-3.30pm, 7pm-1am Tue-Sat. **Average** €25. **Credit** AmEx, MC, V. **Map** p263 B1 ❶

This centrally located *osteria* offers an excellent value lunch, and a good variety of wines, but lacks atmosphere at dinner time. The attractive tables outside are a pleasant place for an *aperitivo*.

Bella Vicenza Pizzeria

Via G De Proti 12 (0444 546 192). **Meals served** 6.30-11pm Wed-Sun. **Average** €15. **Credit** AmEx, DC, MC, V. **Map** p263 B2 ❷

This basic but adequate eaterie offers great-value pizzas from €4 to €8, plus limited other dishes.

De Gobbi

Via Olmo 52, Creazzo (0444 520 509). **Meals served** 12-2.30pm, 7.30-10.30pm Mon-Thur, Sun; 7.30-10.30pm Sat. Closed 3wks Aug. **Average** €30. **Credit** AmEx, DC, MC, V. **Map** p263 C2 ❸

A few kilometres outside Vicenza; great *bollito misto*.

Osteria Il Cursore

Stradella Pozzetto 10 (0444 323 504). **Open** 11.30am-3pm, 6pm-1am Mon, Wed-Sun; Closed 3wks July-Aug. **Meals served** noon-3pm, 7.30-10.30pm Mon, Wed-Sat; 6.30-10.30pm Sun. **Average** €28. **Credit**, AmEx, MC, V. **Map** p263 B2 ❹

This old-fashioned *vicentino* drinking den is across the arched ponte San Michele. If you're looking for a quick snack, there are bar nibbles; otherwise, for larger appetites, the kitchen turns out excellent versions of local specialities such as *bigoli con sugo di anatra* (fat spaghetti with duck sauce) or *baccalà alla vicentina*.

Osteria I Monelli

Contrà Ponte San Paolo 13 (0444 540 400). **Open** 10.30am-3.30pm, 6.30pm-2am Tue-Sun. **Meals served** 12.30-3pm, 7.30-11pm Tue-Sun. Closed 2wks July. **Average** €35. **Credit** DC, MC, V. **Map** p263 B2 ❺

A lively *osteria* near piazza delle Erbe serving excellent quality food, primarily meat dishes, including *filetto di struzzo* (ostrich steak).

Pasticceria Sorarù

Piazzetta Palladio 17 (0444 320 915). **Open** 8.30am-1pm, 3.30-8pm Mon, Tue, Thur-Sun. **No credit cards**.

One of Italy's most charming *pasticcerie*, Sorarù is worth a look even if you don't have a sweet tooth. The columns, marble counters and ornate wooden shelves backed with mirrors are all 19th-century originals; the cakes, firmly in the Austro-Hungarian tradition, are a tad fresher.

Remo
Contrà Caimpenta 14 (0444 911 007/fax 0444 911 856). **Meals served** noon-2.30pm, 7.30-10.30pm Tue-Sat; noon-2.30pm Sun. Closed Aug, 2wks Dec-Jan. **Average** €35. **Credit** AmEx, DC, MC, V.
This country restaurant in an old farmhouse offers some of the best cooking you'll find anywhere in the Vicenza area. The boiled and roasted meats trolley is a fixture, and Remo's *baccalà alla vicentina* is spectacular. Excellent sweets and house wine.

Ristorante Tre Visi Vecchia Roma
Corso Palladio 25 (0444 324 868/www.trevisi. vicenza.com). **Meals served** 12.30-2.30pm, 7-10.30pm Tue-Sat; 12.30-3pm Sun. Closed 2wks July. **Average** €35. **Credit** AmEx, MC, V. **Map** p263 A2 ⑥
A good place to pop into when Palladio's genius gets a bit too much. Try for the outside courtyard.

Where to stay

Albergo San Raffaele
Viale X Giugno 10 (0444 545 767/fax 0444 542 259/www.albergosanraffaele.it). **Rates** €43 single; €65 double. **Credit** AmEx, DC MC, V.
Situated on the hill just below the Santuario di Monte Berico (*see p266*), this hotel has fantastic views over the city and is a real bargain for those on

a budget. Rooms are clean and simple, but comfortable; free parking included.

Camping Vicenza
Strada Pelosa 239 (0444 582 311/fax 0444 582 434). **Closed** Oct-Mar. **Rates** €3-€7.40 per person; €6-€14.60 per camper/tent. **Credit** AmEx, DC, MC, V.
Situated near the Vicenza Est exit of the Milan–Venice motorway, this upmarket campsite is well equipped; but be warned that it is a serious hike from the city centre.

Hotel Castello
Contrà Piazza Castello 24 (0444 323 585/fax 0444 323 583/hotelcastelloitaly.com). **Rates** €90 single; €120 double. **Credit** AmEx, DC, MC, V. **Map** p263 A2 ⑦
This unpretentious hotel with 1980s-style interiors is in the city centre close to corso Palladio and all the main sights. Free parking is provided.

Hotel Cristina
Corso San Felice 32 (0444 323 751/fax 0444 543 656/www.hcristina.it). **Rates** €80-€88 single; €103-€113 double. **Credit** AmEx, DC, MC, V. **Map** p263 A2 ⑧
Located just a few steps outside the Porta Castello gate, the recently restructured Hotel Cristina offers special weekend packages for tourists.

Hotel Giardini
Viale Giuriolo 10 (tel/fax 0444 326 458/www. hotelgiardini.com). **Closed** 2wks Aug. **Rates** €83 single; €114 double. **Credit** AmEx, DC, MC, V. **Map** p263 C1 ⑨
This small, modern hotel is located across piazza Matteotti from Palladio's Teatro Olimpico (*see p267*).

Teatro Olimpico. *See p267.*

The Veneto

Resources

Tourist information

IAT
Piazza Matteotti 12 (0444 320 854/fax 0444 327 072/www.vicenzae.org). **Open** 9am-1pm, 2-6pm daily. **Map** p263 C1.
Piazza dei Signori 8 (0444 544 122/www.vicenzae. org). **Open** 10am-2pm, 2.30-6.30pm daily. **Map** p263 B2.

Getting there

By car
Take the A4 *La Serenissima* motorway from Venice towards Milan.

By train
There are regular trains to and from Venice (55mins) and Verona (30mins). As of August 2006 the left luggage office at the station has closed indefinitely.

By bus
FTV (0444 223 111/www.ftv.vi.it) buses run from Padua to Vicenza, near the railway station.

Getting around

By bus
Vicenza's buses are operated by AIM (0444 394 909/www.aimvicenza.it). A ticket valid for any number of trips in the space of 90 minutes costs €1.05.

By taxi
Radiotaxi Vicenza (0444 920 600/www.taxivicenza.com) operate a 24-hour service of metered cabs. During the night the service is automated.

Around Vicenza

The countryside surrounding Vicenza is dense with particularly magnificent villas, including many by Palladio. Names of villas change when they pass from one family to another; we refer to their most common names. Many villas are private homes so opening hours are subject to change; some are not open to the public at all. All transport instructions apply from central Vicenza; unless otherwise stated, buses depart from the rural FTV bus service terminal (information 0444 223 115/fax 0444 327 422/ www.ftv.vi.it) in front of Vicenza station.
See also p271 **Villa jaunts**.

Palladian villas

What follows is a critical selection of the most important visitable villas designed entirely or mostly by Palladio. *See also* *p266* **Andrea Palladio**.

Villa Godi Valmarana ora Malinverni
Via Palladio 44, Lugo di Vicenza (0445 860 561/fax 0445 860 806/www.villagodi.com). Bus to Thiene; change at Thiene to hourly bus for Lugo di Vicenza. **Open** *June-Sept* 3-7pm Tue, Sat, Sun. *Nov-Mar* 2-6pm Tue, Sat, Sun. **Admission** €6. **No credit cards.**
Palladio's first villa, built before he ever set foot in Rome and completed by 1542. In some ways it's one of his most radical, pared-back designs. It has some good 16th-century frescoes as well as a former owner's collection of 19th-century art, artefacts and fossils (including a palm tree 5m/16ft high). Groups can book visits outside the times given above.

Villa Piovene Porto Godi
Via Palladio 51, Lugo di Vicenza (0445 860 613). Bus to Thiene; change at Thiene to hourly bus for Lugo di Vicenza. **Open** *Gardens only* Apr-Oct 2.30-7pm daily. Nov-Mar 2-5pm daily. **Admission** €4.50. **No credit cards.**
Parhaps one of the architect's last commissions; the formulaic Palladian style – the portico, the colonnaded wings, the theatrical double staircase – is proof for some that self-parody was beginning to set in. Only the central block is plausibly by Palladio; the rest may be by his follower Vincenzo Scamozzi.

Villa Pisani
Via Risaie 1, Bagnolo frazione di Lonigo (0444 831 104/fax 0444 835 517). Bus for Cologna Veneta. **Open** Apr-Nov by appointment. **Admission** €6; €4 concessions. **No credit cards.**
Villa Pisani was an early commission (begun in 1540), and shows Palladio honing his style and experimenting. It's hard to appreciate how revolutionary this must have seemed at the time. The revolution continues inside, where the division of rooms and design details such as the thermal windows are purely classical in inspiration.

Villa Pojana
Via Castello 41, Poiana Maggiore (tel/fax 0444 898 554). Bus for Noventa Vicentina. **Open** by appointment only *Apr-Oct* 10am-6pm Sat, Sun. **Admission** €4; €2.50 concessions. **No credit cards.**
Villa Pojana, one of the architect's most original creations, demonstrates Palladio's skill as an architect of smaller dwellings. Completed around 1550, the villa offers no projecting temple portico for once, and the façade is dominated by a serliana arch (a central arched opening flanked by two rectangular ones) topped by telephone-dial openings. The interior has frescoes by Bernardino India and Anselmo Canera.

Villa Saraceno
Via Finale 8, Finale di Agugliaro (tel/fax 0444 891 371/ www.landmarktrust.org.uk). Bus for Noventa Vicentina; change at Ponte Botti for local service. **Open** *Apr-Sept* 2-4pm Wed. *Oct-Mar* by appointment. **Admission** by donation.
In 1988 the lovely Villa Saraceno (1550) was bought up by the British Landmark Trust and restored, opening as self-catering accommodation in 1994 and

Villa jaunts

The countryside around Vicenza abounds in splendid Palladian villas. These driving itineraries (you can try by public transport, but you may find that hiring a car for the day is more conducive to enjoyment) take in several villas apiece, in trips from Vicenza. Vicenza tourist offices (*see p270*) provide excellent road maps and their own villa information. The majority of villas are private homes, so opening hours are subject to change at short notice; phoning in advance is recommended.

North-east of Vicenza

It's quite a hike up to Lugo di Vicenza, home to magnificent Palladian villas, so allow a generous half-day for this drive. Head north-east out of Vicenza on SS53. Four kilometres out of town, beyond a motorway flyover, the SP29 branches right towards Quinto Vicento, where you can pop in to visit Palladio's **Villa Thiene** (*see p272*), now the town hall.

Backtrack on the SS53 towards Vicenza for about 500m, then join the A31 motorway, heading north towards Thiene. Where the motorway ends, veer right and follow the SP68 to Caltrano, then Lugo di Vicenza. In the centre of the village via Giacomo Matteotti becomes via Palladio, which has two fine villas by the architect: **Villa Godi Valmarana ora Malinverni** and **Villa Piovene Porto Godi** (for both, *see p270*). For a luxury lunch break or indulgent dinner, get back on the SP68, head for Zugliano, then Sarcedo, and continue on the SP63 to Montecchio Precalcino, home to the excellent **Locanda di Piero** (*see p272*). From here Vicenza is about 10km due south on the SP248.

North-west of Vicenza

If you're making this an afternoon drive, you could set out after a lunch at the **Antica Trattoria Monterosso** (*see p272*) in Alta Villa Vicentina. Take the SR11 south-west out of Vicenza, following the railway line towards Verona. The restaurant is in the village centre, in via Roma, alongside the motorway.

Back on the SR11, continue west to Montecchio Maggiore, home to the charming **Villa Cordellina Lombardi** and its gardens. From here, the SP246 goes north to Valdagno; about 7km outside Montecchio is Trissino. Here you can visit the gardens and interiors of **Villa Trissino Marzotto** (by appointment only), and eat (and even stay) at the **Ca' Masieri** restaurant and hotel (for all, *see p272*).

From here, return to Vicenza by the same route, or, for a different experience, continue on to Valdagno, the main town in the Agno valley and home to Villa Cengia Barbieri, a late 18th-century villa by Carlo Barrera. The town is dominated by the vast Marzotto woollen mill complex, which overshadows many of the other features, including the 17th-century Villa Valle, now the town hall.

In an instance of the enlightened paternalism popular among northern Italian industrialists in the early 20th century, Gaetano Marzotto had an 'ideal' workers' city constructed in 1927-37. This *Città sociale*, as it's known, was designed by Francesco Bonfanti and Gino Zardin with an eye for the spiritual, cultural, physical and moral well-being of Marzotto's employees: there are health centres and nursery schools, an indoor swimming pool and an 1,800-seater theatre – the largest theatre in the Veneto when it was built.

A further 10km along the SP246 is the spa town of Recoaro Terme, whose waters have been famous for centuries and are still a major attraction. The Terme di Recoaro (0445 76006/0445 76016) offers mud baths, inhalation and massage

South of Vicenza

This whole-day circuit takes in four villas and a wonderful rural restaurant. From Vicenza, head due south on the SP247 towards Noventa Vicentina for about 15km. Palladio's beautifully restored **Villa Saraceno** (see p270) is located on via Finale, off the SP247 to the left, 2km before Noventa. Three kilometres beyond Noventa Vicentina lies Pioana Maggiore, home to Palladio's beguilingly modern-looking **Villa Pojana** (*see p270*).

Next take the SP4 north out of Poiana Maggiore, taking a right onto the SP14 towards Lonigo after about 2km. Just outside Lonigo, perched on a hill overlooking the town is **Villa Pisani Ferri 'Rocca Pisana'** (*see p272*) designed by Palladio's protégé Vincenzo Scamozzi. Those with rumbling tummies and a generous overdraft facility should try luxurious **La Peca** (*see p272*), just off via San Daniele, the main street of the town.

Next follow the SP500 directly south out of town in the direction of Cologna Veneta for about one kilometre. Take the first right at the tiny hamlet of Bagnolo-Frazione di Lonigo. The next left leads to the classic Palladian **Villa Pisani** (*see p270*).

The Veneto

offering a unique chance to stay in a Palladian villa. Like many of Palladio's villas, it was built for a gentleman farmer, with an attic-granary lit by large grilled windows, so that the wheat was kept ventilated. As this guide went to press, Landmark was fighting to prevent the planned extension of the A31 motorway being built nearby.

For weekly rental (sleeps 16) call Landmark Trust UK (01628 825 925/www.landmarktrust.org.uk).

Villa Thiene

Piazza IV Novembre 2, Quinto Vicentino (0444 584 211/fax 0444 357 388). Bus 5 (for Quinto or Lanzé) from Vicenza (piazza Matteotti). **Open** 9.30am-12.45pm, 5.30-6.45pm Mon, Thur; 9.30am-12.45pm Fri. Groups by appointment only. **Admission** free.

Now the town hall of the unremarkable town of Quinto Vicentino, imposing Villa Thiene is only a fraction of what was to be an even more immense villa, designed by Palladio in 1546. The interior was frescoed in the mid 16th century by Giovanni De Mio and Bernardino India. Visitors can only visit a couple of rooms and the gardens, subject to permission.

Other villas

His influence is unmistakeable and lasting, but Andrea Palladio was not the only gainfully employed architect in Vicenza. Below is a selection of the *other* most important country villas in Vicenza province.

Villa Cordellina Lombardi

Via Lovara 36, Montecchio Maggiore (0444 908 141/www.provincia.vicenza.it/pdv/ville). Bus to Recoaro. **Open** *Apr-Oct* 9am-1pm Tue-Fri; 9am-noon, 3-6pm Sat, Sun. Closed Nov-Mar. **Admission** €2.10. **No credit cards.**

This beautifully restored villa, built between 1735 and 1760 in the grand Palladian style, contains some flamboyant frescoes by Giambattista Tiepolo. Painted in 1743, they include one of the painter's favourite Enlightenment allegories, *The Light of Reason Driving out the Fog of Ignorance.* There is also a charming French-style park, and a garden. The villa is often host to corporate events, in which case it will not be open to the public, so call ahead.

Villa Pisani Ferri 'Rocca Pisana'

Via Rocca 1, Lonigo (0444 831 625). Bus to Lonigo. **Open** Mar-early Nov 3pm-5.30pm Mon-Sat, by appointment. **Admission** €5. **No credit cards.**

This magnificent villa, built in 1576 on the ruins of a medieval castle, was designed by Palladio's star pupil, Vincenzo Scamozzi. Like La Rotonda (*see p268*), La Rocca has four main windows facing the four points of the compass and a dome with a hole. But whereas the Rotonda hole is covered with glass, the hole here is open, allowing air to circulate.

Villa Trissino Marzotto

Piazza GG Trissino 2, Trissino (0445 962 029). Bus to Recoaro. **Open** by appointment only. **Admission** *Villa* €5. *Garden* €5. **No credit cards.**

This elaborate complex is set in one of the most charming of Italy's private parks. The upper villa and the park were designed by Francesco Muttoni between 1718 and 1722. The garden is a typically 18th-century mixture of art and nature; the lower villa – destroyed by lightning in 1841 – acts as a theatrical focal point.

Where to stay & eat

Antica Trattoria Monterosso

Via Roma 40, Altavilla Vicentina (0444 371 362) **Meals served** noon-2.30pm, 7.30-10pm Mon-Sat **Average** €25. **Closed** 2wks Aug. **Credit** AmEx, DC, MC, V.

Five kilometres south-west of Vicenza this simple trattoria in the small town of Altavilla Vicentina serves Veneto cuisine to budget-conscious diners.

Ca' Masieri

Via Masieri 15, Località Masieri, Trissino (restaurant 0445 962 100/hotel 0445 490 122/www.camasieri. com) **Meals served** 7.30-10pm Mon; 12.30-2.30pm, 7.30-10pm Tue-Sat. Closed Dec. **Average** €50. **Rates** €60 single; €110 double; €140 suite **Credit** AmEx, DC, MC, V.

Located 2km West of Trissino town, This charming 18th-century stone *relais* offers serious meat, game and fish cooking at fairly serious prices with indoor and al fresco dining; it also has 12 rooms, and a swimming pool. Breakfast included.

La Peca

Via Alberto Giovannelli 2, Lonigo (0444 830 214) **Meals served** noon-2pm, 8-10pm Tue-Sat; noon-2pm Sun. **Average** €80. **Closed** 2wks June; 1wk Aug **Credit** AmEx, DC, MC, V.

The place to splash out on a luxurious meal, which might include such delights as king prawn soup with avocado and lime, laurel smoked eel and liquorice mousse. Booking highly recommended.

Locanda di Piero

Via Roma 32-4, Montecchio Precalcino (0445 864 827/www.lalocandadipiero.it). **Meals served** 7.30-10pm Mon; noon-2.15pm, 7.30-10pm Tue-Fri; 7.30-10pm Sat. **Average** €60 **Closed** 2wks Mar, 2weeks Aug **Credit** AmEx, DC, MC, V.

Fifteen kilometres north of Vicenza, this is the ultimate gastro-treat: the Michelin-starred Locanda di Piero does a cordon bleu take on the local tradition.

Tourist information

IAT

Piazza Garibaldi 15, Lonigo (0444 830 948/ fax 0444 430 385/www.prolonigo.it). **Open** 9am-11am Mon-Fri.

IAT

Via Roma 15, Recoaro Terme (0445 75 070/ www.vicenzae.org). **Open** 8.30am-12.30pm, 3-7pm Mon-Sat; 10am-noon, 3-6pm Sun.

Treviso & the Northern Veneto

The Dolomites' own millionaires' row.

North of Venice, the Veneto is a land of extremes, incorporating regimental rows of beach huts, fenlands spattered with small industries and dramatic Alpine mountain ranges. For the tourist, there is a plethora of day-trip opportunities: craggy mountains, Alpine meadows, mighty forests, towered hills and walled towns with one or two points of interest. For outdoor types, a day may not be enough to enjoy what the Dolomites have to offer in this dramatic corner of northern Veneto.

Treviso

Twenty-five kilometres (16 miles) north of its ostentatious neighbour, Treviso likes to fashion itself 'little Venice'. This pretty town, with its painstakingly restored *palazzi* (damaged during intensive World War II bombing) and stunning frescoed churches, is an underrated beauty. It offers all of Venice's romantic canal-side walks, Renaissance architecture, great art and shopping, but all on a much smaller scale and without the tourist mass to mar your visit.

While the Venetians are responsible for the walls guarding the old town, Treviso was important long before they muscled in during the 14th century. Originally the Roman town of Tarvisium, the city was also the seat of a Lombard duchy. The Venetian walls, dating back to 1509, protect three sides of the old town. The fourth is protected by Sile River, which provides some of the water in the canals – the rest comes from a series of streams that converge outside the walls. Once the canals were used by the city's dyers, tanners and paper mills; today their mossy walls and small bridges offer a slightly bucolic touch to the casual *osterie* ranged alongside.

Treviso is famous in the Veneto for its number of millionaires, the product of its family-run businesses. The most famous – Benetton – has branched out from the home-knitted jumpers of Giuliana Benetton to less fashionable assets, like a sizeable chunk of Italy's motorway system. The oversized Benetton store in piazza Indipendenza is a reminder of the family's connections to the

city… just as the '*polenta si, couscous no*' stickers around the town indicate that all that cash has led to increased immigration but no increase of interracial harmony in this very conservative and very Catholic city.

Around the corner from the Benetton store are piazza dei Signori and the Palazzo dei Trecento, the town hall which dates back to 1217. Across from the palazzo in piazza Duomo, the **Duomo** (open 9am-noon, 3.30-6.30pm daily) contains an *Annunciation* (1570) by Titian and a beautiful *Adoration of the Magi* (1520) by Pordenone. Two other churches in nearby piazza San Vito – **San Vito** and **Santa Lucia** (both open 8am-noon daily) – offer splendid frescoes by Tommaso da Modena (1325-79), considered by some to be the greatest 14th-century artist after Giotto.

The church of **Santa Caterina**. *See p274.*

Moving mountains

Behind Cortina d'Ampezzo's glam sophistication and breath taking natural surroundings lies a bleak heritage of wartime suffering. The town had been part of the Habsburg empire from 1511, but when Italy entered World War I in 1915, the Austro-Hungarians abandoned it swiftly, beating a hasty retreat into the mountains where their defences stopped the advance of the Italian forces. As winter approached, both sides began digging into a platform high up stark, rugged Monte Lagazuoi (2,752m). Temperatures that fell to −30°C and snow nine metres deep meant that thousands of men died not in combat but from hypothermia, disease and starvation.

The tunnels, open emplacements and trenches that witnessed those chilling events are now being restored and opened to the public in an EU-financed project run by Cortina in partnership with the Austrian town of Innsbrück. Spread over a swathe of bitterly contested mountainside to the west of Cortina, the open-air Museo della Grande Guerra (Great War Museum) comprises three sites (Monte Lagazuoi, Monte Cinque Torri and the Tre Sassi Fort) within a five-mile radius, each furnished with well sign posted walking tracks and information panels.

Five kilometres (three miles) out of Cortina on the SS48, is the Pocol Sacrario Militare, a war memorial erected in 1935; the 48m (157ft) tower stands on top of a two-floor mausoleum where the remains of 9,707 Italian soldiers and 37 Austro-Hungarian troops are interred. To the right of the entrance is the small church built in 1916 by the Italian Alpini regiment. Continuing west, Monte Cinque Torri lies to the south of the road. If the hike up looks daunting you can hop on the chairlift from the road, whizzing up to the high Italian defences in minutes. Otherwise various paths will take you to the top, from where there's a breath-taking view of the whole front line as you walk along miles of trenches.

Further along the SS48, turn off right for the Valparola pass and the Fortezza Tre Sassi, an Austro-Hungarian fortress initially

More works by Da Modena, including his masterpiece *The Life of St Ursula* are tucked away in **Santa Caterina** in piazza Giacomo Matteotti (open during exhibitions only). The privately run **Casa dei Carraresi** (0422 513 161) at via Palestra 33-5 is an exhibition space with world-class pretensions. For a fresco fest, head to the church of **San Francesco** (open 7am-noon, 3-7pm daily). Work on the ceiling of the main chapel includes the wonderful *St Francis with Stigmata*, by an anonymous 14th-century painter, though some argue it should be attributed to Da Modena. Da Modena pops up yet again with a series of frescoes in the chapter house of the Dominican monastery adjoining the Romanesque-Gothic church of **San Nicolò** (via San Nicolò, open 8am-noon, 3.30-6pm daily).

Where to stay & eat

Toni del Spin (via Inferiore 7, 0422 543 829, closed Mon lunch, all Sun & mid July-mid Aug, average €30) is a pretty, intimate *osteria* serving local specialities at reasonable prices. **Trattoria Due Mori** (via Bailo 9, 0422 540 383, closed Wed, average €25) dishes up no-frills fare and alfresco seating in the centre of town. A cute spot with a young crowd can be found at **Osteria ai Filodrammatici** (via Filodrammatici 5, 0422 580 011, closed Sun lunch & Mon, average €20). **Muscoli** (via Pescheria 23, 0422 583 390, closed Sun, closed Wed in Apr-Oct, average €15) is the place to go for a reviving *ombra* (glass of wine) and outstanding nibbles. **Albergo Il Focolare** (piazza Ancilotto 4, 0422 56 601, www.albergoil focolare.net, €85 double, breakfast €6) offers good service right in the heart of town.

Resources

Tourist information

IAT *Piazza Monte di Pietà 8 (0422 547 632/fax 0422 419 092/www.provincia.treviso.it).* **Open** 9am-12.30pm Mon; 9am-12.30pm, 2-6pm Tue-Fri; 9am-12.30pm, 3-6pm Sat; 9.30am-12.30pm, 3-6pm Sun.

Getting there

By car
Take the Treviso Sud exit from the A27 motorway; alternatively, take the SS13 from Venice–Mestre.

By train
Regular Venice–Treviso services (25 minutes).

built at the end of the 18th century and bombarded during the Great War. The building is now a museum housing interesting artefacts from the period.

Hovering above the fortezza is Monte Lagazuoi, reachable on the SS48. The Falzarego-Lagazuoi cable car races you up the mountain; alternatively, you can clamber to the top. Here you will find miles of tunnels burrowed deep into the mountain, fitted out with exhibits and sound commentaries. The guide ropes and steps that have been added recently make the pathways easier to navigate, though the pitch-black tunnels are nevertheless not for the claustrophobic. It is also possible to visit some of the trenches and frontline positions.

Though all the walks are relatively 'easy' (at least for experienced walkers), you will need nerves of steel to cross the suspension bridge on Mount Lagazuoi, which connects the Austrian ledge to the Vonbank position. Ropes are highly recommended for the section preceding the bridge… just to add a hint of danger to your jaunt.

Practicalities

The Museo della Grande Guerra (www.grande guerra.dolomiti.org) is open all year, and free. Hire audio guides for the mountain excursions at cable car and chairlift ticket offices. Admission to the Tre Sassi Fort costs €4.

Tickets for the Cinque Torri chairlift and Lagazuoi cable car cost €8.50 uphill, €6 downhill and €11.50 round trip. The Freepass day ticket costs €16 and comprises entry to the Tre Sassi museum, plus cable car/chairlift return trips on the two mountains. No credit cards.

All the sites scan be reached by bus from Cortina; the tourist office (see p280) has timetables. You are advised to take torches if you're planning to explore the tunnels on Monte Lagazuoi.Guided tours are available all year round; contact the Gruppo Guide Alpine Cortina (corso Italia 69, 0436 868 505, www.dolomiti.org/guidecortina) for information. Guides are particularly recommended during winter months when skis or snow shoes are necessary to see the sites.

By bus

ACTV and ATVO (for both, see p286) buses run regularly from Venice's bus terminus in piazzale Roma.

West from Treviso

The plains and hills of the Po basin west of Treviso are brimming with day-trip potential. Between Treviso and Castelfranco are two fine villas by Andrea Palladio (see p266 **Andrea Palladio**): the magnificent **Villa Barbaro a Maser** and **Villa Emo** (for both, see p277). Villa Barbaro, among the most famous of all Palladian villas and not just those in this region, is an out-and-out exercise in rural utopianism.

It derives partly from Palladio's intellectual communion with the Barbaro brothers for whom it was designed and built between 1550 and 1557, and partly from the quality of the decoration. For only in this villa did the architect find a painter, Paolo Veronese, capable of matching his genius.

The light, airy rooms house the artist's sumptuous *trompe l'œil* frescoes. Two traditional parts of the Veneto farmhouse have been dressed up in a new classical disguise: those two arcaded wings flanking

the main porticoed building are actually *barchesse*, or farmhouse wings; while the mirror-image, sundial-adorned chapel fronts on either end are in fact dovecotes. Behind these is a nymphaeum – a semicircular pool surrounded by statues.

A tad more rustic, Villa Emo was one of the first properties built as part of a Venetian scheme to encourage landowners to develop uncultivated land and exert greater government control over the *terra firma*. Still owned by the Emo family, it contains joyous frescoes by Giambattista Zelotti, one of the major fresco artists of the late Italian Renaissance.

In **Castelfranco Veneto**, the **Duomo** (open 9.30-11.45am, 3.15-5.45pm Mon-Sat) is home to *Madonna and Child with Saints Liberal and Francis* (1504), one of the few surviving masterpieces of local boy done good Giorgio Barbarella, better known as Giorgione. The moats and 13th-century fortified red-brick wall provide a picturesque backdrop to the town.

Another local boy is featured in the tiny village of **Possagno**. Inside the family home of sculptor Antonio Canova (1757-1822) is the **Gipsoteca Canoviana** (see p277). The museum has many of Canova's works, including the striking black-tack-studded

Villa Barbaro a Maser: among the most famous Palladian villas. *See p277.*

plaster models for the finished statues. Canova's neo-classical statues have been praised as among the best since Michelangelo, and damned as precursors of Totalitarian Art; the Gipsoteca lets you make up your own mind. Modernist architect Carlo Scarpa is responsible for the museum's extension, built between 1955-7.

Scarpa, the quintessential Venetian, shared his city's traditional fascination with the East, fusing the ancient and modern in functional but striking spaces. His other trademarks were the use of natural elements as raw material and his ability to combine inner and outer space. For further treats, head to the cemetery (open 9am-7pm daily) in **San Vito d'Altivole**. Among the more mundane remembrances is the massive *Tomba Brion* – 2,200 square metres (23,656 square feet) of pure Scarpa, who spent the nine years before his death in 1978 constructing the monster. He is also buried here.

Robert Browning fell so deeply in love with the picture-postcard landscape of **Asolo** that he named his last collection of verse after the town (*Asolando*, 1889). Set among rolling hills covered with cypress trees, olive groves and vineyards, the town is a place for luxuriating, rather than sight-seeing – a dedicated tourist can cover the town in 20 minutes.

Asolo is perfect for window-shopping, a long lunch and a leisurely walk with the town's illustrious ghosts: Caterina Cornaro, the exiled Venetian-born Queen of Cyprus, who set up court in Asolo in 1489, and the 19th-century actress Eleonora Duse. When you're through with luxuriating, Asolo is also a good base for exploring the other small gems of the area.

To the west of Asolo, **Bassano del Grappa** sits astride the Brenta river just as it emerges from the mountains. Monte Grappa, a few kilometres outside of town, offers its name to both the town and Italy's fiery after-dinner drink. Technically a pomace brandy, grappa began life as a way to get the most out of the grapes used for wine-making. After the grapes are pressed, 20 per cent of their total weight still remains, in the form of skins, seeds, stems and so on: this is known as the pomace. Instead of throwing it out, the frugal inhabitants of the Veneto distil it and use it as a sort of internal central heating system during the winter.

These days upscale restaurants come around after dinner with a grappa trolley, but the traditional method of drinking it – pouring a slug into a cup of espresso for a *caffè corretto* – still works just fine. The oldest and most famous name in grappa is Nardini (Ponte Vecchio 2), whose distillery is located in Bassano's main street, just outside the old city gates. Another famous name, Poli, can be found at via Gamba 6, at the foot of Bassano's showpiece, the Ponte degli Alpini. Though the

The Veneto

original bridge was probably constructed in the 1150s, what we see now is a faithful copy of Palladio's magnificent covered wooden bridge built in 1586. The copy dates back no further than 1948 – Palladio's having been blown up by retreating German troops at the end of World War II.

Bassano is one of Italy's wealthiest cities, a fact easily confirmed by window-shopping in the city centre. The shops are decidedly high-end, with a rich selection of Italian fashion, jewellery, ceramics and gourmet food. In piazza Garibaldi – one of the town's two main squares – is the **Museo Civico** (*see below*), located inside the beautiful convent and cloistered gardens of the 14th-century church of San Francesco.

The museum contains a fine collection of ceramics – Bassano is also known for its ceramics industry – and an archaeological section devoted to the city's Roman origins. The other square – piazza Libertà – is dominated by the medieval Palazzo Municipale, which is covered with faded frescoes. The **Museo degli Alpini** (*see below*), with its interesting collection of World War I memorabilia, stands at the far end of the ponte degli Alpini.

Gipsoteca Canoviana
Piazza Canova 74, Possagno (0423 544 323/ www.museocanova.it). **Open** 9am-12.30pm, 3-6pm Tue-Sun. **Admission** €5; €3.50 concessions. **No credit cards.**

Museo Civico
Piazza Garibaldi 12, Bassano (0424 519 450/www. museobassano.it). **Open** 9am-6.30pm Tue-Sat; 3.30-6.30pm Sun. **Admission** €4.50; €3 concessions. **No credit cards.**

Museo degli Alpini
Via Angarano 2, Bassano (0424 503 662). **Open** 9am-8pm Tue-Sun. **Admission** free.

Villa Barbaro a Maser
Via Cornuda 7, Maser (0423 923 004/fax 0423 923 002/www.villadimaser.it). **Open** *Mar-Oct* 3-6pm Tue, Sat, Sun. *Nov-Feb* 2.30-5pm Sat, Sun. Other days by appointment for groups only (min 20 persons). **Admission** €5; €4.50 groups (by appointment). **No credit cards. Photo** *p276*.

Villa Emo
Via Stazione 5, Fanzolo di Vedelago (0423 476 414/ fax 0423 487 043). **Open** *Apr-Oct* 3-7pm daily. *Nov-Mar* 2-6pm Sat, Sun. **Admission** €5.50; €3 concessions. **No credit cards.**

Where to stay & eat

In Asolo, the **Hotel Duse** (via Browning 190, 0423 55 241, www.hotelduse.com, €100-€120 double, breakfast €6) is a comfortable three-star

option in the centre of town. The **Villa Cipriani** (via Canova 298, 0423 523 411, www.sheraton.com/villacipriani, €307-€605 double) and the **Albergo al Sole** (via Collegio 33, 0423 951 332, www.albergoal sole.com, €170-€255 double) are best for full-immersion luxury.

Meanwhile, **Ca' Derton** (piazza d'Annunzio 11, 0423 529 648, closed Mon lunch, Sun dinner & 2wks Aug, average €45) is a firm favourite with Italian foodies. Nearby in the same piazza, **Ristorante Due Mori** (piazza d'Annunzio 5, 0423 952 256, closed Wed, average €35) has more casual but equally delicious repast.

Considering it is such a wealthy city, Bassano can often make up only rather disappointing overnight stay, with few charming hotels and welcoming *osterie*. **Al Castello** (piazza Terraglio 19, 0424 228 665, www.hotelalcastello.it, €70-€90 double) is a reasonably priced three-star. In the centre of town, **Birraria Ottone** (via Matteotti 50, 0424 522 206, closed Mon dinner & Tue, average €25), serving mainly regional and Austrian dishes, is a good bet.

Tourist information

APT Bassano *Largo Corona d'Italia 35 (0424 524 351/fax 0424 525 301/www.comunebassano .vi.it.vicenzae.org).* **Open** 9am-1pm, 2-6pm daily.
IAT Asolo *Piazza Garibaldi 73, Asolo (0423 529 046/fax 0423 524 137).* **Open** 9am-12.30pm Mon-Wed; 9am-12.30pm, 3-6pm Thur-Sun.
IAT Castelfranco Veneto *Via Francesco Maria Preti 66, Castelfranco Veneto (0423 491 416/fax 0423 771 085).* **Open** 9.30am-12.30pm Mon-Wed, Sun; 9.30am-12.30pm, 3-6pm Thur-Sat.

Getting there

For Treviso airport information, *see p285*.

By car
From Treviso, SS53 will take you directly to Castelfranco Veneto. For Asolo, take SS348 to Montbelluna, then take SS248, which continues to Bassano del Grappa and Marostica. Possagno is located a short distance from Asolo on minor roads.

By train
Frequent Venice–Bassano trains also stop at Castelfranco.

By bus
Bus operator La Marca (0422 577 311) runs services from Treviso to Castelfranco and Bassano, and to Villa Barbaro a Maser. The bus for Montebelluna from Castelfranco station passes by Villa Emo.

The Veneto

The hills are alive…

…with the sound of 'Action!' Cortina and the mountains and forests of the Dolomites have provided the backdrop for countless cinematic gems (and howlers). Though ostensibly set in Colorado, Renny Harlin's *Cliffhanger* cliff-edge scenes were predominantly shot in the more dramatic Dolomites. Practised climbers bad-mouthed the film for its inaccurate depiction of the sport, but Sly Stallone saving the day offers spectacular shots of these craggy peaks.

Also set in north America, Jean-Jacques Annaud's *The Bear* was filmed in the Dolomites natural park. Not nearly as gory as *Grizzly*, this is an eco-friendly fable about an orphan bear cub hooking up with an older male for company and protection against us nasty humans.

Two big films taking even bigger advantage of Cortina and her environs are *The Pink Panther* and *For Your Eyes Only*. The first sees the hapless Inspector Clouseau (Peter Sellars) pursuing the elusive Phantom (David Niven); watching these movies, anyone who has ever tried to reach Cortina using public transport might gasp at the sight of a working train station in the town, while skiers will weep at the sight of the unpopulated slopes.

For Your Eyes Only really makes full use of all that Cortina has to offer. The town centre, with snow sculptures from the town's annual competition, was 'enhanced' with truckloads of snow brought down from the slopes. The Olympic stadia (Cortina hosted the Winter Olympics in 1956) take centre stage. Part of the plot revolves around a figure skater; we catch her dancing in the Olympic ice stadium. Further stunning stunts are shot on local ski-runs and the dramatically sculptural Olympic ski-jump. With a cliffhanger shot on top of the Tofana mountain, the film is a hymn to the dazzling beauty of this Dolomite diamond.

North from Treviso

The famous Bellini cocktail began life up the A27 motorway from Treviso, in the area of hills and valleys known as the Altamarca Trevigiana. Sheltered from cold northerlies by the nearby Dolomites and enjoying warmer air sweeping up the Adriatic, the area between Conegliano and Valdobbiadene is home to the sparkling *prosecco* necessary for Harry's (*see p171* **Harry's Bar**) signature bubbly-and-peach-juice drink, as well as Italy's oldest *strada del vino* – an itinerary around vineyards and wine outlets), the obviously named *Strada del Prosecco*.

The town of **Conegliano** is another in the string of pleasant, unchallenging Veneto towns. The 14th-century **Duomo** is home to a painting of the *Virgin and Child with Saints and Angels* by the town's most famous son, Giambattista Cima, known as Cima da Conegliano. Conegliano's cultural treasures end here, but visit the **Sala dei Battuti** (open Apr-Sept 3.30-7pm Sun; Oct-Mar 3-6.30pm Sun) next to the Duomo: dedicated to a brotherhood of flagellants, it's decorated with some truly odd 15th- and 16th-century biblical frescoes.

The hills change to mountains near **Vittorio Veneto** and the air seems a little fresher, the light a little sharper. Originally two smaller towns called Ceneda and Serravalle, Vittorio Veneto was formed and named in 1866, to commemorate the unification of Italy under King Vittorio Emanuele II. Serravalle boasts a well-preserved medieval *borgo* (quarter), which is unfortunately situated right on the busy *strada statale*. It's worth braving the exhaust fumes for a brief walk through the

The Veneto

borgo and an admiring glance at the frescoed Loggia Serravallese, which dates from 1462.

Both Conegliano and Vittorio Veneto offer access to Valdobbiadene; the road from Vittorio Veneto (take the SS51 out of town then follow signs) has the advantage of passing through Follina. Here, nestled among the hills of the *prealpi* and the sleepy town centre is one of the jewels of the Veneto, the **Abbazia Santa Maria** (open 6.30am-noon, 2.30-9.30pm daily). The Romanesque abbey dates back to the 12th century and features one of the most peaceful cloisters you'll ever see. A few kilometres before Follina, the **Castello Brandolini** (0438 9761, www.castelbrando.it) is an intriguing mixture of ancient castle (it dates back to a Roman fortress) and modern health spa. Even if wellness isn't your thing, the trip up the elevator is worth the €1 it costs for the views of the valley.

The town of **Valdobbiadene** is the headquarters for the production of *prosecco*, an autochthonous (it means 'native') grape which fills 33 million bottles a year. The townspeople – in conjunction with the area's wine producers – are diligent in their efforts to uphold the reputation of the dry, slightly bitter bubbly, most notably in an annual *Mostra nazionale degli spumanti*, which takes place in September – visit www.mostranazionalespumanti.it for more information. The tourist office in the town (*see p281*) will also provide a complete list of producers on request. Azienda Bisol, in the neighbouring village of Santo Stefano (via Fol 33, 0423 900 138), produces one of the best *prosecchi* you can get. Hydro-electric power has long been vital to Italy's economy, and the many reservoirs and generating stations that you can see along the *Strada d'Alemagna* – the main road (SS51) from Vittorio Veneto to Belluno – are a vivid reminder of this.

It is hard not to rhapsodise about the area. Lago di Santa Croce is a semi-artificial mirror reflecting jagged Dolomite peaks, the thick forests of Bosco di Cansiglio, and the truly stupendous natural bowl formed by the high valley of the Alpago. There's no shortage of awe-inspiring views, or trails (maps available from the APT in Belluno, *see p280*) to view them from. On top of all the natural beauty there are plenty of reasonable hotels and some wonderful restaurants serving everything from home-cured sausages to Michelin-starred culinary creations.

Like Treviso, the medieval town of **Belluno** invites comparisons with Venice. 'The Venice of the Alps' occupies a rocky terrace overlooking the Piave and Ardo rivers. How high the town is perched is wonderfully illustrated by the escalator that carries visitors from the Lamboi car park to the main piazza. The escalator emerges on to a scene that is pure enchantment. Against a beautiful backdrop of mountains and tranquillity, the 15th-century Palazzo dei Rettori (once home to the town's Venetian rulers; not open to the public) and 16th-century **Duomo** (open 7am-12.30pm, 3.30-7.30pm daily) recall the architecture along the Grand Canal. The **Baptistry** (variable hours) across from the Duomo contains an early 18th-century carving of John the Baptist by Andrea Brustolon. Just outside the old city walls is the new heart of the town , piazza dei Martiri. Still called Campadel by locals, this pleasant, open square, with plenty of benches for relaxing and breathing in the mountain air, had its name changed in 1945, in memory of the four partisans hanged from its lamp-posts.

In the mountains beyond Belluno is the jet-set capital of the Dolomites, **Cortina d'Ampezzo** – beautiful, but expensive. Summer sport pursuits range from the obvious climbing and hiking to riding and fishing. For those with thighs of thunder and butts of steel, mountain bikes can be hired from 2UE & 2UE (via Roma 70, 0436 4121, www.dueduecortina.com). Half a day will set you back €14. Family cards are available, plus a bike shuttle service. For would-be Reinhold Messners, check out the *Scuola roccia* rock climbing school (corso Italia 69B, 0436 868 505, www.guidecortina.com), which offers individual lessons, group excursions and guided solo climbs.

If you're heading for Cortina, stop off at **Borca di Cadore** to check out architect Carlo Scarpa's amazing church (open 9am-noon, 4-6pm daily), built in 1959. Borca itself is a time warp experience. Constructed by the state-owned ENI fuel company as a holiday camp for its sickly workers, this village has remained virtually unchanged since the 1950s. If you're looking for a mountain retreat that bears no resemblance to Heidi's homestead, check in to one of the village apartments or main hotel. To book, contact the Centro Vacanze at Borca di Cadore (Dolomiti Gestioni, on the SS51, 0435 487 500, open 8.30am-12.30pm, 2-6pm Mon-Sat). Borca is also home to one of Italy's most spectacular health spas, Corte Spa (via Enrico Mattei Km88, 0435 482 527, www.cortespa.it). It offers pampering from stone massage to mud treatments and an indoor pool with panoramic Alpine views, so you'll feel (and look) part of the jet set after a session here.

To the west of Belluno, **Feltre** was once a Roman fortress on the banks of the river Piave. Today it is a perfectly preserved 16th-century town. Among the cobbled streets and frescoed *palazzi*, the sharp-eyed visitor will notice that many of the lapidaries are chipped clean. *La Serenissima* was a munificent patron to Feltre, and financed a well-endowed rebuilding programme after the town was destroyed in 1510 by the troops of the Holy Roman Emperor Maximilian I. Many of the stone markers praised Venice for its aforementioned munificence. When Napoleon rolled in (an event marked by one of the few unchipped lapidaries in town) he took umbrage at all the praise directed towards his enemies, and ordered the words destroyed. Despite Napoleon's enmity, paintings and statues of the lion of St Mark are everywhere. Many of the *palazzi* along Feltre's high street, via Mezzaterra, are frescoed by local artist Lorenzo Luzzo (1467-1512); frescoes on simple merchants' houses down the town's narrow alleyways are often just as striking.

Where to stay & eat

For good-value local cuisine in Conegliano, try the **Trattoria Stella** (via Accademia 3, 0438 22 178, closed Sun & 3wks Aug, average €25). Alternatively, for something more upmarket, head for **Ristorante al Salisà** (via XX Settembre 2, 0438 24 288, closed Tue dinner, Wed, average €35) and take the chance to indulge in a bottle from its excellent wine list.

On the same street you will find the **Hotel Canon d'Oro** (via XX Settembre 131, 0438 34 246, www.hotelcanondoro.it, €80-€175 double). The **Hotel dei Chiostri** in Follina (piazza Municipio 20, 0438 971 805, www.hoteldei chiostri.com, €130-€155 double) is a super-swanky hotel right across the street from the Abbazia (*see p279*); its sister hotel, the upscale **Villa Abbazia** (piazza IV Novembre 3, 0438 971 277, www.hotelabbazia.it, €200-€255 double) is one of the fanciest hotels in the region.

At the lovely **Trattoria alla Cima** in Valdobbiadene (via Cima 13, 0423 972 711, closed Mon dinner, Tue, average €30) you can enjoy excellent grilled meats, an incomparable view of the vineyards and the opportunity to eavesdrop on *prosecco* producers discussing the latest oenological news. East of Belluno, the **Locanda San Lorenzo** in the small town of Puos d'Alpago (via IV Novembre 79, 0437 454 048, www.locandasanlorenzo.it, closed Wed & 3wks Jan-Feb, average €55) offers some of the Veneto's best food, and doubles as an excellent hotel (€95 double). A few kilometres away, the even smaller town of Plois di Pieve d'Alpago (generally shortened to Pieve d'Alpago) is home to Michelin-starred **Dolada** (via Dolada 21, 0437 479 141, www.dolada.it, average €65), also a three-star hotel (€103 double, breakfast €13).

In Cortina, the **Baita Fraina** (località Fraina 1, 0436 3634, closed Mon, 2wks Jan, 2wks July, average €30) offers hearty fare on a panoramic terrace. The **Hotel Menardi** (via Majon 110,

0436 24 00, www.hotelmenardi.it, €103 double) has excellent modern facilities in a rustic setting.

Belluno's rustic **Al Borgo** restaurant (via Anconetta 8, 0437 926 755, closed Mon dinner, Tue & 2wks Jan, average €30) offers smoked ham and sausages, and unusual, filling pasta dishes. For accommodation try the centrally located **Albergo delle Alpi** (via Tasso 13, 0437 940 545, www.dellealpi.it, €110 double).

In Feltre, the **Belle Epoque** (piazza Maggiore, 0439 80193, closed Mon & 2 wks Jan, average €25) serves up comforting food under the porticos of the town's main square.

Tourist information

For information on ski resorts in the region, consult www.dolomitisuperski.it. For the Cortina area, see www.impianticortina.it.

IAT Belluno *Piazza Duomo 2 (0437 940 083/fax 0437 958 716/www.infodolomiti.it).* **Open** 9am-12.30pm, 3.30-6.30pm daily. Closed Sunday afternoons Oct-Mar.

IAT Conegliano Via XX Settembre 61 (0438 21 230/fax 0438 428 777/www.turismo.provincia. treviso.it). **Open** 9.30am-12.30pm daily; 3-6pm Thur, Fri, Sat.

IAT Cortina *Piazzetta San Francesco 8 (0436 3231/fax 0436 3235/www.infodolomiti.it).* **Open** 9am-12.30pm, 3.30-6.30pm daily.

IAT Feltre *Piazzetta Trento e Trieste 9 (0439 2540/fax 0439 2839/www.infodolomiti.it).* **Open** 9am-12.30pm, 3.30-6.30pm daily.

IAT Valdobbiadene *Piazza Marconi 1 (0423 976 975/www.valdobbiadene.com).* **Open** 9.30am-12.30pm, 3-6pm daily.

Getting there

By car

From Treviso take the SS13 to Conegliano, then the SS51 (*Strada d'Alemagna*) to Vittorio Veneto and Belluno. The three towns can also be reached by the A27 motorway. For the Alpago, turn off SS51 on to SS422d. To get to Feltre from Belluno, take SS50. For Cortina and Borca, continue on SS51.

By train

Fast Venice–Udine trains stop at Conegliano; local Venice–Belluno trains call at Conegliano and Vittorio Veneto as well. There's a local train service from Treviso to Feltre. For Cortina and Borca di Cadore, take the train to Calalzo, where there are bus connections to the towns.

By bus

Services from Venice's piazzale Roma to Belluno run during the summer, stopping at Conegliano and Vittorio Veneto. La Marca (0422 577 311) runs services from Treviso's bus station to the three towns, as well as Feltre. Buses to Plois di Pieve d'Alpago and Puos d'Alpago run from Belluno – call Dolomiti Bus, 0437 941 167, for information.

There's an ATVO (0421 383 671) bus from piazzale Roma to Cortina d'Ampezzo at 7.50am (daily through summer; Saturdays and Sundays only for most of the rest of the year, except peak skiing weeks; consult the excellent website www.atvo.it – in English – for details); the journey takes three-and-a-half hours. The return service leaves Cortina at 3.15pm and will, on request, proceed to Venice airport after reaching piazzale Roma at 6.15pm.

East from Treviso

Friuli-Venezia Giulia, the Veneto's neighbour to the east, is best known for Trieste, the very Mittel European port where James Joyce once taught English. But it is **Aquileia** that draws the attention of art historians.

Legend has it that an eagle (*aquila*) soared overhead as the outline of the new town of Aquileia was being ploughed up in 181 BC, giving the town its name. In short order, it became one of the most important cities in the Roman Empire, with a population of more than 100,000. By the fourth century Aquileia was one of Italy's most important patriarchates, but constant harrying by barbarian tribes forced the bishop to shift his residence to nearby Grado.

The 11th-century **Basilica Teodoriana** (piazza Capitolo 1, open 8.30am-12.30pm, 2.30-5.30pm daily) contains 700 square metres (2,333 square feet) of mosaic paving – remains from a fourth-century church that stood on the site –

with a mishmash of imagery both Christian (Jonah and the whale, the Good Shepherd) and pagan (tortoises and cockerels). In the apse, frescoes dated 1031 show the patriarch Poppo, who founded the basilica in the 11th century, with Emperor Conrad II and his wife and son, before the Virgin Mary. Twelfth-century frescoes depicting the lives of Christ and Mary are to be found in the crypt beneath the presbytery – entrance is by **Museo Archeologico** (*see below*) ticket; the crypt is a more interesting sight than the museum itself.

Museo Archeologico
Via Roma 1, Aquileia (0431 91 016/www.museo archeo-aquileia.it). **Open** 8.30am-2pm Mon; 8.30am-7.30pm Tue-Sun. **Admission** €4; €2 concessions. **No credit cards**.

Tourist information
IAT *Piazza Capitolo 4 (tel & fax 0431 919 491/ www.aquileia.it).* **Open** *Jan-Oct* 9.30am-3.30pm daily. *Nov, Dec* 9.30am-3.30pm Fri-Sun.

Getting there

By car
Coming from Venice take the A4 Venice–Trieste motorway. Exit at Palmanova (17km from Aquileia) and follow the southbound SS352 road.

By train
Some Venice–Trieste trains stop at nearby Cervignano station; regular SAF buses do the 8km trip from the station to Aquileia regularly through the day.

Belluno's **city walls**. See p279.

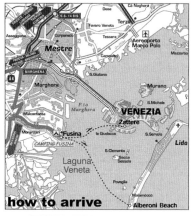

Directory

Directory

Arriving & Leaving

By air – Venice

Venice Marco Polo Airport – SAVE SpA
Viale G Galilei 30/1, Tessera (switchboard 041 260 6111/flight & airport information 041 260 9260/www.veniceairport.it).

To & from Venice airport

By boat

Docks are seven minutes' walk from arrivals; porter service costs €4.50. A shuttle bus runs every ten mins, 6am-8pm, and costs €1.
Società Alilaguna
(041 523 5775/www.alilaguna. com). **No credit cards.**
Alilaguna's colour-coded services link the airport to Venice. Most useful and least likely to alter its timetable at short notice is Linea Rossa (Red line), an hourly service (6.15am-12.15am from the airport to Venice; 4.20am-10.40pm in the other direction). Tickets (€12) can be purchased at Alilaguna's counter in the arrivals hall or on board. Allow 70mins from or to San Marco. The service also stops at Murano, the Lido and Arsenale; after San Marco it proceeds to Zattere. Other lines (Blue, Orange, Yellow and Gold) run throughout the day to different stops in Venice, including Fondamente Nove and Guglie. See the website for up-to-date timetables.
Consorzio Motoscafi Venezia
Marco Polo Airport, arrivals hall (041 541 5084). **No credit cards.**
A water-taxi ride to your hotel in Venice will take about 25-30 minutes and cost upwards of €90.
Bucintoro Agency
Marco Polo Airport, arrivals hall (041 521 0632/www.bucintoro viaggi.com). **No credit cards.**
If your flight arrives between 8am and 7pm, book online at least 24 hours in advance (not weekends),

By bus

ATVO
Marco Polo Airport, arrivals hall (0421 383 672/www.atvo.it).
Open 8am-midnight daily.
Tickets €3, €5.50 return.
No credit cards.
A 20 minute express service (number 35) between the airport and piazzale Roma. Buy tickets from the ATVO counter or their piazzale Roma office. Buses leave hourly or more often (8.20am-12.10am from airport; 5am-8.40pm from piazzale Roma) After 8.40pm buses from piazzale Roma to San Donà and Lido di Jesolo stop at the airport on request.
ACTV
Marco Polo Airport, arrivals hall (0421 383 672/timetable information 041 24 24/www.actv. it). **Open** 8am-midnight daily.
Tickets €2. **No credit cards.**
Bus 5 travels between the airport and piazzale Roma, leaving the airport at 4.08am and 5.10am, piazzale Roma at 4.40am, then both ends at 5.40am, 6.15am, 6.40am, and then every half-hour until midnight; journey time 35-40 minutes. Buy tickets (€2) on board, at the ACTV counter or from their piazzale Roma office.

By taxi

Cooperativa Artigiana Radio Taxi
Marco Polo Airport, arrivals hall (041 541 6363/info 041 595 1402/switchboard 041 595 2080/ taxiapt@radiotaxive.mysem.it).
Credit AmEx, MC, V.
To or from piazzale Roma takes about 20 minutes and costs about €30. Credit cards only accepted for payments at the arrivals hall.

By bus

Buses to Venice all arrive at piazzale Roma in Venice. For bus services on mainland Venice and the Lido, *see p289*; to other destinations in the Veneto, see relevant chapters.

By rail

Most trains arrive at Santa Lucia station in Venice (map p321 D4), though a few will only take you as far as Mestre on the mainland; if so, change to a local train (every ten minutes or less during the day) for the short hop across the lagoon. *See also p290*.

By road

Venice is connected to other large Italian and European cities by fast motorway links, but prohibitive parking fees make this one of the least practical modes of arrival. However, many Venetian hotels offer their guests discounts at car parks. Main car parks are listed below.

Autorimessa Comunale
Santa Croce 496, piazzale Roma (041 272 7301/www.asmvenezia. it). Vaporetto Piazzale Roma.
Open 24hrs daily. **Rates** €20 per 24hrs or part thereof. **Credit** AmEx, DC, MC, V. **Map** p320 C5.
Covered parking for over 2,300 cars, automatic number plate reader and 200 CCTV cameras. Reservation online recommended.

Marco Polo Park
Marco Polo Airport, (041 541 5913/www.veniceairport.it). Bus 5 from piazzale Roma/free shuttle bus from main entrance of Venice airport. **Open** 24hrs daily. **Rates** €12 daily (discounts for longer periods). **Credit** AmEx, DC, MC, V.
Unsupervised. No reservations.

Parcheggio Sant'Andrea
Santa Croce 465B, piazzale Roma (041 272 7304/www.asmvenezia. it). Vaporetto Piazzale Roma.

Open 24hrs daily. **Rates** €4 .50 2hrs. **Credit** AmEx, MC, V. **Map** p320 C5.
Short-stay car park; 130 spaces.

Parking Stazione

Viale Stazione 10, Mestre (041 938 021). Bus 2 from piazzale Roma or train to Mestre station. **Open** 24hrs daily. **Rates** €5 per day Mon-Fri; €10 per day Sat, Sun, public holidays. **Credit** AmEx, DC, MC, V.

Park Terminal Fusina

Via Moranzani 79, Fusina (041 547 0160/fax 014 547 9133/ www.terminalfusina.it). Vaporetto 16 from Zattere to Fusina (runs hourly *Nov-Mar* 8am-6pm daily; *Apr-May, Oct* 8am-8pm daily; *June-Sept* 8am-10pm daily). **Open** 24hrs daily. **Rates** €8 up to 12 hours; €13 up to 24 hours. **Credit** MC, V.
Park on the mainland and catch a vaporetto to the centre of Venice.

Venezia Tronchetto Parking

Isola Nuova del Tronchetto 1, (041 520 7555/www.venice parking.it). Vaporetto Tronchetto. **Open** 24hrs daily. **Rates** €3 per hour, €20 7-24 hours, €20 per day. (20% discount with Venicecard (*see p68* **Discount cards**) and on stays over 3 days) **Credit** AmEx, MC, V. **Map** p320 A3.
3,500 covered stalls with CCTV. Online booking recommended.

By air – Treviso

Treviso Sant'Angelo Airport – Aer Tre SpA

Via Noalese, Treviso (airport information 0422 315 111/ www.trevisoairport.it).

To & from Treviso airport

ATVO
(Timetable information 0422 315 327/www.atvo.it)
Bus services run from Venice's piazzale Roma and back to coincide with flights – if the flight arrives late, the bus will wait. The journey takes about 70 minutes, and costs €5 one way, €9 round trip (valid for seven days). Buses from piazzale Roma leave ridiculously early so ensure your timely arrival. Alternatively, take a train to Treviso (35 minutes) and then a bus or taxi (Cooperativa Radiotaxi Padova, 049 651 333) to the airport. **ACTT** (0422 3271) bus 6 does the 20-minute trip from in front of Treviso train station to the airport at 10 and 40 minutes past the hour and costs €1.

By air – Verona

Valerio Catullo Airport

Verona Villafranca (045 809 5666/www.aeroportoverona.it).

To & from Verona airport

A bus (0458 057911) runs every 20 minutes to the train station from 6.35am to 11.35pm. The 20-minute journey costs €4.20 (pay on bus).

Airlines

Many airlines have offices in the Venice departures hall, as does SAVE (041 260 6432, fax 041 260 6429, open 5.30am-9pm daily, credit AmEx, DC, MC, V) which handles other lines.

Alitalia

(06 2222/www.alitalia.it). **Open** 5.30am-8pm daily. **Credit** AmEx, DC, MC, V.

British Airways

SAVE ticket counter (199 712 266/www.britishairways.com). **Open** 5.30am-9pm daily. **Credit** AmEx, DC, MC, V.

Easyjet

SAVE ticket counter (848 887 766/www.easyjet.com). **Open** 5.30am-9pm daily. **Credit** AmEx, DC, MC, V.

Ryanair

Treviso Airport (0422 315 331). **Open** *Office* 7am-10pm daily. *Premium rate booking line 899 678 910.* **Credit** MC, V.

Cutting costs

The privilege of seeing Venice from the waterways does not come cheap: a single ticket costs a whopping €5, but is valid for 60 minutes from the time of validating, allowing for multiple journeys. The fare for a shuttle journey (ie one stop across the Grand Canal, the hop across to the Giudecca, or from Sant'Elena to the Lido) is a bargain €2. Tickets can be bought on board.

If you're in Venice for longer than a few hours and plan to make good use of public transport, invest in a 24hr ticket (€12) or a three-day ticket (€25). Unlimited public transport is also included for holders of the Venice Card (*see p68* **Discount cards**).

For even longer stays, a Cartavenezia and *abbonamento* are a sound investment.

Available from main Hellovenezia offices (*see p286*), this three-year travel ID card allows you to pay the same, much lower, rates as Veneto residents; although technically only for residents, a c/o address in Venice will suffice. A one-off charge of €8 is made for the card, for which you will need one passport photo and valid photo ID.

You must buy an *abbonamento* (monthly season ticket: €26; €18 students) when applying for the Cartavenezia. After the first month, you can buy another *abbonamento*, single tickets for €1, or a *carnet* (ten tickets) for €9. All tickets must be validated at the time of first use in the yellow stamping machines at vaporetto stops, otherwise you may be liable for a fine.

Getting Around

Public transport – including *vaporetti* (water buses) and buses – in Venice itself and in some mainland areas – is run by **ACTV** (Azienda Comunale per il Trasporto di Venezia).

ACTV's **Hellovenezia** outlets sell tickets for events, vaporetto tickets and *abbonamenti* (passes and season tickets; *see p285* **Cutting costs**). If you're lucky, you can also pick up a free transport timetable booklet, but these are published at the beginning of the season and tend to run out after a month or two (you can download them at www.hellovenezia.it/orari). The extremely helpful **Hellovenezia** (041 24 24) call

centre can provide you with information on ACTV vaporetto and bus schedules, and on events and tourist sights, in English.

ATVO runs more extensive bus services to numerous destinations on the mainland. These services, along with those of many other local companies, are described in The Veneto section of this guide which begins on p235.

Hellovenezia

Santa Croce 509, piazzale Roma (information 041 24 24/www.hello venezia.it). Vaporetto Piazzale Roma. **Map** p320 C5. *Public transport tickets* **Open** 7am-8pm daily. **No credit cards.** *Event tickets* **Open** 8am-6.30pm daily. **Credit** MC, V.

ATVO

Santa Croce 497, piazzale Roma (0421 383 671/www.atvo.it). Vaporetto Piazzale Roma. **Open** 6.30am-7.30pm daily. **Credit** MC, V. **Map** p320 C5.

By bicycle

Bikes are banned – and otiose – in Venice itself. One of the best ways to explore the Lido is by bicycle, but be prepared to fight off hordes of journalists and film critics during the Film Festival in early September (*see chapter* **Film**).

Giorgio Barbieri

Gran viale Santa Maria Elisabetta 79A, Lido (041 526 1490). **Open** Mar-Oct 8.30am-8pm daily. Closed Nov-Feb. **Rates** €3hr; €9 a day. **No credit cards. Map** p317 B3.

On foot: wet

Photos and film footage misrepresent *acqua alta* (high water) making these episodes of flooding look more dramatic than they really are. Except in truly exceptional tides, all that happens is that a couple of inches of water laps into the lowest parts of the city for an hour or two, then recedes. The *acqua alta* season is between September and April. How often a high tide occurs depends on several factors: a high tide in itself is not enough. What's needed is a stiff breeze forcing water up the Adriatic, rain inland, plus particularly high pressure. Some years it doesn't happen at all. When it does, sirens sound five ten-second blasts two hours before the water reaches the maximum.

During the *acqua alta* season, trestles and wooden planks are stacked up along flood-prone thoroughfares, ready to be transformed into raised walkways by the city rubbish department workers. On the very rare occasions when the tide rises more than 120cm (47 inches) above its average level, even the walkways float.

Acqua alta has an etiquette all of its own. It is most evident on the raised walkways where Venetians wait their turn patiently, then proceed along the narrow planks slowly and with consideration for other users. They

expect tourists to do the same, or risk an angry telling-off for their lack of manners.

The etiquette extends beyond the walkways. The *calli* and *campi* may be waterlogged, but they continue to function as a municipal road network; locals are understandably peeved if thoughtless tourists doing Gene Kelly impersonations prevent them from reaching their destination in as dry a state as possible. Remember too, that during *acqua alta* you can't see where the pavement stops and the canal begins.

A map posted at each vaporetto stop shows flood-prone areas and routes covered by raised walkways. If you don't want to get your feet wet, stick to higher ground. Alternatively, sit out those couple of damp hours in your dry hotel room or bar. If, on the other hand, you particularly want to enjoy the *acqua alta* experience, head to St Mark's Square, the lowest lying area in Venice, where even the most amateur photographer can be guaranteed to capture some atmospheric, if predictable, pictures of reflections of the basilica in the floodwater.

The tide office (*Centro maree*) provides *acqua alta* forecasts in Italian only (recorded message 041 241 1996/www.comune. venezia.it/maree/previsione.asp).

Lido on Bike

Gran Viale 21B, Lido (041 526 8019/www.lidoonbike.it). **Open** *Mar-Sept* 8am-8pm daily. **Rates** €3 per hr for the first 3hrs; €9 per day (8am-8pm); €42 per wk; €80 2wks; €120 1mth. *Tandems* €5 per hr/€18 per day. *Two-people 'carriages'* €6 per hr/4-people €12 per hr. **Credit** MC, V. **Map** p317 B3.
ID must be left with this shop for the entire hire period.

By boat

Vaporetti

Venice's water buses (*see p290* **Vaporetti**) run to a very tight schedule, with sailing times for each line that makes a pick up marked clearly at vaporetto stops. Strikes are frequent, but always announced in advance; look out for yellow notices posted inside vaporetto stops bearing the title *sciopero* (strike). Alternatively, check the ACTV website (www.actv.it), or call the Hellovenezia centre (041 24 24) for updates.

Regular services run from about 5am to around midnight, after which a frequent night service follows the route taken by Line 82 during the day.

Venice

The main lines follow the Grand Canal, or circle the island. It is worth picking up a timetable, (although they frequently run out) from the central Hellovenezia office (*see p286*), tourist offices (*see p302*) or any large ACTV booth. A simple but handy map is available at any ACTV ticket office.

Taking a boat in the wrong direction is alarmingly easy. Remember – if you're standing with your back to the station and want to head down the Grand Canal, take Line 1 (slow) or Line 82 (faster) heading left. During peak season, ACTV runs express *vaporetti* 3 and 4 to San Marco from Tronchetto, piazzale Roma and the train station (Ferrovia).

Southern islands

To get to the islands in the lagoon south of Venice (San Servolo, San Lazzaro degli Armeni) take the 20 from San Zaccaria. Lines 1, 51, 52, 61 (and 82 in summer) all terminate at the Lido.

Northern islands

Murano: the DM line (Diretto Murano) departs every half-hour from Tronchetto, piazzale Roma and Ferrovia for Murano. Between 10.15am and 4.55pm Line 5 leaves San Zaccaria for Murano every 20 minutes (with a break between 12.15 and 1.15pm); the journey takes just under half an hour. Lines 41 & 42 depart every ten minutes or so throughout the day (4.20am-11.22pm) from Fondamenta Nove, and are replaced at night by the hourly *Notturno murano* service. En route to Murano, 41 & 42 also stop at Cimitero on the island of San Michele.

All other services to islands in the northern lagoon depart from Fondamente Nove. The LN (Laguna Nord) Line leaves roughly every 30 minutes throughout the day from Fondamente Nove, stopping at Faro (Murano), Mazzorbo, Burano, Treporti and Punta Sabbioni. In the late evening (9.33pm, 10.28pm and 11.14pm) the LN also stops at Torcello. At other times take the half-hourly shuttle from Burano (ten minutes); check the timetable or call 800 845 065. Line 13 leaves hourly from Fondamente Nove to Faro (Murano), Vignole, Sant'Erasmo Capannone, Sant'Erasmo Chiesa and Sant'Erasmo Punta Vela. Some boats continue for Treporti.

Tickets

Single-trip (€6), 12-hour (€13), 24-hour (€15), 36-hour (€20), 48-hour (€25) and 72-hour (€30) vaporetto tickets can be purchased at most vaporetto stops, at tabacchi and at Hellovenezia offices (see p286).

On board you can only buy a single ticket (€6, valid 60 minutes). There's also a 72-hour card (€15) for 14-29 year olds who must purchase a €4 Rolling Venice card in order to be eligible. Tickets must be validated prior to boarding by stamping them in the yellow machines at the jetty entrance. *See also p285* **Cutting costs.**

Traghetti

The best way to cross the Grand Canal when you're far from a bridge is to hop on a *traghetto*. These unadorned *gondole* are rowed back and forth at fixed points along the canal. At 50¢ this is the cheapest gondola ride in the city; Venetians make the three-minute hop standing up.

Traghetti ply between the following points:
San Marcuola–Fontego dei Turchi: *Closed at time of going to press due to restoration.* **Map** p321 F3.
Santa Sofia–Pescheria: 7.30am-7.45pm Mon-Sat; 8.45am-7pm Sun. **Map** p322 B4.
Riva del Carbon–riva del Vin: 8am-2pm Mon-Sat. **Map** p322 B5.
Ca' Garzoni-San Tomà: 7.30am-7.45pm Mon-Sat; 8.30am-7.15pm Sun. **Map** p325 F1.
San Samuele–Ca' Rezzonico: 7.40am-1.30pm Mon-Sat. **Map** p325 F1.
Santa Maria del Giglio–Santa Maria della Salute: 9.30am-6pm daily. **Map** p326 A2.

Water taxis

Water taxis are hugely expensive: expect to pay upwards of €90 from the airport directly to any single destination in Venice, and more for multiple stops. The minimum possible cost for a 15-minute trip from hotel to restaurant, for a single person is €70, with most journeys averaging €110 once numbers of passengers and baggage have been taken into account. Between the hours of 10pm and 7am there is a surcharge of €10. Taxi pick-up points can

Directory

On foot: dry

Unless a vaporetto can take you door to door or you're splashing out on a taxi, you're going to have to rely on shanks' pony to get around Venice. Walking is still very much the principle means of transport, so sturdy and comfortable shoes are far more essential here than in other cities, where a broken high heel simply requires the hailing of a cab.

With millions of tourists coursing through its narrow thoroughfares every year, it's easy to understand why the Venetians take a dim view of tourists who obstruct narrow streets as they stand to gawp, or – worse still – spread out their picnics on busy bridges. A few 'road rules' will help you manoeuvre through the streets of Venice. Think of your body as a vehicle. Traffic tends to flow in loosely divided lanes (keep to the right) with potential for passing. A quick acceleration to the left with a polite 'scusate' or 'permesso' will help part the crowds. Slow down and pull off to the right side or into an untrafficked side-street to consult a map or admire a building, instead of suddenly stopping, causing disruption to the traffic flow.

As in any city, rush hour for Venetians is in the mornings and afternoons going to and from work. During the high season this blends into an all-day-long traffic jam clogging the main arteries of the city, especially near San Marco and Rialto, and along the road that joins them. Be adventurous and explore the more remote parts of the island if you want to avoid these situations.

be found at piazzale Roma, outside the station, next to the Rialto Vaporetto stop, and next to Valaresso Vaporetto stop, in front of the Giardini ex Reali, but it's more reliable to call and order yourself. Avoid asking your hotel to book a taxi for you, as they frequently add a 10% mark up. Beware of unlicensed taxis, which charge even more than authorised ones. The latter have a black number on a yellow background.

Venezia Motoscafi

041 716 922 (24 hour); 041 716 000/041 71 124/041 715 544/ 041 716 949/www.veneziana motoscafi.it. **Open** 24hrs daily. **No credit cards**.

Gondole

What can you say about the Venetian gondola? They're over-hyped, overpriced, hopelessly kitsch… and hopelessly romantic. Even the hardest-hearted cynics may find themselves melting at this unique and most unforgettable experience.Official gondola stops can be found at the following locations:
Fondamenta Bacino Orseolo (map p326 B1).

In front of the Hotel Danieli on the **riva degli Schiavoni** (map p326 C2).
By the **Vallaresso** vaporetto stop (map p326 B2).
By the **railway station** (map p321 E3).
By the **piazzale Roma** bus terminus (map p320 C4).
By the **Santa Maria del Giglio** vaporetto stop (map p326 B2).
At the jetty at the end of the **piazzetta San Marco** (map p326 C2).
At **campo Santa Sofia** (map p322 A4) near the Ca' d'Oro vaporetto stop.
By the **San Tomà** vaporetto stop (map p325 F1).
By the Hotel Bauer in **campo San Moisè** (map p326 B2).
On the **riva del Carbon** at the southern end of the Rialto bridge (map p322 B5).
Fares are set by the Istituzione per la Conservazione della gondola e tutela del gondoliere (Gondola Board; 041 528 5075/www.gondola venezia.it); in the event that a gondolier tries to overcharge you – and it does happen: be prepared to stick to your guns – complain to the Ente. Prices below are for the hire of the gondola, regardless of the number of passengers (up to six). Having your own personal crooner will push the fare up.
8am-7pm: €80 for 40mins; €40 for each additional 20mins.
7pm-8am: €100 for 50mins; €50 for each additional 20mins.

By bus

Orange coloured ACTV buses operate to both Mestre and Marghera on the mainland, as well as serving the Lido, Pellestrina and Chioggia. Services for the mainland depart from piazzale Roma (map p320 C5).

From midnight until 5am, buses N1 (leaving every 30 minutes) and N2 (leaving every hour) depart from Mestre for piazzale Roma and vice versa. There are also regular night buses to the Lido (departing at least hourly) to Malamocco, Alberoni and Pellestrina.

Tickets

Bus tickets, costing €1 (also available in blocks of 10 tickets for €9), are valid for 60 minutes, during which you may use several buses, though you can't make a return journey on the same ticket. They can be purchased from ACTV ticket booths or from *tabacchi* (*see p301*) anywhere in the city. They should be bought before boarding the bus and then stamped on board.

By car

For car parks, *see p284*.

Avis

*Santa Croce 496G, piazzale Roma
(041 523 7377/www.avisauto
noleggio.it).* **Open** *Apr-Oct* 8am-
6.30pm Mon-Fri; 8.30am-1.30pm
Sat, Sun. *Nov-Mar* 8.30am-
12.30pm, 2.30-6pm Mon-Fri;
8.30am-12.30pm Sat, Sun. NB
opening hours currently under
review. **Credit** AmEx, DC, MC,
V. **Map** p320 C5.
Other locations: Arrivals hall,
Marco Polo Airport (041 541 5030).
Open 8am-midnight daily.

Europcar

*Santa Croce 496H, piazzale Roma
(041 523 8616/www.europcar.it).*
Open 8.30am-6.30pm Mon-Sat;
9am-1pm Sun. **Credit** AmEx, DC,
MC, V. **Map** p320 C5.
Other locations: Arrivals hall,
Marco Polo Airport (041 541 5654).
Open 8am-midnight daily.

Hertz

*Santa Croce 496F, piazzale
Roma (041 528 4091).* **Open**
8am-6pm Mon-Fri; 8am-1pm Sat,
Sun. **Credit** AmEx, DC, MC, V.
Map p320 C5.
Other locations: Arrivals hall,
Marco Polo Airport (041 541 6075).
Open 8am-midnight daily.

Maggiore National

*Mestre railway station (041 935
300/www.maggiore.it).* **Open** 8am-
1pm, 2.30-6pm Mon-Fri; 8am-1pm
Sat. **Credit** AmEx, DC, MC, V.
Other locations: Arrivals hall,
Marco Polo Airport (041 541 5040).
Open 8am-11.30pm daily.

Mattiazzo

*Santa Croce 496E, piazzale Roma
(041 522 0084/www.mattiazzo.it).*
Open 8am-8pm daily. **Credit**
AmEx, DC, MC, V. **Map** p320 C5.
Chauffeur-driven limousine hire.

By train

Santa Lucia (map p321 D4)
is Venice's main station. Most
long-distance trains stop here;
though some only go as far as
Mestre on the mainland. Local
trains leave Mestre for Santa
Lucia every ten minutes or so.

Tickets & information

The information office in
the main hall of Santa Lucia
railway station is open 7am-
9pm daily. Buy tickets from
windows (open 6am-9pm
daily, all major credit cards
accepted), vending machines
in the station, or travel agents
around the city bearing the
Trenitalia logo.

The Club Eurostar office
(open 7.30am-5pm Mon-Fri,
7.30am-4.30pm Sat, 041 785
547), located in a glass hut
near platform 2, dispenses
information about high-speed
Eurostar trains (not to be
confused with the British
cross-channel service).

The national rail information
and booking number is 89 20
21, or 199 166 177 from mobile
phones (both 7am-9pm daily).
From a land line, press 1 after
the recorded message, then say
'altro' to speak to an operator
(who may not speak English).

The user-friendly website
www.trenitalia.com gives
complete information on
schedules, in English as well
as Italian. Tickets can be
booked through the website
with a credit card and picked
up from automated dispensers
or the ticket windows in the
station. Some Eurostar routes
are ticketless; take your email
booking printout with you.
The website details special
offers and discount cards for
the under-26s (*Carta verde*)
and over-60s (*Carta argento*).

The slowest trains are R
(Regionale) and IR
(Interregionale); supplements
are charged for high-speed
trains: ES (Eurostar), IC
(Intercity) or EC (Eurocity –
crosses a national border). Seat
bookings are obligatory (and
included in the price) on ES
trains; tickets can be bought
until departure time (but may
sell out). Reserving a seat on IC
costs €3 and is well worth it to
avoid standing, especially on
Friday and Sunday evenings.
If your ES train arrives more
than 26 minutes late, you are
entitled to a 50% refund (in
Trenitalia vouchers), or 30%
for an IC (with a booked seat)
more than 31 minutes late.
They can be claimed at booths
marked '*rimborsi*' or at
information offices at your
destination; it's a long process.

**You must stamp your
ticket** – and any supplement
– in the yellow machines on
each platform before boarding.
Failure to do so can result in a
fine, though looking foreign,
confused and contrite may get
you off the hook. If you forget
to stamp your ticket, locate the
inspector as soon as possible
and s/he will waive the fine.

Vaporetti

Even locals tend to lump them together, but
not all Venetian ferries are, strictly speaking,
vaporetti. For information about private hire
see the ACTV website (www.actv.it).
Vaporetto a 230-passenger boat, larger and
slower, with more room for luggage; older
models have much sought-after outside
seats at the front. Run routes along the
Grand Canal including no.1 and no.82.

Motoscafo a 160-passenger boat, sleeker,
smaller and faster, with outside seats only
at the back. Run routes encircling the island,
including no.41/42, no.51/52 and
no.61/62.
Motonave a large capacity (600-1,200,
depending on the model) charming double-
decker steamers that cross the lagoon
regally to Lido, Torcello and Punta Sabbioni.

Resources A-Z

Accommodation

It's best not to come to Venice without a hotel reservation. But if your spontaneous romantic weekend getaway so demands, the **Associazione Veneziana Albergatori** (Venice Hoteliers' Association, 041 522 8004, tollfree from inside Italy only 800 843 006, www.vanews.it) can make on-the-spot reservations. Booths can be found at the locations listed below:
Santa Lucia train station (041 715 288). **Open** 8am-9pm daily
Arrivals hall, Marco Polo airport (041 541 5017). **Open** 10am-11pm.
Autorimessa Comunale (*see p284*; 041 522 8640) **Open** 9am-10pm daily.

Addresses

Postal addresses in Venice consist of the name of the *sestiere* (*see p66*) plus the house number. With only this information, you will never reach your destination.

For convenience, we have also given the name of the *calle* (street) or *campo* (square) etc where each place is located. But finding your way around remains a challenge, especially as matters are sometimes complicated by there being an official Italian and several unofficial Venetian dialect names in use for the same location. When asking for directions, make sure you ascertain the nearest vaporetto stop, church, large square or other easily identifiable local landmark.

Age restrictions

You must be 16 legally to buy cigarettes and alcohol. Alcohol can be consumed in bars from the age of 16. Anyone aged 18 or over can ride a 50cc moped

or scooter; so can 14- to 18-year-olds if they have a special licence. You must be over 18 to drive and over 21 to hire a car.

Business

If you are planning to do business in Venice, a call to your embassy's commercial sector in Rome (*see p293*) is always a good idea.

Conferences

Venice has many facilities on offer for business conferences and congresses. Palladian villas and other historic landmarks in the surrounding areas also make great venues for all sorts of events.

For information on trade fairs in Venice, contact **Venezia Fiere** (San Polo 2120, campo Santa Polo, 041 714 066/fax 041 713 151/ www.veneziafiere.it).

Most of the organisers listed below are able to book transportation and hotels as well as the usual facilities.

Codess Cultura

San Polo 2120, campo San Polo (041 710 200/fax 041 717 771/www.codesscultura.it). **Map** p321 F5.

Endar

Castello 4966, fondamenta de l'Osmarin (041 523 8440/fax 041 528 6846/www.endar.it). **Map** p327 D1.

Nexa

San Marco 3870, corte dell'Albero (041 521 0255/fax 041 528 5041/ www.nexaweb.it). **Map** p326 A1.

Studio Systema

San Polo 699, calle del Paradiso (041 520 1959/fax 041 520 1960). **Map** p322 A5.

Venezia Congressi

San Marco 4606, calle del Teatro Goldoni (041 522 8400/fax 041 523 8995/www.veneziacongressi. com). **Map** p326 B1.

Couriers

Local

Bartolini *041 531 8944/fax 041 531 8943/www.bartolini.it*
Executive *041 508 4811/041 990 879/www.executivegroup.com*
Pony Express *041 532 1077/ fax 041 531 1905/www.pony.it*

National and international

DHL *199 199 345/www.dhl.it*
Federal Express *(toll free) 800 123 800/www.fedex.com/it*
UPS *(toll free) 800 877 877*

Interpreters

Most of the conference organisers listed above will also be able to provide you with interpreters.

Lexicon Translations

Via Caneve 77, Mestre (041 534 8005/www.lexiconline.it).

TER Centro Traduzioni

Cannaregio 1076C, ramo San Zuane (041 524 2538/fax: 041 524 4021/www.ter-traduzioni. com). **Map** p322 A3.

Customs

If you arrive from an EU country you are not required to declare goods imported into or exported from Italy as long as they are for personal use.

For people arriving from non-EU countries the following limits apply: 200 cigarettes or 100 cigarillos or 50 cigars or 250 grams of tobacco; one litre of spirits or two litres of wine; one bottle of perfume (50 ml/1.76 oz), 250 millilitres of eau de toilette plus gift items not exceeding €175 (€95 for children under 15).

Anything above these limits will be subject to taxation at the port of entry. For more information call customs (*dogana*) at Marco Polo airport on 041 269 9311 or consult www.agenziadogane.it.

Directory

Disabled travellers

The very things that make Venice unique – narrow streets, bridges (almost 400), no barriers between pavements and canals – make the city an extra-difficult destination for travellers with impaired mobility or vision. Despite this, Venice should not be crossed off the holiday list altogether, as there has been an effort in recent years to make the city more negotiable for disabled travellers.

Information

The Comune di Venezia's **Informahandicap** service (*see below*) is a vital one-stop shop for information.

APT offices (*see p302*) provide a map (which can be downloaded at www.comune. venezia.it/informahandicap/ files/va-carta-ita.jpg) showing bridges with wheelchair ramps (there are just five in the centre of Venice, plus one on the Giudecca) and accessible public toilets, though the APT will be the first to tell you that these latter don't always work. It also indicates which parts of the city are accessible to wheelchair users. Keys for operating automated ramps are also available at APT offices.

Informahandicap

Ca' Farsetti, San Marco 4136, riva del Carbon (041 274 8144/ www.comune.venezia.it/handicap). Vaporetto Vallaresso. **Open** 9am-1pm, 3-5pm Thur. **Map** p322 A5. *Centro Culturale Candiani, piazzale Candiani 5, Mestre (041 274 6144).* **Open** 3-5pm Tue, Thur; 9am-1pm Wed, Fri. Set up by the city council, this service has an excellent website with travel information for the disabled, although only some pages have an English translation. Super helpful English-speaking staff can answer queries over the phone and send information on accessible hotels, restaurants and museums in Venice and the

Veneto. Give them a call or send your inquiries to informahandicap @comune.venezia.it.

CO.IN.

067 162 3919 (9am-5pm Mon-Fri) www.coinsociale.it. This Rome-based organisation provides a telephone information line, with English speaking operators to advise visitors on the accessibility of hotels, museums and other disabled facilities.

Transport

Public transport is one area where Venice scores higher than many other destinations, as standard *vaporetti* and *motonavi* have a reasonably large, flat deck area and there are no steps or steep inclines on the route between quayside and boat, enabling easy travel along the Grand Canal, on lines 1 and 82. Lines that circle the city use *motoscafi* (*see p290* **Vaporetti**); some of their older models have not yet been adapted to accommodate wheelchairs, although the onboard ACTV personnel are unerringly helpful. The vaporetto lines that currently guarantee disabled access (though peak times should be avoided if possible) are 1, 82, 3, 4, 13, T, LN and N. Some of the buses that run between Mestre and Venice also have wheelchair access.

For further information consult the Informahandicap site or call these numbers:
Bus and vaporetti: ACTV 041 24 24.
Trains: Trenitalia 041 785 570.
Planes: Marco Polo Airport 041 260 9260.

Drugs

As this guide went to press, Italy's draconian drug laws were again under review.

The current laws state that anyone caught in possession of any quantity of drugs of any kind must be taken before a magistrate. There is no distinction between possession

for personal use and intent to supply. All offenders are therefore subject to stiff penalties, including lengthy prison sentences. Foreigners can expect to be swiftly deported. Holders of Italian driving licences may have them temporarily suspended. Proposals for new legislation define the difference between *leggere* (light) and *pesanti* (heavy) drugs, with different punishments depending on the circumstances of each case.

Couriering or dealing can land you in prison for up to 20 years. If you are a foreigner, you will be made to serve your prison sentence and then be expelled from the country.

It is an offence to buy drugs or even to give them away. Sniffer dogs are a fixture at most ports of entry into Italy and are on patrol at Marco Polo airport. Customs police will take a dim view of visitors entering with even the tiniest quantities of narcotics, and are likely to allow them to stay no longer than it takes a magistrate to expel them from the country.

Electricity

Italy's electricity system runs on 220/230v. To use British or US appliances, you will need two-pin adaptor plugs: these are best bought before leaving home, as they tend to be expensive in Italy and are not always easy to find. If you do need to buy one here, try any electrical retailer (look for *casalinghi* or *elettrodomestici* in the yellow pages).

Embassies & consulates

There are a handful of diplomatic missions in Venice. However, for most information, and in emergencies, you will probably have to contact offices in Rome or Milan.

British Consulate

*Piazzale Donatori di Sangue 2,
Mestre (041 505 5990). Bus 7
from piazza Roma.* **Open** 10am-
1pm Mon-Fri.
The British consulate has moved
to the mainland. Outside of these
hours refer to the duty officer at
the Milan consulate on 02 723 001.

South African Consulate

*Santa Croce 466G, piazzale
Roma (041 524 1599). Vaporetto
Piazzale Roma.* **Open** 9am-12pm,
2pm-6pm Mon-Fri. **Map** p321 D5.
In emergencies contact the Milan
consulate (*see below*).

Embassies in Rome

Australian 06 852 721
British 06 4220 0001
Canadian 06 854 441
Irish 06 697 9121
New Zealand 06 441 7171
South African 06 852 541
US 06 46 741

Consulates in Milan

Australian 02 777 041
British 02 723 001
Irish 02 5518 7569
Canadian 02 675 81
New Zealand 02 499 0201
South Africa 02 885 8581
US 02 290 351

Emergencies

See also p300 **Safety
& security** *and p294*
Insurance.
  Thefts or losses should
be reported immediately at
the nearest police station
(either the Polizia di Stato
or the nominally military
Carabinieri). Report the loss
of your passport to the nearest
consulate or embassy (*see
above*). Report the loss of
a credit card or travellers'
cheques to your credit card
company (*see p297*).

National emergency numbers

Ambulance 118
Carabinieri 112
Car breakdowns (Automobile
Club d'Italia) 803 116

CISS traffic news 1518
Coastguard 1530
Fire brigade 115
Guardia di Finanza 117
Guardia Forestale 1515
Infant emergency 114
Medical Emergency 118
Polizia di Stato 113

Local emergency numbers

Carabinieri *Castello 4693A,
campo San Zaccaria (041 274
111). Vaporetto San Zaccaria.*
Map p327 D1.
Coastguard (Capitaneria di
Porto) 041 240 5711
Fire brigade 041 257 4700
Polizia di Stato *Questura,
Santa Croce 500, piazzale Roma
(041 271 5511/www.polizia
distato.it). Vaporetto Piazzale
Roma.* **Map** p320 C4.

Domestic emergencies

To report a malfunction in any
of the main public services, call
the following:
Electricity (ENEL) 800 900 800
Gas (Italgas) 800 900 777
Telephone (Telecom Italia) 187
Water (Vesta) 041 729 1111/
www.vestaspa.net

Health & hospitals

The *pronto soccorso* (casualty
department) of all public
hospitals will provide free
emergency treatment for
travellers (bring your EHIC
card with you if possible), but

it is worth taking out private
health insurance (*see p294*).
  If you are an EU citizen
and need minor treatment,
take your EHIC card with
you to any doctor for a free
consultation. Drugs they
prescribe can be bought
at chemists at prices set by
the health ministry. Tests or
appointments with specialists
in the public system (*Sistema
sanità nazionale*, SSN) will be
charged at fixed rates (*il ticket*)
and a receipt issued.
  For urgent medical advice
from local health authority
doctors during the night, call
041 529 4060 in Venice, 041 526
7743 on the Lido and 041 951
332 in Mestre (8pm-8am Mon-
Fri; 10pm Sat-8am Mon).

Contraception

Condoms are on sale near the
checkout in supermarkets, or
over the counter at chemists.
The contraceptive pill is freely
available with a prescription at
any pharmacy.

Dentists

Dental treatment in Italy is
expensive; your insurance may
not cover it. For urgent dental
issues, go to the **Ambulatorio
Odontostomatologico** at the
Ospedale Civile (*see p294*).

Travel advice

For up-to-date information on travel to a specific country
– including the latest news on safety and security, health
issues, local laws and customs – contact your home
country government's department of foreign affairs.
Most have websites packed with useful advice for
would-be travellers.

Australia
www.dfat.gov.au/travel

Canada
www.voyage.gc.ca

New Zealand
www.safetravel.govt.nz

Republic of Ireland
www.irlgov.ie/iveagh

UK
www.fco.gov.uk/travel

USA
www.state.gov/travel

Directory

Hospitals

The public relations department of Venice's **Ospedale Civile** (041 529 4588) can provide general information on being hospitalised in Venice.

The hospitals below all have 24-hour *pronto soccorso* (casualty) facilities. For an ambulance boat, call 118.

Ospedale Civile
Castello 6777, campo Santi Giovanni e Paolo (041 529 4111/ casualty 041 529 4517). Vaporetto Ospedale. **Map** p322 C4.
Housed in the 15th-century Scuola di San Marco, Venice's main hospital has helpful staff and doctors who are quite likely to speak English.

Ospedale al Mare
Lungomare D'Annunzio 1, Lido (041 529 4111/casualty 10am-8pm 041 529 5234). Vaporetto Lido. **Map** p317 B1.
Smaller than the Ospedale Civile, and offering a smaller range of services, but with fine sea views.

Ospedale Umberto I
Via Circonvallazione 50, Mestre (041 260 7111).
A modern hospital situated on the mainland.

Ospedale di Padova
Via Giustiniani 2, Padova (049 821 1111).

Ospedale di Verona
Piazzale Stefani 1, Verona (045 807 1111).

Pharmacies

Pharmacies (*farmacie*), identified by a green or red cross above the door, are run by qualified chemists who will dispense informal advice on, and assistance for, minor ailments, as well as filling doctors' prescriptions. Over-the-counter drugs such as aspirin are substantially more expensive in Italy than in the UK or US. As of 2006 they can be purchased in some supermarkets.

Most chemists are open 9am-12.30pm, 3.45-7.30pm Mon-Fri and 9am-12.45pm Sat. A small number remain open on Saturday afternoon, Sunday and at night on a duty rota system, details of which are posted outside every pharmacy and published in the local press (*see p296*).

Most pharmacies carry homeopathic medicines. All will check your blood pressure. If you require regular medication, bring adequate supplies of your drugs with you. Ask your GP for the generic rather than the brand name of your medicine: it may only be available in Italy under a different name.

Insurance

EU citizens are entitled to reciprocal medical care in Italy provided they leave their own country with an EHIC (European Health Insurance Card) card, which, in the UK, can be applied for on-line (www.dh.gov.uk) or by post using forms that you can pick up at any post office.

If your insurance is used for anything but emergencies (which are treated free anyway in casualty departments, *see above*), it will entail your dealing with the intricacies of the Italian state health system – something you want to avoid. For short-term visits, it is advisable to take out private travel/health insurance.

Non-EU citizens should review their private health insurance plans to see if they cover expenses incurred while travelling. If they don't, travel insurance should be obtained before setting out from home. If you are a student, you may want to check with your student travel organisation: some offer basic health cover with the purchase of their IDs.

If you decide to rent a car, motorcycle or moped while in Italy, make sure you pay the extra charge to upgrade to comprehensive insurance cover.

Internet

A number of Italian service providers offer free internet access, including **Caltanet** (www.caltanet.it), **Libero** (www.libero.it), **Tiscali** (www.tiscalinet.it), **Kataweb** (www.kataweb.com) and **Fastweb** (www.fastweb.it).

Venice lags behind in the wi-fi sector, with only unofficial hotspots (ie open private networks) to be found by the tech-savvy on the streets of Venice (try campo del Ghetto Nuovo and along fondamenta della Misericordia, both in Cannaregio). This is partly due to anti-terrorism/anti-paedophile legislation which decrees that anyone using public internet access must have their ID verified.

For this reason you will need to present ID to use any of the growing number of internet cafés in Venice, none of which are cheap. Some internet cafés have wi-fi, which can be accessed for a limited period with a password you pay for; others will let you plug in your laptop to their sockets with an ethernet cable.

Internet Point Santo Stefano
San Marco 2958, campo Santo Stefano (041 894 6122/www. teleradiofuga.com). Vaporetto Accademia or San Samuele. **Open** 10.15am-11pm daily. **Rates** €3 for 20mins; *foreign students* €2 for 20mins; *students studying in Venice & Italian students* €1.50 for 20mins. **No credit cards. Map** p325 F2.
This internet café offers student discounts (proper student ID required) and deals for residents. Services include fax, photocopying, scanner, printing, CD burning and international calling booths that use credit cards.

Left luggage

Most hotels will look after your luggage for a reasonable amount of time, even after you have checked out.

Marco Polo airport

Arrivals hall (near Post Office) (041 260 5043). **Open** 5am-9pm daily. **Rates** €4.50 per item per day. **No credit cards.**

Piazzale Roma bus terminus

041 523 1107. **Open** 6am-9pm daily. **Rates** €3.50 per item per day. **No credit cards.** **Map** p320 C5.

Santa Lucia railway station

041 785 531. **Open** 6am-midnight daily. **Rates** €3.80 per item per 5hrs; 60¢ every additional hour. **No credit cards.** **Map** p321 D4.

Legal aid

If you are in need of legal advice, your first stop should always be your consulate or embassy (*see p292*). For diplomatic missions not listed here, look for *Ambasciate* in the phone book.

Libraries

Most of the libraries listed below have on-line catalogues. For help with in-depth research at national level consult the **Servizio bibliotecario nazionale** website at www.sbn.it.

Archivio di Stato

San Polo 3002, campo dei Frari (041 522 2281/www.archivi. beniculturali.it). Vaporetto San Tomà. **Open** 8.20am-6pm Mon-Thur; 8.30am-2pm Fri, Sat. **Map** p321 E5.
The state archives house all official documents relating to the administration of the Venetian Republic, and a host of other historic manuscripts. Material must be requested between 11am and 1pm. ID is required; a letter of presentation is a good idea but not mandatory.

Archivio Storico delle Arti Contemporanee (ASAC)

Vega-Lybra, via delle Industrie 17A, 30175 Porto Marghera (041 521 8700/fax 041 521 8747/www.labiennale.org/it/asac).
The archive of the Venice Biennale contemporary art festival (*see p215*) has moved to Marghera and is currently accessible only by appointment. Applications to consult the archive should be made in writing to the above address or by fax or email (segreteria.asac@labiennale.org). More information can be found on their web page.

Biblioteca Centrale Istituto Universitario di Architettura di Venezia

Santa Croce 191, fondamenta Tolentini (041 257 1106/iuavbc. iuav.it). Vaporetto Piazzale Roma. **Open** 9am-midnight Mon-Fri; 2pm-midnight first Mon of the month. **Map** p321 D5.
The library of one of Italy's top architecture faculties has a vast collection of works on the history of architecture, town planning, art, engineering and social sciences. ID is necessary to enter the library; the library's borrowing facilities are only available to students of the university.

Biblioteca Fondazione Giorgio Cini

Isola di San Giorgio Maggiore (041 271 0255/www.cini.it). Vaporetto San Giorgio. **Open** (see website for variations) 9am-4.30pm Mon-Fri. **Map** p327 D4.
The Giorgio Cini Foundation houses several libraries, each of which has different opening times (see the website for details). Among them one is dedicated to art history, one to the history of Venice and others to literature, theatre, music and Vivaldi. They contain a large archive of microfilms and photographs as well as individual archive collections of scholars and historical figures. Documents may not be borrowed and you will be asked to deposit a valid document at the entrance.

Biblioteca Fondazione Scientifica Querini Stampalia

Castello 5252, campo Santa Maria Formosa (041 271 1411/www.querinistampalia.it). Vaporetto Rialto or San Zaccaria. **Open** 10am-midnight Tue-Sat; 10am-7pm Sun. **Map** p322 C5.

The Querini Stampalia library is attached to the museum of the same name (*see p93*) and has a fine collection of books with an emphasis on Venice and all things Venetian. You will need to fill out an application and present valid ID to access the library.

Biblioteca Generale dell'Università di Ca' Foscari

Dorsoduro 1392, Zattere (041 234 5811/www.biblio.unive.it). Vaporetto San Basilio. **Open** 9am-11pm Mon-Fri; 9am-2pm Sat. **Map** p325 D2.
The university library is strong on the humanities and economics. ID is necessary to enter the library; note that only students of the university can borrow books.

Biblioteca Museo Correr

San Marco 52, piazza San Marco (041 240 5211/www.comune. venezia.it/museicivici). Vaporetto Vallaresso. **Open** 8.30am-1.30pm Mon, Wed, Fri; 8.30am-5pm Tue, Thur. **Map** p326 B2.
Part of the Museo Correr (*see p83*), this small library contains prints, manuscripts and books about Venetian history and art history. To access the library you will need to obtain a membership card by filling out an application form, and submitting it, together with ID and a letter of presentation from your university or faculty advisor, prior to your visit.

Biblioteca Nazionale Marciana

San Marco 7, piazzetta San Marco (041 240 7211/www. marciana.venezia.sbn.it). Vaporetto Vallaresso. **Open** 8.10am-7pm Mon-Fri; 8.10am-1.30pm Sat. **Map** p326 C2.
The city's main public library, the Marciana has medieval manuscripts and editions of the classics dating back to the 15th century. The library is, in fact, now housed in the Zecca (*see p87*); however, the original Biblioteca Marciana can still be visited through the Museo Correr (*see p83*). ID will get you access to the reading rooms; if you can prove that you are connected to any of the universities in the Veneto you might be granted permission to borrow books.

Lost property

Your mislaid belongings may end up at one of the *uffici oggetti smarriti* listed below. You could also try the police (*see p293* **Emergencies**), or get in touch with VESTA, the city's rubbish collection department (041 729 1111).

ACTV
Santa Croce, piazzale Roma (041 272 2179). Vaporetto Piazzale Roma. **Open** 7am-7.30pm daily. **Map** p320 C5.
For items found on *vaporetti* or buses.

Comune (City Council)
San Marco 4136, riva del Carbon (041 274 8225). Vaporetto Rialto. **Open** 8.30am-12.30pm Mon-Fri; 2.30-4.30 pm Mon, Thur. **Map** p322 A5.

FS/Stazione Santa Lucia
Santa Lucia railway station, next to track 14 (041 785 531). Vaporetto Ferrovia. **Open** 6am-midnight daily. **Map** p321 D4.
All items found on trains in the Venice area and in the station itself are brought to this deposit.

Marco Polo Airport
Arrivals Hall (lost bags) (041 260 9222). Bus 5 to Aeroporto. **Open** 9am-8pm daily.
Arrivals Hall (lost objects) (041 260 9260) **Open** 24hrs daily.

Media

National dailies

Sometimes lengthy, turgid and featuring indigestible political stories, Italian newspapers can be a frustrating read. On the plus side, papers are delightfully unpretentious and happily blend serious news, leaders by internationally known commentators, and well-written, often surreal, crime and human-interest stories.

Sports coverage in the dailies is extensive and thorough, but if you're not sated, there are the mass-circulation sports papers *Corriere dello Sport, La Gazzetta dello Sport* and *Tuttosport.*

Corriere della Sera
www.corriere.it
To the centre of centre-left, this solid, serious but often dull Milan-based daily is good on crime and foreign news. Online there is an English section called 'Italian Life' which has international news and Italocentric editorials.

Il Manifesto
www.ilmanifesto.it
Although the Cold War may be a distant memory, there is still some corner of central Rome where hearts beat Red.

La Repubblica
www.repubblica.it
The centre-ish, left-ish *La Repubblica* is good on the Mafia and the Vatican, and comes up with the occasional scoop on its business pages.

Il Sole-24 Ore
www.ilsole24ore.com
This business, finance and economics daily has a great arts supplement on Sunday.

Venice dailies

Il Gazzettino
www.gazzettino.it
Il Gazzettino is one of Italy's most successful local papers. It provides national and international news on the front pages and local news inside, with different editions for towns around the Veneto region.

Il Venezia
www.ilvenezia.it
New kid on the block (from 2006), this stylish daily covers local and international news with a centre-left-ish outlook and costs 50¢, although it is available free in bars and cafés. Also contains TV and local listings and a page of useful phone numbers and contacts.

La Nuova Venezia
www.nuovavenezia.quotidianies presso.it
This popular, small-circulation daily – known to locals as *La Nuova* – contains lively editorials, crime stories, Venetian news and event listings.

Foreign press

The *Financial Times, Wall Street Journal, USA Today, International Herald Tribune* and most European dailies can be found on the day of issue at news stands all around town – especially those at the station, within striking distance of St Mark's and the Rialto, and at the large *edicole* at the Accademia and Lido vaporetto stops. Dailies from the UK are generally available the following day, and US papers and magazines sometimes take a day or two to appear.

Magazines

News weeklies *Panorama* (roughly centre right) and *L'Espresso* (centre left-ish) provide a general round-up of the week's events, while *Sette* and *Venerdì* – respectively the colour supplements of *Corriere della Sera* (Thursday) and *La Repubblica* (Friday) – have nice photos, though the quality of the journalism often leaves much to be desired.

For *Hello!*-style scandal, try *Gente* and *Oggi* with their weird mix of sex, glamour and religion, or the generally execrable scandal sheets *Eva 3000, Novella 2000* and *Cronaca Vera. Internazionale* (www.internazionale.it) provides an excellent digest of interesting bits and pieces gleaned from around the world the previous week. *Diario della Settimana* (www.diario.it) is informed and urbane and has a flair for investigative journalism.

But the biggest-selling magazine of them all is *Famiglia Cristiana*, which alternates Vatican line toeing with Vatican baiting, depending on the state of relations between the Holy See and the idiosyncratic Paoline monks who produce it. It is available from news-stands or in most churches.

Listings & classified ads

Aladino
www.aladinoannunci.com
Weekly classified ads for everything from flats for rent to *gondole* for sale, available in *edicole*, their website offers free ads and has an English version.

Boom
A weekly small-ads paper delivered free through letterboxes or available at street dispensers. *Boom* is the place to look for flats, jobs and lonely hearts.

Gente Veneta
This weekly broadsheet, produced by the local branch of the Catholic church, blends cultural and religious listings with reports on Venetian social problems.

2night magazine
www.2night.it
Trendy pocket-sized magazine, which comes out each month, containing art and nightlife listings for the whole Veneto, in Italian.

Venezia News
This info-packed bilingual magazine, which comes out on the first of each month, encompasses music, film, theatre, art and sports listings, plus interviews and features.

Television

Italy has six major networks (three are owned by state broadcaster RAI, three belong to Silvio Berlusconi's Mediaset group). Dancing girls, variety shows, music and beauty competitions predominate. The standard of news and current affairs programmes varies; most, though, offer reasonable international news coverage. Ubiquitous MTV is a terrestrial channel in Italy.

Local radio

Radio Venezia
FM 92.4
Pop music, pop music, pop music. Did we mention pop music?

Radio Capital
FM 98.5
Heavy on advertising, but generous with information on events and news in the city. You'll hear 1980s and '90s classics with a sprinkling of current hits.

Radio Padova
FM 103.9 & 88.4
Popular chart music and concert information for the Veneto area.

Money

Italy's currency is the euro (€). There are euro banknotes of €5, €10, €20, €100, €200 and €500, and coins worth €1 and €2 as well as 1¢ (*centesimo*), 2¢, 5¢, 10¢, 20¢ and 50¢. Notes and coins from any euro-zone country are valid.

ATMs

Most banks have cash dispensers and the vast majority of these accept cards with the Maestro, Cirrus and Visa Electron symbols. Most cashpoint machines dispense cash to a daily limit of €250.

Banking hours

Most banks are open 8.20am-1.20pm and 2.45-3.45pm Mon-Fri. All banks are closed on public holidays and work reduced hours the day before a holiday, usually closing at 11am. Banks are listed under *Banche ed istituti di credito* in the yellow pages.

Foreign exchange

Banks usually offer more generous exchange rates than bureaux de change (*cambio*). Commission rates in banks vary considerably. Note that 'No commission' signs in exchange offices usually mean that the exchange rate is dire.
   You will need your passport, or other valid photo ID if you want to change travellers' cheques or draw money on your credit card.

American Express
San Marco 1471, salizada San Moisè (041 520 0844). Vaporetto Vallaresso. **Open** 9am-5.30pm Mon-Fri. **Map** p326 B2.
Exchange with no commission, travellers' cheque refund, card replacements, 24-hour money transfers, plus extra services such as hotel reservations, car rentals, train and plane tickets and tour organisation.

Travelex
San Marco 5126, riva del Ferro (041 528 7358/www.travelex.it). Vaporetto Rialto. **Open** 9am-7pm Mon-Fri; 9am-5.50pm Sat; 9.30am-4.50pm Sun. **Credit** MC, V. **Map** p322 B5.
Cash and travellers' cheques exchanged with no commission. Mastercard and Visa cardholders can also withdraw cash.
Other locations: San Marco 142, piazza San Marco (041 522 4751); Marco Polo Airport, arrivals (041 541 6833).

Credit cards

Most hotels of two stars and over will take most major credit cards. Report lost credit or charge cards to the appropriate emergency number listed below. All the lines are toll-free, operate 24 hours a day and have English-speaking operators.
American Express 800 864 046
American Express (travellers' cheques) 800 872 000
Diners' Club 800 864 064
Mastercard 800 870 866
Visa 800 819 014

Postal services

Each district has its own sub-post office, open 8.30am-2pm Mon-Fri, 8.30am-1pm Sat. There is also a branch at Marco Polo Airport open 8.30am-2pm Mon-Fri, 8.30am-1pm Sat (041 541 5900).

Posta Centrale (Central Post Office)
San Marco 5554, salizada del Fontego dei Tedeschi (041 528 5813). Vaporetto Rialto. **Open** 8.30am-6.30pm Mon-Sat. **Map** p322 B5.

Directory

The main post office is housed in the 16th-century Fontego dei Tedeschi, once a base for German merchants in the city and formerly frescoed by Giorgione. You can purchase stamps, and send packages or MoneyGrams, faxes or telegrams. The office also provides information for stamp collectors and a *fermo posta* (poste restante) service. Expect long queues, especially in the afternoon. This post office and the one at piazzale Roma (*see below*) take turns in opening 8.30am-2pm Mon-Fri; 8.30am-1pm Sat during the month of August and over the Christmas period.

Posta Piazzale Roma

Santa Croce 510, fondamenta Santa Chiara (041 522 1976). Vaporetto Piazzale Roma. **Open** 8.30am-6.30pm Mon-Fri; 8.30am-1pm Sat. **Map** p320 C4.
Another main post office, offering the same services, often has shorter queues for posting. This post office and the one at Rialto (*see above*) take turns in opening 8.30am-2pm Mon-Fri; 8.30am-1pm Sat during the month of August and over the Christmas period.

Stamps & charges

Italy's postal service (www. poste.it) is generally reliable and you can be more or less sure that your letters will arrive in reasonable time. Postage supplies – such as large mailing boxes and packing tape – are now available at most post offices.
Italy's standard postal service, *posta prioritaria*, works very well: it promises to get postcards and letters to their destination within 24 hours in Italy, three days for EU countries and four or five for the rest of the world; more often than not, it delivers. A letter of 20g or less in Italy is 60¢, within the EU 62¢, and to the rest of the world 80¢ or €1 (Oceania); stamps can be bought at post offices and *tabacchi* (*see p301*) and posted in any letter box.
The Postacelere 1 Plus service (up to 3kg €10)

promises (but doesn't always achieve) 24-hour delivery to major cities in Italy.
Paccocelere has one-three- and five-day services (for packages) within Italy. Paccocelere Internazionale, EMS Corriere Espresso Internazionale and Quick Pack Europe move packages internationally, charging according weight and destination.
Letterboxes are red and distributed throughout the city. They have two slots: *Per la città* (for Venezia, Mestre and Marghera), and *Tutte le altre destinazioni* (for all other destinations).

Telegrams

The main post office provides a telegram service during business hours; it's not cheap and not always quick, however. Telegrams to any destination can be sent and dictated over the phone by dialing 186 from a private phone or 49186 from a mobile phone, which will be billed automatically for the service. Or you can speed things up by sending a telegram via the post office's website (www.poste.it; in Italian and English).

Faxes

The main post office will send faxes during regular business hours. The service is costly, however. Some photocopy shops, *tabacchi* and internet cafés offer fax services too; ask for prices before you send your fax, as they vary significantly. Most hotels will send a fax for their guests.

Religion

Mass (*messa*) times vary from church to church and are posted by front doors: services are usually held between 9am and 11am and again at 6.30pm on Sundays (6.45pm in St

Mark's basilica, *see p78*); most churches have Mass on Saturdays at 6pm. *Un'ospite di Venezia*, a free brochure, has mass times. The church of San Zulian (041 523 5383; map p326 B1) has Mass in English 11.30am and 7pm on Sundays throughout the year. Listed below are the non-Catholic denominations in the city:

Anglican

St George's, Dorsoduro 870, campo San Vio (041 520 0571). Vaporetto Accademia. **Services** Sung Mass 10.30am Sun. **Map** p325 F2.

Greek Orthodox

San Giorgio dei Greci, Castello 3419, fondamenta dei Greci (041 522 5446). Vaporetto San Zaccaria. **Services** 9.30am, 10.30am Sun. **Map** p327 D1.

Jewish

Cannaregio 1146, campo del Ghetto Vecchio (041 715 012/ www.jewishcommunityofvenice.org). Vaporetto Guglie. **Services** after sunset Fri; Sat am. **Map** p321 E2.
For security reasons, those wishing to attend services at the Synagogue must present themselves, with ID to the main office of the Jewish Community (as above) or call them on 041 715 012. Free Shabbat meals are held for attendees after the service at the restaurant Gam Gam.

Lutheran

Cannaregio 4448, campo Santi Apostoli (041 524 2040). Vaporetto Ca' D'Oro. **Services** 10am on 2nd & 4th Sun of mth. **Map** pC B4.

Methodist and Evangelical Waldesian

Castello 5170, fondamenta Cavagnis (041 522 7549/www. chiesavaldese.org). Vaporetto Rialto or San Zaccaria. **Service** 11am Sun. **Map** p323 D5.

Relocation

Accommodation

Student-type shares are abundant in Venice and can be found on paper announcements around the city, through the notice boards at Ca' Foscari and IUAV universities (*see p300*) or through local listings magazines (*see p297*).

For short-term rentals expect to pay upwards of €600 a week for a very basic apartment in Venice. Online you can try www.venice apartment.com, www.venice-rentals.com or www.interflats. it. For longer stays, an agency is your best bet; most agencies will take the equivalent of one month's rent as their commission. Most landlords will demand at least one month's (it can sometimes be as much as three months') rent as a deposit.

Giaretta
San Marco 514, campo della Guerra (041 520 9747/www. giaretta.com). Vaporetto Rialto. **Open** 9am-1pm, 3-7pm Mon-Fri. **Map** p326 C1.
Well organised and pleasant, Giaretta offer pricey, long-term rentals and sales.

Immobil Veneta
San Polo 3132, campiello San Rocco (041 524 0088/www. immobilvenetasnc.com). Vaporetto San Tomà. **Open** 9am-noon, 3.30-7pm Mon-Fri. **Map** p321 E5.
A reliable agency with short-term apartment rentals, monthly rentals and apartments for sale.

Bureaucracy

You may need any or all of the following documents if you plan to work or study in Venice. Be prepared for multiple office visits, long, unruly queues and irritable people who have been waiting longer than you.

Permesso di soggiorno (permit to stay)
The crucial document for anyone staying in Italy for more than a short period, the *permesso di soggiorno* can be obtained from the Questura in Marghera (*see below*). Get there

by 7am. Take your passport and two photocopies of every page containing data; four passport photos; proof that you are enrolled in a course or that you are in
Italy on a scholarship and have health insurance (for students); and a statement from your employer. Freelancers and students should take a certified bank or tax statement showing you have means of support; everyone needs to take their *contratto di locazione* (apartment contract) or a *lettera di ospitalità* (hospitality letter); and a €14.62 *marca da bollo* (official stamp) available from *tabacchi* (*see p301*) or the post office. EU citizens are given their *permesso* directly; as this guide went to press, the waiting period for renewal for non-EU citizens was 12 months.
Questura *via Nicolodi 23, Marghera (ufficio stranieri 041 271 5802/041 271 5761/ switchboard 041 271 5511). Bus 6/ from piazzale Roma.* **Open** 8.30-9.30am Tue, Thur, Fri; 8.30-10.30am, 2.30-3.30pm Wed.

Carta d'Identità (identity card)
This official Italian ID card is not necessary for foreigners, who can use their own national IDs and passports as a means of identification. It can be obtained from the Ufficio anagrafe of the town hall. Take ID, your *permesso di soggiorno* and three passport photographs.
Ufficio anagrafe *San Marco 4061, calle del Carbon (041 274 8221). Vaporetto Rialto.* **Open** 8.45am-1pm Mon, Wed, Fri; 8.45am-5pm Tue, Thur. **Map** p326 B1.

Codice fiscale & partito IVA (tax code & VAT number)
A *codice fiscale* is required to work legally in Italy, or to open your own business. You will need one to open a bank account or get a phone line, and for treatment under the

Italian national health service. You may even need one to get an Italian SIM card for your mobile phone. Take your passport or equivalent. The same office issues the *partito IVA* (VAT number). Company owners or freelancers may need a VAT number for invoicing. There is a form to be filled in, but no charge.
Agenzia delle Entrate *ufficio locale Venezia 1 San Marco 3538, campo Sant'Angelo (041 271 8111). Vaporetto Sant'Angelo.* **Open** 8.45am-12.45pm Mon, Wed, Fri; 8.45am-12.45pm, 2.45-4.45pm Tue, Thur. **Map** p326 A1.

Certificato di residenza (residence permit)
Necessary if you want to buy a car or import your belongings without paying customs duties, the *certificato di residenza* can unfortunately cause diplomatic stand-offs with your landlord.

To obtain it, the tax on rubbish collection (*nettezza urbana*) must have been paid for the property you reside in – which means that either you have to volunteer to pay it (and landlords renting out property but not paying taxes on the income run the risk of being discovered), or you have to persuade the owner to. In either case, you'll need to present your passport and *permesso di soggiorno*.
Ufficio anagrafe *San Marco 4142, calle Loredan (041 274 8221). Vaporetto Rialto.* **Open** 8.45am-1pm Mon, Wed, Fri; 8.45am-5pm Tue, Thur. **Map** p326 A1.

Permesso di lavoro (work permit)
Non-EU citizens must have a work permit to be legally employed in Italy. Getting one is a minefield best traversed by a lawyer, although employers may help you to arrange it. For further information, contact the Uffico Provinciale del Lavoro, via Ca' Venier 8, Mestre (041 259 1302/fax 041 250 1331).

Directory

Work

Falling in love with Venice is easy; living in the city without independent means of support is difficult. Openings for casual employment in Venice are few, though language schools (*Scuole di lingua*) sometimes seek native English speakers, especially those with TEFL experience. Women *di bella apparenza* (as the ads put it) – and with some knowledge of Italian – might try contacting conference organisers (*see p291*), or the smart boutiques in the Frezzerie area around San Marco, which sometimes advertise for *commesse* (sales assistants). The more exclusive hotels may have openings for experienced babysitters.

The main Ca' Foscari university building at Dorsoduro 3246, calle Foscari (vaporetto San Tomà) often has employment opportunities posted on the notice boards; or try the following agencies:

Manpower

Via Piave 120, Mestre (041 935 900/fax 041 936 666/www.man power.it). Bus 2 from piazzale Roma. **Open** 9am-11am; 2.30-4.30pm Mon-Fri.

Temporary

Via Manin 38A, Mestre (041 979 048/www.temporary.it). Bus 7 from piazzale Roma. **Open** 9am-1pm, 2-6pm Mon-Fri.

Safety & security

Venice is, on the whole, an exceptionally safe place at any time of day or night, and violent crime is almost unknown. Lone women would be advised to steer clear of dark alleyways (as far as is possible in labyrinthine Venice) late at night, though even there they are more likely to be harassed than attacked (*see p303* **Women**). Bag-snatchers are a rarity, mostly because of the logistical difficulties Venice presents

for making a quick getaway. However, pickpockets operate in crowded thoroughfares, especially around San Marco and the Rialto, and on public transport, so make sure you leave passports, plane/train tickets and at least one means of getting hold of money in your hotel room safe.

If you are the victim of theft or serious crime, call one of the emergency numbers listed under Emergencies, *see p293*. The following rules will help avoid unfortunate incidents:

• Don't carry wallets in back pockets, particularly on buses or boats. If you have a bag or camera with a long strap, wear it across your chest and not dangling from one shoulder.

• Keep bags closed, with your hand on them. If you stop at a pavement café or restaurant, do not leave bags or coats on the ground or the back of a chair.

• Avoid attracting unwanted attention by pulling out large wads of cash to pay for things at street stalls or in busy bars. Keep some small bills and change easily accessible.

• Crowds in general offer easy camouflage for canny pickpockets. Be especially careful when boarding buses or boats, and entering and leaving museums.

If you have your bag or wallet stolen, or are otherwise made a victim of of crime, go as soon as possible to a police station to report a *scippo* ('bagsnatching', *see p293* **Emergencies**). A *denuncia* (written statement) of the incident will be made for you.

Give police as much information as possible, including your passport number, holiday address and flight numbers. The *denuncia* will be signed, dated and stamped with an official police seal. It is unlikely that your things will be found, but you will need the *denuncia* for making an insurance claim.

Smoking

Smoking is banned anywhere with public access, including bars, restaurants, stations, offices, lobbies of apartment blocks and on all public transport except in clearly designated smoking rooms. For where to buy cigarettes, *see p301* **Tabacchi**.

Study

Studying at either of Venice's two main universities is likely to involve lectures and exams in Italian, making a good knowledge of the Italian language a prerequisite; however, there are some exceptions, especially at the more international IUAV. To find out about entrance requirements, consult the faculty websites at **www. iuav.it** (Istituto Universitario di Architettura di Venezia) or **www.unive.it** (Università degli Studi di Venezia Ca' Foscari), both in English.

EU citizens have the same right to study at Italian universities as Italian nationals. You will need to have your school diplomas translated and authenticated at the Italian consulate in your own country before presenting them to the *ufficio studenti stranieri* (foreign students' department) of any university.

Both universities run exchange programmes and participate in the EU's Erasmus scheme. The **Venice International University** (041 271 9511/www.univiu. org) is a consortium of seven universities, the Cassa di Risparmio Foundation of Venice and the Province of Venice. Students registered at one of the Venice International member universities (see their website for a list) are eligible to apply for VIU undergraduate activities. There are also Master's and PhD programmes available for foreign students.

Directory

Language courses

ASCI-Onlus – Associazione Socio-Culturale Internazionale

Corso del Popolo 117, Mestre (041 504 0433/www.ascionlus.com). Bus 4/ to Mestre. **Open** 3.30-8.30pm Mon-Thur. **No credit cards.**
This association offers courses in languages including Italian, French, German, Spanish, Arabic, Hindi and Chinese. Also available are lessons in art, photography, belly dancing and much more.

Centro Linguistico Interfacoltà

Palazzo Bonvicini, Santa Croce 2161, ramo dell'Agnello (041 234 9711/www.unive.it/cli). *Vaporetto San Stae.* **Open** (office hours) 10am-noon Mon, Wed, Fri; 10am-noon, 3-5pm Tue, Thur. **No credit cards. Map** p321 F4.
This school, affiliated with the University of Ca' Foscari, offers good short courses in Italian, French, Spanish and German, plus access to audiovisual equipment.

Tabacchi

Tabacchi or *tabaccherie* (identified by a white T on a black or blue background) are the only places where you can legally buy tobacco products.

They also sell stamps, telephone cards, individual or season tickets for public transport, lottery tickets and the stationery required when dealing with bureaucracy.

Most of Venice's *tabacchi* pull their shutters down by 7.30pm. If you're gasping for nicotine late in the evening or on Sunday, you'll have to try one of the automatic cigarette vending machines in campo Santa Margherita, piazzale Roma, next to the train station, on strada Nuova near Ponte della Guglie and near Santi Apostoli, fondamenta della Misericordia, Scuola di San Giorgio degli Schiavoni (*see p101*) and via XXII Marzo, although these only 'open' at 9pm to prevent sales to minors.

Telephones

Directory enquiries

This is a jungle, and charges for information given over the phone are steep. The major services are: 1254 (Italian and international numbers); 892 412 (international numbers, in English and Italian, from mobile phones); Italian directory information can be had for free on www.info412.it; www.paginebianche.it.

Phone numbers

Italian landline numbers must be dialled *with* their prefixes, even if you are phoning within the local area. Numbers in Venice and its province begin 041; numbers in Padua province begin 049; in Vicenza they begin 0444; in Verona 045.

Numbers generally have seven or eight digits after the prefix; some older ones have six, and some switchboards five. If you try a number and can't get through, it may have been changed to an eight-digit number. Check the directory (*elenco telefonico*) or ring directory enquiries (*see above*).

Numeri verdi ('green numbers') are free and start 800 or 147. Numbers beginning 840 and 848 are charged at a nominal rate. These numbers can be called from within Italy only, and some are available only within certain regions.

Cellphone numbers always begin with a 3.

Rates

Italy's telephone company (Telecom Italia) is still costly despite tough competition.

The minimum charge for a local call from a private phone is about 8¢ (10¢ from a public phone). Calling a mobile from a fixed line is almost triple and phoning abroad remains dear. Keep costs down by:

• phoning off-peak (6.30pm-8am Mon-Fri, 1pm Sat-8am Mon).
• not using phones in hotels, which usually carry extortionate surcharges.
• using international phone cards, available at *tabacchi* (*see p301*). Operators such as Happiness, Planet, Welcome and Europa offer €5 and €10 cards, which can be used from public, cell or landline phones and will cut costs significantly.
• not calling cellphones from landlines and vice versa.

Public phones

There are some public phones in Venice along the tourist routes but many are out of service. Most public phones operate only with phone cards (*schede telefoniche*). Newer models take major credit cards, while the few remaining old-style ones take 10¢, 20¢ and 50¢ coins. Phonecards costing €2.50, €5 and €7.50 can be purchased at post offices, *tabacchi* and some newsstands.

To use your card, tear off one corner as marked, insert it into the appropriate slot and dial. Your credit balance will be displayed on the phone. Note that your phonecard expires on a date written in very small print on the card, after which you have lost your outstanding credit.

International calls

To make an international call from Venice dial 00, then the country code (Australia 61, Canada and USA 1, Ireland 353, New Zealand 64, UK 44, South Africa 27), then the area code (usually without the initial 0) and the number. International directory enquiries are on 170. When calling an Italian landline from abroad, the whole prefix, including the 0, must be dialled, so dial 00 39 041... for Venice from the UK.

Directory

For operator-assisted calls abroad or reverse-charge calls (collect) dial 170. Other services include:
4114 alarm call.
186 telegrams.
4161 speaking clock.
4197 interrupts a conversation on an engaged line.

Mobile phones

Standard European handsets will work in Italy, but your service provider may need to activate international roaming before you leave; beware of extortionate roaming charges. Tri-band US handsets should also work; check with the manufacturer. If your phone is not locked to your home SIM card/service provider, you can buy an Italian pay-as-go SIM card, (they may ask you for your *codice fiscale, see p299*) available from mobile phone shops for around €10, allowing you to make cheaper calls within Italy.

Vodafone Gestioni SpA

San Marco 5170, campo San Bartolomeo (041 523 9016/ www.vodafone.it). Vaporetto Rialto. **Open** 10am-7.30pm Mon-Sat; 10am-1pm, 2-7pm Sun **Credit** AmEx, DC, MC, V. **Map** p322 B5.

Time

Italy is one hour ahead of London, six ahead of New York, eight behind Sydney and 12 behind Wellington.

Tipping

There are no hard and fast rules on tipping in Italy, though Venetians know that foreigners tip generously back home, and expect them to be liberal. Some upmarket restaurants (and a growing number of cheaper ones) will add a service charge to your bill: ask *il servizio è incluso?* If not, leave whatever you think the service merited (Italians leave five to ten per cent).

Bear in mind that all restaurants charge a cover charge (*coperto*), which is a quasi-tip in itself.

Toilets

Public toilets (servizi igienici pubblici) are numerous and relatively clean in Venice but you have to pay (€1) to use them, unless you have invested in a Venice Card (*see p68* **Discount cards**). Follow blue and green signs marked WC. By law all cafés and bars should allow anyone to use their facilities; however, many Venetian bar owners don't.

Tourist information

Several free publications provide comprehensive tourist information in Venice, available at APT (*see below*) and VeLa (*see p286*) offices, and some bars. Most hotels will provide you with a copy of *Un'ospite di Venezia/A Guest in Venice*, a bilingual booklet compiled by hoteliers, which contains useful addresses, night pharmacies, Mass times and transport timetables. It is published every fortnight in high season and once a month in winter.

The local press is another source of useful information on events (*see p296*), as are the posters plastered on walls all over the city. *Leo*, available at the APT, has well-written features and a tear-out, easy to consult, listing booklet of events by day.

Information offices

See chapters in **The Veneto** section for information offices outside Venice.

Azienda di Promozione Turistica (APT)

San Marco 71F, piazza San Marco (041 529 8740/www. turismovenezia.it). Vaporetto Vallaresso. **Open** 9am-3.30pm daily. **Map** p326 B2.

The APT website is worth looking at before you arrive in Venice. The offices provide information on sights and events, a list of hotels, and walking itineraries with maps for sale. They'll also put you in touch with registered guides and give details of official fees for guided tours (also available on their website).
The Palazzina Santi branch (map p326 B2) has a selection of books and sells concert tickets. In high season supplementary kiosks are set up around the city. Direct any complaints to the Tourist Mediation Counter 041 529 8710, fax 041 523 0399 or complaint.apt @turismovenezia.it.
Other locations: *Palazzina Santi, San Marco 2, Giardinetti Reali (041 522 5150).* **Open** 10am-6pm daily
Venice-Santa Lucia railway station (041 529 8727). **Open** 8am-6.30pm daily
Marco Polo Airport arrivals hall (tel/fax 041 541 5887). **Open** 9.30am-7.30pm daily
Autorimessa Comunale, Santa Croce 465B, piazzale Roma (041 529 8711). **Open** 9.30am-1pm, 1.30-4.30pm daily
Viale Santa Maria Elisabetta 6A, Lido (041 526 5721). **Open** June-Sept 9am-12pm, 3-6pm daily

Tours & guides

The APT site (*see above*) provides information on guides by language and area. **Venice Walks and Tours** (www. tours-italy.com) offers a selection of themed tours.

Cooperativa guide turistiche

San Marco 750, calle Morosini de la Regina (041 520 9038/fax 041 521 0762/www.guidevenezia.it). Vaporetto San Zaccaria. **Open** June-Aug 9am-1pm, 2-6pm Mon-Fri; 9am-1pm Sat. Sept-May 9am-5pm Mon-Fri; 9am-1pm Sat. **Rates** €121 for 2hr tour for groups of up to 30 people; €4 for every extra person. **No credit cards. Map** p326 C1.
This cooperative has around 100 guides on its books, and offers made-to-measure tours in English and a multitude of other languages. In high season book at least a week in advance.

American Express

San Marco 1471, salizada San Moisè (041 520 0844). Vaporetto Vallaresso. **Open** 9am-5.30pm Mon-Fri. **Map** p326 B2.
American Express offers daily guided tours in several languages from €20 per person.

Visas

For EU citizens, a passport or a national identity card valid for travel abroad are sufficient. Non-EU citizens must have full passports. Citizens of the US, Canada, Australia and New Zealand do not need visas for stays of up to three months. In theory, visitors are required to declare their presence to the local police within a few days of arrival, unless they are staying in a hotel, where this will be done for them. In practice, you will not need to report to the police station unless you decide to extend your stay and you apply for a *permesso di soggiorno* (permit to stay, *see p299*).

Water & drinking

Forget *Death in Venice*-style cholera scares: tap water is regularly checked, safe to drink and tastes good. Fountains throughout the city provide a constant source of free tap water. For information visit www.vestaspa.net.

When to go

Holidays

See also chapter **Festivals & Events**.

On public holidays (*giorni festivi*) public offices, banks and post offices are closed. So, in theory, are shops – but in tourism-oriented Venice, this rule is often waived. Some bars and restaurants may observe holidays: if in doubt, call ahead. You won't find much open on Christmas Day and New Year's Day.

Public transport is reduced to a skeleton service on 1 May, Christmas Day and New Year's Day, and may be rerouted or curtailed for local festivities, especially those including regattas (*see chapter* **Festivals & Events**); details are posted at vaporetto stops and at the bus terminus in piazzale Roma.

Holidays falling on a Saturday or Sunday are not celebrated on the following Monday. By popular tradition, if a public holiday falls on a Tuesday or Thursday, many people will also take the Monday or Friday off as well, a practice known as *fare il ponte* (doing a bridge). The public holidays are:
1 January New Year's Day (Capodanno).
6 January Epiphany (Befana).
Easter Monday (Pasquetta).
25 April Liberation Day (Festa della Liberazione) and patron saint's day (San Marco).
1 May Labour Day (Festa del Lavoro).
15 August Assumption (Ferragosto).
1 November All Saints' Day (Ognissanti).
21 November Festa della Salute (Venice only).
8 December Immaculate Conception (L'Immacolata).
25 December Christmas Day (Natale).
26 December Boxing Day (Santo Stefano).

Weather

Venice's unique position gives the city a bizarre mix of weather conditions. During the winter, high levels of humidity often make winter days seem colder than their average few degrees above zero, and summer days become humid as soon as the thermometer rises above 25°C.

Strong north-easterlies in winter, coming off the snow-covered Alps (snow in the city is rare) have bone-chilling effects but make the weather crisp and clear, with blue skies and great views. In the still

summer months, high humidity can make it stiflingly hot; a warm southerly wind called the *scirocco* makes the heat more intense.

Autumn and spring are generally mild with occasional pea-soup fog; November and March are the rainiest months, while *acqua alta* (*see p296* **On foot: wet**) is mainly an autumn and winter event.

Women

Although Venice is relatively a very safe place for women travellers, it is always best to apply common sense while travelling alone.

At night, keep away from quieter, more outlying areas and from the Tronchetto car park. Stick to main through-routes to avoid getting lost in dark alleyways; if in doubt, cut walking to a minimum by taking the vaporetto to as near to your destination as possible.

Tampons (*assorbenti interni*) and sanitary towels (*assorbenti esterni*) are expensive in Italy, although it may be cheaper buying them in supermarkets than in pharmacies.

Women who experience gynaecological emergencies should make for the *pronto soccorso* (emergency ward) at the Ospedale Civile (*see p294*).

Family planning

Consultori familiari are run by the local health authority, and EU citizens with an EHIC (*see p294*) form are entitled to use them, paying the same low charges for services and prescriptions as locals. Non-EU citizens may use the service and, depending on their insurance plan, claim refunds. The *consultori* are staffed by good gynaecologists – book ahead for a visit.

The contraceptive pill is available on prescription. Abortions are legal when performed in public hospitals.

Directory

Glossary

Amphitheatre (*ancient*) oval open-air theatre.
Apse large recess at the high-altar end of a church.
Baldachin canopy supported by columns.
Barrel vault a ceiling with arches shaped like half-barrels.
Baroque artistic period from the 17th-18th centuries, in which the decorative element became increasingly florid, culminating in the rococo (*qv*).
Basilica ancient Roman rectangular public building; rectangular Christian church.
Byzantine Christian artistic and architectural style drawing on ancient models developed in the fourth century in the Eastern empire (capital Byzantium/Constantinople/Istanbul) and through the Middle Ages.
Campanile bell tower.
Campo Venetian for piazza or square.
Capital head of a column, generally decorated according to classical orders (*qv*).
Caryatid column carved in female shape.
Chiaroscuro from Italian *chiaro* (light) and *scuro* (dark); juxtaposition of light and shade to bring out relief and volume.
Cloister exterior courtyard surrounded on all sides by a covered walkway.
Coffered ceiling decorated with sunken square or polygonal panels.
Cupola dome-shaped roof or ceiling.
Decumanus (*ancient*) main road, usually running east-west.
Ex-voto an offering given to fulfil a vow; often a small model in silver of the limb/organ/loved one cured as a result of prayer.
Fan vault vault formed of concave semi-cones, meeting at the apex; from beneath, it gives appearance of four backwards-leaning fans meeting.

Festoon painted or carved swag or swathe decorated with fruit and/or flowers.
Fresco painting technique in which pigment is applied to wet plaster.
Gothic architectural and artistic style of the late Middle Ages (from the 12th century), of soaring, pointed arches.
Greek cross (church) in the shape of a cross with arms of equal length.
Grisailles painting in shades of grey to mimic sculpture.
Iconostasis rood screen; screen in Eastern-rite churches separating nave from the sanctuary.
Intarsia form of mosaic made from pieces of different-coloured wood; also know as **intaglio**.
Latin cross (church) in the shape of a cross with one arm longer than the other.
Loggia gallery open on one side.
Lunette semi-circular surface, usually above window or door.
Mannerism post-High Renaissance style of the later 16th century; characterised in painting by elongated, contorted human figures.
Monoforate with one opening (cf biforate, triforate, polyforate *qv*), usually used of windows.
Narthex enclosed porch in front of a church.
Nave main body of a church; the longest section of a Latin cross church (*qv*).
Ogival (arches, windows etc) curving in to a point at the top.
Opus sectile pavement made of (usually) geometrically shaped marble slabs.
Orders classical rules governing the proportions of columns, their entablatures (*qv*) and their capitals (*qv*), the most common being the less ornate Doric, the curlicue Ionic and the Corinthian in which

capitals are decorated with stylised acanthus leaves.
Palazzo large and/or important building (not necessarily a palace).
Pendentives four concave triangular sections on top of piers supporting a dome.
Piano nobile showiest floor of a palazzo (*qv*), containing mainly reception rooms with very high ceilings.
Pilaster column-shaped projection from a wall.
Polyforate with more than one opening (cf monoforate).
Polyptych painting composed of several panels (cf dyptych with two panels, triptych with three).
Porphyry hard igneous rock ranging from dark green to dark purple; this latter was most commonly used, and known as *rosso antico*.
Presbytery the part of a church containing the high altar.
Reredos decorated wall or screen behind an altar.
Rococo highly decorative style fashionable in the 18th century.
Romanesque architectural style of the early Middle Ages (c500 to 1200), drawing on Roman and Byzantine (*qv*) influences.
Rusticated large masonry blocks with deep joints between them used to face buildings or monuments.
Sarcophagus (*ancient*) stone or marble coffin.
Stele upright slab of stone with decorative relief sculpture and/or commemorative inscription.
Transept shorter arms of a Latin cross church (*qv*).
Trilobate with three arches.
Triumphal arch arch in front of an apse (*qv*), usually over the high altar.
Trompe l'œil decorative painting effect to make surface appear three-dimensional.

Vocabulary

Italian is pronounced as it is spelled. Stresses usually fall on the penultimate syllable; a stress on the final syllable is indicated by an accent.

There are three 'you' forms: the formal singular *lei*, the informal singular *tu*, and the plural *voi*. Masculine nouns and their accompanying adjectives generally end in 'o' (plural 'i'), female nouns and their adjectives end in 'a' (plural 'e'). For restaurant vocabulary, *see p160*. For café and bar terms, *see p173*.

Venetian

The distinctive nasal Venetian drawl is more than just an accent: locals have their own vocabulary too, some of it from Byzantine roots. Venetians tend to ignore consonants, running vowels together in long diphthongs (explaining how *vostro schiavo* – 'your servant' became *ciao*.) *Xè* is pronounced 'zay'; *gò* sounds like 'go' in 'got.' For further information consult www.veneto.org/language.

Pronunciation

Vowels

a – as in ask; **e** – like a in age (closed e) or e in sell (open e); **i** – like ea in east; **o** – as in hotel (closed o) or in hot (open o); **u** – as in boot

Consonants

c before a, o or u, like c in cat; **c** before an e or an i is like the ch in check (sh as in ship in Venetian); **ch** is like c in cat; **g** before a, o or u is like g in get; **g** before an e or an i is like the j in jig; **gh** is like the g in get; **gl** followed by an i is like lli in million; **gn** is like ny in canyon; **qu** is as in quick; **r** is always rolled; **s** has two sounds, as in soap or rose; **sc** before an e or an i is like the sh in shame; **sch** is like the sc in scout; **z** has two different sounds, like ts and dz

Useful phrases

(Italian/*Venetian*)

Hello and goodbye – ciao; used informally in other parts of Italy; in any and all social situations in Venice; **Good morning, hello** – buongiorno; **Good afternoon, good evening** – buonasera; **I'm sorry** – mi dispiace/*me dispiaxe*; **I don't understand** – non capisco, non ho capito/*no gò capìo* **Do you speak English?** – parla inglese?; **Please** – per favore, per piacere; **Thank you** – grazie; **You're welcome** – prego; **Open** – aperto/*verto*; **Closed** – chiuso **When does it open?** – quando apre?; **It's closed** – è chiuso/*xè serà*; **What's the time?** – che ore sono?; **Excuse me** – mi scusi (polite), scusami (informal) *scusime/me scusa*; **Entrance** – entrata; **exit** – uscita; **Do you have a light?** – hai d'accendere?/*ti gà da accender, ti gà fógo?*; **Would you like an ice-cream?** – Vuoi un gelato?/*ti vol un geàto?*

Transport

Car – macchina; **bus** – autobus; **taxi** – tassì, taxi; **train** – treno; **plane** – aereo; **stop** (bus or vaporetto) – fermata; **station** – stazione; **platform** – binario; **ticket/s** – biglietto, biglietti; **one way** – solo andata; **return** – andata e ritorno; **I'd like a ticket to...** – Vorrei un biglietto per...

Communications

Phone – telefono; **cellphone** – cellulare; **fax** – fax; **postcard** – cartolina; **stamp** – francobollo; **e-mail** – e-mail, (messaggio di) posta elettronica.

Directions

Where is...? – dov'è...?/*dove xè?*; **(Turn) left** – (giri a) sinistra; **(It's on the) right** – (è sulla/a) destra; **Straight on** – sempre dritto; **Could you tell me the way to...?** – mi può indicare la strada per...?; **Is it near/far?** – è vicino/lontano?

Accommodation

I'd like to book a single/twin/double bedroom – vorrei prenotare una camera singola/doppia/matrimoniale; **I'd prefer a room with a bath/shower/window over the** courtyard/canal – preferirei una camera con vasca da bagno/doccia/finestra sul cortile/canale

Eating & drinking

I'd like to book a table for four at eight – vorrei prenotare una tavola per quattro alle otto; **That was poor/good/delicious** – era mediocre/buono/ottimo; **The bill** – il conto; **I think there's a mistake in this bill** – credo che il conto sia sbagliato – **Is service included?** – è incluso il servizio?.

Shopping

I'd like to try on the blue sandals/black shoes/brown boots – vorrei provare i sandali blu/le scarpe nere/ gli stivali marroni; **I take (shoe) size** – porto il numero...; **I take (dress) size** – porto la taglia...; **It's too loose/too tight/just right** – mi sta largo/stretto/bene; **100 grammes of** – un etto di; **200 grammes of** – due etti di; **One kilo of** – un kilo di; **two kilos of** – due kili di; **A litre** – un litro; **Ha delle monete?** – do you have small change?

Days & times

Monday – lunedì; **Tuesday** – martedì; **Wednesday** – mercoledì; **Thursday** – giovedì; **Friday** – venerdì; **Saturday** – sabato; **Sunday** – domenica; **yesterday** – ieri; **today** – oggi/*ancùo*; **tomorrow** – domani; **morning** – mattina; **afternoon** – pomeriggio; **evening** – sera; **this evening** – stasera; **night** – notte; **tonight** – stanotte Numbers, money & shopping **0** zero; **1** uno; **2** due; **3** tre; **4** quattro; **5** cinque; **6** sei; **7** sette; **8** otto; **9** nove; **10** dieci; **11** undici; **12** dodici; **13** tredici; **14** quattordici; **15** quindici; **16** sedici; **17** diciassette; **18** diciotto; **19** diciannove; **20** venti; **21** ventuno; **22** ventidue; **30** trenta; **40** quaranta; **50** cinquanta; **60** sessanta; **70** settanta; **80** ottanta; **90** novanta; **100** cento; **1,000** mille; **2,000** duemila **Shop** – negozio/*botega*. **How much does it cost/is it?** – quanto costa, quant'è?/*quanto xè?* **Do you accept credit cards?** – si accettano le carte di credito?

Further Reference

Books

Non-fiction

Paolo Barbaro *Venice Revealed: an Intimate Portrait*
Fascinating facts on the city's physical structure.
Robert Davis and Garry Marvin *Venice: the Tourist Maze*
A well-documented study of Venice's role as a tourist mecca.
Deborah Howard *The Architecture of Venice*
Howard's *Architecture* is the definitive account.
WD Howells *Venetian Life*
US consul's (1861-5) account of Venetian life before mass tourism.
Peter Humfrey *Painting in Renaissance Venice*
Informative and compact enough to carry with you.
Frederick C Lane *Venice: a Maritime Republic*
The best single-volume scholarly history of Venice.
Mary Laven *Virgins of Venice: Broken Vows and Cloistered Lives in the Renaissance Convent*
The title says it all.
Michelle Lovric *Venice: Tales of the City*
Compendium of writers on Venice.
Mary McCarthy *Venice Observed*
Witty account of Venetian art.
Damiano Martin *The Da Fiore Cookbook*
How to cook like they do at Da Fiore (see *pxxx*).
Francesco Da Mosto *Francesco's Venice*
Coffee-table guide by a scion of an aristocratic Venetian family.
Jan Morris *Venice*
Impressionistic history.
John Julius Norwich *A History of Venice; Paradise of Cities*
Engagingly rambling.
John Pemble *Venice Rediscovered*
On the 19th-century obsession with things Venetian.
David Rosand *Painting in 16th-Century Venice*
Read before your trip.
John Ruskin *The Stones of Venice*
Ruskin's hymn to the Gothic.
Gary Wills *Venice: Lion City*
Fascinating blend of history and art criticism.

Fiction & literature

Lord Byron *Childe Harold's Pilgrimage; Beppo*
Venice as a dream (*Harold*) and at Carnevale (*Beppo*).
Giacomo Casanova *My Life*
The great seducer's escapades in mid 18th-century Venice.
Michael Dibdin *Dead Lagoon*
Aurelio Zen returns to Venice.
Ernest Hemingway *Across the River and into the Trees*
Aka *Across the Canal and into the Bar*.
Henry James *The Wings of the Dove*
Melodrama concealed behind a wall of elegant prose.
Donna Leon *Acqua Alta* (and many others)
Series featuring detective *commissario* Guido Brunetti.
Thomas Mann *Death in Venice*
Disease, decadence, indecision, voyeurism.
Ezra Pound *The Cantos*
Full of abstruse Venetian details.
William Rivière *A Venetian Theory of Heaven*
Novel set among the English community in Venice.
William Shakespeare *The Merchant of Venice; Othello*
The bard's Venetian offerings.
Sally Vickers *Miss Garnett's Angel*
Elderly English lady's staid life is overturned by angelic encounters.

Film

Casanova (Lasse Halstrom, 2005)
Heath Ledger plays a sugary no-sex-please version of the legendary lover.
The Comfort of Strangers (Paul Schrader, 1990)
Based on an Ian McEwan novel.
Death in Venice (Luchino Visconti, 1971)
Dirk Bogarde chases boy around cholera-plagued Venice.
Don't Look Now (Nicholas Roeg, 1973)
Chilling tale of a couple in Venice after the death of their daughter.
Eve (Joseph Losey, 1962)
Budding novelist is ensnared by temptress.
The Merchant of Venice (Michael Radford, 2004)
Al Pacino is Shylock in this star-studded adaptation.
Senso (Luchino Visconti, 1954)
Tale of sadism and passion.

Music

Lorenzo Da Ponte (1749-1838)
Penned *libretti* for Mozart's *Marriage of Figaro, Don Giovanni* and *Così fan tutte*.
Andrea Gabrieli (c1510-1586)
Organist of St Mark's basilica, Gabrieli senior's madrigals were Venetian favourites.
Giovanni Gabrieli (c1556-1612)
composed sacred and choral music, particularly motets; *In ecclesiis* is perhaps his masterpiece.
Antonio Vivaldi (1678-1741)
There's no escaping his *Four Seasons* in Venice.

Websites

www.beniculturali.it Culture ministry's useful site.
www.venezia.net apartment rents to information on hiring a carnevale costume (English).
www.venetia.it History, useful phone numbers and good links (English).
http://english.comune.venezia.it City council's site with useful practical information (English).
www.regione.veneto.it/cultura Cultural offerings around the Veneto. Museum info in English.
www.meetingvenice.it Hotel booking service in the city and surrounding areas, plus news on events and tourist attractions (English).
www.agendavenezia.it Good up-to-date diary of events in Venice (English).
www.veniceword.com News magazine with current events and entertainment (English).
www.venetianlegends.it A great collection (in English) of ghost stories and grisly legends.
www.artive.arti.beniculturali.it Information (English in parts) on state-owned museums.
www.insula.it Exhaustive information on keeping Venice above water (English).
www.veneto.org Idiosyncratic site on the history and language of the Veneto region; excellent links.

Index

Page numbers in **bold** indicate section(s) giving key information on a topic; *italics* indicate photographs.

Advertisers' Index

Please refer to relevant pages for full contact details

	Church
	Airport
H	Hospital
	Vaporetto stop
	Palazzo

Maps

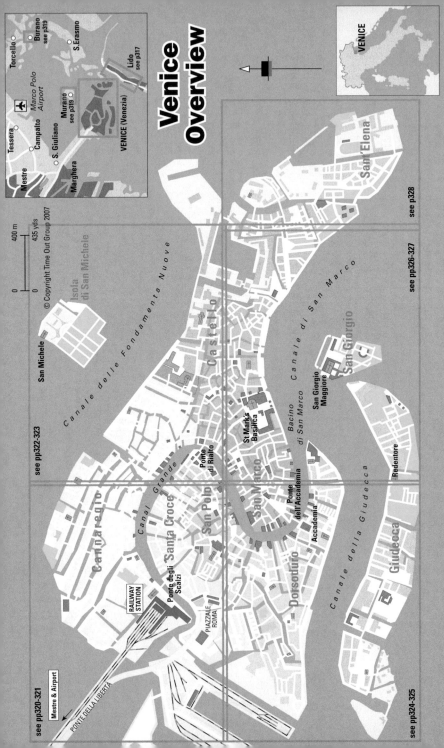

Venice Overview

see pp320-321

see pp322-323

see pp324-325

see pp326-327

see p328

VENICE

Mestre & Airport

PONTE DELLA LIBERTÀ

RAILWAY STATION

PIAZZALE ROMA

Ponte degli Scalzi

Canal Grande

Cannaregio

Santa Croce

San Polo

Dorsoduro

Ponte dell'Accademia

Accademia

San Marco

Ponte di Rialto

St Mark's Basilica

Castello

Canale delle Fondamenta Nuove

Isola di San Michele

San Michele

Bacino di San Marco

Canale di San Marco

San Giorgio Maggiore

San Giorgio

Sant'Elena

Redentore

Giudecca

Canale della Giudecca

© Copyright Time Out Group 2007

0   400 m
0   435 yds

Torcello

Burano
see p319

S.Erasmo

Tessera

Mestre

Campalto

Marghera

S. Giuliano

Murano
see p319

Lido
see p317

Marco Polo
Airport

VENICE (Venezia)

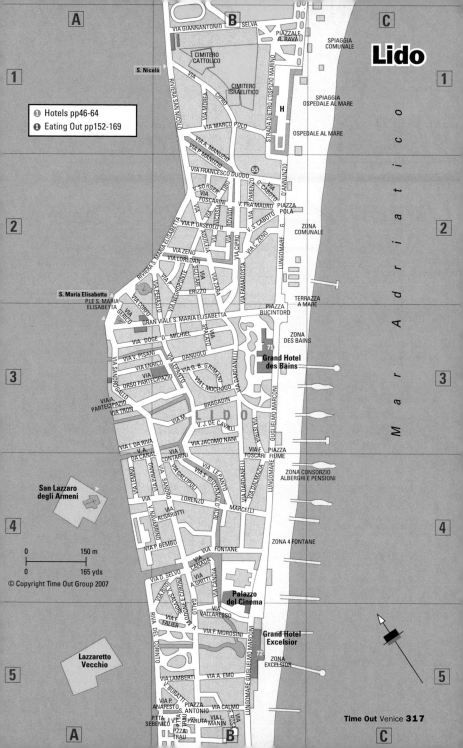

Lido

● Hotels pp46-64
● Eating Out pp152-169

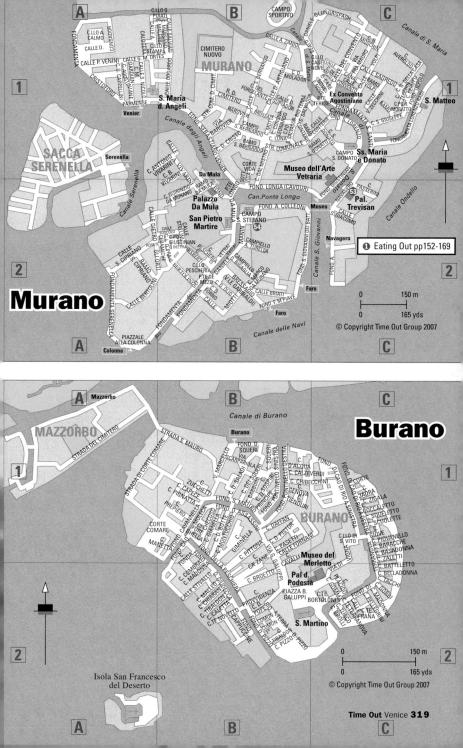

Murano

CAMPO SPORTIVO
Canale di S. Maria
C.llo G. PUATI
C.llo A. CALMO
Calle D.
CALLE P. VENINI
FONDAMENTA
CRISTOFORO
CIMITERO NUOVO
MURANO
CALLE A. ZANIOL
C. MOSCHIN
Averoldo C.
S. Matteo
SACCA SERENELLA
Serenella
S. Maria d. Angeli
Venier
Canale degli Angeli
Ex Convento Agostiniane
Ss. Maria e Donato
Palazzo Da Mula
San Pietro Martire
Museo dell'Arte Vetraria
Pal. Trevisan
Can.Ponte Longo
Museo
Navagero
Canale Ondello

❶ Eating Out pp152-169

Canale delle Navi
PIAZZALE ALLA COLONNA
Colonna

0   150 m
0   165 yds

© Copyright Time Out Group 2007

Burano

Mazzorbo
Canale di Burano
MAZZORBO
Burano
STRADA DEL CIMITERO
STRADA S. MAURO
BURANO
Museo del Merletto
Pal d. Podestà
PIAZZA B. GALUPPI
S. Martino

Isola San Francesco del Deserto

0   150 m
0   165 yds

© Copyright Time Out Group 2007

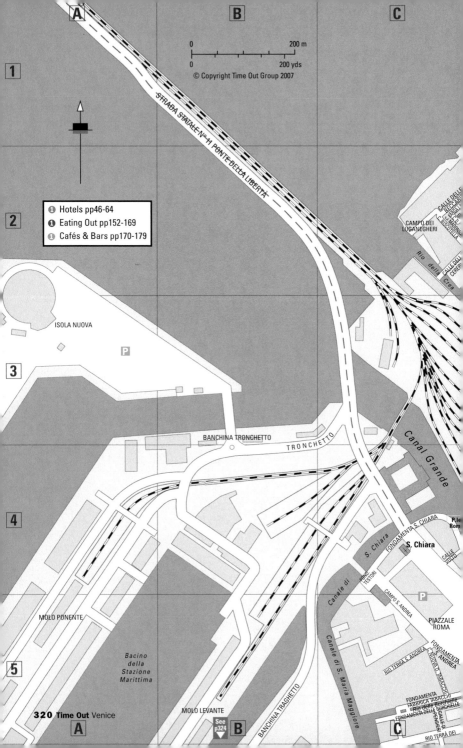

A **B** **C**

1

200 m

200 yds

© Copyright Time Out Group 2007

STRADA STATALE N°11 PONTE DELLA LIBERTÀ

2

❶ Hotels pp46-64
❶ Eating Out pp152-169
❶ Cafés & Bars pp170-179

CAMPO DEI LUGANEGHERI

CALLE DELLE BECCARIE
CALLE BRAGADIN
CALLE MADONNA
CALLE DEL BRUSCHELLE
Rio delle Crea
CALLE DEGLI CEREERI

ISOLA NUOVA

3

P

BANCHINA TRONCHETTO

TRONCHETTO

Canal Grande

4

FONDAMENTA S. CHIARA

S. Chiara
S. Chiara

P.le Rom

CALLE VIOTTO

Canale di S. Chiara

FERRO TESTORI

CAMPO S. ANDREA

P

MOLO PONENTE

Canale di S. Maria Maggiore

PIAZZALE ROMA

FONDAMENTA S. ANDREA
CALLE COSSETTI
RIO TERRA S. ANDREA

5

Bacino della Stazione Marittima

FONDAMENTA FABBRICA TABACCHI
Rio delle Burchielle
FONDAMENTA DELLE BURCHIELLE
CALLE DEL BRESSAN

MOLO LEVANTE

See p324 ▶

BANCHINA TRAGHETTO

FONDAMENTA DEI PENSIERI
RIO TERRA DEI

A **B** **C**

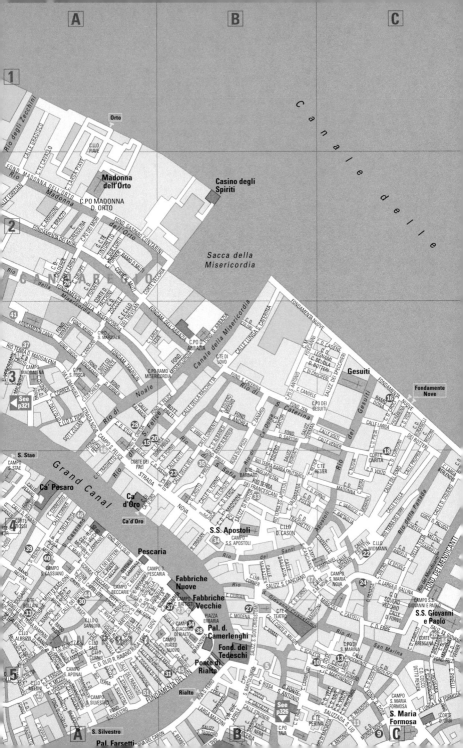

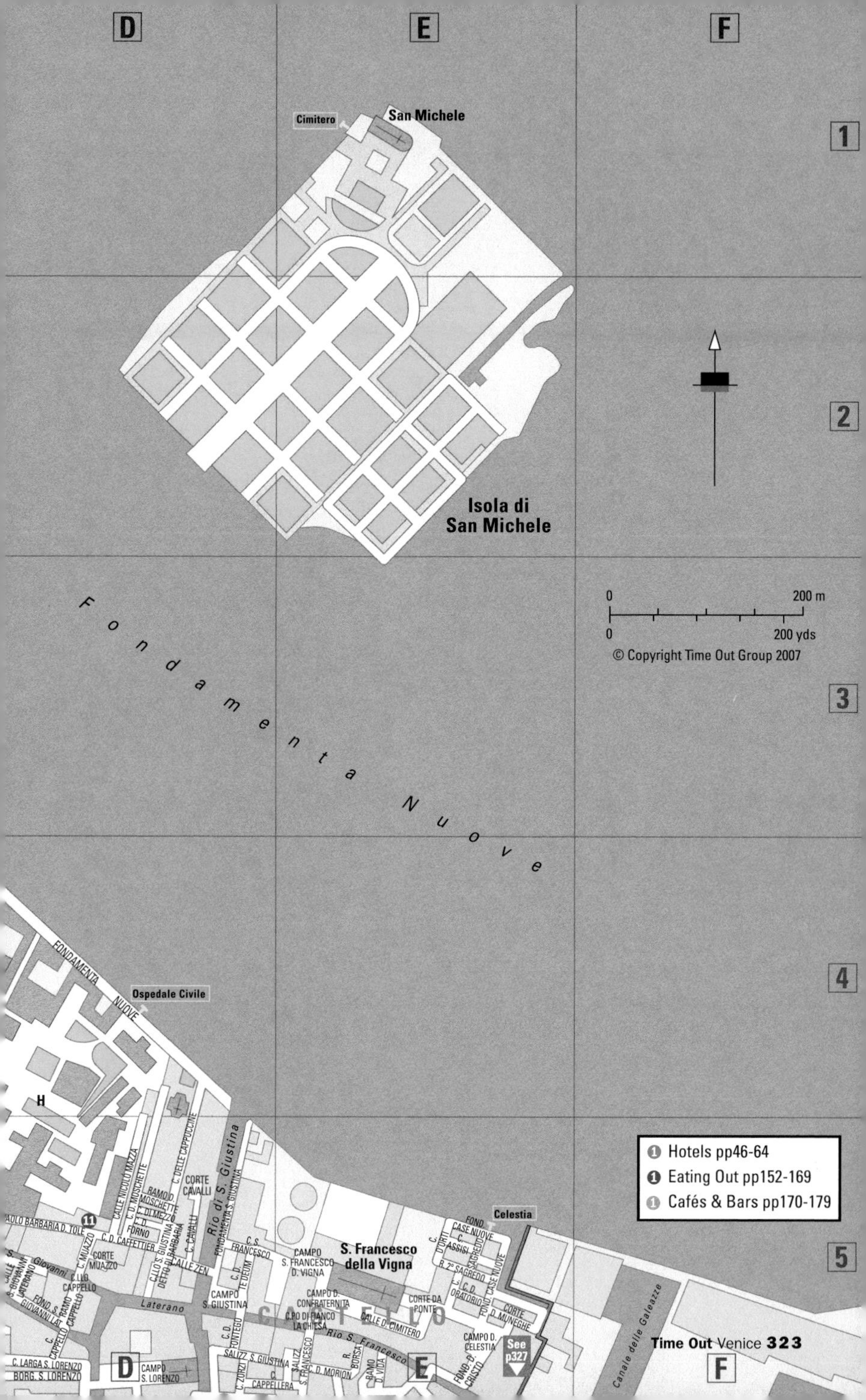

1

Cimitero

San Michele

2

Isola di
San Michele

| 0 | | | 200 m |

| 0 | | | 200 yds |

© Copyright Time Out Group 2007

3

F o n d a m e n t a   N u o v e

FONDAMENTA
NUOVE

Ospedale Civile

4

H

11

S. Francesco
della Vigna

Celestia

5

Laterano

Canale delle Galeazze

- ❶ Hotels pp46-64
- ❶ Eating Out pp152-169
- ❶ Cafés & Bars pp170-179

See
p327

Time Out Venice **323**

D

E

F

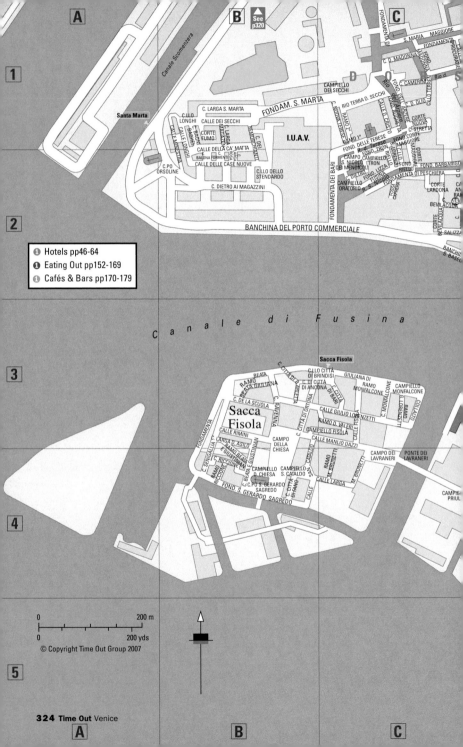

A   **B**   ▲ See p320   **C**

1

Canale Scomenzera

Santa Marta

FONDAM. S. MARTA

C. LLO
LONGHI
CALLE DEI SECCHI
C. LARGA S. MARTA
C.LLO
CORTE
FUMO
C. LARGA
C.ZA BENEDE

C. LONGHI
CALLE A. BENEDE
CALLE DELLA CA' MATTA
CALLE DELLE CASE NUOVE
BALDNA FORMENTI

C.PO
ORSOLINE

I.U.A.V.

C. DIETRO AI MAGAZZINI
C.LLO DELLO
STENDARDO

CAMPIELLO
DEI SECCHI
RIO TERRA D. SECCHI
C. D. MADONNA
C. D. OLIO

FOND. DELLE TERESE
R. TERESE
FOND. TRON
RIELLO
FOND.
FOND. S. NICCOLO
CAMPO
S. NICOLO
DEI MENDICOLI

CAMPIELLO
ORATORIO P. S. NICCOLA
FONDAMENTA DI PESCHIERA

FONDAMENTA DEI BARI

CAMPIELLO
MAGGIORE
CORTE
NUOVA
C.STRETTA

CAMERINI
FOND.
FOND.BARBARIGO

S. MARIA MAGGIORE
FONDAMENTA
D.

D

O

S

CORTE
LARDONA
C. 48
BEVILACQUA
CORTE
BEVILACQUA
SALIZZ
BANCHIN
S. BASE

2

BANCHINA DEL PORTO COMMERCIALE

❶ Hotels pp46-64
❶ Eating Out pp152-169
❶ Cafés & Bars pp170-179

3

C a n a l e   d i   F u s i n a

Sacca Fisola

BEATA
RAMO
BEATA GIULIANA
C.LLO CITTA
DI BRINDISI
C. DI CITTA
DI ANCONA
C. CITTA DI B. ARLETTA
GIULIANA DI
RAMO
MONFALCONE
C. MONFALCONE
CAMPIELLO
MONFALCONE
RAMO

C. DE LA SCUOLA
C. RAVENNA
CALLE GIULIO LOR
RAMO D. VALERI
C. CITTA D'OROVA
BENZETTI
RAMO
D'OLBRIO
PALAZZO

**Sacca
Fisola**
FONDAMENTA
CALLE RIMINI
C. LARGA D. ASILO
RAMO BEATA
E GIUSTINIANI
C. RICCOGNANA
RAMO
RICCIONE
C. RICCOGNANA
C.CO P.O S. GERARDO
SAGREDO
FOND. S. GERARDO SAGREDO
CAMPO
DELLA
CHIESA
CAMPIELLO
D. CHIESA
CAMPIELLO
S. CATALDO
C. CATALDO
RAMO
M. BRUNETTI
CALLE MANLIO DAZZI
CAMPIELLO FISOLA
CALLE LARGA
C. CITTA
BRANO
CALLE
C. CITTA BRANO
M. BRUNETTI
CAMPO DEI
LAVRANERI
PONTE DEI
LAVRANERI
CAMPIE
PRIUL

SENIGALLIA
C. BEATA E GIUSTINIAN

4

0   200 m
0   200 yds
© Copyright Time Out Group 2007

5

A   **B**   **C**

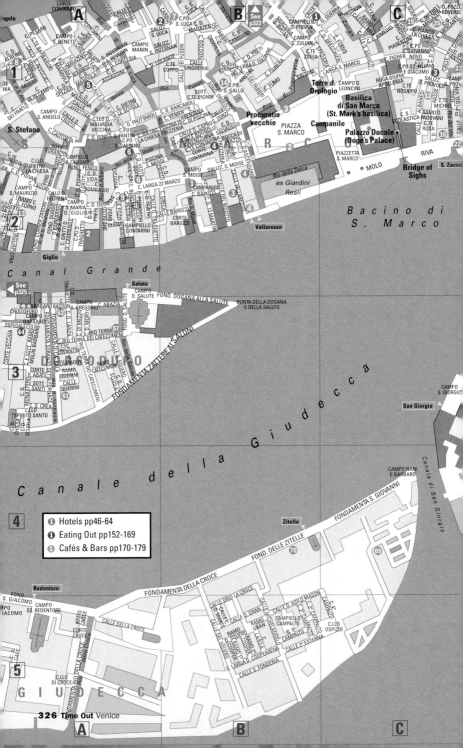

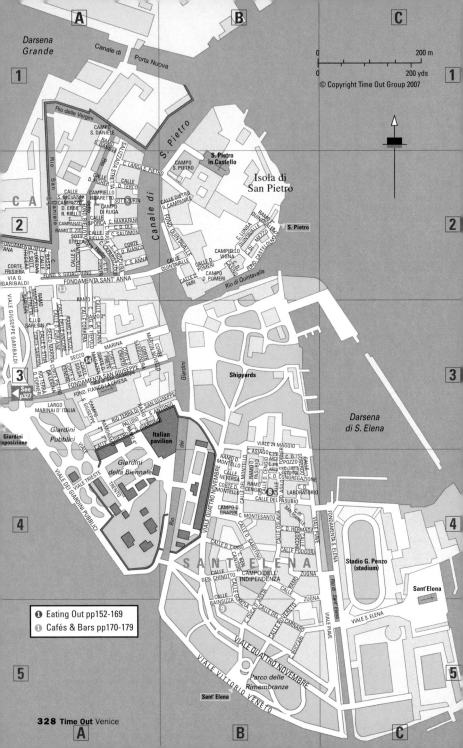

Street Index

MORANDI C.	322 C4
MORI Cpo d.	322 A2
MORI Fond. d.	322 A2
MORO Fond. d.	322 A3
MOSTO BALBI C. d.	321 E3
MOSTO Cte	321 F3
MUNUGHE C. d.	321 F2
MUTI Cte d.	322 A2
MUTI Ramo d.	322 A2
NIELLO C.	**321 E3**
NOVA Strada	322 A3
NOVA Strada	322 B4
NUOVA C.	322 C4
NUOVA C.	321 E1
NUOVA C.	321 F2
NUOVE Fond.	322 B3
NUOVE Fond.	322 C3
OCA C. d.	**322 B4**
OLIO C. d.	322 A3
OLIO C. d.	321 F3
ORAGAN C.	322 B4
ORMESINI Fond.	321 F2
ORMESINI C. d.	321 F2
ORTO C.	321 E2
PAGLIA C. d.	**321 F3**
PALI Cte d.	322 A4
PALUDO Cte d.	322 C4
PANADA	322 C4
PAZIENZA Cllo	321 D2
PEGOLOTTO Cte	321 F3
PEGOLOTTO Sott. d.	321 F3
PENITENTI C. LARGA d.	321 D1
PERLIERI C. d.	321 D1
PESARO C.	321 E3
PESARO Cllo	321 D2
PESARO Cllo	321 E3
PESCARIA Fond.	321 E3
PIAVE C. LARGA	322 A2
PIAVE Cllo	322 A1
PICIUTTA Cte	321 F1
PIETA C. d.	322 C3
PIGNATE C.	322 A2
PIGNATER d. TABACCO C.	321 F2
PISANI Cte	321 F1
PISTOR C. d.	322 B4
PISTOR Sal.	322 B4
PORPORA C.	321 E2
PORTON C. d.	321 F2
PORTON C. d.	321 F2
POSTA C.	322 B4
POZZO Sott. Cllo	321 E3
PRESTIN C.	322 C4
PRETI C. d.	321 F3
PRETI Sott.	322 B3
PRIMA C.	321 D2
PRIULI C.	322 B4
PRIULI DETTA d. CAVALLETTI C.	321 D3
PRIULI Fond.	322 B4
PROCURATIE C. d.	321 E3
PROPRIA C.	322 C4
QUERINI C.	**321 F3**
RABBIA C. d.	**321 F3**
RACCHETTA C. d.	322 B3
REMIER Cllo	321 F3
RETIER C.	322 B4
RIFORMATI C. d.	321 F1
RIFORMATI Fond. d.	321 F1
RIZZO C.	321 E1
RIZZO C.	321 E2
RIZZO Cte	321 F1
ROTONDA C. d.	321 F1
ROZZINI C.	322 C3
RUBINI C.	321 F2
S. ALVISE Cpo d.	**321 F1**
S. ANDREA Fond.	322 B3
S. ANTONIO C.	321 F3
S. ANTONIO Cpo	322 B3
SS. APOSTOLI Cpo	322 B4
SS. APOSTOLI RIO TERA	322 B4
S. CANCIANO Cpo	322 B4
S. CANCIANO Sal.	322 B4
S. CATERINA Fond.	322 B3
S. FELICE C.	322 A4
S. FELICE Cpo	322 A3
S. FELICE Fond.	322 B3
S. FOSCA Cpo	322 A3
S. GEREMIA Cpo	321 E3
S. GEREMIA Sal..	321 E3
S. GIOBBE Cpo	322 A3
S. GIOBBE Fond. DI	321 D2
S. GIOVANNI C. d.	321 E2
S. GIOVANNI CRISOSTOMO Sal.	322 B5
S. GIOVANNI Ramo d.	321 E2
S. GIROLAMO C.	321 E1
S. GIROLAMO Fond.	321 E2
S. LEONARDO Cpo	321 F3
S. LEONARDO RIO TERA	321 F3
S. LUCIA Fond.	321 D4
S. MARCUOLA Cpo	321 F3
S. MARIA NOVA Cllo	322 C4
S. MARIA NOVA Cpo	322 C4
S. MARZIALE Cpo	322 A3
SABBIONI Rio Terà d.	321 E3
SACCA SAN GIROLANO Fond.	321 D1
SACCHIERE Cte	321 F1
SALAMON C.	322 A3
SAON C. d.	320 C2
SARTORI C. d.	322 B3
SARTORI Fond. d.	322 B3
SAVORGNAN Fond.	321 E2
SCALA MATTA Cte	321 E2
SCALZI Fond. d.	321 E3
SCARLATTO C. d.	321 D2
SCUOLA d. BOTTERI C.	322 C3
SCUOLE Cllo d.	321 E2
SCURO C. d. Sott.	321 E2
SELLE C.	321 F2
SENSA Fond. d.	321 F2
SERIMAN Sal.	322 B3
SORANZO C.	321 F3
SPECCHIERI Sal. d.	322 C3
SPEZIER C. d.	321 E3
SQUERO C. d.	322 B4
SQUERO C. d.	322 C4
SQUERO C. d.	321 E2
SQUERO VECCHIO C. d.	322 C5
SQUERO VECCHIO Ramo	322 B3
STELLA C.	322 C4
STORTO Cllo P.TE	321 F3
STUA C. d.	322 A3
TAGLIAPIETRA C. d.	**322 B4**
TAGLIAPIETRE Ramo d.	321 E3
TEATRO Cte	322 B5
TESTA C. d.	322 C4
TINTOR C. d.	321 D2
TINTORETTO C. Cte	322 A2
TINTORIA C.	321 E2
TRACANNA C. d.	321 F2
TRAGHETTO C. d.	322 A4
TRAGHETTO C.d.	322 B4
TRAPOLIN Fond.	322 A3
TREVISAN C. d.	322 A3
TREVISAN Cllo d.	322 A3
VALBARANA C.	**322 B4**
VARISCO C.	322 C4
VECCHIA Cte	322 A2
VELE C. d.	322 B4
VENDRAMIN C. LARGA	321 F3
VENDRAMIN C.	322 A3
VENDRAMIN Fond.	322 A3
VENIER C.	322 C3
VENIER Fond.	321 E3
VERDE C. d.	322 B4
VERDE C. d.	321 D2
VERGOLA C.	321 E3
VIDA C.	322 C3
VITELLI C.RE d.	321 E2
VOLTI C.	322 C3
VOLTO C. d.	322 C4
WIDMANN C.	**322 C4**
ZANARDI C.	**322 B3**
ZANCANI C.	322 A3
ZAPPA Cte	321 F2
ZEN Fond.	322 B3
ZOCCOLO C.	322 A3
ZOLFO C.	321 F2
ZOLFO Ramo d.	321 F2
ZOTTI C.	322 B4
ZUDIO C.	321 F2
ZULIAN Sott.	322 A3

SAN POLO

ALBANESI C. d.	**321 E5**
ALBANESI C. d.	321 F5
ALBRIZZI C.	322 A5
ALBRIZZI Cllo	322 A5
AMOR d. AMICI C.	321 F5
ANGELO C.	322 A5
ARCO C.	322 A5
BADEOR Cte	**321 F5**
BALBO Ramo	325 E1
BALLO Cte	321 D5
BANCO SALVIATI C.	322 A5
BARBARIZZA C.	322 A5
BATTISTI Cpo C.	322 B4
BECCARIE C.	322 A4
BECCARIE Cpo d.	322 A4
BERNARDO C.	321 F5
BERNARDO Ramo	321 F5
BIANCA CAPPELLO C.	322 A5
BO C. d.	322 A5
BOLLANI Cte	322 A5
BOTTA C.	322 A4
BOTTERI C. d.	322 A4
BOTTERI C. d.	322 A4
BUSINELLO C.	322 A5
BUSINELLO Fond.	322 A5
CAFFETTIER C.	**321 F5**
CALDERER Cte	321 E5
CALICE C. d.	321 F4
CAMPANIEI C.	325 F1
CAMPANILE C. d.	322 A4
CAMPANILE C. d.	322 A5
CAMPAZZO C.	321 E5
CAMPAZZO Ramo	321 E5
CAPPELLER C. d.	322 A4
CASSETTI Ramo	321 F5
CAVALLI C. d.	322 A5
CHIESA C. d.	322 A5
CHIESA CAMPO d.	321 F5
CHIOVERE Cllo	321 E5
CHIOVERE C. d.	321 E5
CIMESIN Ramo	321 E5
CINQUE C. d.	322 A5
COLLALTO C.	321 F5
CONTARIN Cte	321 F5
CONTARINI Fond.	321 F5
CORNER C.	321 F5
CORTI C. d.	321 F5
CRISTI C. d.	322 A4
CRISTO C. d.	325 E1
CRISTO C. d.	321 F5
CURNIS Cllo	322 A5
DANDOLO C.	**325 F1**
DIETRO CASTELFORTE C.	321 E5
DIETRO L'ARCHIVIO C.	321 E5
DOANETTA C.	321 F5
DOGANA DI TERRA C.	322 A5
DOLERA C.	322 A5
DONA O SPEZIER C.	321 F5
DONZELLA C. 1 d.	322 A4
DONZELLA C. d.	322 A4
DONZELLA C.	322 A5
ERBARIA Pza	**322 B5**
ERBE C.	321 F5
FIGHER C. d.	**322 A5**
FONDERIA C.	321 E5
FORNER Cllo	321 E5
FORNER Fond. d.	325 F1
FORNER Ramo	321 F4
FORNO C. d.	322 A5
FORNO C. d.	321 F5
FRARI Cpo d.	321 F5
FRARI Fond.	321 F5
FRUTTAROLA C. d.	322 A5
FRUTTAROLA Fond.	322 A5
GAFFARO Fond. d.	**321 D5**
GALEZZA C.	322 A5
GALIZZI C.	322 A5
GALLIPOLI C. STRETTA	321 E5
GAMBERO C. d.	322 B5
LACA C. d.	**321 E5**
LARGA C.	321 F5
LARGA C.	321 F5
LATE Fond.	321 E5
LUGANEGHER C.	322 A5
LUGANEGHER C. d.	322 A5
MADONNA C. d.	**322 B5**
MADONNA C. d.	321 F5
MADONNA C. d.	321 F5
MADONNETTA Sott. C.	321 F5
MAGAZEN C.	321 F5
MAGAZEN Fond.	321 D5
MALCANTON Fond.	321 D5
MALVASIA C.	321 F5
MELONI Cllo	322 A5
MEZZO C. d.	322 A5
MEZZO C. d.	321 E5
MIANI C.	322 A4
MICHIEL Cte	322 A4
MISERICORDIA C. d.	321 D5
MORO C.	321 F5
MUTI C. d.	322 A4
MUTI O BAGLIONI C.	322 A4
NARANZERIA	**322 B5**
NOMBOLI C. d.	321 F5
NUOVA Cte	321 E5
OLIO C. d.	**322 A5**
OLIO C. d.	321 E5
OLIO Fond. d.	322 A5
OREFICI Ruga d.	322 B5
OSTERIA d. CAMPANA	322 A4
PARADISO C. d.	**322 A5**
PARRUCCHETTA Rio Terà d.	321 F5
PASSION C. d.	321 F5

Map

Pianta generale e avvertenze

General map and notes

Linee centrocittà

1 **N** **82**

in entrambi i sensi
two ways

Linee giracittà

41 **51** **61**   **42** **52** **62**

in senso antiorario
anticlockwise

in senso orario
clockwise

Linee lagunari

LN **20** **DM** **T**

in entrambi i sensi
two ways

Linee stagionali

3 **4** **5**

monodirezionali
one way

Legenda

Effettua la fermata
Does stop here

Non effettua la fermata
Does not stop here

Autobus actv   Ospedale   Ferrovia   Parcheggio   Taxi
Actv bus   Hospital   Railway   Park

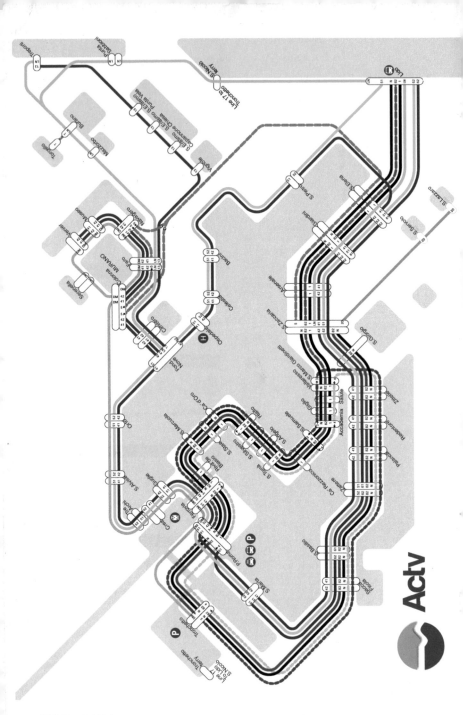